D1289329

A SECRET PILGRIMAGE TO MECCA AND MEDINA

A SECRET PILGRIMAGE TO MECCA AND MEDINA

Richard F. Burton

Introduced by
Tim Mackintosh-Smith

LONDON
THE FOLIO SOCIETY
2004

A Secret Pilgrimage to Mecca and Medina was first published by Longman, Brown, Green and Longmans in 1855–6, under the title *Personal Narrative of a Pilgrimage to El-Medinah and Meccah.* The text of this edition follows that of the 1879 edition published by William Mullan & Son, with minor emendations, and with the omission from the Appendices of A. Sprenger's 'Notes on My Journey'.

Plans redrawn by Reginald Piggott
Typography by Bernard Roberts

Frontispiece: Richard Francis Burton, 1865

Second printing 2005

Typeset in Monotype Baskerville at The Folio Society.
Printed at Cambridge University Press, Cambridge,
on Cordier Wove paper and bound by them in
buckram printed and blocked with a
design by David Eccles.

CONTENTS

ILLUSTRATIONS

BETWEEN PAGES 328 AND 329

BETWEEN PAGES 376 AND 377

Prayers around the Kaabah, Mecca. Photograph by Mohammed Sadiq Bey, *c.*1881.
(*Bibliothèque de l'Institut de France, Paris/RMN, Paris*)

Mecca, with Ajyad Fort. Photograph by Christiaan Snouck Hurgronje, 1889.
(*The British Library*)

BETWEEN PAGES 408 AND 409

Sherif Yahya with a slave and two Sherifs, Mecca. Photograph by Christiaan Snouck Hurgronje, 1889.
(*The British Library*)

Pilgrims at Mount Arafat. Photograph by Christiaan Snouck Hurgronje, 1889.
(*© Royal Geographical Society*)

Pilgrim camp at Mount Arafat. Photograph by Mohammed Sadiq Bey, *c.*1881.
(*Bibliothèque de l'Institut de France, Paris/RMN, Paris*)

Pilgrim camp at Sarif, on the road to Mecca. Photograph by Christiaan Snouck Hurgronje, 1889.
(*The British Library*)

BETWEEN PAGES 440 AND 441

Pilgrims at the Muzdalifah, near Muna. Photograph by Christiaan Snouck Hurgronje, 1889.
(*Library of Congress*)

Pilgrim camp at Muna, outside Mecca. Photograph by Christiaan Snouck Hurgronje, 1889.
(*© Royal Geographical Society*)

Pilgrim camp at the tomb of the Prophet's wife, Maymunah, Sarif. Photograph by Christiaan Snouck Hurgronje, 1889.
(*Library of Congress*)

The Safa Gate, Mecca. Photograph by Mohammed Sadiq Bey, *c.*1881.
(*Bibliothèque de l'Institut de France, Paris/RMN, Paris*)

INTRODUCTION

Trinity College, Oxford, never thought of Richard Burton (1821–90) as one of its more successful products; at least not when I was an undergraduate there and, like Burton, an escapee from the Classics to the liberating climes of Arabic. Even 140 years on, his claim to collegiate fame was that he had left Trinity degreeless, tooting on a tin trumpet as he drove a dogcart over the sacred flower beds. Burton was not a man to emulate.

Most decidedly not, agreed the Indian Army, his next stab at conformity, when his secret report on the boy brothels of Karachi became public. They had needed someone to penetrate under cover these 'unspeakable haunts of the Persian Vice'. Ruffian Dick, the White Nigger (as he was known to his brother officers) was the man for the job—fearless, a superb linguist, master of disguise, almost looked like a native; probably a touch of the tar-brush, if the truth were known. The problem was, said the whisperers, that there were certain details in the document . . . that the penetration might have been too, well, *intimate*. Brilliant Burton was swiftly, silently sidelined.

India, however, if it deepened that disdain for the Establishment which he had already expressed in his memorable departure from Oxford, also confirmed his love for 'the Orient', that refuge from cloying Classics and dull dons. 'What scenes he saw!'—this of himself in his Indian days—'What adventures he went through! But who would believe him, even if he ventured to detail them?' Probably, after the affair of the brothel report, rather too many people. Far fewer of those who knew Burton would have fallen for the opening of the autobiographical Postscript to *Falconry in the Valley of the Indus*, written soon after his debacle: 'After some years of careful training for the Church in the north and south of France, Florence, Naples and the University of Pisa . . . ' The fisticuffs and fornication of his Continental youth are judiciously edited out. But even without them it would be hard to picture Burton, a man with 'the brow of a god'—Swinburne was surely thinking of Pan, for those temples look ready to break out in horns—'and the jaw of a devil', living a life of mattins and Madeira cake. Ruffian, now unspeakable, Dick in a dog collar? That, apparently, was the fate his father had in store for him. But Burton's allusion to it is tongue-in-cheek, a farewell to Europe and conformity. His true destiny was a life, a fury, of travel and writing. Many of the journeys entailed disguise and penetration, those skills the Indian Army had used, and spurned; every book or article he wrote was a raspberry blown at the dons.

The travel was diverse. Sind and Goa in his Indian years; Arabia in 1853, the subject of this, the book that made him famous; the forbidden, dangerous and ultimately disappointing city of Harar in Abyssinia; the grim trek to find the source of the Nile; Salt Lake City, disguised as a Mormon elder. Marriage could not stop him; his wife, adoring, networking Isabel, wheedled a slot for him in the consular service. He sweated for Her Britannic Majesty in Fernando Po, alone, then with Isabel in Santos, Brazil. Hardly plums, either job, but they enabled Burton to add west and central Africa, the Amazon and Paraguay to the labels on his travelling trunk. That original Orient of escape had extended, to anywhere but Europe. There was a blissful but all too brief posting to Damascus, then a long twilight in Trieste—eighteen years as HM spectacularly underworked Consul. The Burtons travelled on, but Ruffian, now rather refined, Dick had made another journey, from explorer to tourist. Europe closed about him, England had him in the end. Isabel laid him in a marble tent in Surrey—an Arab tent, or an English idea of one.

The writing, however, never slowed. That Lucifer-fall in India had released a potential literary energy of extraordinary magnitude. Four books appeared in the two years after he left the Subcontinent—two on Sind, one on Goa, and *Falconry*. Thereafter, Burton's pump-action pen turned journeys into tomes with a speed that would make the slickest hack dizzy with envy, and produced not only Travel but also works on swords, bayonets, vampires, cannibals, Jews, gypsies; on scalping (scalps come off, he said, 'with a sound which, I am told, is not unlike "flop"') and farting (unpublished and sadly, I think, lost); and in his Trieste days, the great translations: Catullus, *The Book of a*

Thousand Nights and a Night—ten volumes, or sixteen with the supplement. This *maximum opus* was lapped up by gentlemen readers —the sort I imagine with astrakhan collars, dubious etchings and terminal footnote fetishes—and it made Burton rich. Arabists have always been snooty about the *Nights*. But it is impossible not to be awed by its thumping monumentality, by those great fat footnotes—by what Borges called its 'gross erudition'.

'Thou art always writing, O my brave!' observed Burton's Arabic teacher in Cairo (p. 49 below). 'What evil habit is this? Surely thou hast learned it in the lands of the Frank. Repent!' He never did. He wrote and wrote; but could he *write*? Lesley Blanch, in her study of Isabel, thought not: 'His actual writing is second rate—the only ordinary thing about him.' The late Sir Wilfred Thesiger considered reading Burton 'hard labour'. The first opinion is, I believe, simply wrong; the second is right to some extent, but misleading.

I must confess that my first reaction on returning to the *Pilgrimage* after an absence of years was one of irritation. Why that epigraph from Gibbon, who says that on Mecca 'our travellers are silent'? Burton was perfectly aware that Gibbon was wrong, that two European accounts of the Pilgrimage—one by a Florentine in the sixteenth century, the other by an Englishman in the seventeenth—had escaped the great historian's notice. Since then, in Burton's own century, Domingo Badia y Leblich the Catalan, alias Ali Bey, and Burckhardt the Swiss had both published personal—and detailed—narratives of the Islamic Holy Land. To these earlier pilgrims Burton eventually gives something of their due; he even reprints as an appendix Burckhardt's description of the Meccan sanctuary. So why such wilful misinformation on the very title page? It looks like a blatant puff —as if Burton were suggesting that he, alone of the infidels, had entered the virgin penetralia of Mecca. And after that misinformation of the first epigraph, obfuscation in the second:

> Dark and the Desert and Destriers me ken,
> And the Glaive and the Joust, and Paper and Pen.

'Destriers' and 'Glaive' are plain 'horses' and 'sword' in the Arabic original. Why on earth travesty them in Gothick fancy dress? 'Joust' is a howler—it should be 'Guest' (the error remains uncorrected even in the fourth edition). I could go on . . .

Perhaps I am a pedant. But on top of all this I must also admit that Burton at our first reacquaintance struck me as deeply unsympathetic. He is perfectly horrible about his teacher in Alexandria, to whom he imputes fickleness, cunning, dishonesty and cowardice purely on the basis of the poor man's looks. Granted, the quackeries of phrenology and physiognomy, on which he bases his diagnosis, had a certain vulgar currency at the time. But nothing can excuse the three-page paroxysm of nastiness about the Indians (pp. 26–8), Rajputs and a few similarly manly others excepted—inspired, note, by Burton's two-week stay in Cairo with a kindly merchant from Lahore. 'In none of the Eastern languages with which I am acquainted', our hero pontificates a few pages on, 'is there a single term conveying the meaning of our "gratitude"' (p. 36). This, at least as far as Arabic goes, is arrant nonsense; unless—as I suspect—Burton didn't know the meaning of the word in English.

I was beginning to wonder how I could ever introduce Burton without putting the reader off him for good, when his sneer relaxed. Perhaps it had been a symptom of culture shock, for now the traveller was acclimatising, the author settling into his book. Fellow-travellers began to appear—not phrenologised 'Orientals' but real, almost Chaucerian, individuals. Burton stopped opining and opened his eyes. And when he walked me, in one long fluent paragraph, through Cairo at night, the last of my antipathy evaporated. I have done that walk myself, seen what he saw. At times—and there are many more to come—'something not of earth' (p. 60) possesses Burton's prose, as it did that night scene. It is the poetic genius which the South Arabians call *hajis*. 'Ordinary' it is not.

Is it 'hard labour'? Burton felicitously translated the Arabic proverb *al-safar saqar* as 'travel is travail'. So, it seems on occasion, is Travel. Burton is no Kinglake (much less a Bryson); at times he can be a Baedeker, a veritable *Pilgerführer*. Speaking, in a footnote to the Memorial Edition, of a martyr's tomb which he failed to locate, he observes that 'the people of Al-Madinah are so wealthy in saints that they can well afford to lose sight of one';

he himself does his best not to miss a single sepulchre, an approach which can bring on severe shrine-strain. 'I have now described, at wearying length I fear . . . ' (p. 314), he admits at one point, after a particularly gruelling morning of holy sightseeing.

Persevere. You will know what it was to travel every step of the way. You will find, glittering among the *longueurs*, gems of description; and of arcane knowledge (how to price a slave-girl, for one)—some picked up along the road, others the result of magpie reading that takes in the great Arabic geographies, Dr Howe's *Report on Idiocy in Massachusetts* of 1848, and quite a lot in between. And you will come across unexpected moments that show how far behind Burton has left the cynical, grimacing self of his opening—for instance, as he shares a laugh with some Turkish ladies over the highly unchic masks they have to wear as part of their pilgrim-kit; as he surveys congregational prayers at his final goal, Mecca, 'never—nowhere—aught so solemn, so impressive as this' (p. 435).

Such raptures are brief. Looking back over the *Pilgrimage*, I suspect Burton never enjoyed himself more than when cross-buttocking a drunken bashi-bazouk in Cairo or, on board the ship to Yambu, beating up the captain or laying into fellow-passengers with his terrible, well-greased quarter-stave. Ruffian Dick was aptly named. But he was, in a phrase he uses elsewhere of the Sharifs (the old nobility of the holy cities), a distinguished ruffian. And, with age, he became a very pragmatic one. During the Trieste years he and Isabel cooked up a 'Pilgrimage to Meccah Syndicate Ltd', a package-tour company catering for pilgrims who preferred pampering to the picaresque. The venture never got off the ground; it was too far ahead of its time.

Burton was never at home—not at Oxford, nor in the army, nor in the times he lived through. With one foot in the buccaneering age and the other in that of mass tourism, he bestrode the Victorian era but never quite belonged in it. This book, a mixture of scholarship, slapdash and slapstick, of tedium, trivia and transcendence, of rhapsody and rant, prejudice and poetry, is the masterpiece of a misfit.

TIM MACKINTOSH-SMITH

Our notions of Meccah must be drawn from the Arabians:
as no unbeliever is permitted to enter the city,
our travellers are silent.

Gibbon, chap. 50

الليل والخيل والبيداء تعرفني
والسيف والضيف والقرطاس والقلم

Dark and the Desert and Destriers me ken,
And the Glaive and the Joust, and Paper and Pen.

Al-Mutanabbi

I
To Alexandria

A Few Words Concerning What Induced me to a Pilgrimage

In the autumn of 1852, through the medium of my excellent friend, the late General Monteith, I offered my services to the Royal Geographical Society of London for the purpose of removing that opprobrium to modern adventure, the huge white blot which in our maps still notes the Eastern and the Central regions of Arabia. Sir Roderick I. Murchison, Colonel P. Yorke, and Dr Shaw, a deputation from that distinguished body, with their usual zeal for discovery and readiness to encourage the discoverer, honoured me by warmly supporting, in a personal interview with the then Chairman of the then Court of Directors to the then Honourable East India Company, my application for three years' leave of absence on special duty from India to Muscat. But they were unable to prevail upon the said Chairman, Sir James Hogg, who, much disliking, if fact must be told, my impolitic habit of telling political truths, and not unwilling to mortify my supporter, his colleague, Colonel W. Sykes, refused his sanction, alleging as a no-reason that the contemplated journey was of too dangerous a nature. In compensation, however, for the disappointment, I was allowed the additional furlough of a year, in order to pursue my Arabic studies in lands where the language is best learned.

What remained for me but to prove, by trial, that what might be perilous to other travellers was safe to me? The *experimentum crucis* was a visit to El-Hejaz, at once the most difficult and the most dangerous point by which a European can enter Arabia. I had intended, had the period of leave originally applied for been granted, to land at Maskat—a favourable starting-place—and there to apply myself, slowly and surely, to the task of spanning the Deserts. But now I was to hurry, in the midst of summer, after a four years' sojourn in Europe, during which many things Oriental had faded from my memory; and, after passing through the ordeal of Egypt, a country where the police is curious as in Rome or Milan, to begin with the Moslem's Holy Land, the jealously guarded and exclusive Haram. However, being liberally supplied with the sinews of travel by the Royal Geographical Society; thoroughly tired of 'progress' and of 'civilisation'; curious to see with my eyes what others are content to hear with ears, namely, Moslem inner life in a really Mohammedan country; and longing, if truth be told, to set foot on that mysterious spot which no vacation tourist has yet described, measured, sketched, and photographed, I resolved to resume my old character of a wandering Dervish, and to make the attempt.

The principal object with which I started was this: to cross the unknown Arabian Peninsula, in a direct line from either El-Medinah to Maskat, or diagonally from Meccah to Makallah on the Indian Ocean. By what 'Circumstance, the miscreator', my plans were defeated, the reader will discover in the course of this volume. The secondary objects were numerous. I was desirous to find out if any market for horses could be opened between Central Arabia and India, where the studs were beginning to excite general dissatisfaction; to obtain information concerning the Great Eastern wilderness, the vast expanse marked Ruba' el-Khali (the Empty Abode) in our maps; to inquire into the hydrography of the Hejaz, its water-shed, the disputed slope of the country, and the existence or non-existence of perennial streams; and finally, to try, by actual observation, the truth of a theory proposed by Colonel W. Sykes, namely, that if history speak truth, in the population of the vast Peninsula there must exist certain physiological differences sufficient to warrant our questioning the common origin of the Arab family.

As regards horses, I am satisfied that from the Eastern coast something might be done—nothing on the Western, where the animals, though thoroughbred, are mere 'weeds', of a foolish price and procurable only by chance. Of the Ruba' el-Khali I have heard enough, from credible relators, to conclude that its horrid depths swarm with a large and half-starving population; that it abounds in Wadys, valleys, gullies, and ravines, partially fertilised by intermittent torrents; and, therefore, that the land is open to the adventurous traveller. Moreover, I am satisfied that, in spite of all geographers, from Ptolemy to Jomard, Arabia, which abounds in Nullahs or Fiumaras, possesses not a single perennial stream worthy the name of river; and the testimony of the natives induces me to think, with Wallin, contrary to Ritter and others, that the Peninsula falls instead of rising towards the south. Finally, I have found proof, to be produced in a future part of this publication, for believing in three distinct races. (1) The aborigines of the country, driven, like the Bheels and other autochthonic Indians, into the eastern and south-eastern wilds bordering upon the ocean. (2) A Syrian or Mesopotamian stock, typified by Shem and Joktan, that drove the Indigenae from the choicest tracts of country; these invaders still enjoy their conquests, representing the great Arabian people. And, (3) An impure Egypto-Arab clan—we personify it by Ishmael, his son Nebajoth, and Edom (Esau, the son of Isaac)—that populated and still populates the Sinaitic Peninsula. And in most places, even in the heart of Meccah, I met with *débris* of heathenry, proscribed by Mohammed, yet still popular, while the ignorant observers of the old customs assign to them a modern and a rationalistic origin.

I have entitled this account of my summer's tour through El-Hejaz, a Personal Narrative, and I have laboured to make its nature correspond with its name, simply because 'it is the personal that interests mankind'. Many may not follow my example; but some perchance will be curious to see what measures I adopted, in order to appear suddenly as an Eastern upon the stage of Oriental life; and, as the recital may be found useful by future adventurers, I make no apology for the egotistical semblance of the narrative. Those who have felt the want of some silent friend to aid them with advice, when it must not be asked, will appreciate what may appear to the uninterested critic mere outpourings of a mind full of self.

On the evening of the 3rd April, 1853, I left London for Southampton. By the advice of a brother officer—little thought at that time the adviser or the advised how valuable was the suggestion!—my Eastern dress was called into requisition before leaving Town, and all my impedimenta were taught to look exceedingly Oriental. Early the next day a 'Persian Prince', accompanied by Captain Henry Grindlay of the Bengal Cavalry, embarked on board the Peninsular and Oriental Company's magnificent screw steamer *Bengal.*

A fortnight was profitably spent in getting into the train of Oriental manners. For what polite Chesterfield says of the difference between a gentleman and his reverse, namely, that both perform the same offices of life, but each in a several and widely different way, is notably as applicable to the manners of the Eastern as of the Western man. Look, for instance, at that Indian Moslem drinking a glass of water. With us the operation is simple enough, but his performance includes no less than five novelties. In the first place, he clutches his tumbler as though it were the throat of a foe; secondly, he ejaculates, 'In the name of Allah the Compassionate, the Merciful!' before wetting his lips; thirdly, he imbibes the contents, swallowing them, not sipping them as he ought to do, and ending with a satisfied grunt; fourthly, before setting down the cup, he sighs forth, 'Praise be to Allah!' of which you will understand the full meaning in the Desert; and, fifthly, he replies, 'May Allah make it pleasant to thee!' in answer to his friend's polite 'Pleasurably and health!' Also he is careful to avoid the irreligious action of drinking the pure element in a standing position, mindful, however, of the three recognised exceptions, the fluid of the Holy Well Zem Zem, water distributed in charity, and that which remains after Wuzu, the lesser ablution. Moreover, in Europe, where both extremities are used indiscriminately, one forgets the use of the right hand, the manipulation of the rosary, the abuse of the chair—your genuine Oriental gathers up his legs, looking almost as comfortable in it as a sailor upon the back of a high-trotting horse—the rolling gait with the toes straight to the front, the grave look and the habit of pious ejaculations.

Our voyage over the summer sea was eventless. In a steamer of 2,000 or 3,000 tons you discover the once dreaded, now contemptible, stormy waters only by the band—a standing nuisance be it remarked—performing

There we lay, all the day,
In the Bay of Biscay, O!

The sight of glorious Trafalgar excites none of the sentiments with which a tedious sail used to invest it. 'Gib' is, probably, better known to you, by Théophile Gautier and Warburton, than the regions about Cornhill; besides which, you anchor under the Rock exactly long enough to land and to breakfast. Malta, too, wears an old familiar face, which bids you order a dinner and superintend the iceing of claret (beginning of Oriental barbarism), instead of galloping about on donkey-back through fiery air in memory of St Paul and White-Cross Knights.

But though our journey was monotonous, there was nothing to complain of. The ship was in every way comfortable; the cook, strange to say, was good; and the voyage lasted long enough, and not too long. On the evening of the thirteenth day after our start, the big-trousered pilot, so lovely in his deformities to western eyes, made his appearance, and the good screw *Bengal* found herself at anchor off the Headland of Clay (*Ra sel-Tín*), the promontory upon which immortal Pharaohs once stood.

Having been invited to start from the house of a kind friend, John Wingfield Larking, I disembarked with him, and rejoiced to see that by dint of a beard and a shaven head I had succeeded, like the Lord of Geesh, in 'misleading the inquisitive spirit of the populace'. The mingled herd of spectators before whom we passed in review on the landing-place, hearing an audible 'Alhamdulillah' ('Praise be to Allah, Lord of the three worlds!'), whispered 'Moslem!' The infant population spared me the compliments usually addressed to hatted heads; and when a little boy, presuming that the occasion might possibly open the hand of generosity, looked in my face and exclaimed 'Bakhshísh' ('Largess!'),[1] he obtained in reply a 'Mafish' ('Not a

[1] 'Bakhshísh', says a modern writer, 'is a fee or present which the Arabs (he here means the Egyptians, who took the word from the Persians through the Turks) claim on all occasions for services you render them, as well as for services they have rendered you. A doctor visits a patient gratis—the patient or his servant will ask for a Bakhshísh; you employ, pay, clothe, and feed a child—the father will demand his Bakhshísh; you may save the life of an Arab, at the risk of your own, and he will certainly claim a Bakhshísh. This Bakhshísh, in fact, is a sort of alms or tribute, which the poor Arab believes himself entitled to claim from every respectable-looking person.'

bless!'),[1] which convinced the bystanders that the sheep-skin covered a real sheep. We then mounted a carriage, fought our way through the donkeys, and in half an hour found ourselves, chibouque in mouth and coffee-cup in hand, seated on the divan of my friend's hospitable home.

Wonderful was the contrast between the steamer and that villa on the Mahmudiyah canal! Startling the sudden change from presto to adagio life! In thirteen days we had passed from the clammy grey fog, that atmosphere of industry which kept us at anchor off the Isle of Wight, through the liveliest air of the Inland Sea, whose sparkling blue and purple haze spread charms even on North Africa's beldame features; and now we are sitting silent and still, listening to the monotonous melody of the East—the soft night-breeze wandering through starlit skies and tufted trees, with a voice of melancholy meaning.

And this is the Arab's Kayf. The savouring of animal existence; the passive enjoyment of mere sense; the pleasant languor, the dreamy tranquillity, the airy castle-building, which in Asia stand in lieu of the vigorous, intensive, passionate life of Europe. It is the result of a lively, impressible, excitable nature, and exquisite sensibility of nerve; it argues a facility for voluptuousness unknown to northern regions, where happiness is placed in the exertion of mental and physical powers; where *Ernst ist das Leben*; where niggard earth commands ceaseless sweat of brow, and damp chill air demands perpetual excitement, exercise, or change, or adventure, or dissipation, for want of something better. In the East, man requires but rest and shade: upon the bank of a bubbling stream, or under the cool shelter of a perfumed tree, he is perfectly happy, smoking a pipe, or sipping a cup of coffee, or drinking a glass of sherbet, but above all things deranging body and mind as little as possible; the trouble of conversations, the displeasures of memory, and the vanity of thought being the most unpleasant interruptions to

[1] Mafish, 'There is none,' equivalent to, 'I have left my purse at home.' Nothing takes the Oriental mind so much as a retort alliterative or jingling. An officer in the Bombay army once saved himself from assault and battery by informing a furious band of natives, that under British rule '*harakat* na hui, *barakat* hui,' '*blessing* hath there been to you; *bane* there hath been none.'

his Kayf. No wonder that 'Kayf' is a word untranslatable in our mother-tongue![1]

Laudabunt alii claram Rhodon aut Mitylenem.

Let others describe this once famous Capital of Egypt, this City of Misnomers, whose dry-docks are ever wet, and whose marble fountain is eternally dry; whose 'Cleopatra's Needle' is not Cleopatra's; whose 'Pompey's Pillar' never had any connection with Pompey; and whose 'Cleopatra's Baths' are, according to veracious travellers, no baths at all. Yet is it a wonderful place, this 'Libyan suburb' of our day, this outpost of civilisation planted upon the skirts of barbarism, this Osiris seated side by side with Typhon, his great old enemy. Still may be said of it, 'it ever beareth something new'; and Alexandria, a threadbare subject in Bruce's time, is even yet, from its perpetual changes, a fit field for modern description.

The better to blind the inquisitive eyes of servants and visitors, my friend Larking lodged me in an outhouse, where I could revel in the utmost freedom of life and manners. And although some Armenian Dragoman, a restless spy like all his race, occasionally remarked *voilà un Persan diablement dégagé*, none, except those who were entrusted with the secret, had any idea of the part I was playing.

The domestics, devout Moslems, pronounced me to be an Ajami, a Persian as opposed to an Arab, not a good Mohammedan like themselves, but, still, better than nothing. I lost no time in securing the assistance of a Shaykh or private tutor, and plunged once more into the intricacies of the Faith, revived my recollections of religious ablution, read the Koran, and again became an adept in the art of prostration. My leisure hours were employed in visiting the baths and coffee-houses, in attending the bazars, and in shopping—an operation which hereabouts consists of sitting upon a chapman's counter, smoking, sipping coffee, and telling your beads the while, to show that you are not of the slaves for whom time is made; in fact, in

[1] In a coarser sense 'Kayf' is applied to all manner of intoxication. Sonnini is not wrong when he says, 'The Arabs give the name of Kayf to the voluptuous relaxation, the delicious stupor, produced by the smoking of hemp.'

pitting your patience against that of your adversary, the vendor.

I found time for a short excursion to a country village on the banks of the canal; nor was an opportunity of seeing El-nahl, the Bee-dance, neglected, for it would be some months before my eyes might dwell on such a pleasant spectacle again.

Delicias videam, Nile jocose, tuas!

Careful also of graver matters, I attended the mosque, and visited the venerable localities in which modern Alexandria abounds. Pilgrimaging Moslems are here shown the tomb of El-nabi Daniyal (Daniel the Prophet), discovered upon a spot where the late Sultan Mahmud dreamed that he saw an ancient man at prayer. Sikandar El-Rumi, the Moslem Alexander the Great, of course left his bones in the place bearing his name, or—as he ought to have done so—bones have been found for him. Alexandria also boasts of two celebrated Walis (holy men). One is Mohammed El-Busiri, the author of a poem called El-Burdah, universally read throughout the world of Islam, and locally recited at funerals, and on other solemn occasions. The other is Abu Abbas El-Andalusi, a sage and saint of the first water, at whose tomb prayer is never breathed in vain.

It is not to be supposed that the people of Alexandria could look upon my phials and pill-boxes without a yearning for their contents. An Indian doctor, too, was a novelty to them; Franks they despised—but a man who had come so far from East and West! Then there was something infinitely seducing in the character of a magician, doctor, and fakir, each admirable of itself, thus combined to make great medicine.

Men, women, and children besieged my door, by which means I could see the people face to face, and especially the fair sex, of which Europeans, generally speaking, know only the worst. Even respectable natives, after witnessing a performance of the Magic Mirror, opined that the stranger was a holy man, gifted with supernatural powers, and knowing everything.

One old person sent to offer me his daughter in marriage—he said nothing about dowry—but I thought proper to decline the honour. And a middle-aged lady proffered me the sum of

100 piastres, 1 Napoleon, if I would stay at Alexandria, and superintend the restoration of her blind left eye.

But the reader must not be led to suppose that I acted Carabin, or Sangrado, without any knowledge of my trade. From youth I have always been a dabbler in medical and mystical study. Moreover, the practice of physic is comparatively easy amongst dwellers in warm latitudes, uncivilised peoples, where there is not that complication of maladies which troubles more polished nations. And further, what simplifies extremely the treatment of the sick in these parts is the undoubted periodicity of disease, reducing almost all to one type—ague. Hence the origin of the Chronothermal system, a discovery which physic owes to my old friend, the late Dr Samuel Dickson.

Many of the complaints of tropical climates, as medical men well know, display palpably intermittent symptoms little known to colder countries; and, speaking from individual experience, I may safely assert that in all cases of suffering, from a wound to ophthalmia, this phenomenon has forced itself upon my notice. So much by way of excuse. I therefore considered myself as well qualified for the work as if I had taken out a *buono per l'estero* diploma at Padua, and not more likely to do active harm than most of the regularly graduated young surgeons who start to 'finish themselves' upon the sturdy frame of the British soldier.

After a month's hard work at Alexandria, I prepared to assume the character of a wandering Dervish; reforming my title from 'Mirza', the Persian Mister, to 'Shaykh' Abdullah. Arab Christians sometimes take the name of Servant of Allah—'which', as a modern traveller observes, 'all sects and religions might be equally proud to adopt'.

The Moslem Prophet said, 'The names most approved of God are Abdullah, Abd-el-rahman (Slave of the Compassionate), and such like.' A reverend man whose name I do not care to quote, some time ago initiated me into his order, the Kadiriyah, under the high-sounding name of Bismillah-Shah—King-in-the-name-of-Allah, a manner of Oriental Praise-God-Barebones: and, after a due period of probation, he graciously elevated me to the proud position of Murshid, or Master,[1] in the

[1] A Murshid is one allowed to admit Murids or apprentices into the order.

mystic craft. I was therefore sufficiently well acquainted with the tenets and practices of these Oriental Freemasons.

No character in the Moslem world is so proper for disguise as that of the Dervish. It is assumed by all ranks, ages, and creeds; by the nobleman who has been disgraced at court, and by the peasant who is too idle to till the ground; by Dives, who is weary of life, and by Lazarus, who begs his bread from door to door. Further, the Dervish is allowed to ignore ceremony and politeness, as one who ceases to appear upon the stage of life; he may pray or not, marry or remain single as he pleases, be respectable in cloth of frieze as in cloth of gold, and no one asks him—the chartered vagabond—Why he comes here? or Wherefore he goes there? He may wend his way on foot or alone, or ride his Arab mare followed by a dozen servants; he is equally feared without weapons, as swaggering through the streets armed to the teeth.

The more haughty and offensive he is to the people, the more they respect him; a decided advantage to the traveller of choleric temperament. In the hour of imminent danger, he has only to become a maniac, and he is safe; a madman in the East, like a notably eccentric character in the West, is allowed to say or do whatever the spirit directs. Add to this character a little knowledge of medicine, a 'moderate skill in magic, and a reputation for caring for nothing but study and books', together with capital sufficient to save you from the chance of starving, and you appear in the East to peculiar advantage. The only danger of the Mystic Path which leads or is supposed to lead to heaven, is, that the Dervish's ragged coat not unfrequently covers the cutthroat, and, if seized in the society of such a 'brother', you may reluctantly become his companion, under the stick or on the stake.

For be it known, Dervishes are of two orders, the Sharai, or those who conform to religion, and the Bi-Sharai, or Luti, whose practices are hinted at by their own tradition that 'he we daurna name' once joined them for a week, but at the end of that time left them in dismay, and returned to whence he came.

II

I Leave Alexandria

The thoroughbred wanderer's idiosyncrasy I presume to be a composition of what phrenologists call inhabitiveness and locality equally and largely developed. After a long and toilsome march, weary of the way, he drops into the nearest place of rest to become the most domestic of men. For awhile he smokes the long 'pipe of permanence' with an infinite zest; he delights in various siestas during the day, relishing withal deep sleep through the dark hours; he enjoys dining at a fixed dinner-hour, and he wonders at the demoralisation of the mind which cannot find means of excitement in chit-chat or small-talk, in a novel or a newspaper. But soon the passive fit has passed away; again a paroxysm of ennui coming on by slow degrees, Viator loses appetite, he walks about his room all night, he yawns at conversations, and a book acts upon him as a narcotic. The man wants to wander, and he must do so or he shall die.

After about a month most pleasantly spent at Alexandria, I perceived the approach of the enemy, and as nothing hampered my incomings and outgoings, I surrendered. The world was all before me, and there was pleasant excitement in plunging single-handed into its chilling depths. My Alexandrian Shaykh, whose heart fell victim to a new Jubbah, or cloak of broadcloth, which I had given in exchange for his tattered Za'abut (woollen cloak), offered me, in consideration of a certain monthly stipend, the affections of a brother and religious refreshment, proposing to send his wife back to her papa, and to accompany me, in the capacity of private chaplain, to the other side of Kaf, the mountain that encircles the world. I politely accepted the *Bruderschaft*, but many reasons induced me to decline his society and services. In the first place, he spoke the detestable Egyptian jargon. Secondly, it was but prudent to lose the spoor between Alexandria and Suez. And, thirdly, my 'brother' had shifting eyes (symptoms of fickleness), close together (indices of cunning);

a flat-crowned head, and large ill-fitting lips; signs which led me to think lightly of his honesty, firmness, and courage. Phrenology and physiognomy, be it observed, disappoint you often amongst civilised people, the proper action of whose brain upon the features is impeded by the external pressure of education, accident, example, habit, and necessity. But they are tolerably safe guides when groping your way through the mind of man in his so-called natural state, a being of impulse in that chrysalis condition of mental development which is rather instinct than reason.

Before my departure, however, there was much to be done.

The land of the Pharaohs is becoming civilised, and unpleasantly so: nothing can be more uncomfortable than its present middle state between barbarism and the reverse. The prohibition against carrying arms is rigid as in Italy; all violence is violently denounced; and beheading being deemed cruel, the most atrocious crimes, as well as those small political offences which in the days of the Mamelukes would have led to a beyship or a bowstring, receive fourfold punishment by deportation to Fayzoghlú, the local Cayenne. If you order your peasant to be flogged, his friends gather in threatening hundreds at your gates; when you scold your boatman, he complains to your consul; the dragomans afflict you with strange wild notions about honesty; a Government order prevents you from using vituperative language to the natives in general; and the very donkey-boys are becoming cognisant of the right of man to remain unbastinado'd. Still the old leaven remains behind: here, as elsewhere in 'Morning-Land', you cannot hold your own without employing the *voie de fait.* The passport system, now dying out of Europe, has sprung up, or rather has revived, in Egypt, with peculiar vigour. Its good effects claim for it our respect; still we cannot but lament its inconvenience. By *we*, I mean real Easterns. As strangers—even those whose beards have whitened in the land—know absolutely nothing of what unfortunate natives must endure, I am tempted to subjoin a short sketch of my adventures in search of a Tezkirah, or passport, at Alexandria.

Through ignorance which might have cost me dear but for friend Larking's weight with the local authorities, I had neglected to provide myself with a passport in England, and it was not without difficulty, involving much unclean dressing and an unlimited expenditure of broken English, that I obtain from HBM's Consul at Alexandria a certificate, declaring me to be an Indo-British subject named Abdullah, by profession a doctor, aged thirty, and not distinguished—at least so the frequent blanks seemed to denote—by any remarkable conformation of eyes, nose, or cheek. For this I disbursed a dollar. And here let me record the indignation with which I did it. That mighty Britain, the mistress of the seas, the ruler of one-sixth of mankind, should charge 5*s.* to pay for the shadow of her protecting wing! That I cannot speak my modernised *civis sum Romanus* without putting my hand into my pocket, in order that these officers of the Great Queen may not take too ruinously from a revenue of seventy millions! Oh the meanness of our magnificence! the littleness of our greatness!

My new passport would not carry me without the Zabit or Police Magistrate's counter-signature, said HBM's Consul. Next day I went to the Zabit, who referred me to the Muhafiz (Governor) of Alexandria, at whose gate I had the honour of squatting at least three hours, till a more compassionate clerk vouchsafed the information that the proper place to apply to was the Diwan Kharijiyyeh (the Foreign Office). Thus a second day was utterly lost. On the morning of the third I started, as directed, for the palace, which crowns the Headland of Clay. It is a huge and couthless shell of building in parallelogramic form, containing all kinds of public offices in glorious confusion, looking with their glaring whitewashed faces upon a central court, where a few leafless wind-wrung trees seem struggling for the breath of life in an eternal atmosphere of clay, dust, and sunblaze.

The first person I addressed was a Kawwas, or police officer, who, coiled comfortably up in a bit of shade fitting his person like a robe, was in full enjoyment of the Asiatic Kayf. Having presented the consular certificate, and briefly stated the nature of my business, I ventured to inquire what was the right course to pursue for a visa.

They have little respect for Dervishes, it appears, at Alexandria!

M'adri—'Don't know,' growled the man of authority, without moving anything but the quantity of tongue absolutely necessary for articulation.

Now there are three ways of treating Asiatic officials—by bribe, by bullying, or by bothering them, with a dogged perseverance, into attending to you and your concerns. The latter is the peculiar province of the poor; moreover, this time I resolved, for other reasons, to be patient. I repeated my question in almost the same words. *Ruh!* ('Be off') was what I obtained for all reply. But this time the questioned went so far as to open his eyes. Still I stood twirling the paper in my hands, and looking very humble and very persevering, till aloud *Ruh ya Kalb!* ('Go, O dog!') converted into a responsive curse the little speech I was preparing about the brotherhood of El-Islam and the mutual duties obligatory on true believers. I then turned away slowly and fiercely, for the next thing might have been a cut with the Kurbaj, or *cravache* of hippo hide, and, by the hammer of Thor! British flesh and blood could never have stood *that.*

After which satisfactory scene—for satisfactory it was in one sense, proving the complete fitness of the Dervish's costume—I tried a dozen other promiscuous sources of information, policemen, grooms, scribes, donkey-boys, and idlers in general. At length, wearied of patience, I offered a soldier some pinches of tobacco, and promised him an Oriental sixpence if he would manage the business for me. The man was interested by the tobacco and the pence; he took my hand, and inquiring the while he went along, led me from place to place, till, mounting a grand staircase, I stood in the presence of Abbas Effendi, Naib or deputy to the Governor.

It was a little, whey-faced, black-bearded Turk, coiled up in the usual conglomerate posture upon a calico-covered divan, at the end of a long, bare, large-windowed room. Without deigning even to nod the head, which hung over his shoulder with transcendent listlessness and affectation of pride, in answer to my salams and benedictions, he eyed me with wicked eyes, and faintly ejaculated *Min ent?* for *Man anta?*—'Who art thou?' Then hearing that I was a Dervish and doctor—he must be an Osmanli Voltairian, that little Turk—the official snorted a contemptuous snort. He condescendingly added, however, that the proper source to seek was *Taht*, which meaning simply 'below', conveyed rather imperfect information in a topographical point of view to an utter stranger.

At length, however, my soldier guide found out that a room in the custom-house bore the honourable appellation of Foreign Office. Accordingly I went there, and, after sitting at least a couple of hours at the bolted door in the noonday sun, was told, with a fury which made me think I had sinned, that the officer in whose charge the department was, had been presented with an olive-branch in the morning, and consequently that business was not to be done that day. The angry-faced official communicated the intelligence to a large group of Anadolian, Caramanian, Bosniac, and Roumelian Turks—sturdy, undersized, broad-shouldered, bare-legged, splay-footed, horny-fisted, dark-browed, honest-looking mountaineers, who were lounging about with long pistols and yataghans stuck in their broad sashes, head-gear composed of immense Tarbushes, with proportionate turbans coiled round them, and bearing two or three suits of substantial clothes, even at this season of the year, upon their shoulders. Like myself, they had waited some hours, but they were not patient under disappointment: they bluntly told the angry official that he and his master were a pair of idlers, and the curses that rumbled and gurgled in their hairy throats as they strode towards the door, sounded like the growling of wild beasts.

Thus was another day truly orientally lost. On the morrow, however, I obtained permission in the character of Dr Abdullah, to visit any part of Egypt I pleased, and to retain possession of my dagger and pistols.

And now I must explain what induced me to take so much trouble about a passport. The home reader naturally inquires, Why not travel under your English name?

For this reason. In the generality of barbarous countries you must either proceed, like Bruce, preserving the 'dignity of manhood', and carrying matters with a high hand, or you must worm your way by timidity and subservience; in fact, by becoming an animal too contemptible for man to let or injure. But to pass through the Moslem's Holy Land, you must either be a born believer, or have become one; in the former case you may demean yourself as you please, in the latter a path is ready prepared for you. My spirit could not bend to own myself a Burma, a renegade—to be pointed at and shunned and catechised, an object of suspicion to the many and of contempt to all. Moreover, it would have obstructed the aim of my wanderings. The convert is always watched with Argus eyes, and men do not willingly give information to a new Moslem, especially a Frank: they suspect his conversion to be feigned or forced, look upon him as a spy, and let him see as little of life as possible. Firmly as was my heart set upon travelling in Arabia, I would have given up the dear project rather than purchase a doubtful and partial success at such a price. Consequently, I had no choice but to appear as a born believer, and part of my birthright in that respectable character was toil and trouble in obtaining a Tezkirah.[1]

Then I had to provide myself with certain necessaries for the way. These were not numerous. The silver-mounted dressing-bag is here supplied by a rag containing a Miswak, or tooth-stick, a bit of soap and a comb, wooden, for bone and tortoiseshell are not, religiously speaking, correct. Equally simple was my wardrobe; a change or two of clothing. It is a great mistake to carry too few clothes, and those who travel as Orientals should always have at least one very grand suit for critical occasions. Throughout the East a badly dressed man is a pauper, and, as in England, a pauper—unless he belongs to an order having a right to be poor—is a scoundrel. The only article of canteen description was a Zemzemiyah, a goat-skin water-bag, which, especially when new, communicates to its contents a ferruginous aspect, and a wholesome, though hardly an attractive, flavour of tanno-gelatine. This was a necessary; to drink out of a tumbler, possibly fresh from pig-eating lips, would have entailed a certain loss of reputation.

For bedding and furniture I had a coarse Persian rug which, besides being couch, acted as chair, table, and oratory; a cotton-

[1] During my journey, and since my return, some Indian papers conducted by jocose editors made merry upon an Englishman 'turning Turk'. Once for all, I beg leave to point above for the facts of the case; it must serve as a general answer to any pleasant little fictions which may hereafter appear.

stuffed chintz-covered pillow, a blanket in case of cold, and a sheet, which did duty for tent and mosquito curtains in nights of heat. Almost all Easterns sleep under a sheet, which becomes a kind of respirator, defending them from the dews and mosquitoes by night and the flies by day. The 'rough and ready' traveller will learn to follow the example, remembering that 'Nature is founder of customs in savage countries'; whereas, amongst the soi-disant civilised, Nature has no deadlier enemy than Custom.

As shade is a convenience not always procurable, another necessary was a huge cotton umbrella of Eastern make, brightly yellow, suggesting the idea of an overgrown marigold. I had also a substantial housewife, the gift of a kind relative, Miss Elizabeth Stisted; it was a roll of canvas, carefully soiled, and garnished with needles and thread, cobblers'-wax, buttons, and other such articles. These things were most useful in lands where tailors abound not; besides which, the sight of a man darning his coat or patching his slippers teems with pleasing ideas of humility.

A dagger, a brass inkstand and pen-holder stuck in the belt, and a mighty rosary, which on occasion might have been converted into a weapon of offence, completed my equipment. I must not omit to mention the proper method of carrying money, which in these lands should never be entrusted to box or bag. A common cotton purse secured in a breast pocket (for Egypt now abounds in that civilised animal the pick-pocket) contained silver pieces and small change. My gold, of which I carried 25 sovereigns, and papers, were committed to a substantial leathern belt of Maghrabi manufacture, made to be strapped round the waist under the dress. This is the Asiatic method of concealing valuables, and one more civilised than ours in the last century, when Roderic Random and his companion 'sewed their money between the lining and the waistband of their breeches, except some loose silver for immediate expense on the road'. The great inconvenience of the belt is its weight, especially where dollars must be carried, as in Arabia, causing chafes and discomfort at night. Moreover, it can scarcely be called safe. In dangerous countries wary travellers will adopt surer precautions. Some prefer a long chain of pure gold divided into links and covered with leather, so as to resemble the twisted girdle which the Arab fastens round his waist. It is a precaution well known to the wandering knights of old. Others, again, in very critical situations, open with a lancet the shoulder, or any other fleshy part of the body and insert a precious stone, which does not show in its novel purse.

A pair of common native *Khurjin*, or saddle-bags, contained my wardrobe; the bed was readily rolled up into a bundle; and for a medicine chest I bought a pea-green box with red and yellow flowers, capable of standing falls from a camel twice a day.

The next step was to find out when the local steamer would start for Cairo, and accordingly I betook myself to the Transit Office. No vessel was advertised; I was directed to call every evening till satisfied. At last the fortunate event took place: a 'weekly departure', which, by-the-bye, occurred once every fortnight or so, was in orders for the next day. I hurried to the office, but did not reach it till past noon—the hour of idleness. A little dark gentleman, so formed and dressed as exactly to resemble a liver-and-tan bull-terrier, who with his heels on the table was dozing, cigar in mouth, over the last *Galignani*, positively refused, after a time—for at first he would not speak at all—to let me take my passage till three p.m. I inquired when the boat started, upon which he referred me, as I had spoken bad Italian, to the advertisement. I pleaded inability to read or write, whereupon he testily cried, *Alle nove! alle nove!*—'at nine! at nine!' Still appearing uncertain, I drove him out of his chair, when he rose with a curse and read eight a.m. An unhappy Eastern, depending upon what he said, would have been precisely one hour too late.

Thus were we lapsing into the real good old East Indian style of doing business. Thus Anglo-Indicus orders his first clerk to execute some commission; the senior, having 'work' upon his hands, sends a junior; the junior finds the sun hot, and passes on the word to a 'peon'; the 'peon' charges a porter with the errand; and the porter quietly sits or dozes in his place, trusting that Fate will bring him out of the scrape, but firmly resolved, though the shattered globe fall, not to stir an inch.

The reader, I must again express a hope, will pardon the egotism of these descriptions—my object is to show him how business is carried on in these hot countries. Business generally. For had I been, not Abdullah the Dervish, but a rich native merchant, it would have been the same. How many complaints of similar treatment have I heard in different parts of the Eastern world! and how little can one realise them without having actually experienced the evil! For the future I shall never see a 'nigger' squatting away half a dozen mortal hours in a broiling sun patiently waiting for something or for some one, without a lively remembrance of my own cooling of the calces at the custom-house of Alexandria.

At length, about the end of May (1853), all was ready. Not without a feeling of regret I left my little room among the white myrtle blossoms and the rosy oleander flowers with the almond smell. I kissed with humble ostentation my good host's hand in presence of his servants—he had become somewhat unpleasantly anxious of late to induce in me the true Oriental feeling, by a slight administration of the bastinado. I bade adieu to my patients, who now amounted to about fifty, shaking hands with all meekly and with religious equality of attention; and, mounted in a 'trap' which looked like a cross between a wheelbarrow and a dog-cart, drawn by a kicking, jibbing, and biting mule, I set out for the steamer, the *Little Asthmatic*.

III

The Nile Steamboat

In the days of the Pitts we have invariably a 'Relation' of Egyptian travellers who embark for a place called 'Roseet' on the 'River Nilus'. Wanderers of the Brucean age were wont to record their impressions of voyage upon land subjects observed between Alexandria and Cairo. A little later we find every one inditing rhapsodies about, and descriptions of, his or her *Dahabiyah* (barge) on the canal. After this came the steamer. And after the steamer will come the railroad, which may disappoint the author tourist, but will be delightful to that class of men who wish to get over the greatest extent of ground with the least inconvenience to themselves and others. Then shall the Mahmudiyah—ugliest and most wearisome of canals—be given up to cotton boats and grain barges, and then will note-books and the headings of chapters clean ignore its existence.

I saw the canal at its worst, when the water was low; and I have not one syllable to say in its favour. Instead of thirty hours, we took three mortal days and nights to reach Cairo, and we grounded with painful regularity four or five times between sunrise and sunset. In the scenery on the banks sketchers and describers have left you nought to see. From Pompey's Pillar to the Maison Carrée, Kariom and its potteries, El-Birkah of the night birds, Bastarah with the alleys of trees, even unto Atfeh, all things are perfectly familiar to us, and have been so years before the traveller actually sees them. The Nil el-Mubarak itself—the Blessed Nile—as notably fails too at this season to arouse enthusiasm. You see nothing but muddy waters, dusty banks, a sand mist, a milky sky, and a glaring sun: you feel nought but a breeze like the blast from a potter's furnace. You can only just distinguish through a veil of reeking vapours the village Shibr Katt from the village Kafr el-Zayyat, and you steam too far from Wardan town to enjoy the Timonic satisfaction of enraging its male population with *Haykal! ya ibn Haykal!*—'O

Haykal! O son of Haykal!' Haykal was a pleasant fellow, who, having basely abused the confidence of the fair ones of Wardan, described their charms in sarcastic verse, and stuck his scroll upon the door of the village mosque, taking at the same time the wise precaution to change his lodgings without delay. The very mention of his name affronts the brave Wardanenses to the last extent, making them savage as Oxford bargees. You are nearly wrecked, as a matter of course, at the Barrage; and you are certainly dumbfoundered by the sight of its ugly little Gothic crenelles. The Pyramids of Cheops and Cephren, 'rearing their majestic heads above the margin of the Desert', only suggest the remark that they have been remarkably well sketched; and thus you proceed till with a real feeling of satisfaction you moor alongside of the tumble-down old suburb Bulak.

To me there was double dulness in the scenery: it seemed to be Sind over again—the same morning mist and noontide glare; the same hot wind and heat clouds, and fiery sunset, and evening glow; the same pillars of dust and devils of sand sweeping like giants over the plain; the same turbid waters of a broad, shallow stream studded with sand-banks and silt-isles, with crashing earth slips and ruins nodding over a kind of cliff, whose base the stream gnaws with noisy tooth. On the banks, saline ground sparkled and glittered like hoar-frost in the sun; and here and there mud villages, solitary huts, pigeon-towers, or watch turrets, whence little brown boys shouted and slung stones at the birds, peeped out from among bright green patches of palm-tree, tamarisk, and mimosa; maize, tobacco, and sugar-cane.

Beyond the narrow tongue of land on the river banks lay the glaring, yellow Desert, with its low hills and sand slopes bounded by innumerable pyramids of Nature's architecture. The boats, with their sharp bows, preposterous sterns, and lateen sails, might have belonged to the Indus. So might the chocolate-skinned, blue-robed peasantry; the women carrying progeny on their hips, with the eternal water-pot on their heads; and the men sleeping in the shade, or following the plough to which probably Osiris first put hand. The lower animals, like the higher, are the same; gaunt, mange-stained camels, muddy buffaloes, scurvied donkeys, sneaking jackals, and fox-like dogs. Even the feathered creatures were perfectly familiar to my eye—paddy birds, pelicans, giant cranes, kites, and wild water-fowl.

I had taken a third-class or deck passage, whereby the evils of the journey were exasperated. A roasting sun pierced the canvas awning like hot water through a gauze veil, and by night the cold dews fell raw and thick as a Scotch mist. The cooking was abominable, and the dignity of Dervish-hood did not allow me to sit at meat with Infidels or to eat the food which they had polluted. So the Pilgrim squatted apart, smoking perpetually, with occasional interruptions to say his prayers and to tell his beads upon the mighty rosary; and he drank the muddy water of the canal out of a leathern bucket, and he munched his bread and garlic with a desperate sanctimoniousness. Those skilled in simples, eastern as well as western, praise garlic highly, declaring that it 'strengthens the body, prepares the constitution for fatigue, brightens the sight, and, by increasing the digestive power, obviates the ill-effects arising from sudden change of air and water'. The traveller inserts it into his dietary in some pleasant form as 'Provence-butter', because he observes that, wherever fever and ague abound, the people, ignorant of cause but observant of effect, make it a common article of food. The old Egyptians highly esteemed this vegetable, which, with onions and leeks, enters into the list of articles so much regretted by the Hebrews (Numbers xi. 5; Koran, chapter 2). The modern people of the Nile, like the Spaniards, delight in onions, which, as they contain between twenty-five and thirty per cent of gluten, are highly nutritive. In Arabia, however, the stranger must use this vegetable sparingly. The city people despise it as the food of a Fellah—a boor. The Wahhabis have a prejudice against onions, leeks, and garlic, because the Prophet disliked their strong smell, and all strict Moslems refuse to eat them immediately before visiting the mosque, or meeting for public prayer.

The *Little Asthmatic* was densely crowded, and discipline not daring to mark out particular places, the scene on board of her was motley enough. There were two Indian officers, who naturally spoke to none but each other, drank bad tea, and smoked their cigars exclusively like Britons. A troop of Kurd policemen, escorting treasure, was surrounded by a group of noisy Greeks; these men's gross practical jokes sounding anything but pleasant to the solemn Moslems, whose saddle-bags and furniture were at every moment in danger of being defiled by abominable drinks and the ejected juices of tobacco. There was one pretty woman on board, a Spanish girl, who looked strangely misplaced—a rose in a field of thistles. Some silent Italians, with noisy interpreters, sat staidly upon the benches. It was soon found out, through the communicative dragoman, that their business was to buy horses for HM of Sardinia: they were exposed to a volley of questions delivered by a party of French tradesmen returning to Cairo, but they shielded themselves and fought shy with Machiavellian dexterity.

Besides these was a German, a 'beer bottle in the morning and a bottle of beer in the evening', to borrow a simile from his own nation; a Syrian merchant, the richest and ugliest of Alexandria; and a few French house-painters going to decorate the Pasha's palace at Shoobrah. These last were the happiest of our voyagers—veritable Children of Paris, Montagnards, Voltairians, and thoroughbred Sans-Soucis. All day they sat upon deck chattering as only their lively nation can chatter, indulging in ultra-gallic maxims, such as *on ne vieillit jamais à table*; now playing écarté for love or nothing, then composing *des ponches un peu chiques*; now reciting adventures of the category *Mirabolant*, then singing, then dancing, then sleeping, and rising to play, to drink, talk, dance, and sing again. One chanted—

> *Je n'ai pas connu mon père*
> *Ce respectable viellard.*
> *Je suis né trois ans trop tard*, etc.;

whilst another trolled out—

> *Qu'est ce que je vois?*
> *Un canard en rôbe de chambre!*

They being new comers, free from the western morgue so soon caught by Oriental Europeans, were particularly civil to me, even wishing to mix me a strong draught; but I was not so fortunate with all on board. A large shopkeeper threatened to *briser* my *figure* for putting my pipe near his pantaloons; but seeing me finger my dagger curiously, though I did not shift my pipe, he forgot to remember his threat.

I had taken charge of a parcel for one M. P——, a student of Coptic, and remitted it to him on board; of this little service the only acknowledgment was a stare and a petulant inquiry why I had not given it to him before. And one of the Englishmen, half publicly, half privily, as though communing with himself, condemned my organs of vision because I happened to touch his elbow. He was a man in my own service; I pardoned him in consideration of the compliment paid to my disguise.

Two fellow-passengers were destined to play an important part in my comedy of Cairo. Just after we had started, a little event afforded us some amusement. On the bank appeared a short, crummy, pursy kind of man, whose efforts to board the steamer were notably ridiculous. With attention divided between the vessel and a carpet-bag carried by his donkey-boy, he ran along the sides of the canal, now stumbling into hollows, then climbing heights, then standing shouting upon the projections with the fierce sun upon his back, till every one thought his breath was completely gone. But no! game to the back-bone, he would have perished miserably rather than lose his fare. 'Perseverance', say the copy-books, 'accomplishes great things': at last he was taken on board, and presently he lay down to sleep. His sooty complexion, lank black hair, features in which appeared *beaucoup de finesse*, that is to say, abundant rascality, an eternal smile and treacherous eyes, his gold[1] ring, dress of showy colours, fleshy stomach, fat legs, round back, and a peculiar manner of frowning and fawning simultaneously, marked him an Indian. When he awoke he introduced himself to me as Miyan Khudabakhsh Namdar, a native of Lahore: he had carried on the trade of a shawl merchant in London and Paris, where he had lived two years, and after a pilgrimage intended to purge away the sins of civilised lands, he had settled at Cairo.

[1] The stricter sort of Moslems, such as the Arabs, will not wear gold ornaments, which are forbidden by their law.

My second friend, Haji Wali, I will introduce to the reader in a future chapter; and my two expeditions to Midian have brought him once more into notice.[1]

Long conversations in Persian and Hindostani abridged the tediousness of the voyage, and when we arrived at Bulak, the polite Khudabakhsh insisted upon my making his house my home. I was unwilling to accept the man's civility, disliking his looks; but he advanced cogent reasons for changing my mind. His servants cleared my luggage through the custom-house, and a few minutes after our arrival I found myself in his abode near the Ezbekiyeh Gardens, sitting in a cool Mashrabiyah—the projecting latticed window of richly carved wood, for which Cairo was once so famous—that gracefully projected over a garden, and sipping the favourite glass of pomegranate syrup.

As the Wakalahs or caravanserais were at that time full of pilgrims, I remained with Khudabakhsh ten days or a fortnight. But at the end of that time my patience was thoroughly exhausted. My host had become a civilised man, who sat on chairs, who ate with a fork, who talked European politics, and who had learned to admire, if not to understand liberty—liberal ideas! and was I not flying from such things? Besides which, we English have a peculiar national quality, which the Indians, with their characteristic acuteness, soon perceived, and described by an opprobrious name. Observing our solitary habits, that we could not, and would not, sit and talk and sip sherbet and smoke with them, they called us *Jangli*—wild men, fresh caught in the jungle and sent to rule over the land of Hind. Certainly nothing suits us less than perpetual society, an utter want of solitude, when one cannot retire into oneself an instant without being asked some puerile question by a companion, or look into a book without a servant peering over one's shoulder; when from the hour you rise to the time you rest, you must ever be talking or listening, you must converse yourself to sleep in a public dormitory, and give ear to your companions' snores and mutterings at midnight.

The very essence of Oriental hospitality, however, is this

[1] See *The Gold Mines of Midian*, and *The Land of Midian* (*Revisited*) (Messrs Paul and Co., London, 1878 and 1879).

family style of reception, which costs your host neither money nor trouble. You make one more at his eating tray, and an additional mattress appears in the sleeping-room. When you depart, you leave if you like a little present, merely for a memorial, with your entertainer; he would be offended if you offered it him openly as a remuneration, and you give some trifling sums to the servants. Thus you will be welcome wherever you go. If perchance you are detained perforce in such a situation—which may easily happen to you, medical man—you have only to make yourself as disagreeable as possible, by calling for all manner of impossible things. Shame is a passion with eastern nations. Your host would blush to point out to you the indecorum of your conduct; and the laws of hospitality oblige him to supply the every want of a guest, even though he be a *détenu.*

But of all Orientals, the most antipathetical companion to an Englishman is, I believe, an East Indian. Like the fox in the fable, fulsomely flattering at first, he gradually becomes easily friendly, disagreeably familiar, offensively rude, which ends by rousing the 'spirit of the British lion'. Nothing delights the Hindi so much as an opportunity of safely venting the spleen with which he regards his victors.[1] He will sit in the presence of a magistrate, or an officer, the very picture of cringing submissiveness. But after leaving the room, he is as different from his former self as a

[1] The *Calcutta Review* (No. 41), noticing *L'Inde sous la Domination Anglaise*, by the Baron Barchou de Penhoën, delivers the following sentiment: 'Whoever states, as the Baron B. de P. states and repeats again and again, that the natives generally entertain a bad opinion of the Europeans generally, states what is decidedly untrue.'

The reader will observe that I differ as decidedly from the Reviewer's opinion.

Popular feeling towards the English in India was 'at first one of fear, afterwards of horror: Hindus and Moslems considered the strangers a set of cow-eaters and fire-drinkers, *tetrae belluae ac molossis suis ferociores*, who would fight like Eblis, cheat their own fathers, and exchange with the same readiness a broadside of shots and thrusts of boarding-pikes, or a bale of goods and a bag of rupees'—*The English in Western India.* We have risen in a degree above such low standard of estimation: still, incredible as it may appear to the Frank himself, it is no less true, that the Frank everywhere in the East is considered a contemptible being, and dangerous withal. As regards Indian opinion concerning our government, my belief is, that in and immediately about the three presidencies, where the people owe everything to and hold everything by our rule, it is popular. At the same time I am convinced that in other places the people would most willingly hail any change. And how can we hope it to be otherwise—we, a nation of strangers, aliens to the country's customs and creed, who, even while resident in India, act the part which absentees do in other lands? Where, in the history of the world, do we read that such foreign dominion ever made itself loved?

counsel in court from a counsel at a concert, a sea captain at a club dinner from a sea captain on his quarter-deck. Then he will discover that the English are not brave, nor clever, nor generous, nor civilised, nor anything but surpassing rogues; that every official takes bribes, that their manners are utterly offensive, and that they are rank infidels. Then he will descant complacently upon the probability of a general Bartholomew's Day in the East, and look forward to the hour when enlightened young India will arise and drive the 'foul invader' from the land.[1] Then he will submit his political opinions nakedly, that India should be wrested from the Company and given to the Queen, or taken from the Queen and given to the French. If the Indian has been a European traveller, so much the worse for you. He has blushed to own—explaining, however, conquest by bribery—that 50,000 Englishmen hold 150 million of his compatriots in thrall, and for aught you know, republicanism may have become his idol. He has lost all fear of the white face, and having been accustomed to unburden his mind in

> The land where, girt by friend or foe,
> A man may say the thing he will—

he pursues the same course in other countries where it is exceedingly misplaced. His doctrines of liberty and equality he applies to you personally and practically, by not rising when you enter or leave the room—at first you could scarcely induce him to sit down—by not offering you his pipe, by turning away when you address him; in fact, by a variety of similar small affronts which none know better to manage skilfully and with almost impalpable gradations. If—and how he prays for it!—an opportunity of refusing you anything presents itself, he does it with an air.

> In rice strength,
> In an Indian manliness,

say the Arabs. And the Persians apply the following pithy tale to their neighbours. 'Brother,' said the leopard to the jackal, 'I crave a few of thy cast-off hairs; I want them for medicine (for an

[1] NOTE TO THIRD EDITION.—This was written three years before the Indian Mutiny. I also sent in to the Court of Directors a much stronger report—for which I duly suffered.

especial purpose, an urgent occasion); where can I find them?' 'Wallah!' replied the jackal, 'I don't exactly know—I seldom change my coat—I wander about the hills. Allah is bounteous.' —'Allah Karim!' said to a beggar when you do not intend to be bountiful—'brother! hairs are not so easily shed.'

Woe to the unhappy Englishman, Pasha, or private soldier, who must serve an Eastern lord! Worst of all, if the master be an Indian who, hating all Europeans, adds an especial spite to Oriental coarseness, treachery, and tyranny. Even the experiment of associating with them is almost too hard to bear. But a useful deduction may be drawn from such observations; and as few have had greater experience than myself, I venture to express my opinion with confidence, however unpopular or unfashionable it may be.

I am convinced that the natives of India cannot respect a European who mixes with them familiarly, or especially who imitates their customs, manners, and dress. The tight pantaloons, the authoritative voice, the pococurante manner, and the broken Hindostani impose upon them—have a weight which learning and honesty, which wit and courage, have not. This is to them the master's attitude: they bend to it like those Scythian slaves that faced the sword but fled from the horsewhip. Such would never be the case amongst a brave people, the Afghan for instance; and for the same reason it is not so with 'White Plume', the North American Indian. 'The free trapper combines in the eye of an Indian (American) girl, all that is dashing and heroic, in a warrior of her own race, whose gait and garb and bravery he emulates, with all that is gallant and glorious in the white man.' There is but one cause for this phenomenon: the *imbelles Indi* are still, with few exceptions, a cowardly and slavish people, who would raise themselves by depreciating those superior to them in the scale of creation. The Afghans and American aborigines, being chivalrous races, rather exaggerate the valour of their foes, because by so doing they exalt their own.

IV

Life in the Wakalah

The Wakalah, as the Caravanserai or Khan is called in Egypt, combines the offices of hotel, lodging-house, and store. It is at Cairo, as at Constantinople, a massive pile of buildings surrounding a quadrangular *Hosh*, or courtyard. On the ground-floor are rooms like caverns for merchandise, and shops of different kinds—tailors, cobblers, bakers, tobacconists, fruiterers, and others. A roofless gallery or a covered verandah, into which all the apartments open, runs round the first and sometimes the second story; the latter, however, is usually exposed to the sun and wind. The accommodations consist of sets of two or three rooms, generally an inner one and an outer; the latter contains a hearth for cooking, a bathing-place, and similar necessaries. The staircases are high, narrow, and exceedingly dirty; dark at night and often in bad repair: a goat or donkey is tethered upon the different landings; here and there a fresh skin is stretched in process of tanning, and the smell reminds the veteran traveller of those closets in the old French inns where cat used to be prepared for playing the part of jugged hare. The interior is unfurnished; even the pegs upon which clothes are hung have been pulled down for fire-wood: the walls are bare but for stains, thick cobwebs depend in festoons from the blackened rafters of the ceiling, and the stone floor would disgrace a civilised prison: the windows are huge apertures carefully barred with wood or iron, and in rare places show remains of glass or paper pasted over the framework. In the courtyard the poorer sort of travellers consort with tethered beasts of burden, beggars howl, and slaves lie basking and scratching themselves upon mountainous heaps of cotton bales and other merchandise.

This is not a tempting picture, yet is the Wakalah a most amusing place, presenting a succession of scenes which would delight the lovers of the Dutch school—a rich exemplification of the grotesque, and what is called by artists the 'dirty picturesque'.

I could find no room in the Wakalah Khan Khalil (the Long's, or Meurice's, of native Cairo); I was therefore obliged to put up with the Jemaliyah, a Greek quarter, swarming with drunken Christians, and therefore about as fashionable as Oxford Street or Covent Garden. Even for this I had to wait a week. The pilgrims were flocking to Cairo, and to none other would the prudent hotel keepers open their doors, for the following sufficient reasons. When you enter a Wakalah, the first thing you have to do is to pay a small sum, varying from 2*s.* to 5*s.*, for the *Miftah* (the key). This is generally equivalent to a month's rent; so the sooner you leave the house the better for it. I was obliged to call myself a Turkish pilgrim in order to get possession of two most comfortless rooms, which I afterwards learned were celebrated for making travellers ill; and I had to pay 18 piastres for the key and 18 ditto per mensem for rent, besides 5 piastres to the man who swept and washed the place. So that for this month my house-hire amounted to nearly fourpence a day.

But I was fortunate enough in choosing the Jemaliyah Wakalah, for I found a friend there. On board the steamer a fellow-voyager, seeing me sitting alone and therefore as he conceived in discomfort, placed himself by my side and opened a hot fire of kind inquiries. He was a man about forty-five, of middle size, with a large round head closely shaven, a bull-neck, limbs sturdy as a Saxon's, a thin red beard, and handsome features beaming with benevolence. A curious dry humour he had, delighting in quizzing, but in so quiet, solemn, and quaint a way that before you knew him you could scarcely divine his drift.

'Thank Allah, we carry a doctor!' said my friend more than once, with apparent fervour of gratitude, after he had discovered my profession. I was fairly taken in by the pious ejaculation, and some days elapsed before the drift of his remark became apparent.

'You doctors,' he explained, when we were more intimate, 'what do you do? A man goes to you for ophthalmia: it is a purge, a blister, and a drop in the eye! Is it for fever? well! a purge and Kinakina (quinine). For dysentery? a purge and extract of opium. Wallah! I am as good a physician as the best of you,' he would add with a broad grin, 'if I only knew the

Dirham-birhams—drams and drachms—and a few break-jaw Arabic names of diseases.'

Haji Wali therefore emphatically advised me to make bread by honestly teaching languages. 'We are doctor-ridden,' said he, and I found it was the case.

When we lived under the same roof, the Haji and I became fast friends. During the day we called on each other frequently, we dined together, and passed the evening in a Mosque, or some other place of public pastime. Coyly at first, but less guardedly as we grew bolder, we smoked the forbidden weed Hashish, conversing lengthily the while about that world of which I had seen so much. Originally from Russia, he also had been a traveller, and in his wanderings he had cast off most of the prejudices of his people. 'I believe in Allah and his Prophet, and in nothing else,' was his sturdy creed; he rejected alchemy, genii, and magicians, and truly he had a most unoriental distaste for tales of wonder. When I entered the Wakalah, he constituted himself my cicerone, and especially guarded me against the cheating of tradesmen. By his advice I laid aside the Dervish's gown, the large blue pantaloons, and the short shirt; in fact, all connection with Persia and the Persians.

'If you persist in being an Ajemi,' said the Haji, 'you will get yourself into trouble; in Egypt you will be cursed; in Arabia you will be beaten because you are a heretic; you will pay the treble of what other travellers do, and if you fall sick you may die by the roadside.'

After long deliberation about the choice of nations, I became a Pathan. Born in India of Afghan parents, who had settled in the country, educated at Rangoon, and sent out to wander, as men of that race frequently are, from early youth, I was well guarded against the danger of detection by a fellow-countryman. To support the character requires a knowledge of Persian, Hindostani, and Arabic, all of which I knew sufficiently well to pass muster; any trifling inaccuracy was charged upon my long residence at Rangoon. This was an important step: the first question at the shop, on the camel, and in the Mosque, is 'What is thy name?' the second, 'Whence comest thou?' This is not generally impertinent, or intended to be annoying; if, however, you see any evil intention in the questioner, you may rather roughly ask him, 'What may be his maternal parent's name'—equivalent to inquiring, *anglice*, in what church his mother was married—and escape your difficulties under cover of the storm. But this is rarely necessary. I assumed the polite, pliant manners of an Indian physician, and the dress of a small Effendi or gentleman, still, however, representing myself to be a Dervish, and frequenting the places where Dervishes congregate.

'What business', asked the Haji, 'have those reverend men with politics or statistics, or any of the information which you are collecting? Call yourself a religious wanderer if you like, and let those who ask the object of your peregrinations know that you are under a vow to visit all the holy places in El-Islam. Thus you will persuade them that you are a man of rank under a cloud, and you will receive much more civility than perhaps you deserve,' concluded my friend with a dry laugh. The remark proved his sagacity; and, after ample experience I had not to repent having been guided by his advice.

Haji Wali, by profession a merchant at Alexandria, had accompanied Khudabakhsh, the Indian, to Cairo, on law-business. He soon explained his affairs to me, and as his case brought out certain Oriental peculiarities in a striking light, with his permission I offer a few of its details.

My friend was defendant in a suit instituted against him in HBM's Consular Court, Cairo, by one Mohammed Shafia, a scoundrel of the first water. This man lived, and lived well, by setting up in business at places where his name was not known; he enticed the unwary by artful displays of capital; and, after succeeding in getting credit, he changed residence, carrying off all he could lay hands upon. But swindling is a profession of personal danger in uncivilised countries, where law punishes pauper debtors by a short imprisonment; and where the cheated prefer to gratify their revenge by the cudgel or the knife. So Mohammed Shafia, after a few narrow escapes, hit upon a prime expedient. Though known to be a native of Bokhara—he actually signed himself so in his letters, and his appearance at once bespoke his origin—he determined to protect himself by a British passport.

Our officials are sometimes careless enough in distributing these documents, and by so doing they expose themselves to certain loss of reputation at Eastern courts;[1] still Mohammed Shafia found some difficulties in effecting his fraud. To recount all his Reynardisms would weary the reader; suffice it to say that by proper management of the subalterns in the consulate, he succeeded without ruining himself. Armed with this new defence, he started boldly for Jeddah on the Arabian coast. Having entered into partnership with Haji Wali, whose confidence he had won by prayers, fastings, and pilgrimages, he openly trafficked in slaves, sending them to Alexandria for sale, and writing with matchless impudence to his correspondent that he would dispose of them in person, but for fear of losing his British passport and protection.

Presently an unlucky adventure embroiled this worthy British subject with Faraj Yusuf, the principal merchant of Jeddah, and also an English protégé. Fearing so powerful an adversary, Mohammed Shafia packed up his spoils and departed for Egypt. Presently he quarrels with his former partner, thinking him a soft man, and claims from him a debt of 165*l.* He supports his pretensions by a document and four witnesses, who are ready to swear that the receipt in question was 'signed, sealed, and delivered' by Haji Wali. The latter adduces his books to show that accounts have been settled, and can prove that the witnesses in question are paupers, therefore not legal; moreover, that each has received from the plaintiff 2 dollars, the price of perjury.

Now had such a suit been carried into a Turkish court of justice, it would very sensibly have been settled by the bastinado, for Haji Wali was a respectable merchant, and Mohammed

[1] For the simple reason that no Eastern power confers such an obligation except for value received. In old times, when official honour was not so rigorous as it is now, the creditors of Eastern powers and principalities would present high sums to British Residents and others for the privilege of being enrolled in the list of their subjects or servants. This they made profitable; for their claims, however exorbitant, when backed by a name of fear, were certain to be admitted, unless the Resident's conscience would allow of his being persuaded by weightier arguments of a similar nature to abandon his protégé.

It is almost needless to remark that nothing of the kind can occur in the present day, and at the same time that throughout the Eastern world it is firmly believed that such things are of daily occurrence. Ill fame descends to distant generations; whilst good deeds, if they blossom, as we are told, in the dust, are at least as short-lived as they are sweet.

Shafia a notorious swindler. But the latter was a British subject, which notably influenced the question. The more to annoy his adversary, he went up to Cairo, and began proceedings there, hoping by this acute step to receive part payment of his demand.

Arrived at Cairo, Mohammed Shafia applied himself stoutly to the task of bribing all who could be useful to him, distributing shawls and piastres with great generosity. He secured the services of an efficient lawyer; and, determining to enlist heaven itself in his cause, he passed the Ramazan ostentatiously; he fasted, and he slaughtered sheep to feed the poor.

Meanwhile Haji Wali, a simple truth-telling man, who could never master the rudiments of that art which teaches man to blow hot and to blow cold with the same breath, had been persuaded to visit Cairo by Khudabakhsh, the wily Indian, who promised to introduce him to influential persons, and to receive him in his house till he could provide himself with a lodging at the Wakalah. But Mohammed Shafia, who had once been in partnership with the Indian, and who possibly knew more than was fit to meet the public ear, found this out; and, partly by begging, partly by bullying, persuaded Khudabakhsh to transfer the influential introductions to himself. Then the Hakim Abdullah—your humble servant—appears upon the scene: he has travelled in Feringistan, he has seen many men and their cities, he becomes an intimate and an adviser of the Haji, and he finds out evil passages in Mohammed Shafia's life. Upon which Khudabakhsh ashamed, or rather afraid of his duplicity, collects his Indian friends. The Hakim Abdullah draws up a petition addressed to Mr Walne, HBM's Consul, by the Indian merchants and others resident at Cairo, informing him of Mohammed Shafia's birth, character, and occupation as a vendor of slaves, offering proof of all assertions, and praying him for the sake of their good name to take away his passport. And all the Indians affix their seals to this paper. Then Mohammed Shafia threatens to waylay and to beat the Haji. The Haji, not loud or hectoringly, but with a composed smile, advises his friends to hold him off.

One would suppose that such a document would have elicited some inquiry.

But Haji Wali was a Persian protégé, and proceedings between the Consulates had commenced before the petition was presented. The pseudo-British subject, having been acknowledged as a real one, must be supported. Consuls, like kings, may err, but must not own to error. No notice was taken of the Indian petition; worse still, no inquiry into the slave-affair was set on foot; and it was discovered that the passport, having been granted by a Consul-General, could not with official etiquette be resumed by a Consul. Yet at the time there was at Alexandria an acting Consul-General, to whom the case could with strict propriety have been referred.

Thus matters were destined to proceed as they began. Mohammed Shafia had offered 5,000 piastres to the Persian Consul's interpreter; this of course was refused, but still somehow or other all the Haji's affairs seemed to go wrong. His statements were mistranslated, his accounts were misunderstood, and the suit was allowed to drag on to a suspicious length. When I left Cairo in July, Haji Wali had been kept away nearly two months from his business and family, though both parties —for the plaintiff's purse was rapidly thinning—appeared eager to settle the difference by arbitration: when I returned from Arabia in October, matters were almost *in statu quo ante*, and when I started for India in January, the proceedings had not closed.

Such is a brief history, but too common, of a case in which the subject of an Eastern state has to contend against British influence. It is doubtless a point of honour to defend our protégés from injustice, but the higher principle should rest upon the base of common honesty. The worst part of such a case is, that the injured party has no redress.

Fiat in*justitia, ruat coelum,*

is the motto of his 'natural protectors', who would violate every law to gratify the false pride of a petty English official. And, saving the rare exceptions where rank or wealth command consideration, with what face, to use the native phrase, would a hapless Turk appeal to the higher powers, our ministers or our Parliament?

After lodging myself in the Wakalah, my first object was to make a certain stir in the world. In Europe your travelling doctor advertises the loss of a diamond ring, the gift of a Russian autocrat; or he monopolises a whole column in a newspaper, feeing perhaps a title for the use of a signature: the large brass plate, the gold-headed cane, the rattling chariot, and the summons from the sermon complete the work. Here, there is no such Royal Road to medical fame. You must begin by sitting with the porter, who is sure to have blear eyes, into which you drop a little nitrate of silver, whilst you instil into his ear the pleasing intelligence that you never take a fee from the poor. He recovers; his report of you spreads far and wide, crowding your doors with paupers. They come to you as though you were their servant, and when cured they turn their backs upon you for ever. Hence it is that European doctors generally complain of ingratitude on the part of their Oriental patients. It is true that if you save a man's life he naturally asks you for the means of preserving it. Moreover, in none of the Eastern languages with which I am acquainted is there a single term conveying the meaning of our 'gratitude', and none but Germans have ideas unexplainable by words. But you must not condemn this absence of a virtue without considering the cause. An Oriental deems that he has a right to your surplus. 'Daily bread is divided' (by heaven), he asserts, and eating yours, he considers it his own.

Thus it is with other things. He is thankful to Allah for the gifts of the Creator, but he has a claim to the good offices of a fellow-creature. In rendering him a service you have but done your duty, and he would not pay you so poor a compliment as to praise you for the act. He leaves you, his benefactor, with a short prayer for the length of your days. 'Thank you,' being expressed by 'Allah increase thy weal!' or the selfish wish that your shadow (with which you protect him and his fellows) may never be less. And this is probably the last you hear of him.

There is a discomfort in such proceedings, a reasonable, a metaphysical coldness, uglily contrasting in theory with the genial warmth which a little more heart would infuse into them. In theory, I say, not in practice. What can be more troublesome than, when you have obliged a man, to run the gauntlet of his and his family's thanksgivings, to find yourself become a master from being a friend, a great man when you were an equal; not to be contradicted, where shortly before every one gave his opinion freely? You must be unamiable if these considerations deter you from benefiting your friend; yet, I humbly opine, you still may fear his gratefulness.

To resume. When the mob has raised you to fame, patients of a better class will slowly appear on the scene. After some coquetting about etiquette, whether you are to visit them, or they are to call upon you, they make up their minds to see you, and to judge with their eyes whether you are to be trusted or not; whilst you, on your side, set out with the determination that they shall at once cross the Rubicon—in less classical phrase, swallow your drug.

If you visit the house, you insist upon the patient's servants attending you; he must also provide and pay an ass for your conveyance, no matter if it be only to the other side of the street. Your confidential man accompanies you, primed for replies to the fifty searching questions of the servants' hall. You are lifted off the saddle tenderly, as nurses dismount their charges, when you arrive at the gate; and you waddle upstairs with dignity. Arrived at the sick room, you salute those present with a general 'Peace be upon you!' to which they respond, 'And unto thee be the peace and the mercy of Allah, and his blessing!' To the invalid you say, 'There is nothing the matter, please Allah, except the health'; to which the proper answer—for here every sign of ceremony has its countersign—is, 'May Allah give thee health!' Then you sit down, and acknowledge the presence of the company by raising your right hand to your lips and forehead, bowing the while circularly; each individual returns the civility by a similar gesture. Then inquiry about the state of your health ensues. Then you are asked what refreshment you will take; you studiously mention something not likely to be in the house, but at last you rough it with a pipe and a cup of coffee. Then you proceed to the patient, who extends his wrist, and asks you what his complaint is. Then you examine his tongue, you feel his pulse, you look learned, and—he is talking all the time—after hearing a detailed list of all his ailments, you gravely discover them, taking for the same as much praise to yourself as does the practising phrenologist for a similar simple exercise of the reasoning faculties.

The disease, to be respectable, must invariably be connected with one of the four temperaments, or the four elements, or the 'humours of Hippocrates'. Cure is easy, but it will take time, and you, the doctor, require attention; any little rudeness it is in your power to punish by an alteration in the pill, or the powder, and, so unknown is professional honour, that none will brave your displeasure.

If you would pass for a native practitioner, you must finally proceed to the most uncomfortable part of your visit, bargaining for fees. Nothing more effectually arouses suspicion than disinterestedness in a doctor. I once cured a rich Hazramaut merchant of rheumatism, and neglected to make him pay for treatment; he carried off one of my coffee cups, and was unceasingly wondering where I came from. So I made him produce 5 piastres, 1*s*., which he threw upon the carpet, cursing Indian avarice. 'You will bring on another illness,' said my friend, the Haji, when he heard of it. Properly speaking, the fee for a visit to a respectable man is 20 piastres, but with the rich patient you begin by making a bargain. He complains, for instance, of dysentery and sciatica. You demand 10*l*. for the dysentery, and 20*l*. for the sciatica. But you will rarely get it.

The Eastern pays a doctor's bill as an Oirishman does his 'rint', making a grievance of it. Your patient will show indisputable signs of convalescence: he will laugh and jest half the day; but the moment you appear, groans and a lengthened visage, and pretended complaints, welcome you. Then your way is to throw out some such hint as

> The world is a carcase, and they who seek it are dogs.

And you refuse to treat the second disorder, which conduct may bring the refractory one to his senses.

Dat Galenus opes, however, is a Western apothegm; the utmost 'Jalinus' can do for you here is to provide you with the necessaries and the comforts of life. Whatever you prescribe must be solid and material, and if you accompany it with something painful, such as rubbing to scarification with a horse-brush, so much the better. Easterns, like our peasants in Europe, wish the doctor to 'give them the value of their money'. Besides which, rough measures act beneficially upon their imagination. So the Hakim of the King of Persia cured fevers by the bastinado; patients are beneficially baked in a bread-oven at Baghdad; and an Egyptian at Alexandria, whose quartan resisted the strongest appliances of European physic, was effectually healed by the actual cautery, which a certain Arab Shaykh applied to the crown of his head.

When you administer with your own hand the remedy—half a dozen huge bread pills, dipped in a solution of aloes or cinnamon water, flavoured with assafoetida, which in the case of the dyspeptic rich often suffice, if they will but diet themselves—you are careful to say, 'In the name of Allah, the Compassionate, the Merciful.' And after the patient has been dosed, 'Praise be to Allah, the Curer, the Healer'; you then call for pen, ink, and paper, and write some such prescription as this:

A.[1]

> In the name of Allah, the Compassionate, the Merciful, and blessings and peace be upon our Lord the Apostle, and his family, and his companions one and all! But afterwards let him take bees-honey and cinnamon and album graecum, of each half a part, and of ginger a whole part, which let him pound and mix with the honey, and form boluses, each bolus the weight of a Miskal, and of it let him use every day a Miskal on the saliva (that is to say, fasting, the first thing in morning). Verily its effects are wonderful. And let him abstain from flesh, fish, vegetables, sweetmeats, flatulent food, acids of all descriptions, as well as the major ablution, and live in perfect quiet. So shall he be cured by the help of the King, the Healer, i.e. the Almighty. And the peace (w'as-salam, i.e. adieu).

[1] A monogram generally placed at the head of writings. It is the initial letter of 'Allah', and the first of the alphabet, used from time immemorial to denote the origin of creation. 'I am Alpha and Omega, the first and the last.'

The diet, I need scarcely say, should be rigorous; nothing has tended more to bring the European system of medicine into contempt among Orientals than our inattention to this branch of the therapeutic art. When a Hindi or a Hindu takes medicine, he prepares himself for it by diet and rest two or three days before adhibition, and as gradually, after the dose, he relapses into his usual habits; if he break through the regime it is concluded that fatal results must ensue. The ancient Egyptians we learn from Herodotus devoted a certain number of days in each month to the use of alteratives, and the period was consecutive, doubtless in order to graduate the strength of the medicine. The Persians, when under salivation, shut themselves up in a warm room, never undress, and so carefully guard against cold that they even drink tepid water. When the Afghan princes find it necessary to employ Chob-Chini (the Jin-seng, or China root so celebrated as a purifier, tonic, and aphrodisiac), they choose the spring season; they remove to a garden, where flowers and trees and bubbling streams soothe their senses; they carefully avoid fatigue and trouble of all kinds, and will not even hear a letter read, lest it should contain bad news.

When the prescription is written out, you affix an impression of your ring seal to the beginning and to the end of it, that no one may be able to add to or to take from its contents. And when you send medicine to a patient of rank, who is sure to have enemies, you adopt some similar precaution against the box or the bottle being opened.

One of the Pashas whom I attended—a brave soldier who had been a favourite with Mohammed Ali, and therefore was degraded by his successor—kept an impression of my ring in wax, to compare with that upon the phials. Men have not forgotten how frequently, in former times, those who became obnoxious to the State were seized with sudden and fatal cramps in the stomach. In the case of the doctor it is common prudence to adopt these precautions, as all evil consequences would be charged upon him, and he would be exposed to the family's revenge.

Cairo, though abounding in medical practitioners, can still support more; but to thrive they must be Indians, Chinese, or

Maghrabis. The Egyptians are thoroughly disgusted with European treatment, which is here about as efficacious as in India — that is to say, not at all. But they are ignorant of the medicine of Hind, and therefore great is its name; deservedly perhaps, for skill in simples and dietetics. Besides which the Indian may deal in charms and spells—things to which the latitude gives such force that even Europeans learn to put faith in them. The traveller who, on the banks of the Seine, scoffs at Sights and Sounds, Table-turning and Spirit-rapping, sees, in the wilds of Tartary and Tibet, a something supernatural and diabolical in the bungling Sie-fa of the Bokte.[1] Some sensible men, who pass for philosophers among their friends, have been caught by the incantations of the turbaned and bearded Cairo magician. In our West African colonies the phrase 'growing black' was applied to colonists, who, after a term of residence, become thoroughly imbued with the superstitions of the land. And there are not wanting old Anglo-Indians, intelligent men, that place firm trust in tales and tenets too puerile even for the Hindus to believe.

As a 'Hindi' I could use animal magnetism, taking care, however, to give the science a specious supernatural appearance. Haji Wali, who, professing positive scepticism, showed the greatest interest in the subject as a curiosity, advised me not to practise pure mesmerism; otherwise that I should infallibly become a 'Companion of Devils'. 'You must call this an Indian secret,' said my friend, 'for it is clear that you are no Mashaikh (holy man), and people will ask, where are your drugs, and what business have you with charms?' It is useless to say that I followed his counsel; yet patients would consider themselves my disciples, and delighted in kissing the hand of the Sahib Nafas[2] or minor saint.

The Haji repaid me for my docility by vaunting me everywhere as the very phoenix of physicians. My first successes were

[1] See M. Huc's *Travels*.

[2] A title literally meaning the Master of Breath, one who can cure ailments, physical as well as spiritual, by breathing upon them—a practice well known to mesmerists. The reader will allow me to observe (in self-defence, otherwise he might look suspiciously upon so credulous a narrator), that when speaking of animal magnetism, as a thing established, I allude to the lower phenomena, rejecting the discussion of all disputed points, as the existence of a magnetic Aura, and of all its unintelligibilities—Prevision, Introvision, and other divisions of Clairvoyance.

in the Wakalah; opposite to me there lived an Arab slave-dealer, whose Abyssinians constantly fell sick. A tender race, they suffer when first transported to Egypt from many complaints, especially consumption, dysentery, and varicose veins. I succeeded in curing one girl. As she was worth at least 15*l.*, the gratitude of her owner was great, and I had to dose half a dozen others in order to cure them of the pernicious and price-lowering habit of snoring. Living in rooms opposite these slave-girls, and seeing them at all hours of the day and night, I had frequent opportunities of studying them. They were average specimens of the steatopygous Abyssinian breed, broad-shouldered, thin-flanked, fine-limbed, and with haunches of a prodigious size. None of them had handsome features, but the short curly hair that stands on end being concealed under a kerchief, there was something pretty in the brow, eyes, and upper part of the nose, coarse and sensual in the pendent lips, large jowl and projecting mouth, whilst the whole had a combination of piquancy with sweetness. Their style of flirtation was peculiar.

'How beautiful thou art, O Maryam!—what eyes!—what—'

'Then why'—would respond the lady—'don't you buy me?'

'We are of one faith—of one creed—formed to form each other's happiness.'

'Then why don't you buy me?'

'Conceive, O Maryam, the blessing of two hearts—'

'Then why don't you buy me?'

and so on. Most effectual gag to Cupid's eloquence! Yet was not the plain-spoken Maryam's reply without its moral. How often is it our fate in the West, as in the East, to see in bright eyes and to hear from rosy lips an implied, if not an expressed, 'Why don't you buy me?' or, worse still, 'Why *can't* you buy me?'

All I required in return for my services from the slave-dealer, whose brutal countenance and manners were truly repugnant, was to take me about the town, and explain to me certain mysteries in his craft, which knowledge might be useful in time to come. I have, however, nothing new to report concerning the present state of bondsmen in Egypt. England has already learned that slaves are not necessarily the most wretched and degraded of men. Some have been bold enough to tell the British public that, in the generality of Oriental countries,[1] the serf fares far better than the servant, or indeed than the poorer orders of freemen. 'The laws of Mahomet enjoin his followers to treat slaves with the greatest mildness, and the Moslems are in general scrupulous observers of the Apostle's recommendation. Slaves are considered members of the family, and in houses where free servants are also kept, they seldom do any other work than filling the pipes, presenting the coffee, accompanying their master when going out, rubbing his feet when he takes his nap in the afternoon, and driving away the flies from him. When a slave is not satisfied, he can legally compel his master to sell him. He has no care for food, lodging, clothes and washing, and has no taxes to pay; he is exempt from military service and soccage, and in spite of his bondage is freer than the freest Fellah in Egypt.' This is, I believe, a true statement, but of course it in nowise affects the question of slavery in the abstract. A certain amount of reputation was the consequence of curing the Abyssinian girls: my friend Haji Wali carefully told the news to all the town, and before fifteen days were over I found myself obliged to decline extending a practice which threatened me with fame.

Servants are most troublesome things to all Englishmen in Egypt, but especially to one travelling as a respectable native, and therefore expected to have slaves. After much deliberation, I resolved to take a Berberi, or native of Upper Egypt, and accordingly summoned a Shaykh—there is a Shaykh for every thing down to thieves in Asia—and made known my want. The list of *sine qua non*s was necessarily rather extensive, good health and a readiness to travel anywhere, a little skill in cooking, sewing, and washing, willingness to fight, and a habit of regular prayers.

After a day's delay the Shaykh brought me a specimen of his choosing, a broad-shouldered, bandy-legged fellow, with the

[1] In the generality, not in all. Nothing, for instance, can be more disgraceful to human nature than the state of praedial slavery, or serfs attached to the glebe, when Malabar was under the dominion of the 'mild Hindu'. And as a rule in the East it is only the domestic slaves who taste the sweets of slavery. Yet there is truth in Sonnini's terrible remark: 'The severe treatment under which the slaves languish in the West Indies is the shameful prerogative of civilisation, and is unknown to those nations among whom barbarism is reported to hold sway.'—*Travels in Upper and Lower Egypt*, vol. ii.

usual bull-dog expression of the Berberis, in his case rendered doubly expressive by the drooping of an eyelid—an accident brought about with acrid juice in order to avoid conscription. He responded sturdily to all my questions. Some Egyptian donkey-boys and men were making a noise in the room at the time, and the calm ferocity with which he ejected them commanded my approval. When a needle, thread, and an unhemmed napkin were handed to him, he sat down, held the edge of the cloth between his big toe and its neighbour, and finished the work in superior style. Walking out, he armed himself with a Kurbaj, which he used, now lightly, then heavily, upon all laden animals, biped and quadruped, that came in the way. His conduct proving equally satisfactory in the kitchen; after getting security from him, and having his name registered by the Shaykh, who becomes responsible, and must pay for any theft his protégé may commit, I closed with him for 80 piastres a month. But Ali the Berberi and I were destined to part. Before a fortnight he stabbed his fellow-servant, a Surat lad, who wishing to return home forced his services upon me; and for this trick he received, with his dismissal, 400 blows on the feet by order of the Zabit, or police magistrate.

After this failure I tried a number of servants, Egyptians, Saidis, and clean and unclean eating Berberis. Recommended by different Shaykhs, all had some fatal defect; one cheated recklessly, another robbed me, a third drank, a fourth was always in scrapes for infringing the Julian edict, and the last, a long-legged Nubian, after remaining two days in the house, dismissed me for expressing a determination to travel by sea from Suez to Yambu'. I kept one man; he complained that he was worked to death; two, they did nothing but fight; and three, they left me, as Mr Elwes said of old, to serve myself.

At last, thoroughly tired of Egyptian domestics, and one servant being really sufficient for comfort, as well as suitable to my assumed rank, I determined to keep only the Indian boy. He had all the defects of his nation; a brave at Cairo, he was an arrant coward at El-Medinah; and the Bedawin despised him heartily for his effeminacy in making his camel kneel to dismount. But the choice had its advantages: his swarthy skin and chubby features made the Arabs always call him an Abyssinian slave, which, as it favoured my disguise, I did not care to contradict; he served well, he was amenable to discipline, and, being completely dependent upon me, he was therefore less likely to watch and especially to prate about my proceedings.

As master and man we performed the pilgrimage together; but, on my return to Egypt after the pilgrimage, Shaykh, become Haji, Nur, finding me to be a Sahib, or English officer, changed for the worse. He would not work, and he reserved all his energy for the purpose of pilfering, which he practised so audaciously upon my friends, as well as upon myself, that he could not be kept in the house.

Perhaps the reader may be curious to see the necessary expenses of a bachelor residing at Cairo. He must observe, however, in the following list that I was not a strict economist, and, besides that, I was a stranger in the country: inhabitants and old settlers would live as well for little more than two-thirds the sum.

		Piastres	Faddeh
House rent at 18 piastres per mensem		0	24
Servant at 80 piastres per mensem		2	26
Breakfast for self and servant	10 eggs	0	5
	Coffee	0	10
	Water-melon	1	0
	Two rolls of bread	0	10
Dinner	2 lb. of meat	2	20
	Two rolls of bread	0	10
	Vegetables	0	20
	Rice	0	5
	Oil and clarified butter	1	0
Sundries	A skin of Nile water	1	0
	Tobacco	1	0
	Hammam (hot bath)	3	20
	Total	12	50

Equal to about 2*s*. 6*d*.

In these days who at Cairo without a Shaykh? I thought it right to conform to popular custom, and accordingly, after having secured a servant, my efforts were directed to finding a teacher; the pretext being that as an Indian doctor I wanted to read Arabic works on medicine, as well as to perfect myself in divinity and pronunciation. My theological studies were in the Shafei school for two reasons: in the first place, it is the least rigorous of the Four Orthodox, and, secondly, it most resembles the Shiah heresy, with which long intercourse with Persians had made me familiar. My choice of doctrine, however, confirmed those around me in their conviction that I was a rank heretic, for the Ajemi, taught by his religion to conceal offensive tenets in lands where the open expression would be dangerous, always represents himself to be a Shafei. This, together with the original mistake of appearing publicly at Alexandria as a Mirza in a Persian dress, caused me infinite small annoyance at Cairo, in spite of all precautions and contrivances. And throughout my journey, even in Arabia, though I drew my knife every time an offensive hint was thrown out, the ill fame clung to me like the shirt of Nessus.

It was not long before I happened to hit upon a proper teacher, in the person of Shaykh Mohammed el-Attar, or the 'Druggist'. He had known prosperity, having once been a Khatib (preacher) in one of Mohammed Ali's mosques. But HH the late Pasha had dismissed him, which disastrous event, with its subsequent train of misfortunes, he dates from the melancholy day when he took to himself a wife. He talks of her abroad as a stern and rigid master dealing with a naughty slave, though, by the look that accompanies his rhodomontade, I am convinced that at home he is the very model of 'managed men'. His dismissal was the reason that compelled him to fall back upon the trade of a druggist, the refuge for the once wealthy, though now destitute, Sages of Egypt.

His little shop in the Jemaliyah Quarter is a perfect gem of Nilotic queerness. A hole about five feet long and six deep, pierced in the wall of some house, it is divided into two compartments, separated by a thin partition of wood, and communicating by a kind of arch cut in the boards. The inner box, germ of a back parlour, acts as store-room, as the pile of empty old baskets tossed in dusty confusion upon the dirty floor shows.

In the front is displayed the stock in trade, a matting full of Persian tobacco and pipe-bowls of red clay, a palm-leaf bag, containing vile coffee and large lumps of coarse, whity-brown sugar wrapped up in browner paper. On the shelves and ledges are rows of well-thumbed wooden boxes, labelled with the greatest carelessness, pepper for rhubarb, arsenic for Tafl, or wash-clay, and sulphate of iron where sal-ammoniac should be.

There is also a square case containing, under lock and key, small change and some choice articles of commerce, damaged perfumes, bad antimony for the eyes, and pernicious rouge. And dangling close above it is a rusty pair of scales, ill poised enough for Egyptian Themis herself to use.

To hooks over the shop front are suspended reeds for pipes, tallow candles, dirty wax tapers and cigarette paper: instead of plate-glass windows and brass-handled doors, a ragged net keeps away the flies when the master is in, and the thieves when he goes out to recite in the Hasanayn mosque his daily chapter, 'Ya Sin'. A wooden shutter which closes down at night-time, and by day two palm-stick stools intensely dirty and full of fleas, occupying the place of the Mastabah or earthen bench,[1] which accommodated purchasers, complete the furniture of my preceptor's establishment.

There he sits, or rather lies (for verily I believe he sleeps through three-fourths of the day), a thin old man, about fifty-eight, with features once handsome and regular; a sallow face, shaven head, deeply wrinkled cheeks, eyes hopelessly bleared, and a rough grey beard ignorant of oil and comb. His turban, though large, is brown with wear; his coat and small-clothes display many a hole; and, though his face and hands must be frequently washed preparatory to devotion, still they have the quality of looking always unclean.

It is wonderful how fierce and gruff he is to the little boys

[1] The Mastabah here is a long earthen bench plastered over with clay, and raised about two feet from the ground, so as to bring the purchaser's head to a level with the shop. Mohammed Ali ordered the people to remove them, as they narrowed the streets; their place is now supplied by Kafas, cages or stools of wicker-work.

and girls who flock to him grasping farthings for pepper and sugar. On such occasions I sit admiring to see him, when forced to exertion, wheel about on his place, making a pivot of that portion of our organisation which mainly distinguishes our species from the other families of the Simiadae, to reach some distant drawer, or to pull down a case from its accustomed shelf. How does he manage to say his prayers, to kneel and to prostrate himself upon that two feet of ragged rug, scarcely sufficient for a British infant to lie upon? He hopelessly owns that he knows nothing of his craft, and the seats before his shop are seldom occupied. His great pleasure appears to be when the Haji and I sit by him a few minutes in the evening, bringing with us pipes, which he assists us to smoke, and ordering coffee, which he insists upon sweetening with a lump of sugar from his little store. There we make him talk and laugh, and occasionally quote a few lines strongly savouring of the jovial: we provoke him to long stories about the love borne him in his student-days by the great and holy Shaykh Abd el-Rahman, and the antipathy with which he was regarded by the equally great and holy Shaykh Nasr el-Din, his memorable single imprisonment for contumacy, and the temperate but effective lecture, beginning with 'O almost entirely destitute of shame!' delivered on that occasion in presence of other undergraduates by the Right Reverend principal of his college.

Then we consult him upon matters of doctrine, and quiz him tenderly about his powers of dormition, and flatter him, or rather his age, with such phrases as, 'The water from thy hand is of the Waters of Zem Zem'; or, 'We have sought thee to deserve the Blessings of the Wise upon our undertakings.' Sometimes, with interested motives it must be owned, we induce him to accompany us to the Hammam, where he insists upon paying the smallest sum, quarrelling with every thing and every body, and giving the greatest trouble. We are generally his only visitors: acquaintances he appears to have few, and no friends; he must have had them once, for he was rich, but is not now, so they have fallen away from the poor old man.

When the Shaykh Mohammed sits with me, or I climb up into his little shop for the purpose of receiving a lesson from him, he is quite at his ease, reading when he likes, or making me read, and generally beginning each lecture with some such preamble as this:

Aywa! aywa! aywa!—'Even so, even so, even so! we take refuge with Allah from the Stoned Fiend! In the name of Allah, the Compassionate, the Merciful, and the Blessings of Allah upon our Lord Mohammed, and his Family and his Companions one and all! Thus saith the author, may Almighty Allah have mercy upon him! "Section I of chapter two, upon the orders of prayer", etc.'

He becomes fiercely sarcastic when I differ with him in opinion, especially upon a point of grammar, or the theology over which his beard has grown grey.

Subhan Allah! ('Allah be glorified!') This is of course ironical: 'Allah be praised for creating such a prodigy of learning as thou art!' What words are these? 'If thou be right, enlarge thy turban (i.e. set up as a learned man)[1] and throw away thy drugs, for verily it is better to quicken men's souls than to destroy their bodies, O Abdullah!'

Oriental-like, he revels in giving good counsel.

'Thou art always writing, O my brave!' (this is said on the few occasions when I venture to make a note in my book); 'what evil habit is this? Surely thou hast learned it in the lands of the Frank. Repent!'

He loathes my giving medical advice gratis.

'Thou hast two servants to feed, O my son! The doctors of Egypt never write A, B, without a reward. Wherefore art thou ashamed? Better go and sit upon the mountain at once (i.e. go to the desert) and say thy prayers day and night!'

And finally he is prodigal of preaching upon the subject of household expenses.

'Thy servant did write down two pounds of flesh yesterday! What words are these, O he?'—*Ya hu*, a common interpellative, not, perhaps, of the politest description. 'Dost thou never say, "Guard us, Allah, from the sin of extravagance"?'

[1] The larger the turban, the greater are the individual's pretensions to religious knowledge and respectability of demeanour. This is the custom in Egypt, Turkey, Persia, and many other parts of the Moslem world.

He delights also in abruptly interrupting a serious subject when it begins to weigh upon his spirits. For instance,

'Now the waters of ablution being of seven different kinds, it results that—hast thou a wife?'

'No.'

'Then verily thou must buy thee a female slave, O youth! This conduct is not right, and men will say of thee—Repentance: I take refuge with Allah!—"of a truth his mouth watereth for the spouses of other Moslems." '

But sometimes he nods over a difficult passage under my very eyes, or he reads it over a dozen times in the wantonness of idleness, or he takes what schoolboys call a long shot most shamelessly at the signification. When this happens I lose my temper, and raise my voice, and shout, 'Verily there is no power nor might save in Allah, the High, the Great!' Then he looks at me, and with passing meekness whispers— 'Fear Allah, O man!'

V

The Ramazan

This year the Ramazan befell in June, and a fearful infliction was that 'blessed month', making the Moslem unhealthy and unamiable. For the space of sixteen consecutive hours and a quarter, we were forbidden to eat, drink, smoke, snuff, and even to swallow our saliva designedly. I say forbidden, for although the highest orders of Turks—the class is popularly described as

Turco fino
Mangia porco e beve vino—

may break the ordinance in strict privacy, popular opinion would condemn any open infraction of it with uncommon severity. In this, as in most human things, how many are there who hold that

Pécher en secret n'est pas pécher,
Ce n'est que l'éclat qui fait le crime?

The middle and lower ranks observe the duties of the season, however arduous, with exceeding zeal: of all who suffered severely from such total abstinence, I found but one patient who would eat even to save his life. And among the vulgar, sinners who habitually drink when they should pray, will fast and perform their devotions through the Ramazan.

Like the Italian, the Anglo-Catholic and the Greek fasts, the chief effect of the 'blessed month' upon True Believers is to darken their tempers into positive gloom. Their voices, never of the softest, acquire, especially after noon, a terribly harsh and creaking tone. The men curse one another, and beat the women. The women slap and abuse the children, and these in their turn cruelly entreat, and use bad language to, the dogs and cats. You can scarcely spend ten minutes in any populous part of the city without hearing some violent dispute. The Karakun, or station-houses, are filled with lords who have administered an undue dose of chastisement to their ladies, and with ladies who have scratched, bitten, and otherwise injured the bodies of their lords. The Mosques are crowded with a sulky, grumbling population, making themselves offensive to one another on earth, whilst working their way to heaven; and in the shade, under the outer walls, the little boys who have been expelled the church attempt to forget their miseries in spiritless play.

In the bazars and streets, pale long-drawn faces, looking for the most part intolerably cross, catch your eye, and at this season a stranger will sometimes meet with positive incivility. A shopkeeper, for instance, usually says when he rejects an insufficient offer, *Yaftah Allah*, 'Allah opens' (the door of daily bread): it is a polite way of informing a man that you and he are not likely to do business; in other words, that you are not in want of his money. During the Ramazan, he will grumble about the bore of Ghashim (Johnny raws), and gruffly tell you not to stand there wasting his time. But as a rule the shops are either shut or destitute of shopmen, merchants will not purchase, and students will not study. In fine, the Ramazan, for many classes, is one-twelfth of the year wantonly thrown away.

The following is the routine of a fast-day. About half an hour after midnight, the gun sounds its warning to faithful men that it is time to prepare for the Sahur (early breakfast). My servant then wakes me, if I have slept; brings water for ablution, spreads the Sufrah or leather cloth, and places before me certain remnants of the evening's meal. It is some time before the stomach becomes accustomed to such hours, but in matters of appetite, habit is everything, and for health's sake one should strive to eat as plentifully as possible. Then sounds the Salam, or Blessings on the Prophet, an introduction to the Call of Morning Prayer. Smoking sundry pipes with tenderness, as if taking leave of a friend; and until the second gun, fired at about half-past two a.m., gives the Imsak—the order to abstain from food—I await the Azan, or summons to prayer, which in this month is called somewhat earlier than usual. Then, after a ceremony termed the Niyat (purpose) of fasting, I say my prayers, and prepare for repose. At seven a.m. the labours of the day begin for the working classes of society: the rich spend the night in revelling, and rest in down from dawn till noon.

The first thing on rising is to perform the Wuzu, or lesser ablution, which invariably follows sleep in a reclining position; without this it would be improper to pray, to enter the Mosques, to approach a religious man, or to touch the Koran. A few pauper patients usually visit me at this hour, report the phenomena of their complaints—which they do, by-the-bye, with unpleasant minuteness of detail—and receive fresh instructions. At nine a.m. Shaykh Mohammed enters, with 'lecture' written upon his wrinkled brow; or I pick him up on the way, and proceed straight to the Mosque El-Azhar.

After three hours' hard reading, with little interruption from bystanders, most of the students being at home, comes the call to midday prayer. The founder of El-Islam ordained but few devotions for the morning, which is the business part of the Eastern day; but during the afternoon and evening they succeed one another rapidly, and their length increases. It is then time to visit my rich patients, and afterwards, by way of accustoming myself to the sun, to wander among the bookshops for an hour or two, or simply to idle in the street. At three p.m. I return home, recite the afternoon prayers, and re-apply myself to study.

This is the worst part of the day. In Egypt the summer nights and mornings are, generally speaking, pleasant, but the forenoons are sultry, and the afternoons are serious. A wind wafting the fine dust and furnace-heat of the desert blows over the city; the ground returns with interest the showers of caloric from above, and not a cloud or a vapour breaks the dreary expanse of splendour on high. There being no such comforts as Indian tatties, and few but the wealthiest houses boasting glass windows, the interior of your room is somewhat more fiery than the street.

Weakened with fasting, the body feels the heat trebly, and the disordered stomach almost affects the brain. Every minute is counted with morbid fixity of idea as it passes on towards the blessed sunset, especially by those whose terrible lot is manual labour at such a season.

A few try to forget their afternoon miseries in slumber, but most people take the Kaylulah, or Siesta, shortly after the meridian, holding it unwholesome to sleep late in the day.

As the Maghrib, the sunset hour, approaches—and how slowly it comes!—the town seems to recover from a trance. People flock to the windows and balconies, in order to watch the moment of their release. Some pray, others tell their beads; while others, gathering together in groups or paying visits, exert themselves to while away the lagging time.

O gladness! at length it sounds, that gun from the citadel. Simultaneously rises the sweet cry of the Muezzin, calling men to prayer, and the second cannon booms from the Abbasiyyah Palace—*Al Fitar! al Fitar!* 'fast-breaking! fast-breaking!' shout the people, and a hum of joy rises from the silent city. Your acute ears waste not a moment in conveying the delightful intelligence to your parched tongue, empty stomach, and languid limbs. You exhaust a pot full of water, no matter its size. You clap hurried hands for a pipe; you order coffee; and, provided with these comforts, you sit down, and calmly contemplate the coming pleasures of the evening.

Poor men eat heartily at once. The rich break their fast with a light meal, a little bread and fruit, fresh or dry, especially water-melon, sweetmeats, or such digestible dishes as Muhallabah, a thin jelly of milk, starch, and rice-flour. They then smoke a pipe, drink a cup of coffee or a glass of sherbet, and recite the evening prayers; for the devotions of this hour are delicate things; and while smoking a first pipe after sixteen hours' abstinence, time easily slips away. Then they sit down to the Fatur (breakfast), *the* meal of the twenty-four hours, and eat plentifully, if they would avoid illness.

There are many ways of spending a Ramazan evening. The Egyptians have a proverb, like ours of the Salernitan school:

> After El-Ghada (early dinner) rest, if it be but for two moments:
> After El-Asha (early supper) walk, if it be but two steps.

The streets are now crowded with a good-humoured throng of strollers; the many bent on pleasure, the few wending their way to mosque, where the Imam recites Tarawih or extra prayers. They saunter about, the accustomed pipe in hand, shopping, for the stalls are open till a late hour; or they sit in crowds at the coffee-house entrance, smoking Shishahs (water-pipes), chatting, and listening to story-tellers, singers, and itinerant preachers. Here, a barefooted girl trills and quavers, accompanied by a noisy tambourine and a 'scrannel pipe' of abominable discordance, in honour of a perverse saint whose corpse insisted upon being buried inside some respectable man's dwelling-house. The scene reminds you strongly of the Sonneurs of Brittany and the Zampognari from the Abruzzian Highlands bagpiping before the Madonna. There, a tall gaunt Maghrabi displays, upon a square yard of dirty paper, certain lines and blots, supposed to represent the venerable Kaabah, and collects coppers to defray the expenses of his pilgrimage.

A steady stream of loungers sets through the principal thoroughfares towards the Ezbekiyeh Gardens, which skirt the Frank quarter: there they sit in the moonlight, listening to Greek and Turkish bands, or making merry with cakes, toasted grains, coffee, sugared drinks, and the broad pleasantries of Kara Gyuz, the local Punch and Judy. Here the scene is less thoroughly Oriental than within the city; but the appearance of Frank dress amongst the varieties of Eastern costume, the moonlit sky, and the light mist hanging over the deep shade of the Acacia trees—whose rich scented yellow-white blossoms are popularly compared to the old Pasha's beard—make it passing picturesque. And the traveller from the far East remarks with wonder the presence of certain ladies, whose only mark of modesty is the Burka, or face-veil: upon this laxity the police looks with lenient eyes, inasmuch as, until very lately, it paid a respectable tax to the State.

Returning to the Moslem quarter, you are bewildered by its variety of sounds. Every one talks, and talking here is always in extremes, either in a whisper, or in a scream; gesticulation excites the lungs, and strangers cannot persuade themselves that men so converse without being or becoming furious.

All the street cries, too, are in the soprano key. 'In thy protection! in thy protection!' shouts a Fellah peasant to a sentinel, who is flogging him towards the station-house, followed by a tail of women, screaming, *Yá Ghárati—yá Dahwati—yá Hasratí—yá Nidámití*—'O my calamity! O my shame!' The boys have elected a Pasha, whom they are conducting in procession, with wisps of straw for Mashals, or cressets, and outrunners, all huzzaing with ten-schoolboy power.

'O thy right! O thy left! O thy face! O thy heel! O thy back, thy back!' cries the panting footman, who, huge torch on shoulder, runs before the grandee's carriage; 'Bless the Prophet, and get out of the way!'

'O Allah bless him!' respond the good Moslems, some shrinking up to the walls to avoid the stick, others rushing across the road, so as to give themselves every chance of being knocked down. The donkey-boy beats his ass with a heavy palm-cudgel —he fears no treadmill here—cursing him at the top of his voice for a 'pander', a 'Jew', a 'Christian', and a 'son of the One-eyed, whose portion is Eternal Punishment'. 'O chick pease! O pips!' sings the vendor of parched grains, rattling the unsavoury load in his basket.

'Out of the way, and say, "There is one God", ' pants the industrious water-carrier, laden with a skin, fit burden for a buffalo. 'Sweet-water, and gladden thy soul, O lemonade!' pipes the seller of that luxury, clanging his brass cups together.

Then come the beggars, intensely Oriental. 'My supper is in Allah's hands, my supper is in Allah's hands! whatever thou givest, that will go with thee!' chants the old vagrant, whose wallet perhaps contains more provision than the basket of many a respectable shopkeeper. *Na'l abuk*,[1] 'O brother of a naughty sister!' is the response of some petulant Greek to the touch of the old man's staff.

'The grave is darkness, and good deeds are its lamp!' sing the blind women, rapping two sticks together: 'Upon Allah! upon Allah! O daughter!' cry the bystanders, when the obstinate 'bint' (daughter) of sixty years seizes their hands, and will not let go without extorting a farthing. 'Bring the sweet (i.e. fire), and take the full (i.e. empty cup, euphemistically),' cry the long-moustached, fierce-browed Arnauts to the coffee-house keeper, who stands by them charmed by the rhyming repartee that flows so readily from their lips.

[1] For *La'n abuk*, 'curse thy father'. So in Europe pious men have sworn *per diem*, instead of *per Deum*, and 'drat' acts for something stronger.

Hanien, 'May it be pleasant to thee!' is the signal for encounter.

'Thou drinkest for *ten*,' replies the other, instead of returning the usual religious salutation.

'I am the cock and thou art the *hen*!' is the rejoinder—a tart one.

'Nay, I am the thick one and thou art the *thin*!' resumes the first speaker, and so on till they come to equivoques which will not bear a literal English translation.

And sometimes, high above the hubbub, rises the melodious voice of the blind muezzin, who, from his balcony in the beetling tower, rings forth, 'Hie ye to devotion! Hie ye to salvation! Devotion is better than sleep! Devotion is better than sleep!' Then good Moslems piously stand up, and mutter, previous to prayer, 'Here am I at Thy call, O Allah! here am I at Thy call!'

Sometimes I walked with my friend to the citadel, and sat upon a high wall, one of the outworks of Mohammed Ali's mosque, enjoying a view which, seen by night when the summer moon is near the full, has a charm no power of language can embody. Or, escaping from 'stifled Cairo's filth', we passed, through the Gate of Victory, into the wilderness beyond the City of the Dead.[1] Seated upon some mound of ruins, we inhaled the fine air of the desert, inspiriting as a cordial, when starlight and dew-mists diversified a scene which, by day, is one broad sea of yellow loam with billows of chalk rock, thinly covered by a spray of sand surging and floating in the fiery wind. There, within a mile of crowded life, all is desolate; the town walls seem crumbling to decay, the hovels are tenantless, and the paths untrodden; behind you lies the Wild, before you the thousand tombstones, ghastly in their whiteness; while beyond them the tall dark forms of the Mameluke Soldans' towers rise from the low and hollow ground like the spirits of kings guarding ghostly subjects in the Shadowy Realm. Or we spent the evening at some Takiyeh (Dervish's Oratory), generally preferring that called the Gulshani, near the Muayyid Mosque outside

[1] Here lies the Swiss Burckhardt who enjoyed a wonderful immunity from censure, until a certain pseudo-orientalist of the present day seized the opportunity of using the 'unscrupulous traveller's' information, and of abusing his memory.

the Mutawalli's saintly door. There is nothing attractive in its appearance. You mount a flight of ragged steps, and enter a low verandah enclosing an open stuccoed terrace, where stands the holy man's domed tomb: the two stories contain small dark rooms in which the Dervishes dwell, and the ground-floor doors open into the verandah. During the fast-month, zikrs (forms of Dervish worship) are rarely performed in the Takiyehs; the inmates pray there in congregations, or they sit conversing upon benches in the shade. And a curious medley of men they are, composed of the choicest vagabonds from every nation of Islam. Beyond this I must not describe the Takiyeh or the doings there, for the path of the Dervish may not be trodden by feet profane.

Curious to see something of my old friends the Persians, I called with Haji Wali upon one Mirza Husayn, who by virtue of his dignity as Shahbandar—Consul-General—ranks with the dozen little quasi-diplomatic kings of Cairo. He suspends over his lofty gate a signboard in which the Lion and the Sun, Iran's proud ensign, are by some Egyptian limner's art metamorphosed into a preternatural tabby-cat grasping a scimitar, with the jolly fat face of a 'gay' young lady, curls and all complete, resting fondly upon her pet's concave back. This high dignitary's reception-room was a courtyard *sub dio:* fronting the door were benches and cushions composing the Sadr or high place; with the parallel rows of Divans spread down the less dignified sides, and a line of naked boards, the lowest seats, ranged along the door wall. In the middle stood three little tables supporting three huge lanterns— as is their size so is the owner's dignity—each of which contained three of the largest spermaceti candles.

The Haji and I entering took our seats upon the side benches with humility, and exchanged salutations with the great man on the Sadr. When the Darbar or levee was full, in stalked the Mirza; and all arose as he calmly divested himself of his shoes and with all due solemnity ascended his proper cushion. He is a short thin man about thirty-five, with regular features and the usual preposterous lamb-skin cap and beard, two peaked black cones at least four feet in length, measured from the tips, resting on a slender basement of pale yellow face. After a quarter of an hour of ceremonies, polite mutterings and low bendings with the right hand on the left breast, the Mirza's pipe was handed to him first, in token of his dignity—at Teheran he was probably an under-clerk in some government office. In due time we were all served with Kaliuns (Persian hookahs) and coffee by the servants, who made royal *congés* whenever they passed the great man; and more than once the janissary, in dignity of belt and crooked sabre, entered the court to quicken our awe.

The conversation was the usual Oriental thing. It is, for instance, understood that you have seen strange things in strange lands.

'Voyaging—is—victory,' quotes the Mirza; the quotation is a hackneyed one, but it steps forth majestic as to pause and emphasis.

'Verily,' you reply with equal ponderousness of pronunciation and novelty of citation, 'in leaving home one learns life, yet a journey is a bit of Jehannum.'

Or if you are a physician, the *lieu commun* will be,

> Little-learned doctors the body destroy:
> Little-learn'd parsons the soul destroy.

To which you will make answer, if you would pass for a man of *belles-lettres*, by the well-known lines,

> Of a truth, the physician hath power with drugs,
> Which, long as the patient hath life, may relieve him;
> But the tale of our days being duly told,
> The doctor is daft, and his drugs deceive him.

After sitting there with dignity, like the rest of the guests, I took my leave, delighted with the truly Persian apparatus of the scene. The Mirza, having no salary, lives by fees extorted from his subjects, who pay rather than lack protection; and his dragoman for a counter-fee will sell their interests shamelessly. He is a hidalgo of blue blood in pride, pompousness, and poverty. There is not a sheet of writing paper in the 'Consulate'—when they want one a farthing is sent to the grocer's—yet the Consul drives out in an old carriage with four outriders, two tall-capped men preceding and two following the crazy vehicle. And the Egyptians laugh heartily at this display, being accustomed by Mohammed Ali to consider all such parade obsolete.

About half an hour before midnight sounds the Abrar, or call to prayer, at which time the latest wanderers return home to prepare for their dawn meal. You are careful on the way to address each sentinel with a 'Peace be upon thee!' especially if you have no lantern, otherwise you may chance to sleep in the guard-house. And, *chemin faisant*, you cannot but stop to gaze at streets as little like what civilised Europe understands by that name as is an Egyptian temple to the new Houses of Parliament.

There are certain scenes, cannily termed 'kenspeckle', which print themselves upon Memory, and which endure as long as Memory lasts—a thunder-cloud bursting upon the Alps, a night of stormy darkness off the Cape, an African tornado; and, perhaps, most awful of all, a solitary journey over the sandy Desert.

Of this class is a stroll through the thoroughfares of old Cairo by night. All is squalor in the brilliancy of noon-day. In darkness you see nothing but a silhouette. When, however, the moon is high in the heavens, and the summer stars rain light upon God's world, there is something not of earth in the view. A glimpse at the strip of pale blue sky above scarcely reveals three ells of breadth; in many places the interval is less: here the copings meet, and there the outriggings of the houses seem to interlace. Now they are parted by a pencil, then by a flood of silvery splendour; while under the projecting cornices and the huge hanging-windows of fantastic wood-work, supported by gigantic corbels, and deep verandahs, and gateways vast enough for Behemoth to pass through, and blind wynds and long *culs-de-sac*, lie patches of thick darkness, made visible by the dimmest of oil lights.

The arch is a favourite form: in one place you see it a mere skeleton of stone opening into some huge deserted hall; in another it is full of fretted stone and carved wood. Not a line is straight; the tall dead walls of the mosques slope over their massy buttresses, and the thin minarets seem about to fall across your path. The cornices project crookedly from the houses, while the great gables stand merely by force of cohesion. And that the Line of Beauty may not be wanting, the graceful bending form of the palm, on whose topmost feathers, quivering in the cool night breeze, the moonbeam glistens, springs from a gloomy mound, or from the darkness of a mass of houses almost level with the ground.

Briefly, the whole view is so fantastic, so ghostly, that it seems rather preposterous to imagine that in such places human beings like ourselves can be born, and live through life, to carry out the command 'increase and multiply', and die.

VI

The Mosque

When the Byzantine Christians, after overthrowing the temples of Paganism, meditated rebuilding and remodelling them, poverty of invention and artistic impotence reduced them to group the spoils in a heterogeneous mass. The seaports of Egypt and the plains of Syria abounding in pillars of granite, syenite, and precious marbles, in Pharaonic, Greek, and Roman statuary, and in all manner of structural ornaments, the architects were at no loss for material. Their Syncretism, the result of chance and precipitancy, of extravagance and incuriousness, fell under eyes too ignorant to be hurt by the hybrid irregularity: it was perpetuated in the so-called Saracenic style, a plagiarism from the Byzantine, and it was reiterated in the Gothic, an offshoot from the Saracenic. This fact accounts in the Gothic style for its manifold incongruities of architecture, and for the phenomenon, not solely attributable to the buildings having been erected piecemeal, of its most classic period being that of its greatest irregularity.

Such 'architectural lawlessness', such disregard for symmetry—the result, I believe, of an imperfect 'amalgamation and enrichment'—may doubtless be defended upon the grounds both of cause and of effect. Architecture is of the imitative arts, and Nature, the Myriomorphous, everywhere delighting in variety, appears to abhor nothing so much as perfect similarity and precise uniformity. To copy her exactly we must therefore seek that general analogy compatible with individual variety; in fact, we should avoid the over-display of order and regularity. And again, it may be asserted that, however incongruous these disorderly forms may appear to the conventional eye, we find it easy to surmount our first antipathy. Perhaps we end in admiring them the more, as we love those faces in which irregularity of feature is compensated for by diversity and piquancy of expression.

There is nothing, I believe, new in the Arab Mosque; it is an unconscious revival of the forms used from the earliest ages to denote by symbolism the worship of the generative and the creative gods. The reader will excuse me if I only glance at a subject of which the investigation would require a volume, and which, discussed at greater length, would be out of place in such a narrative as this.

The first mosque in El-Islam was erected by Mohammed at Kuba, near El-Medinah: shortly afterwards, when he entered Meccah as a conqueror, he destroyed the 360 idols of the Arab Pantheon, and thus purified that venerable building from its abominations. He had probably observed in Syria the two forms appropriated by the Christians to their places of worship, the cross and the parallelogramic Basilica; he therefore preferred for the prayers of the 'Saving Faith' a square, some authors say, with, others without, a cloister. At length in the reign of El-Walid (about AH 90), the cupola, the niche, and the minaret made their appearance; and what is called the Saracenic style became for ever the order of the Moslem world.

The Hindus I believe to have been the first who symbolised by an equilateral triangle their peculiar cult, the Yoni-Lingam: in their temple architecture it became either a conoid or a perfect pyramid. Egypt denoted it by the obelisk, peculiar to that country; and the form appeared in different parts of the world: thus in England it was a mere upright stone, and in Ireland a round tower. This we might expect to see. D'Hancarville and Brotier have successfully traced the worship itself, in its different modifications, to all people: the symbol would therefore be found everywhere. The old Arab minaret is a plain conoid or polygonal tower, without balcony or stages, widely different from the Turkish, Modern Egyptian, and Hejazi combinations of cylinder and prism, happily compared by a French traveller to *une chandelle coiffée d'un éteignoir*. And finally the ancient minaret, made solid as all Gothic architecture is, and provided with a belfry, became the spire and steeple of our ancestors.

From time immemorial, in hot and rainy lands, a hypaethral court, either round or square, surrounded by a covered portico, was used for the double purpose of church and mart—a place where God and Mammon were worshipped turn by turn. In some places we find rings of stones, like the Persian Pyroetheia; in others, circular concave buildings representing the vault of heaven, where Fire, the divine symbol, was worshipped; and in Arabia, columnar aisles which, surmounted by the splendid blue vault, resemble the palm-grove. The Greeks adopted this idea in the fanes of Creator Bacchus; and at Puzzuoli, near Naples, it may be seen in the building vulgarly called the Temple of Serapis. It was equally well known to the Celts: in some places the Temenos was a circle, in others a quadrangle. And such to the present day is the Mosque of El-Islam.

Even the Riwak or porches surrounding the area in the Mosque are revivals of older forms. 'The range of square buildings which enclose the temple of Serapis are not, properly speaking, parts of the fane, but apartments of the priests, places for victims, and sacred utensils, and chapels dedicated to subordinate deities, introduced by a more complicated and corrupt worship, and probably unknown to the founders of the original edifice.'

The cloisters in the Mosque became cells, used as lecture rooms, and stores for books bequeathed to the college. They are unequal, because some are required to be of larger, others to be of smaller dimensions. The same reason causes difference of size when the building is distributed into four hyposteles opening upon the area: the porch in the direction of the Kaabah, where worshippers mostly congregate, demands greater depth than the other three. The wings were not unfrequently made unequal, either from want of building materials, or because the same extent of accommodation was not required in both.

The columns were of different substances; some of handsome marble, others of rough stone meanly plastered over; with dissimilar capitals, vulgarly cut shafts of various sizes, here with a pediment, there without, now turned upside-down, then joined together by halves in the centre, and almost invariably nescient of intercolumnar rule. This is the result of Byzantine Syncretism, carelessly and ignorantly grafted upon Arab ideas of the natural and the sublime. Loving and admiring the great, or rather the big in plan, they care little for the execution of mere details, and they have not the acumen to discern the effect which clumsy workmanship, crooked lines, and visible joints—parts apparently insignificant—exercise upon the whole of an edifice. Their use of colours was a false taste, commonly displayed by mankind in their religious houses, and statues of the gods. The Hindus paint their pagodas inside and outside; and rub vermilion, in token of honour, over their deities. The Persian Colossi of Kaiomars and his consort on the Balkh road, and the Sphinx of Egypt, as well as the temples of the Nile, still show traces of artificial complexion. The fanes in classic Greece have been dyed. In the Forum Romanum, one of the finest buildings still bears stains of the Tyrian purple. And to mention no other instances, in the churches and belfries of Modern Italy, we see alternate bands of white and black material so disposed as to give them the appearance of giant zebras.

The origin of Arabesque ornament must be referred to one of the principles of El-Islam. The Moslem, forbidden by his law to decorate his Mosque with statuary and pictures, supplied their place with quotations from the Koran, and inscriptions, 'plastic metaphysics' of marvellous perplexity. His alphabet lent itself to the purpose, and hence probably arose that almost inconceivable variety of lace-like fretwork, of incrustations, of arabesques, and of geometric flowers, in which his eye delights to lose itself.

The Meccan Mosque became a model to the world of El-Islam, and the nations that embraced the new faith copied the consecrated building, as religiously as Christendom produced imitations of the Holy Sepulchre. The Mosque of Omar at Jerusalem, of Amru at Babylon on the Nile, and of Taylun at Cairo, were erected with some trifling improvements, such as arched cloisters and inscribed cornices, upon the plan of the Kaabah. From Egypt and Palestine the ichnography spread far and wide. It was modified, as might be expected, by national taste; what in Arabia was simple and elegant became highly ornate in Spain, florid in Turkey, and effeminate in India. Still divergence of detail had not, even after the lapse of twelve centuries, materially altered the fundamental form.

Perhaps no Eastern city affords more numerous or more

accessible specimens of Mosque architecture than Cairo. Between 300 and 400 places of worship; some stately piles, others ruinous hovels, many new, more decaying and earthquake-shaken, with minarets that rival in obliquity the Pisan monster, are open to the traveller's inspection. And Europeans by following the advice of their hotel-keeper have penetrated, and can penetrate, into any one they please.

If architecture be really what I believe it to be, the highest expression of a people's artistic feeling—highest because it includes all others—to compare the several styles of the different epochs, to observe how each monarch building his own Mosque, and calling it by his own name, identified the manner of the monument with himself, and to trace the gradual decadence of art through 1,200 years, down to the present day, must be a work of no ordinary interest to Orientalists. The limits of my plan, however, compel me to place only the heads of the argument before the reader. May I be allowed to express a hope that it will induce some learned traveller to investigate a subject in every way worthy his attention?

The Jami Taylun (ninth century) is simple and massive, yet elegant, and in some of its details peculiar. One of the four colonnades still remains to show the original magnificence of the building; the other porches are walled up, and inhabited by paupers. In the centre of a quadrangle about 100 paces square is a domed building springing from a square which occupies the proper place of the Kaabah. This Jami (cathedral) is interesting as a point of comparison. If it be an exact copy of the Meccan temple, as it stood in AD 879, it shows that the latter has greatly altered in this our modern day.

Next in date to the Taylun Mosque is that of the Sultan El-Hakim, third Caliph of the Fatimites, and founder of the Druze mysteries. The minarets are remarkable in shape, as well as size: they are unprovided with the usual outer gallery, they are based upon a cube of masonry, and they are pierced above with apertures apparently meaningless. A learned Cairene informed me that these spires were devised by the eccentric monarch to disperse, like large censers, fragrant smoke over the city during the hours of prayer.

The Azhar and Hasanayn[1] Mosques are simple and artless piles, celebrated for sanctity, but remarkable for nothing save ugliness. Few buildings, however, are statelier in appearance, or give a nobler idea of both founder and architect than that which bears Sultan Hasan's name.

The stranger stands awe-struck before walls high-towering without a single break, a hypaethral court severe in masculine beauty, a gateway that might suit the palace of the Titans, and a lofty minaret of massive grandeur. This Mosque, with its fortress aspect, owns no more relationship to the efforts of a later age than does Canterbury Cathedral to an Anglo-Indian Gothic. For dignified beauty and refined taste, the mosque and tomb of Kaid Bey and the other Mameluke kings are admirable. Even in their present state picturesqueness presides over decay, and the traveller has seldom seen aught more striking than the rich light of the stained glass pouring through the first shades of evening upon the marble floor.

The modern Mosques must be visited, to see Egyptian architecture in its decline and fall. That of Sittna Zaynab (our Lady Zaynab), founded by Murad Bey, the Mameluke, and interrupted by the French invasion, shows, even in its completion, some lingering traces of taste. But nothing can be more offensive than the building which every tourist flogs donkey in his hurry to see—old Mohammed Ali's Folly in the citadel. Its Greek architect has toiled to caricature a Mosque, to emulate the glories of our English Oriental Pavilion. Outside, as Monckton Milnes sings,

> The shining minarets, thin and high,

are so thin, so high above the lumpy domes, that they look like the spindles of crouching crones, and are placed in full sight of Sultan Hasan the Giant, so as to derive all the disadvantages of the contrast. Is the pointed arch forgotten by man, that this hapless building should be disgraced by large and small

[1] So called because supposed to contain relics of Hasan and Husayn, the martyred grandsons of Mohammed. The tradition is little credited, and the Persians ostentatiously avoid visiting the place. 'You are the first Ajemi that ever said the Fatihah at this holy spot,' quoth the Mujawir, or guardian of the tomb, after compelling me, almost by force, to repeat the formula, which he recited with the prospect of a few piastres.

parallelograms of glass and wood so placed and so formed as to give its exterior the appearance of a European theatre *coiffé* with Oriental cupolas? Inside, money has been lavished upon alabaster full of flaws; round the bases of pillars run gilt bands; in places the walls are painted with streaks to resemble marble, and the wood-work is overlaid with tinsel gold. After a glance at these abominations, one cannot be surprised to hear the old men of Egypt lament that, in spite of European education, and of prizes encouraging geometry and architecture, modern art offers a melancholy contrast to antiquity.

It is said that HH Abbas Pasha proposes to erect for himself a mosque that shall far surpass the boast of the last generation. I venture to hope that his architect will light the 'sacred fire' from Sultan Hasan's, not from Mohammed Ali's Turco-Grecian splendours. The former is like the genuine Osmanli of past ages, fierce, cold, with a stalwart frame, index of a strong mind—there was a sullen grandeur about the man. The latter is the pert and puny modern Turk in pantaloons, frock-coat, and fez, ill-dressed, ill-conditioned, and ill-bred, body and soul.

We will now enter the Mosque El-Azhar. At the dwarf wooden railing we take off our slippers, hold them in the left hand, sole to sole, that no dirt may fall from them, and cross the threshold with the right foot, ejaculating, 'Bismillah', etc. Next we repair to the Mayza'ah, or large tank, for ablution, without which it is unlawful to appear in the House of Allah. We then seek some proper place for devotion, place our slippers on some other object in front of us to warn the lounger; and perform a two-bow prayer in honour of the Mosque. This done, we may wander about, and inspect the several objects of curiosity.

The moon shines splendidly upon a vast open court, paved with stones which are polished like glass by Faithful feet. There is darkness in the body of the building, a large oblong hall, at least twice too lengthy for its height, supported by a forest of pillars, thin, poor-looking, crooked marble columns, planted avenue-like, upon torn and dirty matting. A few oil lamps shed doubtful light over scanty groups, who are debating some point of grammar, or are listening to the words of wisdom that fall from the mouth of a Waiz (lecturer). Presently they will leave the hypostyle, and throw themselves upon the flags of the quadrangle, where they may enjoy the open air, and avoid some fleas.

It is now 'long vacation': so the holy building has become a kind of caravanserai for travellers; perhaps a score of nations meet in it; there is a confusion of tongues, and the din at times is deafening. Around the court runs a tolerably well-built colonnade, whose entablature is garnished with crimson arabesques, and in the inner wall are pierced apartments, now closed with plank doors.

Of the Riwak, as the porches are called, the Azhar contains twenty-four, one for each recognised nation in El-Islam, and of these fifteen are still open to students. Inside them we find nothing but matting, and a pile of large dingy wooden boxes, which once contained the college library: they are now, generally speaking, empty.

There is nothing worth seeing in the cluster of little dark chambers that form the remainder of the Azhar. Even the Zawiyat el-Umyan (or the Blind-men's Oratory), a place whence so many town and gown rows have emanated, is rendered interesting only by the fanaticism of its inmates, and the certainty that, if recognised in this sanctum, we shall run the gauntlet under the staves of its proprietors, the angry blind.

The Azhar is the grand collegiate Mosque of this city—the Christ Church, in fact, of Cairo—once celebrated throughout the world of El-Islam. It was built, I was told, originally in poor style by Jauhar el-Kaid,[1] originally the slave of a Moorish merchant, in consequence of a dream that ordered him to erect a place whence the light of science should shine upon El-Islam. It gradually increased by Wakf (entailed bequests) of lands, money, and books; and pious rulers made a point of adding to its size and wealth. Of late years it has considerably declined, the result of sequestrations, and of the diminished esteem in which the

[1] Lane (*Modern Egyptians*) has rectified Baron von Hammer's mistake concerning the word 'Azhar'; our English Orientalist translates it the 'splendid Mosque'. I would venture to add that the epithet must be understood in a spiritual and not in a material sense. Wilkinson attributes the erection of the building to Jauhar El-Kaid, general under El-Moez, about AD 970. Wilson ascribes it partly to El-Moez the Fatimire (AD 973), partly to his general and successor, El-Hakim (?).

purely religious sciences are now held in the land of Egypt. Yet it is calculated that between 2,000 and 3,000 students of all nations and ages receive instruction here gratis. Each one is provided with bread, in a quantity determined by the amount of endowment, at the Riwak set apart for his nation, with some article of clothing on festival days, and with a few piastres once a year. The professors, who are about 150 in number, may not take fees from their pupils; some lecture on account of the religious merit of the action, others to gain the high title of 'Teacher in El-Azhar'.[1] Six officials receive stipends from the government—the Shaykh el-Jami or dean, the Shaykh el-Sakka, who regulates the provision of water for ablution, and others that may be called heads of departments.

The following is the course of study in the Azhar. The schoolboy of four or five years' standing has been taught, by a liberal application of the maxim 'The Green Rod is of the Trees of Paradise', to chant the Koran without understanding it, the elementary rules of arithmetic; and, if he is destined to be a learned man, the art of writing. He then registers his name in El-Azhar, and applies himself to the branches of study most cultivated in El-Islam, namely Nahw (Syntax), Fikh (the Law), Hadis (the Traditions of the Prophet), and Tafsir, or Exposition of the Koran.

The young Egyptian reads at the same time Sarf, or Inflexion, and Nahw (Syntax). But as Arabic is his mother-tongue, he is not required to study the former so deeply as are the Turks, the Persians, and the Indians. If he desire, however, to be a proficient, he must carefully peruse five books in Sarf, and six in Nahw.

Master of grammar, our student now applies himself to its proper end and purpose, Divinity. Of the four schools, those of Abu Hanifah and El-Shafei are most common in Cairo; the followers of Ibn Malik abound only in Southern Egypt and the Berberah country, and the Hanbali is almost unknown. The

[1] As the attending of lectures is not compulsory, the result is that the lecturer is always worth listening to. May I commend this consideration to our college reformers at home? In my day men were compelled to waste—notoriously to waste—an hour or two every morning, for the purpose of putting a few pounds sterling into the pocket of some droning Don.

theologian begins with what is called a Matn or text, a short, dry, and often obscure treatise, a mere string of precepts; in fact, the skeleton of the subject. This he learns by repeated perusal, till he can quote almost every passage *literatim*. He then passes to its Sharh, or commentary, generally the work of some other savant, who explains the difficulty of the text, amplifies its Laconicisms, enters into exceptional cases, and deals with principles and reasons, as well as with mere precept. A difficult work will sometimes require Hashiyah, or marginal notes; but this aid has a bad name:

> Who readeth with note,
> But learneth by rote,

says a popular doggerel. The reason is, that the student's reasoning powers being little exercised, he learns to depend upon the *dixit* of a master rather than to think for himself. It also leads to the neglect of another practice, highly advocated by the Eastern pedagogue:

> The lecture is one,
> The dispute (upon the subject of the lecture)
> is one thousand.

In order to become a Fakih, or divine of distinguished fame, the follower of Abu Hanifah must peruse about ten volumes, some of huge size, written in a diffuse style: the Shafei's reading is not quite so extensive. Theology is much studied, because it leads directly to the gaining of daily bread, as priest or tutor; and other scientific pursuits are neglected for the opposite reason.

The theologian in Egypt, as in other parts of El-Islam, must have a superficial knowledge of the Prophet's traditions. Of these there are eight well-known collections, but only the three first are generally read.

Schoolboys are instructed, almost when in their infancy, to intone the Koran; at the university they are taught a more exact system of chanting. The style called Hafs is the most common in Egypt, as it is indeed throughout the Moslem world. And after learning to read the holy volume, some savants are ambitious enough to wish to understand it: under these circumstances they must dive into the Ilm el-Tafsir, or the Exegesis of the Koran.

Our student is now a perfect Fakih or Mulla. But the poor fellow has no scholarship or fellowship—no easy tutorship, no fat living to look forward to. After wasting seven years, or twice seven years, over his studies, and reading till his brain is dizzy, his digestion gone, and his eyes half blind, he must either starve upon college alms, or squat, like my old Shaykh Mohammed, in a druggist's shop, or become pedagogue and preacher in some country place, on the pay of 8*l.* per annum.

With such prospects, it is wonderful how the Azhar can present any attractions; but the southern man is essentially an idler, and many become Olema, like Capuchins, in order to do nothing. A favoured few rise to the degree of Mudarris (professors), and thence emerge Kazis and Muftis. This is another inducement to matriculate; every undergraduate having an eye upon the Kazi-ship, with as much chance of obtaining it as the country parocco has of becoming a cardinal. Others again devote themselves to laical pursuits, degenerate into Wakils (lawyers), or seek their fortunes as Katibs—public or private accountants.

To conclude this part of the subject, I cannot agree with Dr Bowring when he harshly says, upon the subject of Moslem education: 'The instruction given by the Doctors of the Law in the religious schools, for the formation of the Mohammedan priesthood, is of the most worthless character.' Would not a superficial, hasty, and somewhat prejudiced Turk say exactly the same thing about the systems of Christ Church and Trinity College?

His opinion is equally open to objection with that of those who depreciate the law itself because it deals rather in precepts than in principle, in ceremonies and ordinances rather than in ethics and aesthetics. Both are what Eastern faiths and Eastern training have ever been—both are eminently adapted for the Oriental mind. When the people learn to appreciate ethics, and to understand psychics and aesthetics, the demand will create a supply. Meanwhile they leave transcendentalism to their poets and philosophers, and they busy themselves with preparing for heaven by practising the only part of their faith now intelligible to them—the Material.

It is not to be supposed that a nation in this stage of civilisation could be so fervently devout as the Egyptians are, without the bad leaven of bigotry. The same tongue which is employed in blessing Allah, is, it is conceived, doing its work equally well in cursing Allah's enemies. Wherefore the Kafir is denounced by every sex, age, class, and condition, by the man of the world as by the boy at school; and out of, as well as in, the Mosque. If you ask your friend who is the person with a black turban, he replies,

'A Christian. Allah make his Countenance cold!'

If you inquire of your servant who are the people singing in the next house, it is ten to one that his answer will be,

'Jews. May their lot be Jehannum!'

It appears unintelligible, still it is not less true, that Egyptians who have lived as servants under European roofs for years, retain the liveliest loathing for the manners and customs of their masters.

Few Franks, save those who have mixed with the Egyptians in Oriental disguise, are aware of their repugnance to, and contempt for, Europeans—so well is the feeling veiled under the garb of innate politeness, and so great is their reserve when conversing with those of strange religions. I had a good opportunity of ascertaining the truth when the first rumour of a Russian war arose. Almost every able-bodied man spoke of hastening to the Jihad, or holy war, and the only thing that looked like apprehension was the too eager depreciation of their foes. All seemed delighted with the idea of French co-operation, for, somehow or other, the Frenchman is everywhere popular. When speaking of England, they were not equally easy: heads were rolled, pious sentences were ejaculated, and finally out came the old Eastern cry,

'Of a truth they are Shaytans, those English.'

The Austrians are despised, because the East knows nothing of them since the days when Osmanli hosts threatened the gates of Vienna. The Greeks are hated as clever scoundrels, ever ready to do El-Islam a mischief. The Maltese, the greatest of cowards off their own ground, are regarded with a profound contempt: these are the protégés which bring the British nation into disrepute at Cairo. And Italians are known only as *istruttori* and *distruttori*: doctors, druggists, and pedagogues.

Yet Egyptian human nature is, like human nature everywhere, contradictory. Hating and despising Europeans, they still long for European rule. This people admire an iron-handed and lion-hearted despotism; they hate a timid and a grinding tyranny.[1] Of all foreigners, they would prefer the French yoke —a circumstance which I attribute to the diplomatic skill and national dignity of our neighbours across the Channel. But whatever European nation secures Egypt will win a treasure. Moated on the north and south by seas, with a glacis of impassable deserts to the eastward and westward, capable of supporting an army of 180,000 men, of paying a heavy tribute, and yet able to show a considerable surplus of revenue, this country in western hands will command India, and by a ship-canal between Pelusium and Suez would open the whole of Eastern Africa.[2]

There is no longer much to fear from the fanaticism of the people, and a little prudence would suffice to command the interests of the Mosque. The chiefs of corporations, in the present state of popular feeling, would offer even less difficulty to an invader or a foreign ruler than the Olema. Briefly, Egypt is the most tempting prize which the East holds out to the ambition of Europe, not excepted even the Golden Horn.

[1] Of this instances abound. Lately an order was issued to tax the villages of the Bedawin settled upon the edge of the Western desert, who, even in Mohammed Ali's time, were allowed to live free of assessment. The Aulad Ali, inhabitants of a little village near the Pyramids, refused to pay, and turned out with their matchlocks, defying the Pasha. The government then insisted upon their leaving their houses, and living under hair-cloth like Bedawin, since they claimed the privileges of Bedawin. The sturdy fellows at once pitched their tents, and when I returned to Cairo (in December 1853) they had deserted their village. I could offer a score of such cases, proving the present debased condition of Egypt.

[2] As this canal has become a question of national interest, its advisability is surrounded with all the circumstance of unsupported assertion and bold denial. The English want a railroad, which would confine the use of Egypt to themselves. The French desire a canal that would admit the hardy cruisers of the Mediterranean into the Red Sea. The cosmopolite will hope that both projects may be carried out. Even in the seventh century Omar forbade Amru to cut the Isthmus of Suez for fear of opening Arabia to Christian vessels. The canal is now a fact. As late as April 1864 Lord Palmerston informed the House of Commons that labourers might be more usefully employed in cultivating cotton than in 'digging a canal through a sandy desert and in making two harbours in deep mud and shallow water'. It is, however, understood that the Premier was the only one of his Cabinet who took this view. Mr Robert Stephenson, CE, certainly regretted before his death the opinion which he had been induced to express by desire.

VII

Preparations to Quit Cairo

At length the slow 'month of blessings' passed away. We rejoiced like Romans finishing their Quaresima, when a salvo of artillery from the citadel announced the end of our Lenten woes. On the last day of Ramazan all gave alms to the poor, at the rate of a piastre and a half for each member of the household—slave, servant, and master.

The next day, first of the three composing the Eed or Lesser Festival, we arose before dawn, performed our ablutions, and repaired to the Mosque, to recite the peculiar prayer of the season and to hear the sermon which bade us be 'merry and wise'. After which we ate and drank heartily; then, with pipes and tobacco-pouches in hand, we sauntered out to enjoy the contemplation of smiling faces and street scenery.

The favourite resort on this occasion is the large cemetery beyond the Bab el-Nasr—that stern, old, massive gateway which opens upon the Suez road. There we found a scene of jollity. Tents and ambulant coffee-houses were full of men equipped in their 'Sunday best', listening to singers and musicians, smoking, chatting, and looking at jugglers, buffoons, snake-charmers, Dervishes, ape-leaders, and dancing boys habited in women's attire. Eating-stalls and lollipop-shops, booths full of playthings, and sheds for lemonade and syrups, lined the roads, and disputed with swings and merry-go-rounds the regards of the little Moslems and Moslemahs.

The chief item of the crowd—fair Cairenes—carried in their hands huge palm branches, intending to ornament therewith the tombs of parents and friends. Yet, even on this solemn occasion, there is, they say, not a little flirtation and love-making; parties of policemen are posted, with orders to interrupt all such irregularities, with a long cane; but their vigilance is notoriously unequal to the task. I could not help observing that frequent pairs —doubtless cousins or other relations—wandered to unusual distances among the sand-hills, and that sometimes the confusion of a distant bastinado struck the ear. These trifles did not, however, by any means interfere with the general joy. Every one wore something new; most people were in the fresh suits of finery intended to last through the year; and so strong is personal vanity in the breasts of Orientals, men and women, young and old, that from Cairo to Calcutta it would be difficult to find a sad heart under a handsome coat. The men swaggered, the women minced their steps, rolled their eyes, and were eternally arranging and coquetting with their head-veils. The little boys strutting about foully abused any one of their number who might have a richer suit than his neighbours. And the girls ogled every one in the ecstasy of conceit, and glanced contemptuously at other little girls their rivals.

Weary of the country, the Haji and I wandered about the city, paying visits, which at this time are like new-year calls in continental Europe. I can describe the operation of calling in Egypt only as the discussion of pipes and coffee in one place, and of coffee and pipes in another. But on this occasion, whenever we meet a friend we throw ourselves upon each other's breast, placing right arms over left shoulders, and vice versa, squeezing like wrestlers, with intermittent hugs, then laying cheek to cheek delicately, at the same time making the loud noise of many kisses in the air. You are bound also to meet even your enemies in the most friendly way—for which mortification you afterwards hate them more cordially than before.

The compliment of the season is, *Kull'am antum bil khayr*—'Every year may you be well!'—in fact, our 'Many happy returns of the day!' After this come abundant good wishes, and kindly prophecies; and, from a religious person, a blessing, and a short prayer. To complete the resemblance between a Moslem and a Christian festival, we have dishes of the day, fish, *Shurayh*, the cross-bun, and a peculiarly indigestible cake called in Egypt Kahk, the plum-pudding of El-Islam.

This year's Eed was made gloomy, comparatively speaking, by the state of politics. Report of war with Russia, with France, with England, who was going to land 3 million men at Suez, and with Infideldom in general, rang through Egypt, and the city of Mars[1] became unusually martial. The government armouries, arsenals, and manufactories were crowded with kidnapped workmen. Those who purposed a pilgrimage feared forcible detention. Wherever men gathered together, in the Mosques, for instance, or the coffee-houses, the police closed the doors, and made forcible capture of the able-bodied. This proceeding, almost as barbarous as our impressment law, filled the main streets with detachments of squalid-looking wretches, marching to be made soldiers, with collars round their necks and irons on their wrists. The dismal impression of the scene was deepened by crowds of women, who, habited in mourning, and scattering dust and mud over their rent garments, followed their sons, brothers, and husbands, with cries and shrieks. The death-wail is a peculiar way of cheering on the patriot departing *pro patria mori*; and the origin of the custom is characteristic of the people.

The principal public amusements allowed to Oriental women are those that come under the general name of Fantasia—birth-feasts, marriage festivals, and funerals. And the early campaigns of Mohammed Ali's family in Syria and El-Hejaz having, in many cases, deprived the bereaved of their sex-right to keen for the dead, they have now determined not to waste the opportunity, but to revel in the luxury of woe at the live man's wake.

Another cloud hung over Cairo. Rumours of conspiracy were afloat. The Jews and Christians, here as ready to take alarm as the English in Italy, trembled at the fancied preparations for insurrection, massacre, and plunder. And even the Moslems whispered that some hundred desperadoes had resolved to fire the city, beginning with the bankers' quarter, and to spoil the wealthy Egyptians. Of course HH Abbas Pasha was absent at the time, and even had he been at Cairo, his presence would have been of little use: the ruler can do nothing towards restoring confidence to a panic-stricken Oriental nation.

[1] With due deference to the many of a different opinion, I believe 'Kahirah' (corrupted through the Italian into 'Cairo') to mean, not the 'victorious', but the 'City of Kahir', or Mars. It was so called because, as Richardson has informed the world, it was founded in AD 968 by Jauhar, before mentioned, when the warlike planet was in the ascendant.

At the end of the Eed, as a counter-irritant to political excitement, the police magistrates began to bully the people. There is a standing order in the chief cities of Egypt, that all who stir abroad after dark without a lantern shall pass the night in the station-house. But at Cairo in certain quarters, the Ezbekiyeh, for instance, a little laxity is usually allowed. Before I left the capital the licence was withdrawn, and the sudden strictness caused many ludicrous scenes.

If by chance you (clad in Oriental garb) had sent on your lantern to a friend's house by your servant, and had leisurely followed it five minutes after the hour of eight, you were sure to be met, stopped, collared, questioned, and captured by the patrol. You probably punched three or four of them, but found the dozen too strong for you. Held tightly by the sleeves, skirts, and collar of your wide outer garment, you were hurried away on a plane of about nine inches above the ground, your feet mostly treading the air. You were dragged along with a rapidity which scarcely permitted you to answer strings of questions concerning your name, nation, dwelling, faith, profession, and self in general—especially concerning the present state of your purse.

If you lent an ear to the voice of the charmer that began by asking a crown to release you, and gradually came down to twopence halfpenny, you fell into a simple trap; the butt-end of a musket applied a posteriori, immediately after the transfer of property, convicted you of wilful waste. But if, more sensibly, you pretended to have forgotten your purse, you were reviled, and dragged, with increased violence of shaking, to the office of the Zabit or police magistrate. You were spun through the large archway leading to the court, every fellow in uniform giving you, as you passed, a Kafa, cuff, on the back of the neck. Despite your rage, you were forced up the stairs to a long gallery full of people in a predicament like your own. Again your name, nation—I suppose you to be masquerading—offence, and other particulars were asked, and carefully noted in a folio by a ferocious-looking clerk.

If you knew no better, you were summarily thrust into the Hasil, or condemned cell, to pass the night with pick-pockets and ruffians, pell-mell. But if an adept in such matters, you insisted upon being conducted before the 'Pasha of the Night', and, the clerk fearing to refuse, you were hurried to the great man's office hoping for justice, and dealing out ideal vengeance to your captors—the patrol. Here you found the dignitary sitting with pen, ink, and paper before him, and pipe and coffee-cup in hand, upon a wide Divan of dingy chintz, in a large dimly lit room, with two guards by his side, and a semicircle of recent seizures vociferating before him. When your turn came, you were carefully collared, and led up to the presence, as if even at that awful moment you were mutinously and murderously disposed.

The Pasha, looking at you with a vicious sneer, turned up his nose, ejaculated 'Ajemi', and prescribed the bastinado. You observed that the mere fact of being a Persian did not give mankind a right to capture, imprison, and punish you; you declared moreover that you were no Persian, but an Indian under British protection.

The Pasha, a man accustomed to obedience, then stared at you, to frighten you, and you, we will suppose, stared at him, till, with an oath, he turned to the patrol, and asked them your offence. They all simultaneously swore by Allah, that you had been found without a lantern, dead-drunk, beating respectable people, breaking into houses, robbing and invading Harams.

You openly told the Pasha that they were eating abominations; upon which he directed one of his guards to smell your breath—the charge of drunkenness being tangible. The fellow, a comrade of your capturers, advanced his nose to your lips; as might be expected, cried, 'Kikh'—'Fie!' or 'Ugh!'—contorted his countenance, and answered, by the beard of 'Effendina'—'Our lord', i.e. HH the Pasha—that he perceived a pestilent odour of distilled waters. This announcement probably elicited a grim grin from the 'Pasha of the Night', who loves Curaçoa, and who is not indifferent to the charms of Cognac. Then by his favour (for you improved the occasion) you were allowed to spend the hours of darkness on a wooden bench, in the adjacent long gallery, together with certain little parasites for which polite language has no name.

In the morning the janissary of your Consulate was sent for; he came, and claimed you; you were led off criminally; again you gave your name and address, and if your offence was merely sending on your lantern, you were dismissed with advice to be more careful in future. And assuredly your first step was towards the Hammam.

But if, on the other hand, you had declared yourself a European, you would either have been dismissed at once, or sent to your consul, who is here judge, jury, and jailer. Egyptian authority has of late years lost half its prestige.

When Mr Lane first settled at Cairo, all Europeans accused of aggression against Moslems were, he tells us, surrendered to the Turkish magistrates. Now, the native powers have no jurisdiction over strangers, nor can the police enter their houses. If the West would raise the character of its Eastern co-religionists, it will be forced to push the system a point further, and to allow all bona fide Christian subjects to register their names at the different Consulates whose protection they might prefer. This is what Russia has so 'unwarrantably and outrageously' attempted. We confine ourselves to a lesser injustice, which deprives Eastern states of their right as independent Powers to arrest, and to judge foreigners, who for interest or convenience settle in their dominions. But we still shudder at the right of arrogating any such claim over the born lieges of Oriental Powers.

What, however, would be the result were Great Britain to authorise her sons resident at Paris, or Florence, to refuse attendance at a French or an Italian court of justice, and to demand that the police should never force the doors of an English subject? I commend this consideration to all those who 'stickle for abstract rights' when the interest and progress of others are concerned, and who become somewhat latitudinarian and concrete in cases where their own welfare and aggrandisement are at stake.

Besides patients, I made some pleasant acquaintances at Cairo. Antun Zananire, a young Syrian of considerable attainments as a linguist, paid me the compliment of permitting me to see the fair face of his Harem. Mr Hatchadur Nury, an Armenian gentleman, well known in Bombay, amongst other acts of kindness, introduced me to one of his compatriots, Khwajah Yusuf, whose advice was most useful to me. The Khwajah had wandered far and wide, picking up everywhere some scrap of strange knowledge, and his history was a romance. Expelled for a youthful peccadillo from Cairo, he started upon his travels, qualified himself for sanctity at Meccah and El-Medinah, became a religious beggar at Baghdad, studied French at Paris, and finally settled down as a professor of languages, under an amnesty, at Cairo. In his house I saw an Armenian marriage. The occasion was memorable: after the gloom and sameness of Moslem society, nothing could be more gladdening than the unveiled face of a pretty woman. Some of the guests were undeniably charming brunettes, with the blackest possible locks, and the brightest conceivable eyes. Only one pretty girl wore the national costume; yet they all smoked chibouques and sat upon the Divans, and, as they entered the room, they kissed with a sweet simplicity the hands of the priest, and of the other old gentlemen present.

Among the number of my acquaintances was a Meccan boy, Mohammed el-Basyuni, from whom I bought the pilgrim-garb called El-Ihram, and the Kafan or shroud, with which the Moslem usually starts upon such a journey as mine. He, being in his way homewards after a visit to Constantinople, was most anxious to accompany me in the character of a companion. But he had travelled too much to suit me; he had visited India, he had seen Englishmen, and he had lived with the Nawab Balu of Surat. Moreover he showed signs of over-wisdom. He had been a regular visitor, till I cured one of his friends of an ophthalmia, after which he gave me his address at Meccah, and was seen no more. Haji Wali described him and his party to be *Nas jarrár* (extractors), and certainly he had not misjudged them. But the sequel will prove how *der Mensch denkt und Gott lenkt*; and, as the boy Mohammed eventually did become my companion throughout the Pilgrimage, I will place him before the reader as summarily as possible.

He is a beardless youth, of about eighteen, chocolate-brown, with high features, and a bold profile; his bony and decided Meccan cast of face is lit up by the peculiar Egyptian eye, which seems to descend from generation to generation. His figure is short and broad, with a tendency to be obese, the result of a strong stomach and the power of sleeping at discretion. He can read a little, write his name, and is uncommonly clever at a bargain.

Meccah had taught him to speak excellent Arabic, to understand the literary dialect, to be eloquent in abuse, and to be profound at Prayer and Pilgrimage. Constantinople has given him a taste for Anacreontic singing, and female society of the questionable kind, a love of strong waters—the hypocrite looked positively scandalised when I first suggested the subject—and an off-hand latitudinarian mode of dealing with serious subjects in general. I found him to be the youngest son of a widow, whose doting fondness had moulded his disposition; he was selfish and affectionate, as spoiled children usually are, volatile, easily offended and as easily pacified (the Oriental), coveting other men's goods, and profuse of his own (the Arab); with a matchless intrepidity of countenance (the traveller); brazen lunged, not more than half brave, exceedingly astute, with an acute sense of honour, especially where his relations were concerned (the individual).

I have seen him in a fit of fury because some one cursed his father; and he and I nearly parted because on one occasion I applied to him an epithet which, etymologically considered, might be exceedingly insulting to a high-minded brother, but which in popular parlance signifies nothing. This *point d'honneur* was the boy Mohammed's strong point.

During the Ramazan I laid in my stores for the journey. These consisted of tea, coffee, loaf-sugar, rice, dates, biscuit, oil, vinegar, tobacco, lanterns, and cooking pots, a small bell-shaped tent, costing 12*s*., and three water-skins for the Desert. The provisions were placed in a *Kafas*, or hamper, artistically made of palm-sticks, and in a huge Sahharah, or wooden box, about three feet each way, covered with leather or skin, and provided with a small lid fitting into the top. The former, together with my green box containing medicines, and saddle-bags full of clothes, hung on one side of the camel, a counterpoise the big Sahharah on the other flank; the Bedawin, like muleteers, always requiring a balance of weight. On the top of the load was placed, transversely, a Shibriyah, or cot, on which Shaykh Nur squatted like a large crow. This worthy had strutted out into the streets armed with a pair of horse-pistols and a sword almost as long as himself. No sooner did the mischievous boys of Cairo—they are as bad as the gamins of Paris and London—catch sight of him than they began to scream with laughter at the sight of the 'Hindi (Indian) in arms' till, like a vagrant owl pursued by a flight of larks, he ran back into the Caravanserai.

Having spent all my ready money at Cairo, I was obliged to renew the supply. My native acquaintances advised me to take at least 80*l.*, and considering the expense of outfit for Desert-travelling, the sum did not appear excessive. I should have found some difficulty in raising the money had it not been for the kindness of a friend at Alexandria, John Thurburn, now, I regret to say, no more, and Mr Sam Shepheard, then of Shepheard's Hotel, Cairo, presently a landed proprietor near Rugby, and now also gone. My Indians scrutinised the diminutive square of paper, the letter of credit, as a raven may sometimes be seen peering, with head askance, into the interior of a suspected marrow-bone. 'Can this be a bona fide draft?' they mentally inquired. And finally they offered, most politely, to write to England for me, to draw the money, and to forward it in a sealed bag directed 'El-Medinah'. I need scarcely say that such a style of transmission would, in the case of precious metals, have left no possible chance of its safe arrival.

When the difficulty was overcome, I bought 50*l.* worth of German dollars (Maria Theresas), and invested the rest in English and Turkish sovereigns. The gold I myself carried; part of the silver I sewed up in Shaykh Nur's leather waist-belt, and part was packed in the boxes, for this reason—when Bedawin begin plundering a respectable man, if they find a certain amount of ready money in his baggage, they do not search his person. If they find none, they proceed to a bodily inspection, and if his waist-belt be empty they are rather disposed to rip open his stomach, in the belief that he must have some peculiarly ingenious way of secreting valuables.

Having passed through this trouble, I immediately fell into another. My hardly earned Alexandrian passport required a double visa, one at the police office, the other at the consul's.

After returning to Egypt, I found it was the practice of travellers who required any civility from Dr Walne, then the English official at Cairo, to enter the 'presence' furnished with an order from the Foreign Office. I had neglected the precaution, and had ample reason to regret having done so. Failing at the British Consulate, and unwilling to leave Cairo without being *en règle*—the Egyptians warned me that Suez was a place of obstacles to pilgrims—I was obliged to look elsewhere for protection.

My friend Haji Wali was the first consulted: after a long discussion, he offered to take me to his consul, the Persian, and to find out for what sum I could become a temporary subject of the Shah. We went to the sign of the Lion and the Sun, and we found the dragoman,[1] a subtle Syrian Christian, who, after a rigid inquiry into the state of my purse (my country was no consideration at all), introduced me to the Great Man. I have described this personage once already, and he merits not a second notice. The interview was truly ludicrous. He treated us with exceeding hauteur, motioned me to sit almost out of hearing, and after rolling his head in profound silence for nearly a quarter of an hour, vouchsafed the information that though my father *might* be a Shirazi, and my mother an Afghan, he had not the honour of my acquaintance. His companion, a large old Persian with Polyphemean eyebrows and a mulberry beard,

[1] The consular dragoman is one of the greatest abuses I know. The tribe is, for the most part, Levantine and Christian, and its connections are extensive. The father will perhaps be interpreter to the English, the son to the French Consulate. By this means, the most privy affairs will become known to every member of the department, except the head, and eventually to that best of spy-trainers, the Turkish government. This explains how a subordinate, whose pay is 200*l.* per annum, and who spends double that sum, can afford, after twelve or thirteen years' service, to purchase a house for 2,000*l.* and to furnish it for as much more. Besides which, the condition, the ideas, and the very nature of these dragomans are completely Oriental. The most timid and cringing of men, they dare not take the proper tone with a government to which, in case of the expulsion of a Consul, they and their families would become subject. And their prepossessions are utterly Oriental. Hanna Massara, dragoman to the Consul-General at Cairo, in my presence, and before others, advocated the secret murder of a Moslem girl who had fled with a Greek, on the grounds that an adulteress must always be put to death, either publicly or under the rose. Yet this man is an 'old and tried servant' of the State.

Such evils might be in part mitigated by employing English youths, of whom an ample supply, if there were any demand, would soon be forthcoming. This measure has been advocated by the best authorities, but without success. Most probably, the reason of the neglect is the difficulty how to begin, or where to end, the Augean labour of consular reform.

put some gruff and discouraging questions. I quoted the verses

> He is a man who benefits his fellow-men,
> Not he who says 'why?' and 'wherefore?'
> and 'how much?'

upon which an imperious wave of the arm directed me to return to the dragoman, who had the effrontery to ask me 4*l.* for a Persian passport. I offered 1*l.* He derided my offer, and I went away perplexed.

On my return to Cairo some months afterwards, he sent to say that had he known me as an Englishman, I should have had the document gratis—a civility for which he was duly thanked.

At last my Shaykh Mohammed hit upon *the* plan. 'Thou art', said he, 'an Afghan; I will fetch hither the principal of the Afghan college at the Azhar, and he, if thou make it worth his while' (this in a whisper), 'will be thy friend.' The case was looking desperate; my preceptor was urged to lose no time.

Presently Shaykh Mohammed returned in company with the principal, a little, thin, ragged-bearded, one-eyed, hare-lipped divine, dressed in very dirty clothes, of nondescript cut. Born at Muscat of Afghan parents, and brought up at Meccah, he was a kind of cosmopolite, speaking five languages fluently, and full of reminiscences of toil and travel. He refused pipes and coffee, professing to be ascetically disposed: but he ate more than half my dinner, to reassure me, I presume, should I have been fearful that abstinence might injure his health. We then chatted in sundry tongues. I offered certain presents of books, which were rejected (such articles being valueless), and the Shaykh Abd el-Wahháb having expressed his satisfaction at my account of myself, told me to call for him at the Azhar Mosque next morning.

Accordingly, at six p.m. Shaykh Mohammed and Abdullah Khan—Khan is a title assumed in India and other countries by all Afghans and Pathans, their descendants, simple as well as gentle—the latter equipped in a gigantic sprigged-muslin turban, so as to pass for a student of theology, repaired to El-Azhar. Passing through the open quadrangle, we entered the large hall which forms the body of the Mosque. In the northern wall was a dwarf door, leading by breakneck stairs to a pigeon-hole, the study of the learned Afghan Shaykh.

We found him ensconced behind piles of musty and greasy manuscripts, surrounded by scholars and scribes, with whom he was cheapening books. He had not much business to transact; but long before he was ready, the stifling atmosphere drove us out of the study, and we repaired to the hall. Presently the Shaykh joined us, and we all rode on to the citadel, and waited in a Mosque till the office hour struck. When the doors were opened we went into the Divan, and sat patiently till the Shaykh found an opportunity of putting in a word.

The officials were two in number; one an old invalid, very thin and sickly-looking, dressed in the Turco-European style, whose hand was being severely kissed by a troop of religious beggars, to whom he had done some small favours; the other was a stout young clerk, whose duty it was to engross, and not to have his hand kissed. My name and other essentials were required, and no objections were offered, for who holier than the Shaykh Abd el-Wahháb ibn Yunus el-Sulaymani?

The clerk filled up a printed paper in the Turkish language, apparently borrowed from the European method for spoiling the traveller; certified me, upon the Shaykh's security, to be one Abdullah, the son of Yusuf (Joseph), originally from Cabool; described my person, and, in exchange for 5 piastres, handed me the document. I received it with joy.

With bows and benedictions, and many wishes that Allah might make it the officials' fate to become pilgrims, we left the office, and returned towards El-Azhar.

When we had nearly reached the Mosque, Shaykh Mohammed lagged behind, and made the sign. I drew near the Afghan, and asked for his hand. He took the hint, and muttering 'It is no matter!'—'It is not necessary!'—'By Allah it is not required!' extended his fingers, and brought the *musculus guineorum* to bear upon 3 dollars. Poor man! I believe it was his necessity that consented to be paid for doing a common act of Moslem charity; he had a wife and children, and the calling of an Alim is no longer worth much in Egypt.

My departure from Cairo was hastened by an accident. I lost

my reputation by a little misfortune which happened in this wise.

At Haji Wali's room in the caravanserai, I met a Yuzbashi, or captain of Albanian Irregulars, who was in Egypt on leave from El-Hejaz. He was a tall, bony, and broad-shouldered mountaineer, about forty years old, with the large *bombé* brow, the fierce eyes, thin lips, lean jaws, and peaky chin of his race. His mustachios were enormously long and tapering, and the rest of his face, like his head, was close shaven. His *Fustan*, the stiff, white, plaited kilt worn by Albanians, was none of the cleanest; nor was the red cap, which he wore rakishly pulled over his frowning forehead, quite free from stains.

Not permitted to carry the favourite pistols, he contented himself with sticking his right hand in the empty belt, and stalking about the house with a most military mien. Yet he was as little of a bully as carpet knight, that same Ali Agha; his body showed many a grisly scar, and one of his shin bones had been broken by a Turkish bullet, when he was playing tricks on the Albanian hills—an accident inducing a limp, which he attempted to conceal by a heavy swagger. When he spoke, his voice was affectedly gruff; he had a sad knack of sneering, and I never saw him thoroughly sober.

Our acquaintance began with a kind of storm, which blew over, and left fine weather. I was showing Haji Wali my pistols with Damascene barrels when Ali Agha entered the room. He sat down before me with a grin which said intelligibly enough—'What business have *you* with weapons?'—snatched the arm out of my hand, and began to inspect it as a connoisseur. Not admiring this procedure, I wrenched it away from him, and, addressing myself to Haji Wali, proceeded quietly with my dissertation. The captain of Irregulars and I then looked at each other. He cocked his cap on one side, in token of excited pugnacity. I twirled my mustachios to display a kindred emotion. Had he been armed, and in El-Hejaz, we should have fought it out at once, for the Arnauts are *terribili colla pistola*, as the Italians say, meaning that upon the least provocation they pull out a horse-pistol, and fire it in the face of friend or foe. Of course, the only way under these circumstances is to anticipate them; but even this desperate prevention seldom saves a stranger, as whenever there is danger, these men go about in pairs.

I never met with a more reckless brood. Upon the line of march Albanian troops are not allowed ammunition; for otherwise there would be half a dozen duels a day. When they quarrel over their cups, it is the fashion for each man to draw a pistol, and to place it against his opponent's breast. The weapons being kept accurately clean, seldom miss fire, and if one combatant draw trigger before the other, he would immediately be shot down by the bystanders. In Egypt these men—who are used as irregulars, and are often quartered upon the hapless villagers, when unable or unwilling to pay taxes—were the terror of the population. On many occasions they have quarrelled with foreigners, and insulted European women. In El-Hejaz their recklessness awes even the Bedawin. The townspeople say of them that 'tripe-sellers, and bath-servants, at Stamboul, they become Pharaohs (tyrants, ruffians) in Arabia'.

At Jeddah the Arnauts have amused themselves with firing at the English consul (Mr Ogilvie) when he walked upon his terrace. And this man-shooting appears a favourite sport with them; at Cairo numerous stories illustrate the sang-froid with which they used to knock over the camel-drivers, if any one dared to ride past their barracks. The Albanians vaunt their skill in using weapons, and their pretensions impose upon Arabs as well as Egyptians; yet I have never found them wonderful with any arm (the pistol alone excepted); and our officers, who have visited their native hills, speak of them as tolerable but by no means first-rate rifle shots.

The captain of Irregulars being unhappily debarred the pleasure of shooting me, after looking fierce for a time, rose, and walked majestically out of the room. A day or two afterwards, he called upon me civilly enough, sat down, drank a cup of coffee, smoked a pipe, and began to converse. But as he knew about a hundred Arabic words, and I as many Turkish, our conversation was carried on under difficulties. Presently he asked me in a whisper for '*Raki*'. I replied that there was none in the house, which induced a sneer, and an ejaculation sounding like 'Himar' (ass), the slang synonym amongst fast Moslems for water-drinker.

After rising to depart, he seized me waggishly, with an eye to a trial of strength. Thinking that an Indian doctor and a temperance man would not be very dangerous, he exposed himself to what is professionally termed a 'cross-buttock', and had his 'nut' come in contact with the stone floor instead of my bed, he might not have drunk for many a day. The fall had a good effect upon his temper. He jumped up, patted my head, called for another pipe, and sat down to show me his wounds, and to boast of his exploits.

I could not help remarking a ring of English gold, with a bezel of bloodstone, sitting strangely upon his coarse, sunstained hand. He declared that it had been snatched by him from a Konsul (consul) at Jeddah, and he volubly related, in a mixture of Albanian, Turkish, and Arabic, the history of his acquisition. He begged me to supply him with a little poison that 'would not lie', for the purpose of quieting a troublesome enemy, and he carefully stowed away in his pouch five grains of calomel, which I gave him for that laudable purpose. Before taking leave he pressed me strongly to go and drink with him; I refused to do so during the day, but, wishing to see how these men sacrifice to Bacchus, promised compliance that night.

About nine o'clock, when the caravanserai was quiet, I took a pipe, and a tobacco-pouch, stuck my dagger in my belt, and slipped into Ali Agha's room. He was sitting on a bed spread upon the ground; in front of him stood four wax candles (all Orientals hate drinking in any but a bright light), and a tray containing a basin of stuff like soup maigre, a dish of cold stewed meat, and two bowls of *Salatah*, sliced cucumber, and curds. The materials peeped out of an iron pot filled with water; one was a long, thin, white-glass flask of *Raki*, the other a bottle of some strong perfume. Both were wrapped up in wet rags, the usual refrigerator.

Ali Agha welcomed me politely, and seeing me admire the preparations, bade me beware how I suspected an Albanian of not knowing how to drink; he made me sit by him on the bed, threw his dagger to a handy distance, signalled me to do the same, and prepared to begin the bout. Taking up a little tumbler, in shape like those from which French postilions used to drink *la goutte*, he inspected it narrowly, wiped out the interior with his forefinger, filled it to the brim, and offered it to his guest with a bow. I received it with a low salam, swallowed its contents at once, turned it upside-down in proof of fair play, replaced it upon the floor, with a jaunty movement of the arm, somewhat like a pugilist delivering a 'rounder', bowed again, and requested him to help himself. The same ceremony followed on his part. Immediately after each glass—and rapidly the cup went about—we swallowed a draught of water, and ate a spoonful of the meat or the *Salatah* in order to cool our palates. Then we reapplied ourselves to our pipes, emitting huge puffs, a sign of being 'fast' men, and looked facetiously at each other—drinking being considered by Moslems a funny and pleasant sort of sin.

The Albanian captain was at least half-seas-over when we began the bout, yet he continued to fill and to drain without showing the least progress towards ebriety. I in vain for a time expected the 'bad-masti' (as the Persians call it), the horse play, and the gross facetiae, which generally accompany southern and eastern tipsiness. Ali Agha, indeed, occasionally took up the bottle of perfume, filled the palm of his right hand, and dashed it in my face: I followed his example, but our pleasantries went no further.

Presently my companion started a grand project, namely, that I should entice the respectable Haji Wali into the room, where we might force him to drink. The idea was facetious: it was making a Bow-street magistrate polk at a casino.

I started up to fetch the Haji: and when I returned with him Ali Agha was found in a new stage of 'freshness'. He had stuck a green-leaved twig upright in the floor, and had so turned over a gugglet of water, that its contents trickled slowly, in a tiny stream under the verdure; whilst he was sitting before it mentally gazing, with an outward show of grim Quixotic tenderness, upon the shady trees and the cool rills of his fatherland. Possibly he had peopled the place with 'young barbarians at play'; for verily I thought that a tear 'which had no business there' was glistening in his stony eye.

The appearance of Haji Wali suddenly changed the scene. Ali Agha jumped up, seized the visitor by the shoulder, compelled him to sit down, and, ecstasied by the good man's horror at the scene, filled a tumbler, and with the usual grotesque grimaces insisted upon its being drunk off. Haji Wali stoutly refused; then Ali Agha put it to his own lips, and drained it with a hurt-feeling and reproachful aspect.

We made our unconvivial friend smoke a few puffs, and then we returned to the charge. In vain the Haji protested that throughout life he had avoided the deadly sin; in vain he promised to drink with us to-morrow—in vain he quoted the Koran, and alternately coaxed, and threatened us with the police. We were inexorable. At last the Haji started upon his feet, and rushed away, regardless of anything but escape, leaving his Tarbush, his slippers, and his pipe in the hands of the enemy. The host did not dare to pursue his recreant guest beyond the door, but returning he carefully sprinkled the polluting liquid on the cap, pipe, and shoes, and called the Haji an ass in every tongue he knew.

Then we applied ourselves to supper, and despatched the soup, the stew, and the *Salatah.* A few tumblers and pipes were exhausted to obviate indigestion, when Ali Agha arose majestically, and said that he required a troop of dancing girls to gladden his eyes with a ballet.

I represented that such persons are no longer admitted into caravanserais. He inquired, with calm ferocity, 'who hath forbidden it?' I replied 'the Pasha'; upon which Ali Agha quietly removed his cap, brushed it with his dexter fore-arm, fitted it on his forehead, raking forwards, twisted his mustachios to the sharp point of a single hair, shouldered his pipe, and moved towards the door, vowing that he would make the Pasha himself come, and dance before us.

I foresaw a brawl, and felt thankful that my boon companion had forgotten his dagger. Prudence whispered me to return to my room, to bolt the door, and to go to bed, but conscience suggested that it would be unfair to abandon the Albanian in his present helpless state.

I followed him into the outer gallery, pulling him, and begging him, as a despairing wife might urge a drunken husband, to return home. And he, like the British husband, being greatly irritated by the unjovial advice, instantly belaboured with his pipe-stick the first person he met in the gallery, and sent him flying down the stairs with fearful shouts of 'O Egyptians! O ye accursed! O genus of Pharaoh! O race of dogs! O Egyptians!'

He then burst open a door with his shoulder, and reeled into a room where two aged dames were placidly reposing by the side of their spouses, who were basket-makers. They immediately awoke, seeing a stranger, and hearing his foul words, they retorted with a hot volley of vituperation.

Put to flight by the old women's tongues, Ali Agha, in spite of all my endeavours, reeled down the stairs, and fell upon the sleeping form of the night porter, whose blood he vowed to drink—the Oriental form of threatening 'spiflication'. Happily for the assaulted, the Agha's servant, a sturdy Albanian lad, was lying on a mat in the doorway close by. Roused by the tumult, he jumped up, and found the captain in a state of fury. Apparently the man was used to the master's mood. Without delay he told us all to assist, and we lending a helping hand, half dragged and half carried the Albanian to his room. Yet even in this ignoble plight, he shouted with all the force of his lungs the old war-cry, 'O Egyptians! O race of dogs! I have dishonoured all Sikandariyah—all Kahirah—all Suways,'[1] and in this vaunting frame of mind he was put to bed. No Welsh undergraduate at Oxford, under similar circumstances, ever gave more trouble.

'You had better start on your pilgrimage at once,' said Haji Wali, meeting me the next morning with a *goguenard* smile.

He was right. Throughout the caravanserai nothing was talked of for nearly a week but the wickedness of the captain of Albanian Irregulars, and the hypocrisy of the staid Indian doctor. Thus it was, gentle reader, that I lost my reputation of being a serious person at Cairo. And all I have to show for it is the personal experience of an Albanian drinking-bout.

I wasted but little time in taking leave of my friends, telling them, by way of precaution, that my destination was Meccah via Jeddah, and firmly determining, if possible, to make El-Medinah via Yambu'. 'Conceal', says the Arab's proverb, 'thy Tenets, thy Treasure, and thy Travelling.'

[1] *Anglice*, Alexandria, Cairo, and Suez—an extensive field of operations.

VIII
From Cairo to Suez

Shaykh Nassár, a Bedawi of Tur (Mount Sinai), being on his way homewards, agreed to let me have two dromedaries for the sum of 50 piastres, or about 10*s*., each. Being desirous to set out with a certain display of respectability, I accepted these terms; a man of humbler pretensions would have travelled with a single animal, and a camel-man running behind him.

But, besides ostentation, I wanted my attendant to be mounted, that we might make a forced march in order to ascertain how much a four years' life of European effeminacy had impaired my powers of endurance. The reader may believe the assertion that there are few better tests than an eighty-four-mile ride in midsummer, on a bad wooden saddle, borne by a worse dromedary, across the Suez Desert. Even the Squire famed for being copper-sheeted might not have disdained a trial of the kind.

I started my Indian boy and heavy luggage for Suez two days before the end of the Eed, laden camels generally taking fifty-five or sixty hours to do the journey, and I spent the intermediate time with Haji Wali. He advised me to mount about three p.m., so that I might arrive at Suez on the evening of the next day; and assisted me in making due preparations of water, tobacco, and provisions.

Early on the morning of departure the Afghan Shaykh came to the caravanserai, and breakfasted with us, 'because Allah willed it'. After a copious meal he bestowed on me a stately benediction, and would have embraced me, but I humbly bent over his hand: sad to relate, immediately that his back was turned, Haji Wali raised his forefinger to a right angle with the palm, and burst into a shout of irreverent laughter.

At three o'clock, Nassár, the Bedawi, came to announce that the dromedaries were saddled. I dressed myself, sticking a pistol in my belt, and passing the crimson silk cord of the Hamail or pocket Koran over my shoulder, in token of being a pilgrim. Then distributing a few trifling presents to friends and servants, and accompanied by the Shaykh Mohammed, and Haji Wali, I descended the stairs with an important gait. In the courtyard squatted the camels (dromedaries they could not be called), and I found that a second driver was going to accompany us. I objected to this, as the extra Bedawi would, of course, expect to be fed by me; but Nassár swore that the man was his brother, and, as you rarely gain by small disputes with these people, he was allowed to have his own way.

Then came the preparatory leave-takings. Haji Wali embraced me heartily, and so did my poor old Shaykh, who, despite his decrepitude and my objections, insisted upon accompanying me to the city gate. I mounted the camel, crossed my legs before the pommel—stirrups are not used in Egypt—and, preceding my friend, descended the street leading towards the Desert.

As we emerged from the huge gateway of the caravanserai all the bystanders, except only the porter, who believed me to be a Persian, and had seen me with the drunken captain, exclaimed, 'Allah bless thee, Y'al Hajj (O Pilgrim), and restore thee to thy country and thy friends!' And passing through the Bab el-Nasr, where I addressed the salutation of peace to the sentry, and to the officer commanding the guard, both gave me God-speed with great cordiality—the pilgrim's blessing in Asia, like the old woman's in Europe, being supposed to possess peculiar efficacy. Outside the gate my friends took a final leave of me, and I will not deny having felt a tightening of heart as their honest faces and forms faded in the distance.

But Shaykh Nassár switches his camel's shoulder, and appears inclined to take the lead. This is a trial of manliness. There is no time for emotion. Not a moment can be spared, even for a retrospect. I kick my dromedary, who steps out into a jog-trot. The Bedawin with a loud ringing laugh attempt to give me the go-by. I resist, and we continue like children till the camels are at their speed, though we have eighty-four miles before us, and above us an atmosphere like a furnace blast. The road is deserted at this hour, otherwise grave Moslem travellers would have believed the police to be nearer than convenient to us.

Presently we drew rein, and exchanged our pace for one more seasonable, whilst the sun began to tell on man and beast. High raised as we were above the ground, the reflected heat struck us sensibly, and the glare of a macadamised road added a few extra degrees of caloric. The Bedawin, to refresh themselves, prepare to smoke. They fill my chibouque, light it with a flint and steel, and cotton dipped in a solution of gunpowder, and pass it over to me. After a few puffs, I return it to them, and they use it turn by turn.

Then they begin to while away the tedium of the road by asking questions, which *passe-temps* is not easily exhausted; for they are never satisfied till they know as much of you as you do of yourself. They next resort to talking about victuals; for with this hungry race, food, as a topic of conversation, takes the place of money in happier lands. And lastly, even this engrossing subject being exhausted for the moment, they take refuge in singing; and, monotonous and droning as it is, their *modinha* has yet an artless plaintiveness, which admirably suits the singer and the scenery. If you listen to the words, you will surely hear allusions to bright verdure, cool shades, bubbling rills, or something which hereabouts man hath not, and yet which his soul desires.

And now while Nassár and his brother are chanting a duet—the refrain being,

> *W'al Arz mablul bi Matar,*
> And the earth wet with rain—

I must crave leave to say a few words, despite the triteness of the subject, about the modern Sinaitic race of Arabs.

Besides the tribes occupying the northern parts of the peninsula, five chief clans are enumerated by Burckhardt. Nassár, and other authorities at Suez, divided them into six, namely:

(1) Karashi, who, like the Gara in Eastern Arabia, claim an apocryphal origin from the great Koraysh tribe.

(2) Salihi, the principal family of the Sinaitic Bedawin.

(3) Arimi: according to Burckhardt, this clan is merely a sub-family of the Sawalihahs.

(4) Saidi. Burckhardt calls them Welad Said, and derives them also from the Sawalihahs.

(5) Aliki; and lastly, the

(6) Muzaynah, generally pronounced M'zaynah. This clan claims to be an offshoot from the great Juhaynah tribe inhabiting the coast and inner barrens about Yambu'. According to oral tradition, five persons, the ancestors of the present Muzaynah race, were forced by a blood-feud to fly their native country. They landed at the Shurum, or creek-ports, and have now spread themselves over the eastern parts of the so-called Sinaitic Peninsula. In El-Hejaz the Muzaynah is an old and noble tribe. It produced Kaab el-Ahbar, the celebrated poet, to whom Mohammed gave the cloak which the Ottomans believe to have been taken by Sultan Selim from Egypt, and to have been converted, under the name of Khirkah Sherif, into the national Oriflamme.

There are some interesting ethnographical points about these Sinaitic clans—interesting at least to those who would trace the genealogy of the great Arabian family. Any one who knows the Bedawin can see that the Muzaynah are pure blood. Their brows are broad, their faces narrow, their features regular, and their eyes of a moderate size; whereas the other Tawarah (Sinaitic) clans are as palpably Egyptian. These have preserved that roundness of face which may still be seen in the Sphinx as in the modern Copt, and their eyes have that peculiar size, shape, and look, which the old Egyptian painters attempted to express by giving to the profile the form of the full organ. Upon this feature, so characteristic of the Nilotic race, I would lay great stress. No traveller familiar with the true Egyptian eye—long, almond-shaped, deeply fringed, slightly raised at the outer corner and dipping in front like the Chinese—can ever mistake it. It is to be seen in half-castes, and, as I have before remarked, families originally from the banks of the Nile, but settled for generations in the Holy Land of El-Hejaz, retain the peculiarity.

I therefore believe the Turi Bedawin to be an impure race, Egypto-Arab, whereas their neighbour the Hejazi is the pure Syrian or Mesopotamian. 'And he (Ishmael) dwelt in the wilderness of Paran (Wady Firan?), and his mother took him a wife out of the land of Egypt' (Genesis xxi. 21). I wonder that some geographers have attempted to identify Massa the son of Ishmael (Genesis xxv. 14) with Meccah, when in verse 18 of the same chapter we read, 'And they (the twelve princes, sons of Ishmael) *dwelt from Havilah unto Shur.*' This asserts, as clearly as language can, that the posterity of, or the race typified by, Ishmael, the Egypto-Arab, occupied only the northern parts of the peninsula.

The late Dr J. Wilson (*Lands of the Bible*), repeated by Eliot Warburton (*Crescent and Cross*), lays stress upon the Tawarah tradition, that they are Beni-Israel converted to El-Islam, considering it a fulfilment of the prophecy that 'a remnant of Israel shall dwell in Edom'. With due deference to so illustrious an Orientalist and Biblical scholar as was Dr Wilson, I believe that most modern Moslems, being ignorant that Jacob was the first called 'prince with God', apply the term Beni-Israel to all the posterity of Abraham, not to Jews only.

A wonderful change has taken place in the Tawarah tribes, whilome portrayed by Sir John Mandeville as 'folke fulle of alle evylle condiciouns'. Niebuhr notes the trouble they gave him, and their perpetual hankering for both murder and pillage. Even in the late Mohammed Ali's early reign, no governor of Suez dared to flog or to lay hands upon a Turi, whatever offence he might have committed within the walls of the town. Now the wild man's sword is taken from him before he is allowed to enter the gates,[1] and my old acquaintance, Giaffar Bey, would think no more of belabouring a Bedawi than of flogging a Fellah. Such is the result of Mohammed Ali's vigorous policy, and such the effects of even semi-civilisation, when its influence is brought to bear direct upon barbarism.

To conclude this subject, the Tawarah still retain many characteristics of the Bedawi race. The most good-humoured and sociable of men, they delight in a jest, and may readily be managed by kindness and courtesy. Yet they are passionate, nice upon points of honour, revengeful, and easily offended where their peculiar prejudices are misunderstood. I have always found them pleasant companions, and deserving of respect, for

[1] In 1879 the Gates of Suez are a thing of the past; and it is not easy to find where they formerly stood.

their hearts are good, and their courage is beyond a doubt. Those travellers who complain of their insolence and extortion may have been either ignorant of their language, or offensive to them by assumption of superiority— in the Desert man meets man—or physically unfitted to acquire their esteem.

We journeyed on till near sunset through the wilderness without ennui. It is strange how the mind can be amused by scenery that presents so few objects to occupy it. But in such a country every slight modification of form or colour rivets observation: the senses are sharpened, and the perceptive faculties, prone to sleep over a confused mass of natural objects, act vigorously when excited by the capability of embracing each detail. Moreover, Desert views are eminently suggestive; they appeal to the Future, not to the Past; they arouse because they are by no means memorial.

To the solitary wayfarer there is an interest in the Wilderness unknown to Cape seas and Alpine glaciers, and even to the rolling Prairie—the effect of continued excitement on the mind, stimulating its powers to their pitch. Above, through a sky terrible in its stainless beauty, and the splendours of a pitiless blinding glare, the Simúm[1] caresses you like a lion with flaming breath. Around lie drifted sand-heaps, upon which each puff of wind leaves its trace in solid waves, flayed rocks, the very skeletons of mountains, and hard unbroken plains, over which he who rides is spurred by the idea that the bursting of a water-skin, or the pricking of a camel's hoof, would be a certain death of torture; a haggard land infested with wild beasts, and wilder men; a region whose very fountains murmur the warning words 'Drink and away!'

What can be more exciting? what more sublime? Man's heart bounds in his breast at the thought of measuring his puny force with Nature's might, and of emerging triumphant from the trial. This explains the Arab's proverb, 'Voyaging is a Victory.'

In the Desert, even more than upon the ocean, there is present death: hardship is there, and piracies, and shipwreck, solitary, not in crowds, where, as the Persians say, 'Death is a

[1] Vulgarly and most erroneously called the Simoon.

Festival'; and this sense of danger, never absent, invests the scene of travel with an interest not its own.

Let the traveller who suspects exaggeration leave the Suez road for an hour or two, and gallop northwards over the sands: in the drear silence, the solitude, and the fantastic desolation of the place, he will feel what the Desert may be. And then the Oases,[1] and little lines of fertility—how soft and how beautiful!—even though the Wady el-Ward (the Vale of Flowers) be the name of some stern flat upon which a handful of wild shrubs blossom while struggling through a cold season's ephemeral existence.

In such circumstances the mind is influenced through the body. Though your mouth glows, and your skin is parched, yet you feel no languor, the effect of humid heat; your lungs are lightened, your sight brightens, your memory recovers its tone, and your spirits become exuberant; your fancy and imagination are powerfully aroused, and the wildness and sublimity of the scenes around you stir up all the energies of your soul—whether for exertion, danger, or strife. Your morale improves: you become frank and cordial, hospitable and single-minded: the hypocritical politeness and the slavery of civilisation are left behind you in the city. Your senses are quickened: they require no stimulants but air and exercise—in the Desert spirituous liquors excite only disgust.

There is a keen enjoyment in mere animal existence. The sharp appetite disposes of the most indigestible food; the sand is softer than a bed of down, and the purity of the air suddenly puts to flight a dire cohort of diseases. Hence it is that both sexes, and

[1] Nothing can be more incorrect than the vulgar idea of an Arabian Oasis, except it be the popular conception of an Arabian Desert. One reads of 'isles of the sandy sea', but one never sees them. The real Wady is, generally speaking, a rocky valley bisected by the bed of a mountain torrent, dry during the hot season. In such places the Bedawin love to encamp, because they find food and drink—water being always procurable by digging. When the supply is perennial, the Wady becomes the site of a village.

The Desert is as unaptly compared to a sandy sea. Most of the wilds of Arabia resemble the tract between Suez and Cairo; only the former are of primary formation, whereas the others are of a later date. Sand-heaps are found in every desert, but sand-plains are a local feature, not the general face of the country. The wilderness east of the Nile is mostly a hard dry earth, which requires only a monsoon to become highly productive: even where silicious sand covers the plain, the waters of a torrent, depositing humus or vegetable mould, bind the particles together, and fit it for the reception of seed.

every age, the most material as well as the most imaginative of minds, the tamest citizen, the parson, the old maid, the peaceful student, the spoiled child of civilisation, all feel their hearts dilate, and their pulses beat strong, as they look down from their dromedaries upon the glorious Desert. Where do we hear of a traveller being disappointed by it? It is another illustration of the ancient truth that Nature returns to man, however unworthily he has treated her. And believe me, when once your tastes have conformed to the tranquillity of such travel, you will suffer real pain in returning to the turmoil of civilisation. You will anticipate the bustle and the confusion of artificial life, its luxury and its false pleasures, with repugnance. Depressed in spirits, you will for a time after your return feel incapable of mental or bodily exertion. The air of cities will suffocate you, and the careworn and cadaverous countenances of citizens will haunt you like a vision of judgment.

As the black shadow mounted in the eastern sky, I turned off the road, and was suddenly saluted by a figure rising from a little hollow with an 'As' Salamo Alaykum' of truly Arab sound. I looked at the speaker for a moment without recognising him. He then advanced with voluble expressions of joy, invited me to sup, seized my camel's halter without waiting for an answer, 'nakh'd' it (i.e. forced it to kneel), led me hurriedly to a carpet spread in a sandy hollow, pulled off my slippers, gave me cold water for ablution, told me that he had mistaken me at a distance for a Sherif, or Prince, of the Arabs, but was delighted to find himself in error; and urged me to hurry over ablution, otherwise that night would come on before we could say our prayers. It was Mohammed el-Basyuni, the Meccan boy of whom I had bought my pilgrim-garb at Cairo. There I had refused his companionship, but here for reasons of his own—one of them was an utter want of money—he would take no excuse. When he prayed, he stood behind me, thereby proving pliancy of conscience, for he suspected me from the first of being at least a heretic. There are many qualifications necessary for an Imam, a leader of prayer; the first condition, of course, is orthodoxy.

After prayer he lighted a pipe, and immediately placed the

snake-like tube in my hand; this is an argument which the tired traveller can rarely resist. He then began to rummage my saddle-bags; he drew forth stores of provisions, rolls, water-melons, boiled eggs, and dates, and whilst lighting the fire, and boiling the coffee, he managed to distribute his own stock, which was neither plentiful nor first-rate, to the camel-men. Shaykh Nassár and his brother looked aghast at this movement, but the boy was inexorable.

They tried a few rough hints, which he noticed by singing a Hindostani couplet that asserts the impropriety of anointing rats' heads with jasmine oil. They suspected abuse, and waxed cross; he acknowledged this by deriding them. 'I have heard of Nasrs and Násirs and Mansúrs, but may Allah spare me the mortification of a Nassár!' said the boy, relying upon my support. And I urged him on, wanting to see how the city Arab treats the countryman. He then took my tobacco-pouch from the angry Bedawin, and in a stage-whisper reproved me for entrusting it to such thieves; insisting, at the same time, upon drinking all the coffee, so that the poor guides had to prepare some for themselves.

He improved every opportunity of making mischief. 'We have eaten water-melon!' cried Nassár, patting its receptacle in token of repletion.

'Dost thou hear, my lord, how they grumble?—the impudent ruffians!' remarked Mohammed—'*We have eaten water-melon!* that is to say, we ought to have eaten meat!'

The Bedawin, completely out of temper, told him not to trust himself among their hills. He seized a sword, and began capering about after the fashion of the East Indian school of arms, and boasted that he would attack single-handed the whole clan, which elicited an ironical 'Allah! Allah!' from the hearers.

After an hour most amusingly spent in this way, I arose, much to the dissatisfaction of my guides, who wished to sleep there, and insisted upon mounting. Shaykh Nassár and his brother had reckoned upon living gratis, for at least three days, judging it improbable that a soft Effendi would hurry himself. When they saw the fair vision dissolve, they began to finesse: they induced the camel-man, who ran by the side of Mohammed's dromedary, to precede the animal—a favourite manoeuvre to prevent overspeed. Ordered to fall back, the fellow pleaded fatigue, and inability to walk. The boy Mohammed immediately asked if I had any objection to dismount one of my guides, and to let his weary attendant ride for an hour or so. I at once assented, and the Bedawi obeyed me with ominous grumblings. When we resumed our march the melancholy Arabs had no song left in them; whereas Mohammed chanted vociferously, and quoted bad Hindostani and worse Persian till silence was forcibly imposed upon him.

The camel-men lagged behind, in order to prevent my dromedary advancing too fast, and the boy's guide, after dismounting, would stride along in front of us, under pretext of showing the way. And so we jogged on, now walking, then trotting, till the dromedaries began to grunt with fatigue, and the Arabs clamoured for a halt.

At midnight we reached the Central Station, and lay down under its walls to take a little rest. The dews fell heavily, wetting the sheets that covered us; but who cares for such trifles in the Desert? The moon shone bright; the breeze blew coolly, and the jackal sang a lullaby which lost no time in inducing the soundest sleep. As the 'Wolf's tail' (the first brushes of grey light which appear as forerunners of dawn) showed in the heavens we arose. Grey mists floating over the hills northwards gave the Dar el-Bayda, the Pasha's Palace, the look of some old feudal castle. There was a haze in the atmosphere, which beautified even the face of Desolation. The swift-flying Kata[1] sprang in noisy coveys from the road, and a stray gazelle paced daintily over the stony plain.

As we passed by the Pilgrims' tree, I added another rag to its coat of tatters. We then invoked the aid of the holy saint El-Dakrur from his cream-coloured abode, mounted our camels, and resumed the march in real earnest. The dawn passed away in its delicious coolness, and sultry morning came on. Then day

[1] The Tetrao Kata or sand-grouse (Pterocles melanogaster; in Sind called the rock pigeon) is a fast-flying bird, not unlike a grey partridge whilst upon the wing. When, therefore, Shanfara boasts 'The ash-coloured Katas can only drink my leavings, after hastening all night to slake their thirst in the morning,' it is a hyperbole to express his exceeding swiftness.

glared in its fierceness, and the noontide sun made the plain glow with terrible heat. Still we pressed onwards.

At three p.m. we turned off the road into a dry water-course which is not far from No. 13 Station. The sand was dotted with the dried-up leaves of the Datura, and strongly perfumed by Shib, a kind of Absinthe, the sweetest herb of the Desert. A Mimosa was there, and although its shade at this season is little better than a cocoa tree's, the Bedawin would not neglect it.

We lay down upon the sand to rest among a party of Maghrabi pilgrims travelling to Suez. These wretches, who were about a dozen in number, appeared to be of the lowest class; their garments consisted of a Burnus-cloak and a pair of sandals; their sole weapon a long knife, and their only stock a bag of dry provisions. Each had his large wooden bowl, but none carried water with him. It was impossible to help pitying their state, nor could I eat, seeing them hungry, thirsty, and wayworn. Nassár served out about a pint of water and a little bread to each man. Then they asked for more. None was to be had, so they cried out that money would do as well. I had determined upon being generous to the extent of a few pence. Custom, as well as inclination, was in favour of the act; but when the alms became a demand, and the demand was backed by fierce looks and a derisive sneer, and a kind of reference to their knives, gentle Charity took the alarm and fled. My pistols kept them at bay, for they were only making an attempt to intimidate, and, though I took the precaution of sitting apart from them, there was no real danger.

The Suez road, by the wise regulations of Mohammed Ali, has become as safe to European travellers as that between Hampstead and Highgate; and even Easterns have little to fear but what their fears create. My Indian servant was full of the dangers he had run, but I did not believe in them. I afterwards heard that the place where the Maghrabis attempted to frighten what they thought a timid Turk was once notorious for plunder and murder. Here the spurs of two opposite hills almost meet upon the plain, a favourable ground for Bedawi ambuscade.

Of the Maghrabis I shall have more to say when relating my voyage in the Pilgrim Ship: they were the only travellers from whom we experienced the least annoyance. Numerous parties of Turks, Arabs, and Afghans, and a few East Indians, were on the same errand as ourselves. All, as we passed them, welcomed us with the friendly salutation that becomes men engaged in a labour of religion.

About half an hour before sunset, I turned off the road leftwards; and, under pretext of watering the dromedaries, rode up to inspect the fort El-Ajrudi. It is a quadrangle with round towers at the gateway and at the corners, newly built of stone and mortar; the material is already full of crevices, and would not stand before a twelve-pounder. Without guns or gunners, it is occupied by about a dozen Fellahs, who act as hereditary Ghafirs (guardians); they were expecting at that time to be reinforced by a party of Bash-Buzuks—irregulars from Cairo. The people of the country were determined that an English fleet would soon appear in the Red Sea, and this fort is by them ridiculously considered the key of Suez. As usual in these Vauban-lacking lands, the well supplying the stronghold is in a detached and distant building, which can be approached by an enemy with the greatest security. Over the gateway was an ancient inscription reversed; the water was brackish, and of bad quality.

We resumed our way: Suez now stood near. In the blue distance the castellated peaks of Jebel Rahah, and the wide sand-tracts over which lies the land-route to El-Hejaz. Before us the sight ever dear to English eyes—a strip of sea gloriously azure, with a gallant steamer walking the waters. On the right-hand side the broad slopes of Jebel Mukattam, a range of hills which flanks the road all the way from Cairo. It was at this hour a spectacle not easily to be forgotten. The near range of chalk and sandstone wore a russet suit, gilt where the last rays of the sun seamed it with light, and the deep folds were shaded with the richest purple; whilst the background of the higher hills, Jebel Taweri, generally known as Abu Diráj (the Father of Steps), was sky-blue streaked with the lightest plum colour. We drew up at a small building called Bir Suways (Well of Suez); and, under pretext of watering the cattle, I sat for half an hour admiring the charms of the Desert. The eye never tires of such loveliness of hue, and the memory of the hideousness of this range, when a sun in front exposed each gaunt and barren feature, supplied the evening view with another element of attraction.

It was already night when we passed through the tumbling six-windowed gateway of Suez; and still remained the task of finding my servant and effects. After wandering in and out of every Wakalah in the village, during which peregrination the boy Mohammed proved himself so useful that I determined at all risks to make him my companion, we accidentally heard that a Hindi had taken lodgings at a hostelry bearing the name of Jirjis el-Zahr, the George; so called after its owner, a Copt, Consular Agent for Belgium. On arriving there our satisfaction was diminished by the intelligence that the same Hindi, after locking the door, had gone out with his friends to a ship in the harbour; in fact, that he had made all preparations for running away. I dismounted and tried to persuade the porter to break open the wooden bolt, but he absolutely refused, and threatened the police. Meanwhile Mohammed had found a party of friends, men of El-Medinah, returning to the pilgrimage after a begging tour through Egypt and Turkey. The meeting was characterised by vociferous inquiries, loud guffaws, and warm embraces.

I was invited to share their supper, and their dormitory—an uncovered platform projecting from the gallery over the square court below—but I had neither appetite nor spirits enough to be sociable. The porter, after much persuasion, showed me an empty room, in which I spread my carpet. That was a sad night. My eighty-four-mile ride had made every bone ache; I had lost much epidermis, and the sun had seared every portion of skin exposed to it. So lamenting my degeneracy and the ill-effects of four years' domicile in Europe, and equally disquieted in mind about the fate of my goods and chattels, I fell into an uncomfortable sleep.

IX
Suez

Early on the morning after my arrival, I arose, and consulted my new acquaintances about the means of recovering the missing property. They unanimously advised a visit to the governor, whom, however, they described to be a 'Kalb ibn kalb' ('dog, son of a dog'), who never returned Moslem's salutations, and who thought all men dirt to be trodden underfoot by the Turks. The boy Mohammed showed his *savoir-faire* by extracting from his huge Sahharah-box a fine embroidered cap, and a grand peach-coloured coat, with which I was instantly invested; he dressed himself with similar magnificence, and we then set out to the 'palace'.

Giaffar Bey—he has been since deposed—then occupied the position of judge, officer commanding, collector of customs, and magistrate of Suez. He was a *Mir-liwa*, or brigadier-general, and had some reputation as a soldier, together with a slight tincture of European science and language. The large old Turk received me most superciliously, disdained all return of salam, and fixing upon me two little eyes like gimlets, demanded my business. I stated that one Shaykh Nur, my Hindi servant, had played me false; therefore I required permission to break into the room supposed to contain my effects. He asked my profession. I replied the medical. This led him to inquire if I had any medicine for the eyes, and being answered in the affirmative, he sent a messenger with me to enforce obedience on the part of the porter. The obnoxious measure was, however, unnecessary. As we entered the caravanserai, there appeared at the door the black face of Shaykh Nur, looking, though accompanied by sundry fellow-countrymen, uncommonly as if he merited and expected the bamboo. He had, by his own account, been seduced into the festivities of a coal-hulk, manned by Lascars; and the vehemence of his self-accusation saved him from the chastisement which I had determined to administer.

I must now briefly describe the party of Meccah and Medinah men into which fate threw me: their names will so frequently appear in the following pages, that a few words about their natures will not be misplaced.

First of all comes Umar Effendi, so called in honour, a Daghistani or Circassian, the grandson of a Hanafi Mufti at El-Medinah, and the son of a Shayk-Rakb, an officer whose duty it is to lead dromedary-caravans. He sits upon his cot, a small, short, plump body, of yellow complexion and bilious temperament, grey-eyed, soft-featured, and utterly beardless—which affects his feelings—he looks fifteen, and he owns to twenty-eight. His manners are those of a student; he dresses respectably, prays regularly, hates the fair sex, like an Arab, whose affections and aversions are always in extremes; is serious, has a mild demeanour, a humble gait, and a soft slow voice. When roused he becomes furious as a Bengal tiger. His parents have urged him to marry, and he, like Camaralzaman, has informed his father that he is 'a person of great age, but little sense'. Urged moreover by a melancholy turn of mind, and the want of leisure for study at El-Medinah, he fled the paternal domicile, and entered himself a pauper *Talib ilm* (student) in the Azhar Mosque. His disconsolate friends and afflicted relations sent a confidential man to fetch him home, by force should it be necessary; he has yielded, and is now awaiting the first opportunity of travelling gratis, if possible, to El-Medinah.

That confidential man is a negro-servant, called Saad, notorious in his native city as El-Jinni, the Demon. Born and bred a slave in Umar Effendi's family, he obtained manumission, became a soldier in El-Hejaz, was dissatisfied with pay perpetually in arrears, turned merchant, and wandered far and wide, to Russia, to Gibraltar, and to Baghdad. He is the pure African, noisily merry at one moment, at another silently sulky; affectionate and abusive, brave and boastful, reckless and crafty, exceedingly quarrelsome, and unscrupulous to the last degree. The bright side of his character is his love and respect for the young master Umar Effendi: yet even him he will scold in a paroxysm of fury, and steal from him whatever he can lay his hands on. He is generous with his goods, but is ever borrowing and never paying money: he dresses like a beggar, with the dirtiest Tarbush upon his tufty poll, and only a cotton shirt over his sooty skin; whilst his two boxes are full of handsome apparel for himself and the three ladies, his wives, at El-Medinah. He knows no fear but for those boxes.

Frequently during our search for a vessel he forced himself into Giaffar Bey's presence, and there he demeaned himself so impudently, that we expected to see him lamed by the bastinado; his forwardness, however, only amused the dignitary. He wanders all day about the bazar, talking freight and passage, for he has resolved, cost what it will, to travel free, and with doggedness like his he must succeed.

Shaykh Hamid el-Samman derives his cognomen, the 'Clarified-Butter-Seller', from a celebrated saint and Sufi of the Kadiriyah order, who left a long line of holy descendants at El-Medinah. This Shaykh squats upon a box full of presents for the 'daughter of his paternal uncle' (his wife), a perfect specimen of the town Arab. His poll is crowned with a rough Shushah or tuft of hair; his face is of a dirty brown, his little goatee straggles untrimmed; his feet are bare, and his only garment is an exceedingly unclean, ochre-coloured blouse, tucked into a leathern girdle beneath it. He will not pray, because he is unwilling to take pure clothes out of his box; but he smokes when he can get other people's tobacco, and groans between the whiffs, conjugating the verb all day, for he is of active mind. He can pick out his letters, and he keeps in his bosom a little dog's-eared MS full of serious romances and silly prayers, old and exceedingly ill written: this he will draw forth at times, peep into for a moment, devoutly kiss, and restore to its proper place with the veneration of the vulgar for a book. He can sing all manner of songs, slaughter a sheep with dexterity, deliver a grand call to prayer, shave, cook, fight; and he excels in the science of vituperation: like Saad, he never performs his devotions, except when necessary to keep up appearances; and, though he has sworn to perish before he forgets his vow to the 'daughter of his uncle', I shrewdly suspect he is no better than he should be. His brow crumples at the word wine, but there is quite another expression about the region of the mouth: Stamboul, where he has lived some months, without learning ten words of Turkish, is a notable place for displacing prejudice. And, finally, he has not more than a piastre or two in his pocket, for he has squandered the large presents given to him at Cairo and Constantinople by noble ladies, to whom he acted as master of the ceremonies at the tomb of the Prophet.

Stretched on a carpet, smoking a Persian Kaliun all day, lies Salih Shakkar, a Turk on the father's and an Arab on the mother's side, born at El-Medinah. This lanky youth may be sixteen years old, but he has the ideas of forty-six; he is thoroughly greedy, selfish, and ungenerous; coldly supercilious as a Turk, and energetically avaricious as an Arab. He prays more often, and dresses more respectably, than the descendant of the Clarified-Butter-Seller; he affects the Constantinople style of toilette, and his light yellow complexion makes people consider him a superior person.

We were intimate enough on the road, when he borrowed from me a little money. But at El-Medinah he cut me pitilessly, as a town man does a continental acquaintance accidentally met in Hyde Park; and of course he tried, though in vain, to evade repaying his debt. He had a tincture of letters, and appeared to have studied critically the subject of largess. 'The Generous is Allah's Friend, ay, though he be a Sinner; and the Miser is Allah's Foe, ay, though he be a Saint,' was a venerable saying always in his mouth. He also informed me that Pharaoh, although the quintessence of impiety, is mentioned by name in the Koran, by reason of his liberality: whereas Nimrod, another monster of iniquity, is only alluded to, because he was a stingy tyrant. It is almost needless to declare that Salih Shakkar was, as the East Indians say, a very 'fly-sucker'.

There were two other men of El-Medinah in the Wakalat Girgis; but I omit description, as we left them, they being penniless, at Suez. One of them, Mohammed Shiklibha, I afterwards met at Meccah, and seldom have I seen a more honest and warm-hearted fellow. When we were embarking at Suez, he fell upon Hamid's bosom, and both of them wept bitterly at the prospect of parting even for a few days.

All the individuals above mentioned lost no time in opening

the question of a loan. It was a lesson in Oriental metaphysics to see their condition. They had a twelve days' voyage, and a four days' journey before them; boxes to carry, custom-houses to face, and stomachs to fill; yet the whole party could scarcely, I believe, muster 2 dollars of ready money. Their boxes were full of valuables, arms, clothes, pipes, slippers, sweetmeats, and other 'notions'; but nothing short of starvation would have induced them to pledge the smallest article.

Foreseeing that their company would be an advantage, I hearkened favourably to the honeyed request for a few crowns. The boy Mohammed obtained 6 dollars; Hamid about 5*l.*, as I intended to make his house at El-Medinah my home; Umar Effendi 3 dollars; Saad the Demon, 2—I gave the money to him at Yambu'—and Salih Shakkar 50 piastres.

But since in these lands, as a rule, no one ever lends coins, or, borrowing, ever returns them, I took care to exact service from the first, to take two rich coats from the second, a handsome pipe from the third, a bala or yataghan from the fourth, and from the fifth an imitation cashmere shawl. After which, we sat down and drew out the agreement. It was favourable to me: I lent them Egyptian money, and bargained for repayment in the currency of El-Hejaz, thereby gaining the exchange, which is sometimes sixteen per cent. This was done, not so much for the sake of profit, as with the view of becoming a Hatim, a well-known Arab chieftain, whose name has come to stand for generosity itself, by a 'never mind' on settling-day.

My companions having received these small sums, became affectionate, and eloquent in my praise: they asked me to make one of their number at meals for the future, overwhelmed me with questions, insisted upon a present of sweetmeats, detected in me a great man under a cloud—perhaps my claims to being a Dervish assisted them to this discovery—and declared that I should perforce be their guest at Meccah and El-Medinah. On all occasions precedence was forced upon me; my opinion was the first consulted, and no project was settled without my concurrence: briefly, Abdullah the Dervish suddenly found himself a person of consequence.

This elevation led me into an imprudence which might have

cost me dear; it aroused the only suspicion about me ever expressed during the summer's tour. My friends had looked at my clothes, overhauled my medicine-chest, and criticised my pistols; they sneered at my copper-cased watch, and remembered having seen a compass at Constantinople. Therefore I imagined they would think little about a sextant. This was a mistake. The boy Mohammed, I afterwards learned, waited only my leaving the room to declare that the would-be Haji was one of the Infidels from India, and a council sat to discuss the case.

Fortunately for me, Umar Effendi had looked over a letter which I had written to Haji Wali that morning, and he had at various times received categorical replies to certain questions in high theology. He felt himself justified in declaring, *ex cathedra*, the boy Mohammed's position perfectly untenable. And Shaykh Hamid, who looked forward to being my host, guide, and debtor in general, and probably cared scantily for catechism or creed, swore that the light of El-Islam was upon my countenance; and, consequently, that the boy Mohammed was a pauper, a fakir, an owl, a cut-off-one (from the pleasures and the comforts of life),[1] a stranger, and a Wahhabi (heretic), for daring to impugn the faith of a brother believer. The scene ended with a general abuse of the acute youth, who was told on all sides that he had no shame, and was directed to fear Allah. I was struck with the expression of my friends' countenances when they saw the sextant; and, determining with a sigh to leave it behind, I prayed five times a day for nearly a week.

We all agreed not to lose an hour in securing places on board some vessel bound for Yambu'; and my companions, hearing that my passport as a British Indian was scarcely *en règle*, earnestly advised me to have it signed by the governor without delay, whilst they occupied themselves about the harbour.

They warned me that if I displayed the Turkish Tezkirah given to me at the citadel of Cairo, I should infallibly be ordered to await the caravan, and lose their society and friendship. Pilgrims arriving at Alexandria, be it known to the reader, are

[1] 'Munkati'—one cut off (from the pleasures and comforts of life). In El-Hejaz, as in England, any allusion to poverty is highly offensive.

divided into bodies, and distributed by means of passports to the three great roads, namely, Suez, Cosseir, and the Hajj route by land round the Gulf of El-Akabah. After the division has once been made, government turns a deaf ear to the representations of individuals.

The Bey of Suez has an order to obstruct pilgrims as much as possible till the end of the season, when they are hurried down that way, lest they should arrive at Meccah too late. As most of the Egyptian high officials have boats, which sail up the Nile laden with pilgrims and return freighted with corn, the government naturally does its utmost to force the delays and discomforts of this line upon strangers. And as those who travel by the Hajj route must spend money in the Egyptian territories at least fifteen days longer than they would if allowed to embark at once for Suez, the Bey very properly assists them in the former, and obstructs them in the latter case.

Knowing these facts, I felt that a difficulty was at hand. The first thing was to take Shaykh Nur's passport, which was *en règle*, and my own, which was not, to the Bey for signature. He turned the papers over and over, as if unable to read them, and raised false hopes high by referring me to his clerk. The under-official at once saw the irregularity of the document, asked me why it had not been *visé* at Cairo, swore that under such circumstances nothing would induce the Bey to let me proceed; and, when I tried persuasion, waxed insolent. I feared that it would be necessary to travel via Cosseir, for which there was scarcely time, or to transfer myself on camel-back to the harbour of Tur, and there to await the chance of finding a place in some half-filled vessel to El-Hejaz—which would have been relying upon an accident.

My last hope at Suez was to obtain assistance from Mr West, then HBM's vice-consul, and since made consul. I therefore took the boy Mohammed with me, choosing him on purpose, and excusing the step to my companions by concocting an artful fable about my having been, in Afghanistan, a benefactor to the British nation. We proceeded to the consulate. Mr West, who had been told by imprudent Augustus Bernal to expect me, saw through the disguise, despite jargon assumed to satisfy official scruples, and nothing could be kinder than the part he took. His clerk was directed to place himself in communication with the Bey's factotum; and, when objections to signing the Alexandrian Tezkirah were offered, the vice-consul said that he would, at his own risk, give me a fresh passport as a British subject from Suez to Arabia. His firmness prevailed: on the second day, the documents were returned to me in a satisfactory state. I take pleasure in owning this obligation to Mr West: in the course of my wanderings, I have often received from him open-hearted hospitality and the most friendly attentions.

Whilst these passport difficulties were being solved, the rest of the party was as busy in settling about passage and passage-money. The peculiar rules of the port of Suez require a few words of explanation.[1] 'About thirty-five years ago (1853), the shipowners proposed to the then government, with the view of keeping up freight, a Farzah, or system of rotation. It might be supposed that the Pasha, whose object notoriously was to retain all monopolies in his own hands, would have refused his sanction to such a measure.

'But it so happened in those days that all the court had ships at Suez: Ibrahim Pasha alone owned four or five. Consequently they expected to share profits with the merchants, and thus to be compensated for the want of port-dues. From that time forward all the vessels in the harbour were registered, and ordered to sail in rotation. This arrangement benefits the owner of the craft *en départ*, giving him in his turn a temporary monopoly, with the advantage of a full market; and freight is so high that a single trip often clears off the expense of building and the risk of losing the ship—a sensible succedaneum for insurance companies. On the contrary, the public must always be a loser by the Farzah.

'Two of a trade do not agree elsewhere; but at Suẹz even the Christian and the Moslem shipowner are bound by a fraternal

[1] The account here offered to the reader was kindly supplied to me by Henry Levick, Esq. (late vice-consul, and afterwards postmaster at Suez), and it may be depended upon as coming from a resident of sixteen years' standing. All the passages marked with inverted commas are extracts from a letter with which that gentleman favoured me. The information is obsolete now (1870), but it may be interesting as a specimen of the things that were.

tie, in the shape of this rotation system. It injures the general merchant, and the Red Sea trader, not only by perpetuating high freight, but also by causing at one period of the year a break in the routine of sales and in the supplies of goods for the great Jeddah market.[1] At this moment (November 1853) the vessel to which the turn belongs happens to be a large one; there is a deficiency of export to El-Hejaz: her owner will of course wait any length of time for a full cargo; consequently no vessel with merchandise has left Suez for the last seventy-two days. Those who have bought goods for the Jeddah market at three months' credit will therefore have to meet their acceptances for merchandise still warehoused at the Egyptian port. This strange contrast to free-trade principle is another proof that protection benefits only one party, the protected, while it is detrimental to the interests of the other party, the public.'

To these remarks of Mr Levick's, I have only to add that the government supports the Farzah with all the energy of protectionists. A letter from Mr (now Sir) John Drummond Hay was insufficient to induce the Bey of Suez to break through the rule of rotation in favour of certain princes from Morocco. The recommendations of Lord Stratford de Redcliffe met with no better fate; and all Mr West's goodwill could not procure me a vessel out of her turn.

We were forced to rely upon our own exertions, and the activity of Saad the Demon. This worthy, after sundry delays and differences, mostly caused by his own determination to travel gratis, and to make us pay too much, finally closed with the owner of the *Golden Thread*. He took places for us upon the poop, the most eligible part of the vessel at this season of the year; he premised that we should not be very comfortable, as we were to be crowded with Maghrabi pilgrims, but that 'Allah makes all things easy!' Though not penetrated with the conviction that this would happen in our case, I paid for two deck passages 18

[1] NOTE TO THIRD EDITION. The Farzah, I may here observe, has been abolished by Said Pasha since the publication of these lines: the effects of free trade are exactly what were predicted by Mr Levick.

The principal trade from Suez is to Jeddah, Cosseir supplying Yambu'. The latter place, however, imports from Suez, wheat, beans, cheese, biscuit, and other provisions for return pilgrims.

Riyals (dollars); and my companions 7 each, whilst Saad secretly entered himself as an able seaman. Mohammed Shiklibha we were obliged to leave behind, as he could not or would not afford the expense, and none of us might afford it for him. Had I known him to be the honest, true-hearted fellow he was—his kindness at Meccah quite won my heart—I should not have grudged the small charity.

Nothing more comfortless than our days and nights in the George Inn. The ragged walls of our rooms were clammy with dirt, the smoky rafters foul with cobwebs, and the floor, bestrewed with kit in terrible confusion, was black with hosts of cockroaches, ants, and flies. Pigeons nestled on the shelf, cooing amatory ditties the livelong day, and cats like tigers crawled through a hole in the door, making night hideous with their caterwaulings. Now a curious goat, then an inquisitive jackass, would walk stealthily into the room, remark that it was tenanted, and retreat with dignified demeanour, and the mosquitoes sang Io Paeans over our prostrate forms throughout the twenty-four hours.

I spare the reader the enumeration of the other Egyptian plagues that infested the place. After the first day's trial, we determined to spend the hours of light in the passages, lying upon our boxes or rugs, smoking, wrangling, and inspecting one another's chests. The latter occupation was a fertile source of disputes, for nothing was more common than for a friend to seize an article belonging to another, and to swear by the Apostle's beard that he admired it, and, therefore, would not return it. The boy Mohammed and Shaykh Nur, who had been intimates the first day, differed in opinion on the second, and on the third came to pushing each other against the wall.

Sometimes we went into the bazar, a shady street flanked with poor little shops, or we sat in the coffee-house, drinking hot saltish water tinged with burnt bean, or we prayed in one of three tumble-down old Mosques, or we squatted upon the pier, lamenting the want of Hammams, and bathing in the tepid sea. I presently came to the conclusion that Suez as a watering-place is duller even than Dover.

The only society we found, excepting an occasional visitor,

was that of a party of Egyptian women, who with their husbands and families occupied some rooms adjoining ours. At first they were fierce, and used bad language, when the boy Mohammed and I, whilst Umar Effendi was engaged in prayer, and the rest were wandering about the town, ventured to linger in the cool passage, where they congregated, or to address a facetious phrase to them. But hearing that I was a Hakim-bashi, for fame had promoted me to the rank of a Physician General at Suez, all discovered some ailments.

They began prudently with requesting me to display the effects of my drugs by dosing myself, but they ended submissively by swallowing the nauseous compounds. To this succeeded a primitive form of flirtation, which mainly consisted of the demand direct. The most charming of the party was one Fattúmah, a plump-personed dame fast verging upon her thirtieth year, fond of a little flattery, and possessing, like all her people, a most voluble tongue.

The refrain of every conversation was 'Marry me, O Fattúmah! O daughter! O female pilgrim!' In vain the lady would reply, with a coquettish movement of the sides, a toss of the head, and a flirting manipulation of her head-veil, 'I am mated, O young man': it was agreed that she, being a person of polyandrous propensities, could support the weight of at least three matrimonial engagements.

Sometimes the entrance of the male Fellahs interrupted these little discussions, but people of our respectability and nation were not to be imposed upon by such husbands. In their presence we only varied the style of conversation—inquiring the amount of Mahr, or marriage settlement, deriding the cheapness of womanhood in Egypt, and requiring to be furnished on the spot with brides at the rate of 10*s*. a head.

More often the amiable Fattúmah—the fair sex in this country, though passing frail, have the best tempers in the world—would laugh at our impertinences. Sometimes vexed by our imitating her Egyptian accent, mimicking her gestures, and depreciating her country-women, she would wax wroth, and order us to be gone, and stretch out her forefinger, a sign that she wished to put out our eyes, or adjure Allah to cut the hearts out of our bosoms. Then the 'Marry me, O Fattúmah, O daughter, O female pilgrim!' would give way to 'Y'al Ago-o-ozah! (O old woman and decrepit!) O daughter of sixty sires, and fit only to carry wood to market': whereupon would burst a storm of wrath, at the tail of which all of us, like children, starting upon our feet, rushed out of one another's way. But—*qui se dispute, s'adore*—when we again met all would be forgotten, and the old tale be told over *de novo*.

This was the amusement of the day. At night we men, assembling upon the little terrace, drank tea, recited stories, read books, talked of our travels, and indulged in various pleasantries. The great joke was the boy Mohammed's abusing all his companions to their faces in Hindostani, which none but Shaykh Nur and I could understand; the others, however, guessed his intention, and revenged themselves by retorts of the style uncourteous in the purest Hejazi.

I proceed to offer a few more extracts from Mr Levick's letter about Suez and the Suezians.

'It appears that the number of pilgrims who pass through Suez to Meccah has of late been steadily on the decrease. When I first came here (in 1838) the pilgrims who annually embarked at this port amounted to between 10,000 and 12,000, the shipping was more numerous, and the merchants' ware more affluent. I have ascertained from a special register kept in the government archives that in the Moslem year 1268 (from 1851 to 1852) the exact number that passed through was 4,893. In AH 1269 it had shrunk to 3,136. The natives assign the falling off to various causes, which I attribute chiefly to the indirect effect of European civilisation upon the Moslem powers immediately in contact with it. The heterogeneous mass of pilgrims is composed of people of all classes, colours, and costumes. One sees among them not only the natives of countries contiguous to Egypt, but also a large proportion of central Asians from Bokhara, Persia, Circassia, Turkey, and the Crimea, who prefer this route by way of Constantinople to the difficult, expensive, and dangerous caravan-line through the desert from Damascus and Baghdad. The West sends us Moors, Algerines, and Tunisians, and Inner Africa a mass of sable Takruri, and others from Bornou, the Sudan, Ghedamah near the Niger, and Jabarti from the Habash.

'The Suez ship-builders are an influential body of men, originally Candiots and Alexandrians. When Mohammed Ali fitted out his fleet for the Hejaz war, he transported a number of Greeks to Suez, and the children now exercise their fathers' craft. There are at present three great builders at this place. Their principal difficulty is the want of material. Teak comes from India, via Jeddah, and Venetian boards, owing to the expense of camel-transport, are a hundred per cent dearer here than at Alexandria. Trieste and Turkey supply spars, and Jeddah, canvas: the sail-makers are Suez men, and the crews a mongrel mixture of Arabs and Egyptians; the Rais, or captain, being almost invariably, if the vessel be a large one, a Yambu' man. There are two kinds of craft, distinguished from each other by tonnage, not by build. The Baghlah (buggalow) is a vessel above fifty tons burden, the Sambuk (a classical term) from fifteen to fifty. The shipowner bribes the Amir el-Bahr, or port-captain, and the Nazir el-Safayn, or the captain commanding the government vessels, to rate his vessel as high as possible; if he pay the price, he will be allowed nine ardebbs (each 300 lb.) to the ton.

'The number of ships belonging to the port of Suez amounts to ninety-two; they vary from twenty-five to 250 tons. The departures in AH 1269 (1852 and 1853) were thirty-eight, so that each vessel, after returning from a trip, is laid up for about two years. Throughout the passage of the pilgrims—that is to say, during four months—the departures average twice a week; during the remainder of the year from six to ten vessels may leave the port. The homeward trade is carried on principally in Jeddah bottoms, which are allowed to convey goods to Suez, but not to take in return cargo there: they must not interfere with, nor may they partake in any way of the benefits of the rotation system.

'During the present year the imports were contained in 41,395 packages, the exports in 15,988. Specie makes up in some manner for this preponderance of imports: a sum of from 30,000*l.* to 40,000*l.* in crown or Maria Theresa dollars annually leaves Egypt for Arabia, Abyssinia, and other parts of Africa. I value the imports at about 350,000*l*.; the export trade to Jeddah at 300,000*l*. per annum. The former consists principally of coffee and gum-arabic; of these there were respectively 17,460 and 15,132 bales, the aggregate value of each article being from 75,000*l*. to 80,000*l*., and the total amount 160,000*l*. In the previous year the imports were contained in 36,840 packages, the exports in 13,498; of the staple articles—coffee and gum-arabic—they were respectively 15,499 and 14,129 bales, each bale being valued at about 5*l*. Next in importance comes wax from Yemen and the Hejaz, mother-of-pearl from the Red Sea, sent to England in rough, pepper from Malabar, cloves brought by Moslem pilgrims from Java, Borneo, and Singapore, cherry pipe-sticks from Persia and Bussora, and Persian or Surat "Timbak" (tobacco). These I value at 20,000*l*. per annum. There were also (AD 1853) of cloves 708 packages, and of Malabar pepper 948; the cost of these two might be 7,000*l*.

'Minor articles of exportation are—general spiceries (ginger, cardamoms, etc.); Eastern perfumes, such as aloes-wood, ottar of rose, ottar of pink, and others; tamarinds from India and Yemen, Banca tin, hides supplied by the nomade Bedawin, senna leaves from Yemen and the Hejaz, and blue chequered cotton Melayahs (women's mantillas), manufactured in southern Arabia. The total value of these smaller imports may be 20,000*l*. per annum.

'The exports chiefly consist of English and native "grey domestics", bleached Madipilams, Paisley lappets, and muslin for turbans; the remainder being Manchester prints, antimony, Syrian soap, iron in bars and common ironmongery, Venetian or Trieste beads, used as ornaments in Arabia and Abyssinia, writing paper, Tarbushes, Papushes (slippers), and other minor articles of dress and ornament.

'The average annual temperature of the year at Suez is 67° Fahrenheit. The extremes of heat and cold are found in January and August; during the former month the thermometer ranges from a minimum of 38° to a maximum of 68°; during the latter the variation extends from 68° to 102°, or even to 104°, when the heat becomes oppressive. Departures from these extremes are rare. I never remember to have seen the thermometer rise above 108° during the severest Khamsin, or to have sunk below 34° in the rawest wintry wind. Violent storms come up from the south in March. Rain is very variable; sometimes three years have passed without a shower, whereas in 1841 torrents poured for nine successive days, deluging the town, and causing many buildings to fall.

'The population of Suez now numbers about 4,800. As usual in Mohammedan countries, no census is taken here. Some therefore estimate the population at 6,000. Sixteen years ago it was supposed to be under 3,000. After that time it rapidly increased till 1850, when a fatal attack of cholera reduced it to about half its previous number. The average mortality is about twelve a month. The endemic diseases are fevers of typhoid and intermittent types in spring, when strong northerly winds cause the waters of the bay to recede,[1] and leave a miasma-breeding swamp exposed to the rays of the sun. In the months of October and November febrile attacks are violent; ophthalmia more so. The eye-disease is not so general here as at Cairo, but the symptoms are more acute; in some years it becomes a virulent epidemic, which ends either in total blindness or in a partial opacity of the cornea, inducing dimness of vision, and a permanent weakness of the eye. In one month three of my acquaintances lost their sight. Dysenteries are also common, and so are bad boils, or rather ulcers. The cold season is not unwholesome, and at this period the pure air of the Desert restores and invigorates the heat-wasted frame.

'The walls, gates, and defences of Suez are in a ruinous state, being no longer wanted to keep out the Sinaitic Bedawin. The houses are about 500 in number, but many of the natives prefer occupying the upper stories of the Wakalahs, the rooms on the ground floor serving for stores to certain merchandise, wood, dates, cotton, etc.

'The Suezians live well, and their bazar is abundantly stocked with meat and clarified butter brought from Sinai, and fowls,

[1] 'During these north winds the sandy bar is exposed, and allows men to cross, which may explain the passage of the Israelites. Similarly at Jeddah, the bars are covered during the south and bare during the north winds.'

corn, and vegetables from the Sharkiyah province; fruit is supplied by Cairo as well as by the Sharkiyah, and wheat conveyed down the Nile in flood to the capital is carried on camel-back across the Desert. At sunrise they eat the Fatur, or breakfast, which in summer consists of a fatireh, a kind of muffin, or of bread and treacle. In winter it is more substantial, being generally a mixture of lentils and rice, with clarified butter poured over it, and a "kitchen" of pickled lime or stewed onions. At this season they greatly enjoy the *Ful mudammas* (boiled horse-beans), eaten with an abundance of linseed oil, into which they steep bits of bread. The beans form, with carbon-generating matter, a highly nutritive diet, which, if the stomach can digest it—the pulse is never shelled—gives great strength. About the middle of the day comes El-Ghada, a light dinner of wheaten bread, with dates, onions, or cheese: in the hot season melons and cooling fruits are preferred, especially by those who have to face the sun. El-Asha or supper, is served about half an hour after sunset: at this meal all but the poorest classes eat meat. Their favourite flesh, as usual in this part of the world, is mutton; beef and goat are little prized.'[1]

The people of Suez are a finer and fairer race than the Cairenes. The former have more the appearance of Arabs: their dress is more picturesque, their eyes are carefully darkened with Kohl, and they wear sandals, not slippers. They are, according to all accounts, a turbulent and somewhat fanatic set, fond of quarrels, and slightly addicted to *pronunciamientos*. The general programme of one of these latter diversions is said to be as follows. The boys will first be sent by their fathers about the town in a disorderly mob, and ordered to cry out 'Long live the Sultan!' with its usual sequel, 'Death to the Infidels!' The Infidels, Christians or others, must hear and may happen to resent this; or possibly the governor, foreseeing a disturbance, orders an ingenuous youth or two to be imprisoned, or to be caned by the police. Whereupon some person, rendered influential by wealth or religious reputation, publicly complains that the Christians are all in all, and that in these evil days El-Islam is going to

[1] Here concludes Mr Levick's letter. For the following observations I alone am answerable.

destruction. On this occasion the speaker conducts himself with such insolence, that the governor perforce consigns him to confinement, which exasperates the populace still more. Secret meetings are now convened, and in them the chiefs of corporations assume a prominent position.

If the disturbance be intended by its main-spring to subside quietly, the conspirators are allowed to take their own way; they will drink copiously, become lions about midnight, and recover their hare-hearts before noon next day. But if mischief be intended, a case of bloodshed is brought about; and then nothing can arrest the torrent of popular rage. The Egyptian, with all his good humour, merriment, and nonchalance, is notorious for doggedness, when, as the popular phrase is, his 'blood is up'. And this, indeed, is his chief merit as a soldier. He has a certain mechanical dexterity in the use of arms, and an Egyptian regiment will fire a volley as correctly as a battalion at Chobham. But when the head, and not the hands, is required, he notably fails. The reason of his superiority in the field is his peculiar stubbornness, and this, together with his powers of digestion and of enduring hardship on the line of march, is the quality that makes him terrible to his old conqueror, the Turk.[1]

[1] NOTE TO THIRD EDITION. I revisited Suez in September 1869, and found it altered for the better. The population had risen from 6,000 to 20,000. The tumble-down gateway was still there, but of the old houses—including the George Inn, whose front had been repaired—I recognised only four, and they looked mean by the side of the fine new buildings. In a few years ancient Suez will be no more. The bazars are not so full of filth and flies, now that pilgrims pass straight through, and hardly even encamp. The sweet water canal renders a Hammam possible; coffee is no longer hot saltish water, and presently irrigation will cover with fields and gardens the desert plain extending to the feet of Jebel Atakah. The noble works of the canal maritime, which should in justice be called the 'Lesseps Canal', shall soon transform Clysma into a modern and civilised city. The railway station, close to the hotel, the new British hospital, the noisy Greek casino, the Frankish shops, the puffing steamers, and the ringing of morning bells, gave me a novel impression. Even the climate has been changed by filling up the Timsch Lakes. Briefly, the nat is now at home in Suez.

NOTE TO FOURTH EDITION. The forecast in the last paragraphs had not been fulfilled. I again visited Suez in 1877–8, and found that it had been ruined by the Canal leaving it out of line. In fact, another Suez is growing up about the New Docks, while the old town is falling to pieces. For this, and other Egyptian matters, see *The Gold Mines of Midian* (C. Kegan Paul: London, 1878).

X

The Pilgrim Ship

The larger craft anchor some three or four miles from the Suez Pier, so that it is necessary to drop down in a skiff or shore-boat.

Immense was the confusion at the eventful hour of our departure. Suppose us gathered upon the beach, on the morning of a fiery July day, carefully watching our hurriedly packed goods and chattels, surrounded by a mob of idlers, who are not too proud to pick up waifs and strays; whilst pilgrims are rushing about apparently mad; and friends are weeping, acquaintances are vociferating adieux; boatmen are demanding fees; shopmen are claiming debts; women are shrieking and talking with inconceivable power, and children are crying—in short, for an hour or so we stand in the thick of a human storm.

To confound confusion, the boatmen have moored their skiff half a dozen yards away from the shore, lest the porters should be unable to make more than double their fare from the Hajis.

Again the Turkish women make a hideous noise, as they are carried off struggling vainly in brawny arms; the children howl because their mothers howl; and the men scold and swear, because in such scenes none may be silent. The moment we had embarked, each individual found that he or she had missed something of vital importance, a pipe, a child, a box, or a watermelon; and naturally all the servants were in the bazars, when they should have been in the boat.

Briefly, despite the rage of the sailors, who feared being too late for a second trip, we stood for some time on the beach before putting off.

From the shore we poled to the little pier, where sat the Bey in person to perform a final examination of our passports. Several were detected without the necessary document. Some were bastinado'd, others were peremptorily ordered back to Cairo, and the rest were allowed to proceed. At about ten a.m. (6th July), we hoisted sail, and ran down the channel leading to the roadstead. On our way we had a specimen of what we might expect from our fellow-passengers, the Maghrabi—men of the Maghrab, or Western Africa. A boat crowded with these ruffians ran alongside of us; and, before we could organise a defence, about a score of them poured into our vessel. They carried things too with a high hand, laughed at us, and seemed quite ready to fight. My Indian boy, who happened to let slip the word *Muarras*, narrowly escaped a blow with a palm-stick, which would have felled a camel. They outnumbered us, and they were armed; so that, on this occasion, we were obliged to put up with their insolence.

Our Pilgrim Ship, the *Silk el-Zahab*, or the *Golden Wire*, was a Sambuk of about fifty tons, with narrow wedge-like bows, a clean water-line, a sharp keel, and undecked, except upon the poop, which was high enough to act sail in a gale of wind. She carried two masts, raking imminently forwards, the main being considerably larger than the mizzen; the former was provided with a huge triangular latine, very deep in the tack, but the second sail was unaccountably wanting. She had no means of reefing, no compass, no log, no sounding lines, no spare ropes, nor even the suspicion of a chart: in her box-like cabin and ribbed hold there was something which savoured of close connexion between her model and that of the Indian Toni or dug-out. Such, probably, were the craft which carried old Sesostris across the Red Sea to Deir; such were the cruisers which once every three years left Ezion-Geber for Tarshish; such the transports of which 130 were required to convey Aelius Gallus, with his 10,000 men.

'Bakhshísh' was the last as well as the first odious sound I heard in Egypt. The owner of the shore-boat would not allow us to climb the sides of our vessel before paying him his fare, and when we did so, he asked for Bakhshísh. If Easterns would only imitate the example of Europeans—I never yet saw an Englishman give Bakhshísh to a soul—the nuisance would soon be done away with. But on this occasion all my companions complied with the request, and at times it is unpleasant to be singular.

The first look at the interior of our vessel showed a hopeless sight: Ali Murad, the greedy owner, had promised to take sixty passengers in the hold, but had stretched the number to ninety-seven. Piles of boxes and luggage in every shape and form filled the ship from stem to stern, and a torrent of Hajis were pouring over the sides like ants into the East Indian sugar-basin. The poop, too, where we had taken our places, was covered with goods, and a number of pilgrims had established themselves there by might, not by right.

Presently, to our satisfaction, appeared Saad the Demon, equipped as an able seaman, and looking most unlike the proprietor of two large boxes full of valuable merchandise. This energetic individual instantly prepared for action. With our little party to back him, he speedily cleared the poop of intruders and their stuff by the simple process of pushing or rather throwing them off it into the pit below. We then settled down as comfortably as we could; three Syrians, a married Turk with his wife and family, the Rais or captain of the vessel, with a portion of his crew, and our seven selves, composing a total of eighteen human beings, upon a space certainly not exceeding ten feet by eight.

The cabin—a miserable box about the size of the poop, and three feet high—was stuffed, like the hold of a slave ship, with fifteen wretches, children and women; and the other ninety-seven were disposed upon the luggage, or squatted on the bulwarks. Having some experience in such matters, and being favoured by fortune, I found a spare bed-frame slung to the ship's side; and giving a dollar to its owner, a sailor—who flattered himself that, because it was his, he would sleep upon it—I instantly appropriated it, preferring any hardship outside, to the condition of a packed herring inside, the place of torment.

Our Maghrabis were fine-looking animals from the Deserts about Tripoli and Tunis; so savage that, but a few weeks ago, they had gazed at the cock-boat, and wondered how long it would be growing to the size of the ship that was to take them to Alexandria. Most of them were sturdy young fellows, round-headed, broad-shouldered, tall, and large-limbed, with frowning eyes, and voices in a perpetual roar. Their manners were rude, and their faces full of fierce contempt or insolent familiarity.

A few old men were there, with countenances expressive of intense ferocity; women as savage and full of fight as men; and handsome boys with shrill voices, and hands always upon their daggers. The women were mere bundles of dirty white rags. The males were clad in Burnus, brown or striped woollen cloaks with hoods; they had neither turban nor Tarbush, trusting to their thick curly hair, or to the prodigious hardness of their scalps, as a defence against the sun; and there was not a slipper nor a shoe amongst the party.

Of course all were armed; but, fortunately for us, none had anything more formidable than a cut-and-thrust dagger about ten inches long. These Maghrabis travel in hordes under a leader who obtains the temporary title of Maula—the master. He has generally performed a pilgrimage or two, and has collected a stock of superficial information which secures for him the respect of his followers, and the profound contempt of the heaven-made ciceroni of Meccah and El-Medinah.

No people endure greater hardships when upon the pilgrimage than these Africans, who trust almost entirely to alms and to other such dispensations of Providence. It is not therefore to be wondered at that they rob whenever an opportunity presents itself. Several cases of theft occurred on board the *Golden Wire*; and as such plunderers seldom allow themselves to be baulked by insufficient defence, they are accused, perhaps deservedly, of having committed some revolting murders.

The first thing to be done, after gaining standing-room, was to fight for greater comfort; and never a Holyhead packet in the olden time showed a finer scene of pugnacity than did our pilgrim ship. A few Turks, rugged old men from Anatolia and Caramania, were mixed up with the Maghrabis; and the former began the war by contemptuously elbowing and scolding their wild neighbours. The Maghrabis, under their leader, Maula Ali, a burly savage, in whom I detected a ridiculous resemblance to the Rev. Charles Delafosse, an old and well-remembered schoolmaster, retorted so willingly that in a few minutes nothing was to be seen but a confused mass of humanity, each item indiscriminately punching and pulling, scratching and biting, butting and trampling, with cries of rage, and all the accompaniments of a proper fray, whatever was obnoxious to such operations.

One of our party on the poop, a Syrian, somewhat incautiously leapt down to aid his countrymen by restoring order. He sank immediately below the surface of the living mass: and when we fished him out, his forehead was cut open, half his beard had disappeared, and a fine sharp set of teeth belonging to some Maghrabi had left their mark in the calf of his leg.

The enemy showed no love of fair play, and never appeared contented unless five or six of them were setting upon a single man. This made matters worse. The weaker of course drew their daggers, and a few bad wounds were soon given and received. In a few minutes five men were completely disabled, and the victors began to dread the consequences of their victory.

Then the fighting stopped, and, as many could not find places, it was agreed that a deputation should wait upon Ali Murad, the owner, to inform him of the crowded state of the vessel. After keeping us in expectation at least three hours, he appeared in a row-boat, preserving a respectful distance, and informed us that any one who pleased might quit the ship and take back his fare. This left the case exactly as it was before; none would abandon his party to go on shore: so Ali Murad rowed off towards Suez, giving us a parting injunction to be good, and not fight; to trust in Allah, and that Allah would make all things easy to us.

His departure was the signal for a second fray, which in its accidents differed a little from the first. During the previous disturbance we kept our places with weapons in our hands. This time we were summoned by the Maghrabis to relieve their difficulties, by taking about half a dozen of them on the poop. Saad the Demon at once rose with an oath, and threw amongst us a bundle of Nebút—goodly ashen staves six feet long, thick as a man's wrist, well greased, and tried in many a rough bout.

He shouted to us, 'Defend yourselves if you don't wish to be the meat of the Maghrabis!' and to the enemy—'Dogs and sons of dogs! now shall you see what the children of the Arab are.' 'I am Umar of Daghistan!' 'I am Abdullah, the son of Joseph!' 'I am Saad the Demon!' we exclaimed, 'renowning it' by this display of name and patronymic.

To do our enemies justice, they showed no sign of flinching; they swarmed towards the poop like angry hornets, and encouraged one another with loud cries of 'Allaho akbar!' But we had a vantage-ground about four feet above them, and their palm-sticks and short daggers could do nothing against our terrible quarterstaves. In vain the 'Jacquerie' tried to scale the poop and to overpower us by numbers; their courage only secured them more broken heads.

At first I began to lay on load with *main morte*, really fearing to kill some one with such a weapon; but it soon became evident that the Maghrabis' heads and shoulders could bear and did require the utmost exertion of strength. Presently a thought struck me. A large earthen jar full of drinking water—in its heavy frame of wood the weight might have been a hundred pounds—stood upon the edge of the poop, and the thick of the fray took place beneath. Seeing an opportunity, I crept up to the jar, and, without attracting attention, rolled it down by a smart push with the shoulder upon the swarm of assailants. The fall caused a shriller shriek to rise above the ordinary din, for heads, limbs, and bodies were sorely bruised by the weight, scratched by the broken potsherds, and wetted by the sudden discharge. A fear that something worse might be coming made the Maghrabis slink off towards the end of the vessel.

After a few minutes, we, sitting in grave silence, received a deputation of individuals in whity-brown Burnus, spotted and striped with what Mephistopheles calls a 'curious juice'. They solicited peace, which we granted upon the condition that they would pledge themselves to keep it. Our heads, shoulders, and hands were penitentially kissed, and presently the fellows returned to bind up their hurts in dirty rags.

We owed this victory entirely to our own exertions, and the meek Umar was by far the fiercest of the party. Our Rais, as we afterwards learned, was an old fool who could do nothing but call for the Fatihah, or opening chapter of the Koran, claim Bakhshísh at every place where we moored for the night, and spend his leisure hours in the Caccia del Mediterraneo. Our crew consisted of half a dozen Egyptian lads, who, not being able to defend themselves, were periodically chastised by the Maghrabi, especially when any attempt was made to cook, to fetch water, or to prepare a pipe.

At length, about three p.m. on the 6th July, 1853, we shook out the sail, and, as it bellied in the favourable wind, we recited the Fatihah with upraised hands which we afterwards drew down our faces.[1] As the *Golden Wire* started from her place, I could not help casting one wistful look upon the British flag floating over the Consulate. But the momentary regret was stifled by the heart-bounding which prospects of an adventure excite, and by the real pleasure of leaving Egypt. I had lived there a stranger in the land, and a hapless life it had been: in the streets every man's face, as he looked upon the Persian, was the face of a foe. Whenever I came in contact with the native officials, insolence marked the event; and the circumstance of living within hail of my fellow-countrymen, and yet finding it impossible to enjoy their society, still throws a gloom over the memory of my first sojourn in Egypt.

The ships of the Red Sea—infamous region of rocks, reefs, and shoals—cruise along the coast by day; and at night lay to in the first cove they find: they do not sail when it blows hard, and as in winter time the weather is often stormy and the light of day does not last long, the voyage is intolerably slow. At sunset we stayed our adventurous course; and, still within sight of Suez, we anchored comfortably under the lee of Jebel Atakah, the Mountain of Deliverance, the butt-end of Jebel Joshi. We were now on classic waters. The eastern shore was dotted with the little grove of palm-trees which clusters around the Uyun Musa, or Moses' Wells; and on the west, between two towering ridges, lay the mouth of the valley (Bádiah, or Wady Tawarik, or Wady Musa), down which, according to Father Sicard, the Israelites fled to the Sea of Sedge. The view was by no means deficient in a sort of barbarous splendour. Verdure there was none, but under the violet and orange tints of the sky the chalky rocks

[1] The hands are raised in order to catch the blessing that is supposed to descend from heaven upon the devotee; and the meaning of drawing the palms down the face, is symbolically to transfer the benediction to every part of the body.

became heaps of topazes, and the brown-burnt ridges masses of amethyst. The rising mists, here silvery white, there deeply rosy, and the bright blue of the waves,[1] lining long strips of golden sand, compensated for the want of softness by a semblance of savage gorgeousness.

Next morning (7th July), before the cerulean hue had vanished from the hills, we set sail. It was not long before we came to a proper sense of our position. The box containing my store of provisions, and, worse still, my opium, was at the bottom of the hold, perfectly unapproachable: we had, therefore, the pleasure of breaking our fast on 'Mare's skin',[2] and a species of biscuit hard as a stone and quite as tasteless. During the day, whilst insufferable splendour reigned above, the dashing of the waters below kept my nest in a state of perpetual drench. At night rose a cold bright moon, with dews falling so thick and clammy that the skin felt as though it would never be dry again. It is, also, by no means pleasant to sleep upon a broken cot about four feet long by two broad, with the certainty that a false movement would throw you overboard, and a conviction that if you do fall from a Sambuk under sail, no mortal power can save you. And as under all circumstances in the East, dozing is one's chief occupation, the reader will understand that the want of it left me in utter, utter idleness.

The gale was light that day, and the sunbeams were fire; our crew preferred crouching in the shade of the sail to taking advantage of what wind there was. In spite of our impatience, we made but little way: near evening time we anchored on a tongue of sand, about two miles distant from the well-known and picturesque heights called by the Arabs Hammam Faraun, Pharaoh's hot baths, which

like giants stand
To sentinel enchanted land.

[1] Most travellers remark that they have never seen a brighter blue than that of the Red Sea. It was the observation of an early age that 'the Rede Sea is not more rede than any other sea, but in some place thereof is the gravelle rede, and therefore men clepen it the Rede Sea'.

[2] Jild el-Faras (or Kamar el-Din), a composition of apricot paste, dried, spread out, and folded into sheets, exactly resembling the article after which it is named. Turks and Arabs use it when travelling; they dissolve it in water, and eat it as a relish with bread or biscuit.

The strip of coarse quartz and sandstone gravel is obviously the offspring of some mountain torrent; it stretches southwards, being probably disposed in that direction by the currents of the sea, as they receive the deposit. The distance of the Hammam Bluffs prevented my visiting them, which circumstance I regretted the less as they have been described by pens equal to the task.

That evening we enjoyed ourselves upon clean sand, whose surface, drifted by the wind into small yellow waves, was easily converted by a little digging and heaping up into the coolest and the most comfortable of couches. Indeed, after the candescent heat of the day, and the tossing of our ill-conditioned vessel, we should have been contented with lodgings far less luxurious. Fuel was readily collected, and while some bathed, others erected a hearth—three large stones and a hole open to leeward—lit the fire, and put the pot on to boil. Shaykh Nur had fortunately a line; we had been successful in fishing; a little rice also had been bought; with this boiled, and rock-cod broiled upon the charcoal, we made a dinner that caused every one to forget the sore grievance of 'Mare's skin' and stone-hard biscuit. A few Maghrabis had ventured on shore, the Rais having terrified the others by threatening them with those bogies, the Bedawin, and they offered us *Kuskusu* in exchange for fish.

As evening fell we determined, before sleeping, to work upon their morale as effectually as we had attacked their physique. Shaykh Hamid stood up and indulged them with the Azan, or call to prayers, pronounced after the fashion of El-Medinah. They performed their devotions in lines ranged behind us as a token of respect, and when worship was over we were questioned about the Holy City till we grew tired of answering. Again our heads and shoulders, our hands and knees were kissed, but this time in devotion, not in penitence. My companions could scarcely understand half the rugged words which the Maghrabis used, as their dialect was fresh from the distant Desert. Still we succeeded in making ourselves intelligible to them, vaunting our dignity as the Sons of the Prophet, and the sanctity of our land which should protect its children from every description of fraud and violence. We benignantly promised to be their guides at El-Medinah, and the boy Mohammed would conduct their devotions at Meccah, always provided that they repented their past misdeeds, avoided any repetition of the same, and promised to perform the duties of good and faithful pilgrims.

Presently the Rais joined our party, and the usual story-telling began. The old man knew the name of each hill, and had a legend for every nook and corner in sight. He dwelt at length upon the life of Abu Zulaymah, the patron saint of these seas, whose little tomb stands at no great distance from our bivouac place, and told us how he sits watching over the safety of pious mariners in a cave among the neighbouring rocks, and sipping his coffee, which is brought in a raw state from Meccah by green birds, and prepared in the usual way by the hands of ministering angels. He showed us the spot where the terrible king of Egypt, when close upon the heels of the children of Israel, was whelmed in the 'hell of waters'; and he warned us that next day our way would be through breakers and reefs, and dangerous currents, over whose troubled depths, since that awful day, the Ifrit of the storm has never ceased to flap his sable wing. The wincing of the hearers proved that the shaft of the old man's words was sharp; but as night was advancing, we unrolled our rugs, and fell asleep upon the sand, all of us happy, for we had fed and drunk, and—the *homo sapiens* is a hopeful animal—we made sure on the morrow that the Ifrit would be merciful and allow us to eat fresh dates at the harbour of Tur.

Fair visions of dates doomed to the Limbo of things which should have been! The grey dawn (8th July) looked down upon us in difficulties. The water is deep near this coast; we had anchored at high tide close to the shore, and the ebb had left us high and dry. When this fact became apparent, a storm was upon the point of breaking. The Maghrabis, but for our interference, would have bastinado'd the Rais, who, they said with some reason, ought to have known better. When this phase of feeling passed away, they applied themselves to physical efforts.

All except the women and children, who stood on the shore encouraging their relatives with shrill quaverings, threw themselves into the water; some pushed, others applied their shoulders to the vessel's side, and all used their lungs with might and main. But the *Golden Wire* was firmly fixed, and their exertions were too irregular. Muscular force failed, upon which they changed their tactics. At the suggestion of their Maula, they prepared to burn incense in honour of the Shaykh Abu Zulaymah. The material not being forthcoming, they used coffee, which perhaps accounts for the shortcomings of that holy man. After this the Rais remembered that their previous exertions had not begun under the auspices of the Fatihah. Therefore they prayed, and then re-applied themselves to work. Still they failed. Finally, each man called aloud upon his own particular saint or spiritual guide, and rushed forward as if he alone sufficed for the exploit. Shaykh Hamid unwisely quoted the name, and begged the assistance, of his great ancestor, the 'Clarified-Butter-Seller'; the obdurate *Golden Wire* was not moved, and Hamid retired in momentary confusion.

It was now about nine a.m., and the water had risen considerably. My morning had been passed in watching the influx of the tide, and the grotesque efforts of the Maghrabis. When the vessel showed some symptoms of unsteadiness, I arose, walked gravely up to her, ranged the pilgrims around her with their shoulders to the sides, and told them to heave with might when they heard me invoke the revered name of my patron saint. I raised my hands and voice; *Ya Piran Pir! Ya Abd el-Kadir Jilani* was the signal. I thus called upon a celebrated Sufi or mystic, whom many East Indian Moslems reverence as the Arabs do their Apostle. Each Maghrabi worked like an Atlas, the *Golden Wire* canted half over, and, sliding heavily through the sand, once more floated off into deep water. This was generally voted a minor miracle, and the Effendi was respected—for a day or two.

The wind was fair, but we had all to re-embark, an operation which went on till noon. After starting, I remarked the natural cause which gives this Birkat Faraun (Pharaoh's Bay) a bad name. Here the gulf narrows; and the winds, which rush down the clefts and valleys of the lofty mountains on the eastern and western shores, meeting tides and counter-currents, cause a perpetual commotion. That day the foam-tipped waves repeatedly washed over my cot, by no means diminishing its discomforts.

In the evening, or rather late in the afternoon, we anchored, to our infinite disgust, under a ridge of rocks, behind which lies the plain of Tur. The Rais deterred all from going on shore by terrible stories about the Bedawin that haunt the place, beside which there was no sand to sleep upon. We remained, therefore, on board that night; and, making sail early the next morning, we threaded through reefs and sand-banks about noon into the intricate and dangerous entrance of Tur.

Nothing can be meaner than the present appearance of the old Phoenician colony, although its position as a harbour, and its plentiful supply of fruit and fresh water, make it one of the most frequented places on the coast. The only remains of any antiquity—except the wells—are the fortifications which the Portuguese and the Turks erected to keep out the Bedawin. The little town lies upon a plain that stretches with a gradual rise from the sea to the lofty mountain-axis of the Sinaitic group. The country around reminded me strongly of maritime Sind; a flat of clay and sand, clothed with sparse turfs of Salsolae, and bearing strong signs of a (geologically speaking) recent origin. The town is inhabited principally by Greek and other Christians, who live by selling water and provisions to ships.

A fleecy cloud hung lightly over the majestic head of Jebel Tur, about eventide, and the outlines of the giant hills stood picked out from the clear blue sky. Our Rais, weather-wise man, warned us that these were indications of a gale, and that, in case of rough weather, he did not intend to leave Tur. I was not sorry to hear this. We had passed a pleasant day, drinking sweet water, and eating the dates, grapes, and pomegranates which the people of the place carry down to the beach for the benefit of hungry pilgrims. Besides which, there were various sights to see, and with these we might profitably spend the morrow. We therefore pitched the tent upon the sand, and busied ourselves with extricating a box of provisions: the labour was rendered lighter by the absence of the Maghrabis, some of whom were wandering about the beach, whilst others had gone off to fill their bags with fresh water. We found their surliness insufferable; even when we were passing from poop to forecastle, landing or boarding, they grumbled forth their dissatisfaction.

Our Rais was not mistaken in his prediction. The fleecy cloud on Tur's tops had given true warning. When morning (9th July) broke, we found the wind strong, and the sea white with foam. Most of us thought lightly of these terrors, but our valorous captain swore that he dared not for his life cross, in such a storm, the mouth of ill-omened Akabah. We breakfasted, therefore, and afterwards set out to visit Moses' Hot Baths, mounted on wretched donkeys with pack-saddles, ignorant of stirrups, and without tails, whilst we ourselves suffered generally from boils, which, as usual upon a journey, make their appearance in localities the most inconvenient.

Our road lay northward across the plain towards a long narrow strip of date ground, surrounded by a ruinous mud wall. After a ride of two or three miles, we entered the gardens, and came suddenly upon the Hammam. It is a prim little Cockney bungalow, built by Abbas Pasha of Egypt for his own accommodation; glaringly whitewashed, and garnished with divans and calico curtains of a gorgeous hue. The guardian had been warned of our visit, and was present to supply us with bathing-cloths and other necessaries. One by one, we entered the cistern, which is now in an inner room. The water is about four feet deep, warm in winter, cold in summer, of a saltish-bitter taste, but celebrated for its invigorating qualities, when applied externally.

On one side of the calcareous rock, near the ground, is the hole opened for the spring by Moses' rod, which must have been like the 'mast of some tall Ammiral'; and near it are the marks of Moses' nails—deep indentations in the stone, which were probably left there by some extinct Saurian. Our cicerone informed us that formerly the finger-marks existed, and that they were long enough for a man to lie in. The same functionary attributed the sanitary properties of the spring to the blessings of the prophet, and, when asked why Moses had not made sweet water to flow, informed us that the Great Lawgiver had intended the spring for bathing, not for drinking. We sat with him, eating the small yellow dates of Tur, which are delicious, melting like honey in the mouth, and leaving a surpassing *arrière goût*.

After finishing sundry pipes and cups of coffee, we gave the bath-man a few piastres; and, mounting our donkeys, started eastward for the Bir Musa, Moses' Well, which we reached in half an hour. It is a fine old work, built round and domed over with roughly squared stones, very like what may be seen in some rustic parts of Southern England. The sides of the pit were so rugged that a man could climb down them, and at the bottom was a pool of water, sweet and abundant. We had intended to stay there, and to dine al fresco, but the hated faces of our companions, the Maghrabis, meeting us at the entrance, nipped that project in the bud. Accordingly we retired from the burning sun to a neighbouring coffee-house, a shed of palm-leaves kept by a Tur man, and there, seated on mats, we demolished the contents of our basket.

Whilst we were eating, some Bedawin came in and joined us, when invited so to do. They were poorly dressed, and all armed with knives and cheap sabres, hanging to leathern bandoleers: in language and demeanour they showed few remains of their old ferocity. As late as Mohammed Ali's time these people were noted wreckers, and formerly they were dreaded pirates: now they are lions with their fangs and claws drawn.

In the even, when we returned to our tent, a Syrian, one of our party on the poop, came out to meet us with the information that several large vessels had arrived from Suez, comparatively speaking, empty, and that the captain of one of them would land us at Yambu' for 3 dollars a head. The proposal was tempting. But presently it became apparent that my companions were unwilling to shift their precious boxes; and, moreover, that I should have to pay for those who could not or would not pay for themselves—that is to say, for the whole party. As such a display of wealth would have been unadvisable, I dismissed the idea with a sigh.

Amongst the large vessels was one freighted with Persian pilgrims, a most disagreeable race of men on a journey or a voyage. They would not land at first, because they feared the Bedawin. They would not take water from the townspeople, because some of these were Christians. Moreover, they insisted upon making their own call to prayer, which heretical proceeding—it admits five extra words—our party, orthodox Moslems, would rather have died than have permitted. When their crier, a small wizen-faced man, began the Azan with a voice

in quel tenore
Che fa il cappon quando talvolta canta,

we received it with a shout of derision, and some, hastily snatching up their weapons, offered him an opportunity of martyrdom. The Maghrabis, too, hearing that the Persians were Rafaz (heretics) crowded fiercely round to do a little Jihad, or Fighting for the Faith. The long-bearded men took the alarm. They were twice the number of our small party, and therefore they had been in the habit of strutting about with nonchalance, and looking at us fixedly, and otherwise demeaning themselves in an indecorous way. But when it came to the point, they showed the white feather.

These Persians accompanied us to the end of our voyage. As they approached the Holy Land, visions of the Nebút caused a change for the better in their manners. At Mahar they meekly endured a variety of insults, and at Yambu' they cringed to us like dogs.

XI

To Yambu'

On the 11th July, 1853, about dawn, we left Tur after a pleasant halt, with the unpleasant certainty of not touching ground for thirty-six hours. I passed the time in steadfast contemplation of the web of my umbrella, and in making the following meteorological remarks.

Morning. The air is mild and balmy as that of an Italian spring; thick mists roll down the valleys along the sea, and a haze like mother-of-pearl crowns the headlands. The distant rocks show Titanic walls, lofty donjons, huge projecting bastions, and moats full of deep shade. At their base runs a sea of amethyst, and as earth receives the first touches of light, their summits, almost transparent, mingle with the jasper tints of the sky. Nothing can be more delicious than this hour. But, as

Les plus belles choses
Ont le pire destin,

so lovely Morning soon fades. The sun bursts up from behind the main, a fierce enemy, a foe that will force every one to crouch before him. He dyes the sky orange, and the sea incarnadine, where its violet surface is stained by his rays; and he mercilessly puts to flight the mists and haze and the little agate-coloured masses of cloud that were before floating in the firmament. The atmosphere is so clear that now and then a planet is visible.

For the two hours following sunrise the rays are endurable; after that they become a fiery ordeal. The morning beams oppress you with a feeling of sickness; their steady glow, reflected by the glaring waters, blinds your eyes, blisters your skin, and parches your mouth: you now become a monomaniac; you do nothing but count the slow hours that must minute by before you can be relieved.

Midday. The wind, reverberated by the glowing hills, is like the blast of a lime-kiln. All colour melts away with the canescence from above. The sky is a dead milk-white, and the mirror-like sea so reflects the tint that you can scarcely distinguish the line of the horizon. After noon the wind sleeps upon the reeking shore; there is a deep stillness; the only sound heard is the melancholy flapping of the sail. Men are not so much sleeping as half senseless; they feel as if a few more degrees of heat would be death.

Sunset. The enemy sinks behind the deep cerulean sea, under a canopy of gigantic rainbow which covers half the face of heaven. Nearest to the horizon is an arch of tawny orange; above it another of the brightest gold; and based upon these a semicircle of tender sea-green blends, with a score of delicate gradations, into the sapphire sky. Across the rainbow the sun throws its rays in the form of giant wheel-spokes tinged with a beautiful pink. The eastern sky is mantled with a purple flush that picks out the forms of the Desert and the Hills. Language is a thing too cold, too poor, to express the harmony and the majesty of this hour, which is as evanescent, however, as it is lovely. Night falls rapidly, when suddenly the appearance of the Zodiacal Light restores the scene to what it was. Again the grey hills and the grim rocks become rosy or golden, the palms green, the sands saffron, and the sea wears a lilac surface of dimpling waves. But after a quarter of an hour all fades once more; the cliffs lie naked and ghastly under the moon, whose light falling upon this wilderness of white crags and pinnacles is most strange—most mysterious.

Night. The horizon is all darkness, and the sea reflects the white visage of the night-sun as in a mirror of steel. In the air we see giant columns of pallid light, distinct, based upon the indigo-coloured waves, and standing with their heads lost in endless space. The stars glitter with exceeding brilliance. At this hour are

> river and hill and wood,
> With all the numberless goings on of life,
> Inaudible as dreams;

while the planets look down upon you with the faces of smiling friends. You feel the 'sweet influence of the Pleiads'. You are bound by the 'bonds of Orion'. Hesperus bears with him a thousand things. In communion with them your hours pass swiftly by, till the heavy dews warn you to cover up your face and sleep. And with one look at a certain little Star in the north, under which lies all that makes life worth living through—surely it is a venial superstition to sleep with your face towards that Kiblah!—you fall into oblivion.

Those thirty-six hours were a trial even to the hard-headed Bedawin. The Syrian and his two friends fell ill. Umar Effendi, it is true, had the courage to say his sunset prayers, but the exertion so altered him that he looked another man. Salih Shakkar in despair ate dates till threatened with a dysentery. Saad the Demon had rigged out for himself a cot three feet long, which, arched over with bent bamboo and covered with cloaks, he had slung on to the larboard side; but the loud grumbling which proceeded from his nest proved that his precaution had not been a cure. Even the boy Mohammed forgot to chatter, to scold, to smoke, and to make himself generally disagreeable. The Turkish baby appeared to be dying, and was not strong enough to wail. How the poor mother stood her trials so well, made every one wonder. The most pleasant trait in my companions' characters was the consideration they showed to her, and their attention to her children. Whenever one of the party drew forth a little delicacy—a few dates or a pomegranate—they gave away a share of it to the children, and most of them took their turns to nurse the baby.

This was genuine politeness—kindness of heart. It would be well for those who sweepingly accuse Easterns of want of gallantry, to contrast this trait of character with the savage scenes of civilisation that take place among the 'Overlands' at Cairo and Suez.[1] No foreigner could be present for the first time without bearing away the lasting impression that the sons of Great Britain are model barbarians. On board the *Golden Wire* Salih Shakkar was the sole base exception to the general geniality of my companions.

As the sun starts towards the west, falling harmlessly upon our heads, we arise, still faint and dizzy, calling for water—which

[1] Written in the days of the vans which preceded the Railway.

before we had not the strength to drink—and pipes, and coffee, and similar luxuries. Our primitive kitchen is a square wooden box, lined with clay, and filled with sand, upon which three or four large stones are placed to form a hearth.

Preparations are now made for the evening meal, which is of the simplest description. A little rice, a few dates, or an onion, will keep a man alive in our position; a single good dinner would justify long odds against his seeing the next evening. Moreover, it is impossible in such cases to have an appetite—fortunately, as our store of provisions is a scanty one. Arabs consider it desirable on a journey to eat hot food once in the twenty-four hours; so we determine to cook, despite all difficulties. The operation, however, is by no means satisfactory; twenty expectants surround the single fire, and there is sure to be a quarrel amongst them every five minutes.

As the breeze, cooled by the dew, begins to fan our parched faces, we recover our spirits amazingly. Songs are sung; tales are told; and rough jests are bandied about till, not unfrequently, Oriental sensitiveness is sorely tried. Or, if we see the prospect of storm or calm, we draw forth, and piously peruse, a 'Hizb el-Bahr'. As this prayer is supposed to make all safe upon the ocean wave, I will not selfishly withhold it from the British reader. To draw forth all its virtues, the reciter should receive it from the hands of his Murshid or spiritual guide, and study it during the Chillah, or forty days of fast, of which, I venture to observe, few Sons of Bull are capable.

'O Allah, O Exalted, O Almighty, O All-pitiful, O All-powerful, Thou art my God, and sufficeth to me the knowledge of it! Glorified be the Lord my Lord, and glorified be the Faith my Faith! Thou givest Victory to whom Thou pleasest, and Thou art the Glorious, the Merciful! We pray Thee for Safety in our goings forth and our standings still, in our Words and our Designs, in our Dangers of Temptation and Doubt, and the secret Designs of our Hearts. Subject unto us this Sea, even as Thou didst subject the Deep to Musa (Moses), and as Thou didst subject the Fire to Ibrahim (Abraham), and as Thou didst subject the Iron to Daud (David), and as Thou didst subject the Wind and the Devils and Genii and Mankind to Sulayman

(Solomon), and as Thou didst subject the Moon and El-Burak to Mohammed, upon whom be Allah's Mercy and His Blessing! And subject unto us all the Seas in Earth and Heaven, in Thy visible and in Thine invisible Worlds, the Sea of this Life, and the Sea of Futurity. O Thou who reignest over every thing, and unto whom all Things return, Khyas! Khyas! Khyas!'[1]

And lastly, we lie down upon our cribs, wrapped up in thickly padded cotton coverlets; we forget the troubles of the past day, and we care nought for the discomforts of that to come.

Late on the evening of the 11th July we passed in sight of the narrow mouth of El-Akabah, whose *famosi rupes* are a terror to the voyagers of these latitudes. Like the Gulf of Cambay, here a tempest is said to be always brewing, and men raise their hands to pray as they cross it. We had no storm that day from without, but a fierce one was about to burst within our ship.

The essence of Oriental discipline is personal respect based upon fear. Therefore it often happens that the commanding officer, if a mild old gentleman, is the last person whose command is obeyed—his only privilege being that of sitting apart from his inferiors. And such was the case with our Rais. On the present occasion, irritated by the refusal of the Maghrabis to stand out of the steerman's way, and excited by the prospect of losing sight of shore for a whole day, he threatened one of the fellows with his slipper. It required all our exertions, even to a display of the dreaded quarterstaves, to calm the consequent excitement. After passing El-Akabah, we saw nothing but sea and sky, and we spent a weary night and day tossing upon the waters, our only exercise: every face brightened as, about sunset on the 12th July, we suddenly glided into the mooring-place.

Marsá (anchorage) Damghah, or rather Dumayghah, is scarcely visible from the sea. An islet of limestone rock defends the entrance, leaving a narrow passage to the south. It is not before he enters that the mariner discovers the extent and the depth of this creek, which indents far into the land, and offers fifteen to twenty feet of fine clear anchorage which no swell can reach. Inside it looks more like a lake, and at night its colour is

[1] These are mystic words, and entirely beyond the reach of dictionaries and vocabularies.

gloriously blue as Geneva itself. I could not help calling to mind, after dinner, the old school lines—

> *Est in secessu longo locus; insula portum*
> *Efficit objectu laterum; quibus omnis ab alto*
> *Frangitur, inque sinus scindit sese unda reductos.*

Nothing was wanted but the *atrum nemus*. Where, however, shall we find such luxuries in arid Arabia?

The Rais, as usual, attempted to deter us from landing, by romancing about the 'Bedoynes and Ascopards', representing them to be 'folke ryghte felonouse and foule and of cursed kynde'. To which we replied by shouldering our Nebúts and scrambling into the cock-boat. On shore we saw a few wretched-looking beings, Juhaynah[1] or Hutaym, seated upon heaps of dried wood, which they sold to travellers; and three boat-loads of Syrian pilgrims who had preceded us. We often envied them their small swift craft, with their double latine sails disposed in 'hare-ears' which, about eventide in the far distance, looked like a white gull alighting upon the purple wave; and they justified our jealousy by arriving at Yambu' two days before us. The pilgrims had bivoacked upon the beach, and were engaged in drinking their after-dinner coffee. They received us with all the rights of hospitality, as natives of El-Medinah should everywhere be received; we sat an hour with them, ate a little fruit, satisfied our thirst, smoked their pipes, and when taking leave blessed them. Then returning to the vessel we fed, and lost no time in falling asleep.

The dawn of the next day saw our sail flapping in the idle air. And it was not without difficulty that in the course of the fore-noon we entered Wijh Harbour, distant from Dumayghah but very few miles. El-Wijh is also a natural anchorage, in no way differing from that where we passed the night, except in being smaller and shallower and less secure. From this place to Cairo the road is safe. The town is a collection of round huts meanly built of round stones, and clustering upon a piece of elevated rock on the northern side of the creek. It is distant about six miles

[1] See *The Land of Midian* (*Revisited*), for a plan of El-Dumayghah and a description of El-Wijh (el-Bahr).

from the inland fort of the same name, which receives the Egyptian caravan, and which thrives, like its port, by selling water and provisions to pilgrims. The little bazar, almost washed by every high tide, provided us with mutton, rice, baked bread, and other necessaries of life, at a moderate rate. Luxuries also were to be found: a druggist sold me an ounce of opium at a Chinese price.

With reeling limbs we landed at El-Wijh, and finding a large coffee-house above and near the beach, we installed ourselves there. But the Persians who preceded us had occupied all the shady places outside, and were correcting their teeth with their case knives; we were forced to content ourselves with the interior. It was a building of artless construction, consisting of little but a roof supported by wooden posts, roughly hewn from date-trees; round the tamped earthen floor ran a raised bench of unbaked brick, forming a divan for mats and sleeping-rugs. In the centre a huge square Mastabah, or platform, answered a similar purpose.

Here and there appeared attempts at long and side walls, but these superfluities had been allowed to admit daylight through large gaps. In one corner stood the apparatus of the Kahwahji, an altar-like elevation, also of earthenwork, containing a hole for a charcoal fire, upon which were three huge coffee-pots dirtily tinned. Near it were ranged the Shishahs, or Egyptian hookahs, old, exceedingly unclean, and worn by age and hard work. A wooden framework, pierced with circular apertures, supported a number of porous earthenware gullehs (*gargoulettes* or monkey jars) full of cold, sweet water; the charge for each was, as usual in El-Hejaz, 5 paras. Such was the furniture of the café, and the only relief to the barrenness of the view was a fine mellowing atmosphere composed of smoke, steam, flies, and gnats, in about equal proportions.

I have been diffuse in my description of the coffee-house, as it was a type of its class: from Alexandria to Aden the traveller will everywhere meet with buildings of the same kind.

Our happiness in this Paradise—for such it was to us after the *Golden Wire*—was nearly sacrificed by Saad the Demon, whose abominable temper led him at once into a quarrel with the master of the café. And the latter, an ill-looking, squint-eyed, low-browed, broad-shouldered fellow, showed himself nowise unwilling to meet the Demon half-way. The two worthies, after a brief bandying of bad words, seized each other's throats leisurely, so as to give the spectators time and encouragement to interfere. But when friends and acquaintances were hanging on to both heroes so firmly that they could not move hand or arm, their wrath, as usual, rose till it was terrible to see.

The little village resounded with the war, and many a sturdy knave rushed in, sword or cudgel in hand, so as not to lose the sport. During the heat of the fray, a pistol which was in Umar Effendi's hand went off—accidentally of course—and the ball passed so close to the tins containing the black and muddy Mocha, that it drew the attention of all parties. As if by magic the storm was lulled. A friend recognised Saad the Demon, and swore that he was no black slave, but a soldier at El-Medinah —'no waiter, but a Knight Templar'. This caused him to be looked upon as rather a distinguished man, and he proved his right to the honour by insisting that his late enemy should feed with him, and when the other decorously hung back, by dragging him to dinner with loud cries.

My alias that day was severely tried. Besides the Persian pilgrims, a number of nondescripts who came in the same vessel were hanging about the coffee-house; lying down, smoking, drinking water, bathing, and picking their teeth with their daggers.

One inquisitive man was always at my side. He called himself a Pathan; he could speak five or six languages, he knew a number of people everywhere, and he had travelled far and wide over Central Asia. These fellows are always good detectors of an incognito. I avoided answering his question about my native place, and after telling him that I had no longer name or nation, being a Dervish, I asked him, when he insisted upon my having been born somewhere, to guess for himself. To my joy he claimed me for a brother Pathan, and in course of conversation he declared himself to be the nephew of an Afghan merchant, a gallant old man who had been civil to me at Cairo.

We then sat smoking together with 'effusion'. Becoming confidential, he complained that he, a Sunni or orthodox Moslem, had been abused, maltreated, and beaten by his fellow-travellers, the heretical Persian pilgrims. I naturally offered to arm my party, to take up our cudgels, and to revenge my compatriot. This thoroughly Sulaymanian style of doing business could not fail to make him sure of his man. He declined, however, wisely remembering that he had nearly a fortnight of the Persians' society still to endure. But he promised himself the gratification, when he reached Meccah, of sheathing his Charay—the terrible Afghan knife—in the chief offender's heart.

At eight a.m. on the 14th July we left El-Wijh, after passing a night, tolerably comfortable by contrast, in the coffee-house. We took with us the stores necessary, for though our Rais had promised to anchor under Jebel Hassáni that evening, no one believed him. We sailed among ledges of rock, golden sands, green weeds, and in some places through yellow lines of what appeared to me at a distance foam after a storm. All day a sailor sat upon the mast-head, looking at the water, which was transparent as blue glass, and shouting out the direction. This precaution was somewhat stultified by the roar of voices, which never failed to mingle with the warning, but we wore every half-hour, and we did not run aground.

About midday we passed by Shaykh Marbat's tomb. It is the usual domed and whitewashed building, surrounded by the hovels of its guardians, standing upon a low flat island of yellow rock, vividly reminding me of certain scenes in Sind. Its dreary position attracts to it the attention of passing travellers; the dead saint has a prayer and a Fatihah for the good of his soul, and the live sinner wends his way with religious refreshment.

Near sunset the wind came on to blow freshly, and we cast anchor together with the Persian pilgrims upon a rock. This was one of the celebrated coral reefs of the Red Sea, and the sight justified Forskal's emphatic description—*luxus lususque naturae.* It was a huge ledge or platform rising but little above the level of the deep: the water-side was perpendicular as the wall of a fort; and, whilst a frigate might have floated within a yard of it, every ripple dashed over the reef, replenishing the little basins and hollows in the surface. The colour of the waves near it was a vivid amethyst.

In the distance the eye rested upon what appeared to be meadows of brilliant flowers resembling those of earth, only far brighter and more lovely. Nor was this Land of the Sea wholly desolate. Gulls and terns here swam the tide; there, seated upon the coral, devoured their prey. In the air, troops of birds contended noisily for a dead flying fish, and in the deep water they chased a shoal, which, in fright and hurry to escape the pursuers, veiled the surface with spray and foam. And as night came on the scene shifted, displaying fresh beauties. Shadows clothed the background, whose features, dimly revealed, allowed full scope to the imagination.

In the fore-part of the picture lay the sea, shining under the rays of the moon with a metallic lustre; while its border, where the wavelets dashed upon the reef, was lit by what the Arabs call the jewels of the deep—brilliant flashes of phosphoric light giving an idea of splendour which Art would vainly strive to imitate. Altogether it was a bit of fairy-land, a spot for nymphs and sea-gods to disport upon: you might have heard, without astonishment, old Proteus calling his flocks with the writhed conch; and Aphrodite seated in her shell would have been only a fit and proper climax for its loveliness.

But—as philosophically remarked by Sir Cauline the Knyghte—

> Every whyte must have its blacke
> And every sweete its soure—

this charming coral reef was nearly being the scene of an ugly accident. The breeze from seaward set us slowly but steadily towards the reef, a fact of which we soon became conscious. Our anchor was not dragging; it had not rope enough to touch the bottom, and vainly we sought for more. In fact the *Golden Wire* was as disgracefully deficient in all the appliances of safety, as any English merchantman in the nineteenth century—a circumstance which accounts for the shipwrecks and for the terrible loss of life perpetually ocurring about the Pilgrimage-season in these seas. Had she struck upon the razor-like edges of the coral-reef, she would have melted away like a sugar-plum in the ripple, for the tide was rising at the time.

Having nothing better to do, we began to make as much noise as possible. Fortunately for us, the Rais commanding the Persian's boat was an Arab from Jeddah; and more than once we had treated him with great civility. Guessing the cause of our distress, he sent two sailors overboard with a cable; they swam gallantly up to us; and in a few minutes we were safely moored to the stern of our useful neighbour.

Which done, we applied ourselves to the grateful task of beating our Rais, and richly had he deserved it. Before noon, when the wind was shifting, he had not once given himself the trouble to wear; and when the breeze was falling he preferred dozing to taking advantage of what little wind remained. With energy we might have been moored that night comfortably under the side of Hassáni Island, instead of floating about on an unquiet sea with a lee-shore of coral reef within a few yards of our counter.

At dawn the next day (15th July) we started. We made Jebel Hassáni about noon, and an hour or so before sunset we glided into Marsa Mahár.

Our resting-place resembled Marsa Dumayghah at an humble distance; the sides of the cove, however, were bolder and more precipitous. The limestone rocks presented a peculiar appearance; in some parts the base and walls had crumbled away, leaving a coping to project like a canopy; in others the wind and rain had cut deep holes, and pierced the friable material with caverns that looked like the work of art. There was a pretty opening of backwood at the bottom of the cove; and palm-trees in the blue distance gladdened our eyes, which pined for the sight of something green.

The Rais, as usual, would have terrified us with a description of the Hutaym tribe that holds these parts, and I knew from Wellsted and Moresby that it is a debased race. But forty-eight hours of cramps on board ship would make a man think lightly of a much more imminent danger.

Wading to shore, we cut our feet with the sharp rocks. I remember to have felt the acute pain of something running into my toe: but after looking at the place and extracting what appeared to be a bit of thorn, I dismissed the subject, little guessing the trouble it was to give me. Having scaled the rocky side of the cove, we found some half-naked Arabs lying in the shade; they were unarmed, and had nothing about them except their villainous countenances wherewith to terrify the most timid. These men still live in limestone caves, like the Thamud tribe of tradition; also they are Ichthyophagi, existing without any other subsistence but what the sea affords. They were unable to provide us with dates, flesh, or milk, but they sold us a kind of fish called Buri or Bui: broiled upon the embers, it proved delicious.

After we had eaten and drunk and smoked, we began to make merry; and the Persians, who, fearing to come on shore, had kept to their conveyance, appeared proper butts for the wit of some of our party: one of us stood up and pronounced the orthodox call to prayer, after which the rest joined in a polemical hymn, exalting the virtues and dignity of the three first Caliphs. Then, as general on such occasions, the matter was made personal by informing the Persians in a kind of rhyme sung by the Meccan gamins, that they were the 'slippers of Ali and the dogs of Omar'. But as they were too frightened to reply, my companions gathered up their cooking utensils, and returned to the *Golden Wire* melancholy, like disappointed candidates for the honours of Donnybrook.

Our next day was silent and weary, for we were all surly, and heartily sick of being on board ship. We should have made Yambu' in the evening but for the laziness of the Rais. Having duly beaten him, we anchored on the open coast, insufficiently protected by a reef, and almost in sight of our destination. In the distance rose Jebel Radhwah or Radhwa, one of the Mountains of Paradise in which honoured Arabia abounds. It is celebrated by poetry as well as by piety.

> Did Radhwah strive to support my woes,
> Radhwah itself would be crushed by the weight,

says Antar. It supplies El-Medinah with hones. I heard much of its valleys and fruits and bubbling springs, but afterwards I learned to rank these tales with the superstitious legends which are attached to it. Gazing at its bare and ghastly heights, one of our party, whose wit was soured by the want of fresh bread, surlily remarked that such a heap of ugliness deserved ejection from heaven—an irreverence too public to escape general denunciation. We waded on shore, cooked there, and passed the night; we were short of fresh water, which, combined with other grievances, made us as surly as bears.

Saad the Demon was especially vicious; his eyes gazed fixedly on the ground, his lips protruded till you might have held up his face by them, his mouth was garnished with bad wrinkles, and he never opened it but he grumbled out a wicked word. He solaced himself that evening by crawling slowly on all-fours over the boy Mohammed, taking scrupulous care to place one knee upon the sleeper's face. The youth awoke in a fiery rage: we all roared with laughter; and the sulky Negro, after savouring the success of his spite, grimly, as but half satisfied, rolled himself, like a hedgehog, into a ball; and, resolving to be offensive even in his forgetfulness, snored violently all night.

We slept upon the sands and arose before dawn (17th July), determined to make the Rais start in time that day. A slip of land separated us from our haven, but the wind was foul, and by reason of rocks and shoals, we had to make a considerable *détour*.

It was about noon on the twelfth day after our departure from Suez, when, after slowly beating up the narrow creek leading to Yambu' harbour, we sprang into a shore-boat, and felt new life when bidding an eternal adieu to the vile *Golden Wire*.

I might have escaped much of this hardship and suffering by hiring a vessel to myself. There would then have been a cabin to retire into at night, and shade from the sun; moreover the voyage would have lasted five, not twelve days. But I wished to witness the scenes on board a pilgrim ship—scenes so much talked of by the Moslem palmer home-returned. Moreover the hire was exorbitant, ranging from 40*l.* to 50*l.*, and it would have led to a greater expenditure, as the man who can afford to take a boat must pay in proportion during his land journey. In these countries you perforce go on as you begin: to 'break one's expenditure', that is to say, to retrench expenses, is considered all but impossible. We have now left the land of Egypt.

XII
The Halt at Yambu'

The heat of the sun, the heavy dews, and the frequent washings of the waves, had so affected my foot, that on landing at Yambu' I could scarcely place it upon the ground. But traveller's duty was to be done; so, leaning upon my 'slave's' shoulder, I started at once to see the town, whilst Shaykh Hamid and the others of our party proceeded to the custom-house.

Yanbu'a el-Bahr, Yambu' or Fountain of the Sea, identified, by Abyssinian Bruce, with the Iambia village of Ptolemy, is a place of considerable importance, and shares with others the title of Gate of the Holy City.[1] It is the third quarter of the caravan road from Cairo to Meccah; and here, as well as at El-Bedr, pilgrims frequently leave behind them, in hired warehouses, goods too heavy to be transported in haste, or too valuable to risk in dangerous times. Yambu', being the port of El-Medinah, as Jeddah is of Meccah, is supported by a considerable transport trade and extensive imports from the harbours on the western coasts of the Red Sea; it supplies its chief town with grain, dates, and henna. Here the Sultan's dominion is supposed to begin, whilst the authority of the Pasha of Egypt ceases; there is no Nizam or Regular Army, however, in the town, and the governor is a Sherif or Arab chief. I met him in the great bazar; he is a fine young man of light complexion and the usual high profile, handsomely dressed, with a cashmere turban, armed to the extent of sword and dagger, and followed by two large fierce-looking Negro slaves leaning upon enormous Nebúts.

The town itself is in nowise remarkable. Built on the edge of a sunburnt plain that extends between the mountains and the sea, it fronts the northern extremity of a narrow winding creek. Viewed from the harbour, it is a long line of buildings, whose painful whiteness is set off by a sky-like cobalt and a sea-like indigo;

[1] The Yambu'a or Iambia village is now known as Yambu'a El-Nakhil. See *The Land of Midian (Revisited)*.

behind it lies the flat, here of a bistre-brown, there of a lively tawny; whilst the background is formed by dismal Radhwah,

Barren and bare, unsightly, unadorned.

Outside the walls are a few little domes and tombs, which by no means merit attention. Inside, the streets are wide; and each habitation is placed at an unsociable distance from its neighbour, except near the port and the bazars, where ground is valuable. The houses are roughly built of limestone and coralline, and their walls full of fossils crumble like almond cake; they have huge hanging windows, and look mean after those in the Moslem quarters of Cairo. There is a Suk, or market-place, of the usual form, a long narrow lane darkened by a covering of palm-leaves, with little shops let into the walls of the houses on both sides. The cafés, which abound here, have already been described in the last chapter; they are rendered dirty in the extreme by travellers, and it is impossible to sit in them without a fan to drive away the flies. The custom-house fronts the landing-place upon the harbour; it is managed by Turkish officials—men dressed in Tarbushes, who repose the livelong day upon the Divans near the windows. In the case of us travellers they had a very simple way of doing business, charging each person of the party 3 piastres for each large box, but by no means troubling themselves to meddle with the contents. This, as far as I could learn, is the only tax which the Sultan's government derives from the northern Hejaz; the people declare it to be, as one might expect at this distance from the capital, liable to gross peculation. When the Wahhabis held Yambu', they assessed it, like all other places; for which reason their name is held in the liveliest abhorrence.

Yambu' also boasts of a Hammam or hot bath, a mere date-leaf shed, tenanted by an old Turk, who, with his surly Albanian assistant, lives by 'cleaning' pilgrims and travellers. Some white-washed mosques and minarets of exceedingly simple form, a Wakalah or two for the reception of merchants, and a saint's tomb, complete the list of public buildings.

In one point Yambu' claims superiority over most other towns in this part of El-Hejaz. Those who can afford the luxury drink sweet rain-water, collected amongst the hills in tanks and cisterns, and brought on camel-back to the town. Two sources are especially praised, the Ayn el-Birkat, and the Ayn Ali, which suffice to supply the whole population: the brackish water of the wells is confined to coarser purposes. Some of the old people here, as at Suez, are said to prefer the drink to which years of habit have accustomed them, and it is a standing joke that, arrived at Cairo, they salt the water of the Nile to make it palatable.

The population of Yambu'—one of the most bigoted and quarrelsome races in El-Hejaz—strikes the eye after arriving from Egypt, as decidedly a new feature. The Shaykh or gentleman is over-armed and over-dressed, as Fashion, the Tyrant of the Desert as well as of the Court, dictates to a person of his consequence.

The civilised traveller from El-Medinah sticks in his waist-shawl a loaded pistol, garnished with crimson silk cord, but he partially conceals the butt-end under the flap of his jacket. The irregular soldier struts down the street a small armoury of weapons: one look at the man's countenance suffices to tell you what he is.

Here and there stalk grim Bedawin, wild as their native wastes, and in all the dignity of pride and dirt; they also are armed to the teeth, and even the presence of the policeman's quarterstaff cannot keep their swords in their scabbards. What we should call the peaceful part of the population never leave the house without the Nebút over the right shoulder, and the larger, the longer, and the heavier the weapon is, the more gallantry does the bearer claim. The people of Yambu' practise the use of this implement diligently; they become expert in delivering a head-blow so violent as to break through any guard, and with it they always decide their trivial quarrels.

The dress of the women differs but little from that of the Egyptians, except in the face-veil,[1] which is generally white. There is

[1] Europeans inveigh against this article—which represents the 'loup' of Louis XIV's time—for its hideousness and jealous concealment of charms made to be admired. It is, on the contrary, the most coquettish article of woman's attire, excepting, perhaps, the Lisam of Constantinople. It conceals coarse skins, fleshy noses, wide mouths, and vanishing chins, whilst it sets off to best advantage what in these lands is almost always lustrous and liquid—the eye. Who has not remarked this at a masquerade ball?

an independent bearing about the Yambu' men, strange in the East; they are proud without insolence, and they look manly without blustering. Their walk partakes somewhat of the nature of a swagger, owing, perhaps, to the shape of the sandals, not a little assisted by the self-esteem of the wearer, but there is nothing offensive in it: moreover, the population has a healthy appearance, and, fresh from Egypt, I could not help noticing their freedom from ophthalmic disease. The children, too, appear vigorous, nor are they here kept in that state of filth to which fear of the Evil Eye devotes them in the Valley of the Nile.

My companions found me in a coffee-house, where I had sat down to rest from the fatigue of halting on my wounded foot through the town. They had passed their boxes through the custom-house, and were now inquiring in all directions, 'Where's the Effendi?' After sitting for half an hour, we rose to depart, when an old Arab merchant, whom I had met at Suez, politely insisted upon paying for my coffee, still a mark of attention in Arabia as it was whilome in France.

We then went to a Wakalah, near the bazar, in which my companions had secured an airy upper room on the terrace opposite the sea, and tolerably free from Yambu's plague, the flies. It had been tenanted by a party of travellers, who were introduced to me as Umar Effendi's brothers; he had by accident met them in the streets the day before their start for Constantinople, where they were travelling to receive the Ikram.[1] The family was, as I have said before, from Daghistan (Circassia), and the male members still showed unequivocal signs of a northern origin, in light yellowish skins, grey eyes fringed with dark lashes, red lips, and a very scant beard. They were broad-shouldered, large-limbed men, distinguished only by a peculiar surliness of countenance; perhaps their expression was the result of their suspecting me; for I observed them narrowly watching every movement during Wuzu and prayers. This was a good opportunity for displaying the perfect nonchalance of a True Believer; and my efforts were, I believe, successful, for afterwards they seemed to treat me as a mere stranger, from whom

[1] A certain stipend allowed by the Sultan to citizens of the Haramayn (Meccah and El-Medinah). It will be treated of at length in a future chapter.

they could expect nothing, and who therefore was hardly worth their notice.

On the afternoon of the day of our arrival we sent for a Mukharrij[1] (hirer of conveyance) and began to treat for camels. One Amm Jemal, a respectable native of El-Medinah who was on his way home, undertook to be the spokesman; after a long palaver (for the Shaykh of the camels and his attendant Bedawin were men that fought for farthings, and we were not far inferior to them), a bargain was struck. We agreed to pay 3 dollars for each beast; half in ready money, the other half after reaching our destination, and to start on the evening of the next day with a grain-caravan, guarded by an escort of irregular cavalry. I hired two animals, one for my luggage and servant, the other for the boy Mohammed and myself, expressly stipulating that we were to ride the better beast, and that if it broke down on the road, its place should be supplied by another as good.

My friends could not dissemble their uneasiness, when informed by the Mukharrij that the Hazimi tribe was out, and that travellers had to fight every day. The Daghistanis also contributed to their alarm. 'We met', said they, 'between 200 and 300 devils on a Razzia near El-Medinah; we gave them the Salam, but they would not reply, although we were all on dromedaries. Then they asked us if we were men of El-Medinah, and we replied "Yes"; and lastly, they wanted to know the end of our journey; so we said "Bir Abbas".' The not returning 'Salam' was a sign on the part of the Bedawin that they were out to fight, and not to make friends; and the dromedary riders, who generally travel without much to rob, thought this behaviour a declaration of desperate designs. The Bedawin asked if they were El-Medinah men; because the former do not like, unless when absolutely necessary, to plunder the people of the Holy City. And the Daghistanis said their destination was Bir Abbas, a neighbouring, instead of Yambu', a distant post, because those who travel on a long journey, being supposed to

[1] The Shaykh, or agent of the camels, without whose assistance it would be difficult to hire beasts. He brings the Bedawin with him; talks them over to fair terms: sees the Arbun, or earnest-money, delivered to them; and is answerable for their not failing in their engagement.

have more funds with them, are more likely to be molested.

The Bedawin who had accompanied the Daghistanis belonged to some tribe unconnected with the Hazimi: the spokesman rolled his head, as much as to say 'Allah has preserved us!' And a young Indian of the party—I shrewdly suspect him of having stolen my penknife that night—displayed the cowardice of a Miyan, by looking aghast at the memory of his imminent and deadly risk. 'Sir,' said Shaykh Nur to me, 'we must wait till all this is over.' I told him to hold his tongue, and sharply reproved the boy Mohammed, upon whose manner the effect of finding himself suddenly in a fresh country had wrought a change for the worse. 'Why, ye were lions at Cairo; and here, at Yambu', you are cats—hens!' It was not long, however, before the youth's impudence returned upon him with increased violence.

We sat through the afternoon in the little room on the terrace, whose reflected heat, together with the fiery winds from the wilderness, seemed to incommode even my companions. After sunset we dined in the open air, a body of twenty: master, servants, children, and strangers. All the procurable rugs and pillows had been seized to make a Divan, and we squatted together round a large cauldron of boiled rice, containing square masses of mutton, the whole covered with clarified butter. Saad the Demon was now in his glory. With what anecdotes the occasion supplied him! His tongue seemed to wag with a perpetual motion; for each man he had a boisterous greeting; and, to judge from his whisperings, he must have been in every one's privacy and confidence. Conversation over pipes and coffee was prolonged to ten p.m., a late hour in these lands; then we prayed the Isha, or vespers, and, spreading our mats upon the terrace, we slept in the open air.

The forenoon of the next day was occupied in making sundry small purchases. We laid in seven days' provisions for the journey; repacked our boxes, polished and loaded our arms, and attired ourselves appropriately for the road. By the advice of Amm Jemal I dressed as an Arab, in order to avoid paying the Jizyat, a capitation tax which, upon this road, the settled tribes extort from stranger travellers; and he warned me not to speak any language but Arabic, even to my 'slave', in the vicinity of a village. I bought for my own conveyance a Shugduf or litter, for which I paid 2 dollars. It is a vehicle appropriated to women and children, fathers of families, married men, Shelebis (Exquisites), and generally to those who are too effeminate to ride. The Shugduf of El-Hejaz differs greatly from that used in Syria and other countries. It is composed of two corded cots five feet long, slung horizontally about half-way down, and parallel with the camel's sides. These cots have short legs, and at the halt may be used as bedsteads; the two are connected together by loose ropes, attached to the inner long sides of the framework, and these are thrown over the camel's pack-saddle. Thick twigs inserted in the ends and the outer long sides of the framework, are bent over the top, bower fashion, to support matting, carpets, and any other protection against the sun. There is an opening in this kind of wicker-work in front (towards the camel's head), through which you creep; and a similar one behind creates a draught of wind. Outside, towards the camel's tail, are pockets containing gullehs, or earthenware bottles of cooled water. Inside, attached to the wicker-work, are large provision pouches, similar to those used in old-fashioned travelling chariots. At the bottom are spread the two beds. The greatest disadvantage of the Shugduf is the difficulty of keeping balance. Two men ride in it, and their weights must be made to tally. Moreover, it is liable to be caught and torn by thorn trees, to be blown off in a gale of wind; and its awkwardness causes the camel repeated falls, which are likely to smash it. Yet it is not necessarily an uncomfortable machine. Those for sale in the bazar are, of course, worthless, being made of badly seasoned wood. But private litters are sometimes pleasant vehicles, with turned and painted framework, silk cordage, and valuable carpets. The often-described Mahmal is nothing but a Syrian Shugduf, royally ornamented.

My reason for choosing a litter was that notes are more easily taken in it than on a dromedary's back; the excuse of lameness prevented it detracting from my manhood, and I was careful when entering any populous place to borrow or hire a saddled beast.

Our party dined early that day, for the camels had been sitting at the gate since noon. We had the usual trouble in loading them: the owners of the animals vociferating about the unconscionable weight, the owners of the goods swearing that a child could carry such weight, while the beasts, taking part with their proprietors, moaned piteously, roared, made vicious attempts to bite, and started up with an agility that threw the half-secured boxes or sacks headlong to the ground. About three p.m. all was ready—the camels formed into Indian file were placed standing in the streets. But, as usual with Oriental travellers, all the men dispersed about the town; and we did not mount before it was late in the afternoon.

I must now take the liberty of presenting to the reader an Arab Shaykh fully equipped for travelling. Nothing can be more picturesque than the costume, and it is with regret that we see it exchanged in the towns and more civilised parts for any other. The long locks or the shaven scalps are surmounted by a white cotton skull-cap, over which is a Kufiyah—a large square kerchief of silk and cotton mixed, and generally of a dull red colour with a bright yellow border, from which depend crimson silk twists ending in little tassels that reach the wearer's waist. Doubled into a triangle, and bound with an Aakal or fillet of rope, a skein of yarn or a twist of wool, the kerchief fits the head close behind; it projects over the forehead, shading the eyes, and giving a fierce look to the countenance.

On certain occasions one end is brought round the lower part of the face, and is fastened behind the head. This veiling the features is technically called Lisam: the chiefs generally fight so, and it is the usual disguise when a man fears the avenger of blood, or a woman starts to take her Sar.[1] In hot weather it is supposed to keep the Simúm, in cold weather the catarrh, from the lungs.

The body dress is simply a Kamis or cotton shirt: tight sleeved, opening in front, and adorned round the waist and collar, and down the breast, with embroidery like network; it extends from neck to foot. Some wear wide trousers, but the Bedawin consider such things effeminate, and they have not yet fallen into the folly of socks and stockings. Over the Kamis is thrown a long-skirted

[1] Generally written 'Thar', the blood-revenge.

and short-sleeved cloak of camel's hair, called an *Aba*. It is made in many patterns, and of all materials from pure silk to coarse sheep's wool; some prefer it brown, others white, others striped: in El-Hejaz the favourite hue is white, embroidered with gold, tinsel, or yellow thread in two large triangles, capped with broad bands and other figures running down the shoulders and sides of the back. It is lined inside the shoulders and breast with handsome stuffs of silk and cotton mixed, and is tied in front by elaborate strings, and tassels or acorns of silk and gold. A sash confines the Kamis at the waist, and supports the silver-hilted Jambiyah or crooked dagger: the picturesque Arab sandal completes the costume. Finally, the Shaykh's arms are a sword and a matchlock slung behind his back; in his right hand he carries a short javelin, or a light crooked stick about two feet and a half long, called a Mashhab, used for guiding camels.

The poorer clans of Arabs twist round their waist, next to the skin, a long plait of greasy leather, to support the back: and they gird the shirt at the middle merely with a cord, or with a coarse sash.

The dagger is stuck in this scarf, and a bandoleer slung over the shoulders carries the cartridge-case, powder-flask, flint and steel, priming-horn, and other necessaries. With the traveller, the waist is an elaborate affair. Next to the skin is worn the money-pouch, concealed by the Kamis; the latter is girt with a waist-shawl, over which is strapped a leathern belt. The latter article should always be well garnished with a pair of long-barrelled and silver-mounted flint pistols, a large and a small dagger, and an iron ramrod with pincers inside; a little leathern pouch fastened to the waist-strap on the right side contains cartridge, wadding, and priming powder. The sword hangs over the shoulder by crimson silk cords and huge tassels: well-dressed men apply the same showy ornaments to their pistols. In the hand may be borne a bell-mouthed blunderbuss; or, better still, a long single-barrel gun with an ounce bore. All these weapons must shine like silver, if you wish to be respected; for the knightly care of arms is here a sign of manliness.

Pilgrims, especially those from Turkey, carry, I have said, a Hamail, to denote their holy errand. This is a pocket Koran, in a handsome gold-embroidered crimson velvet or red morocco case, slung by red silk cords over the left shoulder. It must hang down by the right side, and should never depend below the waist-belt. For this I substituted a most useful article. To all appearance a Hamail, it had inside three compartments; one for my watch and compass, the second for ready money, and the third contained penknife, pencils, and slips of paper, which I could hold concealed in the hollow of my hand. These were for writing and drawing: opportunities of making a fair copy into the diary-book are never wanting to the acute traveller. He must, however, beware of sketching before the Bedawin, who would certainly proceed to extreme measures, suspecting him to be a spy or a sorcerer.

Nothing so effectually puzzles these people as the Frankish habit of putting everything on paper; their imaginations are set at work, and then the worst may be expected from them. The only safe way of writing in presence of a Bedawi would be when drawing out a horoscope or preparing a charm: he also objects not, if you can warm his heart upon the subject, to seeing you take notes in a book of genealogies. You might begin with, 'And you, men of Harb, on what origin do you pride yourselves?' And while the listeners became fluent upon the, to them, all-interesting theme, you could put down whatever you please upon the margin. The townspeople are more liberal, and years ago the Holy Shrines have been drawn, surveyed, and even lithographed, by Eastern artists: still, if you wish to avoid all suspicion, you must rarely be seen with pen or with pencil in hand.

At six p.m., descending the stairs of our Wakalah, we found the camels standing loaded in the street, and shifting their ground in token of impatience. My Shugduf, perched upon the back of a tall strong animal, nodded and swayed about with his every motion, impressing me with the idea that the first step would throw it over the shoulders or the crupper. The camelman told me I must climb up the animal's neck, and so creep into the vehicle. But my foot disabling me from such exertion, I insisted upon their bringing the beast to squat, which they did grumblingly.

We took leave of Umar Effendi's brothers and their dependants, who insisted upon paying us the compliment of accompanying us to the gate. Then we mounted and started, which was a signal for all our party to disperse once more. Some heard the report of a vessel having arrived from Suez, with Mohammed Shiklibha and other friends on board; these hurried down to the harbour for a parting word. Others, declaring they had forgotten some necessaries for the way, ran off to spend one last hour in gossip at the coffee-house. Then the sun set, and prayers must be said.

The brief twilight had almost faded away before all had mounted.

With loud cries of 'Wassit, ya hu!'—'Go in the middle of the road, O He!'—and 'Jannib, y'al Jammal!'—'Keep to the side, O camel-man!'—we threaded our way through long, dusty, narrow streets, flanked with whitewashed habitations at considerable intervals, and large heaps of rubbish, sometimes higher than the houses. We were stopped at the gate to ascertain if we were strangers, in which case, the guard would have done his best to extract a few piastres before allowing our luggage to pass; but he soon perceived by my companions' accent, that they were sons of the Holy City—consequently, that the case was hopeless. While standing here, Shaykh Hamid vaunted the strong walls and turrets of Yambu', which he said were superior to those of Jeddah: they kept Saud, the Wahhabi, at bay in AD 1802, but would scarcely, I should say, resist a field battery in AD 1853. The moon rose fair and clear, dazzling us with light as we emerged from the shadowy streets; and when we launched into the Desert, the sweet air delightfully contrasted with the close offensive atmosphere of the town. My companions, as Arabs will do on such occasions, began to sing.

XIII
From Yambu' to Bir Abbas

On the 18th July, about seven p.m., we passed through the gate of Yambu', and took a due easterly course. Our route lay over the plain between the mountains of Radhwah on the left, and the sea on the right hand; the land was desert—that is to say, a hard level plain, strewed with rounded lumps of granite and greenstone schist, with here and there a dwarf Acacia, and a tuft of rank camel grass. By the light of a glorious moon, nearly at the full, I was able to see the country tolerably well.

Our party consisted of twelve camels, and we travelled in Indian file, head tied to tail, with but one outrider, Umar Effendi, whose rank required him to mount a dromedary with showy trappings. Immediately in front of me was Amm Jemal, whom I had to reprove for asking the boy Mohammed, 'Where have you picked up that Hindi (Indian)?' 'Are we, the Afghans, the Indian-slayers, become Indians?' I vociferated with indignation, and brought the thing home to his feelings, by asking him how he, an Arab, would like to be called an Egyptian—a Fellah?

The rest of the party was behind, sitting or dozing upon the rough platforms made by the lids of the two huge boxes slung to the sides of their camels. Only one old woman, El-Sitt Maryam (the lady Mary), returning to El-Medinah, her adopted country, after a visit to a sister at Cairo, allowed herself the luxury of a half-dollar Shibriyah or cot, fastened crosswise over the animal's load. Moreover, all the party, except Umar Effendi, in token of poverty, were dressed in the coarsest and dirtiest of clothes—the general suit consisting of a shirt torn in divers places and a bit of rag wrapped round the head. They carried short chibouques without mouth-pieces, and tobacco-pouches of greasy leather.

Though the country hereabouts is perfectly safe, all had their arms in readiness, and the unusual silence that succeeded to the singing—even Saad the Demon held his tongue—was sufficient to show how much they feared for their property. After a slow march of two hours facing the moon, we turned somewhat towards the north-east, and began to pass over undulating ground, in which a steady rise was perceptible.

We arrived at the halting-place at three in the morning, after a short march of about eight hours, during which we could not have passed over more than sixteen miles. The camels were made to kneel; the boxes were taken off and piled together as a precaution against invisible robbers; my little tent, the only one in the party, was pitched; we then spread our rugs upon the ground and lay down to sleep.

We arose at about nine a.m. (19th July), and after congratulating one another upon being once more in the 'dear Desert', we proceeded in exhilarated mood to light the fire for pipes and breakfast. The meal—a biscuit, a little rice, and a cup of milkless tea—was soon despatched, after which I proceeded to inspect our position.

About a mile to the westward lay the little village El-Musahhal, a group of miserable mud hovels. On the south was a strip of bright blue sea, and all around, an iron plain producing nought but stones and grasshoppers, and bounded northward by a grisly wall of blackish rock. Here and there a shrub fit only for fuel, or a tuft of coarse grass, crisp with heat, met the eye. All was sun-parched; the furious heat from above was drying up the sap and juice of the land, as the simmering and quivering atmosphere showed; moreover the heavy dews of these regions, forming in large drops upon the plants and stones, concentrate the morning rays upon them like a system of burning-glasses. After making these few obvervations I followed the example of my companions, and returned to sleep.

At two p.m. we were roused to a dinner as simple as the breakfast had been. Boiled rice with an abundance of the clarified butter in which Easterns delight, some fragments of Kahk, or soft biscuit, and stale bread and a handful of stoned and pressed date-paste, called Ajwah, formed the menu. Our potations began before dinner with a vile-tasted but wholesome drink called Akit, dried sour milk dissolved in water; at the meal we drank the leather-flavoured element, and ended with a large cupful of scalding tea. Enormous quantities of liquid were consumed, for the sun seemed to have got into our throats, and the perspiration trickled as after a shower of rain.

Whilst we were eating, a Bedawi woman passed close by the tent, leading a flock of sheep and goats, seeing which I expressed a desire to drink milk. My companions sent by one of the camel-men a bit of bread, and asked in exchange for a cupful of laban. Thus I learned that the Arabs, even in this corrupt region, still adhere to the meaningless custom of their ancestors, who chose to make the term 'Labbán' (milk-seller) an opprobrium and a disgrace. Possibly the origin of the prejudice might be the recognising of a traveller's guest-right to call for milk gratis. However this may be, no one will in the present day sell this article of consumption, even at civilised Meccah, except Egyptians, a people supposed to be utterly without honour.

As a general rule in the Hejaz, milk abounds in the spring, but at all other times of the year it is difficult to be procured. The Bedawi woman managed, however, to send me back a cupful.

At three p.m. we were ready to start, and all saw, with unspeakable gratification, a huge black nimbus rise from the shoulder of Mount Radhwah, and range itself, like a good genius, between us and our terrible foe, the sun. We hoped that it contained rain, but presently a blast of hot wind, like the breath of a volcano, blew over the plain, and the air was filled with particles of sand. This is the dry storm of Arabia; it appears to depend upon some electrical phenomena which it would be desirable to investigate.

When we had loaded and mounted, my camel-men, two in number, came up to the Shugduf and demanded Bakhshísh, which, it appears, they are now in the habit of doing each time the traveller starts. I was at first surprised to find the word here, but after a few days of Bedawi society, my wonder diminished. The men were Beni-Harb of the great Hejazi tribe, which has kept its blood pure for the last thirteen centuries—how much more we know not—but they have been corrupted by intercourse with pilgrims, retaining none of their ancestral qualities but greed of gain, revengefulness, pugnacity, and a frantic kind of bravery, displayed on rare occasions.

Their nobility, however, did not prevent my quoting the Prophet's saying, 'Of a truth, the worst names among the Arabs are the Beni-Kalb (dog-sons) and the Beni-Harb (Fight-sons)', whilst I taunted them severely with their resemblance to the Fellahs of Egypt. They would have resented this with asperity, had it proceeded from their own people, but the Turkish pilgrim—the character in which they knew me, despite my Arab dress—is a privileged person.

The outer man of these Fight-sons was contemptible; small chocolate-coloured beings, stunted and thin, with mops of coarse bushy hair burned brown by the sun, straggling beards, vicious eyes, frowning brows, screaming voices, and well-made, but attenuated, limbs. On their heads were Kufiyahs in the last stage of wear: a tattered shirt, indigo-dyed, and girt with a bit of common rope, composed their clothing; and their feet were protected from the stones by soles of thick leather, kept in place by narrow thongs tied to the ankle. Both were armed, one with a matchlock, and a Shintiyan, or common sword-blade, in a leathern scabbard, slung over the shoulder, the other with a Nebút, and both showed at the waist the Arab's invariable companion, the dagger.

These ragged fellows, however, had their pride. They would eat with me, and not disdain, like certain self-styled Caballeros, to ask for more; but of work they would do none. No promise of Bakhshísh, potent as the spell of that word is, would induce them to assist in pitching my tent: they even expected Shaykh Nur to cook for them, and I had almost to use violence, for even the just excuse of a sore foot was insufficient to procure the privilege of mounting my Shugduf while the camel was sitting. It was, they said, the custom of the country from time immemorial to use a ladder when legs would not act. I agreed with them, but objected that I had no ladder. At last, wearied with their thick-headedness, I snatched the nose-string of the camel, and by main force made it kneel.

Our party was now strong enough. We had about 200 beasts carrying grain, attended by their proprietors, truculent looking as the *contrabandistas* of the Pyrenees. The escort was composed of seven Irregular Turkish cavalry, tolerably mounted, and supplied each with an armoury in epitome. They were privily derided by our party, who, being Arabs, had a sneaking fondness for the Bedawin, however loth they might be to see them amongst the boxes.

For three hours we travelled in a south-easterly direction upon a hard plain and a sandy flat, on which several waters from the highlands find a passage to the sea westward. Gradually we were siding towards the mountains, and at sunset I observed that we had sensibly neared them. We dismounted for a short halt; and, strangers being present, my companions before sitting down to smoke said their prayers—a pious exercise in which they did not engage for three days afterwards, when they met certain acquaintances at El-Hamra.

As evening came on, we emerged from a scrub of Acacia and tamarisk and turned due east, traversing an open country with a perceptible rise. Scarcely was it dark before the cry of 'Harami' (thieves) rose loud in the rear, causing such confusion as one may see in a boat in the Bay of Naples when suddenly neared by a water-spout. All the camel-men brandished their huge staves, and rushed back vociferating in the direction of the robbers. They were followed by the horsemen; and truly, had the thieves possessed the usual acuteness of the profession, they might have driven off the camels in our van with safety and convenience. But these contemptible beings were only half a dozen in number, and they had lighted their matchlocks, which drew a bullet or two in their direction. Thereupon they ran away.

This incident aroused no inconsiderable excitement, for it seemed ominous of worse things about to happen to us when entangled in the hills, and the faces of my companions, perfect barometers of fair and foul tidings, fell to zero. For nine hours we journeyed through a brilliant moonlight, and as the first grey streak appeared in the eastern sky we entered a scanty Misyal, or Fiumara, strewed with pebbles and rounded stones, about half a mile in breadth, and flanked by almost perpendicular hills of primitive formation. I began by asking the names of peaks and other remarkable spots, when I found that a folio volume would not contain a three months' collection: every hill and dale, flat, valley, and water-course here has its proper name or rather names.

The ingenuity shown by the Bedawin in distinguishing between localities the most similar, is the result of a high organisation of the perceptive faculties, perfected by the practice of observing a recurrence of landscape features few in number and varying but little amongst themselves. After travelling two hours up this torrent-bed, winding in an easterly direction, and crossing some Harrah, or ridges of rock, Ria, steep descents, Kitaah, patch of stony flat and bits of Sahil, dwarf plain, we found ourselves, about eight a.m., after a march of about thirty-four miles, at Bir Said (Said's Well), our destination.

I had been led to expect at the 'well' a pastoral scene, wild flowers, flocks, and flowing waters, so I looked with a jaundiced eye upon a deep hole full of slightly brackish water dug in a tamped hollow; a kind of punch-bowl with granite walls, upon whose grim surface a few thorns of exceeding hardihood braved the sun for a season. Not a house was in sight—it was as barren and desolate a spot as the sun ever 'viewed in his wide career'. But this is what the Arabian traveller must expect. He is to traverse, for instance, a Vale of Flowers. He indulges in sweet recollections of Indian lakes beautiful with the Lotus, and Persian plains upon which Narcissus is the meanest of grasses. He sees a plain like swish-work, where knobs of granite act daisies; and where, at every fifty yards, some hapless bud or blossom is dying of inanition among the stones.

The sun scorched our feet as we planted the tent, and, after drinking our breakfast, we passed the usual day of perspiration and semi-lethargy. In discomfort man naturally hails a change, even though it be one from bad to worse. When our enemy began slanting towards the west, we felt ready enough to proceed on our journey. The camels were laden shortly after three p.m., the 20th July, and we started, with water jars in our hands, through a storm of Simúm.

We travelled five hours in a north-easterly course up a diagonal valley, through a country fantastic in its desolation—a mass of huge hills, barren plains, and desert vales. Even the sturdy Acacias here failed, and in some places the camel grass could not find earth enough for its root. The road wound among mountains, rocks and hills of granite, and over broken ground, flanked by huge blocks and boulders piled up as if man's art had aided Nature to disfigure herself. Vast clefts seamed like scars the hideous face of earth; here they widened into dark caves, there they were choked with glistening drift sand.

Not a bird or a beast was to be seen or heard; their presence would have argued the vicinity of water; and, though my companions opined that Bedawin were lurking among the rocks, I decided that these Bedawin were the creatures of their fears. Above, a sky like polished blue steel, with a tremendous blaze of yellow light, glared upon us without the thinnest veil of mist cloud. Below, the brass-coloured circle scorched the face and dazzled the eyes, mocking them the while with offers of water that was but air. The distant prospect was more attractive than the near view, because it borrowed a bright azure tinge from the intervening atmosphere; but the jagged peaks and the perpendicular streaks of shadow down the flanks of the mountainous background showed that yet in store for us was no change for the better.

Between ten and eleven p.m., we reached human habitations—a phenomenon unseen since we left El-Musahhal—in the shape of a long straggling village. It is called El-Hamra, from the redness of the sands near which it is built, or El-Wasitah, the half-way, because it is the middle station between Yambu' and El-Medinah. It is therefore considerably out of place in Burckhardt's map; and those who copy from him make it much nearer the seaport than it really is. We wandered nearly an hour in search of an encamping station, for the surly villagers ordered us off every flatter bit of ground, without, however, deigning to show us where the jaded beasts might rest.

At last, after long wrangling, we found the usual spot; the camels were unloaded, the boxes and baggage were disposed in a circle for greater security against the petty pilferers in which this part of the road abounds, and my companions spread their rugs so as to sleep upon their valuables. I was invited to follow the general example; but I absolutely declined the vicinity of so many steaming and snoring fellow-travellers. Some wonder was excited by the Afghan Haji's obstinacy and recklessness; but resistance to these people is sometimes *bien placé*, and a man from Cabool is allowed to say and to do strange things. In answer to their warnings of nightly peril, I placed a drawn sword by my side and a cocked pistol under my pillow, the saddle-bag: a carpet spread upon the cool loose sand formed by no means an uncomfortable couch, and upon it I enjoyed a sound sleep till day-break.

Rising at dawn (21st July), I proceeded to visit the village. It is built upon a narrow shelf at the top of a precipitous hill to the north, and on the south runs a sandy Fiumara about half a mile broad. On all sides are rocks and mountains rough and stony; so you find yourself in another of those punch-bowls which the Arabs seem to consider choice sites for settlements. The Fiumara, hereabouts very winding, threads the high grounds all the way down from the plateau of El-Medinah: during the rainy season it becomes a raging torrent, carrying westwards to the Red Sea the drainage of a hundred hills. Water of good quality is readily found in it by digging a few feet below the surface at the angles where the stream forms the deepest hollows, and in some places the stony sides give out bubbling springs.

El-Hamra itself is a collection of stunted houses or rather hovels, made of unbaked brick and mud, roofed over with palm-leaves, and pierced with air-holes, which occasionally boast a bit of plank for a shutter. It appears thickly populated in the parts where the walls are standing, but, like all settlements in the Holy Land, El-Hejaz, it abounds in ruins. It is well supplied with provisions, which are here cheaper than at El-Medinah—a circumstance that induced Saad the Demon to overload his hapless camel with a sack of wheat.

In the village are a few shops where grain, huge plantains, ready-made bread, rice, clarified butter, and other edibles are to be purchased. Palm orchards of considerable extent supply it with dates. The bazar is, like the generality of such places in the villages of Eastern Arabia, a long lane, here covered with matting, there open to the sun, and the narrow streets—if they may be so called—are full of dust and glare.

Near the encamping ground of caravans is a fort for the

officer commanding a troop of Albanian cavalry, whose duty it is to defend the village, to hold the country, and to escort merchant travellers. The building consists of an outer wall of hewn stone, loopholed for musketry, and surmounted by Shararif—*remparts coquets*—about as useful against artillery as the sugar gallery round a Twelfth-cake. Nothing would be easier than to take the place: a false attack would draw off the attention of the defenders, who in these latitudes know nothing of sentry-duty, whilst scaling-ladders or a bag full of powder would command a ready entrance into the other side. Around the El-Hamra fort are clusters of palm-leaf huts, where the soldiery lounge and smoke, and near it is the usual coffee-house, a shed kept by an Albanian. These places are frequented probably on account of the intense heat inside the fort.

We passed a comfortless day at the Red Village. Large flocks of sheep and goats were being driven in and out of the place, but their surly shepherds would give no milk, even in exchange for bread and meat. The morning was spent in watching certain Bedawin, who, matchlock in hand, had climbed the hills in pursuit of a troop of cranes: not one bird was hit of the many fired at—a circumstance which did not say much for their vaunted marksmanship.

Before breakfast I bought a moderately sized sheep for a dollar. Shaykh Hamid butchered it, according to rule, and my companions soon prepared a feast of boiled mutton. But that sheep proved a bone of contention. The boy Mohammed had, in a fit of economy, sold its head to a Bedawi for 3 piastres, and the others, disappointed in their anticipations of 'haggis', lost temper. With the Demon's voluble tongue and impudent countenance in the van, they opened such a volley of raillery and sarcasm upon the young 'tripe-seller', that he in his turn became excited—furious. I had some difficulty to keep the peace, for it did not suit my interests that they should quarrel.

But to do the Arabs justice, nothing is easier for a man who knows them than to work upon their good feelings. 'He is a stranger in your country—a guest!' acted as a charm; they listened patiently to Mohammed's gross abuse, only promising to answer him when in *his* land, that is to say, near Meccah. But what especially soured our day was the report that Saad, the great robber-chief, and his brother were in the field; consequently that our march would be delayed for some time: every half-hour some fresh tattle from the camp or the coffee-house added fuel to the fire of our impatience.

A few particulars about this Schinderhans of El-Hejaz[1] may not be unacceptable. He is the chief of the Sumaydah and the Mahamid, two influential sub-families of the Hamidah, the principal family of the Beni-Harb tribe of Bedawin. He therefore aspired to rule all the Hamidah, and through them the Beni-Harb, in which case he would have been, *de facto*, monarch of the Holy Land. But the Sherif of Meccah, and Ahmed Pasha, the Turkish governor of the chief city, for some political reason degraded him, and raised up a rival in the person of Shaykh Fahd, another ruffian of a similar stamp, who calls himself chief of the Beni-Amr, the third sub-family of the Hamidah family. Hence all kinds of confusion. Saad's people, who number it is said 5,000, resent, with Arab asperity, the insult offered to their chief, and beat Fahd's, who do not amount to 800. Fahd, supported by the government, cuts off Saad's supplies. Both are equally wild and reckless, and—nowhere doth the glorious goddess, Liberty, show a more brazen face than in this eastern

Inviolate land of the brave and the free—

both seize the opportunity of shooting troopers, of plundering travellers, and of closing the roads.

This state of things continued till I left the Hejaz, when the Sherif of Meccah proposed, it was said, to take the field in person against the arch-robber. And, as will afterwards be seen in these pages, Saad had the audacity to turn back the Sultan's Mahmal or litter—the ensign of Imperial power—and to shut the road against its *cortège*, because the Pashas of El-Medinah and of the Damascus Caravan would not guarantee his restitution to his former dignity.

That such vermin is allowed to exist proves the imbecility of the Turkish government. The Sultan pays pensions in corn and cloth to the very chiefs who arm their varlets against him; and

[1] He is now dead, and he has been succeeded by a son worse than himself.

the Pashas, after purloining all they can, hand over to their enemies the means of resistance. It is more than probable that Abd el-Mejid has never heard a word of truth concerning El-Hejaz, and that fulsome courtiers persuade him that men there tremble at his name. His government, however, is desirous, if report speaks truth, of thrusting El-Hejaz upon the Egyptian, who on his side would willingly pay a large sum to avert such calamity.

The Holy Land drains off Turkish gold and blood in abundance, and the lords of the country hold in it a contemptible position. If they catch a thief, they dare not hang him. They must pay black-mail, and yet be shot at in every pass. They affect superiority over the Arabs, hate them, and are despised by them.

Such in El-Hejaz are the effects of the charter of Gulkhaneh, a panacea, like Holloway's Pills, for all the evils to which Turkish, Arab, Syrian, Greek, Egyptian, Persian, Armenian, Kurd, and Albanian flesh is heir to. Such the results of the Tanzimát, the silliest copy of Europe's folly—bureaucracy and centralisation—that the pen of empirical statecraft ever traced.[1] Under a strong-handed and strong-hearted despotism, like Mohammed Ali's, El-Hejaz, in one generation, might be purged of its pests. By a proper use of the blood-feud; by vigorously supporting the weaker against the stronger classes; by regularly defeating every Bedawi who earns a name for himself; and, above all, by the exercise of unsparing, unflinching justice, the few thousands of half-naked bandits, who now make the land a fighting field, would soon sink into utter insignificance.

But to effect such end, the Turks require the old stratocracy, which, bloody as it was, worked with far less misery than the charter and the new code. What Milton calls

> The solid rule of civil government

has done wonders for the race that nurtured and brought to perfection an idea spontaneous to their organisation. The world

[1] The greatest of all its errors was that of appointing to the provinces, instead of the single Pasha of the olden time, three different governors, civil, military, and fiscal, all depending upon the supreme council at Constantinople. Thus each province has three plunderers instead of one, and its affairs are referred to a body that can take no interest in it.

The head of the Prophet's Mosque, Medina, and servants attached to the tomb of the Prophet

View from outside the walls of Medina, showing a pilgrim camp

The Prophet's Mosque, Medina, from the north

Interior view of the Prophet's Mosque, Medina

has yet to learn that the admirable exotic will thrive amongst the country gentlemen of Monomotapa or the ragged nobility of El-Hejaz.[1]

Saad, the Old Man of the Mountains, was described to me as a little brown Bedawi; contemptible in appearance, but remarkable for courage and ready wit. He has for treachery a keen scent which he requires to keep in exercise. A blood-feud with Abd el-Muttalib, the present Sherif of Meccah, who slew his nephew, and the hostility of several Sultans, has rendered his life eventful. He lost all his teeth by poison, which would have killed him, had he not, after swallowing the potion, corrected it by drinking off a large pot-full of clarified butter. Since that time he has lived entirely upon fruits, which he gathers for himself, and coffee which he prepares with his own hands. In Sultan Mahmud's time he received from Constantinople a gorgeous purse, which he was told to open, as it contained something for his private inspection. Suspecting treachery, he gave it for this purpose to a slave, bidding him carry it to some distance; the bearer was shot by a pistol cunningly fixed, like Rob Roy's, in the folds of the bag.

Whether this far-known story be 'true or only well found', it is certain that Shayhk Saad now fears the Turks, even when they bring gifts. The Sultan sends, or is supposed to send him, presents of fine horses, robes of honour, and a large quantity of grain. But the Shaykh, trusting to his hills rather than to steeds, sells them; he gives away the dresses to his slaves, and he distributes the grain among his clansmen. Of his character, men as usual tell two tales: some praise his charity, and call him the friend of the poor, as certainly as he is a foe to the rich. Others, on the contrary, describe him as cruel, cold-blooded, and notably, even among Arabs, revengeful and avaricious.

The truth probably lies between these two extremes, but I observed that those of my companions who spoke most highly of the robber chief when at a distance seemed to be in the *sudori freddi* whilst under the shadow of his hills.

El-Hamra is the third station from El-Medinah in the Darb el-Sultani, the Sultan's or High Road, the westerly line leading to Meccah along the sea-coast. When the robbers permit, the

[1] These remarks were written in 1853: I see no reason to change them in 1878.

pilgrims prefer this route on account of its superior climate, the facility of procuring water and supplies, the vicinity of the sea, and the circumstance of its passing through Bedr, the scene of the Prophet's principal military exploits (AH 2).

After midday on the 21st July, when we had made up our minds that Fate had determined we should halt at El-Hamra, a caravan arrived from Meccah; and the new travellers had interest to procure an escort, and permission to proceed without delay towards El-Medinah. The good news filled us with joy. A little after four p.m. we urged our panting camels over the fiery sands to join the Meccans, who were standing ready for the march, on the other side of the torrent-bed. An hour afterwards we started in an easterly direction.

My companions having found friends and relations in the Meccan caravan—the boy Mohammed's elder brother, about whom more anon, was of the number—were full of news and excitement. At sunset they prayed with unction: even Saad and Hamid had not the face to sit their camels during the halt, when all around were washing, sanding themselves,[1] and busy with their devotions. We then ate our suppers, remounted, and started once more.

Shortly after night set in, we came to a sudden halt. A dozen different reports rose to account for this circumstance, which was occasioned by a band of Bedawin, who had manned a gorge, and sent forward a 'parliamentary', ordering us forthwith to stop. They at first demanded money to let us pass; but at last, hearing that we were Sons of the Holy Cities, they granted us transit on the sole condition that the military—whom they, like Irish peasants, hate and fear—should return to whence they came. Upon this, our escort, 200 men, wheeled their horses round and galloped back to their barracks.

We moved onwards, without, however, seeing any robbers; my camel-man pointed out their haunts, and showed me a small bird hovering over a place where he supposed water trickled

[1] When water cannot be obtained for ablution before prayers, Moslems clap the palms of their hands upon the sands, and draw them down the face and both fore-arms. This operation, which is performed once or twice—it varies in different schools—is called Tayammum.

from the rock. The fellow had attempted a sneer at my expense when the fray was impending. 'Why don't you load your pistols, Effendi,' he cried, 'and get out of your litter, and show fight?' 'Because', I replied as loudly, 'in my country, when dogs run at us, we thrash them with sticks.' This stopped Mansur's mouth for a time, but he and I were never friends. Like the lowest orders of Orientals, he required to be ill-treated; gentleness and condescension he seemed to consider a proof of cowardice or of imbecility. I began with kindness, but was soon compelled to use hard words at first, and then threats, which, though he heard them with frowns and mutterings, produced manifest symptoms of improvement.

Oignez vilain, il vous poindra!
Poignez vilain, il vous oindra!

says the old French proverb, and the lesson is more valuable in the East even than in the West.

Our night's journey had no other incident. We travelled over rising ground with the moon full in our faces; and, about midnight, we passed through another long straggling line of villages, called Jadaydah,[1] or El-Khayf. The principal part of it lies on the left of the road going to El-Medinah; it has a fort like that of El-Hamra, springs of tolerable drinking water, a Nakhil or date-ground, and a celebrated (dead) saint, Abd el-Rahim el-Burai. A little beyond it lies the Bughaz, or defile, where in AD 1811 Tussun Bey and his 8,000 Turks were totally defeated by 25,000 Harbi Bedawin and Wahhabis. This is a famous attacking-point of the Beni-Harb.

In former times both Jezzar Pasha, the celebrated 'butcher' of Syria, and Abdullah Pasha of Damascus, were baffled at the gorge of Jadaydah; and this year the commander of the Syrian caravan, afraid of risking an attack at a place so ill-omened, avoided it by marching upon Meccah via the Desert-road of Nejd. At four a.m., having travelled about twenty-four miles due east, we encamped at Bir Abbas.

[1] I write this word as my companions pronounced it. Burckhardt similarly gives it 'Djedeyde', and Ali Bey 'Djideïda'. Giovanni Finati wrongly calls the place 'Jedeed Bughaz', which Mr Bankes, his editor, rightly translates the 'new opening or pass'.

XIV

From Bir Abbas to El-Medinah

The 22nd July was a grand trial of temper to our little party. The position of Bir Abbas exactly resembles that of El-Hamra, except that the bulge of the hill-girt Fiumara is at this place about two miles wide. There are the usual stone-forts and palm-leaved hovels for the troopers, stationed here to hold the place and to escort travellers, with a coffee-shed, and a hut or two, called a bazar, but no village. Our encamping ground was a bed of loose sand, with which the violent Simoom filled the air; not a tree or a bush was in sight; a species of hardy locust and swarms of flies were the only remnants of animal life: the scene was a caricature of Sind. Although we were now some hundred feet, to judge by the water-shed, above the level of the sea, the midday sun scorched even through the tent; our frail tenement was more than once blown down, and the heat of the sand made the work of repitching it painful.

Again my companions, after breakfasting, hurried to the coffee-house, and returned one after the other with dispiriting reports. Then they either quarrelled desperately about nothing, or they threw themselves on their rugs, pretending to sleep in very sulkiness. The lady Maryam soundly rated her surly son for refusing to fill her chibouque for the twelfth time that morning, with the usual religious phrases—

'Ali direct thee into the right way, O my son!'

Meaning that he was going to the bad, and—

'O my calamity, thy mother is a lone woman, O Allah!'

Equivalent to the European parental plaint about grey hairs being brought down in sorrow to the grave.

Before noon a small caravan which followed us came in with two dead bodies—a trooper shot by the Bedawin, and an Albanian killed by sunstroke, or by the fiery wind. Shortly after midday a caravan, travelling in an opposite direction, passed by us; it was composed chiefly of Indian pilgrims, habited in correct costume, and hurrying towards Meccah in hot haste. They had been allowed to pass unmolested, because probably 1*l.* could not have been collected from a hundred pockets, and Saad the Robber sometimes does a cheap good deed. But our party, having valuables with them, did not seem to gather heart from this event.

In the evening we all went out to see some Arab Shaykhs who were travelling to Bir Abbas in order to receive their salaries. Without such *douceurs*, it is popularly said and believed, no stone walls could enable a Turk to hold El-Hejaz against the hill-men. Such was our system in Afghanistan—most unwise, teaching *in limine* the subject to despise rulers subject to black-mail. Besides which, these highly paid Shaykhs do no good. When a fight takes place or a road is shut, they profess inability to restrain their clansmen; and the richer they are, of course the more formidable they become.

The party looked well; they were Harb, dignified old men in the picturesque Arab costume, with erect forms, fierce thin features, and white beards, well armed, and mounted upon high-bred and handsomely equipped dromedaries from El-Shark, the Eastern Region. Preceded by their half-naked clansmen, carrying spears twelve or thirteen feet long, garnished with single or double tufts of black ostrich feathers, and ponderous matchlocks, which were discharged on approaching the fort, they were not without a kind of barbaric pomp.

Immediately after the reception of these Shaykhs, there was a parade of the Arnaut Irregular Horse. About 500 of them rode out to the sound of the Nakus or little kettle-drum, whose puny notes strikingly contrasted with this really martial sight. The men, it is true, were mounted on lean Arab and Egyptian nags, ragged-looking as their clothes; and each trooper was armed in his own way, though all had swords, pistols, and matchlocks, or firelocks of some kind. But they rode hard as Galway 'buckeens', and there was a gallant reckless look about the fellows which prepossessed me strongly in their favour. Their animals, too, though notable 'screws', were well trained, and their accoutrements were intended for use, not show.

I watched their manoeuvres with curiosity. They left their

cantonments one by one, and, at the sound of the tom-tom, by degrees formed a plump or herse—*column* it could not be called—all huddled together in confusion. Presently the little kettle-drum changed its note and the parade its aspect. All the serried body dispersed as would Light Infantry, now continuing their advance, then hanging back, then making a rush, and all the time keeping up a hot fire upon the enemy. At another signal they suddenly put their horses to full speed, and, closing upon the centre, again advanced in a dense mass.

After three-quarters of an hour parading, sometimes charging singly, often in bodies, to the right, to the left, and straight in front, halting when requisite, and occasionally retreating, Parthian-like, the Arnauts turned *en masse* towards their lines. As they neared them, all broke off and galloped in, *ventre à terre*, discharging their shotted guns with much recklessness against objects assumed to denote the enemy. But ball-cartridge seemed to be plentiful hereabouts; during the whole of this and the next day, I remarked that bullets, notched for noise, were fired away in mere fun.

Barbarous as these movements may appear to the Cavalry Martinet of the 'good old school', yet to something of the kind will the tactics of that arm, I humbly opine, return, when the perfect use of the rifle, the revolver, and field artillery shall have made the present necessarily slow system fatal. Also, if we adopt the common-sense opinion of a modern writer—the late Captain Nolan—and determine that 'individual prowess, skill in single combats, good horsemanship, and sharp swords render cavalry formidable', these semi-barbarians are wiser in their generation than the civilised, who never practise arms (properly so called), whose riding-drill never made a good rider, whose horses are over-weighted, and whose swords are worthless.

They have yet another point of superiority over us; they cultivate the individuality of the soldier, whilst we strive to make him a mere automaton. In the days of European chivalry, battles were a system of well-fought duels. This was succeeded by the age of discipline, when, to use the language of Rabelais, 'Men seemed rather a consort of organ-pipes, or mutual concord of the wheels of a clock, than an infantry and cavalry, or army of soldiers'.

Our aim should now be to combine the merits of both systems; to make men individually excellent in the use of weapons, and still train them to act naturally and habitually in concert. The French have given a model to Europe in the Chasseurs de Vincennes—a body capable of most perfect combination, yet never more truly excellent than when each man is fighting alone. We, I suppose, shall imitate them at some future time.

A distant dropping of firearms ushered in the evening of our first melancholy day at Bir Abbas. This, said my companions, was a sign that the troops and the hill-men were fighting. They communicated the intelligence, as if it ought to be an effectual check upon my impatience to proceed; it acted, however, in the contrary way. I supposed that the Bedawin, after battling out the night, would be less warlike the next day; the others, however, by no means agreed in opinion with me.

At Yambu' the whole party had boasted loudly that the people of El-Medinah could keep their Bedawin in order, and had twitted the boy Mohammed with their superiority in this respect to his townsmen, the Meccans. But now that a trial was impending I saw none of the fearlessness so conspicuous when peril was only possible. The change was charitably to be explained by the presence of their valuables; the Sahharahs, like conscience, making cowards of them all. But the young Meccan, who, having sent on his box by sea from Yambu' to Jeddah, felt merry, like the empty traveller, would not lose the opportunity to pay off old scores. He taunted the Medinites till they stamped and raved with fury. At last, fearing some violence, and feeling answerable for the boy's safety to his family, I seized him by the nape of his neck and the upper posterior portion of his nether garments, and drove him before me into the tent.

When the hubbub had subsided, and all sat after supper smoking the pipe of peace in the cool night air, I rejoined my companions, and found them talking, as usual, about old Shaykh Saad. The scene was appropriate for the subject. In the distance rose the blue peak said to be his eyrie, and the place was pointed out with fearful meaning. As it is inaccessible to strangers, report has converted it into another garden of Irem. A glance, however, at its position and formation satisfied me that the bubbling springs, the deep forests, and the orchards of apple-trees, quinces, and pomegranates with which my companions furnished it, were a myth, whilst some experience of Arab ignorance of the art of defence suggested to me strong doubts about the existence of an impregnable fortress on the hill-top. The mountains, however, looked beautiful in the moonlight, and distance gave them a semblance of mystery well suited to the themes which they inspired.

That night I slept within my Shugduf, for it would have been mere madness to lie on the open plain in a place so infested by banditti. The being armed is but a poor precaution near this robbers' den. If you wound a man in the very act of plundering, an exorbitant sum must be paid for blood-money. If you kill him, even to save your life, then adieu to any chance of escaping destruction. Roused three or four times during the night by jackals and dogs prowling about our little camp, I observed that my companions, who had agreed amongst themselves to keep watch by turns, had all fallen into a sound sleep. However, when we awoke in the morning, the usual inspection of goods and chattels showed that nothing was gone.

The next day (23rd July) was a forced halt, a sore stimulant to the traveller's ill-humour; and the sun, the sand, the dust, the furious Simúm, and the want of certain small supplies, aggravated our grievance. My sore foot had been inflamed by a dressing of onion skin which the lady Maryam had insisted upon applying to it. Still, being resolved to push forward by any conveyance that could be procured, I offered 10 dollars for a fresh dromedary to take me on to El-Medinah. Shaykh Hamid also declared he would leave his box in charge of a friend and accompany me. Saad the Demon flew into a passion at the idea of any member of the party escaping the general evil; and he privily threatened Mohammed to cut off the legs of any camel that ventured into camp. This, the boy—who, like a boy of the world as he was, never lost an opportunity of making mischief—instantly communicated to me, and it brought on a furious dispute. Saad was reproved, and apologised for by the rest of the party; and presently he himself was pacified, principally, I believe, by the intelligence that no camel was to be hired at Bir Abbas.

One of the Arnaut garrison, who had obtained leave to go to El-Medinah, came to ask us if we could mount him, as otherwise he should be obliged to walk the whole way. With him we debated the propriety of attempting a passage through the hills by one of the many by-paths that traverse them: the project was amply discussed, and duly rejected.

We passed the day in the usual manner; all crowded together for shelter under the tent. Even Maryam joined us, loudly informing Ali, her son, that his mother was no longer a woman but a man; whilst our party generally, cowering away from the fierce glances of the sun, were either eating or occasionally smoking, or were occupied in cooling and drinking water.

About sunset-time came a report that we were to start that night. None could believe that such good was in store for us; before sleeping, however, we placed each camel's pack apart, so as to be ready for loading at a moment's notice; and we took care to watch that our Bedawin did not drive their animals away to any distance.

At last, about eleven p.m., as the moon was beginning to peep over the eastern wall of rock, was heard the glad sound of the little kettle-drum calling the Albanian troopers to mount and march. In the shortest possible time all made ready; and, hurriedly crossing the sandy flat, we found ourselves in company with three or four caravans, forming one large body for better defence against the dreaded Hawamid.[1]

By dint of much manoeuvring, arms in hand—Shaykh Hamid and the Demon took the prominent parts: we, though the last comers, managed to secure places about the middle of the line. On such occasions all push forward recklessly, as an English mob in the strife of sight-seeing; the rear, being left unguarded, is the place of danger, and none seek the honour of occupying it.

We travelled that night up the Fiumara in an easterly direction, and at early dawn (24th July) we found ourselves in an ill-famed gorge called Shuab el-Hajj (the Pilgrimage Pass). The loudest talkers became silent as we neared it, and their countenances showed apprehension written in legible characters. Presently from the high precipitous cliff on our left, thin blue curls

[1] Hawamid is the plural of Hamidah, Shaykh Saad's tribe.

of smoke—somehow or other they caught every eye—rose in the air; and instantly afterwards rang the sharp cracks of the hill-men's matchlocks echoed by the rocks on the right. My Shugduf had been broken by the camel's falling during the night, so I called out to Mansur that we had better splice the framework with a bit of rope: he looked up, saw me laughing, and with an ejaculation of disgust disappeared. A number of Bedawin were to be seen swarming like hornets over the crests of the hills, boys as well as men carrying huge weapons, and climbing with the agility of cats. They took up comfortable places on the cut-throat eminence, and began firing upon us with perfect convenience to themselves.

The height of the hills and the glare of the rising sun prevented my seeing objects very distinctly, but my companions pointed out to me places where the rock had been scarped, and where a kind of rough stone breastwork—the Sangah of Afghanistan—had been piled up as a defence, and a rest for the long barrel of the matchlock. It was useless to challenge the Bedawin to come down and fight us like men upon the plain; they will do this on the eastern coast of Arabia, but rarely, if ever, in El-Hejaz. And it was equally unprofitable for our escort to fire upon a foe ensconced behind stones. Besides which, had a robber been killed, the whole country would have risen to a man; with a force of 3,000 or 4,000, they might have gained courage to overpower a caravan, and in such a case not a soul would have escaped.

As it was, the Bedawin directed their fire principally against the Albanians. Some of these called for assistance to the party of Shaykhs that accompanied us from Bir Abbas; but the dignified old men, dismounting and squatting in council round their pipes, came to the conclusion that, as the robbers would probably turn a deaf ear to their words, they had better spare themselves the trouble of speaking. We had therefore nothing to do but to blaze away as much powder, and to veil ourselves in as much smoke, as possible; the result of the affair was that we lost twelve men, besides camels and other beasts of burden. Though the bandits showed no symptoms of bravery, and confined themselves to slaughtering the enemy from their hill-top, my companions seemed to consider this questionable affair a most gallant exploit.

After another hour's hurried ride through the Wady Sayyalah, appeared Shuhada, to which we pushed on,

> Like nighted swain on lonely road,
> When close behind fierce goblins tread.

Shuhada is a place which derives its name, the Martyrs, because here are supposed to be buried forty braves that fell in one of Mohammed's many skirmishes. Some authorities consider it the cemetery of the people of Wady Sayyalah. The once populous valley is now barren, and one might easily pass by the consecrated spot without observing a few ruined walls and a cluster of rude Bedawin graves, each an oval of rough stones lying beneath the thorn trees on the left of and a little off the road. Another half-hour took us to a favourite halting-place, Bir el-Hindi, so called from some forgotten Indian who dug a well there. But we left it behind, wishing to put as much space as we could between our tents and the nests of the Hamidah.

Then quitting the Fiumara, we struck northwards into a well-trodden road running over stony rising ground. The heat became sickening; here, and in the East generally, at no time is the sun more dangerous than between eight and nine a.m. Still we hurried on. It was not before eleven that we reached our destination, a rugged plain covered with stones, coarse gravel, and thorn trees in abundance; and surrounded by inhospitable rocks, pinnacle-shaped, of granite below, and in the upper parts fine limestone. The well was at least two miles distant, and not a hovel was in sight; a few Bedawi children belonging to an outcast tribe fed their starveling goats upon the hills. This place is called Suwaykah; it is, I was told, that celebrated in the history of the Arabs. Yet not for this reason did my comrades look lovingly upon its horrors: their boxes were safe, and with the eye of imagination they could now behold their homes. That night we must have travelled about twenty-two miles; the direction of the road was due east, and the only remarkable feature in the ground was its steady rise.

We pitched the tent under a villainous Mimosa, the tree whose shade is compared by poetic Bedawin to the false friend who deserts you in your utmost need. I enlivened the hot dull day by a final affair with Saad the Demon. His alacrity at Yambu' obtained for him the loan of a couple of dollars: he had bought grain at El-Hamra, and now we were near El-Medinah: still there was not a word about repayment. And knowing that an Oriental debtor discharges his debt as he pays his rent—namely, with the greatest unwillingness—and that, on the other hand, an Oriental creditor will devote the labour of a year to recovering a sixpence, I resolved to act as a native of the country, placed in my position, would; and by dint of sheer dunning and demanding pledges to recover my property.

About noon Saad the Demon, after a furious rush, bareheaded, through the burning sun, flung the two dollars down upon my carpet: however, he presently recovered temper, and, as subsequent events showed, I had chosen the right part. Had he not been forced to repay his debt, he would have despised me as a freshman, and would have coveted more. As it was, the boy Mohammed bore the brunt of unpopular feeling, my want of liberality being traced to his secret and perfidious admonitions. He supported his burden the more philosophically, because, as he notably calculated, every dollar saved at El-Medinah would be spent under his stewardship at Meccah.

At four p.m. (24th July) we left Suwaykah, all of us in the crossest of humours, and travelled in a north-easterly direction. So out of temper were my companions, that at sunset, of the whole party, Umar Effendi was the only one who would eat supper. The rest sat upon the ground, pouting, grumbling, and—they had been allowed to exhaust my stock of Latakia—smoking Syrian tobacco as if it were a grievance. Such a game at naughty children I have seldom seen played even by Oriental men.

The boy Mohammed privily remarked to me that the camelmen's beards were now in his fist—meaning that we were out of their kinsmen, the Harb's, reach. He soon found an opportunity to quarrel with them; and, because one of his questions was not answered in the shortest possible time, he proceeded to abuse them in language which sent their hands flying in the direction of their swords. Despite, however, this threatening demeanour, the youth, knowing that he now could safely go to any lengths, continued his ill words, and Mansur's face was so comically furious, that I felt too much amused to interfere.

At last the camel-men disappeared, thereby punishing us most effectually for our sport. The road lay up rocky hill and down stony vale; a tripping and stumbling dromedary had been substituted for the usual *monture:* the consequence was that we had either a totter or a tumble once per mile during the whole of that long night. In vain the now fiery Mohammed called for the assistance of the camel-men with the full force of his lungs:

'Where be those owls, those oxen of the oxen, those beggars, those cut-off ones, those foreigners, those Sons of Flight?[1] withered be their hands! palsied be their fingers! the foul moustached fellows, basest of the Arabs that ever hammered tent-peg, sneaking cats, goats of El-Akhfash![2] Truly I will torture them the torture of the oil,[3] the mines of infamy! the cold of countenance (fools)!'

The Bedawin brotherhood of the camel-men looked at him wickedly, muttering the while—

'By Allah! and by Allah! and by Allah! O boy, we will flog thee like a hound when we catch thee in the Desert!'

All our party called upon him to desist, but his temper had got completely the upper hand over his discretion, and he expressed himself in such classic and idiomatic Hejazi, that I had not the heart to stop him. Some days after our arrival at El-Medinah, Shaykh Hamid warned him seriously never again to go such perilous lengths, as the Beni-Harb were celebrated for shooting or poniarding the man who ventured to use to them even the mild epithet 'O jackass!' And in the quiet of the city the boy Mohammed, like a sobered man shuddering at dangers braved when drunk, hearkened with discomposure and penitence to his friend's words. The only immediate consequence of

[1] A popular but not a bad pun—'Harb' (Fight) becomes, by the alteration of the H, 'Harb' (Flight).

[2] The old Arabic proverb is 'a greater wiseacre than the goat of Akhfash'; it is seldom intelligible to the vulgar.

[3] That is to say, 'I will burn them (metaphorically) as the fiery wick consumes the oil'—a most idiomatic Hejazi threat.

his abuse was that my broken Shugduf became a mere ruin, and we passed the dark hours perched like two birds upon the only entire bits of framework the cots contained.

The sun had nearly risen (25th July) before I shook off the lethargic effects of such a night. All around me were hurrying their camels, regardless of rough ground, and not a soul spoke a word to his neighbour.

'Are there robbers in sight?' was the natural question.

'No!' replied Mohammed; 'they are walking with their eyes, they will presently see their homes!' Rapidly we passed the Wady el-Akik, of which,

> O my friend, this is Akik, then stand by it,
> Endeavouring to be distracted by love, if not really a lover,[1]

and a thousand other such pretty things, have been said by the Arab poets. It was as 'dry as summer's dust', and its 'beautiful trees' appeared in the shape of vegetable mummies. Half an hour after leaving the 'Blessed Valley' we came to a huge flight of steps roughly cut in a long broad line of black scoriaceous basalt. This is termed the Mudarraj or flight of steps over the western ridge of the so-called El-Harratayn. It is holy ground; for the Apostle spoke well of it. Arrived at the top, we passed through a lane of dark lava, with steep banks on both sides, and after a few minutes a full view of the city suddenly opened upon us.

We halted our beasts as if by word of command. All of us descended, in imitation of the pious of old, and sat down, jaded and hungry as we were, to feast our eyes with a view of the Holy City.

'O Allah! this is the Haram (sanctuary) of Thy Apostle; make it to us a Protection from Hell-fire, and a Refuge from Eternal Punishment! O open the Gates of Thy Mercy, and let us pass through them to the Land of Joy!' and 'O Allah, bless the last of Prophets, the Seal of Prophecy, with Blessings in number as the Stars of Heaven, and the Waves of the Sea, and the Sands of the Waste—bless him, O Lord of Might and Majesty, as long as the Corn-field and the Date-grove continue to feed Man-

[1] The esoteric meaning of this couplet is, 'Man! this is a lovely portion of God's creation; then stand by it, and here learn to love the perfections of thy Supreme Friend.'

kind!'[1] And again, 'Live for ever, O Most Excellent of Prophets! —live in the Shadow of Happiness during the Hours of Night and the Times of Day, whilst the Bird of the Tamarisk (the dove) moaneth like the childless Mother, whilst the West-wind bloweth gently over the Hills of Nejd, and the Lightning flasheth bright in the Firmament of El-Hejaz!'

Such were the poetical exclamations that rose all around me, showing how deeply tinged with imagination becomes the language of the Arab under the influence of strong passion or religious enthusiasm. I now understood the full value of a phrase in the Moslem ritual, 'And when his' (the pilgrim's) 'eyes shall *fall upon the Trees of El-Medinah*, let him raise his Voice and bless the Apostle with the choicest of Blessings.' In all the fair view before us nothing was more striking, after the desolation through which we had passed, than the gardens and orchards about the town. It was impossible not to enter into the spirit of my companions, and truly I believe that for some minutes my enthusiasm rose as high as theirs. But presently when we remounted, the traveller returned strong upon me: I made a rough sketch of the town, put questions about the principal buildings, and in fact collected materials for the next chapter.

The distance traversed that night was about twenty-two miles, in a direction varying from easterly to north-easterly. We reached El-Medinah on the 25th July, thus taking nearly eight days to travel over little more than 130 miles. This journey is performed with camels in four days, and a good dromedary will do it without difficulty in half that time.[2]

[1] That is to say, 'throughout all ages and all nations'. The Arabs divide the world into two great bodies, first themselves, and, secondly, Ajam, i.e. all that are not Arabs. Similar bi-partitions are the Hindus and Mlenchhas, the Jews and Gentiles, the Greeks and Barbarians, etc., etc.

[2] The following is a synopsis of our stations:

		Miles	
(1)	From Yambu', the 18th July, to Musahhal, NE	16	64 miles
(2)	From Musahhal, the 19th July, to Bir Said, S and E	34	
(3)	From Bir Said, the 20th July, to El-Hamra, NE	14	
(4)	From El-Hamra, the 21st July, to Bir Abbas, E	24	68 miles
(5)	From Bir Abbas, the 23rd July, to Suwaykah, E	22	
(6)	From Suwaykah, the 24th July, to El-Medinah, N and E	22	
	Total English miles	132	

XV

Through the Suburb of El-Medinah to Hamid's House

As we looked eastward, the sun arose out of the horizon of low hill, blurred and dotted with small tufted trees, which gained from the morning mists a giant stature, and the earth was stained with purple and gold. Before us lay a spacious plain, bounded in front by the undulating ground of Nejd: on the left was a grim pile of rocks, the celebrated Mount Ohod, with a clump of verdure and a white dome or two nestling at its base. Rightwards, broad streaks of lilac-coloured mists, here thick with gathered dew, there pierced and thinned by the morning rays, stretched over the date-groves and the gardens of Kuba, which stood out in emerald green from the dull tawny surface of the plain. Below, distant about two miles, lay El-Medinah; at first sight it appeared a large place, but a closer inspection proved the impression to be erroneous.

A tortuous road from the Harrah to the city wound across the plain, and led to a tall rectangular gateway, pierced in the ruinous mud-wall which surrounds the suburb. This is the Ambari entrance. It is flanked on the left (speaking as a sketcher) by the domes and minarets of a pretty Turkish building, a Takiyeh, erected by the late Mohammed Ali for the reception of Dervish-travellers; on the right by a long low line of whitewashed buildings garnished with ugly square windows, an imitation of civilised barracks. Beginning from the left hand, as we sat upon the ridge, the remarkable features of the town thus presented themselves in succession. Outside, among the palm-trees to the north of the city, were the picturesque ruins of a large old Sebil, or public fountain; and, between this and the enceinte, stood a conspicuous building, in the Turkish pavilion style—the Governor's palace. On the north-west angle of the town-wall is a tall whitewashed fort, partly built upon an outcropping mass of rock: its ramparts and embrasures give it a modern and European appearance, which contrasts strangely with its truly Oriental history.

In the suburb El-Manakhah, the kneeling-place of camels, the brand-new domes and minarets of the Five Mosques stand brightly out from the dull grey mass of house and ground. And behind, in the most easterly part of the city, remarkable from afar, is the gem of El-Medinah—the four tall substantial towers, and the flashing green Dome under which the Apostle's remains rest. Half concealed by this mass of buildings and by the houses of the town, are certain white specks upon a green surface, the tombs that adorn the venerable cemetery, El-Bakia. From that point southwards begins the mass of palm-groves celebrated in El-Islam as the Trees of El-Medinah. The foreground is well fitted to set off such a view: fields of black basaltic scoriae showing clear signs of a volcanic origin, are broken up into huge blocks and boulders, through which a descent, tolerably steep for camels, winds down into the plain.

After a few minutes' rest I remounted, and slowly rode on towards the gate. Even at this early hour the way was crowded with an eager multitude coming out to meet the Caravan. My companions preferred walking, apparently for the better convenience of kissing, embracing, and shaking hands with relations and friends. Truly the Arabs show more heart on these occasions than any Oriental people I know; they are of a more affectionate nature than the Persians, and their manners are far more demonstrative than those of the Indians.

The respectable Maryam's younger son, a pleasant contrast to her surly elder, was weeping aloud for joy as he ran round his mother's camel, he standing on tiptoe, she bending double in vain attempts to exchange a kiss; and generally, when near relatives or intimates, or school companions, met, the fountains of their eyes were opened. Friends and comrades greeted one another, regardless of rank or fortune, with affectionate embraces, and an abundance of queries, which neither party seemed to think of answering.

The general mode of saluting was to throw one arm over the

shoulder and the other round the side, placing the chin first upon the left and then upon the right collar-bone, and rapidly shifting till a *jam satis* suggested itself to both. Inferiors recognised their superiors by attempting to kiss hands, which were violently snatched away; whilst mere acquaintances gave one another a cordial *poignée de mains*, and then raising the finger-tips to their lips, kissed them with apparent relish.

Passing through the Bab Ambari we defiled slowly down a broad dusty street, and traversed the Harat (Quarter) El-Ambariyah, the principal in the Manakhah suburb. The thoroughfare is by no means remarkable after Cairo; only it is rather wider and more regular than the traveller is accustomed to in Asiatic cities.

I was astonished to see on both sides of the way, in so small a place, so large a number of houses too ruinous to be occupied. Then we crossed a bridge, a single little round arch of roughly hewn stone, built over the bed of a torrent, El-Sayh, which in some parts appeared about fifty feet broad, with banks showing a high and deeply indented water-mark. Here the road abuts upon an open space called the Barr el-Manakhah, or more concisely El-Barr, the Plain. Straightforward a line leads directly into the Bab el-Misri, the Egyptian gate of the city. But we turned off to the right; and, after advancing a few yards, we found ourselves at the entrance of our friend Hamid's house.

The Shaykh had preceded us early that morning, in order to prepare an apartment for his guests, and to receive the first loud congratulations and embraces of his mother and the 'daughter of his uncle'. Apparently he had not concluded this pleasing duty when we arrived, for the camels were kneeling at least five minutes at his door, before he came out to offer the usual hospitable salutation. I stared to see the difference of his appearance this morning.

The razor had passed over his head and face; the former was now surmounted by a muslin turban of goodly size, wound round a new embroidered cap; and the latter, besides being clean, boasted of neat little moustaches turned up like two commas, whilst a well-trimmed goat's beard narrowed until it resembled what our grammars call an exclamation point.

The dirty, torn shirt, with the bits of rope round the loins, had been exchanged for a Jubbah or outer cloak of light pink merinos, a long-sleeved Caftan of rich flowered stuff, a fine shirt of Halaili, silk and cotton, and a sash of plaid pattern, elaborately fringed at both ends, and, for better display, wound round two-thirds of his body. His pantaloons were also of Halaili, with tasteful edgings about the ankles like a pantilette's, while his bare and sunburnt feet had undergone a thorough purification before being encased in new Mizz[1] (inner slippers), and Papush (outer slippers) of bright lemon-coloured leather of the newest and most fashionable Constantinopolitan cut. In one of his now delicate hands the Shaykh bore a mother-of-pearl rosary, token of piety; in the other a handsome pipe with a jasmine stick, and an expensive amber mouth-piece; his tobacco-pouch, dangling from his waist like the little purse in the bosom pocket of his coat, was of broadcloth richly embroidered with gold.

In course of time I saw that all my companions had metamorphosed themselves in an equally remarkable manner. As men of sense, they appeared in tatters where they were, or when they wished to be, unknown, and in fine linen where and when the world judged their prosperity by their attire. Their grand suits of clothes, therefore, were worn only for a few days after returning from the journey, by way of proof that the wearer had wandered to some purpose; they were afterwards laid up in lavender, and reserved for choice occasions, as old ladies in Europe store up their state dresses.

The Shaykh, whose manners had changed with his garments, from the vulgar and boisterous to a certain staid courtesy, took my hand, and led me up to the Majlis (parlour), which was swept and garnished, with all due apparatus, for the forthcoming reception-ceremony. And behind us followed the boy Mohammed, looking more downcast and ashamed of himself than I can possibly describe; he was still in his rags, and he felt keenly that every visitor staring at him would mentally inquire—

'Who may that snob be?'

[1] The Mizz are the tight-fitting inner slippers of soft Cordovan leather, worn as stockings inside the slipper; they are always clean, so they may be retained in the Mosque or on the Diwan (divan or sofa).

With the deepest dejectedness he squeezed himself into a corner, aud Shaykh Nur, who was foully dirty, as an Indian *en voyage* always is, would have joined him in his shame, had I not ordered the 'slave' to make himself generally useful.

It is customary for all relations and friends to call upon the traveller the very day he returns, that is to say if amity is to endure. The pipes therefore stood ready filled, the Diwans were duly spread, and the coffee was being boiled upon a brazier in the passage.

Scarcely had I taken my place at the cool window-sill—it was the best in the room—when the visitors began to pour in, and the Shaykh rose to welcome and embrace them. They sat down, smoked, chatted politics, asked all manner of questions about the other wayfarers and absent friends; drank coffee; and, after half an hour's visit, rose abruptly, and, exchanging embraces, took leave. The little men entered the assembly, after an accolade at the door, noiselessly, squatted upon the worst seats with polite *congés* to the rest of the assembly; smoked, took their coffee, as it were, under protest, and glided out of the room as quietly as they crept in.

The great people, generally busy and consequential individuals, upon whose countenances were writ large the words 'well to do in the world', appeared with a noise that made each person in the room rise reverentially upon his feet; sat down with importance, monopolised the conversation; and, departing in a dignified manner, expected all to stand on the occasion.

The Jihad (Holy War), as usual, was the grand topic of conversation. The Sultan had ordered the Czar to become a Moslem. The Czar had sued for peace, and offered tribute and fealty. But the Sultan had exclaimed—

'No, by Allah! El-Islam!'

The Czar could not be expected to take such a step without a little hesitation, but 'Allah smites the faces of the Infidels!' Abd el-Mejid would dispose of the 'Moskow' in a short time; after which he would turn his victorious army against all the idolaters of Feringistan, beginning with the English, the French, and the Arwạm or Greeks. Amongst much of this nonsense—when applied to for my opinion, I was careful to make it popular—I heard news foreboding no good to my journey towards Muscat. The Bedawin had decided that there was to be an Arab contingent, and had been looking forward to the spoils of Europe: this caused quarrels, as all the men wanted to go, and not a ten-year-old would be left behind. The consequence was, that this amiable people was fighting in all directions. At least so said the visitors, and I afterwards found out that they were not far wrong.

The Samman is a great family, in numbers as in dignity; from eight a.m. till midday therefore the Majlis was crowded with people, and politeness delayed our breakfasts until an unconscionable hour.

To the plague of strangers succeeded that of children. No sooner did the parlour become, comparatively speaking, vacant, than they rushed in *en masse*, treading upon our toes, making the noise of a nursery of madlings, pulling to pieces everything they could lay their hands upon, and using language that would have alarmed an old man-o'-war's-man. In fact, no one can conceive the plague but those who have studied the *enfans terribles* which India sends home in cargoes.

One urchin, scarcely three years old, told me, because I objected to his perching upon my wounded foot, that his father had a sword at home with which he would cut my throat from ear to ear, suiting the action to the word. By a few taunts, I made the little wretch furious with rage; he shook his infant fist at me, and then opening his enormous round black eyes to their utmost stretch, he looked at me, and licked his knee with portentous meaning. Shaykh Hamid, happening to come in at the moment, stood aghast at the doorway, chin in hand, to see the Effendi subject to such indignity; and it was not without trouble that I saved the offender from summary nursery discipline. Another scamp caught up one of my loaded pistols before I could snatch it out of his hand, and clapped it to his neighbour's head; fortunately, it was on half-cock, and the trigger was stiff. Then a serious and majestic boy about six years old, with an inkstand in his belt, in token of his receiving a literary education, seized my pipe and began to smoke it with huge puffs.

I ventured laughingly to institute a comparison between the

length of his person and the pipe-stick, when he threw it upon the ground, and stared at me fixedly with flaming eyes and features distorted by anger. The cause of this 'bouldness' soon appeared. The boys, instead of being well beaten, were scolded with fierce faces, a mode of punishment which only made them laugh.

They had their redeeming points, however; they were manly angry boys, who punched one another like Anglo-Saxons in the house, whilst abroad they were always fighting with sticks and stones. And they examined our weapons—before deigning to look at anything else—as if eighteen instead of five had been the general age.

At last I so far broke through the laws of Arab politeness as to inform my host in plain words—how inconceivably wretched the boy Mohammed was thereby rendered!—that I was hungry, thirsty, and sleepy, and that I wanted to be alone before visiting the Haram. The good-natured Shaykh, who was preparing to go out at once in order to pray before his father's grave, immediately brought me breakfast; lighted a pipe, spread a bed, darkened the room, turned out the children, and left me to the society I most desired—my own. I then overheard him summon his mother, wife, and other female relatives into the store-room, where his treasures had been carefully stowed away. During the forenoon, in the presence of the visitors, one of Hamid's uncles had urged him, half jocularly, to bring out the Sahharah. The Shaykh did not care to do anything of the kind. Every time a new box is opened in this part of the world, the owner's generosity is appealed to by those whom a refusal offends, and he must allow himself to be plundered with the best possible grace. Hamid therefore prudently suffered all to depart before exhibiting his spoils; which, to judge by the exclamations of delight which they elicited from feminine lips, proved highly satisfactory to those most concerned.

After sleeping, we all set out in a body to the Haram, as this is a duty which must not be delayed by the pious. The boy Mohammed was in better spirits—the effect of having borrowed from Hamid, amongst other articles of clothing, an exceedingly gaudy embroidered coat. As for Shaykh Nur, he had brushed up his Tarbush, and, by means of some cast-off dresses of mine, had made himself look like a respectable Abyssinian slave, in a nondescript toilette, half Turkish, half Indian. I propose to reserve the ceremony of Ziyarat, or Visitation, for another chapter, and to conclude this with a short account of our style of living at the Shaykh's hospitable house.

Hamid's abode is a small corner building, open on the north and east to the Barr el-Manakhah: the ground floor shows only a kind of vestibule, in which coarse articles, like old Shugdufs, mats and bits of sacking, are lying about; the rest is devoted to purposes of sewerage. Ascending dark winding steps of ragged stone covered with hard black earth, you come to the first floor, where the men live. It consists of two rooms to the front of the house, one a Majlis, and another converted into a store. Behind them is a dark passage, into which the doors open; and the back part of the first story is a long windowless room, containing a Hanafiyah, or large copper water-pot, and other conveniences for purification. On the second floor is the kitchen, which I did not inspect, it being as usual occupied by the Harem.

The Majlis has dwarf windows, or rather apertures in the northern and eastern walls, with rude wooden shutters and reed blinds; the embrasures being garnished with cushions, where you sit, morning and evening, to enjoy the cool air. The ceiling is of date-sticks laid across palm-rafters stained red, and the walls are of rough scoriae, burnt bricks, and wood-work cemented with lime. The only signs of furniture in the sitting-room are a Diwan round the sides and a carpet in the centre. A huge wooden box, like a seaman's chest, occupies one of the corners. In the southern wall there is a Suffah, or little shelf of common stone, sunk under a single arch; upon this are placed articles in hourly use, perfume-bottles, coffee-cups, a stray book or two, and sometimes a turban, to be out of the children's way. Two hooks on the western wall, hung jealously high up, hold a pair of pistols with handsome crimson cords and tassels, and half a dozen cherry-stick pipes. The centre of the room is never without one or more Shishahs (water-pipes), and in the corner is a large copper brazier containing fire, with all the utensils for making coffee either disposed upon its broad brim or lying about the floor. The passage, like the stairs, is spread over with hard black earth, and is regularly watered twice a day during the hot weather.

The household consisted of Hamid's mother, wife, some nephews and nieces, small children who ran about in a half-wild and more than half-nude state, and two African slave-girls. When the Damascus Caravan came in, it was further reinforced by the arrival of his three younger brothers.

Though the house was not grand, it was made lively by the varied views out of the Majlis' windows. From the east, you looked upon the square El-Barr, the town-walls and houses beyond it, the Egyptian gate, the lofty minarets of the Haram, and the distant outlines of Jebel Ohod. The north commanded a prospect of Mohammed's Mosque, one of the Khamsah Masajid, or the five suburban Mosques; of part of the fort-wall; and, when the Damascus Caravan came in, of the gay scene of the 'Prado' beneath. The Majlis was tolerably cool during the early part of the day: in the afternoon the sun shone fiercely upon it. I have described the establishment at some length as a specimen of how the middle classes are lodged at El-Medinah. The upper ranks affect Turkish and Egyptian luxuries in their homes, as I had an opportunity of seeing at Umar Effendi's house in the Barr; and in these countries the abodes of the poor are everywhere very similar.

Our life in Shaykh Hamid's house was quiet, but not disagreeable. I never once set eyes upon the face of woman, unless the African slave-girls be allowed the title. Even these at first attempted to draw their ragged veils over their sable charms, and would not answer the simplest question; by degrees they allowed me to see them, and they ventured their voices to reply to me; still they never threw off a certain appearance of shame. Their voices are strangely soft and delicate, considering the appearance of the organs from which they proceed. Possibly this may be a characteristic of the African races; it is remarkable amongst the Somali women. I never saw, nor even heard, the youthful mistress of the household, who stayed all day in the upper rooms. The old lady, Hamid's mother, would stand upon the stairs, and converse aloud with her son, and, when few people were about the house, with me. She never, however, as afterwards happened to an ancient dame at Meccah, came and sat by my side.

When lying during midday in the gallery, I often saw parties of women mount the stairs to the Gynaeconitis, and sometimes an individual would stand to shake a muffled hand[1] with Hamid, to gossip awhile, and to put some questions concerning absent friends; but they were most decorously wrapped up, nor did they ever deign to *déroger*, even by exposing an inch of cheek.

At dawn we arose, washed, prayed, and broke our fast upon a crust of stale bread, before smoking a pipe, and drinking a cup of coffee. Then it was time to dress, to mount, and to visit the Haram or one of the Holy Places outside the city. Returning before the sun became intolerable, we sat together, and with conversation, Shishahs and chibouques, coffee, and cold water perfumed with mastich-smoke, we whiled away the time till our 'Ariston', a dinner which appeared at the primitive hour of eleven a.m. The meal, here called El-Ghada, was served in the Majlis on a large copper tray, sent from the upper apartments. Ejaculating 'Bismillah'—the Moslem 'grace'—we all sat round it, and dipped equal hands in the dishes set before us. We had usually unleavened bread, different kinds of meat and vegetable stews; and, at the end of the first course, plain boiled rice eaten with spoons; then came the fruits, fresh dates, grapes, and pomegranates.

After dinner I used invariably to find some excuse—such as the habit of a Kaylulah (midday siesta) or the being a Saudawi—a person of melancholy temperament—to have a rug spread in the dark passage behind the Majlis; and there to lie reading, dozing, smoking or writing, *en cachette*, in complete *déshabille*, all through the worst part of the day, from noon to sunset.

Then came the hour for receiving or paying visits. We still kept up an intimacy with Umar Effendi and Saad the Demon, although Salih Shakkar and Amm Jemal, either disliking our society, or perhaps thinking our sphere of life too humble for their dignity, did not appear once in Hamid's house. The evening

[1] After touching the skin of a strange woman, it is not lawful in El-Islam to pray without ablution. For this reason, when a fair dame shakes hands with you, she wraps up her fingers in a kerchief, or in the end of her veil.

prayers ensued, either at home, or in the Haram, followed by our Asha or deipnon, another substantial meal like the dinner, but more plentiful, of bread, meat, vegetables, plain rice and fruits, concluding with the invariable pipes and coffee.

To pass our soirée, we occasionally dressed in common clothes, shouldered a Nebút, and went to the café; sometimes on festive occasions we indulged in a Taatumah (or Itmiyah), a late supper of sweetmeats, pomegranates, and dried fruits. Usually we sat upon mattresses spread upon the ground in the open air at the Shaykh's door; receiving evening visits, chatting, telling stories, and making merry, till each, as he felt the approach of the drowsy god, sank down into his proper place, and fell asleep.

Whatever may be the heat of the day, the night at El-Medinah, owing, I suppose, to its elevated position, is cool and pleasant. In order to allay the dust, the ground before the Shaykh's door was watered every evening, and the evaporation was almost too great to be safe—the boy Mohammed suffered from a smart attack of lumbago, which, however, yielded readily to frictions of olive oil in which ginger had been boiled.

Our greatest inconvenience at night-time was the pugnacity of the animal creation. The horses of the troopers tethered in the Barr were sure to break loose once in twelve hours. Some hobbled old nag, having slipped the head-stall, would advance with kangaroo-leaps towards a neighbour against whom it had a private grudge. Their heads would touch for a moment; then came a snort and a whinny, a furious kick, and, lastly, a second horse loose and dashing about with head and tail viciously cocked. This was the signal for a general breaking of halters and heel-ropes; after which, a stampede scoured the plain, galloping, rearing, kicking, biting, snorting, pawing, and screaming, with the dogs barking sympathetically, and the horse-keepers shouting in hot pursuit.

It was a strange sight to see by moonlight the forms of these 'demon steeds' exaggerated by the shades; and, on more than one occasion, we had all to start up precipitately from our beds, and yield them to a couple of combatants who were determined to fight out their quarrel *à l'outrance*, wherever the battle-field might be.

The dogs at El-Medinah are not less pugnacious than the horses.[1] They are stronger and braver than those that haunt the streets at Cairo; like the Egyptians, they have amongst themselves a system of police regulations, which brings down all the *posse comitatus* upon the unhappy straggler who ventures into a strange quarter of the town. They certainly met in El-Barr upon common ground, to decide the differences which must arise in so artificial a state of canine society.

Having had many opportunities of watching them, I can positively assert that they were divided into two parties, which fought with a skill and an *acharnement* that astounded me. Sometimes when one side gave way, and as the retreat was degenerating into a *sauve qui peut*, some proud warrior, a dog-hero, would sacrifice himself for the public weal, and with gnashing teeth and howls of rage encounter the assaults of the insolent victors until his flying friends had time to recover heart. Such a one my companions called 'Mubariz', the single combatant, the champion of the Arab's classical and chivalrous age. At other times, some huge animal, an Ajax of his kind, would plunge into the ring with frantic yells, roll over one dog, snap at a second, worry a third for a minute or two, and then dash off to a distant part, where a thicker field required his presence. This uncommon sagacity has been remarked by the Arabs, who look on amused at their battles.

Current in El-Hejaz are also certain superstitions about the dog resembling ours; only, as usual, more poetical and less grotesque. Most people believe that when the animal howls without apparent cause in the neighbourhood of a house, it forbodes death to one of the inmates; for the dog they say can distinguish the awful form of Azrael, the Angel of Death, hovering over the doomed abode, whereas man's spiritual sight is dull and dim by reason of his sins.

When the Damascus Caravan entered El-Medinah, our day

[1] Burckhardt (*Travels in Arabia*, vol. ii, p. 268) remarks that El-Medinah is the only town in the East from which dogs are excluded. This was probably as much a relic of Wahhabi-ism (that sect hating even to look at a dog), as arising from apprehension of the mosque being polluted by canine intrusion. I have seen one or two of these animals in the town, but I was told that, when they enter it in any numbers, the police magistrate issues orders to have them ejected.

became a little more amusing. From the windows of Shaykh Hamid's house there was a perpetual succession of strange scenes. A Persian nobleman, also, had pitched his tents so near the door, that the whole course of his private life became public and patent to the boy Mohammed, who amused his companions by reporting all manner of ludicrous scenes. The Persian's wife was rather a pretty woman, and she excited the youth's fierce indignation, by not veiling her face when he gazed at her—thereby showing that, as his beard was not grown, she considered him a mere boy.

'I will ask her to marry me,' said Mohammed, 'and thereby rouse her shame!'

He did so, but, unhappy youth! the fair Persian never even ceased fanning herself.

The boy Mohammed was for once confounded.

XVI
A Visit to the Prophet's Tomb

Having performed the greater ablution, and used the tooth-stick as directed, and dressed ourselves in white clothes, which the Apostle loved, we were ready to start upon our holy errand. As my foot still gave me great pain, Shaykh Hamid sent for a donkey. A wretched animal appeared, raw-backed, lame of one leg, and wanting an ear, with accoutrements to match, a pack-saddle without stirrups, and a halter instead of a bridle. Such as the brute was, however, I had to mount it, and to ride through the Misri gate, to the wonder of certain Bedawin, who, like the Indians, despise the ass.

> Honourable is the riding of a horse to the rider,
> But the mule is a dishonour, and the ass is a disgrace,

says their song. The Turkish pilgrims, however, who appear to take a pride in ignoring all Arab points of prejudice, generally mount donkeys when they cannot walk. The Bedawin therefore settled among themselves, audibly enough, that I was an Osmanli, who of course could not understand Arabic, and they put the question generally—

'By what curse of Allah had they been subjected to ass-riders?'

But Shaykh Hamid is lecturing me upon the subject of the mosque.

The Masjid El-Nabawi, or the Prophet's Mosque, is one of the Haramayn, or the two sanctuaries of El-Islam, and is the second of the three most venerable places of worship in the world; the other two being the Masjid El-Haram at Meccah (connected with Abraham) and the Masjid El-Aksa of Jerusalem (the peculiar place of Solomon). A Hadis or traditional saying of Mohammed asserts, 'One prayer in this my mosque is more efficacious than a thousand in other places, save only the Masjid El-Haram.' It is therefore the visitor's duty, as long as he stays at El-Medinah, to pray there *the five times per diem*, to pass the day in it reading the Koran, and the night, if possible, in watching and devotion.

A visit to the Masjid El-Nabawi, and the holy spots within it, is technically called Ziyarat or Visitation. An essential difference is made between this rite and Hajj or pilgrimage. The latter is obligatory by Koranic order upon every Moslem once in his life: the former is only a meritorious action. Tawaf, or circumambulation of the House of Allah at Meccah, must never be performed at the Apostle's tomb. This should not be visited in the Ihram or pilgrim-dress; men should not kiss it, touch it with the hand, or press the bosom against it, as at the Kaabah; or rub the face with dust collected near the sepulchre; and those who prostrate themselves before it, like certain ignorant Indians, are held to be guilty of deadly sin. On the other hand, to spit upon any part of the Mosque, or to treat it with contempt, is held to be the act of an Infidel.

Thus the learned and religious have settled, one would have thought, accurately enough the spiritual rank and dignity of the Masjid El-Nabawi. But mankind, especially in the East, must always be in extremes. The orthodox school of El-Malik holds El-Medinah, on account of the sanctity of, and the religious benefits to be derived from, Mohammed's tomb, more honourable than Meccah. Some declare that the Apostle preferred his place of refuge, blessing it as Abraham did Meccah. Moreover as a tradition declares that every man's body is drawn from the ground in which he is buried, El-Medinah evidently had the honour of supplying material for the Prophet's person. Others, like Omar, were uncertain which to prefer. The Wahhabis, on the other hand, rejecting the Intercession of the Prophet on the Day of Judgment, considering the grave of a mere mortal unworthy of notice, and highly disgusted by the idolatrous respect paid to it by certain foolish Moslems, plundered the sacred building with sacrilegious violence, and forbade visitors from distant countries to enter El-Medinah.

The general consensus of El-Islam admits the superiority of the Bayt Allah (House of God) at Meccah to the whole world; and declares El-Medinah to be more venerable than every part of Meccah, and consequently all the earth, except only the Bayt

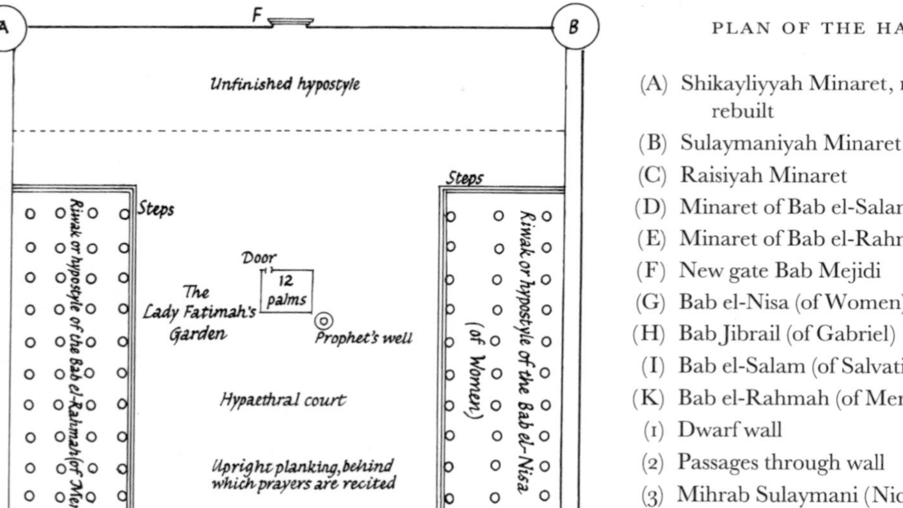

The long walls are 420 feet
The short walls are 340 feet
The Hujrah is an irregular square of 55 feet
The space marked with dots and called El-Rauzah is about 80 feet long
Between the Hujrah and the eastern wall 20 feet
Between the Hujrah and the southern wall 25 or 26 feet

PLAN OF THE HARAM OR PROPHET'S MOSQUE AT EL-MEDINAH

(A) Shikayliyyah Minaret, now being rebuilt
(B) Sulaymaniyah Minaret
(C) Raisiyah Minaret
(D) Minaret of Bab el-Salam
(E) Minaret of Bab el-Rahmah
(F) New gate Bab Mejidi
(G) Bab el-Nisa (of Women)
(H) Bab Jibrail (of Gabriel)
(I) Bab el-Salam (of Salvation)
(K) Bab el-Rahmah (of Mercy)
(1) Dwarf wall
(2) Passages through wall
(3) Mihrab Sulaymani (Niche of Sultan Sulayman)
(4) The Prophet's pulpit
(5) The Prophet's niche
(6) Osman's niche
(7) The Hujrah, the chamber in which the Prophet died and was buried. An irregular square of 50 or 55 feet
(8) The passage encircling the tombs
(9) The door in the grating called Bab el-Muwajihah
(10) Bab el-Taubah (of Repentance)
(11) Bab el-Shami (Syrian)
(12) The gate of our Lady Fatimah
(13) The Prophet's tomb
(14) Abubekr's tomb
(15) Omar's tomb
(16) Vacant place intended for the sepulture of Isa bin Maryam
(17) Makam Sayyidna Isa (Place of our Lord Isa)
(18) Shubak el-Nabi (Prophet's window)
(19) Abubekr's window
(20) Omar's window
(21) The Mahbat Jibrail, or place where Gabriel used to descend, vulgarly called Gabriel's Gate
(22) Fatimah's tomb, supposed to be in her house
(23) The Dakkat el-Aghawah, a low enclosure where the eunuchs sit
(24) The place where the Koran is continually read

The dotted lines denote the visitor's course: the larger points denote the stations of prayer

(25) The Weeping Pillar
(26) The Pillar of Ayisha
(27) The Pillar of the Fugitives
(28) The Pillar of Repentance, or of Abu Lubabah
(29) The Mukabbariyah, consisting of a stone seat supported by four columns. Here the Muballigh (who is to the interior of the Mosque what the Muezzin is to the exterior) warns people five times a day to prayer

Allah. This last is a *juste milieu* view by no means in favour with the inhabitants of either place. In the meanwhile the Meccans claim unlimited superiority over the Madani: the Madani over the Meccans.

Passing through muddy streets—they had been freshly watered before evening time—I came suddenly upon the Mosque. Like that at Meccah, the approach is choked up by ignoble buildings, some actually touching the holy 'enceinte', others separated by a lane compared with which the road round St Paul's is a Vatican square. There is no outer front, no general prospect of the Prophet's Mosque; consequently, as a building, it has neither beauty nor dignity.

And entering the Bab el-Rahmah—the Gate of Pity—by a diminutive flight of steps, I was astonished at the mean and tawdry appearance of a place so universally venerated in the Moslem world. It is not, like the Meccan Temple, grand and simple, the expression of a single sublime idea: the longer I looked at it, the more it suggested the resemblance of a museum of second-rate art, an old Curiosity-shop, full of ornaments that are not accessories, and decorated with pauper splendour.

The Masjid el-Nabi is a parallelogram about 420 feet in length by 340 broad, the direction of the long walls being nearly north and south. As usual in El-Islam, it is a hypaethral building with a spacious central area, called El-Sahn, El-Hosh, El-Haswah, or El-Ramlah, surrounded by a peristyle with numerous rows of pillars like the colonnades of an Italian cloister. The arcades or porticoes are flat-ceilinged, domed above with the small *Media Naranja*, or half-orange cupola of Spain, and divided into four parts by narrow passages, three or four steps below the level of the pavement. Along the whole inner length of the northern short wall runs the Mejidi Riwak, so called from the then reigning Sultan. The western long wall is occupied by the Riwak of the Rahmah Gate; the eastern by that of the Bab el-Nisa, the Women's Entrance.

Embracing the inner length of the southern short wall, and deeper by nearly treble the amount of columns than the other porticoes, is the main colonnade, called El-Rauzah (the Garden), the adytum containing all that is venerable in the building.

These four Riwaks, arched externally, are supported internally by pillars of different shape and material, varying from fine porphyry to dirty plaster. The southern, where the sepulchre or cenotaph stands, is paved with handsome slabs of white marble and marquetry work, here and there covered with coarse matting, and above this by unclean carpets, well worn by faithful feet.

But this is not the time for *Tafarruj*, or lionising. Shaykh Hamid warns me, with a nudge, that other things are expected of a Zair (visitor). He leads me to the Bab el-Salam, fighting his way through a troop of beggars, and inquires markedly if I am religiously pure. Then, placing our hands a little below and on the left of the waist, the palm of the right covering the back of the left, in the position of prayer, and beginning with the dexter feet,[1] we pace slowly forwards down the line called the Muwajihat el-Sharifah, or the Illustrious Fronting, which, divided off like an aisle, runs parallel with the southern wall of the Mosque. On my right hand walks the Shaykh, who recites aloud the following prayer, making me repeat it after him. It is literally rendered, as, indeed, are all the formulae, and the reader is requested to excuse the barbarous fidelity of the translation.

'In the Name of Allah and in the Faith of Allah's Apostle! O Lord, cause me to enter the Entering of Truth, and cause me to issue forth the Issuing of Truth, and permit me to draw near to Thee, and make me a Sultan Victorious!' Then follow blessings upon the Apostle, and afterwards: 'O Allah! open to me the Doors of Thy Mercy, and grant me Entrance into it, and protect me from the Stoned Devil!'

During this preliminary prayer we had passed down two-thirds of the Muwajihat el-Sharifah. On the left hand is a dwarf wall, about the height of a man, painted with arabesques, and pierced with four small doors which open into the Muwajihat. In this barrier are sundry small erections, the niche called the Mihrab Sulaymani, the Mambar, or pulpit, and the Mihrab el-Nabawi.

The two niches are of beautiful mosaic, richly worked with

[1] In this Mosque, as in all others, it is proper to enter with the right foot and to retire with the left.

various coloured marbles, and the pulpit is a graceful collection of slender columns, elegant tracery, and inscriptions admirably carved. Arrived at the western small door in the dwarf wall, we entered the celebrated spot called El-Rauzah, after a saying of the Apostle's, 'Between my Tomb and my Pulpit is a Garden of the Gardens of Paradise.' On the north and west sides it is not divided from the rest of the portico; on the south runs the dwarf wall, and on the east it is limited by the west end of the lattice-work containing the tomb.

Accompanied by my Muzawwir I entered the Rauzah, and was placed by him with the Mukabbariyah[1] behind me, fronting Meccah, with my right shoulder opposite to, and about twenty feet distant from, the dexter pillar of the Apostle's Pulpit. There, after saying the afternoon prayers, I performed the usual two bows in honour of the temple, and at the end of them recited the 109th and the 112th chapters of the Koran—the 'Kul, ya ayyuha'l-Kafiruna', and the 'Surat el-Ikhlas', called also the 'Kul, Huw' Allah', or the Declaration of Unity; and may be thus translated:

'Say, He is the one God!
'The eternal God!
'He begets not, nor is He begot!
'And unto Him the like is not.'

After which was performed a single Sujdah (Prostration) of Thanks, in gratitude to Allah for making it my fate to visit so holy a spot.

This being the recognised time to give alms, I was besieged by beggars, who spread their napkins before us on the ground, sprinkled with a few coppers to excite generosity. But not wishing to be distracted by them, before leaving Hamid's house I had changed 2 dollars, and had given the coin to the boy Mohammed, who accompanied me, strictly charging him to make that sum last through the Mosque.

My answer to the beggars was a reference to my attendant, backed by the simple action of turning my pockets inside-out;

[1] This is a stone desk on four pillars, where the Muballighs (clerks) recite the Ikamah, the call to divine service. It was presented to the mosque by Kaid Bey, the Mameluke Sultan of Egypt.

and, whilst he was battling with the beggars, I proceeded to cast my first *coup-d'œil* upon the Rauzah.

The Garden is the most elaborate part of the Mosque. Little can be said in its praise by day, when it bears the same relation to a second-rate church in Rome as an English chapel-of-ease to Westminster Abbey. It is a space of about eighty feet in length, tawdrily decorated so as to resemble a garden. The carpets are flowered, and the pediments of the columns are cased with bright green tiles, and adorned to the height of a man with gaudy and unnatural vegetation in arabesque. It is disfigured by handsome branched candelabras of cut crystal, the work, I believe, of a London house, and presented to the shrine by the late Abbas Pasha of Egypt.

The only admirable feature of the view is the light cast by the windows of stained glass in the southern wall. Its peculiar background, the railing of the tomb, a splendid filigree-work of green and polished brass, gilt or made to resemble gold, looks more picturesque near than at a distance, when it suggests the idea of a gigantic bird-cage. But at night the eye, dazzled by oil-lamps suspended from the roof, by huge wax candles, and by smaller illuminations falling upon crowds of visitors in handsome attire, with the richest and the noblest of the city sitting in congregation when service is performed, becomes less critical. Still the scene must be viewed with Moslem bias, and until a man is thoroughly imbued with the spirit of the East, the last place the Rauzah will remind him of, is that which the architect primarily intended it to resemble—a garden.

Then with Hamid, professionally solemn, I reassumed the position of prayer, and retraced my steps. After passing through another small door in the dwarf wall that bounds the Muwajihah, we did not turn to the right, which would have led us to the Bab el-Salam; our course was in an opposite direction, towards the eastern wall of the temple. Meanwhile we repeated, 'Verily Allah and His Angels bless the Apostle! O ye who believe, bless him, and salute him with Honour!' At the end of this prayer, we arrived at the Mausoleum, which requires some description before the reader can understand the nature of our proceedings there.

The Hujrah or Chamber as it is called, from the circumstance of its having been Ayisha's room, is an irregular square of from fifty to fifty-five feet in the south-east corner of the building, and separated on all sides from the walls of the Mosque by a passage about twenty-six feet broad on the south side, and twenty on the east. The reason of this isolation has been before explained, and there is a saying of Mohammed's, 'O Allah, cause not my Tomb to become an Object of Idolatrous Adoration! May Allah's Wrath fall heavy upon the People who make the Tombs of their Prophets Places of Prayer!'

Inside there are, or are supposed to be, three tombs facing the south, surrounded by stone walls without any aperture, or, as others say, by strong planking. Whatever this material may be, it is hung outside with a curtain, somewhat like a large four-post bed. The external railing is separated by a dark narrow passage from the inner, which it surrounds; and is of iron filigree painted of a vivid grass green—with a view to the garden. Here carefully inserted in the verdure, and doubly bright by contrast, is the gilt or burnished brass work forming the long and graceful letters of the Suls character, and disposed into the Moslem creed, the Profession of Unity, and similar religious sentences.

On the south side, for greater honour, the railing is plated over with silver, and silver letters are interlaced with it. This fence, which connects the columns and forbids passage to all men, may be compared to the baldacchino of Roman churches. It has four gates: that to the south is the Bab el-Muwajihah; eastward is the gate of our Lady Fatimah; westward the Bab el-Taubah (of Repentance), opening into the Rauzah or garden; and to the north, the Bab el-Shami or Syrian gate. They are constantly kept closed, except the fourth, which admits, into the dark narrow passage above alluded to, the officers who have charge of the treasures there deposited; and the eunuchs who sweep the floor, light the lamps, and carry away the presents sometimes thrown in here by devotees.

In the southern side of the fence are three windows, holes about half a foot square, and placed from four to five feet above the ground; they are said to be between three and four cubits distant from the Apostle's head. The most westerly of these is supposed to front Mohammed's tomb, wherefore it is called the Shubak el-Nabi, or the Prophet's window. The next, on the right as you front it, is Abubekr's, and the most easterly of the three is Omar's.

Above the Hujrah is the Green Dome, surmounted outside by a large gilt crescent springing from a series of globes. The glowing imaginations of the Moslems crown this gem of the building with a pillar of heavenly light, which directs from three days' distance the pilgrims' steps towards El-Medinah. But alas! none save holy men (and perhaps, odylic sensitives), whose material organs are piercing as their spiritual vision, may be allowed the privilege of beholding this poetic splendour.

Arrived at the Shubak el-Nabi, Hamid took his stand about six feet or so out of reach of the railing, and at that respectful distance from, and facing[1] the Hazirah (or presence), with hands raised as in prayer, he recited the following supplication in a low voice, telling me in a stage whisper to repeat it after him with awe, and fear, and love:

'Peace be upon Thee, O Apostle of Allah, and the Mercy of Allah and his Blessings! Peace be upon Thee, O Apostle of Allah! Peace be upon Thee, O Friend of Allah! Peace be upon Thee, O best of Allah's Creation! Peace be upon Thee, O pure Creature of Allah! Peace be upon Thee, O Chief of Prophets! Peace be upon Thee, O Seal of the Prophets! Peace be upon Thee, O Prince of the Pious! Peace be upon Thee, O Apostle of the Lord of the (three) Worlds! Peace be upon Thee, and upon Thy Family, and upon Thy pure Wives! Peace be upon Thee, and upon all

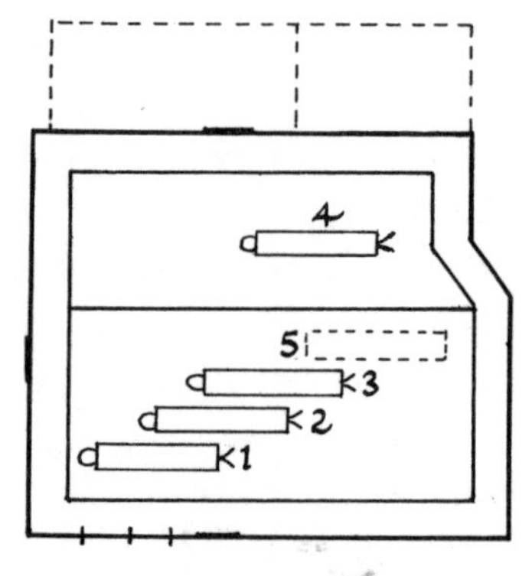

(1) Mohammed
(2) Abubekr
(3) Omar
(4) Fatimah's tomb
(5) The dotted space left empty for Isa

[1] The ancient practice of El-Islam during the recitation of the following benedictions was to face Meccah, the back being turned towards the Tomb, and to form a mental image of the Prophet, supposing him to be in front. El-Kirmani and other doctors prefer this as the more venerable custom, but in our days it is completely exploded; and the purist would probably be soundly bastinadoed by the eunuchs for attempting it.

Thy Companions! Peace be upon Thee, and upon all the Prophets, and upon those sent to preach Allah's Word! Peace be upon Thee, and upon all Allah's righteous Worshippers! Peace be upon Thee, O thou Bringer of Glad Tidings! Peace be upon Thee, O Bearer of Threats! Peace be upon Thee, O thou bright Lamp! Peace be upon Thee, O thou Apostle of Mercy! Peace be upon Thee, O Ruler of Thy Faith! Peace be upon Thee, O Opener of Grief! Peace be upon Thee! and Allah bless Thee! and Allah repay Thee for us, O Thou Apostle of Allah! the choicest of Blessings with which He ever blessed Prophet! Allah bless Thee as often as Mentioners have mentioned Thee, and Forgetters have forgotten Thee! And Allah bless Thee among the First and the Last, with the best, the highest, and the fullest of Blessings ever bestowed on Man; even as we escaped Error by means of Thee, and were made to see after Blindness, and after Ignorance were directed into the Right Way. I bear Witness that there is no god but *the* God (Allah), and I testify that Thou art His Servant, and His Apostle, and His Faithful Follower, and Best Creature. And I bear Witness, O Apostle of Allah! that Thou hast delivered thy Message, and discharged Thy Trust, and advised Thy Faith, and opened Grief, and published Proofs, and fought valiantly for Thy Lord, and worshipped Thy God till Certainty came to Thee (i.e. to the hour of death). And we Thy Friends, O Apostle of Allah! appear before Thee Travellers from distant Lands and far Countries, through Dangers and Difficulties, in the Times of Darkness, and in the Hours of Day, longing to give Thee Thy Rights (i.e. to honour thee by benediction and visitation), and to obtain the Blessings of Thine Intercession, for our Sins have broken our Backs, and Thou intercedest with the Healer. And Allah said,[1] "And though they have injured themselves, they came to Thee, and begged Thee to secure their Pardon, and they found God an Acceptor of Penitence, and full of Compassion." O Apostle of Allah, Intercession! Intercession! Intercession! O Allah, bless Mohammed and Mohammed's Family, and give Him Superiority and high Rank, even as Thou didst promise Him, and graciously allow us to conclude this Visitation. I deposit on this spot, and near Thee, O Apostle of God, my everlasting

[1] This is the usual introduction to a quotation from the Koran.

Profession (of faith) from this our Day, to the Day of Judgment, that there is no god but Allah, and that our Lord Mohammed is His Servant, and His Apostle. Amen! O Lord of the (three) Worlds!'

After which, performing Ziyarat for ourselves, we repeated the Fatihah or 'opening' chapter of the Koran.

'In the name of Allah, the Merciful, the Compassionate!

'Praise be to Allah, who the (three) Worlds made.

'The Merciful, the Compassionate.

'The King of the Day of Faith.

'Thee (alone) do we worship, and of Thee (alone) do we ask Aid.

'Guide us to the Path that is straight—

'The Path of those for whom thy Love is great, not those on whom is Hate, nor they that deviate.

'Amen! O Lord of Angels, Jinns, and Men!'[1]

After reciting this mentally with upraised hands, the forefinger of the right hand being extended to its full length, we drew our palms down our faces and did alms-deeds, a vital part of the ceremony. Thus concludes the first part of the ceremony of visitation at the Apostle's tomb.

Hamid then stepped about a foot and a half to the right, and I followed his example, so as to place myself exactly opposite the second aperture in the grating called Abubekr's window. There, making a sign towards the mausoleum, we addressed its inmate, as follows:

'Peace be upon Thee, O Abubekr, O Thou Truthful One! Peace be upon Thee, O Caliph of Allah's Apostle over his People! Peace be upon Thee, O Companion of the Cave, and Friend in Travel! Peace be upon Thee, O Thou Banner of the Fugitives and the Auxiliaries! I testify Thou didst ever stand firm in the right Way, and wast a Smiter of the Infidel, and a Benefactor to Thine own people. Allah grant Thee through His Apostle Weal! We pray Almighty God to cause us to die in Thy Friendship, and to raise us up in Company with His Apostle and Thyself, even as He hath mercifully vouchsafed to us this Visitation.'

[1] I have endeavoured in this translation to imitate the imperfect rhyme of the original Arabic. Such an attempt, however, is full of difficulties: the Arabic is a language in which, like Italian, it is almost impossible not to rhyme.

After which we closed one more step to the right, and standing opposite Omar's window, the most easterly of the three, after making a sign with our hands, we addressed the just Caliph in these words:

'Peace be upon Thee, O Omar! O Thou Just One! Thou Prince of True Believers! Peace be upon Thee, who spakest with Truth, and who madest thy Word agree with the Strong Book (the Koran)! O Thou Faruk (the Separator)! O Thou Faithful One! who girdedst thy Loins with the Apostle, and the First Believers, and with them didst make up the full Number forty, and thus causedst to be accomplished the Prophet's Prayer, and then didst return to Thy God a Martyr leaving the World with Praise! Allah grant Thee, through his Apostle and His Caliph and his Followers, the best of Good, and may Allah feel in Thee plenary Satisfaction!'

Shaykh Hamid, after wrenching a beggar or two from my shoulders, then permitted me to draw near to the little window, called the Apostle's, and to look in. Here my proceedings were watched with suspicious eyes. The Persians have sometimes managed to pollute the part near Abubekr's and Omar's graves by tossing through the aperture what is externally a handsome shawl intended as a present for the tomb. After straining my eyes for a time, I saw a curtain, or rather hangings, with three inscriptions in long gold letters, informing readers that behind them lie Allah's Apostle and the two first Caliphs.

The exact place of Mohammed's tomb is moreover distinguished by a large pearl rosary, and a peculiar ornament, the celebrated *Kaukab el-Durri*, or constellation of pearls, suspended to the curtain breast-high. This is described to be a 'brilliant star set in diamonds and pearls', placed in the dark that man's eye may be able to bear its splendours: the vulgar believe it to be a 'jewel of the jewels of Paradise'. To me it greatly resembled the round glass stoppers used for the humbler sort of decanters; but I thought the same of the Koh-i-Nur. Moreover I never saw it quite near enough to judge fairly, and I did not think fit to pay an exorbitant sum for the privilege of entering the inner passage of the baldacchino. Altogether the *coup-d'œil* had nothing to recommend it by day. At night, when the lamps, hung in this passage, shed a dim light upon the mosaic-work of the marble floors, upon the glittering inscriptions, and the massive hangings, the scene is more impressive.

Never having seen the Tomb, I must depict it from books —by no means an easy task. Most of the historians are silent after describing the inner walls of the Hujrah. El-Kalkashandi declares *in eo lapidem nobilem continere sepulchra Apostoli, Abubecr et Omar, circumcinctum peribole in modum conclavis fere usque ad tectum assurgente, quae velo serico nigro obligatur.* This author, then, agrees with my Persian friends, who declare the sepulchre to be a marble slab. Ibn Jubayr, who travelled in AH 580, relates that the Prophet's coffin is a box of ebony (*abnus*) covered with sandal-wood, and plated with silver; it is placed, he says, behind a curtain, and surrounded by an iron grating. El-Samanhudi, quoted by Burckhardt, declares that the curtain covers a square building of black stones, in the interior of which are the tombs of Mohammed and his two immediate successors. He adds that the tombs are deep holes; and that the coffin which contains the Apostle is cased with silver, and has on the top a marble slab inscribed 'Bismillah! Allahumma salli alayh!' ('In the name of Allah! Allah have Mercy upon Him!')

The Apostle's body, it should be remembered, lies, or is supposed to lie, stretched at full length on the right side, with the right palm supporting the right cheek, the face fronting Meccah, as Moslems are always buried, and consequently the body lies with the head almost due west and the feet due east. Close behind him is placed Abubekr, whose face fronts the Apostle's shoulder; and, lastly, Omar holds the same position with respect to his predecessor.

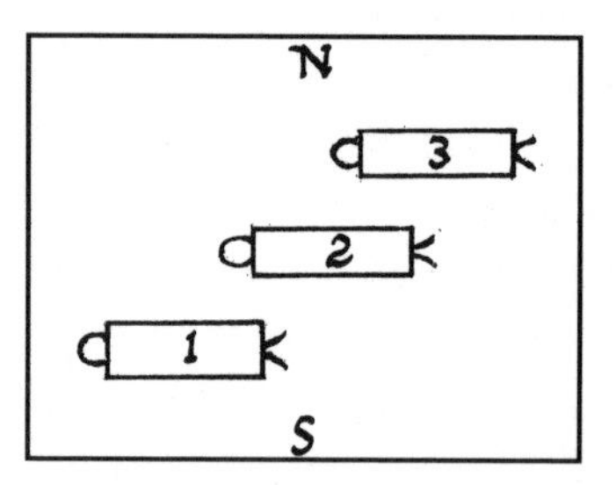

The places they are usually supposed to occupy, then, would be thus disposed. But Moslem historians are not agreed even upon so simple a point as this. Many prefer this position, in line ; some thus, in unicorn, ; and others the right angle, .

The vulgar story of the suspended coffin has been explained in two ways. Niebuhr supposes it to have arisen from the rude drawings sold to strangers. Mr William Bankes (Giovanni Finati, vol. ii, p. 289) believes that the mass of rock popularly described as hanging unsupported below the mosque of Omar at Jerusalem was confounded by Christians, who could not have seen either of these Moslem shrines, with the Prophet's Tomb at El-Medinah.

It is popularly asserted that in the Hujrah there is now spare place for only a single grave, reserved for Isa bin Maryam after his second coming. The historians of El-Islam are full of tales proving that though many of their early saints, as Osman the Caliph and Hasan the Imam, were desirous of being buried there; and that although Ayisha, to whom the room belonged, willingly acceded to their wishes, son of man has as yet been unable to occupy it.

After the Fatihah pronounced at Omar's tomb, and the short inspection of the Hujrah, Shaykh Hamid led me round the south-east corner of the baldacchino. Turning towards the north, we stopped at what is commonly called the *Mahbat Jibrail* (Place of the Archangel Gabriel's Descent with the Heavenly Revelations), or simply El-Malaikah—the Angels. It is a small window in the eastern wall of the mosque; we turned our backs upon it, and fronting the Hujrah, recited the following prayer:

'Peace be upon You, O Angels of Allah, the Mukarrabin (cherubs), and the Musharrifin (seraphs), the pure, the holy, honoured by the Dwellers in Heaven, and by those who abide upon the Earth. O beneficent Lord! O Long-suffering! O Almighty! O Pitier! O thou compassionate One! perfect our Light, and pardon our Sins, and accept Penitence for our Offences, and cause us to die among the Holy! Peace be upon Ye, Angels of the Merciful, one and all! And the Mercy of God and His Blessings be upon You!' After which I was shown the spot in the Hujrah where Sayyidna Isa shall be buried by Mohammed's side.

Then turning towards the west, at a point where there is a break in the symmetry of the Hujrah, we arrived at the sixth station, the sepulchre or cenotaph of the Lady Fatimah. Her grave is outside the enceinte and the curtain which surrounds her father's remains; so strict is Moslem decorum, and so exalted its opinion of the 'Virgin's' delicacy. The eastern side of the Hujrah, here turning a little westward, interrupts the shape of the square, in order to give this spot the appearance of disconnection with the rest of the building. The tomb, seen through a square aperture like those above described, is a long catafalque, covered with a black pall. Though there is great doubt whether the Lady be not buried with her son Hasan in the Bakia cemetery, this place is always visited by the pious Moslem. The following is the prayer opposite the grave of the amiable Fatimah:

'Peace be upon Thee, Daughter of the Apostle of Allah! Peace be upon Thee, Daughter of the Prophet of Allah! Peace be upon Thee, thou Daughter of Mustafa! Peace be upon Thee, thou Mother of the Shurafa (seed of Mohammed)! Peace be upon Thee, O Lady amongst Women! Peace be upon Thee, O fifth of the Ahl el-Kisa![1] Peace be upon Thee, O Zahra and Batul (Pure Virgin)! Peace be upon Thee, O Daughter of the Apostle! Peace be upon Thee, O Spouse of our Lord Ali el-Murtaza! Peace be upon Thee, O Mother of Hasan and Husayn, the two Moons, the two Lights, the two Pearls, the two Princes of the Youth of Heaven, and Coolness of the Eyes (i.e. joy and gladness) of true Believers! Peace be upon Thee, and upon Thy Sire, El-Mustafa, and Thy Husband, our Lord Ali! Allah honour his Face, and Thy Face, and Thy Father's face in Paradise, and Thy two Sons, the Hasanayn! And the Mercy of Allah and His Blessings!'

We then broke away as we best could from the crowd of female 'askers', who have established their Lares and Penates under the shadow of the Lady's wing; and, advancing a few paces, we fronted to the north, and recited a prayer in honour of Hamzah, and of the martyrs who lie buried at the foot of Mount Ohod. We then turned to the right, and, fronting the easterly wall, prayed for the souls of the blessed whose mortal spirits repose within El-Bakia's hallowed circuit.

After this we returned to the southern wall of the Mosque,

[1] The 'People of the Garment', so called, because on one occasion the Apostle wrapped his cloak around himself, his daughter, his son-in-law, and his two grandsons, thereby separating them in dignity from other Moslems.

and, facing towards Meccah, we recited the following supplication: 'O Allah! (three times repeated) O Compassionate! O Beneficent! O Requiter (of good and evil)! O Prince! O Ruler! O ancient of Benefits! O Omniscient! O Thou who givest when asked, and who aidest when Aid is required, accept this our Visitation, and preserve us from Dangers, and make easy our Affairs, and expand our Chests (gladden our hearts), and receive our Prostration, and requite us according to our good Deeds, and turn not our evil Deeds against us, and place not over us one who feareth not Thee, and one who pitieth not us, and write Safety and Health upon us and upon Thy Slaves, the Hujjaj (pilgrims), and the Ghuzzat (fighters for the faith), and the Zawwar (visitors to the tomb), and the Home-dwellers and the Wayfarers of the Moslems, by Land and by Sea, and pardon those of the Faith of our Lord Mohammed One and All!'

From the southern wall we returned to the Apostle's Window, where we recited the following tetrastich and prayer:

O Mustafa! verily, I stand at Thy door,
A man, weak and fearful, by reason of my sins:
If Thou aid me not, O Apostle of Allah!
I die—for, in the world there is none generous as thou art!

'Of a Truth, Allah and His Angels bless the Apostle! O Ye who believe, bless Him and salute Him with salutation! O Allah! verily I implore Thy Pardon, and supplicate Thine Aid in this World as in the next! O Allah! O Allah! abandon us not in this Holy Place to the consequences of our Sins without pardoning them, or to our Griefs without consoling them, or to our Fears, O Allah! without removing them. And Blessings and Salutation to Thee, O Prince of Apostles, Commissioned (to preach the word), and laud be to Allah, the Lord of the (three) Worlds!'

We turned away from the Hujrah, and after gratifying a meek-looking but exceedingly importunate Hindi beggar, who insisted on stunning me with the Chapter Y. S., we fronted southwards, and taking care that our backs should not be in a line with the Apostle's face, stood opposite the niche called Mihrab Osman. There Hamid proceeded with another supplication. 'O Allah! (three times repeated), O Safeguard of the

Fearful, and Defender of those who trust in Thee, and Pitier of the Weak, the Poor, and the Destitute! accept us, O Beneficent! and pardon us, O Merciful! and receive our Penitence, O Compassionate! and have Mercy upon us, O Forgiver!—for verily none but Thou canst remit Sin! Of a Truth Thou alone knowest the hidden and veilest Man's Transgressions: veil, then, our Offences, and pardon our Sins, and expand our Chests, and cause our last Words at the Supreme Hour of Life to be the Words, "There is no god but Allah, and our lord Mohammed is the Apostle of Allah!" O Allah! cause us to live according to this Saying, O thou Giver of life; and make us to die in this Faith, O thou Ruler of Death! And the best of Blessings and the completest of Salutations upon the sole Lord of Intercession, our Lord Mohammed and His Family, and His Companions One and All!'

Lastly, we returned to the Garden, and prayed another two-bow prayer, ending, as we began, with the worship of the Creator.

Unfortunately for me, the boy Mohammed had donned that grand embroidered coat. At the end of the ceremony the Aghas, or eunuchs of the Mosque, a race of men considered respectable by their office, and prone to make themselves respected by the freest administration of club-law, assembled in El-Rauzah to offer me the congratulation *Ziyaratak Mubarak*—'Blessed be thy Visitation'—and to demand fees. Then came the Sakka, or water-carrier of the mosque well, Zem Zem, offering a tinned saucer filled from the holy source. And lastly I was beset by beggars.

Some were mild beggars and picturesque who sat upon the ground immersed in the contemplation of their napkins; others, angry beggars who cursed if they were not gratified; and others noisy and petulant beggars, especially the feminine party near the Lady's tomb, who captured me by the skirt of my garment, compelling me to ransom myself. There were, besides, pretty beggars, boys who held out the right hand on the score of good looks; ugly beggars, emaciated rascals whose long hair, dirt, and leanness entitled them to charity; and lastly, the blind, the halt, and the diseased, who, as Sons of the Holy City, demanded from the Faithful that support with which they could not provide themselves. Having been compelled by my companions, highly against my inclination, to become a man of rank, I was obliged to pay in proportion, and my almoner in the handsome coat, as usual, took a kind of pride in being profuse. This first visit cost me double what I had intended—4 dollars—nearly 1*l.*, and never afterwards could I pay less than half that sum.

Having now performed all the duties of a good Zair, I was permitted by Shaykh Hamid to wander about and see the sights. We began our circumambulation at the Bab el-Salam, the Gate of Salvation, the south-western entrance long wall of the Mosque. It is a fine archway handsomely encrusted with marble and glazed tiles; the many gilt inscriptions on its sides give it, especially at night-time, an appearance of considerable splendour. The portcullis-like doors are of wood, strengthened with brass plates, and nails of the same metal. Outside this gate is a little Sabil, or public fountain, where those who will not pay for the water, kept ready in large earthen jars by the Sakka of the Mosque, perform their ablutions gratis. Here all the mendicants congregate in force, sitting on the outer steps and at the entrance of the Mosque, up and through which the visitors must pass.

About the centre of the western wall is the Bab el-Rahmah, the Gate of Mercy, which admits the dead bodies of the Faithful when carried to be prayed over in the Mosque. There is nothing remarkable in its appearance; in common with the other gates it has huge folding doors, iron-bound, an external flight of steps, and a few modern inscriptions.

The Bab Mejidi, or Gate of the Sultan Abd el-Mejid, stands in the centre of the northern wall; like its portico, it is unfinished, but its present appearance promises that it will eclipse all except the Bab el-Salam.

The Bab el-Nisa, or Gate of Women, is in the eastern wall opposite the Bab el-Rahmah, with which it is connected by the Farsh el-Hajar, a broad band of stone, two or three steps below the level of the portico, and slightly raised above the Sahan or the hypaethral portion of the Mosque. And lastly, in the southern portion of the same eastern wall is the Bab Jibrail, the Gate of the Archangel Gabriel.

All these entrances are arrived at by short external flights of steps leading from the streets, as the base of the temple, unlike that of Meccah, is a little higher than the foundations of the buildings around it. The doors are closed by the attendant eunuchs immediately after the night prayers, except during the blessed month El-Ramazan and in the pilgrimage season, when pious visitors pay considerable fees there to pass the night in meditation and prayer.

The minarets are five in number; but one, the Shikayliyyah, at the north-west angle of the building, has been levelled, and is still in process of being rebuilt. The Munar Bab el-Salam stands by the gate of that name: it is a tall handsome tower surmounted by a large ball or cone[1] of brass gilt or burnished. The Munar Bab el-Rahmah, about the centre of the western wall, is of more simple form than the others: it has two galleries, with the superior portion circular, and surmounted by the conical 'extinguisher'-roof so common in Turkey and Egypt. On the north-east angle of the Mosque stands the Sulaymaniyah Munar, so named after its founder, Sultan Sulayman the Magnificent. It is a well-built and substantial stone-tower divided into three stages; the two lower portions are polygonal, the upper cylindrical, and each terminates in a platform with a railed gallery carried all round for the protection of those who ascend.

And lastly, from the south-east angle of the Mosque, supposed to be upon the spot where Belal, the Apostle's loud-lunged crier, called the first Moslems to prayer, springs the Munar Raisiyah, so called because it is appropriated to the Ruasa or chiefs of the Muezzins. Like the Sulaymaniyah, it consists of three parts: the first and second stages are polygonal; and the third, a cylinder, is furnished like the lower two with a railed gallery. Both the latter minarets end in solid ovals of masonry, from which project a number of wooden triangles. To these and to the galleries on all festive occasions, such as the arrival of the Damascus Caravan, are hung oil-lamps—a poor attempt at

[1] By some wonderful process the 'Printer's Devil' converted, in the first edition, this ball or cone into 'bull or cow'.

illumination, which may rationally explain the origin of the Medinite superstition concerning the column of light which crowns the Prophet's tomb. There is no uniformity in the shape or the size of these four minarets, and at first sight, despite their beauty and grandeur, they appear somewhat bizarre and misplaced. But after a few days I found that my eye grew accustomed to them, and I had no difficulty in appreciating their massive proportions and lofty forms.

Equally irregular are the Riwaks, or porches, surrounding the hypaethral court. Along the northern wall there will be, when finished, a fine colonnade of granite, paved with marble. The eastern Riwak has three rows of pillars, the western four, and the southern, under which stands the tomb, of course has its columns ranged deeper than all the others. These supports of the building are of different material; some of fine marble, others of rough stone, plastered over and painted with the most vulgar of arabesques—vermilion and black in irregular patches, and broad streaks like the stage-face of a London clown. Their size, moreover, is different, the southern colonnade being composed of pillars palpably larger than those in the other parts of the Mosque. Scarcely any two shafts have similar capitals; many have no pedestal, and some of them are cut with a painful ignorance of art. I cannot extend my admiration of the minarets to the columns—in *their* 'architectural lawlessness' there is not a redeeming point.

Of these unpraisable pillars three are celebrated in the annals of El-Islam, for which reason their names are painted upon them, and five others enjoy the honour of distinctive appellations. The first is called El-Mukhallak, because, on some occasion of impurity, it was anointed with a perfume called Khaluk. It is near the Mihrab el-Nabawi, on the right of the place where the Imam prays; and it notes the spot where, before the invention of the Pulpit, the Apostle, leaning upon the Ustuwanat el-Hannanah—the Weeping Pillar—used to recite the Khutbah or Friday sermon.

The second stands third from the Pulpit, and third from the Hujrah. It is called the Pillar of Ayisha, also the Ustuwanat el-Kurah, or the Column of Lots, because the Apostle, according to the testimony of his favourite wife, declared that if men knew the value of the place, they would cast lots to pray there: in some books it is known as the Pillar of the Muhajirin or Fugitives, and others mention it as El-Mukhallak—the Perfumed.

Twenty cubits distant from Ayisha's Pillar, and the second from the Hujrah, and the fourth from the pulpit, is the Pillar of Repentance, or of Abu Lubabah. It derives its name from the following circumstance. Abu Lubabah was a native of El-Medinah, one of the Auxiliaries and a companion of Mohammed, originally it is said a Jew, according to others of the Beni Amr bin Auf of the Aus tribe. Being sent for by his kinsmen or his allies, the Benu Kurayzah, at that time capitulating to Mohammed, he was consulted by the distracted men, women, and children, who threw themselves at his feet, and begged of him to intercede for them with the offended Apostle. Abu Lubabah swore he would do so: at the same time, he drew his hand across his throat, as much as to say, 'Defend yourselves to the last, for if you yield, such is your doom.' Afterwards repenting, he bound himself with a huge chain to the date-tree in whose place the column now stands, vowing to continue there until Allah and the Apostle accepted his penitence—a circumstance which did not take place till the tenth day, when his hearing was gone and he had almost lost his sight.

The less celebrated pillars are the Ustuwanat el-Sarir, or Column of the Cot, where the Apostle was wont to sit meditating on his humble couch-frame of date-sticks. The Ustuwanat Ali notes the spot where the fourth Caliph used to pray and watch near his father-in-law at night. At the Ustuwanat el-Wufud, as its name denotes, the Apostle received envoys, couriers, and emissaries from foreign places. The Ustuwanat el-Tahajjud now stands where Mohammed, sitting upon his mat, passed the night in prayer. And lastly is the Makam Jibrail (Gabriel's place), for whose other name, Mirbaat el-Bair, the Pole of the Beast of Burden, I have been unable to find an explanation.

The four Riwaks, or porches, of the Medinah Mosque open upon a hypaethral court of parallelogramic shape. The only remarkable object in it is a square of wooden railing enclosing a place full of well-watered earth, called the Garden of our Lady

Fatimah. It now contains a dozen date-trees—in Ibn Jubayr's time there were fifteen. Their fruit is sent by the eunuchs as presents to the Sultan and the great men of El-Islam; it is highly valued by the vulgar, but the Olema do not think much of its claims to importance. Among the palms are the venerable remains of a Sidr, or Lote tree (*Rhamnus Nabeca*, Forsk), whose produce is sold for inordinate sums. The enclosure is entered by a dwarf gate in the south-eastern portion of the railing, near the well, and one of the eunuchs is generally to be seen in it: it is under the charge of the Mudir, or chief treasurer. These gardens are not uncommon in Mosques, as the traveller who passes through Cairo can convince himself. They form a pretty and an appropriate feature in a building erected for the worship of Him 'who spread the Earth with Carpets of Flowers and drew shady Trees from the dead Ground'. A tradition of the Apostle also declares that 'acceptable is Devotion in the Garden and in the Orchard'.

At the south-east angle of this enclosure, under a wooden roof supported by pillars of the same material, stands the Zem Zem, generally called the Bir el-Nabi, or the Apostle's well. My predecessor declares that the brackishness of its produce has stood in the way of its reputation for holiness. Yet a well-educated man told me that it was as 'light' (wholesome) water as any in El-Medinah—a fact which he accounted for by supposing a subterraneous passage which connects it with the great Zem Zem at Meccah. Others, again, believe that it is filled by a vein of water springing directly under the Apostle's grave: generally, however, among the learned it is not more revered than our Lady's Garden, nor is it ranked in books among the holy wells of El-Medinah.

Between this Zem Zem well and the eastern Riwak is the Stoa, or Academia, of the Prophet's city. In the cool mornings and evenings the ground is strewed with professors, who teach the young idea, as an eminent orientalist hath it, to shout rather than to shoot. A few feet to the south of the palm garden is a movable wooden planking painted green, and about three feet high; it serves to separate the congregation from the Imam when he prays here; and at the north-eastern angle of the enclosure is a

Shajar Kanadil, a large brass chandelier which completes the furniture of the court.

After this inspection, the shadows of evening began to gather round us. We left the Mosque, reverently taking care to issue forth with the left foot, and not to back out of it as is the Sunnat or practice derived from the Apostle, when taking leave of the Meccan Temple.

To conclude this long chapter. Although every Moslem, learned and simple, firmly believes that Mohammed's remains are interred in the Hujrah at El-Medinah, I cannot help suspecting that the place is doubtful as that of the Holy Sepulchre at Jerusalem. It must be remembered that a tumult followed the announcement of the Apostle's death, when the people, as often happens, believing him to be immortal, refused to credit the report, and even Omar threatened destruction to any one that asserted it.

Moreover the body was scarcely cold when the contest about the succession arose between the fugitives of Meccah and the auxiliaries of El-Medinah: in the ardour of which, according to the Shiahs, the house of Ali and Fatimah—within a few feet of the spot where the tomb of the Apostle is now placed—was threatened with fire, and Abubekr was elected Caliph that same evening. If any one find cause to wonder that the last resting-place of a personage so important was not fixed for ever, he may find many a parallel case in El-Medinah. To quote no other, three several localities claim the honour of containing the Lady Fatimah's mortal spoils, although one might suppose that the daughter of the Apostle and the mother of the Imams would not be laid in an unknown grave. My reasons for incredulity are the following:

From the earliest days the shape of the Apostle's tomb has never been generally known in El-Islam. For this reason it is that graves are made convex in some countries, and flat in others. Had there been a Sunnat, such would not have been the case.

The accounts of the learned are discrepant. El-Samanhudi, perhaps the highest authority, contradicts himself. In one place he describes the coffin; in another he expressly declares that he entered the Hujrah when it was being repaired by Kaid Bey, and saw in the inside three deep graves, but no traces of tombs. Either, then, the mortal remains of the Apostle had, despite Moslem superstition, mingled with the dust (a probable circumstance after nearly 900 years' interment), or, what is more likely, they had been removed by the Shiah schismatics who for centuries had charge of the sepulchre.[1]

And lastly, I cannot but look upon the tale of the blinding light which surrounds the Prophet's tomb, current for ages past and still universally believed upon the authority of the attendant eunuchs, who must know its falsehood, as a priestly gloss intended to conceal a defect.

I here conclude the subject, committing it to some future and more favoured investigator. In offering the above remarks, I am far from wishing to throw a doubt upon an established point of history. But where a suspicion of fable arises from popular 'facts', a knowledge of man and of his manners teaches us to regard it with favouring eye.

I was careful to make a ground-plan of the Prophet's Mosque, as Burckhardt was prevented by severe illness from so doing. It will give the reader a fair idea of the main points, though, in certain minor details, it is not to be trusted. Some of my papers and sketches, which by precaution I had placed among my medicines, after cutting them into squares, numbering them, and rolling them carefully up, were damaged by the breaking of a bottle. The plan of El-Medinah is slightly altered from Burckhardt's.

Nothing can be more ludicrous than the views of the Holy City, as printed in our popular works. They are of the style 'bird's-eye', and present a curious perspective. They despise distance like the Chinese, pictorially audacious; the Harrah, or ridge in the foreground appears to be 200 yards, instead of three or four miles, distant from the town. They strip the place of its suburb El-Manakhah, in order to show the enceinte, omit the fort, and the gardens north and south of the city, enlarge the Mosque twenty-fold for dignity, and make it occupy the whole

[1] I have lately been assured by Mohammed el-Halabi, Shaykh el-Olema of Damascus, that he was permitted by the Aghawat to pass through the gold-plated door leading into the Hujrah, and that he saw no trace of a sepulchre.

centre of the city instead of a small corner in the south-east quarter. They place, for symmetry, towers only at the angles of the walls, instead of all along the curtain; and they gather up and press into the same field all the venerable and interesting features of the country, those behind the artist's back, and at his sides, as well as what appears in front.

Such are the Turkish lithographs. At Meccah, some Indians support themselves by depicting the holy shrines; their works are a truly Oriental mixture of ground-plan and elevation, drawn with pen and ink, and brightened with the most vivid colours —grotesque enough, but less unintelligible than the more ambitious imitations of European art.

XVII

An Essay towards the History of the Prophet's Mosque

Ibn Abbas has informed the world that when the eighty individuals composing Noah's family issued from the ark, they settled at a place distant ten marches and twelve parasangs (thirty-six to forty-eight miles) from Babel or Babylon. There they increased and multiplied, and spread into a mighty empire. At length under the rule of Namrud (Nimrod), son of Kanaan (Canaan), son of Ham, they lapsed from the worship of the true God: a miracle dispersed them into distant parts of the earth, and they were further broken up by the one primeval language being divided into seventy-two dialects.

A tribe called Aulad Sam bin Nuh (the children of Shem), or Amalikah and Amalik, from their ancestor Amlak bin Arfakhshad bin Sam bin Nuh, was inspired with a knowledge of the Arabic tongue: it settled at El-Medinah, and was the first to cultivate the ground and to plant palm-trees. In course of time these people extended over the whole tract between the seas of El-Hejaz (the Red Sea) and El-Oman (north-western part of the Indian Ocean), and they became the progenitors of the Jababirah[1] (tyrants or giants) of Syria, as well as the Farainah (Pharaohs) of Egypt. Under these Amalik such was the age of man that during the space of 400 years a bier would not be seen, nor keening be heard, in their cities.

In this wild tradition we find a confirmation of the sound geographical opinion which makes Arabia *une des pépinières du genre humain* (M. Jomard). It must be remembered that the theatre of all earliest civilisation has been a fertile valley with a navigable stream, like Egypt, Sind, and Mesopotamia. The existence of such a spot in Arabia would have altered every page of her history; she would then have become a centre, not a source of

[1] These were the giants who fought against Israel in Palestine.

civilisation. Strabo's Malothes River in Yemen is therefore a myth. As it is, the immense population of the Peninsula—still thick, even in the 'deserts'—has, from the earliest ages, been impelled by drought, famine, or desire of conquest, to emigrate into happier regions. All history mentions two main streams which took their rise in the wilds. The first set to the north-east, through Persia, Mekran, Belochistan, Sind and the Afghan Mountains, as far as Samarcand, Bokhara, and Tibet. The other, flowing towards the north-west, passed through Egypt and Barbary into Etruria, Spain, the Isles of the Mediterranean, and southern France.

There are two minor emigrations chronicled in history, and written in the indelible characters of physiognomy and philology. One of these set in an exiguous but perennial stream towards India, especially Malabar, where, mixing with the people of the country, the Arab merchants become the progenitors of the Moplah race. The other was a partial emigration, also for commercial purposes, to the coast of Berberah, in Eastern Africa, where, mixing with the Galla tribes, the people of Hazramaut became the sires of the extensive Somali and Sawahil nations, perhaps of the so-called Kafirs. Thus we have from Arabia four different lines of emigration, tending north-east and south-east, north-west and south-west.

At some future time I hope to develop this curious but somewhat obscure portion of Arabian history. It bears upon a most interesting subject, and serves to explain, by the consanguinity of races, the marvellous celerity with which the faith of El-Islam spread from the Pillars of Hercules to the confines of China—embracing part of Southern Europe, the whole of Northern and a portion of Central Africa, and at least three-fourths of the continent of Asia.

The last king of the Amalik, Arkam bin el-Arkam, was, according to most authors, slain by an army of the children of Israel sent by Moses after the Exodus, with orders thoroughly to purge Meccah and El-Medinah of its Infidel inhabitants. All the tribe was destroyed, with the exception of the women, the children, and a youth of the royal family, whose extraordinary beauty persuaded the invaders to spare him pending a reference to the Prophet. When the army returned, they found that Moses had died during the expedition, and they were received with reproaches by the people for having violated his express command. The soldiers, unwilling to live with their own nation under this reproach, returned to El-Hejaz, and settled there.

Moslem authors are agreed that after the Amalik the Bene Israel ruled in the Holy Land of Arabia, but the learned in history are not agreed upon the cause of their emigration. According to some, when Moses was returning from a pilgrimage to Meccah, a multitude of his followers, seeing in El-Medinah the signs of the city which, according to the Taurat, or Pentateuch, should hear the preaching of the last Prophet, settled there, and were joined by many Bedawin of the neighbourhood who conformed to the law of Moses. Ibn Shaybah also informs us that when Moses and Aaron were wending northwards from Meccah, they, being in fear of certain Jews settled at El-Medinah, did not enter the city, but pitched their tents on Mount Ohod. Aaron being about to die, Moses dug his tomb, and said, 'Brother, thine hour is come! turn thy face to the next world!' Aaron entered the grave, lay at full length, and immediately expired; upon which the Jewish lawgiver covered him with earth, and went his way towards the Promised Land.

Abu Hurayrah asserted that the Bene Israel, after long searching, settled in El-Medinah, because, when driven from Palestine by the invasion of Bukht el-Nasr (Nebuchadnezzar), they found in their books that the last Prophet would manifest himself in a town of the towns of Arabiyah, called Zat Nakhl, or the Place of Palm-trees. Some of the sons of Aaron occupied the city; other tribes settled at Khaybar, and in the neighbourhood, building Utum, or square, flat-roofed, stone castles for habitation and defence. They left an order to their descendants that Mohammed should be favourably received, but Allah hardened their hearts unto their own destruction. Like asses they turned their backs upon Allah's mercy,[1] and the consequence is, that they have been rooted out of the land.

The Tarikh Tabari declares that when Bukht el-Nasr, after

[1] When the Arabs see the ass turn tail to the wind and rain, they exclaim 'Lo! he turneth his back upon the mercy of Allah!'

destroying Jerusalem, attacked and slew the king of Egypt, who had given an asylum to a remnant of the house of Israel, the persecuted fugitives made their way into El-Hejaz, settled near Yasrib (El-Medinah), where they founded several towns, Khaybar, Fadak, Wady el-Subu, Wady el-Kura, Kurayzah, and many others. It appears, then, by the concurrence of historians, that the Jews at an early time either colonised, or supplanted the Amalik at, El-Medinah.

At length the Israelites fell away from the worship of the one God, who raised up against them the Arab tribes of Aus and Khazraj, the progenitors of the modern Ansar. Both these tribes claimed a kindred origin, and Yemen as the land of their nativity. The circumstances of their emigration are thus described. The descendants of Yarab bin Kahtan bin Shalik bin Arfakhshad bin Sam bin Nuh, kinsmen to the Amalik, inhabited in prosperity the land of Saba. Their sway extended two months' journey from the dyke of Mareb, near the modern capital of Yemen, as far as Syria, and incredible tales are told of their hospitality and the fertility of their land. As usual, their hearts were perverted by prosperity. They begged Allah to relieve them from the troubles of extended empire and the duties of hospitality by diminishing their possessions. The consequence of their impious supplications was the well-known Flood of Irem.

The chief of the descendants of Kahtan bin Saba, one of the ruling families in Yemen, was one Amru bin Amin Ma el-Sama, called 'El-Muzaykayh' from his rending in pieces every garment once worn. His wife Tarikat Himyariah, being skilled in divination, foresaw the fatal event, and warned her husband, who, unwilling to break from his tribe without an excuse, contrived the following stratagem. He privily ordered his adopted son, an orphan, to dispute with him, and strike him in the face at a feast composed of the principal persons in the kingdom. The disgrace of such a scene afforded him a pretext for selling off his property, and, followed by his thirteen sons—all borne to him by his wife Tarikah—and others of the tribe, Amru emigrated northwards. The little party, thus preserved from the Yemenian Deluge, was destined by Allah to become the forefathers of the Auxiliaries of his chosen Apostle.

All the children of Amru thus dispersed into different parts of Arabia. His eldest son, Salabah bin Amru, chose El-Hejaz, settled at El-Medinah, then in the hands of the impious Bene Israel, and became the father of the Aus and Khazraj. In course of time, the new comers were made by Allah an instrument of vengeance against the disobedient Jews. Of the latter people, the two tribes Kurayzah and Nazir claimed certain feudal rights (well known to Europe) upon all occasions of Arab marriages. The Aus and the Khazraj, after enduring this indignity for a time, at length had recourse to one of their kinsmen who, when the family dispersed, had settled in Syria. Abu Jubaylah, thus summoned, marched an army to El-Medinah, avenged the honour of his blood, and destroyed the power of the Jews, who from that moment became Mawali, or clients to the Arabs.

For a time the tribes of Aus and Khazraj, freed from the common enemy, lived in peace and harmony. At last they fell into feuds and fought with fratricidal strife, until the coming of the Prophet effected a reconciliation between them. This did not take place, however, before the Khazraj received, at the battle of Buas (about AD 615), a decided defeat from the Aus.

It is also related, to prove how El-Medinah was predestined to a high fate, that nearly three centuries before the siege of the town by Abu Jubaylah, the Tobba el-Asghar marched northward, at the requisition of the Aus and Khazraj tribes, in order to punish the Jews; or, according to others, at the request of the Jews to revenge them upon the Aus and Khazraj. After capturing the town, he left one of his sons to govern it, and marched onwards to conquer Syria and El-Irak.

Suddenly informed that the people of El-Medinah had treacherously murdered their new prince, the exasperated Tobba returned and attacked the place; and, when his horse was killed under him, he swore that he would never decamp before razing it to the ground. Whereupon two Jewish priests, Kaab and Assayd, went over to him and informed him that it was not in the power of man to destroy the town, it being preserved by Allah, as their books proved, for the refuge of His Prophet, the descendant of Ishmael.

The Tobba Judaised. Taking 400 of the priests with him,

he departed from El-Medinah, performed pilgrimage to the Kaabah of Meccah, which he invested with a splendid covering;[1] and, after erecting a house for the expected Prophet, he returned to his capital in Yemen, where he abolished idolatry by the ordeal of fire. He treated his priestly guests with particular attention, and on his death-bed he wrote the following tetrastich:

> I testify of Ahmed that he of truth
> Is a Prophet from Allah, the Maker of souls.
> Be my age extended into his age,
> I would be to him a Wazir and a cousin.

Then sealing the paper he committed it to the charge of the High Priest, with a solemn injunction to deliver the letter, should an opportunity offer, into the hands of the great Prophet; and that, if the day be distant, the missive should be handed down from generation to generation till it reached the person to whom it was addressed. The house founded by him at El-Medinah was committed to a priest of whose descendants was Abu Ayyub the Ansari, the first person over whose threshold the Apostle passed when he ended the Flight. Abu Ayyub had also charge of the Tobba's letter, so that after three or four centuries it arrived at its destination.

El-Medinah was ever well inclined to Mohammed. In the early part of his career, the emissaries of a tribe called the Benu Abd el-Ashhal came from that town to Meccah, in order to make a treaty with the Kuraysh, and the Apostle seized the opportunity of preaching El-Islam to them. His words were sec-

[1] If this be true, it proves that the Jews of El-Hejaz had in those days a superstitious reverence for the Kaabah; otherwise the Tobba, after conforming to the law of Moses, would not have shown it this mark of respect. Moreover there is a legend that the same Rabbis dissuaded the Tobba from plundering the sacred place when he was treacherously advised so to do by the Benu Hudayl Arabs.

I have lately perused *The Worship of Baalim in Israel*, based upon the work of Dr R. Dozy, *The Israelites in Mecca*. By Dr H. Oort. Translated from the Dutch, and enlarged, with Notes and Appendices, by the Right Rev. John William Colenso, DD (Longmans). I can see no reason why Meccah or Beccah should be made to mean 'a slaughter'; why the Kaabah should be founded by the Simeonites; why the Hajj should be the Feast of Trumpets; and other assertions in which everything seems to be taken for granted except etymology, which is tortured into confession. If Meccah had been founded by the Simeonites, why did the Persians and the Hindus respect it?

onded by Ayyas bin Maaz, a youth of the tribe, and opposed by the chiefs of the embassy; who, however, returned home without pledging themselves to either party. Shortly afterwards a body of the Aus and the Khazraj came to the pilgrimage of Meccah: when Mohammed began preaching to them, they recognised the person so long expected by the Jews, and swore to him an oath which is called in Moslem history the First Fealty of the Steep.[1]

After the six individuals who had thus pledged themselves returned to their native city, the event being duly bruited abroad caused such an effect that, when the next pilgrimage season came, twelve, or according to others forty persons, led by Asad bin Zararah, accompanied the original converts, and in the same place swore the Second Fealty of the Steep. The Prophet dismissed them in company with one Musab bin Umayr, a Meccan, charged to teach them the Koran and their religious duties, which in those times consisted only of prayer and the Profession of Unity. They arrived at El-Medinah on a Friday, and this was the first day on which the city witnessed the public devotions of the Moslems.

After some persecutions, Musab had the fortune to convert a cousin of Asad bin Zararah, a chief of the Aus, Saad bin Maaz, whose opposition had been of the fiercest. He persuaded his tribe, the Benu Abd el-Ashhal, to break their idols and openly to profess El-Islam. The next season, Musab having made many converts, some say seventy, others 300, marched from El-Medinah to Meccah for the pilgrimage; and there induced his followers to meet the Prophet at midnight upon the Steep near Muna. Mohammed preached to them their duties towards Allah and himself, especially insisting upon the necessity of warring down infidelity. They pleaded ancient treaties with the Jews of El-Medinah, and showed apprehension lest the Apostle, after bringing them into disgrace with their fellows, should desert them and return to the faith of his kinsmen, the Kuraysh.

Mohammed, smiling, comforted them with the assurance

[1] 'Bayet el-Akabat el-úlá.' It is so called because this oath was sworn at a place called El-Akabah (the Mountain Road), near Muna. A Mosque was afterwards built there to commemorate the event.

that he was with them, body and soul, for ever. Upon this they asked him what would be their reward if slain. He replied, 'Gardens 'neath which the streams flow'—that is to say, Paradise.

Then, in spite of the advice of El-Abbas, Mohammed's uncle, who was loud in his denunciations, they bade the Preacher stretch out his hand, and upon it swore the oath known as the Great Fealty of the Steep. After comforting them with an Ayat, or Koranic verse, which promised heaven, the Apostle divided his followers into twelve bodies; and, placing a chief at the head of each, dismissed them to their homes. He rejected the offer made by one of the party—namely, to slay all the idolaters present at the pilgrimage—saying that Allah had favoured him with no such order. For the same reason he refused their invitation to visit El-Medinah, which was the principal object of their mission; and he then took an affectionate leave of them.

Two months and a half after the events above detailed, Mohammed received the inspired tidings that El-Medinah of the Hejaz was his predestined asylum. In anticipation of the order, for as yet the time had not been revealed, he sent forward his friends, among whom were Omar, Talhah, and Hamzah, retaining with him Abubekr and Ali. The particulars of the Flight, that eventful accident to El-Islam, are too well known to require mention here; besides which they belong rather to the category of general than of Medinite history.

Mohammed was escorted into El-Medinah by one Buraydat el-Aslami and eighty men of the same tribe, who had been offered by the Kuraysh 100 camels for the capture of the fugitives. But Buraydat, after listening to their terms, accidentally entered into conversation with Mohammed; and no sooner did he hear the name of his interlocutor, than he professed the faith of El-Islam. He then prepared for the Apostle a standard by attaching his turban to a spear, and anxiously inquired what house was to be honoured by the presence of Allah's chosen servant.

'Whichever', replied Mohammed, 'this she-camel is ordered to show me.'

At the last halting-place, he accidentally met some of his disciples returning from a trading voyage to Syria; they dressed him and his companion Abubekr in white clothing which, it is said, caused the people of Kuba to pay a mistaken reverence to the latter. The Moslems of El-Medinah were in the habit of repairing every morning to the heights near the city, looking out for the Apostle; and, when the sun waxed hot, they returned home. One day, about noon, a Jew, who discovered the retinue from afar, suddenly warned the nearest party of Ansar, or Auxiliaries of El-Medinah, that the fugitive was come. They snatched up their arms and hurried from their houses to meet him.

Mohammed's she-camel advanced to the centre of the then flourishing town of Kuba. There she suddenly knelt upon a place which is now consecrated ground; at that time it was an open space, belonging, they say, to Abu Ayyub the Ansari, who had a house there near the abodes of the Benu Amr bin Auf. This event happened on the first day of the week, the 12th of the month Rabia El-Awwal, in the first year of the Flight: for which reason Monday, which also witnessed the birth, the mission, and the death of the Prophet, is an auspicious day to El-Islam.

After halting two days in the house of Kulsum bin Hadmah at Kuba, and there laying the foundation of the first Mosque, upon the lines where his she-camel trod, the Apostle was joined by Ali, who had remained at Meccah, for the purpose of returning certain trusts and deposits committed to Mohammed's charge. He waited three days longer: on Friday morning (the 16th Rabia El-Awwal, AH 1 = the 2nd July, AD 622), about sunrise, he mounted El-Kaswa, and, accompanied by a throng of armed Ansar on foot and on horseback, he took the way to the city. At the hour of public prayer, he halted in the Wady or valley near Kuba, upon the spot where the Masjid el-Jumah now stands, performed his devotions, and preached an eloquent sermon. He then remounted. Numbers pressed forward to offer him hospitality; he blessed them, and bade them stand out of the way, declaring that El-Kaswa would halt of her own accord at the predestined spot. He then advanced to where the Apostle's pulpit now stands. There the she-camel knelt, and the rider exclaimed, as one inspired,

'This is our place, if Almighty Allah please!'

Descending from El-Kaswa, he recited, 'O Lord, cause me to

alight a good Alighting, and Thou art the Best of those who cause to alight!' Presently the camel rose unaided, advanced a few steps, and then, according to some, returning, sat down upon her former seat; according to others, she knelt at the door of Abu Ayyub el-Ansari, whose abode in those days was the nearest to the halting-place. The descendant of the Jewish High Priest in the time of the Tobbas, with the Apostle's permission, took the baggage off the camel, and carried it into his house. Then ensued great rejoicings. The Abyssinians came and played with their spears. The maidens of the Benu Najjar tribe sang and beat their kettle-drums. And all the wives of the Ansar celebrated with shrill cries of joy the auspicious event; whilst the males, young and old, freemen and slaves, shouted with effusion.

'Allah's Messenger is come! Allah's Messenger is here!'

Mohammed caused Abu Ayyub and his wife to remove into the upper story, contenting himself with the humbler lower rooms. This was done for the greater convenience of receiving visitors without troubling the family; but the master of the house was thereby rendered uncomfortable in mind. His various remarks about the Apostle's diet and domestic habits, especially his avoiding leeks, onions, and garlic, are gravely chronicled by Moslem authors. Mohammed never would eat those strong-smelling vegetables on account of his converse with the angels, even as modern Spiritualists refuse to smoke tobacco; at the same time he allowed his followers to do so, except when appearing in his presence, entering a Mosque, or joining in public prayers.

After spending seven months, more or less, at the house of Abu Ayyub, Mohammed, now surrounded by his wives and family, built, close to the Mosque, huts for their reception. The ground was sold to him by Sahal and Suhayl, two orphans of the Benu Najjar,[1] a noble family of the Khazraj. Some time afterwards one Harisat bin el-Numan presented to the Prophet all his houses in the vicinity of the temple. In those days the habitations of the Arabs were made of a framework of Jerid or palm-sticks, covered over with a cloth of camel's hair, a curtain

[1] The name of the tribe literally means sons of a carpenter; hence the error of the learned and violent Humphrey Prideaux, corrected by Sale.

of similar stuff forming the door. The more splendid had walls of unbaked brick, and date-leaf roofs plastered over with mud or clay. Of this description were the abodes of Mohammed's family. Most of them were built on the north and east of the Mosque, which had open ground on the western side; and the doors looked towards the place of prayer. In course of time, all, except Abubekr and Ali, were ordered to close their doors, and even Omar was refused the favour of having a window opening into the temple.

Presently the Jews of El-Medinah, offended by the conduct of Abdullah bin Salam, their most learned priest and a descendant from the Patriarch Joseph, who had become a convert to the Moslem dispensation, began to plot against Mohammed. They were headed by Hajj bin Akhtah, and his brother Yasir bin Akhtah, and were joined by many of the Aus and the Khazraj. The events that followed this combination of the Munafikun, or Hypocrites, under their chief, Abdullah, belong to the domain of Arabian history.

Mohammed spent the last ten years of his life at El-Medinah. He died on Monday, some say at nine a.m., others at noon, others a little after, on the 12th Rabia El-Awwal in the eleventh year of the Hijrah. When his family and companions debated where he should be buried, Ali advised El-Medinah, and Abubekr, Ayisha's chamber, quoting a saying of the deceased that prophets and martyrs are always interred where they happen to die. The Apostle was placed, it is said, under the bed where he had given up the ghost, by Ali and the two sons of Abbas, who dug the grave.

With the life of Mohammed the interest of El-Medinah ceases, or rather is concentrated in the history of its temple. Since then the city has passed through the hands of the Caliphs, the Sherifs of Meccah, the Sultans of Constantinople, the Wahhabis, and the Egyptians. It has now reverted to the Sultan, whose government is beginning to believe that, in these days when religious prestige is of little value, the great Khan's title, 'Servant of the Holy Shrines', is purchased at too high a price. As has before been observed, the Turks now struggle for existence in El-Hejaz with a soldiery ever in arrears, and officers unequal to the task of managing an unruly people. The pensions are but partly paid, and they are not likely to increase with years. It is probably a mere consideration of interest that prevents the people rising *en masse*, and reasserting the liberties of their country. And I have heard from authentic sources that the Wahhabis look forward to the day when a fresh crusade will enable them to purge the land of its abominations in the shape of silver and gold.

The Masjid el-Nabi, or Prophet's Mosque, is the second in El-Islam in point of seniority, and the second, or, according to others, the first in dignity ranking with the Kaabah itself. It is erected around the spot where the she-camel, El-Kaswa, knelt down by the order of Heaven. At that time the land was a palm-grove and a Mirbad, or place where dates are dried. Mohammed, ordered to erect a place of worship there, sent for the youths to whom it belonged, and certain Ansar, or Auxiliaries, their guardians; the ground was offered to him in free gift, but he insisted upon purchasing it, paying more than its value. Having caused the soil to be levelled and the trees to be felled, he laid the foundation of the first Mosque.

In those times of primitive simplicity its walls were made of rough stone and unbaked bricks: trunks of date-trees supported a palm-stick roof, concerning which the Archangel Gabriel delivered an order that it should not be higher than seven cubits, the elevation of Moses' temple. All ornament was strictly forbidden. The Ansar, or men of El-Medinah, and the Muhajirin, or Fugitives from Meccah, carried the building materials in their arms from the cemetery El-Bakia, near the well of Ayyub, north of the spot where Ibrahim's Mosque now stands, and the Apostle was to be seen aiding them in their labours, and reciting for their encouragement,

> O Allah! there is no good but the good of futurity,
> Then have mercy upon my Ansar and Muhajirin!

The length of this Mosque was fifty-four cubits from north to south, and sixty-three in breadth, and it was hemmed in by houses on all sides save the western. Till the seventeenth month of the new aera the congregation faced towards the northern wall. After that time a fresh revelation turned them in the direction of Meccah, southwards: on which occasion the Archangel Gabriel descended and miraculously opened through the hills and wilds a view of the Kaabah, that there might be no difficulty in ascertaining its true position.

After the capture of Khaybar in AH 7, the Prophet and his first three successors restored the Mosque, but Moslem historians do not consider this a second foundation. Mohammed laid the first brick, and Abu Hurayrah declares that he saw him carry heaps of building materials piled up to his breast. The Caliphs, each in the turn of his succession, placed a brick close to that laid by the Prophet, and aided him in raising the walls. El-Tabrani relates that one of the Ansar had a house adjacent which Mohammed wished to make part of the place of prayer; the proprietor was promised in exchange for it a home in Paradise, which he gently rejected, pleading poverty. His excuse was admitted, and Osman, after purchasing the place for 10,000 dirhams, gave it to the Apostle on the long credit originally offered.

This Mosque was a square of 100 cubits. Like the former building, it had three doors: one on the south side, where the Mihrab el-Nabawi, or the Prophet's niche, now is; another in the place of the present Bab el-Rahmah; and the third at the Bab Osman, now called the Gate of Gabriel. Instead of a Mihrab or prayer niche, a large block of stone directed the congregation; at first it was placed against the northern wall of the Mosque, and it was removed to the southern when Meccah became the Kiblah.

In the beginning the Prophet, whilst preaching the Khutbah or Friday sermon, leaned when fatigued against a post. The Mambar, or pulpit, was the invention of a Medinah man of the Benu Najjar. It was a wooden frame, two cubits long by one broad, with three steps, each one span high; on the topmost of these the Prophet sat when he required rest. The pulpit assumed its present form about AH 90, during the artistic reign of El-Walid.

In this Mosque Mohammed spent the greater part of the day with his companions, conversing, instructing, and comforting the poor. Hard by were the abodes of his wives, his family, and his principal friends. Here he prayed, at the call of the Azan, or devotion-cry, from the roof. Here he received worldly envoys and embassies, and the heavenly messages conveyed by the Archangel Gabriel. And within a few yards of the hallowed spot, he died, and found a grave.

The theatre of events so important to El-Islam could not be allowed—especially as no divine decree forbade the change—to remain in its pristine lowliness. The first Caliph contented himself with merely restoring some of the palm pillars, which had fallen to the ground: Omar, the second successor, surrounded the Hujrah, or Ayisha's chamber, in which the Prophet was buried, with a mud-wall; and in AH 17, he enlarged the Mosque to 140 cubits by 120, taking in ground on all sides except the eastern, where stood the abodes of the Mothers of the Moslems—Mohammed's fifteen widows. Outside the northern wall he erected a Suffah, called El-Batha—a raised bench of wood, earth, or stone, upon which the people might recreate themselves with conversation and quoting poetry, for the Mosque was now becoming a place of peculiar reverence to men.

The second Masjid was erected AH 29, by the third Caliph, Osman, who, regardless of the clamours of the people, overthrew the old walls and extended the building greatly towards the north, and a little towards the west; but he did not remove the eastern limit on account of the private houses. He made the roof of Indian teak (*saj*), and the walls of hewn and carved stone. These innovations caused some excitement, which he allayed by quoting a tradition of the Prophet, with one of which he appears perpetually to have been prepared. The saying in question was, according to some, 'Were this my Mosque extended to Safa (a hill in Meccah) it verily would still be my Mosque'; according to others, 'Were the Prophet's Mosque extended to Zu'l Halifah (a place five miles from El-Medinah) it would still be his.' But Osman's skill in the quotation of tradition did not prevent the new building being in part a cause of his death. It was finished on the 1st Muharram, AH 30.

At length, El-Islam, grown splendid and powerful, determined to surpass other nations in the magnificence of its public buildings. In AH 88, El-Walid the First, twelfth Caliph of the Benu Ummayah race, after building, or rather restoring, the noble Jami' el-Ammawi (cathedral of the Ommiades) at Damascus, determined to display his liberality at El-Medinah. The governor of the place, Umar bin Abd el-Aziz, was directed to buy for 7,000 Dinars (ducats) all the hovels of raw brick that hedged in the eastern side of the old Mosque. They were inhabited by descendants of the Prophet and of the early Caliphs, and in more than one case the ejection of the holy tenantry was effected with considerable difficulty. Some of the women—ever the most obstinate on such occasions—refused to take money, and Umar was forced to the objectionable measure of turning them out of doors with exposed faces in full day. The Greek Emperor, applied to by the magnificent Caliph, sent immense presents, silver lamp chains, valuable curiosities, forty loads of small cut stones for *pietra-dura*, and a sum of 80,000 Dinars, or, as others say, 40,000 Miskals of gold. He also despatched forty Coptic and forty Greek artists to carve the marble pillars and the casings of the walls, and to superintend the gilding and the mosaic work. One of these Christians was beheaded for sculpturing a hog on the Kiblah wall; and another, in an attempt to defile the roof, fell to the ground, and his brains were dashed out. The remainder Islamised, but this did not prevent the older Arabs murmuring that their Mosque had been turned into a Kanisah, a Christian idol-house.

The Hujrah, or chamber, where, by Mohammed's permission, Azrael, the Angel of Death, separated his soul from his body, whilst his head was lying in the lap of Ayisha, his favourite wife, was now for the first time taken into the Mosque. The raw-brick enceinte which surrounded the three graves was exchanged for one of carved stone, enclosed by an outer precinct with a narrow passage between. These double walls were either without a door, or had only a small blocked-up wicket on the northern side, and from that day (AH 90), no one, says El-Samanhudi, has been able to approach the sepulchre. A minaret was erected at each corner of the Mosque. The building was enlarged to 200 cubits by 167, and was finished in AH 91. When El-Walid, the Caliph, visited it in state, he inquired of his lieutenant why greater magnificence had not been displayed in the erection; upon which Umar, the governor, informed him, to his astonishment, that the walls alone had cost 45,000 ducats.

The fourth Mosque was erected in AH 191, by El-Mehdi, third prince of the Beni Abbas or Baghdad Caliphs—celebrated in history only for spending enormous sums upon a pilgrimage. He enlarged the building by adding ten handsome pillars of carved marble, with gilt capitals, on the northern side. In AH 202, El-Maamun made further additions to this Mosque. It was from El-Mehdi's Masjid that El-Hakim b'amr Illah, the third Fatimite Caliph of Egypt, and the deity of the Druse sect, determined to steal the bodies of the Prophet and his two companions. About AH 412, he sent emissaries to El-Medinah: the attempt, however, failed, and the would-be violators of the tomb lost their lives. It is generally supposed that El-Hakim's object was to transfer the Visitation to his own capital; but in one so manifestly insane it is difficult to discover the spring of action. Two Christians, habited like Maghrabi pilgrims, in AH 550, dug a mine from a neighbouring house into the temple. They were discovered, beheaded, and burned to ashes. In relating these events the Moslem historians mix up many foolish preternaturalisms with credible matter. At last, to prevent a recurrence of such sacrilegious attempts, El-Malik el-Adil Nur el-Din of the Baharite Mameluke Sultans, or, according to others, Sultan Nur el-Din Shahid Mahmud bin Zangi who, warned by a vision of the Apostle, had started for El-Medinah only in time to discover the two Christians, surrounded the holy place with a deep trench filled with molten lead. By this means Abubekr and Omar, who had run considerable risks of their own, have ever since been enabled to occupy their last homes undisturbed.

In AH 654, the fifth Mosque was erected in consequence of a fire, which some authors attribute to a volcano that broke out close to the town in terrible eruption; others, with more fanaticism, and less probability, to the schismatic Beni Husayn, then the guardians of the tomb. On this occasion the Hujrah was saved, together with the old and venerable copies of the Koran there deposited, especially the Cufic MSS, written by Osman, the third Caliph. The piety of three sovereigns, El-Mustasim (last Caliph of Baghdad), El-Muzaffar Shems el-Din Yusuf, chief of Yemen, and El-Zahir Beybars, Baharite Sultan of Egypt, completed the work in AH 688. This building was enlarged and beautified by the princes of Egypt, and lasted upwards of 200 years.

The sixth Mosque was built, almost as it now stands, by Kaid Bey, nineteenth Sultan of the Circassian Mameluke kings of Egypt, in AH 888: it is now therefore more than four centuries old. El-Mustasim's Mosque had been struck by lightning during a storm; thirteen men were killed at prayers, and the destroying element spared nothing but the interior of the Hujrah.[1] The railing and dome were restored; niches and a pulpit were sent from Cairo, and the gates and minarets were distributed as they are now. Not content with this, Kaid Bey established Wakf (bequests) and pensions, and introduced order among the attendants on the tomb. In the tenth century, Sultan Sulayman the Magnificent paved with fine white marble the Rauzah or garden, which Kaid Bey, not daring to alter, had left of earth, and erected the fine minaret that bears his name.

During the dominion of the later Sultans, and of Mohammed Ali, a few trifling presents, of lamps, carpets, wax candles and chandeliers, and a few immaterial alterations, have been made. The present head of El-Islam is, as I have before said, rebuilding one of the minarets and the northern colonnade of the temple.

Such is the history of the Mosque's prosperity.

During the siege of El-Medinah by the Wahhabis, the principal people seized and divided amongst themselves the treasures of the tomb, which must have been considerable. When the town surrendered, Saad, accompanied by his principal officers, entered the Hujrah, but, terrified by dreams, he did not penetrate behind the curtain, or attempt to see the tomb. He plundered, however, the treasures in the passage, the *Kaukab el-Durri* (or pearl star), and the ornaments sent as presents

[1] 'On this occasion,' says El-Samanhudi, quoted by Burckhardt, 'the interior of the Hujrah was cleared, and three deep graves were found in the inside, full of rubbish, but the author of this history, who himself entered it, saw no traces of tombs.' Yet in another place he, an eye-witness, had declared that the coffin containing the dust of Mohammed was cased with silver.

from every part of El-Islam. Part of these he sold, it is said, for 150,000 Riyals (dollars), to Ghalib, Sherif of Meccah, and the rest he carried with him to Daraiyah, his capital.

An accident prevented any further desecration of the building. The greedy Wahhabis, allured by the appearance of the golden or gilt globes and crescents surmounting the green dome, attempted to throw down the latter. Two of their number, it is said, were killed by falling from the slippery roof, and the rest, struck by superstitious fears, abandoned the work of destruction. They injured, however, the prosperity of the place by taxing the inhabitants, by interrupting the annual remittances, and by forbidding visitors to approach the tomb. They are spoken of with abhorrence by the people, who quote a peculiarly bad trait in their characters, namely, that in return for any small religious assistance of prayer or recitation, they were in the habit of giving a few grains of gunpowder, or something equally valuable, instead of 'stone-dollars'.[1]

When Abdullah, son of Saad, had concluded in AD 1815 a treaty of peace with Tussun Pasha, the Egyptian General bought back from the townspeople, for 10,000 Riyals, all the golden vessels that had not been melted down, and restored the treasure to its original place. This I have heard denied; at the same time it rests upon credible evidence. Amongst Orientals the events of the last generation are usually speaking imperfectly remembered, and the Olema are well acquainted with the history of vicissitudes which took place 1,200 years ago, when profoundly ignorant of what their grandfathers witnessed. Many incredible tales also I heard concerning the present wealth of the El-Medinah Mosque: this must be expected when the exaggeration is considered likely to confer honour upon the exaggerator.

The establishment attached to the El-Medinah Mosque is greatly altered since Burckhardt's time, the result of the increasing influence of the Turkish half-breeds. It is still extensive, because in the first place the principle of divided labour is a favourite throughout the East, and secondly because the Sons of the Holy Cities naturally desire to extract as much as they can from the Sons of other Cities with the least amount of work.

[1] The Bedawi calls a sound dollar Kirsh Hajar, or Riyal Hajar, a 'stone-dollar'.

The substance of the following account was given to me by Umar Effendi, and I compared it with the information of others upon whom I could rely.

The principal of the Mosque, or Shaykh el-Haram, is no longer a neuter. The present is a Turkish Pasha, Usman, appointed from Constantinople with a salary of about 30,000 piastres a month. His Naib or deputy is a black eunuch, the chief of the Aghawat, upon a pay of 5,000 piastres. The present principal of this college is one Tayfur Agha, a slave of Esma Sultanah, sister to the late Sultan Mahmud. The chief treasurer is called the Mudir el-Haram; he keeps an eye upon the Khaznadar, or treasurer, whose salary is 2,000 piastres. The Mustaslim is the chief of the Katibs, or writers who settle the accounts of the Mosque; his pay is 1,500 and under him is a Nakib or assistant upon 1,000 piastres. There are three Shaykhs of the eunuchs, who receive from 700 to 1,000 piastres a month each. The eunuchs, about 120 in number, are divided into three orders. The Bawwabin, or porters, open the doors of the Mosque. The Khubziyah sweep the purer parts of the temple, and the lowest order, popularly called Battalin, clean away all impurities, beat those found sleeping, and act as beadles, a duty here which involves considerable use of the cane. These men receive as perquisites presents from each visitor when they offer him the usual congratulation, and for other small favours, such as permitting strangers to light the lamps, or to sweep the floor. Their pay varies from 250 to 500 piastres a month: they are looked upon as honourable men, and are generally speaking married, some of them indulging in three or four wives—which would have aroused Juvenal's bile.

The Agha's character is curious and exceptional as his outward conformation. Disconnected with humanity, he is cruel, fierce, brave, and capable of any villainy. His frame is unnaturally long and lean, especially the arms and legs, with high shoulders, protruding joints, and a face by contrast extraordinarily large; he is unusually expert in the use of weapons, and sitting well home, he rides to admiration, his hoarse thick voice investing him with all the circumstance of command.

Besides the eunuchs, there are a number of free servants, called Farrashin, attached to the Mosque; almost all the middle and lower class of citizens belong to this order. They are divided into parties of thirty each, and are changed every week, those on duty receiving a Ghazi, or 22 piastres, for their services. Their business is to dust, and spread the carpets, to put oil and wicks into the lamps which the eunuchs let down from the ceiling, and, generally speaking, diligently to do nothing.

Finally, the menial establishment of the Mosque consists of a Shaykh el-Sakka (chief of the water-carriers), under whom are from forty-five to fifty men who sprinkle the floors, water the garden, and, for a consideration, supply a cupful of brackish liquid to visitors.

The literary establishment is even more extensive than the executive and the menial. There is a Kazi, or chief judge, sent every year from Constantinople. After twelve months at El-Medinah, he passes on to Meccah, and returns home after a similar term of service in the second Holy city. Under him are three Muftis, of the Hanafi, the Shafei, and the Maliki schools—the fourth, or Hanbali, is not represented here or at Cairo. Each of these officers receives as pay about 250 piastres a month. The Ruasa, as the Muezzins (prayer-callers) here call themselves, are extensively represented; there are forty-eight or forty-nine of the lowest order, presided over by six Kubar or Masters, and these again are under the Shaykh el-Ruasa, who alone has the privilege of calling to prayers from the Raisiyah minaret. The Shaykh receives 150 piastres, the chiefs about 100, and the common criers 60; there are forty-five Khatibs, who preach and pray before the congregation on Fridays for 120 piastres a month; they are under the Shaykh el-Khutaba. About the same sum is given to seventy-five Imams, who recite the five ordinary prayers of every day in the Mosque; the Shaykh el-Aimmat is their superior.

Almost all the citizens of El-Medinah who have not some official charge about the temple qualify themselves to act as Muzawwirs. They begin as boys to learn the formula of prayer, and the conducting of visitors; and partly by begging, partly by boldness, they often pick up a tolerable livelihood at an early age. The Muzawwir will often receive strangers into his house, as was done to me, and direct their devotions during the whole time of their stay. For such service he requires a sum of money proportioned to his guests' circumstances, but this fee does not end the connexion. If the Muzawwir visit the home of his Zair, he expects to be treated with the utmost hospitality, and to depart with a handsome present. A religious visitor will often transmit to his cicerone at Meccah and at El-Medinah yearly sums to purchase for himself a prayer at the Kaabah and the Prophet's tomb. The remittance is usually wrapped up in paper, and placed in a sealed leathern bag, somewhat like a portfolio, upon which is worked the name of the person entitled to receive it. It is then given in charge either to a trustworthy pilgrim, or to the public treasurer, who accompanies the principal caravans.

I could procure no exact information about the amount of money forwarded every year from Constantinople and Cairo to El-Medinah; the only point upon which men seemed to agree was that they were defrauded of half their dues. When the Sadaka and Aukaf (the alms and bequests) arrive at the town, they are committed by the Surrah, or financier of the caravan, to the Muftis, the chief of the Khatibs, and the Kazi's clerk. These officers form a committee, and after reckoning the total of the families entitled to pensions, divide the money amongst them, according to the number in each household, and the rank of the pensioners. They are divided into five orders:

The Olema, or learned, and the Mudarrisin, who profess, lecture, or teach adults in the Haram.

The Imams and Khatibs.

The descendants of the Prophet.

The Fukaha, poor divines, pedagogues, gerund-grinders, who teach boys to read the Koran.

The Awam, or *nobile vulgus* of the Holy City, including the Ahali, or burghers of the town, and the Mujawirin, or those settled in the place.

Umar Effendi belonged to the second order, and he informed me that his share varied from 3 to 15 Riyals per annum.

XVIII
El-Medinah

It is equally difficult to define, politically and geographically, the limits of El-Hejaz. Whilst some authors, as Abulfeda, fix its northern frontier at Aylah (Fort El-Akabah) and the Desert, making Yemen its southern limit, others include in it only the tract of land lying between Meccah and El-Medinah. The country has no natural boundaries, and its political limits change with every generation; perhaps, therefore, the best distribution of its frontier would be that which includes all the property called Holy Land, making Yambu' the northern and Jeddah the southern extremes, while a line drawn through El-Medinah Suwayrkiyah, and Jebel Kora—the mountain of Taif—might represent its eastern boundary. Thus El-Hejaz would be an irregular parallelogram, about 200 miles in length, with a maximum breadth of 150 miles.

Two meanings are assigned to the name of this venerated region. Most authorities make it mean the Separator, the Barrier, between Nejd and Tehamah, or between Yemen and Syria. According to others, it signifies the 'colligated', i.e. by mountains. It is to be observed that the people of the country, especially the Bedawin, distinguish the lowlands from the high regions by different names; the former are called Tehamat el-Hejaz—the sea-coast of El-Hejaz, as we should say in India, 'below the Ghauts'; the latter is known peculiarly as El-Hejaz.

Medinat el-Nabi, the Prophet's City, or, as it is usually called for brevity, El-Medinah, *the* City, is situated on the borders of Nejd, upon the vast plateau of high land which forms central Arabia. The limits of the sanctuary called the Hudud el-Haram, as defined by the Apostle, may still serve to mark out the city's plain. Northwards, at a distance of about three miles, is Jebel Ohod, or, according to others, Jebel Saur, a hill somewhat beyond Ohod; these are the last ribs of the vast territory and primitive chine which, extending from Taurus to near Aden, and from Aden again to Maskat, fringes the Arabian trapezium.

To the south-west the plain is bounded by ridges of scoriaceous basalt, and by a buttress of rock called Jebel Ayr, like Ohod, about three miles distant from the town. Westward, according to some authors, is the Mosque Zu'l-Halifah. On the east there are no natural landmarks, nor even artificial, like the Alamayn at Meccah; an imaginary line, therefore, is drawn, forming an irregular circle, of which the town is the centre, with a diameter of from ten to twelve miles. Such is the sanctuary. Geographically considered, the plain is bounded, on the east, with a thin line of low dark hills, traversed by the Darb el-Sharki, or the Eastern road, through El-Nejd to Meccah: southwards, the plateau is open, and almost perfectly level as far as the eye can see.

Within the sanctuary all Muharramat, or sins, are forbidden; but the several schools advocate different degrees of strictness. The Imam Malik, for instance, allows no latrinae nearer to El-Medinah than Jebel Ayr, a distance of about three miles. He also forbids slaying wild animals, but at the same time he specifies no punishment for the offence. Some do not allow the felling of trees, alleging that the Apostle enjoined their preservation as an ornament to the city, and a pleasure to visitors. El-Khattabi, on the contrary, permits people to cut wood, and this is certainly the general practice. All authors strenuously forbid within the boundaries slaying man (except invaders, Infidels, and the sacrilegious), drinking spirits, and leading an immoral life. As regards the dignity of the sanctuary, there is but one opinion; a number of Hadis testify to its honour, praise its people, and threaten dreadful things to those who injure it or them. It is certain that, on the last day, the Prophet will intercede for, and aid, all those who die and are buried at El-Medinah. Therefore, the Imam Malik made but one pilgrimage to Meccah, fearing to leave his bones in any other cemetery but El-Bakia. There is, however, much debate concerning the comparative sanctity of El-Medinah and Meccah. Some say Mohammed preferred the former, blessing it as Abraham did Meccah.

El-Medinah dates its origin doubtless from ancient times, and the cause of its prosperity is evident in the abundant supply of water, a necessary generally scarce in Arabia. The formation of the plateau is in some places salt sand, but usually a white chalk, and a loamy clay, which even by the roughest manipulation makes tolerable bricks. Lime also abounds. The town is situated upon a gently shelving part of the plain, the lowest portion of which, to judge from the versant, is at the southern base of Mount Ohod, hence called El-Safilah, and the highest at the Awali, or plains about Kuba, and the East.

The southern and south-eastern walls of the suburb are sometimes carried away by violent Sayl, or torrents, which, after rain, sweep down from the western as well as from the eastern highlands. The water-flow is towards El-Ghabbah, lowlands in the northern and western hills, a little beyond Mount Ohod. This basin receives the drainage of the mountains and the plain; according to some absorbing it, according to others collecting it till of sufficient volume to flow off to the sea.

Water, though abundant, is rarely of good quality. In the days of the Prophet, the Madani consumed the produce of wells, seven of which are still celebrated by the people. Historians relate that Omar, the second Caliph, provided the town with drinking-water from the northern parts of the plains by means of an aqueduct. The modern city is supplied by a source called the Ayn el-Zarka or Azure Spring, which arises some say at the foot of Mount Ayr, others, with greater probability, in the date-groves of Kuba. Its waters were first brought to El-Medinah by Marwan, governor in El-Muawiyah's day. It now flows down a subterraneous canal, about thirty feet below the surface; in places the water is exposed to the air, and steps lead to it for the convenience of the inhabitants: this was the work of Sultan Sulayman the Magnificent. After passing through the town it turns to the north-west, its course being marked by a line of circular walls breast high, like the Kariz of Afghanistan, placed at unequal distances, and resembling wells: it then loses itself in the Nakhil or palm-groves. During my stay at El-Medinah, I always drank this water, which appeared to me, as the citizens declared it to be, sweet and wholesome.[1]

[1] Burckhardt confounds the Ayn el-Zarka with the Bir el-Khatim, or Kuba well, of whose produce only the surplus mixes with it, and he complains loudly of the 'detestable

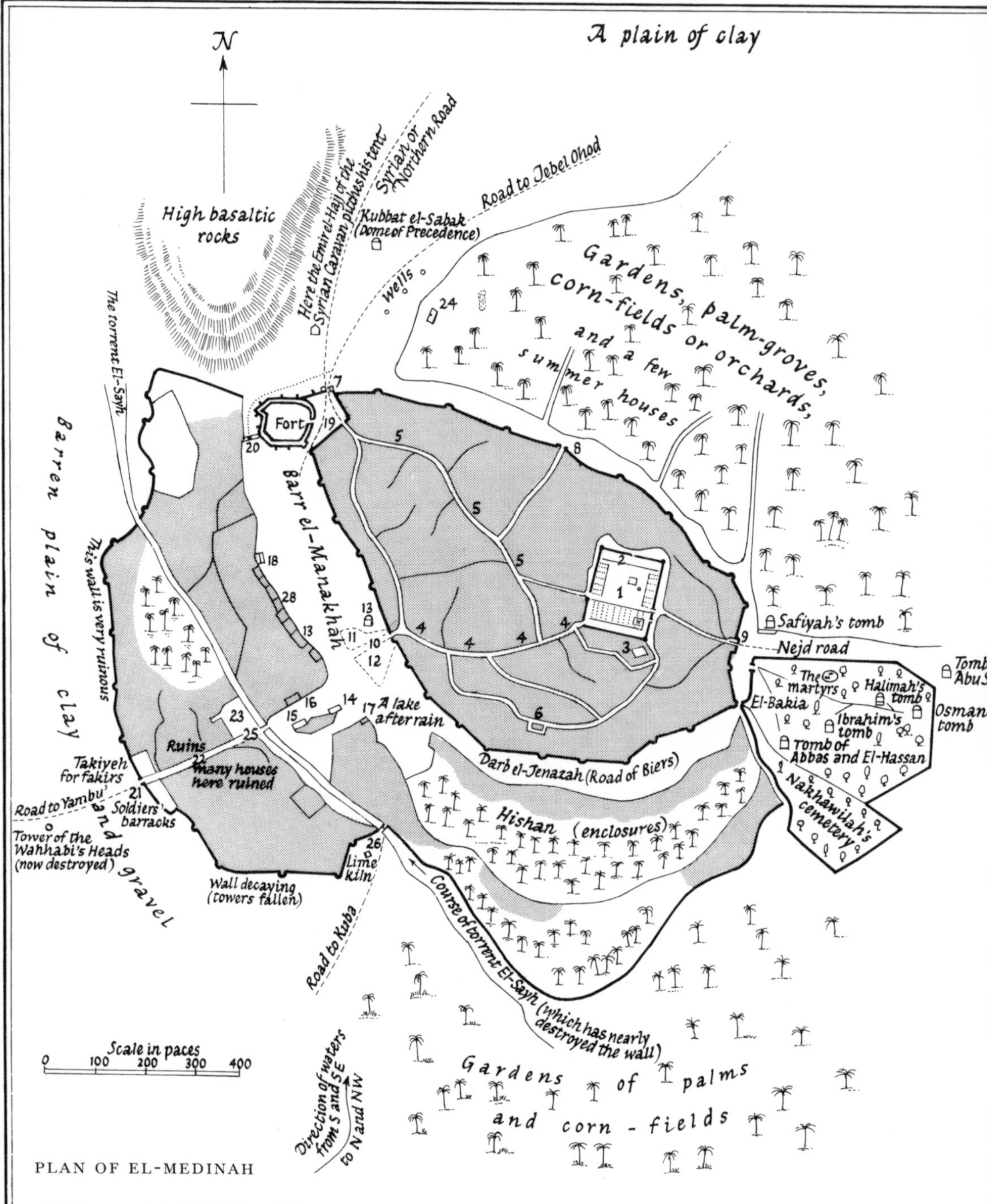

PLAN OF EL-MEDINAH

(1) Haram or Masjid El-Nabawi (Prophet's Mosque)
(2) Unfinished porch to north
(3) Palace of principal officers of the Mosque
(4) Street leading to the Bab el-Salam
(5) Great street el-Belah
(6) Wakalah
(7) Bab el-Shami (Syrian Gate)
(8) Bab el-Ziyafah (Gate of Hospitality)
(9) Bab el-Juma (Friday Gate)
(10) Bab el-Misri (Egyptian Gate)
(11) Suk el-Khuzayriyah (greengrocers' market) and coffee-houses
(12) Suk el-Habbabah (grain bazar) and coffee-houses
(13) Sebil (public fountain)
(14) Musalla el-Nabi (Prophet's Prayer Place)
(15) Omar's Mosque
(16) Large house formerly belonging to the governor
(17) Shaykh Hamid's house
(18) Houses occupied by wealthy and noble citizens
(19) Outer ward to castle
(20) Bab el-Saghir (Little Gate)
(21) Bab el-Ambari (Western Gate)
(22) El-Ambariyah
(23) Large house formerly inhabited by Pasha
(24) Pasha's present abode
(25) Bridge over El-Sayh
(26) Bab Kuba

There are many wells in the town, as water is found at about twenty feet below the surface of the soil: few produce anything fit for drinking, some being salt, and others bitter. As usual in the hilly countries of the East, the wide beds and Fiumaras, even in the dry season, will supply travellers for a day or two with an abundance of water, filtrated through, and, in some cases, flowing beneath the sand.

The climate of the plain is celebrated for a long, and, comparatively speaking, a rigorous winter; a popular saying records the opinion of the Apostle 'that he who patiently endures the cold of El-Medinah and the heat of Meccah, merits a reward in Paradise'. Ice is not seen in the town, but may frequently be met with, it is said, on Jebel Ohod; fires are lighted in the houses during winter, and palsies attack those who at this season imprudently bathe in unwarmed water. The fair complexions of the people prove that this account of the brumal rigours is not exaggerated. Chilly and violent winds from the eastern desert are much dreaded, and though Ohod screens the town on the north and north-east, a gap in the mountains to the north-west fills the air at times with raw and comfortless blasts. The rains begin in October, and last with considerable intervals through six months; the clouds, gathered by the hill-tops and the trees near the town, discharge themselves with violence, and about the equinoxes thunder-storms are common. At such times the Barr el-Manakhah, or the open space between the town and the suburbs, is a sheet of water, and the land near the southern and the south-eastern wall of the faubourg becomes a pool. Rain, however, is not considered unhealthy here; and the people, unlike the Meccans and Cairenes, expect it with pleasure, because it improves their date-trees and fruit plantations.

In winter it usually rains at night, in spring during the morning, and in summer about evening time. This is the case throughout El-Hejaz, as explained by the poet Lebid in these lines, which describe the desolate site of an old encampment:

---

water of Medinah'. But he was ill at the time, otherwise he would not have condemned it so strongly after eulogising the salt-bitter produce of the Meccan Zem Zem.

It (the place) hath been fertilised by the first spring-
showers of the constellations, and hath been swept by
The incessant torrents of the thunder-clouds,
falling in heavy and in gentle rains,
From each night-cloud, and heavily dropping
morning-cloud,
And the even-cloud, whose crashings are re-echoed
from around.

And the European reader will observe that the Arabs generally reckon three seasons, including our autumn, in their summer. The hot weather at El-Medinah appeared to me as extreme as the hibernal cold is described to be, but the air was dry, and the open plain prevented the faint and stagnant sultriness which distinguishes Meccah. Moreover, though the afternoons were close, the nights and the mornings were cool and dewy. At this season the citizens sleep on the house-tops, or on the ground outside their doors. Strangers must follow this example with considerable circumspection; the open air is safe in the Desert, but in cities it causes, to the unaccustomed, violent catarrhs and febrile affections.

I collected the following notes upon the diseases and medical treatment of the northern Hejaz. El-Medinah has been visited four times by the Rih el-Asfar (yellow wind), or Asiatic Cholera, which is said to have committed great ravages, sometimes carrying off whole households. In the Rahmat el-Kabirah, the Great Mercy, as the worst attack is piously called, whenever a man vomited, he was abandoned to his fate; before that, he was treated with mint, lime-juice, and copious draughts of coffee.

It is still the boast of El-Medinah that the Taun, or plague, has never passed her frontier. The Judari, or smallpox, appears to be indigenous to the countries bordering upon the Red Sea; we read of it there in the earliest works of the Arabs,[1] and even

[1] Conjecture, however, goes a little too far when it discovers smallpox in the Tayr Ababil, the swallow birds, which, according to the Koran, destroyed the host of Abrahat el-Ashram. Major Price (*Essay*) may be right in making Ababil the plural of Abilah, a vesicle; but it appears to me that the former is an Arabic and the latter a Persian word, which have no connexion whatever. M. C. de Perceval, quoting the Sirat el-Rasul, which says that at the time smallpox first appeared in Arabia, ascribes the destruction of

to the present time it sometimes sweeps through Arabia and the Somali country with desolating violence. In the town of El-Medinah it is fatal to children, many of whom, however, are in these days inoculated:[1] amongst the Bedawin, old men die of it, but adults are rarely victims, either in the city or in the desert. The nurse closes up the room whilst the sun is up, and carefully excludes the night-air, believing that, as the disease is 'hot', a breath of wind would kill the patient. During the hours of darkness, a lighted candle or lamp is always placed by the side of the bed, or the sufferer would die of madness, brought on by evil spirits or fright. Sheep's wool is burnt in the sick-room, as death would follow the inhaling of any perfume. The only remedy I have heard of is pounded Kohl (antimony) drunk in water, and the same is drawn along the breadth of the eyelid, to prevent blindness. The diet is Adas (lentils),[2] and a peculiar kind of date, called Tamir el-Birni. On the twenty-first day the patient is washed with salt and tepid water.

Ophthalmia is rare. In the summer, quotidian and tertian fevers (Hummah Salis) are not uncommon, and if accompanied by emetism, they are frequently fatal. The attack generally begins with the Naffazah, or cold fit, and is followed by El-Hummah, the hot stage. The principal remedies are cooling drinks, such as Sikanjebin (oxymel) and syrups. After the fever the face and body frequently swell, and indurated lumps appear on the legs and stomach. There are also low fevers, called simply Hummah; they are usually treated by burning charms in the patient's room. Jaundice and bilious complaints are common, and the former is popularly cured in a peculiar way. The sick man looks into a pot full of water, whilst the exorciser, reciting a certain spell, draws the heads of two needles from the patient's

---

the host of Yemen to an epidemic and a violent tempest. The strangest part of the story is that, although it occurred at Meccah, about two months before Mohammed's birth, and, therefore, within the memory of many living at the time, the Apostle alludes to it in the Koran as a miracle.

[1] In Yemen, we are told by Niebuhr, a rude form of inoculation—the mother pricking the child's arm with a thorn—has been known from time immemorial. My Medinah friends assured me that only during the last generation, this practice has been introduced amongst the Bedawin of El-Hejaz.

[2] This grain is cheaper than rice on the banks of the Nile—a fact which enlightened England, now paying a hundred times its value for Revalenta Arabica, apparently ignores.

ears along his eyes, down his face, lastly dipping them into water which at once becomes yellow. Others have Mirayat, Magic Mirrors,[1] on which the patient looks, and loses the complaint.

Dysenteries frequently occur in the fruit season, when the greedy Arabs devour all manner of unripe peaches, grapes, and pomegranates. The popular treatment is by the actual cautery; the scientific affect the use of drastics and astringent simples, and the Bizr el-Kutn (cotton-seed), toasted, pounded, and drunk in warm water. Almost every one here, as in Egypt, suffers more or less from haemorrhoids; they are treated by dietetics—eggs and leeks—and by a variety of drugs, Myrobalans, Lisan-el-Hamal (*Arnoglossum*), etc. But the patient looks with horror at the scissors and knife, so that they seldom succeed in obtaining a radical cure. The Filaria Medinensis, locally called Farantit, is no longer common, at the place which gave it its European name. At Yambu', however, the people suffer much from the Vena appearing in the legs. The complaint is treated here as in India and Abyssinia: when the tumour bursts, and the worm shows, it is extracted by being gradually wound round a splinter of wood.

Hydrophobia is rare, and the people have many superstitions

[1] This invention dates from the most ancient times, and both in the East and the West has been used by the weird brotherhood to produce the appearances of the absent and the dead, to discover treasure, to detect thieves, to cure disease, and to learn the secrets of the unknown world. The Hindus called it Anjan, and formed it by applying lampblack, made of a certain root, and mixed with oil, to the palm of a footling child, male or female. The Greeks used oil poured into a boy's hand. Cornelius Agrippa had a crystal mirror, which material also served the Count de St Germain and Cagliostro. Dr Dee's 'show-stone' was a bit of cannel coal. The modern Sindians know the art by the name of Gahno or Vinyano; there, as in southern Persia, ink is rubbed upon the seer's thumb-nail. The people of northern Africa are considered skilful in this science; and I have a Maghrabi magic formula for inking the hand of a 'boy, a black slave-girl, a virgin, or a pregnant woman', which differs materially from those generally known. The modern Egyptians call it Zarb el-Mandal, and there is scarcely a man in Cairo who does not know something about it. In selecting subjects to hold the ink, they observe the right hand, and reject all who have not what is called in palmistry the *linea media naturalis* straight and deeply cut. Even the barbarous Finns look into a glass of brandy, and the natives of Australia gaze at a kind of shining stone. Lady Blessington's crystal ball is fresh in the memory of the present generation, and most men have heard of Electro-Biology and the Cairo magician.

Upon this latter subject, a vexed one, I must venture a few remarks. In the first account of the magician by Mr Lane, we have a fair and dispassionate recital of certain magical, mystical, or mesmeric phenomena, which 'excited considerable curiosity and interest throughout the civilised world'. As usual in such matters, the civilised world was wholly ignorant of what was going on at home; otherwise, in London, Paris, and New York, about it. They suppose that a bit of meat falls from the sky, and that a dog eating it becomes mad. I was assured by respectable persons, that when a man is bitten, they shut him up with food, in a solitary chamber, for four days, and that if at the end of that time he still howls like a dog, they expel the Ghul (demon) from him, by pouring over him boiling water mixed with ashes—a certain cure I can easily believe. The only description of leprosy known in El-Hejaz is that called El-Baras: it appears in white patches on the skin, seldom attacks any but the poorer classes, and is considered incurable. Wounds are treated by Marham, or ointments, especially by the Balesan, or Balm of Meccah; a cloth is tied round the limb, and not removed till the wound heals, which, amongst this people of simple life, generally takes place by first intention.

Ulcers are common in El-Hejaz, as indeed all over Arabia. We read of them in ancient times. In AD 504, the poet and warrior, Amr el-Kays, died of this dreadful disease and it is related that when Mohammed Abu Si Mohammed, in AH 132, conquered Yemen with an army from El-Hejaz, he found the people suffering from sloughing and mortifying sores, so terrible

---

they might have found dozens studying the science. But a few years before, Dr Herkbts had described the same practice in India, filling three goodly pages; but he called his work *Qanoon-i-Islam*, and, consequently, despite its excellences, it fell still-born from the press. Lady H. Stanhope frequently declared 'the spell by which the face of an absent person is thrown upon a mirror to be within the reach of the humblest and most contemptible of magicians': but the civilised world did not care to believe a prophetess. All, however, were aroused by Mr Lane's discovery, and determined to decide the question by the ordeal of reason.

Accordingly, in AD 1844, Mr Lane, aided by Lord Nugent and others, discovered that a 'coarse and stupid fraud' had been perpetrated upon him by Usman Effendi, the Scotchman. In 1845, Sir G. Wilkinson remarked of this rationalism, 'The explanation lately offered, that Usman Effendi was in collusion with the magician, is neither fair on him nor satisfactory, as he was not present when those cases occurred which were made so much of in Europe,' and he proposed 'leading questions and accidents' as the word of the riddle. Eothen attributed the whole affair to 'shots', as schoolboys call them, and ranks success under the head of Paley's 'tentative miracles'. A writer in the *Quarterly* explained them by suggesting the probability of divers (impossible) optical combinations, and, lest the part of belief should have been left unrepresented, Miss Martineau was enabled to see clear signs of mesmeric action, and, by the decisive experiment of self, discovered the magic to be an 'affair of mesmerism'. Melancholy to relate, after all this philosophy, the herd of travellers at Cairo is still divided in opinion about the magician, some holding his performance to be all humbug, others darkly hinting that there may be something in it.

to look upon that he ordered the sufferers to be burnt alive. Fortunately for the patients, the conqueror died suddenly before his inhuman mandate was executed. These sores here, as in El-Yemen, are worst when upon the shin bones; they eat deep into the leg, and the patient dies of fever and gangrene. They are treated on first appearance by the actual cautery, and, when practicable, by cutting off the joint; the drugs popularly applied are Tutiya (tutty) and verdigris. There is no cure but rest, a generous diet, and change of air.

By the above short account it will be seen that the Arabs are no longer the most skilful physicians in the world. They have, however, one great advantage in their practice, and they are sensible enough to make free use of it. As the children of almost all the respectable citizens are brought up in the Desert, the camp becomes to them a native village. In cases of severe wounds or chronic diseases, the patient is ordered off to the Black Tents, where he lives as a Bedawi, drinking camel's milk, a diet for the first three or four days highly cathartic, and doing nothing. This has been the practice from time immemorial in Arabia, whereas Europe is only beginning to systematise the adhibition of air, exercise, and simple living. And even now we are obliged to veil it under the garb of charlatanry—to call it a milk-cure in Switzerland, a water-cure in Silesia, a grape-cure in France, a hunger-cure in Germany, and other sensible names which act as dust in the public eyes.

El-Medinah consists of three parts, a town, a fort, and a suburb little smaller than the body of the place. The town itself is about one-third larger than Suez, or nearly half the size of Meccah. It is a walled enclosure forming an irregular oval with four gates. The Bab el-Shami, or Syrian Gate, in the north-west side of the enceinte, leads towards Jebel Ohod, Hamzah's burial-place, and the mountains. In the eastern wall, the Bab el-Juma, or Friday Gate, opens upon the Nejd road and the cemetery, El-Bakia.

Between the Shami and the Juma gates, towards the north, is the Bab el-Ziyafah (of Hospitality); and westwards the Bab el-Misri (Egyptian) opens upon the plain called the Barr el-Manakhah. The eastern and the Egyptian gates are fine massive buildings, with double towers close together, painted with broad bands of red, yellow, and other colours, not unlike that old entrance of the Cairo citadel which opens upon the Rumayliyah plain. They may be compared with the gateway towers of the old Norman castles—Arques, for instance. In their shady and well-watered interiors, soldiers keep guard, camel-men dispute, and numerous idlers congregate, to enjoy the luxuries of coolness and companionship. Beyond this gate, in the street leading to the Mosque, is the great bazar. Outside it lie the Suk el-Khuzayriyah, or greengrocers' market, and the Suk el-Habbabah, or the grain bazar, with a fair sprinkling of coffee-houses. These markets are long masses of palm-leaf huts, blackened in the sun and wind, of a mean and squalid appearance, detracting greatly from the appearance of the gates. Amongst them there is a little domed and whitewashed building, which I was told is a Sabil or public fountain.

In the days of the Prophet the town was not walled. Even in El-Idrisi's time (twelfth century), and as late as Bartema's (eighteenth century), the fortifications were mounds of earth, made by order of Kasim el-Daulat el-Ghori, who re-populated the town and provided for its inhabitants. Now, the enceinte is in excellent condition. The walls are well built of granite and lava blocks, in regular layers, cemented with lime; they are provided with Mazghal (or Matras), long loopholes, and Shararif or trefoil-shaped crenelles: in order to secure a flanking fire, semicircular towers, also loopholed and crenellated, are disposed in the curtain at short and irregular intervals. Inside, the streets are what they always should be in these torrid lands, deep, dark, and narrow, in few places paved—a thing to be deprecated—and generally covered with black earth well watered and trodden to hardness. The most considerable lines radiate towards the Mosque.

There are few public buildings. The principal Wakalahs are four in number; one is the Wakalat Bab Salam near the Haram, another the Wakalat Jabarti, and two are inside the Misri gate; they all belong to Arab citizens. These caravanserais are used principally as stores, rarely for dwelling-places like those of Cairo; travellers, therefore, must hire houses at a considerable expense, or pitch tents to the detriment of health and to their extreme discomfort. The other public buildings are a few mean coffee-houses and an excellent bath in the Harat Zarawan inside the town: far superior to the unclean establishments of Cairo, it borrows something from the luxury of Stamboul.

The houses are, for the East, well built, flat-roofed and double-storied; the materials generally used are a basaltic scoria, burnt brick, and palm wood. The best enclose spacious court-yards and small gardens with wells, where water basins and date-trees gladden the owners' eyes. The latticed balconies, first seen by the European traveller at Alexandria, are here common, and the windows are mere apertures in the wall, garnished, as usual in Arab cities, with a shutter of planking.

El-Medinah fell rapidly under the Wahhabis, but after their retreat, it soon rose again, and now it is probably as comfortable and flourishing a little city as any to be found in the East. It contains between fifty and sixty streets, including the alleys and culs-de-sac. There is about the same number of Harat or quarters; but I have nothing to relate of them save their names. Within the town few houses are in a dilapidated condition. The best authorities estimate the number of habitations at about 1,500 within the enceinte, and those in the suburb at 1,000. I consider both accounts exaggerated; the former might contain 800, and the Manakhah perhaps 500; at the same time I must confess not to have counted them, and Captain Sadlier (in AD 1819) declares that the Turks, who had just made a kind of census, reckoned 6,000 houses and a population of 18,000 souls. Assuming the population to be 16,000 (Burckhardt raises it as high as 20,000), of which 9,000 occupy the city, and 7,000 the suburbs and the fort, this would give little more than twelve inhabitants to each house, a fair estimate for an Arab town, where the abodes are large and slaves abound.

I afterwards received the following information from Mr Charles Cole, HBM's Vice-Consul at Jeddah, a gentleman well acquainted with Western Arabia, and having access to official information.

'The population of El-Medinah is from 16,000 to 18,000, and the Nizam troops in garrison 400. Meccah contains about

45,000 inhabitants, Yambu' from 6,000 to 7,000, Jeddah about 2,500 (this I think is too low), and Taif 8,000. Most of the troops are stationed at Meccah and Jeddah. In El-Hejaz there is a total force of five battalions, each of which ought to contain 800 men; they may amount to 3,500, with 500 artillery, and 4,500 irregulars, though the muster-rolls bear 6,000. The government pays in paper for all supplies (even water for the troops), and the paper sells at the rate of 40 piastres per cent.'

The castle joins on to the north-west angle of the city enceinte, and the wall of its eastern outwork is pierced for a communication through a court strewed with guns and war-like apparatus, between the Manakhah Suburb and the Bab el-Shami, or the Syrian Gate.

Having been refused entrance into the fort, I can describe only its exterior. The outer wall resembles that of the city, only its towers are more solid, and the curtain appears better calculated for work. Inside, a donjon, built upon a rock, bears proudly enough the banner of the Crescent and the Star; its whitewashed walls make it a conspicuous object, and guns pointed in all directions, especially upon the town, project from their embrasures. The castle is said to contain wells, bomb-proofs, provisions, and munitions of war: if so, it must be a kind of Gibraltar to the Bedawin and the Wahhabis. The garrison consisted of a Nisf Urtah,[1] or half battalion (400 men) of Nizam infantry, commanded by a Pasha; his authority also extends to a Sanjak, or about 500 Kurdish and Albanian Bash-Buzuks, whose duty it is to escort caravans, to convey treasures, and to be shot at in the Passes. The Madani, who, as usual with Orientals, take a personal pride in their castle, speak of it with much exaggeration. Commanded by a high line of rocks on the north-west, and built as it is in most places without moat, glacis, earthwork, or outworks, a few shells and a single battery of siege guns would soon render it untenable. In ancient times it has more than once been held by a party at feud with the town, for whose mimic battles the Barr el-Manakhah was a fitting field.

[1] The Urtah or battalion here varies from 800 to 1,000 men. Of these four form one Alai or regiment, and thirty-six Alai an Urdu or camp. This word Urdu, pronounced 'Ordoo', is the origin of our 'horde'.

Northward from the fort, on the road to Ohod, but still within fire, is a long many-windowed building, formerly Daud Pasha's palace. In my time it had been bought by Abbas Pasha of Egypt.

The suburbs lie to the south and west of the town. Southwards they are separated from the enceinte by a wide road, called the Darb el-Jenazah, the Road of Biers, so called because the corpses of certain schismatics, who may not pass through the city, are carried this way to their own cemetery near the Bab el-Juma, or Eastern Gate. Westwards, between El-Medinah and its faubourg, lies the plain of El-Manakhah, about three-quarters of a mile long, by 300 yards broad.

The straggling suburbs occupy more ground than the city: fronting the enceinte they are without walls; towards the west, where open country lies, they are enclosed by mud or raw brick ramparts, with little round towers, all falling to decay. A number of small gates lead from the suburb into the country. The only large one, a poor copy of the Bab el-Nasr at Cairo, is the Ambari or western entrance, through which we passed into El-Medinah. The suburb contains no buildings of any consequence, except the Khaskiyah, or official residence of the Muhafiz (governor), a plain building near the Barr el-Manakhah, and the Khamsah Masajid, or the Five Mosques, which every Zair is expected to visit. They are:

The Prophet's Mosque in the Manakhah.

Abubekr's near the Ayn el-Zarka.

Ali's Mosque in the Zukak el-Tayyar of the Manakhah. Some authors call this the Musalla el-'Id, because the Prophet here prayed the Festival Prayer.

Omar's Mosque, near the Bab Kuba of the Manakhah, and close to the little torrent called El-Sayh.

Belal's Mosque, celebrated in books; I did not see it, and some Madani assured me that it no longer exists.

A description of one of these buildings will suffice, for they are all similar. Mohammed's Mosque in the Manakhah stands upon a spot formerly occupied, some say, by the Jami Ghamamah. Others believe it to be founded upon the Musalla el-Nabi, a place where the Apostle recited the first Festival prayers after his arrival at El-Medinah, and used frequently to pray, and to address those of his followers who lived far from the Haram, or Sanctuary. It is a trim modern building of cut stone and lime in regular layers, of parallelogramic shape, surmounted by one large and four small cupolas. These are all whitewashed; and the principal is capped with a large crescent, or rather a trident rising from a series of gilt globes: the other domes crown the several corners. The minaret is of the usual Turkish shape, with a conical roof, and a single gallery for the Muezzin. An Acacia-tree or two on the eastern side, and behind it a wall-like line of mud houses, finish the *coup-d'œil;* the interior of this building is as simple as the exterior. And here I may remark that the Arabs have little idea of splendour, either in their public or in their private architecture.

Whatever strikes the traveller's eye in El-Hejaz is always either an importation or the work of foreign artists. This arises from the simple tastes of the people, combined, doubtless, with their notable thriftiness. If strangers will build for them, they argue, why should they build for themselves? Moreover, they have scant inducement to lavish money upon grand edifices. Whenever a disturbance takes place, domestic or from without, the principal buildings are sure to suffer. And the climate is inimical to their enduring. Both ground and air at El-Medinah, as well as at Meccah, are damp and nitrous in winter, in summer dry and torrid: the lime is poor; palm-timber soon decays; even foreign wood-work suffers, and a few years of neglect suffice to level the proudest pile with the dust.

The suburbs to the south of El-Medinah are a collection of walled villages, with plantations and gardens between. They are laid out in the form, called here, as in Egypt, Hosh—court-yards, with single-storied tenements opening into them. These enclosures contain the cattle of the inhabitants; they have strong wooden doors, shut at night to prevent 'lifting', and they are capable of being stoutly defended. The inhabitants of the suburb are for the most part Bedawin settlers, and a race of schismatics who will be noticed in another chapter. Beyond these suburbs, to the south, as well as to the north and north-east, lie gardens and extensive plantations of palm-trees.

XIX

A Ride to the Mosque of Kuba

The principal places of pious visitation in the vicinity of El-Medinah are the Mosques of Kuba, the Cemetery El-Bakia, and the martyr Hamzah's tomb, at the foot of Mount Ohod. These the Zair is directed by all the Olema to visit, and on the holy ground to pray Allah for a blessing upon himself, and upon his brethren of the faith.

Early one Saturday morning, I started for Kuba with a motley crowd of devotees. Shaykh Hamid, my Muzawwir, was by my side, mounted upon an ass more miserable than I had yet seen. The boy Mohammed had procured for me a Meccan dromedary, with splendid trappings, a saddle with burnished metal peaks before and behind, covered with a huge sheep-skin dyed crimson, and girthed over fine saddle-bags, whose enormous tassels hung almost to the ground. The youth himself, being too grand to ride a donkey, and unable to borrow a horse, preferred walking. He was proud as a peacock, being habited in a style somewhat resembling the plume of that gorgeous bird, in the coat of many colours—yellow, red, and golden flowers, apparently sewed on a field of bright green silk—which cost me so dear in the Haram. He was armed, as indeed all of us were, in readiness for the Bedawin, and he anxiously awaited opportunities of discharging his pistol. Our course lay from Shaykh Hamid's house in the Manakhah, along and up the Fiumara, 'El-Sayh', and through the Bab Kuba, a little gate in the suburb wall, where, by-the-bye, my mounted companion was nearly trampled down by a rush of half-wild camels. Outside the town, in this direction, southward, is a plain of clay, mixed with chalk, and here and there with sand, whence protrude blocks and little ridges of basalt. As far as Kuba, and the Harrah ridge to the west, the earth is sweet and makes excellent gugglets.

Immediately outside the gate I saw a kiln, where they were burning tolerable bricks. Shortly after leaving the suburb, an

Indian, who joined our party upon the road, pointed out on the left of the way what he declared was the place of the celebrated Khandak, or Moat, the Torres Vedras of Arabian History.

Presently the Nakhil, or palm plantations, began. Nothing lovelier to the eye, weary with hot red glare, than the rich green waving crops and the cool shade, the 'food of vision', as the Arabs call it, and 'pure water to the parched throat'. For hours I could have sat and looked at it. The air was soft and balmy; a perfumed breeze, strange luxury in El-Hejaz, wandered amongst the date fronds; there were fresh flowers and bright foliage; in fact, at midsummer, every beautiful feature of spring.

Nothing more delightful to the ear than the warbling of the small birds, that sweet familiar sound; the splashing of tiny cascades from the wells into the wooden troughs, and the musical song of the water-wheels. Travellers—young travellers—in the East talk of the 'dismal grating', the 'mournful monotony', and the 'melancholy creaking of these dismal machines'. To the veteran wanderer their sound is delightful from association, reminding him of fields and water-courses, and hospitable villages, and plentiful crops. The expatriated Nubian, for instance, listens to the water-wheel with as deep emotion as the *Ranz des Vaches* ever excited in the hearts of Switzer mercenary at Naples, or 'Lochaber no more', among a regiment of Highlanders in the West Indies.

The date-trees of El-Medinah merit their celebrity. Their stately columnar stems, here, seem higher than in other lands, and their lower fronds are allowed to tremble in the breeze without mutilation. These enormous palms were loaded with ripening fruits; and the clusters, carefully tied up, must often have weighed upwards of 80 lb. They hung down between the lower branches by a bright yellow stem, as thick as a man's ankle.

Books enumerate 139 varieties of trees; of these between sixty and seventy are well known, and each is distinguished, as usual among Arabs, by its peculiar name. The best kind is El-Shelebi; it is packed in skins, or in flat round boxes covered with paper, somewhat in the manner of French prunes, and sent as presents to the remotest parts of the Moslem world. The fruit is about two inches long, with a small stone, and has a peculiar aromatic flavour and smell; it is seldom eaten by the citizens on account of the price, which varies from 2 to 10 piastres per lb. The tree, moreover, is rare, and is said to be not so productive as the other species. The Ajwah date is eaten, but not sold, because a tradition of the Prophet declares that whoso breaketh his fast every day with six or seven of these fruits, need fear neither poison nor magic. The third kind, El-Hilwah, also a large date, derives a name from its exceeding sweetness: of this palm the Moslems relate that the Prophet planted a stone, which in a few minutes grew up and bore fruit. Next comes El-Birni, of which was said, 'It causeth sickness to depart, and there is no sickness in it.'

The Wahshi on one occasion bent its head, and salamed to Mohammed as he ate its fruit, for which reason even now its lofty tuft turns earthwards. The Sayhani (Crier) is so called, because when the founder of El-Islam, holding Ali's hand, happened to pass beneath, it cried, 'This is Mohammed the Prince of Prophets, and this is Ali the Prince of the Pious, and the Progenitor of the immaculate Imams.'[1] Of course the descendants of so intelligent a vegetable hold high rank in the kingdom of palms, and the vulgar were in the habit of eating the Sayhani and of throwing the stones about the Haram. The Khuzayriyah is thus named because it preserves its green colour, even when ripe; it is dried and preserved as a curiosity. The Jebeli is the common fruit: the poorest kinds are the Laun and the Hilayah, costing from 4 to 7 piastres per mudd.[2]

I cannot say that the dates of El-Medinah are finer than those

[1] So in AD 1272 the Crucifix spoke to St Thomas Aquinas. Superstitions are of no age or country.

[2] At El-Medinah,

12	Dirhams (drams)	make	1	Wukkiyah (oz.).
20	Wukkiyah	"	1	Ratl (lb.).
30	Wukkiyah and 3 (drams)	"	1	Wukkah (less than 2 lb.).
4	Wukkah	"	1	Mudd.
24	Mudd	"	1	Ardebb.

This Ratl is the larger pound applied to particular articles of commerce—such as meat, vegetables, and clarified butter: coffee, rice, soap, etc., are sold by the smaller Ratl of Meccah, equal to 140 Dirhams. In Egypt the Ratl is 144 Dirhams or 12 Wukkiyahs, about 1 lb. 2 oz. and 8 dwt troy.

of Meccah, although it is highly heretical to hold such tenet. The produce of the former city was the favourite food of the Prophet, who invariably broke his fast with it: a circumstance which invests it with a certain degree of relic-sanctity. The citizens delight in speaking of dates as an Irishman does of potatoes, with a manner of familiar fondness: they eat them for medicine as well as food; Rutab, or wet dates, being held to be the most saving, as it is doubtless the most savoury of remedies. The fruit is prepared in a great variety of ways: the favourite dish is a broil with clarified butter, extremely distasteful to the European palate. The date is also left upon the tree to dry, and then called Balah: this is eaten at dessert as the Nukliyat—the *quatre mendiants* of Persia. Amongst peculiar preparations must be mentioned the Kulladat el-Sham (necklace of Sham). The unripe fruit is dipped in boiling water to preserve its gamboge colour, strung upon a thick thread and hung out in the air to dry. These strings are worn all over El-Hejaz as necklaces by children, who seldom fail to munch the ornament when not in fear of slappings; and they are sent as presents to distant countries.

January and February are the time for the masculation of the palm. The Nakhwali, as he is called, opens the female flower, and having inserted the inverted male blossom, binds them together: this operation is performed, as in Egypt, upon each cluster. The fruit is ripe about the middle of May, and the gathering of it forms the Arabs' *vendemmia*. The people make merry the more readily because their favourite diet is liable to a variety of accidents: droughts injure the tree, locusts destroy the produce, and the date crop, like most productions which men are imprudent enough to adopt singly as the staff of life, is often subject to complete failure.

One of the reasons for the excellence of Medinah dates is the quantity of water they obtain: each garden or field has its well; and even in the hottest weather the Persian wheel floods the soil every third day. It has been observed that the date-tree can live in dry and barren spots; but it loves the beds of streams and places where moisture is procurable. The palms scattered over the other parts of the plain, and depending solely upon rain water, produce less fruit, and that too of an inferior quality.

Verdure is not usually wholesome in Arabia, yet invalids leave the close atmosphere of El-Medinah to seek health under the cool shades of Kuba. The gardens are divided by what might almost be called lanes, long narrow lines with tall reed fences on both sides. The graceful branches of the Tamarisk, pearled with manna, and cottoned over with dew, and the broad leaves of the castor plant, glistening in the sun, protected us from the morning rays. The ground on both sides of the way was sunken, the earth being disposed in heaps at the foot of the fences, an arrangement which facilitates irrigation, by giving a fall to the water, and in some cases affords a richer soil than the surface. This part of the Medinah plain, however, being higher than the rest, is less subject to the disease of salt and nitre. On the way here and there the earth crumbles and looks dark under the dew of morning; but nowhere has it broken out into that glittering efflorescence which denotes the last stage of the attack. The fields and gardens are divided into small oblongs separated from one another by little ridges of mould which form diminutive water-courses. Of the cereals there are luxuriant maize, wheat, and barley, but the latter two are in small quantities. Here and there patches of Barsim, or Egyptian clover, glitter brightly in the sunbeams. The principal vegetables are Badanjan (Egg-plant), the Bamiyah (a kind of esculent *hibiscus*, called Bhendi in India), and Mulukhiyah (*Corchoris olitorius*), a mucilaginous spinage common throughout this part of the East. These three are eaten by citizens of every rank; they are, in fact, the potatoes and the greens of Arabia. I remarked also onions and leeks in fair quantities, a few beds of carrots and beans; some Fijl (radishes), Lift (turnips), gourds, cucumbers, and similar plants. Fruit trees abound. There are five descriptions of vines, the best of which is El-Sherifi, a long white grape of a flavour somewhat resembling the produce of Tuscany. Next to it, and very similar, is El-Birni. The Hejazi is a round fruit, sweet, but insipid, which is also the reproach of the Sawadi, or black grape. And lastly, the Raziki is a small white fruit, with a diminutive stone.

The Nebek, Lote or Jujube, is here a fine large tree with a dark green leaf, roundish and polished like the olive; it is armed with a short, curved, and sharp thorn,[1] and bears a pale straw-coloured berry, about the size of the gooseberry, with red streaks on the side next the sun. Little can be said in favour of the fruit, which has been compared successively by disappointed 'Lotus eaters' to a bad plum, an unripe cherry, and an insipid apple. It is, however, a favourite with the people of El-Medinah, who have reckoned many varieties of the fruit: Hindi (Indian), Baladi (native), Tamri (date-like), and others. There are a few peaches, hard like the Egyptian, and almost tasteless, fit only for stewing, but greedily eaten in a half-ripe state; large coarse bananas, lime-trees, a few water-melons, figs, and apples, but neither apricots nor pears.

There are three kinds of pomegranates; the best is the Shami (Syrian); it is red outside, very sweet, and costs 1 piastre; the Turki is large, and of a white colour: and the Misri has a greenish rind, and a somewhat sub-acid and harsh flavour; the latter are sold at one-fourth the price of the best. I never saw in the East, except at Meccah, finer fruits than the Shami: almost stoneless, like those of Maskat, they are delicately perfumed, and as large as an infant's head. El-Medinah is celebrated, like Taif, for its Rubb Rumman, a thick pomegranate syrup, drunk with water during the hot weather, and esteemed cooling and wholesome.

After threading our way through the gardens, an operation requiring less time than to describe them, we saw, peeping through the groves, Kuba's simple minaret. Then we came in sight of a confused heap of huts and dwelling-houses, chapels and towers with trees between, and foul lanes, heaps of rubbish, and barking dogs—the usual material of a Hejazi village.

Having dismounted, we gave our animals in charge of a dozen infant Bedawin, the produce of the peasant gardeners, who shouted 'Bakhshísh' the moment they saw us. To this they were urged by their mothers, and I willingly parted with a few paras for the purpose of establishing an intercourse with fellow-creatures so fearfully and wonderfully resembling the tailless

[1] This thorn (the *Rhamnus Nabeca* or *Zizyphus Spina Christi*) is supposed to be that which crowned the Saviour's head. There are Mimosas in Syria; but no tree, save the fabled Zakhum, could produce the terrible apparatus with which certain French painters of the modern school have attempted to heighten the terrors of the scene.

baboon. Their bodies, unlike those of Egyptian children, were slim[1] and straight, but their ribs stood out with curious distinctness; the colour of the skin was that oily lamp-black seen upon the face of a European sweep; and the elf-locks, thatching the cocoa-nut heads, had been stained by the sun, wind, and rain to that reddish-brown hue which Hindu romances have appropriated to their Rakshasas or demons.

Each anatomy carried in his arms a stark-naked miniature of himself, fierce-looking babies with faces all eyes, and the strong little wretches were still able to extend the right hand and exert their lungs with direful clamour. Their mothers were fit progenitors for such progeny: long, gaunt, with emaciated limbs, wall-sided, high-shouldered, and straight-backed, with pendulous bosoms, spider-like arms, and splay feet. Their long elf-locks, wrinkled faces, and high cheek-bones, their lips darker than the epidermis, hollow staring eyes, sparkling as if to light up the extreme ugliness around, and voices screaming as though in a perennial rage, invested them with all the 'charms of Sycorax'. These 'Houris of Jehannum' were habited in long night-gowns dyed blue to conceal want of washing, and the squalid children had about a yard of the same material wrapped round their waists for all toilette. This is not an overdrawn portrait of the farmer race of Arabs, the most despised by their fellow-countrymen, and the most hard-favoured, morally as well as physically, of all the breed.

Before entering the Mosque of El-Kuba it will be necessary to call to mind some passages of its past history. When the Apostle's she-camel, El-Kaswa, as he was approaching El-Medinah after the flight from Meccah, knelt down here, he desired his companions to mount the animal. Abubekr and Omar did so; still she sat upon the ground; but when Ali obeyed the order, she arose. The Apostle bade him loose her halter, for she was directed by Allah, and the Mosque walls were built upon the line over which she trod. It was the first place of public prayer in El-Islam. Mohammed laid the first brick, and with an Anzah,

[1] Travellers always remark the curious pot-bellied children on the banks of the Nile. This conformation is admired by the Egyptians, who consider it a sign of strength, and a promise of fine growth.

or iron-shod javelin, marked out the direction of prayer: each of his successors followed his example. According to most historians, the land belonged to Abu Ayyub the Ansari, the Apostle's host; for which reason the Bayt Ayyub, his descendants, still perform the service of the Mosque, keep the key, and share with the Bawwabs, or porters, the alms and fees here offered by the Faithful. Others declared that the ground was the property of one Linah, a woman who was in the habit of tethering her ass there. The Apostle used to visit it every Saturday on foot, and always made a point of praying the dawn-prayer there on the 17th Ramazan.

A number of traditions testify to its dignity: of these two are especially significant. The first assures all Moslems that a prayer at Kuba is equal to a Lesser Pilgrimage at Meccah in religious efficacy; and the second declares that such devotion is more acceptable to the Deity than prostrations at the Bayt el-Mukaddas (Jerusalem). Moreover, sundry miracles took place here, and a verset of the Koran descended from heaven. For which reasons the Mosque was much respected by Omar, who, once finding it empty, swept it himself with a broom of thorns, and expressed his wonder at the lukewarmness of Moslem piety. It was originally a square building of very small size; Osman enlarged it in the direction of the minaret, making it sixty-six cubits each way. It is no longer 'mean and decayed' as in Burckhardt's time: the Sultan Abd el-Hamid, father of the Sultan Mahmud, erected a minaret of Turkish shape and a neat structure of cut stone, whose crenelles make it look more like a place of defence than of prayer. It has, however, no pretensions to grandeur. To the south a small and narrow Riwak (porch), with unpretending columns, looks out northwards upon a little open area simply sanded over; and this is the whole building.

The large Mastabah or stone bench at the entrance of the Mosque was crowded with sitting people: we therefore lost no time, after ablution and the Niyat (the Intention) peculiar to this Visitation, in ascending the steps, in pulling off our slippers, and in entering the sacred building. We stood upon the Musalla el-Nabi (the Prophet's place of prayer): after Shaykh Nur and Hamid had forcibly cleared that auspicious spot of a devout

Indian, and had spread a rug upon the dirty matting, we performed a two-bow prayer, in front of a pillar into which a diminutive marble Mihrab or niche had been inserted by way of memento. Then came the Dua, or supplication, which was as follows:

'O Allah! bless and preserve, and increase, and perpetuate, and benefit, and be propitious to, our Lord Mohammed, and to his Family, and to his Companions, and be Thou their Preserver! O Allah! this is the Mosque Kuba, and the Place of the Prophet's Prayers. O Allah! pardon our Sins, and veil our Faults, and place not over us one who feareth not Thee, and who pitieth not us, and pardon us, and the true Believers, Men and Women, the Quick of them and the Dead; for verily Thou, O Lord, art the Hearer, the near to us, the Answerer of our Supplications.' After which we recited the Testification and the Fatihah, and we drew our palms as usual down our faces.

We then moved away to the south-eastern corner of the edifice, and stood before a Mihrab in the southern wall. It is called Takat el-Kashf or Niche of Disclosure, by those who believe that as the Prophet was standing undecided about the direction of Meccah, the Archangel Gabriel removed all obstructions to his vision. There again we went through the two-bow prayer, the Supplication, the Testification, and the Fatihah, under difficulties, for people mobbed us excessively.

During our devotions, I vainly attempted to decypher a Cufic inscription fixed in the wall above and on the right of the Mihrab—my regret, however, at this failure was transitory, the character not being of an ancient date. Then we left the Riwak, and despite the morning sun which shone fiercely with a sickly heat, we went to the open area where stands the Mabrak el-Nakah, or the Place of kneeling of the she-Dromedary. This, the exact spot where El-Kaswa sat down, is covered with a diminutive dome of cut stone, supported by four stone pillars: the building is about eight feet high and a little less in length and breadth. It has the appearance of being modern. On the floor, which was raised by steps above the level of the ground, lay, as usual, a bit of dirty matting, upon which we again went through the ceremonies above detailed.

Then issuing from the canopy into the sun, a little outside the Riwak and close to the Mabrak, we prayed upon the Makan el-Ayat, or the Place of Signs. Here was revealed to Mohammed a passage in the Koran especially alluding to the purity of the place and of the people of Kuba, 'a Temple founded in Purity from its first Day'; and again: 'there live Men who love to be cleansed, and verily Allah delights in the Clean.' The Prophet exclaimed in admiration, 'O ye Sons of Amr! what have ye done to deserve all this Praise and Beneficence?' when the people offered him an explanation of their personal cleanliness which I do not care to repeat. The temple of Kuba from that day took a fresh title—Masjid el-Takwa, or the Mosque of Piety.

Having finished our prayers and ceremonies at the Mosque of Piety, we fought our way out through a crowd of importunate beggars, and turning a few paces to the left, halted near a small chapel adjoining the south-west angle of the larger temple. We there stood at a grated window in the western wall, and recited a supplication, looking the while reverently at a dark dwarf archway under which the Lady Fatimah used to sit grinding grain in a hand-mill. The Mosque in consequence bears the name of Sittna Fatimah. A surly-looking Khadim, or guardian, stood at the door demanding 1 dollar in the most authoritative Arab tone—we therefore did not enter.

At El-Medinah and at Meccah the traveller's hand must be perpetually in his pouch: no stranger in Paris or London is more surely or more severely taken in. Already I began to fear that my 80*l.* would not suffice for all the expenses of sight-seeing, and the apprehension was justified by the sequel. My only friend was the boy Mohammed, who displayed a fiery economy that brought him into considerable disrepute with his countrymen. They saw with emotion that he was preaching parsimony to me solely that I might have more money to spend at Meccah under his auspices. This being palpably the case, I threw all the blame of penuriousness upon the young Machiavel's shoulders, and resolved, as he had taken charge of my finances at El-Medinah, so at Meccah to administer them myself.

After praying at the window, to the great disgust of the Khadim, who openly asserted that we were 'low fellows', we passed through some lanes lined with beggars and Bedawi children, till we came to a third little Mosque situated due south of the larger one. This is called the Masjid Arafat, and is erected upon a mound also named Tall Arafat, because on one occasion the Prophet, being unable to visit the Holy Mountain at the pilgrimage season, stood there, saw through the intervening space, and in spirit performed the ceremony. Here also we looked into a window instead of opening the door with a silver key, and the mesquin appearance of all within prevented my regretting the necessity of economy. In India or Sind every village would have a better mosque.

Our last visit was to a fourth chapel, the Masjid Ali, so termed because the Apostle's son-in-law had a house upon this spot. After praying there—and terribly hot the little hole was!—we repaired to the last place of visitation at Kuba—a large deep well called the Bir el-Aris, in a garden to the west of the Mosque of Piety, with a little oratory adjoining it. A Persian wheel was going drowsily round, and the cool water fell into a tiny pool, whence it whirled and bubbled away in childish mimicry of a river. The music sounded sweet in my ears; I stubbornly refused to do any more praying—though Shaykh Hamid, for form's sake, reiterated, with parental emphasis, 'how very wrong it was'—and sat down, as the Prophet himself did not disdain to do, with the resolution of enjoying on the brink of the well a few moments of unwonted Kayf.

The heat was overpowering, though it was only nine o'clock, the sound of the stream was soothing, that water-wheel was creaking a lullaby, and the limes and pomegranates, gentle rustling, shed voluptuous fragrance through the morning air. I fell asleep, and—wondrous the contrast!—dreamed that I was once more standing

By the wall whereon hangeth the crucified vine,

looking upon the valley of the Lianne, with its glaucous seas and grey skies, and banks here and there white with snow.

The Bir el-Aris, so called after a Jew of El-Medinah, is one which the Apostle delighted to visit. He would sit upon its brink with his bare legs hanging over the side, and his companions used to imitate his example. This practice caused a sad disaster. In the sixth year of his caliphate, Osman, according to Abulfeda and Yakut, dropped from his finger the prophetic ring which, engraved in three lines with 'Mohammed—Apostle—(of) Allah', had served to seal the letters sent to neighbouring kings, and had descended to the first three successors. The precious article was not recovered after three days' search, and the well was thenceforward called Bir el-Khatim—of the Seal Ring. It is also called the Bir el-Taflat—of Saliva—because the Prophet honoured it by expectoration, as, by-the-bye, he seems to have done to almost all the wells in El-Medinah. The effect of the operation upon the Bir el-Aris, say the historians, was to sweeten the water, which before was salt. Their testimony, however, did not prevent my detecting a pronounced medicinal taste in the lukewarm draught drawn for me by Shaykh Hamid.

In Mohammed's day the total number of wells is recorded to have been twenty: most of them have long since disappeared; but there still remain seven, whose waters were drunk by the Prophet, and which, in consequence, the Zair is directed to visit. They are known by the classical title of Saba Abar, or the seven wells, and their names are included in this couplet:

> Aris and Ghars, and Rumah and Buzaat
> And Busat, with Bayruha and Ihn.

After my sleep, which was allowed to last until a pipe or two of Latakia had gone round the party, we remounted our animals. Returning towards El-Medinah, my companions pointed out to me, on the left of the village, a garden called El-Madshuniyah. It contains a quarry of the yellow loam or bole-earth, called by the Arabs Tafl, the Persians Gil-i-Sarshui, and the Sindians Metu. It is used as soap in many parts of the East, and, mixed with oil, it is supposed to cool the body, and to render the skin fresh and supple. It is related that the Prophet cured a Bedawi of the Beni Haris tribe of fever by washing him with a pot of Tafl dissolved in water, and hence the earth of El-Medinah derived its healing fame. As far as I could learn from the Madani, this clay is no longer valued by them, either medicinally or cosmetically.

XX

The Visitation of Hamzah's Tomb

On the morning of Sunday, the 23rd Zu'l Kaadah (28th August, 1853), arrived from El-Sham, or Damascus, the great Caravan popularly called Hajj el-Shami, the Damascus pilgrimage, as the Egyptian Cafila is El-Misri, or the Cairo pilgrimage. It is the main stream which carries off all the small currents that at this season of general movement flow from Central Asia towards the great centre of the Islamitic world, and in 1853 it amounted to about 7,000 souls.

The arrival was anxiously expected by the people for several reasons. In the first place, it brought with it a new curtain for the Prophet's Hujrah, the old one being in a tattered condition; secondly, it had charge of the annual stipends and pensions of the citizens; and thirdly, many families expected members returning under its escort to their homes. The popular anxiety was greatly increased by the disordered state of the country round about; and, moreover, the great caravan had been one day late, generally arriving on the morning of the 22nd Zu'l Kaadah.[1]

During the night three of Shaykh Hamid's brothers, who had entered as Muzawwirs with the Hajj, came suddenly to the house: they leaped off their camels, and lost not a moment in

[1] I reprint the following from the *Illustrated News* in proof that the literati of England have still something to learn:

'On the 1st instant the annual ceremony of the departure of the Suré-emini with the Imperial gifts for the *Prophet's tomb at Mecca* took place in front of the palace at Constantinople. The *Levant Herald* states that the presents, which consist, beside the large money donation, of rich shawls and gold-woven stuffs, were brought out of the Imperial apartments and packed in the presence of the Sultan, on two beautiful camels, which, after the delivery of the usual prayers, were then led in grand procession, accompanied by all the high officers of state, to the landing-place at Cabatash, where the Suré-emini and camels were embarked on a Government steamer and ferried over to Scutari. There the holy functionary will remain some days, till the "faithful" of the capital and those who have come from the interior have joined him, when the caravan will start for Damascus. At this latter city the grand rendezvous takes place, and, that accomplished, the great caravan sets out for Mecca under the Emir-el-Hadj of the year. The Imperial presents on this occasion cost more than 20,000*l.*'

going through the usual scene of kissing, embracing, and weeping bitterly for joy.

I arose in the morning, and looked out from the windows of the Majlis. The Barr el-Manakhah, from a dusty waste dotted with a few Bedawi hair-tents, had assumed all the various shapes and the colours of a kaleidoscope. The eye was bewildered by the shifting of innumerable details, in all parts totally different from one another, thrown confusedly together in one small field; and, however jaded with sight-seeing, it dwelt with delight upon the variety, the vivacity, and the intense picturesqueness of the scene. In one night had sprung up a town of tents of every size, colour, and shape; round, square, and oblong; open and closed—from the shawl-lined and gilt-topped pavilion of the Pasha, with all the luxurious appurtenances of the Haram, to its neighbour the little dirty green 'rowtie' of the tobacco-seller. They were pitched in admirable order: here ranged in a long line, where a street was required; there packed in dense masses, where thoroughfares were unnecessary.

But how describe the utter confusion in the crowding, the bustling, and the vast variety and volume of sound? Huge white Syrian dromedaries, compared with which those of El-Hejaz appeared mere pony-camels, jingling large bells, and bearing Shugdufs (litters) like miniature green tents, swaying and tossing upon their backs; gorgeous Takhtrawan, or litters carried between camels or mules with scarlet and brass trappings; Bedawin bestriding naked-backed Daluls (dromedaries), and clinging like apes to the hairy humps; Arnaut, Kurd, and Turkish Irregular Cavalry, fiercer looking in their mirth than Roman peasants in their rage; fainting Persian pilgrims, forcing their stubborn camels to kneel, or dismounted grumbling from jaded donkeys; Kahwajis, sherbet sellers, and ambulant tobacconists crying their goods; country-people driving flocks of sheep and goats with infinite clamour through lines of horses fiercely snorting and biting and kicking and rearing; townspeople seeking their friends; returned travellers exchanging affectionate salutes; devout Hajis jostling one another, running under the legs of camels, and tumbling over the tents' ropes in their hurry to reach the Haram; cannon roaring from the citadel; shopmen, water-carriers, and fruit vendors fighting over their bargains; boys bullying heretics with loud screams; a well-mounted party of fine old Arab Shaykhs of the Hamidah clan, preceded by their varlets, performing the Arzah or war dance—compared with which the Pyrenean bear's performance is grace itself—firing their duck-guns upwards, or blowing the powder into the calves of those before them, brandishing their swords, leaping frantically the while, with their bright-coloured rags floating in the wind, tossing their long spears tufted with ostrich feathers high in the air, reckless where they fall; servants seeking their masters, and masters their tents, with vain cries of 'Ya Mohammed';[1] grandees riding mules or stalking on foot, preceded by their crowd-beaters, shouting to clear the way; here the loud shrieks of women and children, whose litters are bumping and rasping against one another; there the low moaning of some poor wretch that is seeking a shady corner to die in: add a thick dust which blurs the outlines like a London fog, with a flaming sun that draws sparkles of fire from the burnished weapons of the crowd, and the brass balls of tent and litter; and—I doubt, gentle reader, that even the length, the jar, and the confusion of this description is adequate to its subject, or that any word-painting of mine can convey a just idea of the scene.

This was the day appointed for our visiting the martyrs of Ohod. After praying the dawn prayers as directed at the Haram, we mounted our donkeys; and, armed with pistols and knives, we set out from the city. Our party was large. Saad the Demon had offered to accompany us, and the bustle around kept him in the best of humours; Umar Effendi was also there, quiet-looking and humble as usual, leading his ass to avoid the trouble of dismounting every second minute.[2]

I had the boy Mohammed and my 'slave', and Shaykh Hamid was attended by half a dozen relations. To avoid the crush of the Barr el-Manakhah, we made a *détour* westwards, over the bridge and down the course of the torrent-bed El-Sayh. We then passed along the southern wall of the castle, traversed

[1] One might as sensibly cry out 'John' in an English theatre.

[2] Respectable men in El-Hejaz, when they meet friends, acquaintances, or superiors, consider it only polite to dismount from a donkey.

its eastern outwork, and issued from the Bab el-Shami. During the greater part of the time we were struggling through a living tide; and among dromedaries and chargers a donkey is by no means a pleasant *monture*.

With some difficulty, but without any more serious accident than a fall or two, we found ourselves in the space beyond and northward of the city. This also was covered with travellers and tents, amongst which, on an eminence to the left of the road, rose conspicuous the bright green pavilion of the Emir El-Hajj, the commandant of the Caravan.[1] Hard by, half its height surrounded by a *Kanat* or tent wall, stood the Syrian or Sultan's Mahmal (litter), all glittering with green and gilding and gold, and around it were pitched the handsome habitations of the principal officers and grandees of the pilgrimage. On the right hand lay extensive palm plantations, and on the left, strewed over the plain, were signs of wells and tanks, built to supply the Hajj with water. We pass two small buildings, one the Kubbat El-Sabak, or Dome of Precedence, where the Prophet's warrior friends used to display their horsemanship; the second the Makan, or burial-place of Sayyidna Zaki el-Din, one of Mohammed's multitudinous descendants. Then we fall into a plain, resembling that of Kuba, but less fertile. While we are jogging over it, a few words concerning Mount Ohod may not be misplaced.

A popular distich says,

> Verily there is healing to the eye that looks
> Unto Ohod and the two Harrahs (ridges) near.

And of this holy hill the Apostle declared, 'Ohod is a Mountain which loves Us and which We love: it is upon the Gate of Heaven'; adding, 'and Ayr is a Place which hates Us and which We hate: it is upon the Gate of Hell.' The former sheltered Mohammed in the time of danger; therefore, on Resurrection Day it will be raised to Paradise: whereas Jebel Ayr, its neighbour,

[1] The title of the Pasha who has the privilege of conducting the Caravan. It is a lucrative as well as an honourable employment, for the Emir enjoys the *droit d'aubaine*, becoming heir to the personal property of all pilgrims who die in the holy cities or on the line of march. And no Persian, even of the poorest, would think of undertaking a pilgrimage by this line of country, without having at least 80*l.* in ready money with him.

having been so ill-judged as to refuse the Prophet water on an occasion while he thirsted, will be cast incontinently into Jehannum.

Moslem divines, be it observed, ascribe to Mohammed miraculous authority over animals, vegetables, and minerals, as well as over men, angels, and jinns. Hence the speaking wolf, the weeping post, the oil-stone, and the love and hate of these two mountains. It is probably one of the many remains of ancient paganism pulled down and afterwards used to build up the edifice of El-Islam. According to the old Persians, the sphere has an active soul. Some sects of Hindus believe 'mother earth', upon whose bosom we little parasites crawl, to be a living being. This was a dogma also amongst the ancient Egyptians, who denoted it by a peculiar symbol—the globe with human legs. Hence the Makrokosmos of the plagiaristic Greeks, the animal on a large scale, whose diminutive was the Mikrokosmos—man. *Tota natura*, repeats Malpighi, *existit in minimis*. Amongst the Romans, Tellus or Terra was a female deity, anthropomorphised according to their syncretic system, which furnished with strange gods their Pantheon, but forgot to append the scroll explaining the inner sense of the symbol. And some modern philosophers, Kepler, Blackmore, and others, have not scrupled to own their belief in a doctrine which as long as 'Life' is a mere word on man's tongue, can neither be proved nor disproved. The Mohammedans, as usual, exaggerate the dogma—a Hadis related by Abu Hurayrah casts on the day of judgment the sun and the moon into Hell-fire.

Jebel Ohod owes its present reputation to a cave which sheltered the Apostle when pursued by his enemies; to certain springs of which he drank, and especially to its being the scene of a battle celebrated in El-Islam.

On Saturday, the 11th Shawwal, in the third year of the Hijrah (26th January, AD 625), Mohammed with 700 men engaged 3,000 Infidels under the command of Abu Sufiyan; ran great personal danger, and lost his uncle Hamzah, the 'Lord of Martyrs'. On the topmost pinnacle, also, is the Kubbat Harun, the dome erected over Aaron's remains. It is now, I was told, in a ruinous condition, and is placed upon the 'pinnacle of seven hills' in a position somewhat like that of certain buildings on St Angelo in the Bay of Naples. Alluding to the toil of reaching it, the Madani quote a facetious rhyme inscribed upon the wall by one of their number who had wasted his breath:

Malun ibn Malun
Man talaa Kubbat Harun!

Anglice, 'The man must be a ruffian who climbs up to Aaron's dome.'

Devout Moslems visit Ohod every Thursday morning after the dawn devotions in the Haram; pray for the Martyrs; and, after going through the ceremonies, return to the Haram in time for midday worship. On the 12th Rajab, Zairs come out in large bodies from the city, encamp on the plain for three or four days, and pass the time in feasting, jollity, and devotion, as usual at pilgrimages and saints' festivals in general.

After half an hour's ride we came to the Mustarah or resting-place, so called because the Prophet sat here for a few minutes on his way to the battle of Ohod. It is a newly built square enclosure of dwarf whitewashed walls, within which devotees pray. On the outside fronting El-Medinah is a seat like a chair of rough stones. Here I was placed by my Muzawwir, who recited an insignificant supplication to be repeated after him. At its end with the Fatihah and accompaniments, we remounted our asses and resumed our way.

Travelling onwards, we came in sight of the second Harrah or ridge. It lies to the right and left of the road, and resembles lines of lava, but I had not an opportunity to examine it narrowly. Then we reached the gardens of Ohod, which reflect in miniature those of Kuba; and presently we arrived at what explained the presence of verdure and vegetable life—a deep Fiumara full of loose sand and large stones denoting an impetuous stream. It flows along the southern base of Ohod, said to be part of the plain of El-Medinah, and collects the drainage of the high lands lying to the south and south-east. The bed becomes impassable after rain, and sometimes the torrents overflow the neighbouring gardens. By the direction of this Fiumara I judged that it must supply the Ghabbah or basin in the hills north of the plain. Good authorities, however, informed me that a large volume of water will not stand there, but flows down the beds that wind through the Ghats westward of El-Medinah, and falls into the sea near the harbour of Wijh.

To the south of the Fiumara is a village on an eminence, containing some large brick houses now in a ruinous state; these are the villas of opulent and religious citizens who visited the place for change of air, recreation, and worship at Hamzah's tomb. Our donkeys presently sank fetlock-deep in the loose sand of the torrent-bed. Then reaching the northern side, and ascending a gentle slope, we found ourselves upon the battle-field.

This spot, so celebrated in the annals of El-Islam, is a shelving strip of land, close to the southern base of Mount Ohod. The army of the Infidels advanced from the Fiumara in crescent shape, with Abu Sufiyan, the general, and his idols in the centre. It is distant about three miles from El-Medinah, in a northerly direction. All the visitor sees is hard gravelly ground, covered with little heaps of various coloured granite, red sandstone, and bits of porphyry, to denote the different places where the martyrs fell, and were buried. Seen from this point, there is something appalling in the look of the Holy Mountain. Its seared and jagged flanks rise like masses of iron from the plain, and the crevice into which the Moslem host retired, when the disobedience of the archers in hastening to plunder enabled Khalid bin Walid to fall upon Mohammed's rear, is the only break in the grim wall. Reeking with heat, its surface produces not one green shrub or stunted tree; neither bird nor beast appeared upon its inhospitable sides, and the bright blue sky glaring above its bald and sullen brow, made it look only the more repulsive. I was glad to turn away my eyes from it.

To the left of the road north of the Fiumara, and leading to the mountains, stands Hamzah's Mosque, which, like the Haram of El-Medinah, is a Mausoleum as well as a fane. It is a small strongly built square of hewn stone, with a dome covering the solitary hypostyle to the south, and the usual minaret. The westward wing is a Zawiyah or oratory, frequented by the celebrated Sufi and Saint, Mohammed el-Samman, the 'Clarified-

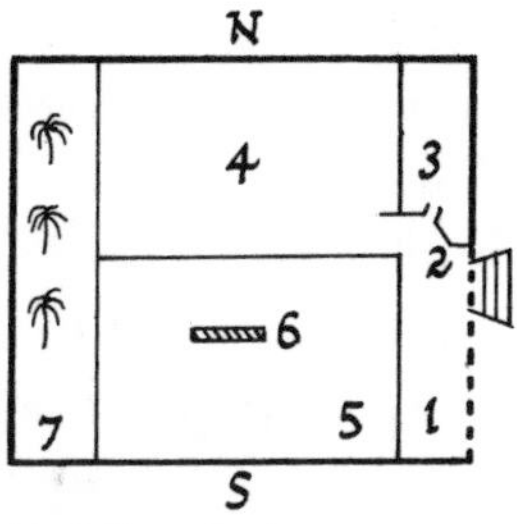

(1) Mastabah
(2) Entrance
(3) Passage leading to Minaret
(4) Hypaethra
(5) Hypostyle
(6) Hamzah's Tomb
(7) The Zawiyah and palm-trees

Butter-Seller', one of whose blood, the reader will remember, stood by my side in the person of Shaykh Hamid. On the eastern side of the building a half wing projects; and a small door opens to the south, upon a Mastabah or stone bench five or six feet high: this completes the square of the edifice. On the right of the road opposite Hamzah's Mosque, is a large erection, now in ruins, containing a deep hole leading to a well, with huge platforms for the accommodation of travellers. Beyond, towards the mountains, are the small edifices presently to be described.

Some Turkish women were sitting veiled upon the shady platform opposite the Martyrs' Mosque. At a little distance their husbands, and the servants holding horses and asses, lay upon the ground, and a large crowd of Bedawin, boys, girls, and old women, had gathered around to beg, draw water, and sell dry dates. They were awaiting the guardian, who had not yet acknowledged the summons. After half an hour's vain patience, we determined to proceed with the ceremonies. Ascending by its steps the Mastabah subtending half the eastern wall, Shaykh Hamid placed me so as to front the tomb. There, standing in the burning sun, we repeated the following prayer:

'Peace be upon Thee, O our Lord Hamzah! O Paternal Uncle of Allah's Apostle! O Paternal Uncle of Allah's Prophet! Peace be upon Thee, O Paternal Uncle of Mustafa! Peace be upon Thee, O Prince of the Martyrs! O Prince of the Happy! Peace be upon Thee, O Lion of Allah! O Lion of His Prophet!'

After which, we asked Hamzah and his companions to lend us their aid in obtaining for us and ours pardon, worldly prosperity, and future happiness. Scarcely had we finished when, mounted on a high-trotting dromedary, appeared the emissary of Mohammed Khalifah, descendant of El-Abbas, who keeps the key of the Mosque, and who receives the fees and donations of the devout. It was to be opened for the Turkish pilgrims. I waited to see the interior. The Arab drew forth from his pouch, with abundant solemnity, a bunch of curiously made keys, and sharply directed me to stand away from and out of sight of the door. When I obeyed, grumblingly, he began to rattle the locks, and to snap the padlocks, opening them slowly, shaking them, and making as much noise as possible. The reason of the precaution—it sounded like poetry if not sense—is this. It is believed that the souls of martyrs, leaving the habitations of their senseless clay, are fond of sitting together in spiritual converse, and profane eye must not fall upon the scene. What grand pictures these imaginative Arabs see! Conceive the majestic figures of the saints—for the soul with Mohammedans is like the old European spirit, a something immaterial in the shape of the body—with long grey beards, earnest faces, and solemn eyes, reposing beneath the palms, and discussing events now buried in the gloom of a thousand years.

I would fain be heard upon this superstition, but shame prevents. When in Nottingham, eggs may not be carried out after sunset; when Ireland hears Banshees, or apparitional old women, with streaming hair, and dressed in blue mantles; when Scotland sees a shroud about a person, showing his approaching death; when France has her *loup-garous, revenants*, and *poules du Vendredi Saint* (i.e. hens hatched on Good Friday supposed to change colour every year): as long as the Holy Coat cures devotees at Trèves, Madonnas wink at Rimini, San Januario melts at Naples, and Addolorate and Estatiche make converts to hysteria at Rome: whilst the Virgin manifests herself to children on the Alps and in France, whilst Germany sends forth Psychography, whilst Europe, the civilised, the enlightened, the sceptical, dotes over clairvoyance and table-turning, and whilst even hard-headed America believes in mediums, in snail-telegraphs, and spirit-rappings[1]—I must hold the men of El-Medinah to be as wise, and their superstition to be as respectable, as that of others.

But the realities of Hamzah's Mosque have little to recommend them. The building is like that of Kuba, only smaller; and the hypostyle is hung with oil-lamps and ostrich eggs, the usual

[1] In fairness I must confess to believing in the reality of these phenomena, but not in their spiritual origin.

Caravan on the road to Mecca

Mecca

The tomb of the Prophet's parents, Janaat el-Maala, Mecca

paltry furniture of an Arab mausoleum. On the walls are a few modern inscriptions and framed poetry, written in a caligraphic hand. Beneath the Riwak lies Hamzah, under a mass of black basaltic stone, resembling that of Aden, only more porous and scoriaceous, convex at the top, like a heap of earth, without the Kiswah, or cover of a saint's tomb, and railed round with wooden bars. At his head, or westward, lies Abdullah bin Jaysh, a name little known to fame, under a plain whitewashed tomb, also convex; and in the courtyard is a similar pile, erected over the remains of Shammas bin Usman, another obscure Companion.

We then passed through a door in the northern part of the western wall, and saw a diminutive palm plantation and a well. After which we left the Mosque, and I was under the 'fatal necessity' of paying a dollar for the honour of entering it. But the guardian promised that the chapters Y. S. and El-Ikhlas should be recited for my benefit, the latter forty times; and if their efficacy be one-twentieth part of what men say it is, the reader cannot quote against me a certain popular proverb concerning an order of men easily parted from their money.

Issuing from the Mosque, we advanced a few paces towards the mountain. On our left we passed by—at a respectful distance, for the Turkish Hajis cried out that their women were engaged in ablution—a large Sehrij or tank, built of cut stone with steps, and intended to detain the overflowing waters of the torrent. The next place we prayed at was a small square, enclosed with dwarf whitewashed walls, containing a few graves denoted by ovals of loose stones thinly spread upon the ground. This is primitive Arab simplicity. The Bedawin still mark the places of their dead with four stones planted at the head, the feet, and the sides; in the centre the earth is either heaped up Musannam (i.e. like the hump of a camel), or more generally left Musattah (level). I therefore suppose that the latter was the original shape of the Prophet's tomb.

Within the enclosure certain martyrs of the holy army were buried. After praying there, we repaired to a small building still nearer to the foot of the mountain. It is the usual cupola springing from four square walls, not in the best preservation. Here the Prophet prayed, and it is called the Kubbat el-Sanaya,

Dome of the Front Teeth, from the following circumstance. Five Infidels were bound by oath to slay Mohammed at the battle of Ohod: one of these, Ibn Kumayyah, threw so many stones, and with such goodwill, that two rings of the Prophet's helmet were driven into his cheek, and blood poured from his brow down his mustachios, which he wiped with a cloak to prevent the drops falling to the ground. Then Utbah bin Abi Wakkas hurled a stone at him, which, splitting his lower lip, knocked out one of his front teeth.

On the left of the Mihrab, inserted low down in the wall, is a square stone, upon which Shaykh Hamid showed me the impression of a tooth: he kissed it with peculiar reverence, and so did I. But the boy Mohammed being by me objurgated—for I remarked in him a jaunty demeanour combined with neglectfulness of ceremonies—saluted it sulkily, muttering the while hints about the holiness of his birthplace exempting him from the trouble of stooping. Already he had appeared at the Haram without his Jubbah, and with ungirt loins—in waistcoat and shirt-sleeves. Moreover, he had conducted himself indecorously by nudging Shaykh Hamid's sides during divine service. Feeling that the youth's 'moral man' was, like his physical, under my charge, and determined to arrest a course of conduct which must have ended in obtaining for me, the master, the reputation of a 'son of Belial', I insisted upon his joining us in the customary two-bow prayers. And Saad the Demon, taking my side of the question with his usual alacrity when a disturbance was in prospect, the youth found it necessary to yield.

After this little scene, Shaykh Hamid pointed out a sprawling inscription blessing the Companions of the Prophet. The unhappy Abubekr's name had been half-effaced by some fanatic Shiah, a circumstance which seemed to arouse all the evil in my companion's nature; and, looking close at the wall I found a line of Persian verse to this effect:

I am weary of my life (Umr),
because it bears the name of Umar.[1]

[1] In Persian characters, the words 'Umr', life, and 'Umar', the name of the hated Caliph, are written in the same way; which explains the pun.

We English wanderers are beginning to be shamed out of our 'vulgar' habit of scribbling names and nonsense in noted spots. Yet the practice is both classical and oriental. The Greeks and Persians left their marks everywhere, as Egypt shows; and the paws of the Sphinx bear scratches which, being interpreted, are found to be the same manner of trash as that written upon the remains of Thebes in AD 1879. And Easterns appear never to enter a building with a white wall without inditing upon it platitudes in verse and prose. Influenced by these considerations, I drew forth a pencil and inscribed in the Kubbat el-Sanaya,

Abdullah, the servant of Allah
(AH) 1269

Issuing from the dome, we turned a few paces to the left, passed northwards, and thus blessed the Martyrs of Ohod:

'Peace be upon Ye, O Martyrs! Peace be upon Ye, O Blessed! ye Pious! ye Pure! who fought upon Allah's Path the good Fight, who worshipped your Lord until He brought you to Certainty.[1] Peace be upon You of whom Allah said (viz., in the Koran), "Verily repute not them slain on God's Path (i.e. warring with Infidels); nay, rather they are alive, and there is no Fear upon them, nor are they sorrowful!" Peace be upon Ye, O Martyrs of Ohod! One and All, and the Mercy of Allah and His Blessings.'

Then again we moved a few paces forward and went through a similar ceremony, supposing ourselves to be in the

[1] That is to say, to the hour of death.

cave that sheltered the Apostle. After which, returning towards the torrent-bed by the way we came, we stood a small distance from a cupola called Kubbat el-Masra. It resembles that of the 'Front-teeth', and notes, as its name proves, the place where the gallant Hamzah fell by the spear of Wahshi the slave. We faced towards it and finished the ceremonies of this Ziyarat by a Supplication, the Testification, and the Fatihah.

In the evening I went with my friends to the Haram. The minaret galleries were hung with lamps, and the inside of the temple was illuminated. It was crowded with Hajis, amongst whom were many women, a circumstance which struck me from its being unusual. Some pious pilgrims, who had duly paid for the privilege, were perched upon ladders trimming wax candles of vast dimensions, others were laying up for themselves rewards in Paradise, by performing the same office to the lamps; many were going through the ceremonies of Ziyarat, and not a few were sitting in different parts of the Mosque apparently overwhelmed with emotion. The boys and the beggars were inspired with fresh energy, the Aghawat were gruffer and surlier than I had ever seen them, and the young men about town walked and talked with a freer and easier demeanour than usual. My old friends the Persians—there were about 1,200 of them in the Hajj caravan—attracted my attention. The doorkeepers stopped them with curses as they were about to enter, and all claimed from each the sum of 5 piastres, whilst other Moslems are allowed to enter the Mosque free. Unhappy men! they had lost all the Shiraz swagger; their mustachios drooped pitiably, their eyes would not look any one in the face, and not a head bore a cap stuck upon it crookedly.

Whenever an Ajemi, whatever might be his rank, stood in the way of an Arab or a Turk, he was rudely thrust aside, with abuse muttered loud enough to be heard by all around. All eyes followed them as they went through the ceremonies of Ziyarat, especially as they approached the tombs of Abubekr and Omar—which every man is bound to defile if he can—and the supposed place of Fatimah's burial. Here they stood in parties, after praying before the Prophet's window: one read from a book the pathetic tale of the Lady's life, sorrows, and mourning death, whilst the others listened to him with breathless attention. Sometimes their emotion was too strong to be repressed.

'Ay Fatimah! Ay Mazlumah! Way! way!—O Fatimah! O thou injured one! Alas! alas!' burst involuntarily from their lips, despite the danger of such exclamations; tears trickled down their hairy cheeks, and their brawny bosoms heaved with sobs. A strange sight it was to see rugged fellows, mountaineers perhaps, or the fierce Iliyat of the plains, sometimes weeping silently like children, sometimes shrieking like hysteric girls, and utterly careless to conceal a grief so coarse and grisly, at the same time so true and real, that I knew not how to behold it.

Then the Satanic scowls with which they passed by or pretended to pray at the hated Omar's tomb! With what curses their hearts are belying those mouths full of blessings! How they are internally canonising Fayruz—the Persian slave who stabbed Omar in the Mosque—and praying for his eternal happiness in the presence of the murdered man! Sticks and stones, however, and not unfrequently the knife and the sabre, have taught them the hard lesson of disciplining their feelings; and nothing but a furious contraction of the brow, a roll of the eye, intensely vicious, and a twitching of the muscles about the region of the mouth, denotes the wild storm of wrath within. They generally, too, manage to discharge some part of their passion in words.

'Hail Omar, thou hog!'

exclaims some fanatic Madani as he passes by the heretic—a demand more outraging than requiring a red-hot, black-north Protestant to bless the Pope.

'O Allah! *hell* him!'

meekly responds the Persian, changing the benediction to a curse most intelligible to, and most delicious in, his fellows' ears. I have heard of a Persian being beaten to death, because, instead of saying 'Peace be with thee, Ya Omar,' he insisted upon saying 'Peace be with thee, Ya Humar (O ass!)' A favourite trick is to change 'Razi Allahu anhu'—May Allah be satisfied with him!—to 'Razi Allahu Aan'. This last word is not to be found in Richardson, but any Luti from Shiraz or Isfahan can make it intelligible to the curious linguist.

An evening hour in the steamy heat of the Haram was equal to half a dozen afternoons; and I left it resolved never to revisit it till the Hajj departed from El-Medinah. It was only prudent not to see much of the Ajamis; and as I did so somewhat ostentatiously, my companions discovered that the Shaykh Abdullah, having slain many of those heretics in some war or other, was avoiding them to escape retaliation. In proof of my generalistic qualities, the rolling down of the water-jar upon the heads of the Maghrabi pilgrims in the *Golden Wire* was quoted, and all offered to fight for me *à l'outrance.*

I took care not to contradict the report.

XXI
The People of El-Medinah

El-Medinah contains but few families descended from the Prophet's Auxiliaries. I heard only of four whose genealogy is undoubted. These were—

(1) The Bayt el-Ansari, or descendants of Abu Ayyub, a most noble race whose tree ramifies through a space of 1,500 years. They keep the keys of the Kuba Mosque, and are Imams in the Haram, but the family is no longer wealthy or powerful.

(2) The Bayt Abu Jud: they supply the Haram with Imams and Muezzins. I was told that there are now but two surviving members of this family, a boy and a girl.

(3) The Bayt el-Shaab, a numerous race. Some of the members travel professionally, others trade, and others are employed in the Haram.

(4) The Bayt el-Karrani, who are mostly engaged in commerce.

There is also a race called el-Nakhawilah, who, according to some, are descendants of the Ansar, whilst others derive them from Yezid, the son of Muawiyah: the latter opinion is improbable, as the Caliph in question was a mortal foe to Ali's family, which is inordinately venerated by these people. As far as I could ascertain, they abuse the Shaykhayn (Abubekr and Omar): all my informants agreed upon this point, but none could tell me why they neglected to bedevil Osman, the third object of hatred to the Shiah persuasion. They are numerous and warlike, yet they are despised by the townspeople, because they openly profess heresy, and are moreover of humble degree. They have their own priests and instructors, although subject to the orthodox Kazi; marry in their own sect, are confined to low offices, such as slaughtering animals, sweeping, and gardening, and are not allowed to enter the Haram during life, or to be carried to it after death. Their corpses are taken down an outer street called the Darb el-Jenazah—Road of Biers—to their own cemetery near

El-Bakia. They dress and speak Arabic, like the townspeople; but the Arabs pretend to distinguish them by a peculiar look denoting their degradation: it is doubtless the mistake of effect for cause, made about all such

Tribes of the wandering foot and weary breast.

A number of reports are current about the horrid customs of these people, and their community of women with the Persian pilgrims who pass through the town. It need scarcely be said that such tales coming from the mouths of fanatic foes are not to be credited. I regret not having had an opportunity to become intimate with any of the Nakhawilah, from whom curious information might be elicited. Orthodox Moslems do not like to be questioned about such hateful subjects; when I attempted to learn something from one of my acquaintance, Shaykh Ula el-Din, of a Kurd family, settled at El-Medinah, a man who had travelled over the East, and who spoke five languages to perfection, he coldly replied that he had never consorted with heretics.

Sayyids and Sherifs,[1] the descendants of the Prophet, here abound. The Benu Husayn of El-Medinah have their headquarters at Suwayrkiyah: the former place contains six or seven families; the latter, ninety-three or ninety-four. Anciently they were much more numerous, and such was their power, that for centuries they retained charge of the Prophet's tomb. They subsist principally upon their Amlak, property in land, for which they have title-deeds extending back to Mohammed's day, and Aukaf, religious bequests; popular rumour accuses them of frequent murders for the sake of succession. At El-Medinah they live chiefly at the Hosh Ibn Saad, a settlement outside the town and south of the Darb el-Jenazah. There is, however, no objection to their dwelling within the walls; and they are taken to the Haram after death, if there be no evil report against the individid-

[1] In Arabia the Sherif is the descendant of Hasan through his two sons, Zayd and Hasan el-Musanna: the Sayyid is the descendant of Husayn through Zayn el-Abidin, the sole of twelve children who survived the fatal field of Kerbela. The former devotes himself to government and war, the latter to learning and religion. In Persia and India, the Sherif is the son of a Sayyid woman and a common Moslem. The Sayyid Nejib el-Taraf (noble on one side) is the son of a Sayyid father and a common Moslemah. The Sayyid Nejib el-Tarafayn (noble on both sides) is one whose parents are both Sayyids.

ual. Their burial-place is the Bakia cemetery. The reason of this toleration is, that some are supposed to be Sunni, or orthodox, and even the most heretical keep their Rafz (heresy) a profound secret. Most learned Arabs believe that they belong, like the Persians, to the sect of Ali; the truth, however, is so vaguely known, that I could find out none of the peculiarities of their faith, till I met a Shirazi friend at Bombay.

The Benu Husayn are spare dark men of Bedawi appearance, and they dress in the old Arab style still affected by the Sherifs—a Kufiyah (kerchief) on the head, and a Benish, a long and wide-sleeved garment resembling our magicians' gown, thrown over the white cotton Kamis (shirt): in public they always carry swords, even when others leave weapons at home. There are about 200 families of Sayyid Alawiyah—descendants of Ali by any of his wives but Fatimah—they bear no distinctive mark in dress or appearance, and are either employed at the temple or engage in trade. Of the Khalifiyyah, or descendants of Abbas, there is, I am told, but one household, the Bayt el-Khalifah, who act as Imams in the Haram, and have charge of Hamzah's tomb. Some declare that there are a few of the Siddikiyah, or descendants from Abubekr; others ignore them, and none could give me any information about the Benu Najjar.

The rest of the population of El-Medinah is a motley race composed of offshoots from every nation in El-Islam. The sanctity of the city attracts strangers, who, purposing to stay but a short time, become residents; after finding some employment, they marry, have families, die, and are buried there with an eye to the spiritual advantages of the place. I was much importuned to stay at El-Medinah. The only known physician was one Shaykh Abdullah Sahib, an Indian, a learned man, but of so melancholic a temperament, and so ascetic in his habits, that his knowledge was entirely lost to the public. 'Why dost thou not', said my friends, 'hire a shop somewhere near the Prophet's Mosque? There thou wilt eat bread by thy skill, and thy soul will have the blessing of being on holy ground.' Shaykh Nur also opined after a short residence at El-Medinah that it was *bara jannati Shahr*, a 'very heavenly City', and little would have induced him to make it his home.

The present ruling race at El-Medinah, in consequence of political vicissitudes, are the Sufat, sons of Turkish fathers by Arab mothers. These half-castes are now numerous, and have managed to secure the highest and most lucrative offices. Besides Turks, there are families originally from the Maghrib, Takruris, Egyptians in considerable numbers, settlers from Yemen and other parts of Arabia, Syrians, Kurds, Afghans, Daghistanis from the Caucasus, and a few Jawis—Java Moslems. The Sindís, I was told, reckon about 100 families, who are exceedingly despised for their cowardice and want of manliness, whilst the Beloch and the Afghan are respected. The Indians are not so numerous in proportion here as at Meccah; still Hindostani is by no means uncommonly heard in the streets. They preserve their peculiar costume, the women persisting in showing their faces, and in wearing tight, exceedingly tight, pantaloons. This, together with other reasons, secures for them the contempt of the Arabs. At El-Medinah they are generally small shopkeepers, especially druggists and sellers of Kumash (cloth), and they form a society of their own. The terrible cases of misery and starvation which so commonly occur among the improvident Indians at Jeddah and Meccah are here rare.

The Hanafi school holds the first rank at El-Medinah, as in most parts of El-Islam, although many of the citizens, and almost all the Bedawin, are Shafeis. The reader will have remarked with astonishment that at one of the fountain-heads of the faith, there are several races of schismatics, the Benu Husayn, the Benu Ali, and the Nakhawilah. At the town of Safra there are said to be a number of the Zuyud schismatics,[1] who visit El-Medinah, and have settled in force at Meccah, and some declare that the Bayazi[2] sect also exists.

The citizens of El-Medinah are a favoured race, although their city is not, like Meccah, the grand mart of the Moslem world or the meeting-place of nations. They pay no taxes, and reject the idea of a Miri, or land-cess, with extreme disdain. 'Are

[1] Plural of Zaydi. These are well-known schismatics of the Shiah persuasion, who abound in Southern Arabia.

[2] The Bayazi sect flourishes near Maskat, whose Imam or Prince, it is said, belongs to the heretical persuasion. It rejects Osman, and advocates the superiority of Omar over the other two Caliphs.

we, the children of the Prophet,' they exclaim, 'to support or to be supported?' The Wahhabis, not understanding the argument, taxed them, as was their wont, in specie and in materials, for which reason the very name of those puritans is an abomination. As has before been shown, all the numerous attendants at the Mosque are paid partly by the Sultan, partly by Aukaf, the rents of houses and lands bequeathed to the shrine, and scattered over every part of the Moslem world. When a Madani is inclined to travel, he applies to the Mudir el-Haram, and receives from him a paper which entitles him to the receipt of a considerable sum at Constantinople. The Ikram (honorarium), as it is called, varies with the rank of the recipient, the citizens being divided into these four orders, viz.,

First and highest, the Sadat (Sayyids) and Imams, who are entitled to twelve purses, or about 60*l.* Of these there are said to be 300 families.

The Khanahdan, who keep open house and receive poor strangers gratis. Their Ikram amounts to eight purses, and they number from 100 to 150 families.

The Ahali (burghers) or Madani properly speaking, who have homes and families, and were born in El-Medinah. They claim six purses.

The Mujawirin, strangers, as Egyptians or Indians, settled at, though not born in, El-Medinah. Their honorarium is four purses.

The Madani traveller, on arrival at Constantinople, reports his arrival to his consul, the Wakil el-Haramayn. This 'Agent of the two Holy Places' applies to the Nazir el-Aukaf, or Intendant of Bequests; the latter, after transmitting the demand to the different officers of the treasury, sends the money to the Wakil, who delivers it to the applicant. This gift is sometimes squandered in pleasure, more often profitably invested either in merchandise or in articles of home-use, presents of dress and jewellery for the women, handsome arms, especially pistols and Balas (yataghans), silk tassels, amber pipe-pieces, slippers, and embroidered purses. They are packed up in one or two large Sahharahs, and then commences the labour of returning home gratis. Besides the Ikram, most of the Madani, when upon these begging trips, are received as guests by great men at Constantinople. The citizens whose turn it is not to travel, await the Aukaf and Sadakat (bequests and alms), forwarded every year by the Damascus caravan; besides which, as has been before explained, the Haram supplies even those not officially employed in it with many perquisites.

Without these advantages El-Medinah would soon be abandoned to cultivators and Bedawin. Though commerce is here honourable, as everywhere in the East, business is slack, because the higher classes prefer the idleness of administering their landed estates, and being servants to the Mosque. I heard of only four respectable houses, El-Isawi, El-Shaab, Abd el-Jawwad, and a family from El-Shark (the Eastern Region). They all deal in grain, cloth, and provisions, and perhaps the richest have a capital of 20,000 dollars. Caravans in the cold weather are constantly passing between El-Medinah and Egypt, but they are rather bodies of visitors to Constantinople than traders travelling for gain. Corn is brought from Jeddah by land, and imported into Yambu' or via El-Rais, a port on the Red Sea, one day and a half's journey from Safra. There is an active provision trade with the neighbouring Bedawin, and the Syrian Hajj supplies the citizens with apparel and articles of luxury—tobacco, dried fruits, sweetmeats, knives, and all that is included under the word 'notions'.

There are few storekeepers, and their dealings are petty, because articles of every kind are brought from Egypt, Syria, and Constantinople. As a general rule, labour is exceedingly expensive, and at the Visitation time a man will demand 15 or 20 piastres from a stranger for such a trifling job as mending an umbrella. Handicraftsmen and artisans—carpenters, masons, locksmiths, potters, and others—are either slaves or foreigners, mostly Egyptians. This proceeds partly from the pride of the people. They are taught from their childhood that the Madani is a favoured being, to be respected however vile or schismatic; and that the vengeance of Allah will fall upon any one who ventures to abuse, much more to strike him. They receive a stranger at the shop window with the haughtiness of Pashas, and take pains to show him, by words as well as by looks, that they consider themselves as 'good gentlemen as the king, only not so rich'. Added to this pride are indolence, and the true Arab prejudice, which, even in the present day, prevents a Bedawi from marrying the daughter of an artisan. Like Castilians, they consider labour humiliating to any but a slave; nor is this, as a clever French author remarks, by any means an unreasonable idea, since Heaven, to punish man for disobedience, caused him to eat daily bread by the sweat of his brow. Besides, there *is* degradation, moral and physical, in handiwork compared with the freedom of the Desert. The loom and the file do not conserve courtesy and chivalry like the sword and spear; man 'extends his tongue', to use an Arab phrase, when a cuff and not a stab is to be the consequence of an injurious expression. Even the ruffian becomes polite in California, where his brother-ruffian carries a revolver, and those European nations who were most polished when every gentleman wore a rapier, have become the rudest since Civilisation disarmed them.

El-Medinah is not a cheap place. Yet the citizens, despite their being generally in debt, manage to live well. Their cookery, like that of Meccah, has borrowed something from Egypt, Turkey, Syria, Persia, and India: as all Orientals, they are exceedingly fond of clarified butter. I have seen the boy Mohammed drink off nearly a tumbler-full, although his friends warned him that it would make him as fat as an elephant. When a man cannot enjoy clarified butter in these countries, it is considered a sign that his stomach is out of order, and all my excuses of a melancholic temperament were required to be in full play to prevent the infliction of fried meat swimming in grease, or that guest-dish, rice saturated with melted—perhaps I should say—rancid butter. The Samn of El-Hejaz, however, is often fresh, being brought in by the Bedawin; it has not therefore the foul flavour derived from the old and impregnated skin-bag which distinguishes the ghi of India.

The house of a Madani in good circumstances is comfortable, for the building is substantial, and the attendance respectable. Black slave-girls here perform the complicated duties of servant-maids in England; they are taught to sew, to cook, and to wash, besides sweeping the house and drawing water for domestic use. Hasinah (the 'Charmer', a decided misnomer) costs from 40 to 50 dollars: if she be a mother, her value is less; but neat-handedness, propriety of demeanour, and skill in feminine accomplishments, raise her to 100 dollars = 25*l.* A little black boy, perfect in all his points, and tolerably intelligent, costs about 1,000 piastres; girls are dearer, and eunuchs fetch double that sum. The older the children become, the more their value diminishes; and no one would purchase, save under exceptional circumstances, an adult slave, because he is never parted with but for some incurable vice. The Abyssinian, mostly Galla, girls, so much prized because their skins are always cool in the hottest weather, are here rare; they seldom sell for less than 20*l.*, and they often fetch 60*l.* I never heard of a Jariyah Bayza, a white slave-girl, being in the market at El-Medinah: in Circassia they fetch from 100*l.* to 400*l.* prime cost, and few men in El-Hejaz could afford so expensive a luxury. The Bazar at El-Medinah is poor, and as almost all the slaves are brought from Meccah by the Jallabs, or drivers, after exporting the best to Egypt, the town receives only the refuse.

The personal appearance of the Madani makes the stranger wonder how this mongrel population of settlers has acquired a peculiar and almost an Arab physiognomy. They are remarkably fair, the effect of a cold climate; sometimes the cheeks are lighted up with red, and the hair in a dark chestnut—at El-Medinah I was not stared at as a white man. The cheeks and different parts of the children's bodies are sometimes marked with Mashali or Tashrih, not the three long stripes of the Meccans, but little scars generally in threes. In some points they approach very near the true Arab type, that is to say, the Bedawin of ancient and noble family. The cheek-bones are high and *saillant*, the eye small, more round than long, piercing, fiery, deep-set, and brown rather than black. The head is small, the ears well-cut, the face long and oval, though not unfrequently disfigured by what is popularly called the lantern-jaw; the forehead high, bony, broad, and slightly retreating, and the beard and mustachios scanty, consisting of two tufts upon the chin, with, generally speaking, little or no whisker. These are the points of resemblance between the city and the country

Arab. The difference is equally remarkable. The temperament of the Madani is not purely nervous, like that of the Bedawin, but admits a large admixture of the bilious and, though rarely, the lymphatic. The cheeks are fuller, the jaws project more than in the pure race, the lips are more fleshy, more sensual and ill-fitting; the features are broader, and the limbs are stouter and more bony. The beard is a little thicker, and the young Arabs of the towns are beginning to imitate the Turks in that abomination to their ancestors—shaving. Personal vanity, always a ruling passion among Orientals, and a hopeless wish to emulate the flowing beards of the Turks and the Persians—perhaps the only nations in the world who ought not to shave the chin—have overruled even the religious objections to such innovation. I was more frequently appealed to at El-Medinah than anywhere else, for some means of removing the opprobrium Kusah, or scant-bearded man. They blacken the beard with gall-nuts, henna, and other preparations, especially the Egyptian mixture, composed of sulphate of iron one part, ammoniure of iron one part, and gall-nuts two parts, infused in eight parts of distilled water. It is a very bad dye.

Much refinement of dress is now found at El-Medinah—Constantinople, the Paris of the East, supplying it with the newest fashions. Respectable men wear either a Benish or a Jubbah; the latter, as at Meccah, is generally of some light and flashy colour, gamboge, yellow, tender green, or bright pink. This is the sign of a 'dressy' man. If you have a single coat, it should be of some modest colour, as a dark violet; to appear always in the same tender green, or bright pink, would excite derision. But the Hejazis, poor and rich, always prefer these tulip tints. The proper Badan, or long coat without sleeves, still worn in truly Arab countries, is here confined to the lowest classes. That ugliest of head-dresses, the red Tunisian cap, called Tarbush, is much used, only the Arabs have too much regard for their eyes and faces to wear it, as the Turks do, without a turban. It is with regret that one sees the most graceful head-gear imaginable, the Kufiyah and the Aakal, proscribed except amongst the Sherifs and the Bedawin.

The women dress, like the men, handsomely. Indoors they

wear, I am told, a Sudayriyah, or boddice of calico and other stuffs, like the Choli of India, which supports the bosom without the evils of European stays. Over this is a *Saub*, or white shirt, of the white stuff called Halaili or Burunjuk, with enormous sleeves, and flowing down to the feet; the Sarwal or pantaloons are not wide, like the Egyptians', but rather tight, approaching to the Indian cut, without its exaggeration. Abroad, they throw over the head a silk or a cotton Milayah, generally chequered white and blue. The Burka (face-veil), all over El-Hejaz, is white, a decided improvement in point of cleanliness upon that of Egypt. Women of all ranks dye the soles of the feet and the palms of the hands black; and trace thin lines down the inside of the fingers, by first applying a plaster of henna and then a mixture, called Shadar, of gall-nuts, alum, and lime. The hair, parted in the centre, is plaited into about twenty little twists called Jadilah. Of ornaments, as usual among Orientals, they have a vast variety, ranging from brass and spangles to gold and precious stones; and they delight in strong perfumes—musk, civet, ambergris, ottar of rose, oil of jasmine, aloe-wood, and extract of cinnamon. Both sexes wear Constantinople slippers. The women draw on Khuff, inner slippers, of bright yellow leather, serving for socks, and covering the ancle, with Papush of the same material, sometimes lined with velvet and embroidered with a gold sprig under the hollow of the foot. In mourning the men show no difference of dress, like good Moslems, to whom such display of grief is forbidden. But the women, who cannot dissociate the heart and the toilette, evince their sorrow by wearing white clothes and by doffing their ornaments. This is a modern custom: the accurate Burckhardt informs us that in his day the women of El-Medinah did not wear mourning.

The Madani generally appear abroad on foot. Few animals are kept here, on account, I suppose, of the expense of feeding them. The Cavalry are mounted on poor Egyptian nags. The horses ridden by rich men are generally Nejdi, costing from 200 to 300 dollars. Camels are numerous, but those bred in El-Hejaz are small, weak, and consequently little prized. Dromedaries of good breed, called Ahrar (the noble) and Namani, from the place of that name, are to be had for any sum between 10 and 400 dollars; they are diminutive, but exceedingly swift, sure-footed, sagacious, thoroughbred, with eyes like the antelope's, and muzzles that would almost enter a tumbler. Mules are not found at El-Medinah, although popular prejudice does not now forbid the people to mount them. Asses come from Egypt and Meccah: I am told that some good animals are to be found in the town, and that certain ignoble Bedawi clans have a fine breed, but I never saw any.

Of beasts intended for food, the sheep is the only common one in this part of El-Hejaz. There are three distinct breeds. The larger animal comes from Nejd and the Anizah Bedawin, who drive a flourishing trade; the smaller is a native of the country. Both are the common Arab species, of a tawny colour, with a long fat tail. Occasionally one meets with what at Aden is called the Berberah sheep, a totally different beast—white, with a black broad face, a dew-lap, and a short fat tail, that looks as if twisted up into a knot: it was doubtless introduced by the Persians. Cows are rare at El-Medinah. Beef throughout the East is considered an unwholesome food, and the Bedawin will not drink cow's milk, preferring that of the camel, the ewe, and the goat. The flesh of the latter animal is scarcely ever eaten in the city, except by the poorest classes.

The manners of the Madani are graver and somewhat more pompous than those of any Arabs with whom I ever mixed. This they appear to have borrowed from their rulers, the Turks. But their austerity and ceremoniousness are skin-deep. In intimacy or in anger the garb of politeness is thrown off, and the screaming Arab voice, the voluble, copious, and emphatic abuse, and the mania for gesticulation, return in all their deformity.

They are great talkers, as the following little trait shows. When a man is opposed to more than his match in disputing or bargaining, instead of patiently saying to himself, *S'il crache il est mort*, he interrupts the adversary with a *Sall' ala Mohammed* —'Bless the Prophet.' Every good Moslem is obliged to obey such requisition by responding, *Allahumma salli alayh*—'O Allah bless him!' But the Madani curtails the phrase to 'A'n', supposing it to be an equivalent, and proceeds in his loquacity. Then perhaps the baffled opponent will shout out *Wahhid*, i.e. 'Attest the unity of the Deity'; when, instead of employing the usual religious phrases to assert that dogma, he will briefly ejaculate 'Al', and hurry on with the course of conversation. As it may be supposed, these wars of words frequently end in violent quarrels; for, to do the Madani justice, they are always ready to fight. The desperate old feud between the Juwwa and the Barra—the town and the suburbs—has been put down with the greatest difficulty. The boys, indeed, still keep it up, turning out in bodies and making determined onslaughts with sticks and stones.

It is not to be believed that in a town garrisoned by Turkish troops, full of travelled traders, and which supports itself by plundering Hajis, the primitive virtues of the Arab could exist. The Meccans, a dark people, say of the Madani, that their hearts are black as their skins are white. This is of course exaggerated; but it is not too much to assert that pride, pugnacity, a peculiar point of honour, and a vindictiveness of wonderful force and patience, are the only characteristic traits of Arab character which the citizens of El-Medinah habitually display. Here you meet with scant remains of the chivalry of the desert. A man will abuse his guest, even though he will not dine without him, and would protect him bravely against an enemy. And words often pass lightly between individuals which suffice to cause a blood-feud amongst Bedawin.

The outward appearance of decorum is conspicuous amongst the Madani. There are no places where Corinthians dwell, as at Meccah, Cairo, and Jeddah. Adultery, if detected, would be punished by lapidation according to the rigour of the Koranic law; and simple immorality by religious stripes, or, if of repeated occurrence, by expulsion from the city. But scandals seldom occur, and the women, I am told, behave with great decency. Abroad, they have the usual Moslem pleasures of marriage, lyings-in, circumcision feasts, holy visitations, and funerals. At home, they employ themselves with domestic matters, and especially in scolding Hasinah and Zaafaran. In this occupation they surpass even the notable English housekeeper of the middle orders of society—the latter being confined to 'knagging', at her slavey, whereas the Arab lady is allowed an unbounded extent of vocabulary. At Shaykh Hamid's house, however, I cannot accuse the women of

Swearing into strong shudders
The immortal gods who heard them.

They abused the black girls with unction, but without any violent expletives. At Meccah, however, the old lady in whose house I was living would, when excited by the melancholy temperament of her eldest son and his irregular hours of eating, scold him in the grossest terms, not unfrequently ridiculous in the extreme. For instance, one of her assertions was that he—the son—was the offspring of an immoral mother; which assertion, one might suppose, reflected not indirectly upon herself. So in Egypt I have frequently heard a father, when reproving his boy, address him by 'O dog, son of a dog!' and 'O spawn of an Infidel—of a Jew—of a Christian!'

Amongst the men of El-Medinah I remarked a considerable share of hypocrisy. Their mouths were as full of religious salutations, exclamations, and hackneyed quotations from the Koran, as of indecency and vile abuse—a point in which they resemble the Persians. As before observed, they preserve their reputation as the sons of a holy city by praying only in public. At Constantinople they are by no means remarkable for sobriety. Intoxicating liquors, especially *Raki*, are made in El-Medinah, only by the Turks: the citizens seldom indulge in this way at home, as detection by smell is imminent among a people of water-bibbers.

The Madani are, like the Meccans, a curious mixture of generosity and meanness, of profuseness and penuriousness. But the former quality is the result of ostentation, the latter is a characteristic of the Semitic race, long ago made familiar to Europe by the Jew. The citizens will run deeply in debt, expecting a good season of devotees to pay off their liabilities, or relying upon the next begging trip to Turkey; and such a proceeding, contrary to the custom of the Moslem world, is not condemned by public opinion. Above all their qualities, personal conceit is remarkable: they show it in their strut, in their looks, and almost in every word. 'I am such a one, the son of such a one,' is a common expletive, especially in times of danger; and this spirit is not wholly to be condemned, as it certainly acts as an incentive to gallant actions. But it often excites them to vie with one another in expensive entertainments and similar vanities. The expression, so offensive to English ears, *Inshallah Bukra*—'Please God, to-morrow'—always said about what should be done to-day, is here common as in Egypt or in India. This procrastination belongs more or less to all Orientals. But Arabia especially abounds in the *Tanakkal al' Allah, ya Shaykh!*—'Place thy reliance upon Allah, O Shaykh!'—enjoined when a man should depend upon his own exertions. Upon the whole, however, though alive to the infirmities of the Madani character, I thought favourably of it, finding among this people more of the redeeming point, manliness, than in most eastern nations with whom I am acquainted.

The Arabs, like the Egyptians, all marry. Yet, as usual, they are hard and facetious upon that ill-treated subject—matrimony. It has exercised the brain of their wits and sages, who have not failed to indite notable things concerning it. Saith Harikar el-Hakim (Dominie Do-all) to his nephew Nadan (Sir Witless), whom he would dissuade from taking to himself a wife, 'Marriage is joy for a month and sorrow for a life, and the paying of settlements and the breaking of back (i.e. under the load of misery), and the listening to a woman's tongue!' And again we have in verse:

> They said, 'Marry!' I replied, 'Far be it from me
> To take to my bosom a sackful of snakes.
> I am free; why then become a slave?
> May Allah never bless womankind.'

And the following lines are generally quoted, as affording a kind of bird's-eye view of female existence:

> From 10 (years of age) unto 20,
> A repose to the eyes of beholders.
> From 20 unto 30,
> Still fair and full of flesh.

From 30 unto 40,
A mother of many boys and girls.
From 40 unto 50,
An old woman of the deceitful.
From 50 unto 60,
Slay her with a knife.
From 60 unto 70,
The curse of Allah upon them, one and all!

Another popular couplet makes a most unsupported assertion:

They declare womankind to be heaven to man;
I say, 'Allah, give me Jehannum, and not this heaven.'

Yet the fair sex has the laugh on its side, for these railers, at El-Medinah as at other places, invariably marry.

The marriage ceremony is tedious and expensive. It begins with a Khitbah or betrothal: the father of the young man repairs to the parent or guardian of the girl, and at the end of his visit exclaims, 'The Fatihah! we beg of your kindness your daughter for our son.' Should the other be favourable to the proposal, his reply is, 'Welcome and congratulation to you: but we must perform Istikharah (religious lot-casting)'; and, when consent is given, both pledge themselves to the agreement by reciting the Fatihah. Then commence negotiations about the Mahr or sum settled upon the bride; and after the smoothing of this difficulty follow feastings of friends and relatives, male and female. The marriage itself is called Akd el-Nikah or Ziwaj. A Walimah or banquet is prepared by the father of the Aris (groom), at his own house, and the Kazi attends to perform the nuptial ceremony, the girl's consent being obtained through her Wakil, any male relation whom she commissions to act for her. Then, with great pomp and circumstance, the Aris visits his Arusah (bride) at her father's house; and finally, with a procession and sundry ceremonies at the Haram, she is brought to her new home.

Arab funerals are as simple as their marriages are complicated. Neither Naddabah (myriologist or hired keener), nor indeed any female, even a relation, is present at burials as in other parts of the Moslem world, and it is esteemed disgraceful for a man to weep aloud. The Prophet, who doubtless had heard of those pagan mournings, where an effeminate and unlimited display of woe was often terminated by licentious excesses, like the Christian's half-heathen wakes, forbade aught beyond a decent demonstration of grief. And his strong good sense enabled him to see through the vanity of professional mourners. At El-Medinah the corpse is interred shortly after decease. The bier is carried through the streets at a moderate pace, by friends and relatives, these bringing up the rear. Every man who passes lends his shoulder for a minute, a mark of respect to the dead, and also considered a pious and a prayerful act. Arrived at the Haram, they carry the corpse in visitation to the Prophet's window, and pray over it at Osman's niche. Finally, it is interred after the usual Moslem fashion in the cemetery El-Bakia.

El-Medinah, though pillaged by the Wahhabis, still abounds in books. Near the Haram are two Madrasah or colleges, the Mahmudiyah, so called from Sultan Mahmud, and that of Bashir Agha: both have large stores of theological and other works. I also heard of extensive private collections, particularly of one belonging to the Nejib el-Ashraf, or chief of the Sherifs, a certain Mohammed Jamal el-Layl, whose father is well known in India. Besides which, there is a large Wakf or bequest of books, presented to the Mosque or entailed upon particular families. The celebrated Mohammed Ibn Abdillah el-Sannusi has removed his collection, amounting it is said to 8,000 volumes, from El-Medinah to his house in Jebel Kubays at Meccah.

The burial-place of the Prophet, therefore, no longer lies open to the charge of utter ignorance brought against it by my predecessor.[1] The people now praise their Olema for learning, and boast a superiority in respect of science over Meccah. Yet many students leave the place for Damascus and Cairo, where the Riwak El-Haramayn (College of the Two Shrines) in the Azhar Mosque-University is always crowded; and though Umar Effendi boasted to me that his city was full of lore, he did not appear the less anxious to attend the lectures of Egyptian

[1] Burckhardt's *Travels in Arabia*, vol. ii, p. 174.

professors. But none of my informants claimed for El-Medinah any facilities of studying other than the purely religious sciences. Philosophy, medicine, arithmetic, mathematics, and algebra cannot be learnt here. I was careful to inquire about the occult sciences, remembering that Paracelsus had travelled in Arabia, and that the Count Cagliostro (Giuseppe Balsamo), who claimed the Meccan Sherif as his father, asserted that about AD 1765 he had studied alchemy at El-Medinah. The only trace I could find was a superficial knowledge of the Magic Mirror.

But after denying the Madani the praise of varied learning, it must be owned that their quick observation and retentive memories have stored up for them an abundance of superficial knowledge, culled from conversations in the market and in the camp. I found it impossible here to display those feats which in Sind, Southern Persia, Eastern Arabia, and many parts of India, would be looked upon as miraculous. Most probably one of the company had witnessed the performance of some Italian conjuror at Constantinople or Alexandria, and retained a lively recollection of every manoeuvre. As linguists they are not equal to the Meccans, who surpass all Orientals excepting only the Armenians; the Madani seldom know Turkish, and more rarely still Persian and Indian. Those only who have studied in Egypt chaunt the Koran well. The citizens speak and pronounce their language purely; they are not equal to the people of the southern Hejaz, still their Arabic is refreshing after the horrors of Cairo and Maskat.

The classical Arabic, be it observed, in consequence of an extended empire, soon split up into various dialects, as the Latin under similar circumstances separated into the Neo-Roman patois of Italy, Sicily, Provence, and Languedoc. And though Niebuhr has been deservedly censured for comparing the Koranic language to Latin and the vulgar tongue to Italian, still there is a great difference between them, almost every word having undergone some alteration in addition to the manifold changes and simplifications of grammar and syntax. The traveller will hear in every part of Arabia that some distant tribe preserves the linguistic purity of its ancestors, uses final vowels with the noun, and rejects the addition of the pronoun which apocope in the verb now renders necessary. But I greatly doubt the existence of such a race of philologists. In El-Hejaz, however, it is considered graceful in an old man, especially when conversing publicly, to lean towards classical Arabic. On the contrary, in a youth this would be treated as pedantic affectation, and condemned in some such satiric quotation as

> There are two things colder than ice,
> A young old man, and an old young man.

XXII

A Visit to the Saints' Cemetery

A splendid comet, blazing in the western sky, had aroused the apprehensions of the Madani. They all fell to predicting the usual disasters—war, famine, and pestilence—it being still an article of Moslem belief that the Dread Star foreshows all manner of calamities. Men discussed the probability of Abd el-Mejid's immediate decease; for here as in Rome,

> When beggars die, there are no comets seen:
> The heavens themselves blaze forth the death of princes:

and in every strange atmospheric appearance about the time of the Hajj, the Hejazis are accustomed to read tidings of the dreaded Rih el-Asfar (cholera).

Whether the event is attributable to the Zu Zuwabah—the Lord of the Forelock—or whether it was a case of *post hoc, ergo propter hoc*, I would not commit myself by deciding; but, influenced by some cause or other, the Hawazim and the Hawamid, sub-families of the Benu-Harb, began to fight about this time with prodigious fury. These tribes are generally at feud, and the least provocation fans their smouldering wrath into a flame.

The Hawamid number, it is said, between 3,000 and 4,000 fighting men, and the Hawazim not more than 700: the latter, however, are considered a race of desperadoes who pride themselves upon never retreating, and under their fiery Shaykhs, Abbas and Abu Ali, they are a thorn in the sides of their disproportionate foe. On the present occasion a Hamidah happened to strike the camel of a Hazimi which had trespassed; upon which the Hazimi smote the Hamidah, and called him a rough name. The Hamidah instantly shot the Hazimi, the tribes were called out, and they fought with asperity for some days. During the whole of the afternoon of Tuesday, the 30th August, the sound of firing amongst the mountains was distinctly heard in the city. Through the streets parties of Bedawin, sword and matchlock in hand, or merely carrying quarterstaves on their shoulders, might be seen hurrying along, frantic at the chance of missing the fray. The townspeople cursed them privily, expressing a hope that the whole race of vermin might consume itself. And the pilgrims were in no small trepidation, fearing the desertion of their camel-men, and knowing what a blaze is kindled in this inflammable land by an ounce of gunpowder. I afterwards heard that the Bedawin fought till night, and separated after losing on both sides ten men.

This quarrel put an end to any lingering possibility of my prosecuting my journey to Maskat, as originally intended. I had on the way from Yambu' to El-Medinah privily made a friendship with one Mujrim of the Benu-Harb. The 'Sinful', as his name, ancient and classical amongst the Arabs, means, understood that I had some motive of secret interest to undertake the perilous journey. He could not promise at first to guide me, as his beat lay between Yambu', El-Medinah, Meccah, and Jeddah. But he offered to make all inquiries about the route, and to bring me the result at noonday, a time when the household was asleep. He had almost consented at last to travel with me about the end of August, in which case I should have slipped out of Hamid's house and started like a Bedawi towards the Indian Ocean. But when the war commenced, Mujrim, who doubtless wished to stand by his brethren the Hawazim, began to show signs of recusancy in putting off the day of departure to the end of September. At last, when pressed, he frankly told me that no traveller—nay, not a Bedawi—could leave the city in that direction, even as far as historic Khaybar, which information I afterwards ascertained to be correct.

It was impossible to start alone, and when in despair I had recourse to Shaykh Hamid, he seemed to think me mad for wishing to wend northwards when all the world was hurrying towards the south. My disappointment was bitter at first, but consolation soon suggested itself. Under the most favourable circumstances, a Bedawi-trip from El-Medinah to Maskat, 1,500 or 1,600 miles, would require at least ten months; whereas, under pain of losing my commission, I was ordered to be at Bombay before the end of March. Moreover, entering Arabia by El-

Hejaz, as has before been said, I was obliged to leave behind all my instruments except a watch and a pocket-compass, so the benefit rendered to geography by my trip would have been scanty. Still remained to me the comfort of reflecting that possibly at Meccah some opportunity of crossing the Peninsula might present itself. At any rate I had the certainty of seeing the strange wild country of the Hejaz, and of being present at the ceremonies of the Holy City.

I must request the reader to bear with a Visitation once more: we shall conclude it with a ride to El-Bakia, the Place of many Roots. This venerable spot is frequented by the pious every day after the prayer at the Prophet's Tomb, and especially on Fridays.

Our party started one morning—on donkeys, as usual, for my foot was not yet strong—along the Darb el-Jenazah round the southern wall of the town. The locomotion was decidedly slow, principally in consequence of the tent-ropes which the Hajis had pinned down literally all over the plain, and falls were by no means infrequent. At last we arrived at the end of the Darb, where I committed myself by mistaking the decaying place of those miserable schismatics the Nakhawilah for El-Bakia, the glorious cemetery of the Saints. Hamid corrected my blunder with tartness, to which I replied as tartly, that in our country—Afghanistan—we burned the body of every heretic upon whom we could lay our hands. This truly Islamitic custom was heard with general applause, and as the little dispute ended, we stood at the open gate of El-Bakia. Then having dismounted I sat down on a low Dakkah or stone bench within the walls, to obtain a general view and to prepare for the most fatiguing of the visitations.

There is a tradition that 70,000, or according to others 100,000 saints, all with faces like full moons, shall cleave on the last day the yawning bosom of El-Bakia. About 10,000 of the *Ashab* (companions of the Prophet) and innumerable Sadat are here buried: their graves are forgotten, because, in the olden time, tombstones were not placed over the last resting-places of mankind. The first of flesh who shall arise is Mohammed, the second Abubekr, the third Omar, then the people of El-Bakia (amongst whom is Osman, the fourth Caliph), and then the *incolae* of the Jannat el-Maala, the Meccan cemetery. The Hadis, 'whoever dies at the two Harams shall rise with the Sure on the Day of Judgment', has made these spots priceless in value. And even upon earth they might be made a mine of wealth. Like the catacombs at Rome, El-Bakia is literally full of the odour of sanctity, and a single item of the great aggregate here would render any other Moslem town famous. It is a pity that this people refuses to exhume its relics.

The first person buried in El-Bakia was Usman bin Mazun, the first of the Muhajirs who died at El-Medinah. In the month of Shaaban, AH 3, the Prophet kissed the forehead of the corpse and ordered it to be interred within sight of his abode. In those days the field was covered with the tree Gharkad; the vegetation was cut down, the ground was levelled, and Usman was placed in the centre of the new cemetery. With his own hands Mohammed planted two large upright stones at the head and the feet of his faithful follower; and in process of time a dome covered the spot. Ibrahim, the Prophet's infant second son, was laid by Usman's side, after which El-Bakia became a celebrated cemetery.

The Burial-place of the Saints is an irregular oblong surrounded by walls which are connected with the suburb at their south-west angle. The Darb el-Jenazah separates it from the enceinte of the town, and the Eastern Desert Road beginning from the Bab el-Juma bounds it on the north. Around it palm plantations seem to flourish. It is small, considering the extensive use made of it: all that die at El-Medinah, strangers as well as natives, except only heretics and schismatics, expect to be interred in it. It must be choked with corpses, which it could never contain did not the Moslem style of burial greatly favour rapid decomposition; and it has all the inconveniences of intramural sepulture. The gate is small and ignoble; a mere doorway in the wall. Inside there are no flower-plots, no tall trees, in fact none of the refinements which lighten the gloom of a Christian burial-place: the buildings are simple, they might even be called mean. Almost all are the common Arab Mosque, cleanly whitewashed, and looking quite new.

The ancient monuments were levelled to the ground by Saad the Wahhabi and his puritan followers, who waged pitiless warfare against what must have appeared to them magnificent mausolea, deeming as they did a loose heap of stones sufficient for a grave. In Burckhardt's time the whole place was a 'confused accumulation of heaps of earth, wide pits, and rubbish, without a single regular tombstone'. The present erections owe their existence, I was told, to the liberality of the Sultans Abd el-Hamid and Mahmud.

A poor pilgrim has lately started on his last journey, and his corpse, unattended by friends or mourners, is carried upon the shoulders of hired buriers into the cemetery. Suddenly they stay their rapid steps, and throw the body upon the ground. There is a lifelike pliability about it as it falls, and the tight cerements so define the outlines that the action makes me shudder. It looks almost as if the dead were conscious of what is about to occur. They have forgotten their tools; one man starts to fetch them, and three sit down to smoke. After a time a shallow grave is hastily scooped out. The corpse is packed in it with such unseemly haste that earth touches it in all directions—cruel carelessness among Moslems, who believe this to torture the sentient frame. One comfort suggests itself. The poor man being a pilgrim has died Shahid—in martyrdom. Ere long his spirit shall leave El-Bakia,

> And he on honey-dew shall feed,
> And drink the milk of Paradise.

I entered the holy cemetery right foot forwards, as if it were a Mosque, and barefooted, to avoid suspicion of being a heretic. For though the citizens wear their shoes in the Bakia, they are much offended at seeing the Persians follow their example.

We began by the general benediction: 'Peace be upon Ye, O People of El-Bakia! Peace be upon Ye, O Admitted to the Presence of the Most High! Receive You what You have been promised! Peace be upon Ye, Martyrs of El-Bakia, One and All! We verily, if Allah please, are about to join Ye! O Allah, pardon us and Them, and the Mercy of God, and His Blessings!' After which we recited the Chapter El-Ikhlas and the Testification, then raised our hands, mumbled the Fatihah, passed our palms down our faces, and went on.

Walking down a rough narrow path, which leads from the western to the eastern extremity of El-Bakia, we entered the humble mausoleum of the Caliph Osman—Osman 'El-Mazlum', or the 'ill-treated', he is called by some Moslems. When he was slain, his friends wished to bury him by the Prophet in the Hujrah, and Ayisha made no objection to the measure. But the people of Egypt became violent; swore that the corpse should neither be buried nor be prayed over, and only permitted it to be removed upon the threat of Habibah (one of the 'Mothers of the Moslems', and daughter of Abu Sufiyan) to expose her countenance. During the night that followed his death, Osman was carried out by several of his friends to El-Bakia, from which, however, they were driven away, and obliged to deposit their burden in a garden, eastward of, and outside, the saints' cemetery. It was called Hisn Kaukab, and was looked upon as an inauspicious place of sepulture, till Marwan included it in El-Bakia. We stood before Osman's monument, repeating, 'Peace be upon Thee, O our Lord Osman, Son of Affan! Peace be upon Thee, O Caliph of Allah's Apostle! Peace be upon Thee, O Writer of Allah's Book! Peace be upon Thee, in whose Presence the Angels are ashamed! Peace be upon Thee, O Collector of the Koran! Peace be upon Thee, O Son-in-law of the Prophet! Peace be upon Thee, O Lord of the Two Lights (the two daughters of Mohammed)! Peace be upon Thee, who fought the Battle of the Faith! Allah be satisfied with Thee, and cause Thee to be satisfied, and render Heaven thy Habitation! Peace be upon Thee, and the Mercy of Allah and His Blessing, and Praise be to Allah, Lord of the (three) Worlds!' This supplication concluded in the usual manner. After which we gave alms, and settled with 10 piastres the demands of the Khadim who takes charge of the tomb: this double-disbursing process had to be repeated at each station.

Then moving a few paces to the north, we faced eastwards, and performed the visitation of Abu Said el-Khazari, a Sahib or companion of the Prophet, whose sepulchre lies outside El-Bakia. The third place visited was a dome containing the tomb of our lady Halimah, the Bedawi wet-nurse who took charge of Mohammed: she is addressed thus: 'Peace be upon Thee, O Halimah the Auspicious! Peace be upon Thee, who performed thy Trust in suckling the Best of Mankind! Peace be upon Thee, O Wet-nurse of El-Mustafa (the chosen)! Peace be upon Thee, O Wet-nurse of El-Mujtaba (the accepted)! May Allah be satisfied with Thee, and cause Thee to be satisfied, and render Heaven thy House and Habitation! and verily we have come visiting Thee, and by means of Thee drawing near to Allah's Prophet, and through Him to God, the Lord of the Heavens and the Earths.'

After which, fronting the north, we stood before a low enclosure, containing ovals of loose stones, disposed side by side. These are the martyrs of El-Bakia, who received the crown of glory at the hands of El-Muslim, the general of the arch-heretic Yezid. The prayer here recited differs so little from that addressed to the martyrs of Ohod, that I will not transcribe it. The fifth station is near the centre of the cemetery at the tomb of Ibrahim, who died, to the eternal regret of El-Islam, some say six months old, others in his second year. He was the son of Mariyah, the Coptic girl, sent as a present to Mohammed by Jarih, the Mukaukas or governor of Alexandria. The Prophet with his own hand piled earth upon the grave, and sprinkled it with water—a ceremony then first performed—disposed small stones upon it, and pronounced the final salutation. For which reason many holy men were buried in this part of the cemetery, every one being ambitious to lie in ground which has been honoured by the Apostle's hands.

Then we visited El-Nafi Maula, son of Omar, generally called Imam Nafi el-Kari, or the Koran chaunter; and near him the great doctor Imam Malik Ibn Anas, a native of El-Medinah, and one of the most dutiful of her sons. The eighth station is at the tomb of Ukayl bin Abi Talib, brother of Ali. Then we visited the spot where lie interred all the Prophet's wives, Khadijah, who lies at Meccah, alone excepted. After the 'Mothers of the Moslems', we prayed at the tombs of Mohammed's daughters, said to be ten in number.

In compliment probably to the Hajj, the beggars mustered

strong that morning at El-Bakia. Along the walls and at the entrance of each building squatted ancient dames, all engaged in anxious contemplation of every approaching face, and in pointing to dirty cotton napkins spread upon the ground before them, and studded with a few coins, gold, silver, or copper, according to the expectations of the proprietress. They raised their voices to demand largess: some promised to recite Fatihahs, and the most audacious seized visitors by the skirts of their garments. Fakihs, ready to write 'Y. S.', or anything else demanded of them, covered the little heaps and eminences of the cemetery, all begging lustily, and looking as though they would murder you, when told how beneficent is Allah—polite form of declining to be charitable. At the doors of the tombs old housewives, and some young ones also, struggled with you for your slippers as you doffed them, and not unfrequently the charge of the pair was divided between two. Inside, when the boys were not loud enough or importunate enough for presents, they were urged on by the adults and seniors, the relatives of the Khadims and hangers-on. Unfortunately for me, Shaykh Hamid was renowned for taking charge of wealthy pilgrims: the result was, that my purse was lightened of 3 dollars. I must add that although at least fifty female voices loudly promised that morning, for the sum of 10 paras each, to supplicate Allah in behalf of my lame foot, no perceptible good came of their efforts.

Before leaving El-Bakia, we went to the eleventh station, the Kubbat el-Abbasiyah, or Dome of Abbas. Originally built by the Abbaside Caliphs in AH 519, it is a larger and a handsomer building than its fellows, and it is situated on the right-hand side of the gate as you enter. The crowd of beggars at the door testified to its importance: they were attracted by the Persians who assemble here in force to weep and pray. Crossing the threshold with some difficulty, I walked round a mass of tombs which occupies the centre of the building, leaving but a narrow passage between it and the walls. It is railed round, and covered over with several Kiswahs of green cloth worked with white letters: it looked like a confused heap, but it might have appeared irregular to me by the reason of the mob around. The eastern portion contains the body of El-Hasan, the son of Ali and grandson of the Prophet; the Imam Zayn el-Abidin, son of El-Husayn, and great-grandson to the Prophet; the Imam Mohammed El-Bakir (fifth Imam), son to Zayn el-Abidin; and his son the Imam Jaafar el-Sadik—all four descendants of the Prophet, and buried in the same grave with Abbas ibn Abd el-Muttalib, uncle to Mohammed. It is almost needless to say that these names are subjects of great controversy. El-Masudi mentions that here was found an inscribed stone declaring it to be the tomb of the Lady Fatimah, of Hasan her brother, of Ali bin Husayn, of Mohammed bin Ali, and of Jaafar bin Mohammed. Ibn Jubayr, describing El-Bakia, mentions only two in this tomb, Abbas and Hasan; the head of the latter, he says, in the direction of the former's feet. Other authors relate that in it, about the ninth century of the Hijrah, was found a wooden box covered with fresh-looking red felt cloth, with bright brass nails, and they believe it to have contained the corpse of Ali, placed here by his son Hasan.

Standing opposite this mysterious tomb, we repeated, with difficulty by reason of the Persians weeping, the following supplication: 'Peace be upon Ye, O Family of the Prophet! O Lord Abbas, the free from Impurity and Uncleanness, and Father's Brother to the Best of Men! And Thou too O Lord Hasan, Grandson of the Prophet! And Thou also O Lord Zayn el-Abidin! Peace be upon Ye, One and All, for verily God hath been pleased to deliver You from all Guile, and to purify You with all Purity. The Mercy of Allah and His Blessings be upon Ye, and verily He is the Praised, the Mighty!' After which, freeing ourselves from the hands of greedy boys, we turned round and faced the southern wall, close to which is a tomb attributed to the Lady Fatimah. I will not repeat the prayer, it being the same as that recited in the Haram.

Issuing from the hot and crowded dome, we recovered our slippers after much trouble, and found that our garments had suffered from the frantic gesticulations of the Persians. We then walked to the gate of El-Bakia, stood facing the cemetery upon an elevated piece of ground, and delivered the general benediction.

'O Allah! O Allah! O Allah! O full of Mercy! O abounding

in Beneficence! Lord of Length (of days), and Prosperity, and Goodness! O Thou, who when asked, grantest, and when prayed for aid, aidest! Have Mercy upon the Companions of thy Prophet, of the Muhajirin, and the Ansar! Have Mercy upon them, One and All! Have Mercy upon Abdullah bin Hantal (and so on, specifying their names), and make Paradise their Resting-place, their Habitation, their Dwelling, and their Abode! O Allah! accept our Ziyarat, and supply our Wants, and lighten our Griefs, and restore us to our Homes, and comfort our Fears, and disappoint not our Hopes, and pardon us, for on no other do we rely; and let us depart in Thy Faith, and after the Practice of Thy Prophet, and be Thou satisfied with us! O Allah! forgive our past Offences, and leave us not to our (evil) Natures during the Glance of an Eye, or a lesser Time; and pardon us, and pity us, and let us return to our Houses and Homes safe (i.e. spiritually and physically), fortunate, abstaining from what is unlawful, re-established after our Distresses, and belonging to the Good, thy Servants upon whom is no Fear, nor do they know Distress. Repentance, O Lord! Repentance, O Merciful! Repentance, O Pitiful! Repentance before Death, and Pardon after Death! I beg Pardon of Allah! Thanks be to Allah! Praise be to Allah! Amen, O Lord of the (three) Worlds!'

After which, issuing from El-Bakia, we advanced northwards, leaving the city gate on the left hand, till we came to a small Kubbah (dome) close to the road. It is visited as containing the tomb of the Prophet's paternal aunts, especially of Safiyah, daughter of Abd el-Muttalib, sister of Hamzah, and one of the many heroines of early El-Islam. Hurrying over our devotions here—for we were tired indeed—we applied to a Sakka for water, and entered a little coffee-house near the gate of the town: after which we rode home.

I have now described, at a wearying length I fear, the spots visited by every Zair at El-Medinah. The guide-books mention altogether between fifty and fifty-five mosques and other holy places, most of which are now unknown even by name to the citizens. The most celebrated of these are the few following, which I describe from hearsay.

About three miles to the north-west of the town, close to the Wady el-Akik, lies the Mosque called El-Kiblatayn—The Two Directions of Prayer. Some give this title to the Masjid el-Takwa at Kuba. Others assert that the Prophet, after visiting and eating at the house of an old woman named Umm Mabshar, went to pray the midday prayer in the Mosque of the Benu Salmah. He had performed the prostration with his face towards Jerusalem, when suddenly warned by revelation he turned southwards and concluded his orisons in that direction. I am told it is a mean dome without inner walls, outer enclosures, or minaret.

The Masjid Benu Zafar (some write the word Tifr) is also called Masjid el-Baghlah—of the She-mule—because, according to El-Matari, on the ridge of stone to the south of this Mosque are the marks where the Prophet leaned his arm, and where the she-mule, Duldul, sent by the Mukaukas as a present with Mariyah the Coptic Girl and Yafur the donkey, placed its hoofs. At the Mosque was shown a slab upon which the Prophet sat hearing recitations from the Koran; and historians declare that by following his example many women have been blessed with offspring.[1] This Mosque is to the east of El-Bakia.

The Masjid el-Jumah—of Friday, or El-Anikah, of the Sand-heaps—is in the valley near Kuba, where Mohammed prayed and preached on the first Friday after his flight from Meccah.

The Masjid el-Fazikh—of Date-liquor—is so called because when Abu Ayyub and others of the Ansar were sitting with cups in their hands, they heard that intoxicating draughts were for the future forbidden, upon which they poured the liquor upon the ground. Here the Prophet prayed six days whilst he was engaged in warring down the Benu Nazir Jews. The Mosque derives its other name, El-Shams—of the Sun—because, being erected on rising ground east of and near Kuba, it receives the first rays of morning light.

To the eastward of the Masjid el-Fazikh lies the Masjid el-Kurayzah, erected on a spot where the Prophet descended to

[1] I cannot say whether this valuable stone be still at the Mosque Beni Tifr. But I perfectly remember that my friend Larking had a mutilated sphinx in his garden at Alexandria, which was found equally efficacious.

attack the Jewish tribe of that name. Returning from the Battle of the Moat, wayworn and tired with fighting, he here sat down to wash and comb his hair, when suddenly appeared to him the Archangel Gabriel in the figure of a horseman dressed in a corslet and covered with dust. 'The Angels of Allah', said the preternatural visitor, 'are still in Arms, O Prophet, and it is Allah's Will that thy Foot return to the Stirrup. I go before Thee to prepare a Victory over the Infidels, the Sons of Kurayzah.' The legend adds that the dust raised by the angelic host was seen in the streets of El-Medinah, but that mortal eye fell not upon horseman's form. The Prophet ordered his followers to sound the battle-call, gave his flag to Ali—the Arab token of appointing a commander-in-chief—and for twenty-five days invested the habitations of the enemy. This hapless tribe was exterminated, sentence of death being passed upon them by Saad ibn Maaz, an Ausi whom they constituted their judge because he belonged to an allied tribe. Six hundred men were beheaded in the market-place of El-Medinah, their property was plundered, and their wives and children were reduced to slavery.

Tantane relligio potuit suadere malorum!

The Masjid Mashrabat Umm Ibrahim, or Mosque of the garden of Ibrahim's mother, is a place where Mariyah the Copt had a garden, and became the mother of Ibrahim, the Prophet's second son. It is a small building in what is called the Awali, or highest part of the El-Medinah plain, to the north of the Masjid Benu Kurayzah, and near the eastern Harrah or ridge.

Northwards of El-Bakia is, or was, a small building called the Masjid el-Ijabah—of Granting—from the following circumstance. One day the Prophet stopped to perform his devotions at this place, which then belonged to the Benu Muawiyah of the tribe of Aus. He made a long Dua or supplication, and then turning to his companions, exclaimed, 'I have asked of Allah three favours, two hath he vouchsafed to me, but the third was refused!' Those granted were that the Moslems might never be destroyed by famine or by deluge. The third was that they might not perish by internecine strife.

The Masjid el-Fath (of Victory), vulgarly called the Four Mosques, is situated in the Wady El-Sayh, which comes from the direction of Kuba, and about half a mile to the east of El-Kiblatayn. The largest is called the Masjid el-Fath, or El-Ahzab —of the troops—and is alluded to in the Koran. Here it is said the Prophet prayed for three days during the Battle of the Moat, also called the affair El-Ahzab, the last fought with the Infidel Kuraysh under Abu Sufiyan. After three days of devotion, a cold and violent blast arose, with rain and sleet, and discomfited the foe. The Prophet's prayer having here been granted, it is supposed by ardent Moslems that no petition put up at the Mosque El-Ahzab is ever neglected by Allah. The form of supplication is differently quoted by different authors. When El-Shafei was in trouble and fear of Harun el-Rashid, by the virtue of this formula he escaped all danger: I would willingly offer so valuable a prophylactory to my readers, only it is of an unmanageable length. The doctors of El-Islam also greatly differ about the spot where the Prophet stood on this occasion; most of them support the claims of the Masjid el-Fath, the most elevated of the four, to that distinction. Below, and to the south of the highest ground, is the Masjid Salman el-Farsi, the Persian, from whose brain emanated the bright idea of the Moat. At the mature age of 250, some say 350, after spending his life in search of a religion, from a Magus (fire-worshipper) becoming successively a Jew and a Nazarene, he ended with being a Moslem, and a companion of Mohammed. During his eventful career he had been ten times sold into slavery. Below Salman's Mosque is the Masjid Ali, and the smallest building on the south of the hill is called Masjid Abubekr. All these places owe their existence to El-Walid the Caliph: they were repaired at times by his successors.

The Masjid el-Rayah—of the Banner—was originally built by El-Walid upon a place where the Prophet pitched his tent during the War of the Moat. Others call it El-Zubab, after a hill upon which it stands. El-Rayah is separated from the Masjid el-Fath by a rising ground called Jebel Sula or Jebel Sawab: the former being on the eastern, whilst the latter lies upon the western declivity of the hill. The position of this place is greatly admired, as commanding the fairest view of the Haram.

About a mile and a half south-east of El-Bakia is a dome called Kuwwat Islam, the Strength of El-Islam. Here the Apostle planted a dry palm-stick, which grew up, blossomed, and bore fruit at once. Moreover, on one occasion when the Moslems were unable to perform the pilgrimage, Mohammed here produced the appearance of a Kaabah, an Arafat, and all the appurtenances of the Hajj. I must warn my readers not to condemn the founder of El-Islam for these puerile inventions.

The Masjid Unayn lies south of Hamzah's tomb. It is on a hill called Jebel el-Rumat, the Shooters' Hill, and here during the battle of Ohod stood the archers of El-Islam. According to some, the Prince of Martyrs here received his death-wound; others place that event at the Masjid el-Askar or the Masjid el-Wady.

Besides these fourteen, I find the names, and nothing but the names, of forty Mosques. The reader loses little by my unwillingness to offer him a detailed list of such appellations as Masjid Benu Abd el-Ashhal, Masjid Benu Harisah, Masjid Benu Haram, Masjid el-Fash, Masjid el-Sukiya, Masjid Benu Bayazah, Masjid Benu Hatmah,

Cum multis aliis quae nunc perscribere longum est.

XXIII
The Damascus Caravan

The Damascus Caravan was to set out on the 27th Zu'l Kaadah (1st September). I had intended to stay at El-Medinah till the last moment, and to accompany the Kafilat el-Tayyarah, or the Flying Caravan, which usually leaves on the 2nd Zu'l Hijjah, two days after that of Damascus.

Suddenly arose the rumour that there would be no Tayyarah, and that all pilgrims must proceed with the Damascus Caravan or await the Rakb. This is a Dromedary Caravan, in which each person carries only his saddle-bags. It usually descends by the road called El-Khabt, and makes Meccah on the fifth day. The Sherif Zayd, Saad the Robber's only friend, had paid him an unsuccessful visit. Schinderhans demanded back his Shaykhship, in return for a safe-conduct through his country: 'Otherwise,' said he, 'I will cut the throat of every hen that ventures into the passes.'

The Sherif Zayd returned to El-Medinah on the 25th Zu'l Kaadah (30th August). Early on the morning of the next day, Shaykh Hamid returned hurriedly from the bazar, exclaiming, 'You must make ready at once, Effendi!—there will be no Tayyarah—all Hajis start to-morrow—Allah will make it easy to you!—have you your water-skins in order?—you are to travel down the Darb el-Sharki, where you will not see water for three days!'

Poor Hamid looked horrorstruck as he concluded this fearful announcement, which filled me with joy. Burckhardt had visited and described the Darb el-Sultani, the road along the east. But no European had as yet travelled down by Harun el-Rashid's and the Lady Zubaydah's celebrated route through the Nejd Desert.

Not a moment, however, was to be lost: we expected to start early the next morning. The boy Mohammed went forth, and bought for 80 piastres a Shugduf, which lasted us throughout the pilgrimage, and for 15 piastres a Shibriyah or cot to be occupied by Shaykh Nur, who did not relish sleeping on boxes. The youth was employed all day, with sleeves tucked up, and working like a porter, in covering the litter with matting and rugs, in mending broken parts, and in providing it with large pockets for provisions inside and outside, with pouches to contain the gugglets of cooled water.

Meanwhile Shaykh Nur and I, having inspected the water-skins, found that the rats had made considerable rents in two of them. There being no workman procurable at this time for gold, I sat down to patch the damaged articles; whilst Nur was sent to lay in supplies for fourteen days. The journey is calculated at eleven days; but provisions are apt to spoil, and the Bedawi camel-men expect to be fed. Besides which, pilferers abound. By my companion's advice I took wheat-flour, rice, turmeric, onions, dates, unleavened bread of two kinds, cheese, limes, tobacco, sugar, tea and coffee.

Hamid himself started upon the most important part of our business. Faithful camel-men are required upon a road where robberies are frequent and stabbings occasional, and where there is no law to prevent desertion or to limit new and exorbitant demands. After a time he returned, accompanied by a boy and a Bedawi, a short, thin, well-built old man with regular features, a white beard, and a cool clear eye; his limbs, as usual, were scarred with wounds. Masud of the Rahlah, a sub-family of the Hamidah family of the Benu-Harb, came in with a dignified demeanour, applied his dexter palm to ours,[1] sat down, declined a pipe, accepted coffee, and after drinking it, looked at us to show that he was ready for negotiation.

We opened the proceedings with 'We want men, and not camels,' and the conversation proceeded in the purest Hejazi. After much discussion, we agreed, if compelled to travel by the Darb el-Sharki, to pay 20 dollars for two camels, and to advance Arbun or earnest-money to half that amount. The Shaykh bound himself to provide us with good animals, which, moreover

[1] This Musafahah, as it is called, is the Arab fashion of shaking hands. They apply the palms of the right hands flat to each other, without squeezing the fingers, and then raise the hand to the forehead.

were to be changed in case of accidents; he was also to supply his beasts with water, and to accompany us to Arafat and back. But, absolutely refusing to carry my large chest, he declared that the tent under the Shugduf was burden enough for one camel; and that the green box of drugs, the saddle-bags, and the provision-sacks, surmounted by Nur's cot, were amply sufficient for the other. On our part, we bound ourselves to feed the Shaykh and his son, supplying them either with raw or with cooked provender, and, upon our return to Meccah from Mount Arafat to pay the remaining hire with a discretionary present.

Hamid then addressed to me flowery praises of the old Bedawi. After which, turning to the latter, he exclaimed, 'Thou wilt treat these friends well, O Masud the Harbi!' The ancient replied with a dignity that had no pomposity in it—'Even as Abu Shawarib—the Father of Mustachios[1]—behaveth to us, so will we behave to him!' He then arose, bade us be prepared when the departure-gun sounded, saluted us, and stalked out of the room, followed by his son, who, under pretext of dozing, had mentally made an inventory of every article in the room, ourselves especially included.

When the Bedawin disappeared, Shaykh Hamid shook his head, advising me to give them plenty to eat, and never to allow twenty-four hours to elapse without dipping hand in the same dish with them, in order that the party might always be Malihin—on terms of salt. He concluded with a copious lecture upon the villainy of Bedawin, and their habit of drinking travellers' water. I was to place the skins on a camel in front, and not behind; to hang them with their mouths carefully tied, and turned upwards, contrary to the general practice; always to keep a good store of liquid, and at night to place it under the safeguard of the tent.

[1] Most men of the Shafei school clip their mustachios exceedingly short; some clean shave the upper lip, the imperial, and the parts of the beard about the corners of the mouth, and the fore-part of the cheeks. I neglected so to do, which soon won for me the epithet recorded above.

Arabs are vastly given to nicknaming God's creatures; their habit is the effect of acute observation, and the want of variety in proper names. Sonnini appears not to like having been called the 'Father of a nose'. But there is nothing disrespectful in these personal allusions. In Arabia you must be father of something, and it is better to be father of a feature, than father of a cooking-pot, or father of a strong smell (Abu-Zirt).

In the afternoon, Umar Effendi and others dropped in to take leave. They found me in the midst of preparations, sewing sacks, fitting up a pipe, patching water-bags, and packing medicines. My fellow-traveller had brought me some pencils and a penknife, as forget-me-nots, for we were by no means sure of meeting again. He hinted, however, at another escape from the paternal abode, and proposed, if possible, to join the Dromedary Caravan. Shaykh Hamid said the same, but I saw, by the expression of his face, that his mother and wife would not give him leave from home so soon after his return.

Towards evening-time the Barr el-Manakhah became a scene of exceeding confusion. The town of tents lay upon the ground. Camels were being laden, and were roaring under the weight of litters and cots, boxes and baggage. Horses and mules galloped about. Men were rushing wildly in all directions on worldly errands, or hurrying to pay a farewell visit to the Prophet's Tomb. Women and children sat screaming on the ground, or ran to and fro distracted, or called their vehicles to escape the danger of being crushed. Every now and then a random shot excited all into the belief that the departure-gun had sounded. At times we heard a volley from the robbers' hills, which elicited a general groan, for the pilgrims were still, to use their own phrase, 'between fear and hope', and, consequently, still far from 'one of the two comforts'.[1] Then would sound the loud 'Jhin-Jhin' of the camels' bells, as the stately animals paced away with some grandee's gilt and emblazoned litter, the sharp plaint of the dromedary, and the loud neighing of excited steeds.

About an hour after sunset all our preparations were concluded, save only the Shugduf, at which the boy Mohammed still worked with untiring zeal; he wisely remembered that he had to spend in it the best portion of a week and a half. The evening was hot, we therefore dined outside the house. I was told to repair to the Haram for the Ziyarat el-Widaa, or the Farewell Visitation; but my decided objection to this step was that we were all to part—how soon!—and when to meet again we knew not. My companions smiled consent, assuring me that

[1] The two comforts are success and despair; the latter, according to the Arabs, being a more enviable state of feeling than doubt or hope deferred.

the ceremony could be performed as well at a distance as in the temple.

Then Shaykh Hamid made me pray a two-prostration prayer, and afterwards, facing towards the Haram, to recite this supplication with raised hands:

'O Apostle of Allah, we beg Thee to entreat Almighty Allah, that He cut off no Portion of the Good resulting to us, from this Visit to Thee and to Thy Haram! May He cause us to return safe and prosperous to our Birthplaces; aid then us in the Progeny he hath given us, and continue to us his Benefits, and make us thankful for our daily Bread! O Allah, let not this be the last of our Visitations to Thy Prophet's Tomb! Yet if Thou summon us before such Blessing, verily in my Death I bear Witness, as in my Life' (here the forefinger of the right hand is extended, that the members of the body may take part with the tongue and the heart) 'that there is no god but Allah, One and without Partner, and verily that our Lord Mohammed is His Servant and His Apostle! O Allah, grant us in this World Weal, and in the future Weal, and save us from the torments of Hell-fire! Praise to Thee, O Lord, Lord of Glory, greater than Man can describe! and Peace be upon the Prophet, and Laud to Allah, the Lord of the (three) Worlds.' This concludes, as usual, with the Testification and the Fatihah. Pious men on such an occasion go to the Rauzah, where they strive, if possible, to shed a tear—a single drop being a sign of acceptance—give alms to the utmost of their ability, vow piety, repentance, and obedience, and retire overwhelmed with grief, at separating themselves from their Prophet and Intercessor. It is customary, too, before leaving El-Medinah, to pass at least one night in vigils at the Haram, and for learned men to read through the Koran once before the Tomb.

Then began the uncomfortable process of paying off little bills. The Eastern creditor always, for divers reasons, waits the last moment before he claims his debt. Shaykh Hamid had frequently hinted at his difficulties; the only means of escape from which, he said, was to rely upon Allah. He had treated me so hospitably, that I could not take back any part of the 5*l.* lent to him at Suez. His three brothers received a dollar or two each, and one or two of his cousins hinted to some effect that such a proceeding would meet with their approbation.

The luggage was then carried down, and disposed in packs upon the ground before the house, so as to be ready for loading at a moment's notice. Many flying parties of travellers had almost started on the highroad, and late in the evening came a new report that the body of the Caravan would march about midnight. We sat up till about two a.m. when, having heard no gun, and having seen no camels, we lay down to sleep through the sultry remnant of the hours of darkness.

Thus, gentle reader, was spent my last night at El-Medinah.

I had reason to congratulate myself upon having passed through the first danger. Meccah is so near the coast, that, in case of detection, the traveller might escape in a few hours to Jeddah, where he would find an English vice-consul, protection from the Turkish authorities, and possibly a British cruiser in the harbour. But at El-Medinah discovery would entail more serious consequences. The next risk to be run was the journey between the two cities, where it would be easy for the local officials quietly to dispose of a suspected person by giving a dollar to a Bedawi.

XXIV
From El-Medinah to El-Suwayrkiyah

Four roads lead from El-Medinah to Meccah. The Darb el-Sultani, or Sultan's Way, follows the line of coast: this general passage has been minutely described by my exact predecessor. The Tarik el-Ghabir, a mountain path, is avoided by the Mahmal and the great Caravans, on account of its rugged passes; water abounds along the whole line, but there is not a single village; and the Sobh Bedawin, who own the soil, are inveterate plunderers. The route called Wady el-Kura is a favourite with Dromedary Caravans; on this road are two or three small settlements, regular wells, and free passage through the Benu Amr tribe. The Darb el-Sharki, or Eastern road, down which I travelled, owes its existence to the piety of Zubaydah Khatun, wife of Harun el-Rashid. That estimable princess dug wells from Baghdad to El-Medinah, and built, we are told, a wall to direct pilgrims over the shifting sands. There is a fifth road, or rather mountain-path, concerning which I can give no information.

At eight a.m. on Wednesday, the 26th Zu'l Kaadah (31st August, 1853), as we were sitting at the window of Hamid's house after our early meal, suddenly appeared, in hottest haste, Masud, our camel-Shaykh. He was accompanied by his son, a bold boy about fourteen years of age, who fought sturdily about the weight of each package as it was thrown over the camel's back; and his nephew, an ugly pock-marked lad, too lazy even to quarrel. We were ordered to lose no time in loading; all started into activity, and at nine a.m. I found myself standing opposite the Egyptian Gate, surrounded by my friends, who had accompanied me thus far on foot, to take leave with due honour. After affectionate embraces and parting mementos, we mounted, the boy Mohammed and I in the litter, and Shaykh Nur in his cot. Then, in company with some Turks and Meccans, for Masud owned a string of nine camels, we passed through the little gate near the castle, and shaped our course towards the north. On our right lay the palm-groves, which conceal this part of the city; far to the left rose the domes of Hamzah's Mosques at the foot of Mount Ohod; and in front a band of road, crowded with motley groups, stretched over a barren stony plain.

After an hour's slow march, bending gradually from north to north-east, we fell into the Nejd highway, and came to a place of renown called El-Ghadir, or the Basin. This is a depression conducting the drainage of the plain towards the Northern Hills. The skirts of Ohod still limited the prospect to the left. On the right was the Bir Rashid (Well of Rashid), and the little whitewashed dome of Ali el-Urays, a descendant from Zayn el-Abidin: the tomb is still a place of visitation. There we halted and turned to take farewell of the Holy City. All the pilgrims dismounted and gazed at the venerable minarets and the Green Dome—spots upon which their memories would for ever dwell with a fond and yearning interest.

Remounting at noon, we crossed a Fiumara which runs, according to my camel-Shaykh, from north to south; we were therefore emerging from the Medinah basin. The sky began to be clouded, and although the air was still full of Simoom, cold draughts occasionally poured down from the hills. Arabs fear this

bitter change
Of fierce extremes, extremes by change more fierce,

and call that a dangerous climate which is cold in the hot season and hot in the cold. Travelling over a rough and stony path, dotted with thorny Acacias, we arrived about two p.m. at the bed of lava heard of by Burckhardt. The aspect of the country was volcanic, abounding in basalts and scoriae, more or less porous: sand veiled the black bed whose present dimensions by no means equal the descriptions of Arabian historians. I made diligent inquiries about the existence of active volcanos in this part of El-Hejaz, and heard of none.

At five p.m., travelling towards the east, we entered a Bughaz, or Pass, which follows the course of a wide Fiumara, walled in by steep and barren hills—the portals of a region too wild even for Bedawin. The torrent-bed narrowed where the turns were abrupt, and the drift of heavy stones, with a water-mark from six to seven feet high, showed that after rains a violent stream runs from east and south-east to west and north-west. The fertilising fluid is close to the surface, evidenced by a spare growth of Acacia, camel grass, and at some angles of the bed by the Daum, or Theban palm. I remarked what are technically called Hufrah, holes dug for water in the sand; and the guide assured me that somewhere near there is a spring flowing from the rocks.

After the long and sultry afternoon, beasts of burden began to sink in numbers. The fresh carcases of asses, ponies, and camels dotted the wayside: those that had been allowed to die were abandoned to the foul carrion-birds, the Rakham (vulture), and the yellow Ukab; and all whose throats had been properly cut, were surrounded by troops of Takruri pilgrims. These half-starved wretches cut steaks from the choice portions, and slung them over their shoulders till an opportunity of cooking might arrive. I never saw men more destitute. They carried wooden bowls, which they filled with water by begging; their only weapon was a small knife, tied in a leathern sheath above the elbow; and their costume an old skull-cap, strips of leather like sandals under the feet, and a long dirty shirt, or sometimes a mere rag covering the loins. Some were perfect savages, others had been fine-looking men, broad-shouldered, thin-flanked, and long-limbed; many were lamed by fatigue and thorns; and looking at most of them, I fancied death depicted in their forms and features.

After two hours' slow marching up the Fiumara eastwards, we saw in front of us a wall of rock; and, turning abruptly southwards, we left the bed, and ascended rising ground. Already it was night; an hour, however, elapsed before we saw, at a distance, the twinkling fires, and heard the watch-cries of our camp. It was pitched in a hollow, under hills, in excellent order; the Pasha's pavilion surrounded by his soldiers and guards disposed in tents, with sentinels, regularly posted, protecting the outskirts of the encampment. One of our men, whom we had sent forward, met us on the way, and led us to an open place, where we unloaded the camels, raised our canvas home, lighted fires, and prepared, with supper, for a good night's rest.

Living is simple on such marches. The pouches inside and outside the Shugduf contain provisions and water, with which you supply yourself when inclined. At certain hours of the day, ambulant vendors offer sherbet, lemonade, hot coffee, and water-pipes admirably prepared. Chibouques may be smoked in the litter; but few care to do so during the Simoom. The first thing, however, called for at the halting-place is the pipe, and its delightfully soothing influence, followed by a cup of coffee, and a 'forty winks' upon the sand, will awaken an appetite not to be roused by other means. How could Waterton, the traveller, abuse a pipe? During the night-halt, provisions are cooked: rice, or Kichri, a mixture of pulse and rice, are eaten with Chutnee and lime-pickle, varied, occasionally, by tough mutton and indigestible goat.

We arrived at Ja el-Sherifah at eight p.m., after a march of about twenty-two miles. This halting-place is the rendez-vous of caravans: it lies 50° south-east of El-Medinah, and belongs rather to Nejd than to El-Hejaz.

At three a.m., on Thursday (1st September), we started up at the sound of the departure-gun, struck the tent, loaded the camels, mounted, and found ourselves hurrying through a gloomy Pass, in the hills, to secure a good place in the Caravan. This is an object of some importance, as, during the whole journey, marching order must not be broken. We met with a host of minor accidents, camels falling, Shugdufs bumping against one another, and plentiful abuse. Pertinaciously we hurried on till six a.m., at which hour we emerged from the Black Pass. The large crimson sun rose upon us, disclosing, through purple mists, a hollow of coarse yellow gravel, based upon a hard whitish clay. About five miles broad by twelve long, it collects the waters of the high grounds after rain, and distributes the surplus through an exit towards the north-west, a gap in the low undulating hills around. Entering it, we dismounted, prayed, broke our fast, and after half an hour's halt proceeded to cross its breadth. The appearance of the Caravan was most striking, as it threaded its slow way over the smooth surface of the Khabt (low plain). To judge by the eye, the host was composed of at least 7,000 souls, on foot, on horseback, in litters, or bestriding

A member of the Beni Shaybah family, guardians of the Kaabah. Burton was required to declare his identity to a youth of this family before being conducted around the building. *Right*, a Sayyid from Mecca. Sayyids and Sherifs were descendants of the Prophet: the former devoted themselves to learning and religion, the latter to government and war

A Circassian slave and his merchant master, Mecca. *Below*, a Meccan doctor

A Meccan citizen. *Above right*, a member of the family of chief Muezzins, Mecca. *Right*, women in street- and home-dress, Jedda

A Meccan bride, or Arusah. *Below*, a Meccan bridegroom, or Aris, here seated on the throne normally occupied by the bride on the final night of marriage celebrations

the splendid camels of Syria. There were eight gradations of pilgrims. The lowest hobbled with heavy staves. Then came the riders of asses, camels, and mules. Respectable men, especially Arabs, were mounted on dromedaries, and the soldiers had horses: a led animal was saddled for every grandee, ready whenever he might wish to leave his litter. Women, children, and invalids of the poorer classes sat upon a Haml Musattah—rugs and cloths spread over the two large boxes which form the camel's load. Many occupied Shibriyahs; a few, Shugdufs, and only the wealthy and noble rode in Takhtrawan (litters), carried by camels or mules. The morning beams fell brightly upon the glancing arms which surrounded the stripped Mahmal, and upon the scarlet and gilt conveyances of the grandees. Not the least beauty of the spectacle was its wondrous variety of detail: no man was dressed like his neighbour, no camel was caparisoned, no horse was clothed in uniform, as it were. And nothing stranger than the contrasts; a band of half-naked Takruri marching with the Pasha's equipage, and long-capped, bearded Persians conversing with Tarbush'd and shaven Turks.

The plain even at an early hour reeked with vapours distilled by the fires of the Simoom: about noon, however, the air became cloudy, and nothing of colour remained, save that milky white haze, dull, but glaring withal, which is the prevailing day-tint in these regions. At midday we reached a narrowing of the basin, where, from both sides, Irk, or low hills, stretch their last spurs into the plain. But after half a mile, it again widened to upwards of two miles. At two p.m. (Friday, the 2nd September), we turned towards the south-west, ascended stony ground, and found ourselves one hour afterwards in a desolate rocky flat, distant about twenty-four miles of unusually winding road from our last station. Mahattah Ghurab, or the Raven's Station, lies 10° south-west from Ja el-Sherifah, in the irregular masses of hill on the frontier of El-Hejaz, where the highlands of Nejd begin.

After pitching the tent, we prepared to recruit our supply of water; for Masud warned me that his camels had not drunk for ninety hours, and that they would soon sink under the privation. The boy Mohammed, mounting a dromedary, set off with the Shaykh and many water-bags, giving me an opportunity of writing out my journal. They did not return home till after nightfall, a delay caused by many adventures. The wells are in a Fiumara, as usual, about two miles distant from the halting-place, and the soldiers, regular as well as irregular, occupied the water and exacted hard coin in exchange for it. The men are not to blame; they would die of starvation but for this resource. The boy Mohammed had been engaged in several quarrels; but after snapping his pistol at a Persian pilgrim's head, he came forth triumphant with two skins of sweetish water, for which we paid 10 piastres. He was in his glory. There were many Meccans in the Caravan, among them his elder brother and several friends: the Sherif Zayd had sent, he said, to ask why he did not travel with his compatriots. That evening he drank so copiously of clarified butter, and ate dates mashed with flour, and other abominations to such an extent, that at night he prepared to give up the ghost.

We passed a pleasant hour or two before sleeping. I began to like the old Shaykh Masud, who, seeing it, entertained me with his genealogy, his battles, and his family affairs. The rest of the party could not prevent expressing contempt when they heard me putting frequent questions about torrents, hills, Bedawin, and the directions of places. 'Let the Father of Mustachios ask and learn,' said the old man; 'he is friendly with the Bedawi, and knows better than you all.' This reproof was intended to be bitter as the poet's satire—

> All fools have still an itching to deride,
> And fain would be upon the laughing side.

It called forth, however, another burst of merriment, for the jeerers remembered my nickname to have belonged to that pestilent heretic, Saad the Wahhabi.

On Saturday, the 3rd September, the hateful signal-gun awoke us at one a.m. In Arab travel there is nothing more disagreeable than the Sariyah or night-march, and yet the people are inexorable about it. 'Choose early Darkness (daljah) for your Wayfarings,' said the Prophet, 'as the Calamities of the Earth (serpents and wild beasts) appear not at Night.' I can scarcely find words to express the weary horrors of the long dark march, during which the hapless traveller, fuming, if a European, with disappointment in his hopes of 'seeing the country', is compelled to sit upon the back of a creeping camel. The day sleep, too, is a kind of lethargy, and it is all but impossible to preserve an appetite during the hours of heat.

At half-past five a.m., after drowsily stumbling through hours of outer gloom, we entered a spacious basin at least six miles broad, and limited by a circlet of low hill. It was overgrown with camel-grass and Acacia (Shittim) trees, mere vegetable mummies; in many places the water had left a mark; and here and there the ground was pitted with mud-flakes, the remains of recently dried pools. After an hour's rapid march we toiled over a rugged ridge, composed of broken and detached blocks of basalt and scoriae, fantastically piled together, and dotted with thorny trees. Shaykh Masud passed the time in walking to and fro along his line of camels, addressing us with a *Khallikum guddam*, 'to the front (of the litter)!' as we ascended, and a *Khallikum wara*, 'to the rear!' during the descent. It was wonderful to see the animals stepping from block to block with the sagacity of mountaineers; assuring themselves of their forefeet before trusting all their weight to advance. Not a camel fell, either here or on any other ridge: they moaned, however, piteously, for the sudden turns of the path puzzled them; the ascents were painful, the descents were still more so; the rocks were sharp; deep holes yawned between the blocks, and occasionally an Acacia caught the Shugduf, almost overthrowing the hapless bearer by the suddenness and the tenacity of its clutch. This passage took place during daylight. But we had many at night, which I shall neither forget nor describe.

Descending the ridge, we entered another hill-encircled basin of gravel and clay. In many places basalt in piles and crumbling strata of hornblende schiste, disposed edgeways, green within, and without blackened by sun and rain, cropped out of the ground. At half-past ten we found ourselves in an Acacia-barren, one of the things which pilgrims dread. Here Shugdufs are bodily pulled off the camel's back and broken upon the hard ground; the animals drop upon their knees, the whole line is deranged, and every one, losing temper, attacks his Moslem brother. The road was flanked on the left by an iron wall of black basalt. Noon brought us to another ridge, whence we descended into a second wooded basin surrounded by hills.

Here the air was filled with those pillars of sand so graphically described by Abyssinian Bruce. They scudded on the wings of the whirlwind over the plain, huge yellow shafts, with lofty heads, horizontally bent backwards, in the form of clouds; and on more than one occasion camels were thrown down by them. It required little stretch of fancy to enter into the Arabs' superstition. These sand-columns are supposed to be Genii of the Waste, which cannot be caught, a notion arising from the fitful movements of the electrical wind-eddy that raises them, and, as they advance, the pious Moslem stretches out his finger, exclaiming, 'Iron! O thou ill-omened one!'

During the forenoon we were troubled by the Simoom, which, instead of promoting perspiration, chokes up and hardens the skin. The Arabs complain greatly of its violence on this line of road. Here I first remarked the difficulty with which the Bedawin bear thirst. *Ya Latif*—'O Merciful (Lord)!'—they exclaimed at times; and yet they behaved like men.[1] I had ordered them to place the water-camel in front, so as to exercise due supervision. Shaykh Masud and his son made only an occasional reference to the skins. But his nephew, a short, thin, pock-marked lad of eighteen, whose black skin and woolly head suggested the idea of a semi-African and ignoble origin, was always drinking; except when he climbed the camel's back, and, dozing upon the damp load, forgot his thirst. In vain we ordered, we taunted, and we abused him: he *would* drink, he *would* sleep, but he would *not* work.

[1] The Eastern Arabs allay the torments of thirst by a spoonful of clarified butter, carried on journeys in a leathern bottle. Every European traveller has some recipe of his own. One chews a musket-bullet or a small stone. A second smears his legs with butter. Another eats a crust of dry bread, which exacerbates the torments, and afterwards brings relief. A fourth throws water over his face and hands or his legs and feet; a fifth smokes, and a sixth turns his dorsal region (raising his coat-tail) to a toasting fire. I have always found that the only remedy is to be patient and not to talk. The more you drink, the more you require to drink—water or strong waters. But after the first two hours' abstinence you have mastered the overpowering feeling of thirst, and then to refrain is easy.

At one p.m. we crossed a Fiumara; and an hour afterwards we pursued the course of a second. Masud called this the Wady el-Khunak, and assured me that it runs from the east and the south-east in a north and north-west direction, to the Medinah plain. Early in the afternoon we reached a diminutive flat, on the Fiumara bank. Beyond it lies a *Mahjar* or stony ground, black as usual in El-Hejaz, and over its length lay the road, white with dust and the sand deposited by the camels' feet. Having arrived before the Pasha, we did not know where to pitch; many opining that the Caravan would traverse the *Mahjar* and halt beyond it. We soon alighted, however, pitched the tent under a burning sun, and were imitated by the rest of the party. Masud called the place Hijriyah. According to my computation, it is twenty-five miles from Ghurab, and its direction is south-east 22°.

Late in the afternoon the boy Mohammed started with a dromedary to procure water from the higher part of the Fiumara. Here are some wells, still called Bir Harun, after the great Caliph. The youth returned soon with two bags filled at an expense of 9 piastres. This being the 28th Zu'l Kaadah, many pilgrims busied themselves rather fruitlessly with endeavours to sight the crescent moon. They failed; but we were consoled by seeing through a gap in the western hills a heavy cloud discharge its blessed load, and a cool night was the result.

We loitered on Sunday, the 4th September, at El-Hijriyah, although the Shaykh forewarned us of a long march. But there is a kind of discipline in these great Caravans. A gun sounds the order to strike the tents, and a second bids you move off with all speed. There are short halts, of half an hour each, at dawn, noon, the afternoon, and sunset, for devotional purposes, and these are regulated by a cannon or a culverin. At such times the Syrian and Persian servants, who are admirably expert in their calling, pitch the large green tents, with gilt crescents, for the dignitaries and their harems. The lasting resting-place is known by the hurrying forward of these Farrash, or tent Lascars, who are determined to be the first on the ground and at the well. A discharge of three guns denotes the station, and when the Caravan moves by night, a single cannon sounds three or four halts at irregular intervals.

The principal officers were the Emir Hajj, one Ashgar Ali Pasha, a veteran of whom my companions spoke slightingly, because he had been the slave of a slave, probably the pipe-bearer of some other grandee. Under him was a Wakil, or lieutenant, who managed the executive. The Emir el-Surrah—called simply El-Surrah, or the Purse—had charge of the caravan-treasure, and remittances to the Holy Cities. And lastly there was a commander of the forces (Bashat el-Askar): his host consisted of about 1,000 irregular horsemen, Bash-Buzuks, half bandits, half soldiers, each habited and armed after his own fashion, exceeedingly dirty, picturesque-looking, brave, and in such a country of no use whatever.

Leaving El-Hijriyah at seven a.m., we passed over the grim stone-field by a detestable footpath, and at nine o'clock struck into a broad Fiumara, which runs from the east towards the north-west. Its sandy bed is overgrown with Acacia, the Senna plant, different species of Euphorbiae, the wild Capparis, and the Daum Palm. Up this line we travelled the whole day. About six p.m., we came upon a basin at least twelve miles broad, which absorbs the water of the adjacent hills. Accustomed as I have been to mirage, a long thin line of salt efflorescence appearing at some distance on the plain below us, when the shades of evening invested the view, completely deceived me. Even the Arabs were divided in opinion, some thinking it was the effects of the rain which fell the day before: others were more acute. It is said that beasts are never deceived by the mirage, and this, as far as my experience goes, is correct. May not the reason be that most of them know the vicinity of water rather by smell than by sight?

Upon the horizon beyond the plain rose dark, fort-like masses of rock which I mistook for buildings, the more readily as the Shaykh had warned me that we were approaching a populous place. At last descending a long steep hill, we entered upon the level ground, and discovered our error by the crunching sound of the camels' feet upon large curling flakes of nitrous salt overlying caked mud. Those civilised birds, the kite and the crow, warned us that we were in the vicinity of man. It was not, however, before eleven p.m. that we entered the confines of El-

Suwayrkiyah. The fact was made patent to us by the stumbling and the falling of our dromedaries over the little ridges of dried clay disposed in squares upon the fields. There were other obstacles, such as garden walls, wells, and hovels, so that midnight had sped before our weary camels reached the resting-place. A rumour that we were to halt here the next day made us think lightly of present troubles; it proved, however, to be false.

During the last four days I attentively observed the general face of the country. This line is a succession of low plains and basins, here quasi-circular, there irregularly oblong, surrounded by rolling hills and cut by Fiumaras which pass through the higher ground. The basins are divided by ridges and flats of basalt and greenstone averaging from 100 to 200 feet in height. The general form is a huge prism; sometimes they are table-topped. From El-Medinah to El-Suwayrkiyah the low beds of sandy Fiumaras abound. From El-Suwayrkiyah to El-Zaribah, their place is taken by Ghadir, or hollows in which water stagnates. And beyond El-Zaribah the traveller enters a region of water-courses trending west and south-west. The versant is generally from the east and south-east toward the west and north-west. Water obtained by digging is good where rain is fresh in the Fiumaras; saltish, so as to taste at first unnaturally sweet, in the plains; and bitter in the basins and lowlands where nitre effloresces and rain has had time to become tainted. The landward faces of the hills are disposed at a sloping angle, contrasting strongly with the perpendicularity of their seaward sides, and I found no inner range corresponding with, and parallel to, the maritime chain.

Nowhere had I seen a land in which Earth's anatomy lies so barren, or one richer in volcanic and primary formations. Especially towards the south, the hills were abrupt and highly vertical, with black and barren flanks, ribbed with furrows and fissures, with wide and formidable precipices and castellated summits like the work of man. The predominant formation was basalt, called the Arabs' Hajar Jehannum, or Hell-stone; here and there it is porous and cellular; in some places compact and black; and in others coarse and gritty, of a tarry colour, and when fractured shining with bright points. Hornblende is common at

El-Medinah and throughout this part of El-Hejaz: it crops out of the ground edgeways, black and brittle. Greenstone, diorite, and actinolite are found, though not so abundantly as those above mentioned. The granites, called in Arabic Suwan, abound. Some are large-grained, of a pink colour, and appear in blocks, which, flaking off under the influence of the atmosphere, form oöidal blocks and boulders piled in irregular heaps. Others are grey and compact enough to take a high polish when cut. The syenite is generally coarse, although there is occasionally found a rich red variety of that stone. I did not see eurite or euritic porphyry except in small pieces, and the same may be said of the petrosilex and the milky and waxy quartz.[1] In some parts, particularly between Yambu' and El-Medinah, there is an abundance of tawny yellow gneiss markedly stratified. The transition formations are represented by a fine calcareous sandstone of a bright ochre colour: it is used at Meccah to adorn the exteriors of houses, bands of this stone being here and there inserted into the courses of masonry. There is also a small admixture of the greenish sandstone which abounds at Aden. The secondary formation is represented by a fine limestone, in some places almost fit for the purposes of lithography, and a coarse gypsum often of a tufaceous nature. For the superficial accumulations of the country, I may refer the reader to any description of the Desert between Cairo and Suez.

[1] NOTE TO THIRD EDITION. This country may have contained gold; but the superficial formation has long been exhausted. At Cairo I washed some sand brought from the eastern shore of the Red Sea, north of El-Wijh, and found it worth my while. I had a plan for working the diggings, but HBM's Consul, Dr Walne, opined that 'gold was becoming too plentiful', and would not assist me. This wise saying has since then been repeated to me by men who ought to have known better than Dr Walne.

XXV
The Bedawin of El-Hejaz

The Arab may be divided into three races—a classification which agrees equally well with genesitic genealogy, the traditions of the country, and the observations of modern physiologists.[1]

The first race, indigens or autochthones, are those sub-Caucasian tribes which may still be met with in the province of Mahrah, and generally along the coast between Muscat and Hadramaut. The Mahrah, the Jenebah, and the Gara especially show a low development, for which hardship and privation only will not satisfactorily account. These are *Arab el-Aribah* for whose inferiority oriental fable accounts as usual by thaumaturgy.

The principal advenae are the Noachians, a Chaldaean or Mesopotamian tribe which entered Arabia about 2200 AC, and by slow and gradual encroachments drove before them the ancient owners and seized the happier lands of the Peninsula. The great Anezah tribe and the Nejdi families are types of this race, which is purely Caucasian, and shows a highly nervous temperament, together with those signs of blood which distinguish even the lower animals, the horse and camel, the greyhound and the goat of Arabia. These advenae would correspond with the *Arab el-Mutarrabah* or Arabicised Arabs of the eastern historians.

The third family, an ancient and a noble race dating from 1900 AC, and typified in history by Ishmael, still occupies the

[1] In Holy Writ, as the indigens are not alluded to—only the Noachian race being described—we find two divisions:
(1) The children of Joktan (great-grandson of Shem), Mesopotamians settled in Southern Arabia, 'from Mesha (Musa or Meccah?) to Sephar (Zafar) a Mount of the East' (Genesis x. 30): that is to say, they occupied the lands from El-Tehamah to Mahrah.
(2) The children of Ishmael, and his Egyptian wife; they peopled only the wilderness of Paran in the Sinaitic Peninsula and the parts adjacent.

Dr Aloys Sprenger (*Life of Mohammed*, p. 18) throws philosophic doubt upon the Ishmaelitish descent of Mohammed, who in personal appearance was a pure Caucasian, without any mingling of Egyptian blood.

so-called Sinaitic Peninsula. These Arabs, however, do not, and never did, extend beyond the limits of the mountains, where, still dwelling in the presence of their brethren, they retain all the wild customs and the untamable spirit of their forefathers. They are distinguished from the pure stock by an admixture of Egyptian blood, and by preserving the ancient characteristics of the Nilotic family. The Ishmaelities are sub-Caucasian, and are denoted in history as the *Arab el-Mustaribah*, the insititious or half-caste Arab.

Oriental ethnography, which, like most eastern sciences, luxuriates in nomenclative distinction, recognises a fourth race under the name of *Arab el-Mustajamah*. These 'barbarised Arabs' are now represented by such a population as that of Meccah.

That Aus and Khazraj, the Himyaritic tribes which emigrated to El-Hejaz, mixed with the Amalikah, the Jurham, and the Katirah, also races from Yemen, and with the Hebrews, a northern branch of the Semitic family, we have ample historical evidence. And they who know how immutable is race in the desert, will scarcely doubt that the Bedawi of El-Hejaz preserves in purity the blood transmitted to him by his ancestors.

I will not apologise for entering into details concerning the *personale* of the Bedawin; a precise physical portrait of race, it has justly been remarked, is the sole deficiency in the pages of Bruce and Burckhardt.

The temperament of the Hejazi is not unfrequently the pure nervous, as the height of the forehead and the fine texture of the hair prove. Sometimes the bilious, and rarely the sanguine, elements predominate: the lymphatic I never saw. He has large nervous centres, and well-formed spine and brain, a conformation favourable to longevity. Bartema well describes his colour as a 'dark leonine': it varies from the deepest Spanish to a chocolate hue, and its varieties are attributed by the people to blood. The skin is hard, dry, and soon wrinkled by exposure. The xanthous complexion is rare, though not unknown in cities, but the leucous does not exist. The crinal hair is frequently lightened by bleaching, and the pilar is browner than the crinal. The voice is strong and clear, but rather barytone than bass: in anger it becomes a shrill chattering like the cry of a wild animal.

The look of a chief is dignified and grave even to pensiveness; the 'respectable man's' is self-sufficient and fierce; the lower orders look ferocious, stupid, and inquisitive. Yet there is not much difference in this point between men of the same tribe, who have similar pursuits which engender similar passions. Expression is the grand diversifier of appearance among civilised people: in the Desert it knows few varieties.

The Bedawi cranium is small, oöidal, long, high, narrow, and remarkable in the occiput for the development of Gall's second propensity; the crown slopes upwards towards the region of firmness, which is elevated; whilst the sides are flat to a fault. The hair, exposed to sun, wind, and rain, acquires a coarseness not natural to it: worn in *Kurun*—ragged elf-locks—hanging down to the breast, or shaved in the form Shushah, a skull-cap of hair, nothing can be wilder than its appearance. The face is made to be a long oval, but want of flesh detracts from its regularity. The forehead is high, broad, and retreating; the upper portion is moderately developed; but nothing can be finer than the lower brow, and the frontal sinuses stand out, indicating bodily strength and activity of character. The temporal fossa are deep, the bones are salient, and the elevated zygomata combined with the lantern-jaw, often give a 'death's-head' appearance to the face. The eyebrows are long, bushy, and crooked, broken, as it were, at the angle where 'Order' is supposed to be, and bent in sign of thoughtfulness. Most popular writers, following De Page, describe the Arab eye as large, ardent, and black. The Bedawi of the Hejaz, and indeed the race generally, has a small eye, round, restless, deep-set, and fiery, denoting keen inspection with an ardent temperament and an impassioned character. Its colour is dark brown or green-brown, and the pupil is often speckled. The habit of pursing up the skin below the orbits, and half closing the lids to exclude glare, plants the outer angles with premature crows'-feet. Another peculiarity is the sudden way in which the eye opens, especially under excitement. This, combined with its fixity of glance, forms an expression now of lively fierceness, then of exceeding sternness; whilst the narrow space between the orbits impresses the countenance in repose with an intelligence not destitute of cunning.

As a general rule, however, the expression of the Bedawi face is rather dignity than that cunning for which the Semitic race is celebrated, and there are lines about the mouth in variance with the stern or the fierce look of the brow. The ears are like those of Arab horses, small, well-cut, 'castey', and elaborate, with many elevations and depressions. The nose is pronounced, generally aquiline, but sometimes straight like those Greek statues which have been treated as prodigious exaggerations of the facial angle. For the most part, it is a well-made feature with delicate nostrils, below which the septum appears: in anger they swell and open like a blood mare's. I have, however, seen, in not a few instances, pert and offensive pugs. Deep furrows descend from the wings of the nose, showing an uncertain temper, now too grave, then too gay. The mouth is irregular. The lips are either *bordés*, denoting rudeness and want of taste, or they form a mere line. In the latter case there is an appearance of undue development in the upper portion of the countenance, especially when the jaws are ascetically thin, and the chin weakly retreats. The latter feature, however, is generally well and strongly made. The teeth, as usual among Orientals, are white, even, short, and broad—indications of strength. Some tribes trim their mustachios according to the Sunnat; the Shafei often shave them, and many allow them to hang Persian-like over the lips. The beard is represented by two tangled tufts upon the chin; where whisker should be, the place is either bare or thinly covered with straggling pile.

The Bedawin of El-Hejaz are short men, about the height of the Indians near Bombay, but weighing on an average a stone more. As usual in this stage of society, stature varies little; you rarely see a giant, and scarcely ever a dwarf. Deformity is checked by the Spartan restraint upon population, and no weakly infant can live through a Bedawi life. The figure, though spare, is square and well knit; fulness of limb seldom appears but about spring, when milk abounds: I have seen two or three muscular figures, but never a fat man. The neck is sinewy, the chest broad, the flank thin, and the stomach in-drawn; the legs, though fleshless, are well made, especially when the knee and ankle are not bowed by too early riding. The shins do not bend cucumber-like to the front as in the African race. The arms are thin, with muscles like whipcords, and the hands and feet are, in point of size and delicacy, a link between Europe and India. As in the Celt, the Arab thumb is remarkably long, extending almost to the first joint of the index, which, with its easy rotation, makes it a perfect prehensile instrument: the palm also is fleshless, small-boned, and elastic. With his small active figure, it is not strange that the wildest Bedawi gait should be pleasing; he neither unfits himself for walking, nor distorts his ankles by turning out his toes according to the farcical rule of fashion, and his shoulders are not dressed like a drill-sergeant's, to throw all the weight of the body upon the heels. Yet there is no slouch in his walk; it is light and springy, and errs only in one point, sometimes becoming a strut.

Such is the Bedawi, and such he has been for ages. The national type has been preserved by systematic intermarriage. The wild men do not refuse their daughters to a stranger, but the son-in-law would be forced to settle among them, and this life, which has its charms for awhile, ends in becoming wearisome. Here no evil results are anticipated from the union of first cousins, and the experience of ages and of a mighty nation may be trusted. Every Bedawi has a right to marry his father's brother's daughter before she is given to a stranger; hence cousin (*Bint Amm*) in polite phrase signifies a wife. Our physiologists[1] adduce the Sangre Azul of Spain and the case of the lower animals to prove that degeneracy inevitably follows breeding-in. Either they have theorised from insufficient facts, or civilisation and artificial living exercise some peculiar influence, or Arabia is a solitary exception to a general rule. The fact which I have mentioned is patent to every Eastern traveller.

After this long description, the reader will perceive with pleasure that we are approaching an interesting theme, the first question of mankind to the wanderer—'What are the women like?'

[1] Dr Howe (*Report on Idiotcy in Massachusetts*, 1848) asserts that 'the law against the marriage of relations is made out as clearly as though it were written on tables of stone'. He proceeds to show that in seventeen households where the parents were connected by blood, of ninety-five children one was a dwarf, one deaf, twelve scrofulous, and forty-four idiots—total fifty-eight diseased!

Truth compels me to state that the women of the Hejazi Bedawin are by no means comely. Although the Benu Amr boast of some pretty girls, yet they are far inferior to the high-bosomed beauties of Nejd. And I warn all men that if they run to El-Hejaz in search of the charming face which appears in my sketch-book as 'a Bedawi girl', they will be bitterly disappointed: the dress was Arab, but it was worn by a fairy of the West.

The Hejazi woman's eyes are fierce, her features harsh, and her face haggard; like all people of the South, she soon fades, and in old age her appearance is truly witch-like. Withered crones abound in the camps, where old men are seldom seen. The sword and the sun are fatal to

A green old age, unconscious of decay.

The manners of the Bedawin are free and simple: 'vulgarity' and affectation, awkwardness and embarrassment, are weeds of civilised growth, unknown to the People of the Desert.[1] Yet their manners are sometimes dashed with a strange ceremoniousness. When two friends meet, they either embrace or both extend the right hands, clapping palm to palm; their foreheads are either pressed together, or their heads are moved from side to side, whilst for minutes together mutual inquiries are made and answered. It is a breach of decorum, even when eating, to turn the back upon a person, and if a Bedawi does it, he intends an insult. When a man prepares coffee, he drinks the first cup: the *Sharbat Kajari* (poison) of the Persians, and the Sulaymani of Egypt, render this precaution necessary. As a friend approaches the camp—it is not done to strangers for fear of startling them—those who catch sight of him shout out his name, and gallop up saluting with lances or firing matchlocks in the air. This is the well-known *Laab el-Barut* or gunpowder play. Bedawin are generally polite in language, but in anger temper is soon shown, and, although life be in peril, the foulest epithets—dog, drunkard, liar, and infidel—are discharged like pistol-shots by both disputants.

The best character of the Bedawi is a truly noble compound

[1] This sounds in English like an 'Irish bull'. I translate Badu, as the dictionaries do, 'a desert'.

of determination, gentleness, and generosity. Usually they are a mixture of worldly cunning and great simplicity, sensitive to touchiness, good-tempered souls, solemn and dignified withal, fond of a jest, yet of a grave turn of mind, easily managed by a laugh and a soft word, and placable after passion, though madly revengeful after injury. It has been sarcastically said of the Benu-Harb that there is not a man

> *Que s'il ne violoit, voloit, tuoit, brûloit*
> *Ne fût assez bonne personne.*

The reader will inquire, like the critics of a certain modern humorist, how the fabric of society can be supported by such material. In the first place, it is a kind of *société léonine* in which the fiercest, the strongest, and the craftiest obtains complete mastery over his fellows, and this gives a keystone to the arch. Secondly, there is the terrible blood-feud, which even the most reckless fear for their posterity. And, thirdly, though the revealed law of the Koran, being insufficient for the desert, is openly disregarded, the immemorial customs of the Kazi el-Arab (the Judge of the Arabs)[1] form a system stringent in the extreme.

The valour of the Bedawi is fitful and uncertain. Man is by nature an animal of prey, educated by the complicated relations of society, but readily relapsing into his old habits. Ravenous and sanguinary propensities grow apace in the Desert, but for the same reason the recklessness of civilisation is unknown there. Savages and semi-barbarians are always cautious, because they have nothing valuable but their lives and limbs. The civilised man, on the contrary, has a hundred wants or hopes or

[1] Throughout the world the strictness of the Lex Scripta is in inverse ratio to that of custom: whenever the former is lax, the latter is stringent, and vice versa. Thus in England, where law leaves men comparatively free, they are slaves to a grinding despotism of conventionalities, unknown in the lands of tyrannical rule. This explains why many, accustomed to live under despotic governments, feel fettered and enslaved in the so-called free countries. Hence, also, the reason why notably in a republic there is less private and practical liberty than under a despotism.

The Kazi el-Arab (Judge of the Arabs) is in distinction to the Kazi el-Shara or the Kazi of the Koran. The former is, almost always, some sharp-witted greybeard, with a minute knowledge of genealogy and precedents, a retentive memory, and an eloquent tongue.

aims, without which existence has for him no charms. Arab ideas of bravery do not prepossess us. Their romances, full of foolhardy feats and impossible exploits, might charm for a time, but would not become the standard works of a really fighting people. Nor would a truly valorous race admire the cautious freebooters who safely fire down upon caravans from their eyries. Arab wars, too, are a succession of skirmishes, in which 500 men will retreat after losing a dozen of their number. In this partisan-fighting the first charge secures a victory, and the vanquished fly till covered by the shades of night. Then come cries and taunts of women, deep oaths, wild poetry, excitement, and reprisals, which will probably end in the flight of the former victor. When peace is to be made, both parties count up their dead, and the usual blood-money is paid for excess on either side. Generally, however, the feud endures till, all becoming weary of it, some great man, as the Sherif of Meccah, is called upon to settle the terms of a treaty, which is nothing but an armistice. After a few months' peace, a glance or a word will draw blood, for these hates are old growths, and new dissensions easily shoot up from them.

But contemptible though their battles be, the Bedawin are not cowards. The habit of danger in raids and blood-feuds, the continual uncertainty of existence, the desert, the chase, the hard life and exposure to the air, blunting the nervous system; the presence and the practice of weapons, horsemanship, sharpshooting, and martial exercises, habituate them to look death in the face like men, and powerful motives will make them heroes. The English, it is said, fight willingly for liberty, our neighbours for glory; the Spaniard fights, or rather fought, for religion and the *Pundonor*; and the Irishman fights for the fun of fighting. Gain and revenge draw the Arab's sword; yet then he uses it fitfully enough, without the gay gallantry of the French or the persistent stay of the Anglo-Saxon. To become desperate he must have the all-powerful stimulants of honour and fanaticism. Frenzied by the insults of his women, or by the fear of being branded as a coward, he is capable of any mad deed. And the obstinacy produced by strong religious impressions gives a steadfastness to his spirit unknown to mere enthusiasm. The history of the Bedawi tells this plainly. Some unobserving travellers, indeed, have mistaken his exceeding cautiousness for stark cowardice. The incongruity is easily read by one who understands the principles of Bedawi warfare; with them, as amongst the Red Indians, one death dims a victory. And though reckless when their passions are thoroughly aroused, though heedless of danger when the voice of honour calls them, the Bedawin will not sacrifice themselves for light motives. Besides, they have, as has been said, another and a potent incentive to cautiousness. Whenever peace is concluded, they must pay for victory.

There are two things which tend to soften the ferocity of Bedawi life. These are, in the first place, intercourse with citizens, who frequently visit and entrust their children to the people of the Black tents; and, secondly, the social position of the women.

The Rev. Charles Robertson, author of a certain *Lecture on Poetry, addressed to Working Men*, asserts that Passion became Love under the influence of Christianity, and that the idea of a Virgin Mother spread over the sex a sanctity unknown to the poetry or the philosophy of Greece and Rome.[1] Passing over the objections of deified Eros and Immortal Psyche, and of the Virgin Mother—symbol of moral purity—being common to every old and material faith, I believe that all the noble tribes of savages display the principle. Thus we might expect to find, wherever the fancy, the imagination, and the ideality are strong, some traces of a sentiment innate in the human organisation. It exists, says Mr Catlin, amongst the North American Indians, and even the Gallas and the Somal of Africa are not destitute of it.

Miss Martineau, when travelling through Egypt, once visited a harem, and there found, among many things, especially in ignorance of books and book-making, materials for a heart-broken wail over the degradation of her sex. The learned lady

[1] Though differing in opinion upon one subject with the Rev. Mr Robertson, the lamented author of this little work, I cannot refrain from expressing the highest admiration of those noble thoughts, those exalted views, and those polished sentiments which, combining the delicacy of the present with the chivalry of a past age, appear in a style

As smooth as woman and as strong as man.

Would that it were in my power to pay a more adequate tribute to his memory!

indulges, too, in sundry strong and unsavoury comparisons between the harem and certain haunts of vice in Europe.

On the other hand, male travellers generally speak lovingly of the harem. Sonnini, no admirer of Egypt, expatiates on 'the generous virtues, the examples of magnanimity and affectionate attachment, the sentiments ardent, yet gentle, forming a delightful unison with personal charms in the harems of the Mamelukes'.

As usual, the truth lies somewhere between the two extremes. Human nature, all the world over, differs but in degree. Everywhere women may be 'capricious, coy, and hard to please' in common conjunctures: in the hour of need they will display devoted heroism. Any chronicler of the Afghan war will bear witness that warm hearts, noble sentiments, and an overflowing kindness to the poor, the weak, and the unhappy are found even in a harem. Europe now knows that the Moslem husband provides separate apartments and a distinct establishment for each of his wives, unless, as sometimes happens, one be an old woman and the other a child. And, confessing that envy, hatred, and malice often flourish in polygamy, the Moslem asks, Is monogamy open to no objections? As far as my limited observations go, polyandry is the only state of society in which jealousy and quarrels about the sex are the exception and not the rule of life.

In quality of doctor I have seen a little and heard much of the harem. It often resembles a European home composed of a man, his wife, and his mother. And I have seen in the West many a 'happy fireside' fitter to make Miss Martineau's heart ache than any harem in Grand Cairo.

Were it not evident that the spiritualising of sexuality by sentiment, of propensity by imagination, is universal among the highest orders of mankind—*c'est l'étoffe de la nature que l'imagination a brodée*, says Voltaire—I should attribute the origin of 'love' to the influence of the Arabs' poetry and chivalry upon European ideas rather than to mediaeval Christianity. Certain Fathers of the Church, it must be remembered, did not believe that women have souls. The Moslems never went so far.

In nomad life, tribes often meet for a time, live together whilst pasturage lasts, and then separate perhaps for a generation. Under such circumstances, youths who hold with the Italian that

Perduto e tutto il tempo
Che in amor non si spende,

will lose heart to maidens, whom possibly, by the laws of the clan, they may not marry, and the light o' love will fly her home. The fugitives must brave every danger, for revenge, at all times the Bedawi's idol, now becomes the lodestar of his existence. But the Arab lover will dare all consequences. 'Men have died and the worms have eaten them, but not for love,' may be true in the West: it is false in the East. This is attested in every tale where love, and not ambition, is the groundwork of the narrative. And nothing can be more tender, more pathetic than the use made of these separations and long absences by the old Arab poets. Whoever peruses the Suspended Poem of Lebid, will find thoughts at once so plaintive and so noble, that even Dr Carlyle's learned verse cannot wholly deface their charm.

The warrior-bard returns from afar. He looks upon the traces of hearth and home still furrowing the desert ground. In bitterness of spirit he checks himself from calling aloud upon his lovers and his friends. He melts at the remembrance of their departure, and long indulges in the absorbing theme. Then he strengthens himself by the thought of Nawara's inconstancy, how she left him and never thought of him again. He impatiently dwells upon the charms of the places which detain her, advocates flight from the changing lover and the false friend, and, in the exultation with which he feels his swift dromedary start under him upon her rapid course, he seems to seek and finds some consolation for woman's perfidy and forgetfulness. Yet he cannot abandon Nawara's name or memory. Again he dwells with yearning upon scenes of past felicity, and he boasts of his prowess—a fresh reproach to her—of his gentle birth, and of his hospitality. He ends with an encomium upon his clan, to which he attributes, as a noble Arab should, all the virtues of man. This is Goldsmith's deserted village in El-Hejaz. But the Arab, with equal simplicity and pathos, has a fire, a force of language, and a depth of feeling, which the Irishman, admirable as his verse is, could never rival.

As the author of the Peninsular War well remarks, women in troubled times, throwing off their accustomed feebleness and frivolity, become helpmates meet for man. The same is true of pastoral life. Here, between the extremes of fierceness and sensibility, the weaker sex, remedying its great want, power, raises itself by courage, physical as well as moral. In the early days of El-Islam, if history be credible, Arabia had a race of heroines. Within the last century, Ghaliyah, the wife of a Wahhabi chief, opposed Mohammed Ali himself in many a bloody field. A few years ago, when Ibn Asm, popularly called Ibn Rumi, chief of the Zubayd clan about Rabigh, was treacherously slain by the Turkish general, Kurdi Usman, his sister, a fair young girl, determined to revenge him. She fixed upon the Arafat-day of pilgrimage for the accomplishment of her designs, disguised herself in male attire, drew her kerchief in the form Lisam over the lower part of her face, and with lighted match awaited her enemy. The Turk, however, was not present, and the girl was arrested to win for herself a local reputation equal to the 'maid' of Salamanca. Thus it is that the Arab has learned to swear that great oath 'by the honour of my women'.

The Bedawin are not without a certain Platonic affection, which they call *Hawa* (or *Ishk*) *uzri*—pardonable love. They draw the fine line between *amant* and *amoureux:* this is derided by the townspeople, little suspecting how much such a custom says in favour of the wild men. Arabs, like other Orientals, hold that, in such matters, man is saved, not by faith, but by want of faith. They have also a saying not unlike ours—

> She partly is to blame who has been tried;
> He comes too near who comes to be denied.

The evil of this system is that they, like certain Southerns—*pensano sempre al male*—always suspect, which may be worldly-wise, and also always show their suspicions, which is assuredly foolish. For thus they demoralise their women, who might be kept in the way of right by self-respect and a sense of duty.

From ancient periods of the Arab's history we find him practising knight-errantry, the wildest form of chivalry. 'The Songs of Antar', says the author of *The Crescent and the Cross*, 'show little of the true chivalric spirit.' What thinks the reader of sentiments like these?[1] 'This valiant man', remarks Antar (who was 'ever interested for the weaker sex'), 'hath defended the honour of women.' We read in another place, 'Mercy, my lord, is the noblest quality of the noble.' Again, 'It is the most ignominious of deeds to take free-born women prisoners.' 'Bear not malice, O Shibub,' quoth the hero, 'for of malice good never came.' Is there no true greatness in this sentiment?—'Birth is the boast of the *fainéant*; noble is the youth who beareth every ill, who clotheth himself in mail during the noontide heat, and who wandereth through the outer darkness of night.' And why does the 'knight of knights' love Ibla? Because 'she is blooming as the sun at dawn, with hair black as the midnight shades, with Paradise in her eye, her bosom an enchantment, and a form waving like the tamarisk when the soft wind blows from the hills of Nejd'? Yes! but his chest expands also with the thoughts of her 'faith, purity, and affection'—it is her moral as well as her material excellence that makes her the hero's 'hope, and hearing, and sight'. Briefly, in Antar I discern

> a love exalted high,
> By all the glow of chivalry;

and I lament to see so many intelligent travellers misjudging the Arab after a superficial experience of a few debased Syrians or Sinaites. The true children of Antar, my Lord Lindsay, have *not* 'ceased to be gentlemen'.

In the days of ignorance, it was the custom for Bedawin, when tormented by the tender passion, which seems to have attacked them in the form of possession, for long years to sigh and wail and wander, doing the most truculent deeds to melt the obdurate fair. When Arabia Islamised, the practice changed its element for proselytism.

The fourth Caliph is fabled to have travelled far, redressing the injured, punishing the injurer, preaching to the Infidel, and

[1] I am not ignorant that the greater part of 'Antar' is of modern and disputed origin. Still it accurately expresses Arab sentiment.

especially protecting women—the chief end and aim of knighthood. The Caliph El-Mustasim heard in the assembly of his courtiers that a woman of Sayyid family had been taken prisoner by a 'Greek barbarian' of Ammoria. The man on one occasion struck her: when she cried 'Help me, O Mustasim!' and the clown said derisively, 'Wait till he cometh upon his pied steed!' The chivalrous prince arose, sealed up the wine-cup which he held in his hand, took oath to do his knightly devoir, and on the morrow started for Ammoria with 70,000 men, each mounted on a piebald charger. Having taking the place, he entered it, exclaiming, 'Labbayki, Labbayki!'—'Here am I at thy call!' He struck off the caitiff's head, released the lady with his own hands, ordered the cupbearer to bring the sealed bowl, and drank from it, exclaiming, 'Now, indeed, wine is good!'

To conclude this part of the subject with another far-famed instance. When El-Mutanabbi, the poet, prophet, and warrior of Hams (AH 354), started together with his son on their last journey, the father proposed to seek a place of safety for the night. 'Art thou the Mutanabbi', exclaimed his slave, 'who wrote these lines—

> ' "I am known to the night, to the wild, and the steed,
> To the guest, and the sword, to the paper and reed!" '[1]

The poet, in reply, lay down to sleep on Tigris' bank, in a place haunted by thieves, and, disdaining flight, lost his life during the hours of darkness.

It is the existence of this chivalry among the 'Children of Antar' which makes the society of Bedawin (damned saints, perchance, and honourable villains) so delightful to the traveller who, like the late Haji Wali (Dr Wallin), understands and is understood by them. Nothing more naïve than his lamentations at finding himself in the loathsome company of Persians, or among Arab townspeople, whose 'filthy and cowardly minds' he contrasts with the 'high and chivalrous spirit of the true Sons of the Desert'. Your guide will protect you with blade and spear, even against his kindred, and he expects you to do the same for

[1] I wish that the clever Orientalist who writes in the *Saturday Review* would not translate 'El-Layl' by *lenes sub nocte susurri:* the Arab bard alluded to no such effeminacies.

him. You may give a man the lie, but you must lose no time in baring your sword. If involved in dispute with overwhelming numbers, you address some elder, *Dakhilak, ya Shaykh!*—'(I am) thy protected, O Sir'—and he will espouse your quarrel with greater heat and energy, indeed, than if it were his own. But why multiply instances?

The language of love and war and all excitement is poetry, and here, again, the Bedawi excels. Travellers complain that the wild men have ceased to sing. This is true if 'poet' be limited to a few authors whose existence everywhere depends upon the accidents of patronage or political occurrences. A far stronger evidence of poetic feeling is afforded by the phraseology of the Arab, and the highly imaginative turn of his commonest expressions. Destitute of the poetic taste, as we define it, he certainly is: as in the Milesian, wit and fancy, vivacity and passion, are too strong for reason and judgment, the reins which guide Apollo's car. And although the Bedawin no longer boast a Lebid or a Maysunah, yet they are passionately fond of their ancient bards. A man skilful in reading El-Mutanabbi and the suspended Poems would be received by them with the honours paid by civilisation to the travelling millionaire. And their elders have a goodly store of ancient and modern war songs, legends, and love ditties which all enjoy.

I cannot well explain the effect of Arab poetry to one who has not visited the Desert. Apart from the pomp of words, and the music of the sound, there is a dreaminess of idea and a haze thrown over the object, infinitely attractive, but indescribable. Description, indeed, would rob the song of indistinctness, its essence. To borrow a simile from a sister art: the Arab poet sets before the mental eye, the dim grand outlines of picture—which must be filled up by the reader, guided only by a few glorious touches, powerfully standing out, and the sentiment which the scene is intended to express—whereas, we Europeans and moderns, by stippling and minute touches, produce a miniature on a large scale so objective as to exhaust rather than to arouse reflection. As the poet is a creator, the Arab's is poetry, the European's versical description. The language, 'like a faithful wife, following the mind and giving birth to its offspring', and free from that 'luggage of particles' which clogs our modern tongues, leaves a mysterious vagueness between the relation of word to word, which materially assists the sentiment, not the sense, of the poem. When verbs and nouns have, each one, many different significations, only the radical or general idea suggests itself. Rich and varied synonyms, illustrating the finest shades of meaning, are artfully used; now scattered to startle us by distinctness, now to form as it were a star about which dimly seen satellites revolve. And, to cut short a disquisition which might be prolonged indefinitely, there is in the Semitic dialect a copiousness of rhyme which leaves the poet almost unfettered to choose the desired expression. Hence it is that a stranger speaking Arabic becomes poetical as naturally as he would be witty in French and philosophic in German. Truly spake Mohammed el Damiri, 'Wisdom hath alighted upon three things—the brain of the Franks, the hands of the Chinese, and the tongues of the Arabs.'

The name of Harami—brigand—is still honourable among the Hejazi Bedawin. Slain in raid or foray, a man is said to die Ghandur, or a brave. He, on the other hand, who is lucky enough, as we should express it, to die in his bed, is called *Fatis* (carrion, the *corps crévé* of the Klephts); his weeping mother will exclaim, 'O that my son had perished of a cut throat!' and her attendant crones will suggest, with deference, that such evil came of the will of Allah. It is told of the Lahabah, a sept of the Auf near Rabigh, that a girl will refuse even her cousin unless, in the absence of other opportunities, he plunder some article from the Hajj Caravan in front of the Pasha's links. Detected twenty years ago, the delinquent would have been impaled; now he escapes with a rib-roasting. Fear of the blood-feud, and the certainty of a shut road to future travellers, prevent the Turks proceeding to extremes. They conceal their weakness by pretending that the Sultan hesitates to wage a war of extermination with the thieves of the Holy Land.

It is easy to understand this respect for brigands. Whoso revolts against society requires an iron mind in an iron body, and these mankind instinctively admires, however misdirected be their energies. Thus, in all imaginative countries, the brigand is a hero; even the assassin who shoots his victim from behind a hedge appeals to the fancy in Tipperary or on the Abruzzian hills. Romance invests his loneliness with grandeur; if he have a wife or a friend's wife, romance becomes doubly romantic, and a tithe of the superfluity robbed from the rich and bestowed upon the poor will win to Gasparoni the hearts of a people. The true Bedawi style of plundering, with its numerous niceties of honour and gentlemanly manners, gives the robber a consciousness of moral rectitude. 'Strip off that coat, O certain person! and that turban,' exclaims the highwayman, 'they are wanted by my lady-cousin.' You will (of course, if necessary) lend ready ear to an order thus politely attributed to the wants of the fair sex. If you will add a few obliging expressions to the bundle, and offer Latro a cup of coffee and a pipe, you will talk half your toilette back to your own person; and if you can quote a little poetry, you will part the best of friends, leaving perhaps only a pair of sandals behind you. But should you hesitate, Latro, lamenting the painful necessity, touches up your back with the heel of his spear. If this hint suffice not, he will make things plain by the lance's point, and when blood shows, the tiger-part of humanity appears. Between Bedawin, to be tamely plundered, especially of the mare, is a lasting disgrace; a man of family lays down his life rather than yield even to overpowering numbers. This desperation has raised the courage of the Bedawin to high repute amongst the settled Arabs, who talk of single braves capable, like the Homeric heroes, of overpowering 300 men.

I omit general details about the often-described Sar, or Vendetta. The price of blood is 800 dollars = 200*l.*, or rather that sum imperfectly expressed by live-stock. All the Khamsah or Aamam, blood relations of the slayer, assist to make up the required amount, rating each animal at three or four times its proper value. On such occasions violent scenes arise from the conflict of the Arab's two pet passions, avarice and revenge. The avenger of blood longs to cut the foe's throat. On the other hand, how let slip an opportunity of enriching himself? His covetousness is intense, as are all his passions. He has always a project of buying a new dromedary, or of investing capital in some marvellous colt; the consequence is, that he is insatiable. Still he receives blood-money with a feeling of shame; and if it be offered to an old woman—the most revengeful variety of our species, be it remarked—she will dash it to the ground, and clutch her knife, and fiercely swear by Allah that she will not 'eat' her son's blood.

The Bedawi considers himself a man only when mounted on horseback, lance in hand, bound for a foray or a fray, and carolling some such gaiety as—

> A steede! a steede of matchlesse speede!
> A sword of metal keene!
> All else to noble minds is drosse,
> All else on earth is meane.

Even in his sports he affects those that imitate war. Preserving the instinctive qualities which lie dormant in civilisation, he is an admirable sportsman. The children, men in miniature, begin with a rude system of gymnastics when they can walk. 'My young ones play upon the backs of camels,' was the reply made to me by a Jahayni Bedawi when offered some Egyptian plaything. The men pass their time principally in hawking, shooting, and riding. The Sakr, I am told, is the only falcon in general use; they train it to pursue the gazelle, which greyhounds pull down when fatigued. I have heard much of their excellent marksmanship, but saw only moderate practice with a long matchlock rested and fired at standing objects. Double-barreled guns are rare amongst them. Their principal weapons are matchlocks and firelocks, pistols, javelins, spears, swords, and the dagger called Jambiyah; the sling and the bow have long been given up. The guns come from Egypt, Syria, and Turkey; for the Bedawi cannot make, although he can repair, this arm. He particularly values a good old barrel seven spans long, and would rather keep it than his coat; consequently, a family often boasts of four or five guns, which descend from generation to generation. Their price varies from 2 to 60 dollars. The Bedawin collect nitre in the country, make excellent charcoal, and import sulphur from Egypt and India; their powder, however, is coarse and weak. For hares and birds they cut up into slugs a bar of lead hammered out to a convenient size, and they cast bullets in moulds. They are fond of ball-practice, firing, as every sensible man does, at short distances, and striving at extreme precision. They are ever backing themselves with wagers, and will shoot for a sheep, the loser inviting his friends to a feast: on festivals they boil the head, and use it as mark and prize. Those who affect excellence are said to fire at a bullet hanging by a thread; curious, however, to relate, the Bedawin of El-Hejaz have but just learned the art, general in Persia and Barbary, of shooting from horseback at speed.

Pistols have been lately introduced into the Hejaz, and are not common amongst the Bedawin. The citizens incline to this weapon, as it is derived from Constantinople. In the Desert a tolerable pair with flint locks may be worth 30 dollars, ten times their price in England.

The spears, called *Kanat*, or reeds, are made of male bamboos imported from India. They are at least twelve feet long, iron shod, with a tapering point, beneath which are one or two tufts of black ostrich feathers. Besides the Mirzak, or javelin, they have a spear called *Shalfah*, a bamboo or a palm-stick garnished with a head about the breadth of a man's hand.

No good swords are fabricated in El-Hejaz. The Khelawiyah and other Desert clans have made some poor attempts at blades. They are brought from Persia, India, and Egypt; but I never saw anything of value.

The *Darakah*, or shield, also comes from India. It is the common Cutch article, supposed to be made of rhinoceros hide, and displaying as much brass knob and gold wash as possible. The Bedawin still use in the remoter parts *Diraa*, or coats of mail, worn by horsemen over buff jackets.

The dagger is made in Yemen and other places: it has a vast variety of shapes, each of which, as usual, has its proper names. Generally they are but little curved (whereas the *Gadaymi* of Yemen and Hazramaut is almost a semicircle), with tapering blade, wooden handle, and scabbard of the same material overlaid with brass. At the point of the scabbard is a round knob, and the weapon is so long, that a man when walking cannot swing his right arm. In narrow places he must enter sideways. But it is the mode always to appear in dagger, and the weapon, like the French soldier's *coupe-choux*, is really useful for such bloodless purposes as cutting wood and gathering grass. In price they vary from 1 to 30 dollars.

The Bedawin boast greatly of sword-play; but it is apparently confined to delivering a tremendous slash, and to jumping away from a return-cut instead of parrying either with sword or shield. The citizens have learned the Turkish scimitar-play, which, in grotesqueness and general absurdity, rivals the East Indian school. None of these Orientals know the use of the point which characterises the highest school of swordsmanship.

The Hejazi Bedawin have no game of chance, and dare not, I am told, ferment the juice of the Daum palm, as proximity to Aden has taught the wild men of Yemen. Their music is in a rude state. The principal instrument is the Tabl, or kettle-drum, which is of two kinds: one, the smaller, used at festivals; the other, a large copper tom-tom, for martial purposes, covered with leather, and played upon, pulpit-like, with fist, and not with stick. Besides which, they have the one-stringed Rubabah, or guitar, that 'monotonous but charming instrument of the Desert'. In another place I have described their dancing, which is an ignoble spectacle.

The Bedawin of El-Hejaz have all the knowledge necessary for procuring and protecting the riches of savage life. They are perfect in the breeding, the training, and the selling of cattle. They know sufficient of astronomy to guide themselves by night, and are acquainted with the names of the principal stars. Their local memory is wonderful. And such is their instinct in the art of Asar, or tracking, that it is popularly said of the Zubayd clan, which lives between Meccah and El-Medinah, a man will lose a she-camel and know her four-year-old colt by its foot. Always engaged in rough exercises and perilous journeys, they have learned a kind of farriery and a simple system of surgery. In cases of fracture they bind on splints with cloth bands, and the patient drinks camel's milk and clarified butter till he is cured. Cuts are carefully washed, sprinkled with meal gunpowder, and sewn up. They dress gunshot wounds with raw camel's flesh, and rely entirely upon nature and diet. When bitten by snakes or stung by scorpions, they scarify the wound with a razor, recite a charm, and apply to it a dressing of garlic. The wealthy have *Fiss* or ring-stones, brought from India, and used with a formula of prayer to extract venom. Some few possess the *Teriyak* (Theriack) of El-Irak—the great counter-poison, internal as well as external, of the East. The poorer classes all wear the *Zaal* or *Hibas* of Yemen; two yarns of black sheep's wool tied round the leg, under the knee and above the ankle. When bitten, the sufferer tightens these cords above the injured part, which he immediately scarifies; thus they act as tourniquets. The ligatures also cure cramps—and there is no other remedy.

The Bedawi's knowledge of medicine is unusually limited in this part of Arabia, where even simples are not required by a people who rise with dawn, eat little, always breathe desert air, and 'at night make the camels their curfew'. The great tonic is clarified butter, and the *Kay*, or actual cautery, is used even for rheumatism. This counter-irritant, together with a curious and artful phlebotomy, blood being taken, as by the Italians, from the toes, the fingers, and other parts of the body, are the Arab panaceas. They treat scald-head with grease and sulphur. Ulcers, which here abound, without, however, assuming the fearful type of the *Helcoma Yemenense*, are cauterised and stimulated by verdigris. The evil of which Fracastorius sang is combated by sudorifics, by unguents of oil and sulphur, and especially by the sand-bath. The patient, buried up to the neck, remains in the sun fasting all day; in the evening he is allowed a little food. This rude course of 'packing' lasts for about a month. It suits some constitutions; but others, especially Europeans, have tried the sand-bath and died of fever. Mules' teeth, roasted and imperfectly pounded, remove cataract. Teeth are extracted by the farrier's pincers, and the worm which throughout the East is supposed to produce toothache, falls by fumigation. And, finally, after great fatigue, or when suffering from cold, the body is copiously greased with clarified butter and exposed to a blazing fire.

Mohammed and his followers conquered only the more civilised Bedawin; and there is even to this day little or no religion amongst the wild people, except those on the coast or in the vicinity of cities. The faith of the Bedawi comes from El-Islam, whose hold is weak. But his customs and institutions, the growth of his climate, his nature, and his wants, are still those of his ancestors, cherished ere Meccah had sent forth a Prophet, and likely to survive the day when every vestige of the Kaabah shall have disappeared. Of this nature are the Hejazi's pagan oaths, his heathenish names (few being Moslem except 'Mohammed'), his ordeal of licking red-hot iron, his Salkh, or scarification—proof of manliness—his blood-revenge, and his eating carrion (i.e. the body of an animal killed without the usual formula). All these I hold to be remnants of some old creed; nor should I despair of finding among the Bedawin bordering upon the Great Desert some lingering system of idolatry.

The Bedawin of El-Hejaz call themselves Shafei; but what is put into the mouths of their brethren in the West applies equally well here. 'We pray not, because we must drink the water of ablution; we give no alms, because we ask them; we fast not the Ramazan month, because we starve throughout the year; and we do no pilgrimage, because the world is the house of Allah.' Their blunders in religious matters supply the citizens with many droll stories. And it is to be observed that they do not, like the Greek pirates or the Italian bandits, preserve a religious element in their plunderings; they make no vows, and they carefully avoid offerings.

The ceremonies of Bedawi life are few and simple—circumcisions, marriages, and funerals. Of the former rite there are two forms, *Taharah*, as usual in El-Islam, and Salkh, an Arab invention, derived from the times of Paganism. During Wahhabi rule it was forbidden under pain of death, but now the people have returned to it. The usual age for *Taharah* is between five and six; among some classes, however, it is performed ten years later. On such occasions feastings and merrymakings take place, as at our christenings.

Women being a marketable commodity in barbarism as in civilisation, the youth in El-Hejaz is not married till his father can afford to buy him a bride. There is little pomp or ceremony save firing of guns, dancing, singing, and eating mutton. The settlement is usually about 30 sound Spanish dollars, half paid down, and the other half owed by the bridegroom to the father, the brothers, or the kindred of his spouse. Some tribes will take animals in lieu of ready money. A man of wrath not contented with his bride, puts her away at once. If peaceably inclined, by a short delay he avoids scandal. Divorces are very frequent among Bedawin, and if the settlement money be duly paid, no evil comes of them.

The funerals of the wild men resemble those of the citizens, only they are more simple, the dead being buried where they die. The corpse, after ablution, is shrouded in any rags procurable; and, women and hired weepers not being permitted to attend, it is carried to the grave by men only. A hole is dug, according to Moslem custom; dry wood, which everywhere abounds, is disposed to cover the corpse, and an oval of stones surrounding a mound of earth keeps out jackals and denotes the spot. These Bedawin have not, like the wild Sindis and Belochis, favourite cemeteries, to which they transport their dead from afar.

The traveller will find no difficulty in living amongst the Hejazi Bedawin. 'Trust to their honour, and you are safe,' as was said of the Crow Indians; 'to their honesty, and they will steal the hair off your head.' Only the wanderer must adopt the wild man's motto, *omnia mea mecum porto*; he must have good nerves, be capable of fatigue and hardship, possess some knowledge of drugs, shoot and ride well, speak Arabic and Turkish, know by reading the customs, and avoid offending against local prejudices, by causing himself, for instance, to be called *Taggaa*. The payment of a small sum secures to him a *Rafik*, and this 'friend', after once engaging in the task, will be faithful. 'We have eaten salt together' (*Nahnu Malihin*) is still a bond of friendship: there are, however, some tribes who require to renew the bond every twenty-four hours, as otherwise, to use their own phrase, 'the salt is not in their stomachs'. Caution must be exercised in choosing a companion who has not too many blood-feuds. There is no objection to carrying a copper watch and a pocket compass, and a Koran could be fitted with secret pockets for notes and pencil. Strangers should especially avoid handsome weapons; these tempt the Bedawi's cupidity more than gold. The other extreme, defencelessness, is equally objectionable. It is needless to say that the traveller must never be seen writing anything but charms, and on no account sketch in public. He should be careful in questioning, and rather lead up to information than ask directly. It offends some Bedawin, besides denoting ignorance and curiosity, to be asked their names or those of their clans: a man may be living incognito, and the tribes distinguish themselves when they desire to do so by dress, personal appearance, voice, dialect, and accentuation, points of difference plain to the initiated. A few dollars suffice for the road, and if you would be 'respectable', a taste which I will not deprecate, some such presents as razors and Tarbushes are required for the chiefs.

The government of the Arabs may be called almost an autonomy. The tribes never obey their Shaykhs, unless for personal considerations, and, as in a civilised army, there generally is some sharp-witted and brazen-faced individual whose voice is louder than the general's. In their leonine society the sword is the great administrator of law.

Relations between the Bedawi tribes of El-Hejaz are of a threefold character: they are either *Ashab, Kiman*, or *Akhwan*.

Ashab, or comrades, are those who are bound by oath to an alliance offensive and defensive: they intermarry, and are therefore closely connected.

Kiman, or foes, are tribes between whom a blood-feud, the cause and the effect of deadly enmity, exists.

Akhawat, or brotherhood, denotes the tie between the stranger and the Bedawi, who asserts an immemorial and inalienable right to the soil upon which his forefathers fed their flocks. Trespass by a neighbour instantly causes war. Territorial increase is rarely attempted, for if of a whole clan but a single boy escape he will one day assert his claim to the land, and be assisted by all the *Ashab*, or allies of the slain. By paying to man, woman, or child, a small sum, varying, according to your means, from a few pence worth of trinkets to a couple of dollars, you share bread and salt with the tribe, you and your horse become *Dakhil* (protected), and every one must afford you brother-help. If traveller or trader attempt to pass through the land without paying *El-Akhawah* or *El-Rifkah*, as it is termed, he must expect to be plundered, and, resisting, to be slain: it is no dishonour to pay it, and he clearly is in the wrong who refuses to conform to custom. The *Rafik*, under different names, exists throughout this part of the world; at Sinai he was called a *Ghafir*, a *Rabia* in Eastern Arabia, amongst the Somal an *Abban*, and by the Gallas a *Mogasa*. I have called the tax black-mail; it deserves a better name, being clearly the rudest form of those transit-dues and octrois which are in nowise improved by 'progress'. The Ahl Bayt, or dwellers in the Black Tents, levy the tax from the Ahl Hayt, or the People of Walls; that is to say, townsmen and villagers who have forfeited right to be held Bedawin. It is demanded from bastard Arabs, and from tribes who, like the Hutaym and the Khelawiyah, have been born basely or have become 'nidering'. And these people are obliged to pay it at home as well as abroad. Then it becomes a sign of disgrace, and the pure clans, like the Benu Harb, will not give their damsels in marriage to 'brothers'.

Besides this *Akhawat*-tax and the pensions by the Porte to chiefs of clans, the wealth of the Bedawi consists in his flocks and herds, his mare, and his weapons. Some clans are rich in horses; others are celebrated for camels; and not a few for sheep, asses, or greyhounds. The Ahamidah tribe, as has been mentioned, possesses few animals; it subsists by plunder and by presents from pilgrims. The principal wants of the country are sulphur, lead, cloths of all kinds, sugar, spices, coffee, corn, and rice. Arms are valued by the men, and it is advisable to carry a stock of Birmingham jewellery for the purpose of conciliating womankind. In exchange the Bedawin give sheep, cattle, clarified butter, milk, wool, and hides, which they use for water-bags, as the Egyptians and other Easterns do potteries. But as there is now a fair store of dollars in the country, it is rarely necessary to barter.

The Arab's dress marks his simplicity; it gives him a nationality, as, according to John Evelyn, 'prodigious breeches' did to the Swiss. It is remarkably picturesque, and with sorrow we see it now confined to the wildest Bedawin and a few Sherifs. To the practised eye, a Hejazi in Tarbush and Caftan is ridiculous as a Basque or a Catalonian girl in a cashmere and a little chip. The necessary dress of a man is his *Saub* (Tobe), a blue calico shirt, reaching from neck to ankles, tight or loose-sleeved, opening at the chest in front, and rather narrow below; so that the wearer, when running, must either hold it up or tuck it into his belt. The latter article, called *Hakw*, is a plaited leathern thong, twisted round the waist very tightly, so as to support the back. The trousers and the *Futah*, or loin-cloth of cities, are looked upon as signs of effeminacy. In cold weather the chiefs wear over the shirt an *Aba*, or cloak. These garments are made in Nejd and the eastern districts; they are of four colours, white, black, red, and brown-striped. The best are of camels' hair, and may cost 15 dollars; the worst, of sheep's wool, are worth only 3; both are cheap, as they last for years. The *Mahramah* (head-cloth) comes from Syria; which, with Nejd, supplies also the Kufiyah or headkerchief. The *Ukal*, fillets bound over the kerchief, are of many kinds; the Bishr tribe near Meccah make a kind of crown like the gloria round a saint's head, with bits of wood, in which are set pieces of mother-of-pearl. Sandals, too, are of every description, from the simple sole of leather tied on with thongs, to the handsome and elaborate chaussure of Meccah; the price varies from a piastre to a dollar, and the very poor walk bare-footed. A leathern bandoleer, called *Majdal*, passed over the left shoulder, and reaching to the right hip, supports a line of brass cylinders for cartridges. The other cross-belt (*El-Masdar*), made of leather ornamented with brass rings, hangs down at the left side, and carries a *Kharizah*, or hide-case for bullets. And finally, the Hizam, or waist-belt, holds the dagger and extra cartridge cases. A Bedawi never appears in public unarmed.

Women wear, like their masters, dark blue cotton Tobes, but larger and looser. When abroad they cover the head with a Yashmak of black stuff, or a poppy-coloured Burka (nose-bag) of the Egyptian shape. They wear no pantaloons, and they rarely affect slippers or sandals. The hair is twisted into *Majdul*, little pig-tails, and copiously anointed with clarified butter. The rich perfume the skin with rose and cinnamon-scented oils, and adorn the hair with El-Shayh (*Absinthium*), sweetest herb of the Desert; their ornaments are bracelets, collars, ear and nose-rings of gold, silver, or silver-gilt. The poorer classes have strings of silver coins hung round the neck.

The true Bedawi is an abstemious man, capable of living for six months on 10 oz. of food per diem; the milk of a single camel, and a handful of dates, dry or fried in clarified butter, suffice for his wants. He despises the obese and all who require regular and plentiful meals, sleeps on a mat, and knows neither luxury nor comfort, freezing during one-quarter and frying for three-quarters of the year. But though he can endure hunger, like all savages, he will gorge when an opportunity offers. I never saw the man who could refrain from water upon the line of march; and in this point they contrast disadvantageously with the hardy Wahhabis of the East, and the rugged mountaineers of Jebel Shammar. They are still 'acridophagi', and even the citizens far prefer a dish of locusts to the *Fasikh*, which act as anchovies, sardines, and herrings in Egypt. They light a fire at night, and as the insects fall dead they quote this couplet to justify their being eaten—

> We are allowed two carrions and two bloods,
> The fish and locust, the liver and the spleen.[1]

Where they have no crops to lose, the people are thankful for a fall of locusts. In El-Hejaz the flights are uncertain; during the last five years El-Medinah has seen but few. They are prepared for eating by boiling in salt water and drying four or five days in the sun: a 'wet' locust to an Arab is as a snail to a Briton. The head is plucked off, the stomach drawn, the wings and the prickly part of the legs are plucked, and the insect is ready for the table. Locusts are never eaten with sweet things, which would be nauseous: the dish is always hot, with salt and pepper, or onions fried in clarified butter, when it tastes nearly as well as a plate of stale shrimps.

The favourite food on the line of march is meat cut into strips and sun-dried. This, with a bag of milk-balls and a little coffee, must suffice for journey or campaign. The Bedawin know neither fermented nor distilled liquors, although *Ikhs ya'l Khammar!* ('Fie upon thee, drunkard!') is a popular phrase, preserving the memory of another state of things. Some clans, though not all, smoke tobacco. It is generally the growth of the country

[1] The liver and the spleen are both supposed to be congealed blood. Niebuhr has exhausted the names and the description of the locust. In El-Hejaz they have many local and fantastic terms: the smallest kind, for instance, is called *Jarad Iblis*, Satan's locust.

called Hejazi or Kazimiyah; a green weed, very strong, with a foul smell, and costing about 1 piastre per lb. The Bedawin do not relish Persian tobacco, and cannot procure Latakia: it is probably the pungency of the native growth offending the delicate organs of the Desert-men, that caused nicotiana to be proscribed by the Wahhabis, who revived against its origin a senseless and obsolete calumny.

The almost absolute independence of the Arabs, and of that noble race the North American Indians of a former generation, has produced a similarity between them worthy of note, because it may warn the anthropologist not always to detect in coincidence of custom identity of origin. Both have the same wild chivalry, the same fiery sense of honour, and the same boundless hospitality: elopements from tribe to tribe, the blood-feud, and the Vendetta are common to the two. Both are grave and cautious in demeanour, and formal in manner—princes in rags or paint. The Arabs plunder pilgrims; the Indians, bands of trappers; both glory in forays, raids, and cattle-lifting; and both rob according to certain rules. Both are alternately brave to desperation, and shy of danger. Both are remarkable for nervous and powerful eloquence; dry humour, satire, whimsical tales, frequent tropes; boasts, and ruffling style; pithy proverbs, extempore songs, and languages wondrous in their complexity. Both, recognising no other occupation but war and the chase, despise artificers and the effeminate people of cities, as the game-cock spurns the vulgar roosters of the poultry-yard. The chivalry of the western wolds, like that of the eastern wilds, salutes the visitor by a charge of cavalry, by discharging guns, and by wheeling around him with shouts and yells. The brave stamps a red hand upon his mouth to show that he has drunk the blood of a foe. Of the Utaybah Harami it is similarly related, that after mortal combat he tastes the dead man's gore.

Of these two chivalrous races of barbarians, the Bedawi claims our preference on account of his treatment of women, his superior development of intellect, and the glorious page of history which he has filled.

XXVI
From El-Suwayrkiyah to Meccah

We have now left the territory of El-Medinah. El-Suwayrkiyah, which belongs to the Sherif of Meccah, is about twenty-eight miles distant from Hijriyah, and by dead reckoning ninety-nine miles along the road from the Prophet's burial-place. Its bearing from the last station was south-west 11°. The town, consisting of about 100 houses, is built at the base and on the sides of a basaltic mass, which rises abruptly from the hard clayey plain. The summit is converted into a rude fortalice—without one, no settlement can exist in El-Hejaz—by a bulwark of uncut stone, piled up so as to make a parapet. The lower part of the town is protected by a mud-wall, with the usual semicircular towers. Inside there is a bazar, well supplied with meat (principally mutton) by the neighbouring Bedawin; and wheat, barley, and dates are grown near the town. There is little to describe in the narrow streets and the mud houses, which are essentially Arab. The fields around are divided into little square plots by earthen ridges and stone walls; some of the palms are fine-grown trees, and the wells appear numerous. The water is near the surface and plentiful, but it has a brackish taste, highly disagreeable after a few days' use, and the effects are the reverse of chalybeate.

The town belongs to the Benu Husayn, a race of schismatics mentioned in the foregoing pages. They claim the allegiance of the Bedawi tribes around, principally Mutayr, and I was informed that their fealty to the Prince of Meccah is merely nominal.

The morning after our arrival at El-Suwayrkiyah witnessed a commotion in our little party: hitherto they had kept together in fear of the road. Among the number was one Ali bin Ya Sin, a perfect 'old man of the sea'. By profession he was a Zem Zemi, or dispenser of water from the Holy Well, and he had a handsome *palazzo* at the foot of Abu Kubays in Meccah, which he periodically converted into a boarding-house. Though past sixty, very decrepit, bent by age, white-bearded, and toothless, he still acted cicerone to pilgrims, and for that purpose travelled once every year to El-Medinah. These trips had given him the cunning of a veteran voyageur. He lived well and cheaply; his home-made Shugduf, the model of comfort, was garnished with soft cushions and pillows, whilst from the pockets protruded select bottles of pickled limes and similar luxuries; he had his travelling Shishah (water-pipe), and at the halting-place, disdaining the crowded, reeking tent, he had a contrivance for converting his vehicle into a habitation. He was a type of the Arab old man. He mumbled all day and three-quarters of the night, for he had *des insomnies*. His nerves were so fine, that if any one mounted his Shugduf, the unfortunate was condemned to lie like a statue. Fidgety and priggishly neat, nothing annoyed him so much as a moment's delay or an article out of place, a rag removed from his water-gugglet, or a cooking-pot imperfectly free from soot; and I judged his avarice by observing that he made a point of picking up and eating the grains scattered from our pomegranates, exclaiming that the heavenly seed (located there by Arab superstition) might be one of those so wantonly wasted.

Ali bin Ya Sin, returning to his native city, had not been happy in his choice of a companion this time. The other occupant of the handsome Shugduf was an ignoble-faced Egyptian from El-Medinah. This ill-suited pair clave together for awhile, but at El-Suwayrkiyah some dispute about a copper coin made them permanent foes. With threats and abuse such as none but an Egyptian could tamely hear, Ali kicked his quondam friend out of the vehicle. But terrified, after reflection, by the possibility that the man, now his enemy, might combine with two or three Syrians of our party to do him a harm, and frightened by a few black looks, the senior determined to fortify himself by a friend. Connected with the boy Mohammed's family, he easily obtained an introduction to me; he kissed my hand with great servility, declared that his servant had behaved disgracefully; and begged my protection, together with an occasional attendance of my 'slave'.

This was readily granted in pity for the old man, who became immensely grateful. He offered at once to take Shaykh Nur into his Shugduf. The Indian boy had already reduced to ruins the frail structure of his Shibriyah by lying upon it lengthways, whereas prudent travellers sit in it cross-legged and facing the camel. Moreover, he had been laughed to scorn by the Bedawin, who seeing him pull up his dromedary to mount and dismount, had questioned his sex, and determined him to be a woman of the Miyan.[1] I could not rebuke them; the poor fellow's timidity was a ridiculous contrast to the Bedawi's style of mounting; a pull at the camel's head, the left foot placed on the neck, an agile spring, and a scramble into the saddle. Shaykh Nur, elated by the sight of old Ali's luxuries, promised himself some joyous hours; but next morning he owned with a sigh that he had purchased splendour at the extravagant price of happiness—the senior's tongue never rested throughout the livelong night.

During our half-halt at El-Sawayrkiyah we determined to have a small feast; we bought some fresh dates, and we paid a dollar and a half for a sheep. Hungry travellers consider 'liver and fry' a dish to set before a Shaykh. On this occasion, however, our enjoyment was marred by the water; even Soyer's dinners would scarcely charm if washed down with cups of a certain mineral-spring found at Epsom.

We started at ten a.m. (Monday, the 5th September) in a south-easterly direction, and travelled over a flat, thinly dotted with desert vegetation. At one p.m. we passed a basaltic ridge; and then, entering a long depressed line of country, a kind of valley, paced down it five tedious hours. The Simoom as usual was blowing hard, and it seemed to affect the travellers' tempers. In one place I saw a Turk, who could not speak a word of Arabic, violently disputing with an Arab who could not understand a word of Turkish. The pilgrim insisted upon adding to the camel's load a few dry sticks, such as are picked up for cooking. The camel-man as perseveringly threw off the extra burthen. They screamed with rage, hustled each other, and at last the Turk dealt the Arab a heavy blow. I afterwards heard

[1] The Hindostani 'sir'. Bedawin address it slightingly to Indians.

that the pilgrim was mortally wounded that night, his stomach being ripped open with a dagger. On inquiring what had become of him, I was assured that he had been comfortably wrapped up in his shroud, and placed in a half-dug grave. This is the general practice in the case of the poor and solitary, whom illness or accident incapacitates from proceeding. It is impossible to contemplate such a fate without horror: the torturing thirst of a wound, the burning sun heating the brain to madness, and—worst of all, for they do not wait till death—the attacks of the jackal, the vulture, and the raven of the wild.

At six p.m., before the light of day had faded, we traversed a rough and troublesome ridge. Descending it, our course lay in a southerly direction along a road flanked on the left by low hills of red sandstone and bright porphyry. About an hour afterwards we came to a basalt field, through whose blocks we threaded our way painfully and slowly, for it was then dark. At eight p.m. the camels began to stumble over the dwarf dykes of the wheat and barley fields, and presently we arrived at our halting-place, a large village called El-Sufayna. The plain was already dotted with tents and lights. We found the Baghdad Caravan, whose route here falls into the Darb el-Sharki. It consists of a few Persians and Kurds, and collects the people of north-eastern Arabia, Wahhabis and others. They are escorted by the Agayl tribe and the fierce mountaineers of Jebel Shammar. Scarcely was our tent pitched, when the distant pattering of musketry and an ominous tapping of the kettle-drum sent all my companions in different directions to inquire what was the cause of quarrel. The Baghdad Cafila, though not more than 2,000 in number, men, women, and children, had been proving to the Damascus Caravan, that, being perfectly ready to fight, they were not going to yield any point of precedence. From that time the two bodies encamped in different places. I never saw a more pugnacious assembly: a look sufficed for a quarrel. Once a Wahhabi stood in front of us, and by pointing with his finger, and other insulting gestures, showed his hatred to the chibouque, in which I was peaceably indulging. It was impossible to refrain from chastising his insolence by a polite and smiling offer of the offending pipe. This made him draw his dagger without a thought; but it was sheathed again, for we all cocked our pistols, and these gentry prefer steel to lead. We had travelled about seventeen miles, and the direction of El-Sufayna from our last halting-place was south-east 5°. Though it was night when we encamped, Shaykh Masud set out to water his moaning camels: they had not quenched their thirst for three days. He returned in a depressed state, having been bled by the soldiery at the well to the extent of 40 piastres, or about 8*s.*

After supper we spread our rugs and prepared to rest. And here I first remarked the coolness of the nights, proving, at this season of the year, a considerable altitude above the sea. As a general rule the atmosphere stagnated between sunrise at ten a.m., when a light wind rose. During the forenoon the breeze strengthened, and it gradually diminished through the afternoon. Often about sunset there was a gale accompanied by dry storms of dust. At El-Sufayna, though there was no night-breeze and little dew, a blanket was necessary, and the hours of darkness were invigorating enough to mitigate the effect of the sand and Simoom-ridden day.

Before sleeping I was introduced to a namesake, one Shaykh Abdullah of Meccah. Having committed his Shugduf to his son, a lad of fourteen, he had ridden forward on a dromedary, and had suddenly fallen ill. His objects in meeting me were to ask for some medicine, and a temporary seat in my Shugduf; the latter I offered with pleasure, as the boy Mohammed was longing to mount a camel. The Shaykh's illness was nothing but weakness brought on by the hardships of the journey: he attributed it to the hot wind, and to the weight of a bag of dollars which he had attached to his waist-belt. He was a man about forty, long, thin, pale, and of a purely nervous temperament; and a few questions elicited the fact that he had lately and suddenly given up his daily opium pill. I prepared one for him, placed him in my litter, and persuaded him to stow away his burden in some place where it would be less troublesome. He was my companion for two marches, at the end of which he found his own Shugduf. I never met amongst the Arab citizens a better-bred or better-informed man. At Constantinople he had learned a little French, Italian, and Greek; and from the properties of a shrub to the varieties of honey, he was full of useful knowledge, and openable as a dictionary. We parted near Meccah, where I met him only once, and then accidently, in the Valley of Muna.

At half-past five a.m., on Tuesday, the 6th September, we arose refreshed by the cool, comfortable night, and loaded the camels. I had an opportunity of inspecting El-Sufayna. It is a village of fifty or sixty mud-walled, flat-roofed houses, defended by the usual rampart. Around it lie ample date-grounds, and fields of wheat, barley, and maize. Its bazar at this season of the year is well supplied: even fowls can be procured.

We travelled towards the south-east, and entered a country destitute of the low ranges of hill which from El-Medinah southwards had bounded the horizon. After a two miles' march, our camels climbed up a precipitous ridge, and then descended into a broad gravel plain. From ten to eleven a.m. our course lay southerly over a high table-land, and we afterwards traversed, for five hours and a half, a plain which bore signs of standing water.

This day's march was peculiarly Arabia. It was a desert peopled only with echoes—a place of death for what little there is to die in it—a wilderness where, to use my companion's phrase, there is nothing but He.[1] Nature, scalped, flayed, discovered all her skeleton to the gazer's eye. The horizon was a sea of mirage; gigantic sand-columns whirled over the plain; and on both sides of our road were huge piles of bare rock, standing detached upon the surface of sand and clay. Here they appeared in oval lumps, heaped up with a semblance of symmetry; there a single boulder stood, with its narrow foundation based upon a pedestal of low, dome-shaped rock. All were of a pink coarse-grained granite, which flakes off in large crusts under the influence of the atmosphere. I remarked one block which could not measure less than thirty feet in height.

Through these scenes we travelled till about half-past four p.m., when the guns suddenly roared a halt. There was not a trace of human habitation around us: a few parched shrubs and the granite heaps were the only objects diversifying the hard

[1] 'La siwa Hu', i.e. where there is none but Allah.

clayey plain. Shaykh Masud correctly guessed the cause of our detention at the inhospitable 'halting-place of the Mutayr'. 'Cook your bread and boil your coffee,' said the old man; 'the camels will rest for awhile, and the gun will sound at nightfall.'

We had passed over about eighteen miles of ground; and our present direction was south-west 20° of El-Sufayna.

At half-past ten that evening we heard the signal for departure, and, as the moon was still young, we prepared for a hard night's work. We took a south-westerly course, through what is called a Waar—stony ground covered with shrub. Darkness fell upon us like a pall. The camels tripped and stumbled, tossing their litters like cockboats in a short sea; at times the Shugdufs were wellnigh torn off their backs. When we came to a ridge worse than usual, old Masud would seize my camel's halter, and, accompanied by his son and nephew bearing lights, encourage the animals with gesture and voice.

It was a strange, wild scene. The black basaltic field was dotted with the huge and doubtful forms of spongy-footed camels, with silent tread, looming like phantoms in the midnight air; the hot wind moaned, and whirled from the torches flakes and sheets of flame and fiery smoke; whilst ever and anon a swift-travelling Takhtrawan, drawn by mules, and surrounded by runners bearing gigantic Mashals, or cressets, threw a passing glow of red light upon the dark road and the dusky multitude.

On this occasion the rule was 'every man for himself'. Each pressed forward into the best path, thinking only of preceding his neighbour. The Syrians, amongst whom our little party had become entangled, proved most unpleasant companions: they often stopped the way, insisting upon their right to precedence. On one occasion a horseman had the audacity to untie the halter of my dromedary, and thus to cast us adrift, as it were, in order to make room for some excluded friend. I seized my sword; but Shaykh Abdullah stayed my hand, and addressed the intruder in terms sufficiently violent to make him slink away. Nor was this the only occasion on which my companion was successful with the Syrians. He would begin with a mild 'Move a little, O my father!' followed, if fruitless, by 'Out of the way, O Father of Syria!' and, if still ineffectual, advancing to a 'Begone, O he!'

This ranged between civility and sternness. If without effect, it was supported by revilings to the 'Abusers of the Salt', the 'Yezid', the 'Offspring of Shimr'. Another remark which I made about my companion's conduct well illustrates the difference between the Eastern and the Western man. When traversing a dangerous place, Shaykh Abdullah the European attended to his camel with loud cries of 'Hai! Hai!' and an occasional switching. Shaykh Abdullah the Asiatic commended himself to Allah by repeated ejaculations of *Ya Sátir! Ya Sattár!*

The morning of Wednesday (7th September) broke as we entered a wide plain. In many places were signs of water: lines of basalt here and there seamed the surface, and wide sheets of the tufaceous gypsum called by the Arabs *Sabkhah* shone like mirrors set in the russet frame-work of the flat. This substance is found in cakes, often a foot long by an inch in depth, curled by the sun's rays and overlying clay into which water had sunk.

After our harassing night, day came on with a sad feeling of oppression, greatly increased by the unnatural glare:

> In vain the sight, dejected to the ground,
> Stoop'd for relief: thence hot ascending streams
> And keen reflection pain'd.

We were disappointed in our expectations of water, which usually abounds near this station, as its name, El-Ghadir, denotes. At ten a.m. we pitched the tent in the first convenient spot, and we lost no time in stretching our cramped limbs upon the bosom of mother Earth. From the halting-place of the Mutayr to El-Ghadir is a march of about twenty miles, and the direction south-west 21°. El-Ghadir is an extensive plain, which probably presents the appearance of a lake after heavy rains. It is overgrown in parts with desert vegetation, and requires nothing but a regular supply of water to make it useful to man. On the east it is bounded by a wall of rock, at whose base are three wells, said to have been dug by the Caliph Harun. They are guarded by a Burj, or tower, which betrays symptoms of decay.

In our anxiety to rest we had strayed from the Damascus Caravan amongst the mountaineers of Shammar. Our Shaykh Masud manifestly did not like the company; for shortly after three p.m. he insisted upon our striking the tent and rejoining the Hajj, which lay encamped about two miles distant in the western part of the basin. We loaded, therefore, and half an hour before sunset found ourselves in more congenial society. To my great disappointment, a stir was observable in the Caravan. I at once understood that another night-march was in store for us.

At six p.m. we again mounted, and turned towards the eastern plain. A heavy shower was falling upon the western hills, whence came damp and dangerous blasts. Between nine p.m. and the dawn of the next day we had a repetition of the last night's scenes, over a road so rugged and dangerous, that I wondered how men could prefer to travel in the darkness. But the camels of Damascus were now worn out with fatigue; they could not endure the sun, and our time was too precious for a halt. My night was spent perched upon the front bar of my Shugduf, encouraging the dromedary; and that we had not one fall excited my extreme astonishment.

At five a.m. (Thursday, the 8th September) we entered a wide plain thickly clothed with the usual thorny trees, in whose strong grasp many a Shugduf lost its covering, and not a few were dragged with their screaming inmates to the ground. About five hours afterwards we crossed a high ridge, and saw below us the camp of the Caravan, not more than two miles distant. As we approached it, a figure came running out to meet us. It was the boy Mohammed, who, heartily tired of riding a dromedary with his friend, and possibly hungry, hastened to inform my companion Abdullah that he would lead him to his Shugduf and his son. The Shaykh, a little offended by the fact that for two days not a friend nor an acquaintance had taken the trouble to see or to inquire about him, received Mohammed roughly; but the youth, guessing the grievance, explained it away by swearing that he and all the party had tried to find us in vain. This wore the semblance of truth: it is almost impossible to come upon any one who strays from his place in so large and motley a body.

At eleven a.m. we had reached our station. It is about twenty-four miles from El-Ghadir, and its direction is south-east 10°. It is called El-Birkat (the Tank), from a large and now ruinous cistern built of hewn stone by the Caliph Harun. The land belongs to the Utaybah Bedawin, the bravest and most ferocious tribe in El-Hejaz; and the citizens denote their dread of these banditti by asserting that to increase their courage they drink their enemy's blood. My companions shook their heads when questioned upon the subject, and prayed that we might not become too well acquainted with them—an ill-omened speech!

The Pasha allowed us a rest of five hours at El-Birkat: we spent them in my tent, which was crowded with Shaykh Abdullah's friends. To requite me for this inconvenience, he prepared for me an excellent water-pipe, a cup of coffee, which, untainted by cloves and cinnamon, would have been delicious, and a dish of dry fruits. As we were now near the Holy City, all the Meccans were busy canvassing for lodgers and offering their services to pilgrims. Quarrels, too, were of hourly occurrence. In our party was an Arnaut, a white-bearded old man, so decrepit that he could scarcely stand, and yet so violent that no one could manage him but his African slave, a brazen-faced little wretch about fourteen years of age. Words were bandied between this angry senior and Shaykh Masud, when the latter insinuated sarcastically, that if the former had teeth he would be more intelligible. The Arnaut in his rage seized a pole, raised it, and delivered a blow which missed the camel-man, but brought the striker headlong to the ground. Masud exclaimed, with shrieks of rage, 'Have we come to this, that every old-woman Turk smites us?' Our party had the greatest trouble to quiet the quarrellers. The Arab listened to us when we threatened him with the Pasha. But the Arnaut, whose rage was 'like red-hot steel', would hear nothing but our repeated declarations, that unless he behaved more like a pilgrim, we should be compelled to leave him and his slave behind.

At four p.m. we left El-Birkat, and travelled eastwards over rolling ground thickly wooded. There was a network of footpaths through the thickets, and clouds obscured the moon; the consequence was inevitable loss of way. About two a.m. we began ascending hills in a south-westerly direction, and presently we fell into the bed of a large rock-girt Fiumara, which runs from east to west. The sands were overgrown with saline and salsolaceous plants; the Coloquintida, which, having no support, spreads along the ground;[1] the Senna, with its small green leaf; the Rhazya stricta; and a large luxuriant variety of the Asclepias gigantea, cottoned over with mist and dew. At six a.m. (9th September) we left the Fiumara, and, turning to the west, we arrived about an hour afterwards at the station. El-Zaribah, the valley, is an undulating plain amongst high granite hills. In many parts it was faintly green; water was close to the surface, and rain stood upon the ground. During the night we had travelled about twenty-three miles, and our present station was south-east 56° from our last.

Having pitched the tent and eaten and slept, we prepared to perform the ceremony of El-Ihram (assuming the pilgrim-garb), as El-Zaribah is the Mikat, or the appointed place.[2] Between the noonday and the afternoon prayers a barber attended to shave our heads, cut our nails, and trim our mustachios. Then, having bathed and perfumed ourselves—the latter is a questionable point—we donned the attire, which is nothing but two new cotton cloths, each six feet long by three and a half broad, white, with narrow red stripes and fringes: in fact, the costume called El-Eddeh in the baths at Cairo. One of these sheets, technically termed the Rida, is thrown over the back, and, exposing the arm and shoulder, is knotted at the right side in the style *Wishah.* The Izar is wrapped round the loins from waist to knee, and, knotted or tucked in at the middle, supports itself. Our heads were bare, and nothing was allowed upon the instep. It is said that some clans of Arabs still preserve this religious but most uncomfortable costume; it is doubtless of ancient date, and to this day, in the regions lying west of the Red Sea, it continues to be the common dress of the people.

After the toilette, we were placed with our faces in the direction of Meccah, and ordered to say aloud, 'I vow this Ihram of Hajj (the pilgrimage) and the Umrah (the little pilgrimage)

[1] Coloquintida is here used, as in most parts of the East, medicinally. The pulp and the seeds of the ripe fruit are scooped out, and the rind is filled with milk, which is exposed to the night air, and drunk in the morning.

[2] Those coming from the north assume the pilgrim-garb at or off the village of Rabigh.

to Allah Almighty!' Having thus performed a two-bow prayer, we repeated, without rising from the sitting position, these words, 'O Allah! verily I purpose the Hajj and the Umrah, then enable me to accomplish the two, and accept them both of me, and make both blessed to me!' Followed the Talbiyat, or exclaiming—

> Here I am! O Allah! here am I—
> No Partner hast Thou, here am I:
> Verily the Praise and the Beneficence are Thine,
> and the Kingdom—
> No Partner hast Thou, here am I![1]

And we were warned to repeat these words as often as possible, until the conclusion of the ceremonies.

Then Shaykh Abdullah, who acted as director of our consciences, bade us be good pilgrims, avoiding quarrels, immorality, bad language, and light conversation. We must so reverence life that we should avoid killing game, causing an animal to fly, and even pointing it out for destruction; nor should we scratch ourselves, save with the open palm, lest vermin be destroyed, or a hair uprooted by the nail. We were to respect the sanctuary by sparing the trees, and not to pluck a single blade of grass. As regards personal considerations, we were to abstain from all oils, perfumes, and unguents; from washing the head with mallow or lote leaves; from dyeing, shaving, cutting, or vellicating a single pile or hair; and though we might take advantage of shade, and even form it with upraised hands, we must by no means cover our sconces. For each infraction of these ordinances we must sacrifice a sheep; and it is commonly said by Moslems that none but the Prophet could be perfect in the intricacies of pilgrimage. Old Ali began with an irregularity: he declared that age

[1] Talbiyat is from the word 'Labbayka' ('Here I am') in the cry—

> Labbayk' Allahumma, Labbayk!
> (Labbayka) La Sharika laka, Labbayk!
> Inna 'l Hamda wa 'n Niamata laka w 'al Mulk
> La Sharika laka, Labbayk!

Some add, 'Here I am, and I honour Thee, I the son of thy two Slaves: Beneficence and Good are all between thy hands.' The Talbiyat is allowed in any language, but is preferred in Arabic. It has a few varieties; the form above given is the most common.

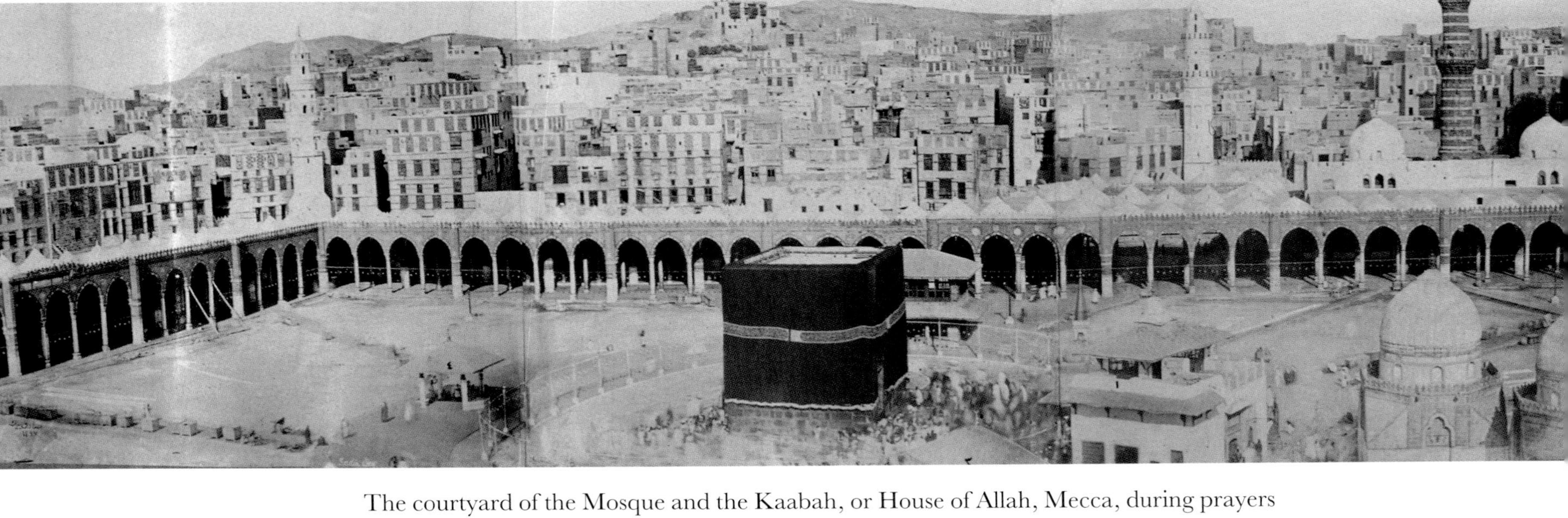

The courtyard of the Mosque and the Kaabah, or House of Allah, Mecca, during prayers

The Tawaf, or circumambulation of the Kaabah, Mecca

Prayers around the Kaabah, Mecca

Mecca, with Ajyad Fort in the background

prevented his assuming the garb, but that, arrived at Meccah, he would clear himself by an offering.

The wife and daughters of a Turkish pilgrim of our party assumed the Ihram at the same time as ourselves. They appeared dressed in white garments; and they had exchanged the Lisam, that coquettish fold of muslin which veils without concealing the lower part of the face, for a hideous mask, made of split, dried, and plaited palm-leaves, with two bulls'-eyes for light. I could not help laughing when these strange figures met my sight, and, to judge from the shaking of their shoulders, they were not less susceptible to the merriment which they had caused.

At three p.m. we left El-Zaribah, travelling towards the south-west, and a wondrously picturesque scene met the eye. Crowds hurried along, habited in the pilgrim-garb, whose whiteness contrasted strangely with their black skins; their newly shaven heads glistening in the sun, and their long black hair streaming in the wind. The rocks rang with shouts of 'Labbayk! Labbayk!' At a pass we fell in with the Wahhabis, accompanying the Baghdad Caravan, screaming 'Here am I'; and, guided by a large loud kettle-drum, they followed in double file the camel of a standard-bearer, whose green flag bore in huge white letters the formula of the Moslem creed. They were wild-looking mountaineers, dark and fierce, with hair twisted into thin Dalik or plaits: each was armed with a long spear, a matchlock, or a dagger. They were seated upon coarse wooden saddles, without cushions or stirrups, a fine saddle-cloth alone denoting a chief. The women emulated the men; they either guided their own dromedaries, or, sitting in pillion, they clung to their husbands; veils they disdained, and their countenances certainly belong not to a 'soft sex'. These Wahhabis were by no means pleasant companions. Most of them were followed by spare dromedaries, either unladen or carrying water-skins, fodder, fuel, and other necessaries for the march. The beasts delighted in dashing furiously through our file, which being lashed together, head and tail, was thrown each time into the greatest confusion. And whenever we were observed smoking, we were cursed aloud for Infidels and Idolaters.

Looking back at El-Zaribah, soon after our departure, I saw a heavy nimbus settle upon the hill-tops, a sheet of rain being stretched between it and the plain. The low grumbling of thunder sounded joyfully in our ears. We hoped for a shower, but were disappointed by a dust-storm, which ended with a few heavy drops. There arose a report that the Bedawin had attacked a party of Meccans with stones, and the news caused men to look exceeding grave.

At five p.m. we entered the wide bed of the Fiumara, down which we were to travel all night. Here the country falls rapidly towards the sea, as the increasing heat of the air, the direction of the water-courses, and signs of violence in the torrent-bed show. The Fiumara varies in breadth from 150 feet to three-quarters of a mile; its course, I was told, is towards the south-west, and it enters the sea near Jeddah. The channel is a coarse sand, with here and there masses of sheet rock and patches of thin vegetation.

At about half-past five p.m. we entered a suspicious-looking place. On the right was a stony buttress, along whose base the stream, when there is one, swings; and to this depression was our road limited by the rocks and thorn-trees which filled the other half of the channel. The left side was a precipice, grim and barren, but not so abrupt as its brother. Opposite us the way seemed barred by piles of hills, crest rising above crest into the far blue distance. Day still smiled upon the upper peaks, but the lower slopes and the Fiumara bed were already curtained with grey sombre shade.

A damp seemed to fall upon our spirits as we approached this Valley Perilous. I remarked that the voices of the women and children sank into silence, and the loud 'Labbayk' of the pilgrims were gradually stilled. Whilst still speculating upon the cause of this phenomenon, it became apparent. A small curl of the smoke, like a lady's ringlet, on the summit of the right-hand precipice, caught my eye; and, simultaneous with the echoing crack of the matchlock, a high-trotting dromedary in front of me rolled over upon the sands—a bullet had split its heart—throwing the rider a goodly somersault of five or six yards.

Ensued terrible confusion; women screamed, children cried, and men vociferated, each one striving with might and main to urge his animal out of the place of death. But the road being narrow, they only managed to jam the vehicles in a solid immovable mass. At every matchlock shot, a shudder ran through the huge body, as when the surgeon's scalpel touches some more sensitive nerve. The irregular horsemen, perfectly useless, galloped up and down over the stones, shouting to and ordering one another. The Pasha of the army had his carpet spread at the foot of the left-hand precipice, and debated over his pipe with the officers what ought to be done. No good genius whispered 'Crown the heights'.

Then it was that the conduct of the Wahhabis found favour in my eyes. They came up, galloping their camels—

Torrents less rapid, and less rash—

with their elf-locks tossing in the wind, and their flaring matches casting a strange lurid light over their features. Taking up a position, one body began to fire upon the Utaybah robbers, whilst 200 or 300, dismounting, swarmed up the hill under the guidance of the Sherif Zayd. I had remarked this nobleman at El-Medinah as a model specimen of the pure Arab. Like all Sherifs, he is celebrated for bravery, and has killed many with his own hand. When urged at El-Zaribah to ride into Meccah, he swore that he would not leave the caravan till in sight of the walls; and, fortunately for the pilgrims, he kept his word.

Presently the firing was heard far in our rear, the robbers having fled. The head of the column advanced, and the dense body of pilgrims opened out. Our forced halt was now exchanged for a flight. It required much management to steer our desert-craft clear of danger; but Shaykh Masud was equal to the occasion. That many were lost was evident by the boxes and baggage that strewed the shingles. I had no means of ascertaining the number of men killed and wounded: reports were contradictory, and exaggeration unanimous. The robbers were said to be 150 in number; their object was plunder, and they would eat the shot camels. But their principal ambition was the boast, 'We, the Utaybah, on such and such a night, stopped the Sultan's Mahmal one whole hour in the Pass.'

At the beginning of the skirmish I had primed my pistols, and sat with them ready for use. But soon seeing that there was nothing to be done, and wishing to make an impression—nowhere does Bobadil now 'go down' so well as in the East—I called aloud for my supper. Shaykh Nur, exanimate with fear, could not move. The boy Mohammed ejaculated only an 'Oh, sir!' and the people around exclaimed in disgust, 'By Allah, he eats!' Shaykh Abdullah, the Meccan, being a man of spirit, was amused by the spectacle. 'Are these Afghan manners, Effendim?' he inquired from the Shugduf behind me. 'Yes,' I replied aloud, 'in my country we always dine before an attack of robbers, because that gentry is in the habit of sending men to bed supperless.' The Shaykh laughed aloud, but those around him looked offended. I thought the bravado this time *mal placé*; but a little event which took place on my way to Jeddah proved that it was not quite a failure.

As we advanced, our escort took care to fire every large dry Asclepias, to disperse the shades which buried us. Again the scene became wondrous wild:

> Full many a waste I've wander'd o'er,
> Clomb many a crag, cross'd many a shore,
>   But, by my halidome,
> A scene so rude, so wild as this,
> Yet so sublime in barrenness,
> Ne'er did my wandering footsteps press,
>   Where'er I chanced to roam.

On either side were ribbed precipices, dark, angry, and towering above, till their summits mingled with the glooms of night; and between them formidable looked the chasm, down which our host hurried with shouts and discharges of matchlocks. The torch-smoke and the night-fires of flaming Asclepias formed a canopy, sable above and livid red below; it hung over our heads like a sheet, and divided the cliffs into two equal parts. Here the fire flashed fiercely from a tall thorn, that crackled and shot up showers of sparks into the air; there it died away in lurid gleams, which lit up a truly Stygian scene.

As usual, however, the picturesque had its inconveniences. There was no path. Rocks, stone-banks, and trees obstructed our passage. The camels, now blind in darkness, then dazzled by a flood of light, stumbled frequently; in some places slipping down a steep descent, in others sliding over a sheet of mud. There were furious quarrels and fierce language between camel-men and their hirers, and threats to fellow-travellers; in fact, we were united in discord. I passed that night crying, 'Hai! Hai!' switching the camel, and fruitlessly endeavouring to fustigate Masud's nephew, who resolutely slept upon the water-bags. During the hours of darkness we made four or five halts, when we boiled coffee and smoked pipes; but man and beasts were beginning to suffer from a deadly fatigue.

Dawn (Saturday, the 10th September) found us still travelling down the Fiumara, which here is about 100 yards broad. The granite hills on both sides were less precipitous; and the borders of the torrent-bed became natural quays of stiff clay, which showed a water-mark of from twelve to fifteen feet in height. In many parts the bed was muddy; and the moist places, as usual, caused accidents. I happened to be looking back at Shaykh Abdullah, who was then riding in old Ali bin Ya Sin's fine Shugduf; suddenly the camel's four legs disappeared from under him, his right side flattening the ground, and the two riders were pitched severally out of the smashed vehicle. Abdullah started up furious, and with great zest abused the Bedawin, who were absent. 'Feed these Arabs,' he exclaimed, quoting a Turkish proverb, 'and they will fire at Heaven!' But I observed that, when Shaykh Masud came up, the citizen was only gruff.

We then turned northward, and sighted El-Mazik, more generally known as Wady Laymun, the Valley of Limes. On the right bank of the Fiumara stood the Meccan Sherif's state pavilion, green and gold: it was surrounded by his attendants, and he had prepared to receive the Pasha of the Caravan. We advanced half a mile, and encamped temporarily in a hill-girt bulge of the Fiumara bed. At eight a.m. we had travelled about twenty-four miles from El-Zaribah, and the direction of our present station was south-west 50°.

Shaykh Masud allowed us only four hours' halt; he wished to precede the main body. After breaking our fast joyously upon limes, pomegranates, and fresh dates, we sallied forth to admire the beauties of the place. We are once more on classic ground—the ground of the ancient Arab poets—

> Deserted is the village—waste the halting-place
> and home
> At Mina, o'er Rijam and Ghul wild beasts
> unheeded roam,
> On Rayyan hill the channel lines have left their
> naked trace,
> Time-worn, as *primal Writ that dints the mountain's*
> *flinty face*[1]—

and this Wady, celebrated for the purity of its air, has from remote ages been a favourite resort of the Meccans. Nothing can be more soothing to the brain than the dark-green foliage of the limes and pomegranates; and from the base of the southern hill bursts a bubbling stream, whose

> *Chiare, fresche e dolci acque*

flow through the gardens, filling them with the most delicious of melodies, the gladdest sound which Nature in these regions knows.

Exactly at noon Masud seized the halter of the foremost camel, and we started down the Fiumara. Troops of Bedawi girls looked over the orchard walls laughingly, and children came out to offer us fresh fruit and sweet water. At two p.m., travelling south-west, we arrived at a point where the torrent-bed turns to the right; and, quitting it, we climbed with difficulty over a steep ridge of granite. Before three o'clock we entered a hill-girt plain, which my companions called Sola. In some places were clumps of trees, and scattered villages warned us that we were approach-

[1] In these lines of Lebid, the 'Mina' alluded to must not, we are warned by the scholiast, be confounded with 'Mina' (vulg. 'Muna'), the Valley of Victims. Ghul and Rayyan are hills close to the Wady Laymun.

The passage made me suspect that inscriptions would be found among the rocks, as the scholiast informs us that 'men used to write upon rocks in order that their writing might remain' (De Sacy's *Moallaka de Lebid*, p. 289). I neither saw nor heard of any. But some months afterwards I was delighted to hear from the late Abbé Hamilton that he had discovered in one of the rock monuments a 'lithographed proof' of the presence of Sesostris (Rhameses II).

ing a city. Far to the left rose the blue peaks of Taif, and the mountain road, a white thread upon the nearer heights, was pointed out to me.

Here I first saw the tree, or rather shrub, which bears the balm of Gilead, erst so celebrated for its tonic and stomachic properties. I told Shaykh Masud to break off a twig, which he did heedlessly. The act was witnessed by our party with a roar of laughter; and the astounded Shaykh was warned that he had become subject to an atoning sacrifice. Of course he denounced me as the instigator, and I could not fairly refuse assistance. The tree has of late years been carefully described by many botanists; I will only say that the bark resembled in colour a cherry-stick pipe, the inside was a light yellow, and the juice made my fingers stick together.

At four p.m. we came to a steep and rocky Pass, up which we toiled with difficulty. The face of the country was rising once more, and again presented the aspect of numerous small basins divided and surrounded by hills. As we jogged on we were passed by the cavalcade of no less a personage than the Sherif of Meccah. Abd el-Muttalib bin Ghalib is a dark, beardless old man with African features derived from his mother. He was plainly dressed in white garments and a white muslin turban, which made him look jet black; he rode an ambling mule, and the only emblem of his dignity was the large green satin umbrella borne by an attendant on foot. Scattered around him were about forty matchlock men, mostly slaves. At long intervals, after their father, came his four sons, Riza Bey, Abdullah, Ali, and Ahmed, the latter still a child. The three elder brothers rode splendid dromedaries at speed; they were young men of light complexion, with the true Meccan cast of features, showily dressed in bright-coloured silks, and armed, to denote their rank, with sword and gold-hilted dagger.

We halted as evening approached, and strained our eyes, but all in vain, to catch sight of Meccah, which lies in a winding valley. By Shaykh Abdullah's direction I recited, after the usual devotions, the following prayer. The reader is forewarned that it is difficult to preserve the flowers of Oriental rhetoric in a European tongue.

'O Allah! verily this is Thy Safeguard (*Amn*) and Thy Sanctuary (*Haram*)! Into it whoso entereth becometh safe (*Amin*). So deny (*Harrim*) my Flesh and Blood, my Bones and Skin, to Hell-fire. O Allah! save me from Thy Wrath on the Day when Thy Servants shall be raised from the Dead. I conjure Thee by this that Thou art Allah, besides whom is none (Thou only), the Merciful, the Compassionate. And have Mercy upon our Lord Mohammed, and upon the Progeny of our Lord Mohammed, and upon his Followers, One and All!' This was concluded with the Talbiyat, and with an especial prayer for myself.

We again mounted, and night completed our disappointment. About one a.m. I was aroused by general excitement. 'Meccah! Meccah!' cried some voices; 'The Sanctuary! O the Sanctuary!' exclaimed others; and all burst into loud 'Labbayk', not unfrequently broken by sobs. I looked out from my litter, and saw by the light of the southern stars the dim outlines of a large city, a shade darker than the surrounding plain. We were passing over the last ridge by a cutting called the *Saniyat Kuda'a*, the winding-place of the cut. The winding path is flanked on both sides by watch-towers, which command the Darb el-Maala or road leading from the north into Meccah. Thence we passed into the Maabidah (northern suburb), where the Sherif's Palace is built. After this, on the left hand, came the deserted abode of the Sherif bin Aun, now said to be a haunted house. Opposite to it lies the Jannat el-Maala, the holy cemetery of Meccah. Thence, turning to the right, we entered the Sulaymaniyah or Afghan quarter. Here the boy Mohammed, being an inhabitant of the Shamiyah or Syrian ward, thought proper to display some apprehension. The two are on bad terms; children never meet without exchanging volleys of stones, and men fight furiously with quarterstaves. Sometimes, despite the terrors of religion, the knife and sabre are drawn. But these hostilities have their code. If a citizen be killed, there is a subscription for blood-money. An inhabitant of one quarter, passing singly through another, becomes a guest; once beyond the walls, he is likely to be beaten to insensibility by his hospitable foes.

At the Sulaymaniyah we turned off the main road into a byway, and ascended by narrow lanes the rough heights of Jebel

Hindi, upon which stands a small whitewashed and crenellated building called a fort. Thence descending, we threaded dark streets, in places crowded with rude cots and dusky figures, and finally at two a.m. we found ourselves at the door of the boy Mohammed's house.

From Wady Laymun to Meccah the distance, according to my calculation, was about twenty-three miles, the direction south-east 45°. We arrived on the morning of Sunday the 7th Zu'l Hijjah (the 11th September, 1853), and had one day before the beginning of the pilgrimage to repose and visit the Haram.[1]

I conclude this chapter with a few remarks upon the watershed of El-Hejaz. The country, in my humble opinion, has a compound slope, southwards and westwards. I have, however,

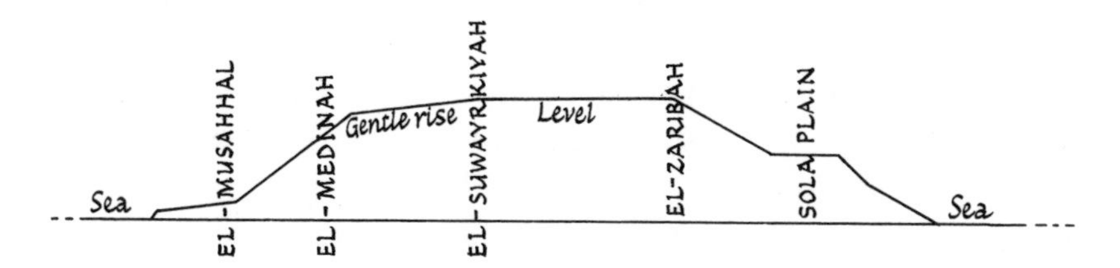

little but the conviction of the modern Arabs to support the assertion that this part of Arabia declines from the north. All declare the course of water to be southerly, and believe the fountain of Arafat to pass underground from Baghdad. The slope, as geographers know, is still a disputed point. Ritter, Jomard, and some old Arab authors, make the country rise towards the

[1] This is a synopsis of our marches, which, protracted on Burckhardt's map, gives an error of ten miles:

				Miles
(1)	From El-Medinah, to Ja el-Sharifah	SE	50°	22
(2)	From Ja el-Sharifah to Ghurab	SW	10°	24
(3)	From Ghurab to El-Hijriyah	SE	22°	25
(4)	From El-Hijriyah to El-Suwayrkiyah	SW	11°	28
(5)	From El-Suwayrkiyah to El-Sufayna	SE	5°	17
(6)	From El-Sufayna to the Beni Mutayr	SW	20°	18
(7)	From the Beni Mutayr to El-Ghadir	SW	21°	20
(8)	From El-Ghadir to El-Birkat	SE	10°	24
(9)	From El-Birkat to El-Zaribah	SE	56°	23
(10)	From El-Zaribah to Wady Laymun	SW	50°	24
(11)	From Wady Laymun to Meccah	SE	45°	23
			Total English miles	248

south, whilst Wallin and others express an opposite opinion. From the sea to El-Musahhal is a gentle rise. The water-marks of the Fiumaras show that El-Medinah is considerably above the coast, though geographers may not be correct in claiming for Jebel Radhwa a height of 6,000 feet; yet that elevation is not perhaps too great for the plateau upon which stands the Apostle's burial-place.

From El-Medinah to El-Suwayrkiyah is another gentle rise, and from the latter to El-Zaribah stagnating water denotes a level.

I believe the report of a perennial lake on the eastern boundary of El-Hejaz, as little as the river placed by Ptolemy between Yambu' and Meccah. No Bedawi could tell me of this feature, which, had it existed, would have changed the whole conditions and history of the country; we know the Greek's river to be a Fiumara, and the lake probably owes its existence to a similar cause, a heavy fall of rain. Beginning at El-Zaribah is a decided fall, which continues to the sea. The Arafat torrent sweeps from east to west with great force, sometimes carrying away the habitations, and even injuring the sanctuary.

XXVII
The First Visit to the House of Allah

The boy Mohammed left me in the street, and having at last persuaded the sleepy and tired Indian porter, by violent kicks and testy answers to twenty cautious queries, to swing open the huge gate of his fortress, he rushed up stairs to embrace his mother. After a minute I heard the *Zaghritah, Lululú*, or shrill cry which in these lands welcomes the wanderer home: the sound so gladdening to the returner sent a chill to the stranger's heart.

Presently the youth returned. His manner had changed from a boisterous and jaunty demeanour to one of grave and attentive courtesy—I had become his guest. He led me into the gloomy hall, seated me upon a large carpeted Mastabah, or platform, and told his *bara Miyan* (great Sir), the Hindostani porter, to bring a light. Meanwhile a certain shuffling of slippered feet above informed my hungry ears that the *Kabirah*, the mistress of the house, was intent on hospitable thoughts. When the camels were unloaded, appeared a dish of fine vermicelli, browned and powdered with loaf-sugar. The boy Mohammed, I, and Shaykh Nur, lost no time in exerting our right hands; and truly, after our hungry journey, we found the *Kunafah* delicious. After the meal we procured cots from a neighbouring coffee-house, and we lay down, weary, and anxious to snatch an hour or two of repose. At dawn we were expected to perform our *Tawaf el-Kudum*, or Circumambulation of Arrival, at the Haram.

Scarcely had the first smile of morning beamed upon the rugged head of the eastern hill, Abu Kubays, when we arose, bathed, and proceeded in our pilgrim-garb to the Sanctuary. We entered by the Bab el-Ziyadah, or principal northern door, descended two long flight of steps, traversed the cloister, and stood in sight of the Bayt Allah.

There at last it lay, the bourn of my long and weary Pilgrimage, realising the plans and hopes of many and many a year. The mirage medium of Fancy invested the huge catafalque and its gloomy pall with peculiar charms. There were no giant fragments of hoar antiquity as in Egypt, no remains of graceful and harmonious beauty as in Greece and Italy, no barbarous gorgeousness as in the buildings of India; yet the view was strange, unique—and how few have looked upon the celebrated shrine! I may truly say that, of all the worshippers who clung weeping to the curtain, or who pressed their beating hearts to the stone, none felt for the moment a deeper emotion than did the Haji from the far-north. It was as if the poetical legends of the Arab spoke truth, and that the waving wings of angels, not the sweet breeze of morning, were agitating and swelling the black covering of the shrine. But, to confess humbling truth, theirs was the high feeling of religious enthusiasm, mine was the ecstasy of gratified pride.

Few Moslems contemplate for the first time the Kaabah, without fear and awe: there is a popular jest against new comers, that they generally inquire the direction of prayer. This being the Kiblah, or fronting place, Moslems pray all around it; a circumstance which of course cannot take place in any spot of El-Islam but the Haram. The boy Mohammed, therefore, left me for a few minutes to myself; but presently he warned me that it was time to begin. Advancing, we entered through the Bab Beni Shaybah, the Gate of the Sons of the Shaybah (old woman). There we raised our hands, repeated the Labbayk, the Takbir, and the Tahlil; after which we uttered certain supplications, and drew our hands down our faces. Then we proceeded to the Shafei's place of worship—the open pavement between the Makam Ibrahim and the well Zem—where we performed the usual two-prostration prayer in honour of the Mosque. This was followed by a cup of holy water and a present to the Sakkas, or carriers, who for the consideration distributed, in my name, a large earthen vaseful to poor pilgrims.

The word 'Zem Zem' has a doubtful origin. Some derive it from the Zam Zam, or murmuring of its waters, others from 'Zam! Zam!' ('fill! fill!' i.e. the bottle), Hagar's impatient exclamation when she saw the stream. Sale translates it 'stay! stay!' and says that Hagar called out in the Egyptian language, to prevent her son wandering. The Hukama, or Rationalists of El-Islam, who invariably connect their faith with the worship of Venus especially, and the heavenly bodies generally, derive Zem Zem from the Persian, and make it signify the 'great luminary'. Hence they say the Zem Zem, as well as the Kaabah, denoting the Cuthite or Ammonian worship of sun and fire, deserve man's reverence. So the Persian poet Khakani addresses these two buildings:

> O Kaabah, thou traveller of the heavens!
> O Venus, thou fire of the world!

Thus Wahid Mohammed, founder of the Wahidiyah sect, identifies the Kiblah and the sun; wherefore he says the door fronts the east. By the names Yemen (right-hand), Sham (left-hand), Kubul, or the east wind (fronting), and Dubur, or the west wind (from the back), it is evident that worshippers fronted the rising sun. According to the Hukama, the original Black Stone represents Venus, 'which in the border of the heavens is a star of the planets', and symbolical of the power of nature, 'by whose passive energy the universe was warmed into life and motion'. The Hindus accuse the Moslems of adoring the Bayt Ullah.

> O Moslem, if thou worship the Kaabah,
> Why reproach the worshippers of idols?

says Rai Manshar. And Musaylimah, who in his attempt to found a fresh faith, gained but the historic epithet of 'Liar', allowed his followers to turn their faces in any direction, mentally ejaculating, 'I address myself to thee, who hast neither side nor figure'; a doctrine which might be sensible in the abstract, but certainly not material enough and pride-flattering to win him many converts in Arabia.

The produce of Zem Zem is held in great esteem. It is used for drinking and religious ablution, but for no baser purposes; and the Meccans advise pilgrims always to break their fast with it. It is apt to cause diarrhoea and boils, and I never saw a stranger drink it without a wry face. Sale is decidedly correct in his assertion: the flavour is a salt-bitter, much resembling an infusion of a teaspoonful of Epsom salts in a large tumbler of tepid water. Moreover, it is exceedingly heavy to the taste. For this reason Turks and other strangers prefer rain-water, collected in cisterns and sold for 5 farthings a gugglet. It was a favourite amusement with me to watch them whilst they drank the holy water, and to taunt their scant and irreverent potations.[1]

The water is transmitted to distant regions in glazed earthen jars covered with basket-work, and sealed by the Zem Zemis. Religious men break their lenten fast with it, apply it to their eyes to brighten vision, and imbibe a few drops at the hour of death, when Satan stands by holding a bowl of purest water, the price of the departing soul. Of course modern superstition is not idle about the waters of Zem Zem. The copious supply of the well is considered at Meccah miraculous; in distant countries it facilitates the pronunciation of Arabic to the student; and everywhere the nauseous draught is highly meritorious in a religious point of view.

We then advanced towards the eastern angle of the Kaabah, in which is inserted the Black Stone; and, standing about ten yards from it, repeated with upraised hands, 'There is no god but Allah alone, Whose Covenant is Truth, and Whose Servant is Victorious. There is no god but Allah, without Sharer; His is the Kingdom, to Him be Praise, and He over all Things is potent.' After which we approached as close as we could to the stone. A crowd of pilgrims preventing our touching it that time, we raised our hands to our ears, in the first position of prayer, and then lowering them, exclaimed, 'O Allah (I do this), in Thy Belief, and in verification of Thy Book, and in Pursuance of thy Prophet's Example—may Allah bless Him and preserve! O Allah, I extend my Hand to Thee, and great is my Desire to Thee! O accept Thou my Supplication, and diminish my Obstacles, and pity my Humiliation, and graciously grant me Thy Pardon!' After which, as we were still unable to reach the stone, we raised our hands to our ears, the palms facing the

[1] The strictures of the *Calcutta Review* (No. 41, art. 1), based upon the taste of Zem Zem, are unfounded. In these days a critic cannot be excused for such hasty judgments: at Calcutta or Bombay he would easily find a jar of Zem Zem water, which he might taste for himself.

stone, as if touching it, recited the various religious formulae, the Takbir, the Tahlil, and the Hamdilah, blessed the Prophet, and kissed the finger-tips of the right hand.

The Apostle used to weep when he touched the Black Stone, and said that it was the place for the pouring forth of tears. According to most authors, the second Caliph also used to kiss it. For this reason most Moslems, except the Shafei school, must touch the stone with both hands and apply their lips to it, or touch it with the fingers, which should be kissed, or rub the palms upon it, and afterwards draw them down the face. Under circumstances of difficulty, it is sufficient to stand before the stone, but the Prophet's Sunnat, or practice, was to touch it. Lucian mentions adoration of the sun by kissing the hand.

Then commenced the ceremony of Tawaf, or circumambulation, our route being the Mataf—the low oval of polished granite immediately surrounding the Kaabah. I repeated, after my Mutawwif, or cicerone, 'In the Name of Allah, and Allah is omnipotent! I purpose to circuit seven Circuits unto Almighty Allah, glorified and exalted!' This is technically called the Niyat (intention) of Tawaf.

Then we began the prayer, 'O Allah (I do this), in Thy Belief, and in Verification of Thy Book, and in Faithfulness to Thy Covenant, and in Perseverance of the Example of the Apostle Mohammed—may Allah bless Him and preserve!' till we reached the place El-Multazem, between the corner of the Black Stone and the Kaabah door.

Here we ejaculated, 'O Allah, Thou hast Rights, so pardon my transgressing them.' Opposite the door we repeated, 'O Allah, verily the House is Thy House, and the Sanctuary Thy Sanctuary, and the Safeguard Thy Safeguard, and this is the Place of him who flies to Thee from (Hell-)Fire!'

At the little building called Makam Ibrahim we said, 'O Allah, verily this is the Place of Abraham, who took Refuge with and fled to Thee from the Fire! O deny my Flesh and Blood, my Skin and Bones to the (eternal) Flames!'

As we paced slowly round the north or Irak corner of the Kaabah we exclaimed, 'O Allah, verily I take Refuge with Thee from Polytheism, and Disobedience, and Hypocrisy, and evil

Conversation, and evil Thoughts concerning Family, and Property, and Progeny!'

When fronting the Mizab, or spout, we repeated the words, 'O Allah, verily I beg of Thee Faith which shall not decline, and a Certainty which shall not perish, and the good Aid of Thy Prophet Mohammed—may Allah bless Him and preserve! O Allah, shadow me in Thy Shadow on that Day when there is no Shade but Thy Shadow, and cause me to drink from the Cup of Thine Apostle Mohammed—may Allah bless Him and preserve!—that pleasant Draught after which is no Thirst to all Eternity, O Lord of Honour and Glory!'

Turning the west corner, or the Rukn el-Shami, we exclaimed, 'O Allah, make it an acceptable Pilgrimage, and a Forgiveness of Sins, and a laudable Endeavour, and a pleasant Action (in Thy sight), and a store which perisheth not, O Thou Glorious! O Thou Pardoner!'

This was repeated thrice, till we arrived at the Yemani, or south corner, where, the crowd being less importunate, we touched the wall with the right hand, after the example of the Prophet, and kissed the finger-tips.

Finally, between the south angle and that of the Black Stone, where our circuit would be completed, we said, 'O Allah, verily I take Refuge with Thee from Infidelity, and I take Refuge with Thee from Want, and from the Tortures of the Tomb, and from the Troubles of Life and Death. And I fly to Thee from Ignominy in this World and the next, and I implore Thy Pardon for the Present and for the Future. O Lord, grant to me in this Life Prosperity, and in the next Life Prosperity, and save me from the Punishment of Fire.'

Thus finished a Shaut, or single course round the house. Of these we performed the three first at the pace called Harwalah, very similar to the French *pas gymnastique*, or Tarammul, that is to say, 'moving the shoulders as if walking in sand'. The four latter are performed in Taammul, slowly and leisurely; the reverse of the Sai, or running. These seven Ashwat, or courses, are called collectively one Usbu. The Moslem origin of this custom is too well known to require mention. After each Taufah, or circuit, we, being unable to kiss or even to touch the Black Stone, fronted towards it, raised our hands to our ears, exclaimed, 'In the Name of Allah, and Allah is omnipotent!' kissed our fingers, and resumed the ceremony of circumambulation, as before, with 'Allah, in Thy Belief,' etc.

At the conclusion of the Tawaf it was deemed advisable to attempt to kiss the stone. For a time I stood looking in despair at the swarming crowd of Bedawin and other pilgrims that besieged it. But the boy Mohammed was equal to the occasion. During our circuit he had displayed a fiery zeal against heresy and schism, by foully abusing every Persian in his path;[1] and the inopportune introduction of hard words into his prayers made the latter a strange patchwork; as

'*Ave Maria purissima*—arrah, don't ye be letting the pig at the pot—*sanctissima*,' and so forth.

He might, for instance, be repeating 'and I take Refuge with Thee from Ignominy in this World', when 'O thou rejected one, son of the rejected!' would be the interpolation addressed to some long-bearded Khorasani—'and in that to come—O hog and brother of a hoggess!'

And so he continued till I wondered that none dared to turn and rend him.

After vainly addressing the pilgrims, of whom nothing could be seen but a mosaic of occiputs and shoulder-blades, the boy Mohammed collected about half a dozen stalwart Meccans, with whose assistance, by sheer strength, we wedged our way into the thin and light-legged crowd. The Bedawin turned round upon us like wild-cats, but they had no daggers. The season being autumn, they had not swelled themselves with milk

[1] In AD 1674 some wretch smeared the Black Stone with impurity, and every one who kissed it retired with a sullied beard. The Persians, says Burckhardt, were suspected of this sacrilege, and now their ill-fame has spread far; at Alexandria they were described to me as a people who defile the Kaabah. It is scarcely necessary to say that a Shiah, as well as a Sunni, would look upon such an action with lively horror. The people of Meccah, however, like the Madani, have turned the circumstance to their own advantage, and make an occasional 'avanie'. Thus, nine or ten years ago, on the testimony of a boy who swore that he saw the inside of the Kaabah defiled by a Persian, they rose up, cruelly beat the schismatics, and carried them off to their peculiar quarter the Shamiyah, forbidding their ingress to the Kaabah. Indeed, till Mohammed Ali's time, the Persians rarely ventured upon a pilgrimage, and even now that man is happy who gets over it without a beating. The defilement of the Black Stone was probably the work of some Jew or Greek, who risked his life to gratify a furious bigotry.

for six months; and they had become such living mummies, that I could have managed single-handed half a dozen of them. After thus reaching the stone, despite popular indignation testified by impatient shouts, we monopolised the use of it for at least ten minutes. Whilst kissing it and rubbing hands and forehead upon it I narrowly observed it, and came away persuaded that it is an aërolite.

It is curious that almost all travellers agree upon one point, namely, that the stone is volcanic. Ali Bey calls it mineralogically a 'block of volcanic basalt, whose circumference is sprinkled with little crystals, pointed and straw-like, with rhombs of tile-red feldspath upon a dark background, like velvet or charcoal, except one of its protuberances, which is reddish'. Burckhardt thought it was 'a lava containing several small extraneous particles of a whitish and of a yellowish substance'.

Having kissed the stone, we fought our way through the crowd to the place called El-Multazem. Here we pressed our stomachs, chests, and right cheeks to the Kaabah, raising our arms high above our heads, and exclaiming, 'O Allah! O Lord of the Ancient House, free my Neck from Hell-fire, and preserve me from every ill Deed, and make me contented with that daily Bread which Thou hast given to me, and bless me in all Thou hast granted!' Then came the Istighfar, or begging of pardon; 'I beg Pardon of Allah the most high, who, there is no other god but He, the Living, the Eternal, and unto Him I repent myself!' After which we blessed the Prophet, and then asked for ourselves all that our souls most desired.

After embracing the Multazem, we repaired to the Shafei's place of prayer near the Makam Ibrahim, and there recited two prostrations, technically called Sunnat el-Tawaf, or the (Apostle's) practice of circumambulation. The chapter repeated in the first was 'Say thou, O Infidels': in the second, 'Say thou He is the one God.' We then went to the door of the building in which is Zem Zem: there I was condemned to another nauseous draught, and was deluged with two or three skinfuls of water dashed over my head *en douche*. This ablution causes sins to fall from the spirit like dust. During the potation we prayed, 'O Allah, verily I beg of Thee plentiful daily Bread, and profitable

Learning, and the healing of every Disease!' Then we returned towards the Black Stone, stood far away opposite, because unable to touch it, ejaculated the Takbir, the Tahlil, and the Hamdilah; and thoroughly worn out with scorched feet and a burning head—both extremities, it must be remembered, were bare, and various delays had detained us till ten a.m.—I left the Mosque.

The boy Mohammed had miscalculated the amount of lodging in his mother's house. She, being a widow and a lone woman, had made over for the season all the apartments to her brother, a lean old Meccan, of true ancient type, vulture-faced, kite-clawed, with a laugh like a hyena, and a mere shell of body. He regarded me with no favouring eye when I insisted as a guest upon having some place of retirement; but he promised that, after our return from Arafat, a little store-room should be cleared out for me. With that I was obliged to be content, and pass that day in the common male drawing-room of the house, a vestibule on the ground floor, called in Egypt a *Takhta-bush.*

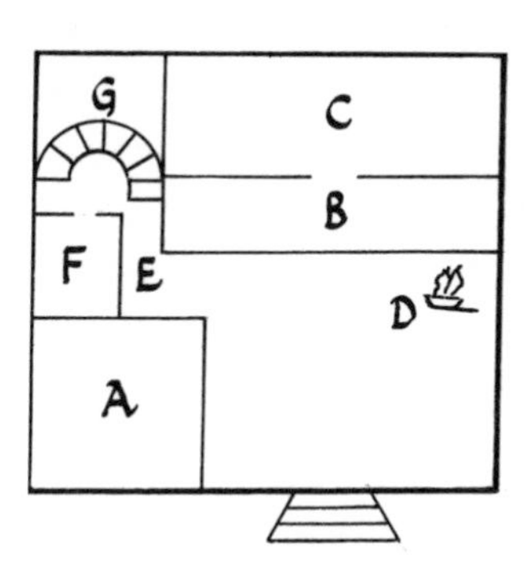

Entering, to the left (A) was a large Mastabah, or platform, and at the bottom (B) a second, of smaller dimensions and foully dirty. Behind this was a dark and unclean store-room (C) containing the Hajis' baggage. Opposite the Mastabah was a firepan for pipes and coffee (D), superintended by a family of lean Indians; and by the side (E) a doorless passage led to a bathing-room (F) and staircase (G).

I had scarcely composed myself upon the carpeted Mastabah, when the remainder was suddenly invaded by the Turkish, or rather Slavo-Turk, pilgrims inhabiting the house, and a host of their visitors. They were large, hairy men, with gruff voices and square figures; they did not take the least notice of me, although, feeling the intrusion, I stretched out my legs with a provoking nonchalance. At last one of them addressed me in Turkish, to which I replied by shaking my head. His question being interpreted to me in Arabic, I drawled out, 'My native place is the land of Khorasan.' This provoked a stern and stony stare from the Turks, and an 'ugh!' which said plainly enough, 'Then you are a pestilent heretic.' I surveyed them with a self-satisfied simper, stretched my legs a trifle farther, and conversed with my water-pipe. Presently, when they all departed for a time, the boy Mohammed raised, by request, my green box of medicines, and deposited it upon the Mastabah; thus defining, as it were, a line of demarcation, and asserting my privilege to it before the Turks. Most of these men were of one party, headed by a colonel of Nizam, whom they called a Bey. My acquaintance with them began roughly enough, but afterwards, with some exceptions, who were gruff as an English butcher when accosted by a lean foreigner, they proved to be kind-hearted and not unsociable men. It often happens to the traveller, as the charming Mrs Malaprop observes, to find intercourse all the better by beginning with a little aversion.

In the evening, accompanied by the boy Mohammed, and followed by Shaykh Nur, who carried a lantern and a praying-rug, I again repaired to the 'Navel of the World'; this time aesthetically, to enjoy the delights of the hour after the 'gaudy, babbling, and remorseful day'. The moon, now approaching the full, tipped the brow of Abu Kubays, and lit up the spectacle with a more solemn light. In the midst stood the huge bier-like erection—

black as the wings
Which some spirit of ill o'er a sepulchre flings—

except where the moonbeams streaked it like jets of silver falling upon the darkest marble. It formed the point of rest for the eye; the little pagoda-like buildings and domes around it, with all their gilding and fretwork, vanished. One object, unique in appearance, stood in view—the temple of the one Allah, the God of Abraham, of Ishmael, and of their posterity. Sublime it was, and expressing by all the eloquence of fancy the grandeur of the One Idea which vitalised El-Islam, and the strength and steadfastness of its votaries.

The oval pavement around the Kaabah was crowded with men, women, and children, mostly divided into parties, which followed a Mutawwif; some walking staidly, and others running, whilst many stood in groups to prayer. What a scene of contrast! Here stalked the Bedawi woman, in her long black robe like a nun's serge, and poppy-coloured face-veil, pierced to show two fiercely flashing orbs. There an Indian woman, with her semi-Tartar features, nakedly hideous, and her thin legs, encased in wrinkled tights, hurried round the fane. Every now and then a corpse, borne upon its wooden shell, circuited the shrine by means of four bearers, whom other Moslems, as is the custom, occasionally relieved. A few fair-skinned Turks lounged about, looking cold and repulsive, as their wont is. In one place a fast Calcutta *Khitmugar* stood, with turban awry and arms akimbo, contemplating the view jauntily, as those 'gentlemen's gentlemen' will do. In another, some poor wretch, with arms thrown on high, so that every part of his person might touch the Kaabah, was clinging to the curtain and sobbing as though his heart would break.

From this spectacle my eyes turned towards Abu Kubays. The city extends in that direction half-way up the grim hill: the site might be compared, at a humble distance, to Bath. Some writers liken it to Florence; but conceive a Florence without beauty! To the south lay Jebel Jiyad the Greater, also partly built over and crowned with a fort, which at a distance looks less useful than romantic: a flood of pale light was sparkling upon its stony surface. Below, the minarets became pillars of silver, and the cloisters, dimly streaked by oil-lamps, bounded the view of the temple with horizontal lines of shade.

Before nightfall the boy Mohammed rose to feed the mosque pigeons, for whom he had brought a pocketful of barley. He went to the place where these birds flock—the line of pavement leading from the isolated arch to the eastern cloisters. During the day women and children are to be seen sitting here, with small piles of grain upon little plaited trays of basket-work. For each they demand a copper piece; and religious pilgrims consider it their duty to provide the reverend blue-rocks with a plentiful meal.

The Hindu Pandits assert that Shiwa and his spouse, under the forms and names of Kapot-Eshwara (pigeon god) and Kapotesi, dwelt at Meccah. The dove was the device of the old Assyrian Empire, because Semiramis was preserved by that bird. The Meccan pigeons, resembling those of Venice, are held sacred probably in consequence of the wild traditions of the Arabs about Noah's dove. Some authors declare that, in Mohammed's time, among the idols of the Meccan Pantheon, was a pigeon carved in wood, and above it another, which Ali, mounting upon the Prophet's shoulder, pulled down. This might have been a Hindu, a Jewish, or a Christian symbol. The Moslems connect the pigeon on two occasions with their faith: first, when that bird appeared to whisper in Mohammed's ear; and, secondly, during the flight to El-Medinah. Moreover, in many countries they are called Allah's Proclaimers, because their movement when cooing resembles prostration.

Almost everywhere the pigeon has entered into the history of religion, which probably induced Mr Lascelles to incur the derision of our grandfathers by pronouncing it a 'holy bird'. At Meccah they are called the doves of the Kaabah, and never appear at table. They are remarkable for propriety when sitting upon the holy building. This may be a minor miracle: I would rather believe that there is some contrivance on the roof. My friend Mr Bicknell remarks: 'This marvel, however, having of late years been suspended, many discern another omen of the approach of the long-predicted period when unbelievers shall desecrate the sacred soil.'

Late in the evening I saw a Negro in the state called Malbus—religious frenzy. To all appearance a Takruri, he was a fine and a powerful man, as the numbers required to hold him testified. He threw his arms wildly about him, uttering shrill cries, which sounded like *lé lé lé lé!* and when held, he swayed his body, and waved his head from side to side, like a chained and furious elephant, straining out the deepest groans. The Africans appear unusually subject to this nervous state which, seen by the ignorant and the imaginative, would at once suggest demoniacal possession. Either their organisation is more impressionable, or more probably, the hardships, privations, and fatigues endured whilst wearily traversing inhospitable wilds, and perilous seas, have exalted their imaginations to a pitch bordering upon frenzy. Often they are seen prostrate on the pavement, or clinging to the curtain, or rubbing their foreheads upon the stones, weeping bitterly, and pouring forth the wildest ejaculations.

That night I stayed in the Haram till two a.m., wishing to see if it would be empty. But the morrow was to witness the egress to Arafat; many, therefore, passed the hours of darkness in the Haram. Numerous parties of pilgrims sat upon their rugs, with lanterns in front of them, conversing, praying, and contemplating the Kaabah. The cloisters were full of merchants, who resorted there to 'talk shop', and to vend such holy goods as combs, tooth-sticks, and rosaries. Before ten p.m. I found no opportunity of praying the usual two prostrations over the grave of Ishmael.

After waiting long and patiently, at last I was stepping into the vacant place, when another pilgrim rushed forward; the boy Mohammed, assisted by me, instantly seized him, and, despite his cries and struggles, taught him to wait. Till midnight we sat chatting with the different ciceroni who came up to offer their services. I could not help remarking their shabby and dirty clothes, and was informed that during pilgrimage, when splendour is liable to be spoiled, they wear out old dresses; and appear *endimanchés* for the Muharram fête, when most travellers have left the city. Presently my two companions, exhausted with fatigue, fell asleep; I went up to the Kaabah, with the intention of 'annexing' a bit of the torn old Kiswat or curtain, but too many eyes were looking on.

At this season of the year the Kiswat is much tattered at the base, partly by pilgrims' fingers, and partly by the strain of the cord which confines it when the wind is blowing. It is considered a mere peccadillo to purloin a bit of the venerable stuff; but as the officers of the temple make money by selling it, they certainly would visit detection with an unmerciful application of the quarterstaff. The piece in my possession was given to me by the boy Mohammed before I left Meccah. Waistcoats cut out of the Kiswat still make the combatants invulnerable in battle, and are considered presents fit for princes. The Moslems generally try to secure a strip of this cloth as a mark for the Koran, or some such purpose.

At last sleep began to weigh heavily upon my eyelids. I awoke my companions, and in the dizziness of slumber they walked with me through the tall, narrow street from the Bab el-Ziyadah to our home in the Shamiyah. The brilliant moonshine prevented our complaining, as other travellers have had reason to do, of the darkness and the difficulty of Meccah's streets. The town, too, appeared safe; there were no watchmen, and yet people slept everywhere upon cots placed opposite their open doors. Arrived at the house, we made some brief preparations for snatching a few hours' sleep upon the Mastabah, a place so stifling, that nothing but utter exhaustion could induce lethargy there.

XXVIII

The Ceremonies of the Yaum El-Tarwiyah, or the First Day

At ten a.m., on the 8th Zu'l Hijjah, AH 1269 (Monday, the 12th September, 1853), habited in our Ihram, or pilgrim-garbs, we mounted the litter. Shaykh Masud had been standing at the door from dawn-time, impatient to start before the Damascus and the Egyptian caravans made the road dangerous. Our delay arose from the tyrannical conduct of the boy Mohammed, who insisted upon leaving his little nephew behind. It was long before he yielded. I then placed the poor child, who was crying bitterly, in the litter between us, and at last we started.

We followed the road by which the caravans entered Meccah. It was covered with white-robed pilgrims, some few wending their way on foot; others riding, and all men barefooted and bareheaded. Most of the wealthier classes mounted asses. The scene was, as usual, one of strange contrasts: Bedawin bestriding swift dromedaries; Turkish dignitaries on fine horses; the most picturesque beggars, and the most uninteresting Nizam. Not a little wrangling mingled with the loud bursts of Talbiyat. Dead animals dotted the ground, and carcases had been cast into a dry tank, the Birkat el-Shami which caused every Bedawi to hold his nose. Here, on the right of the road, the poorer pilgrims, who could not find houses, had erected huts, and pitched their ragged tents.

Traversing the suburb El-Ma'b'dah (Ma'abahah), in a valley between the two barren prolongations of Kayka'an and Khandamah, we turned to the north-east, leaving on the left certain barracks of Turkish soldiery, and the Negro militia here stationed, with the *Saniyat Kuda'a* in the background.

Then, advancing about 3,000 paces over rising ground, we passed by the conical head of Jebel Nur (anciently Hira), and entered the plain of many names. It contained nothing but a few whitewashed walls, surrounding places of prayer, and a number of stone cisterns, some well preserved, others in ruins. All, however, were dry, and water-vendors crowded the roadside. Gravel and lumps of granite grew there like grass, and from under every larger stone, as Shaykh Masud took a delight in showing, a small scorpion; with tail curled over its back, fled, Parthian-like, from the invaders of its home. At eleven a.m., ascending a Mudarraj, or flight of stone steps, about thirty yards broad, we passed without difficulty, for we were in advance of the caravans, over the Akabah, or Steeps, and the narrow, hill-girt entrance, to the low gravel basin in which Muna lies.

Muna, more classically called Mina, is a place of considerable sanctity. Its three standing miracles are these: The pebbles thrown at the Devil return by angelic agency to whence they came; during the three Days of Drying Meat rapacious beasts and birds cannot prey there; and, lastly, flies do not settle upon the articles of food exposed so abundantly in the bazars.[1] During pilgrimage houses are let for an exorbitant sum, and it becomes a World's Fair of Moslem merchants. At all other seasons it is almost deserted, in consequence, says popular superstition, of the *Rajm* or (diabolical) lapidation. Distant about three miles from Meccah, it is a long, narrow, straggling village, composed of mud and stone houses of one or two stories, built in the common Arab style. Traversing a narrow street, we passed on the left the Great Devil, which shall be described at a future time. After a quarter of an hour's halt, spent over pipes and coffee, we came to an open space, where stands the mosque El-Khayf. Here, according to some Arabs, Adam lies, his head being at one end of the long wall, and his feet at another, whilst the dome covers his omphalic region. Grand preparations for fireworks were being made in this square; I especially remarked a fire-ship, which savoured strongly of Stamboul. After passing through the town, we came to Batn el-Muhassir, The Basin of the Troubler (Satan), at the beginning of a descent leading to

[1] According to Mohammed, the pebbles of the accepted are removed by angels; as, however, each man or woman must throw forty-nine or seventy stones, it is fair to suspect the intervention of something more material. Animals are frightened away by the bustling crowd, and flies are found in myriads.

Muzdalifah (the Approacher), where the road falls into the valley of the Arafat torrent.

At noon we reached the Muzdalifah, also called Mashar El-Har'am, the Place dedicated to Religious Ceremonies.[1] It is known in El-Islam as the Minaret without the Mosque, opposed to Masjid Nimrah, which is the Mosque without the Minaret. Half-way between Muna and Arafat, it is about three miles from both. There is something peculiarly striking in the distant appearance of the tall, solitary tower, rising abruptly from the desolate valley of gravel, flanked with buttresses of yellow rock. No wonder that the ancient Arabs loved to give the high-sounding name of this oratory to distant places in their giant Caliph-empire.

Here, as we halted to perform the midday prayer, we were overtaken by the Damascus Caravan. It was a grand spectacle. The Mahmal, no longer naked as upon the line of march, flashed in the sun all green and gold. Around the moving host of white-robed pilgrims hovered a crowd of Bedawin, male and female, all mounted on swift dromedaries, and many of them armed to the teeth. As their drapery floated in the wind, and their faces were veiled with the Lisam, it was frequently difficult to distinguish the sex of the wild being, flogging its animal to speed. These people, as has been said, often resort to Arafat for blood-revenge, in hopes of finding the victim unprepared. Nothing can be more sinful in El-Islam than such deed—it is murder, 'made sicker' by sacrilege; yet the prevalence of the practice proves how feeble is the religion's hold upon the race. The women are as unscrupulous: I remarked many of them emulating the men in reckless riding, and striking with their sticks every animal in the way.

Travelling eastward up the Arafat Fiumara, after about half an hour we came to a narrow pass called El-Akhshabayn, or the Two Rugged Hills. Here the spurs of the rock limit the road to about 100 paces, and it is generally a scene of great confusion. After this we arrived at El-Bazan (the Basin), a widening of the plain; and another half-hour brought us to the Alamayn (the

[1] Many, even since Sale corrected the error, have confounded this Mashar El-*Harám* with the Masjid El-*Hărăm* of Meccah.

Two Signs), whitewashed pillars, or rather thin, narrow walls, surmounted with pinnacles, which denote the precincts of the Arafat plain.

Here, in full sight of the Holy Hill, standing quietly out from the deep blue sky, the host of pilgrims broke into loud 'Labbayks'. A little beyond, and to our right, was the simple enclosure called the Masjid Nimrah. We then turned from our eastern course northwards, and began threading our way down the main street of the town of tents which clustered about the southern foot of Arafat. At last, about three p.m., we found a vacant space near the Matbakh, or kitchen, formerly belonging to a Sherif's palace, but now a ruin with a few shells of arches.

Arafat is about six hours' very slow march, or twelve miles, on the Taif road, due east of Meccah. We arrived there in a shorter time, but our weary camels, during the last third of the way, frequently threw themselves upon the ground. Human beings suffered more. Between Muna and Arafat I saw no less than five men fall down and die upon the highway: exhausted and moribund, they had dragged themselves out to give up the ghost where it departs to instant beatitude. The spectacle showed how easy it is to die in these latitudes; each man suddenly staggered, fell as if shot; and, after a brief convulsion, lay still as marble. The corpses were carefully taken up, and carelessly buried that same evening, in a vacant space amongst the crowds encamped upon the Arafat plain.

The boy Mohammed, who had long chafed at my pertinacious claim to dervishhood, resolved on this occasion to be grand. To swell the party, he had invited Umar Effendi, whom we accidently met in the streets of Meccah, to join us; but failing therein, he brought with him two cousins, fat youths of sixteen and seventeen, and his mother's ground-floor servants. These were four Indians: an old man; his wife, a middle-aged woman of the most ordinary appearance; their son, a sharp boy, who spoke excellent Arabic; and a family friend, a stout fellow about thirty years old. They were Panjabis, and the bachelor's history was instructive. He was gaining an honest livelihood in his own country, when suddenly one night Hazrat Ali, dressed in green, and mounted upon his charger Duldul—at least, so said the narrator—appeared, crying in a terrible voice, 'How long wilt thou toil for this world, and be idle about the life to come?' From that moment, like an English murderer, he knew no peace; Conscience and Hazrat Ali haunted him. Finding life unendurable at home, he sold everything; raised the sum of 20*l.*, and started for the Holy Land. He reached Jeddah with a few rupees in his pocket; and came to Meccah, where, everything being exorbitantly dear and charity all but unknown, he might have starved, had he not been received by his old friend. The married pair and their son had been taken as house-servants by the boy Mohammed's mother, who generously allowed them shelter and 1 lb. of rice per diem to each, but not a farthing of pay. They were even expected to provide their own turmeric and onions. Yet these poor people were anxiously awaiting the opportunity to visit El-Medinah, without which their pilgrimage would not, they believed, be complete. They would beg their way through the terrible Desert and its Bedawin—an old man, a boy, and a woman! What were their chances of returning to their homes?

Such, I believe, is too often the history of those wretches whom a fit of religious enthusiasm, likest to insanity, hurries away to the Holy Land. I strongly recommend the subject to the consideration of our Indian government as one that calls loudly for their interference. No Eastern ruler parts, as we do, with his subjects; all object to lose productive power. To an 'empire of opinion' this emigration is fraught with evils. It sends forth a horde of malcontents that ripen into bigots; it teaches foreign nations to despise our rule; and it unveils the present nakedness of once wealthy India. And we have both prevention and cure in our own hands.

As no Moslem, except the Maliki, is bound to pilgrimage without a sum sufficient to support himself and his family, all who embark at the different ports of India should be obliged to prove their solvency before being provided with a permit. Arrived at Jeddah, they should present the certificate at the British vice-consulate, where they would become entitled to assistance in case of necessity.

The vice-consul at Jeddah ought also to be instructed to assist our Indian pilgrims. Mr Cole, when holding that appointment, informed me that, though men die of starvation in the streets, he was unable to relieve them. The highways of Meccah abound in pathetic Indian beggars, who affect lank bodies, shrinking frames, whining voices, and all the circumstance of misery, because it supports them in idleness.

There are no less than 1,500 Indians at Meccah and Jeddah, besides 700 or 800 in Yemen. Such a body requires a consul.[1] By the representation of a vice-consul when other powers send an officer of superior rank to El-Hejaz, we voluntarily place ourselves in an inferior position. And although the Meccan Sherif might for a time object to establishing a Moslem agent at the Holy City with orders to report to the consul at Jeddah, his opposition would soon fall to the ground.

With the Indians' assistance the boy Mohammed removed the handsome Persian rugs with which he had covered the Shugduf, pitched the tent, carpeted the ground, disposed a Diwan of silk and satin cushions round the interior, and strewed the centre with new chibouques, and highly polished Shishahs. At the doorway was placed a large copper fire-pan, with coffee-pots singing a welcome to visitors. In front of us were the litters, and by divers similar arrangements our establishment was made to look fine. The youth also insisted upon my removing the Rida, or upper cotton cloth, which had become way-soiled, and he supplied its place by a rich cashmere, left with him, some years before, by a son of the king of Delhi.

Arafat, anciently called Jebel Ilal, the Mount of Wrestling in Prayer, and now Jebel el-Rahmah, the Mount of Mercy, is a mass of coarse granite split into large blocks, with a thin coat of withered thorns. About one mile in circumference, it rises abruptly to the height of 180 or 200 feet, from the low gravelly plain—a dwarf wall at the southern base forming the line of demarcation. It is separated by Batn Arnah, a sandy vale, from the spurs of the Taif hills. Nothing can be more picturesque than the view it affords of the azure peaks behind, and the vast encampment scattered over the barren yellow plain below. On the north lay the regularly pitched camp of the guards that

[1] There is a consul for Jeddah now, 1879, but till lately he was an unpaid.

defend the unarmed pilgrims. To the eastward was the Sherif's encampment, with the bright Mahmals and the gilt knobs of the grandees' pavilions; whilst on the southern and western sides, the tents of the vulgar crowded the ground, disposed in *Dowar*, or circles. After many calculations, I estimated the number to be not less than 50,000, of all ages and sexes; a sad falling off, it is true, but still considerable.

Ali Bey (AD 1807) calculates 83,000 pilgrims; Burckhardt (1814), 70,000. I reduce it, in 1853, to 50,000; and in AD 1854, owing to political causes, it fell to about 25,000. Of these at least 10,000 are Meccans, as every one who can leave the city does so at pilgrimage-time. The Arabs have a superstition that the numbers at Arafat cannot be counted, and that if less than 600,000 mortals stand upon the hill to hear the sermon, the angels descend and complete the number. Even this year my Arab friends declared that 150,000 spirits were present in human shape. It may be observed that when the good old Bertrand de la Brocquière, esquire-carver to Philip of Burgundy, declares that the yearly Caravan from Damascus to El-Medinah must always be composed of 700,000 persons, and that this number being incomplete, Allah sends some of his angels to make it up, he probably confounds the Caravan with the Arafat multitude.

The Holy Hill owes its name[1] and honours to a well-known legend. When our first parents forfeited Heaven by eating wheat, which deprived them of their primeval purity, they were cast down upon earth. The serpent descended at Ispahan, the peacock at Cabool, Satan at Bilbays (others say Semnan and Seistan), Eve upon Arafat, and Adam at Ceylon. The latter, determining to seek his wife, began a journey, to which earth owes its present mottled appearance. Wherever our first father placed his foot—which was large—a town afterwards arose; between the strides will always be country. Wandering for many years, he came to the Mountain of Mercy, where our

[1] The word is explained in many ways. One derivation has already been mentioned. Others assert that when Gabriel taught Abraham the ceremonies, he ended by saying 'A '*arafta* manásik'ak?'—'Hast thou learned thy pilgrim rites?' To which the friend of Allah replied, '*Araftu!*'—'I have learned them.'

common mother was continually calling upon his name, and their *recognition* gave the place the name of Arafat. Upon its summit, Adam, instructed by the archangel Gabriel, erected a *Mada'a*, or place of prayer; and between this spot and the Nimrah mosque the couple abode till death. Others declare that, after recognition, the first pair returned to India, whence for forty-four years in succession they visited the Sacred City at pilgrimage-time.

From the Holy Hill I walked down to look at the camp arrangements. The main street of tents and booths, huts and shops, was bright with lanterns, and the bazars were crowded with people and stocked with all manner of eastern delicacies. Some anomalous spectacles met the eye. Many pilgrims, especially the soldiers, were in laical costume. In one place a half-drunken Arnaut stalked down the road, elbowing peaceful passengers and frowning fiercely in hopes of a quarrel. In another part, a huge dimly lit tent, reeking hot, and garnished with cane seats, contained knots of Egyptians, as their red Tarbushes, white turbans, and black Za'abuts showed, noisily intoxicating themselves with forbidden hemp. There were frequent brawls and great confusion; many men had lost their parties, and, mixed with loud 'Labbayks', rose the shouted names of women as well as men. I was surprised at the disproportion of female nomenclature—the missing number of fair ones seemed to double that of the other sex—and at a practice so opposed to the customs of the Moslem world. At length the boy Mohammed enlightened me. Egyptian and other bold women, when unable to join the pilgrimage, will pay or persuade a friend to shout their names in hearing of the Holy Hill, with a view of ensuring a real presence at the desired spot next year. So the welkin rang with the indecent sounds of 'O Fatimah! O Zaynab! O Khayz'ran!'[1] Plunderers, too, were abroad. As we returned to the tent we found a crowd assembled near it; a woman had seized a thief as he was beginning operations, and had the courage to hold

[1] The latter name, Ratan, is servile. Respectable women are never publicly addressed by Moslems except as daughter, female pilgrim, after some male relation, 'O mother of Mohammed', 'O sister of Umar', or *tout bonnement*, by a man's name. It would be ill-omened and dangerous were the true name known. So most women, when travelling, adopt an alias. Who ever knew an Afghan fair who was not Nur Jan, or Sahib Jan?

Sherif Yahya (third from left), flanked by two lesser Sherifs and his slave, who holds a gun. His father was Sherif Ahmed and his grandfather Abd el-Muttalib, the Sherif of Mecca, both of whom Burton met on his way to the holy city

Pilgrims arrive at Mount Arafat

Pilgrim camp at Mount Arafat

Pilgrim camp at Sarif. In the background is the winding road to Mecca

his beard till men ran to her assistance. And we were obliged to defend by force our position against a knot of grave-diggers, who would bury a little heap of bodies within a yard or two of our tent.

One point struck me at once, the difference in point of cleanliness between an encampment of citizens and Bedawin. Poor Masud sat holding his nose in ineffable disgust, for which he was derided by the Meccans. I consoled him with quoting the celebrated song of Maysunah, the beautiful Bedawi wife of the Caliph Muawiyah. Nothing can be more charming in its own Arabic than this little song; the Bedawin never hear it without screams of joy.

> O take these purple robes away,
> Give back my cloak of camel's hair,
> And bear me from this tow'ring pile
> To where the Black Tents flap i' the air.
> The camel's colt with falt'ring tread,
> The dog that bays at all but me,
> Delight me more than ambling mules—
> Than every art of minstrelsy;
> And any cousin, poor but free,
> Might take me, fatted ass! from thee.[1]

The old man, delighted, clapped my shoulder, and exclaimed 'Verily, O Father of Mustachios, I will show thee the black tents of my tribe this year!'

At length night came, and we threw ourselves upon our rugs, but not to sleep. Close by, to our bane, was a prayerful old gentleman, who began his devotions at a late hour and concluded

[1] The British reader will be shocked to hear that by the term 'fatted ass' the intellectual lady alluded to her husband. The story is, that Muawiyah, overhearing the song, sent back the singer to her cousins and beloved wilds. Maysunah departed with her son Yezid, and did not return to Damascus till the 'fatted ass' had joined his forefathers.

Yezid inherited, with his mother's talents, all her contempt for his father; at least the following quatrain, addressed to Muawiyah, and generally known in El-Islam, would appear to argue anything but reverence:

> I drank the water of the vine; that draught had power to rouse
> Thy wrath, grim father! now, indeed, 'tis joyous to carouse!
> I'll drink!—Be wroth!—I reck not!—Ah! dear to this heart of mine
> It is to scoff a sire's command—to quaff forbidden wine.

them not before dawn. He reminded me of the undergraduate my neighbour at Trinity College, Oxford, who would spout Aeschylus at two a.m. Sometimes the chant would grow drowsy, and my ears would hear a dull retreating sound; presently, as if in self-reproach, it would rise to a sharp treble, and proceed at a rate perfectly appalling. The coffee-houses, too, were by no means silent; deep into the night I heard the clapping of hands accompanying merry Arab songs, and the loud shouts of laughter of the Egyptian hemp-drinkers. And the guards and protectors of the camp were not 'Charleys' or night-nurses.

XXIX
The Ceremonies of the Yaum Arafat, or the Second Day

THE morning of the 9th Zu'l Hijjah (Tuesday, the 13th September) was ushered in by military sounds: a loud discharge of cannon warned us to arise and to prepare for the ceremonies of this eventful day.

After ablution and prayer, I proceeded with the boy Mohammed to inspect the numerous consecrated sites on the Mountain of Mercy. In the first place, we repaired to a spot on rising ground to the south-east, and within 100 yards of the hill. It is called Jami el-Sakhrah—the Assembling Place of the Rock—from two granite boulders upon which the Prophet stood to perform Talbiyat. There is nothing but a small enclosure of dwarf and whitewashed stone walls, divided into halves by a similar partition, and provided with a niche to direct prayer towards Meccah. Entering by steps, we found crowds of devotees and guardians, who for a consideration offered mats and carpets. After a two-bow prayer and a long supplication opposite the niche, we retired to the inner compartment, stood upon a boulder and shouted the 'Labbayk'.

Thence, threading our way through many obstacles of tent and stone, we ascended the broad flight of rugged steps which winds up the southern face of the rocky hill. Even at this early hour it was crowded with pilgrims, principally Bedawin and Wahhabis, who had secured favourable positions for hearing the sermon. Already their green flag was planted upon the summit close to Adam's Place of Prayer. The wilder Arabs insist that Wukuf (standing) should take place upon the Hill. This is not done by the more civilised, who hold that all the plain within the Alamayn ranks as Arafat. About half-way up I counted sixty-six steps, and remarked that they became narrower and steeper. Crowds of beggars instantly seized the pilgrims' robes, and strove to prevent our entering a second enclosure. This place, which resembles the former, except that it has but one compartment and no boulders, is that whence Mohammed used to address his followers; and here, to the present day, the Khatib, or preacher, in imitation of the 'Last of the Prophets', sitting upon a dromedary, recites the Arafat sermon. Here, also, we prayed a two-bow prayer, and gave a small sum to the guardian.

Thence ascending with increased difficulty to the hill-top, we arrived at a large stuccoed platform, with prayer-niche and a kind of obelisk, mean and badly built of lime and granite stone, whitewashed, and conspicuous from afar. It is called the Makam, or Mada'a Sayyidna Adam. Here we performed the customary ceremonies amongst a crowd of pilgrims, and then we walked down the little hill. Close to the plain we saw the place where the Egyptian and Damascus Mahmals stand during the sermon; and, descending the wall that surrounds Arafat by a steep and narrow flight of coarse stone steps, we found on our right the fountain which supplies the place with water. It bubbles from the rock, and is exceedingly pure, as such water generally is in El-Hejaz.

Our excursion employed us longer than the description requires—nine o'clock had struck before we reached the plain. All were in a state of excitement. Guns fired incessantly. Horsemen and camel-riders galloped about without apparent object. Even the women and the children stood and walked, too restless even to sleep. Arrived at the tent, I was unpleasantly surprised to find a new visitor in an old acquaintance, Ali bin Ya Sin the Zem Zemi. He had lost his mule, and, wandering in search of its keepers, he unfortunately fell in with our party. I had solid reasons to regret the mishap—he was far too curious and observant to suit my tastes. On the present occasion, he, being uncomfortable, made us equally so. Accustomed to all the terrible neatness of an elderly damsel in Great Britain, a few specks of dirt upon the rugs, and half a dozen bits of cinder upon the ground, sufficed to give him attacks of nerves.

That day we breakfasted late, for night must come before we could eat again. After midday prayer we performed ablutions; some the greater, others the less, in preparation for the Wukuf, or Standing. From noon onwards the hum and murmur of the multitude increased, and people were seen swarming about in all directions.

A second discharge of cannon (at about 3.15 p.m.) announced the approach of El-Asr, the afternoon prayer, and almost immediately we heard the Naubat, or band preceding the Sherif's procession, as he wended his way towards the mountain. Fortunately my tent was pitched close to the road, so that without trouble I had a perfect view of the scene. First swept a cloud of mace-bearers, who, as usual on such occasions, cleared the path with scant ceremony. They were followed by the horsemen of the Desert, wielding long and tufted spears. Immediately behind them came the Sherif's led horses, upon which I fixed a curious eye. All were highly bred, and one, a brown Nejdi with black points, struck me as the perfection of an Arab. They were small, and all were apparently of the northern race. Of their old crimsom-velvet caparisons the less said the better; no little Indian Nawab would show aught so shabby on state occasions.

After the chargers paraded a band of black slaves on foot bearing huge matchlocks; and immediately preceded by three green and two red flags, came the Sherif, riding in front of his family and courtiers. The prince, habited in a simple white Ihram, and bareheaded, mounted a mule; the only sign of his rank was a large green and gold embroidered umbrella, held over him by a slave. The rear was brought up by another troop of Bedawin on horses and camels. Behind this procession were the tents, whose doors and walls were scarcely visible for the crowd; and the picturesque background was the granite hill, covered, wherever standing-room was to be found, with white-robed pilgrims shouting 'Labbayk', and waving the skirts of their glistening garments violently over their heads.

Slowly and solemnly the procession advanced towards the hill. Exactly at the hour El-Asr the two Mahmals had taken their station side by side on a platform in the lower slope. That of Damascus could be distinguished as the narrower and the more ornamented of the pair. The Sherif placed himself with his standard-bearers and retinue a little above the Mahmals, within hearing of the preacher. The pilgrims crowded up to the foot of the mountain; the loud 'Labbayk' of the Bedawin and Wahhabis fell to a solemn silence, and the waving of white robes ceased—a sign that the preacher had begun the Khutbat el-Wakfah, or Sermon of the Standing (upon Arafat). From my tent I could distinguish the form of the old man upon his camel, but the distance was too great for ear to reach.

But how came I to be at the tent?

A short confession will explain. They will shrive me who believe in inspired Spenser's lines—

> And every spirit as it is more pure,
> And hath in it the more of heavenly light,
> So it the fairer body doth procure
> To habit in.

The evil came of a 'fairer body'. I had prepared *en cachette* a slip of paper, and had hid in my Ihram a pencil destined to put down the heads of this rarely heard discourse. But unhappily that red cashmere shawl was upon my shoulders. Close to us sat a party of fair Meccans, apparently belonging to the higher classes, and one of these I had already several times remarked. She was a tall girl, about eighteen years old, with regular features, a skin somewhat citrine-coloured, but soft and clear, symmetrical eyebrows, the most beautiful eyes, and a figure all grace. There was no head thrown back, no straightened neck, no flat shoulders, nor toes turned out—in fact, no 'elegant' barbarisms: the shape was what the Arabs love, soft, bending, and relaxed, as a woman's figure ought to be. Unhappily she wore, instead of the usual veil, a Yashmak of transparent muslin, bound round the face; and the chaperone, mother, or duenna, by whose side she stood, was apparently a very unsuspicious or complaisant old person. Flirtilla fixed a glance of admiration upon my cashmere. I directed a reply with interest at her eyes. She then by the usual coquettish gesture, threw back an inch or two of head-veil, disclosing broad bands of jetty hair, crowning a lovely oval. My palpable admiration of the new charm was rewarded by a partial removal of the Yashmak, when a dimpled mouth and a rounded chin stood out from the envious muslin. Seeing that my companions were safely employed, I ventured upon the dangerous ground of raising hand to forehead. She smiled almost imperceptibly, and turned away. The pilgrim was in ecstasy.

The sermon was then half over. I resolved to stay upon the plain and see what Flirtilla would do. *Grâce* to the cashmere, we came to a good understanding. The next page will record my disappointment—that evening the pilgrim resumed his soiled cotton cloth, and testily returned the red shawl to the boy Mohammed.

The sermon always lasts till near sunset, or about three hours. At first it was spoken amid profound silence. Then loud, scattered 'Amins' (Amens) and volleys of 'Labbayk' exploded at uncertain intervals. At last the breeze brought to our ears a purgatorial chorus of cries, sobs, and shrieks. Even my party thought proper to be affected: old Ali rubbed his eyes, which in no case unconnected with dollars could by any amount of straining be made to shed even a crocodile's tear; and the boy Mohammed wisely hid his face in the skirt of his Rida. Presently the people, exhausted by emotion, began to descend the hill in small parties; and those below struck their tents and commenced loading their camels, although at least an hour's sermon remained. On this occasion, however, all hurry to be foremost, as the 'race from Arafat' is enjoyed by none but the Bedawin.

Although we worked with a will, our animals were not ready to move before sunset, when the preacher gave the signal of Israf, or permission to depart. The pilgrims,

> swaying to and fro,
> Like waves of a great sea, that in mid shock
> Confound each other, white with foam and fear,

rushed down the hill with a 'Labbayk' sounding like a blast, and took the road to Muna. Then I saw the scene which has given to the part of the ceremonies the name of El-Daf'a min Arafat—the Hurry from Arafat. Every man urged his beast with might and main: it was sunset; the plain bristled with tent-pegs, litters were crushed, pedestrians were trampled, camels were overthrown: single combats with sticks and other weapons took place; here a woman, there a child, and there an animal were lost: briefly, it was a chaotic confusion.

To my disgust, old Ali insisted upon bestowing his company upon me. He gave over his newly found mule to the boy Mohammed, bidding him take care of the beast, and mounted with me in the Shugduf. I had persuaded Shaykh Masud, with a dollar, to keep close in rear of the pretty Meccan; and I wanted to sketch the Holy Hill.

The senior began to give orders about the camel—I, counter-orders. The camel was halted. I urged it on: old Ali directed it to be stopped. Meanwhile the charming face that smiled at me from the litter grew dimmer and dimmer; the more I stormed, the less I was listened to—a string of camels crossed our path—I lost sight of the beauty.

Then we began to advance. Again, my determination to sketch seemed likely to fail before the Zem Zemi's little snake's eye. After a few minutes' angry search for expedients, one suggested itself. 'Effendi!' said old Ali, 'sit quiet; there is danger here.' I tossed about like one suffering from evil conscience or the colic. 'Effendi!' shrieked the senior, 'what art thou doing? Thou wilt be the death of us.' 'Wallah!' I replied with a violent plunge, 'it is all thy fault! There!' (another plunge) '—put thy beard out of the other opening, and Allah will make it easy to us.' In the ecstasy of fear my tormentor turned his face, as he was bidden, towards the camel's head. A second halt ensued, when I looked out of the aperture in rear, and made a rough drawing of the Mountain of Mercy.

At the Akhshabayn, double lines of camels, bristling with litters, clashed with a shock more noisy than the meeting of torrents. It was already dark: no man knew what he was doing. The guns roared their brazen notes, re-echoed far and wide by the harsh voices of the stony hills. A shower of rockets bursting in the air threw into still greater confusion the timorous mob of women and children. At the same time martial music rose from the masses of Nizam, and the stouter-hearted pilgrims were not sparing of their 'Labbayk', and 'Eed kum Mubarak'—'May your Festival be happy!'

After the Pass of the Two Rugged Hills, the road widened,

and old Ali, who, during the bumping, had been in a silent convulsion of terror, recovered speech and spirits. This change he evidenced by beginning to be troublesome once more. Again I resolved to be his equal. Exclaiming, 'My eyes are yellow with hunger!' I seized a pot full of savoury meat which the old man had previously stored for supper, and, without further preamble, began to eat it greedily, at the same time ready to shout with laughter at the mumbling and grumbling sounds that proceeded from the darkness of the litter.

We were at least three hours on the road before reaching Muzdalifah, and being fatigued, we resolved to pass the night there. The Mosque was brilliantly illuminated, but my hungry companions apparently thought more of supper and sleep than devotion. Whilst the tent was raised, the Indians prepared our food, boiled our coffee, filled our pipes, and spread our rugs. Before sleeping, each man collected for himself seven Jamrah—bits of granite the size of a small bean. Then, weary with emotion and exertion, all lay down except the boy Mohammed, who preceded us to find encamping ground at Muna. Old Ali, in lending his mule, made the most stringent arrangements with the youth about the exact place and the exact hour of meeting—an act of simplicity at which I could not but smile. The night was by no means peaceful or silent. Lines of camels passed us every ten minutes, and the shouting of travellers continued till near dawn. Pilgrims ought to have nighted at the Mosque, but, as in Burckhardt's time, so in mine, baggage was considered to be in danger thereabouts, and consequently most of the devotees spent the sermon-hours in brooding over their boxes.

XXX

The Ceremonies of the Yaum Nahr, or the Third Day

At dawn on the Eed el-Kurban (the 10th Zu'l Hijjah, Wednesday, the 14th September) a gun warned us to lose no time; we arose hurriedly, and started up the Batn Muhassir to Muna. By this means we lost at Muzdalifah the Salat el-Eed, or Festival Prayers, the great solemnity of the Moslem year, performed by all the community at daybreak. My companion was so anxious to reach Meccah, that he would not hear of devotions.

About eight a.m. we entered the village, and looked for the boy Mohammed in vain. Old Ali was dreadfully perplexed; a host of high-born Turkish pilgrims were, he said, expecting him; his mule was missing—could never appear—he must be late—should probably never reach Meccah—what *would* become of him?

I began by administering admonition to the mind diseased; but signally failing in a cure, I amused myself with contemplating the world from my Shugduf, leaving the office of directing it to the old Zem Zemi. Now he stopped, then he pressed forward; here he thought he saw Mohammed, there he discovered our tent; at one time he would 'nakh' the camel to await, in patience, his supreme hour; at another, half mad with nervousness, he would urge the excellent Masud to hopeless inquiries. Finally, by good fortune, we found one of the boy Mohammed's cousins, who led us to an enclosure called Hosh el-Uzam, in the southern portion of the Muna Basin, at the base of Mount Sabir. There we pitched the tent, refreshed ourselves, and awaited the truant's return. Old Ali, failing to disturb my equanimity, attempted, as those who consort with philosophers often will do, to quarrel with me. But, finding no material wherewith to build a dispute in such fragments as 'Ah'—'Hem!'—'Wallah!' he hinted desperate intentions against the boy Mohammed. When, however, the youth appeared, with even more jauntiness of mien that usual, Ali bin Ya Sin lost heart, brushed by him, mounted his mule, and, doubtless cursing us under the tongue, rode away, frowning viciously, with his heels playing upon the beast's ribs.

Mohammed had been delayed, he said, by the difficulty of finding asses. We were now to mount for 'the Throwing', as a preliminary to which we washed 'with seven waters' the seven pebbles brought from Muzdalifah, and bound them in our Ihrams. Our first destination was the entrance to the western end of the long line which composes the Muna village. We found a swarming crowd in the narrow road opposite the Jamrat el-Akabah, or, as it is vulgarly called, the Shaytan el-Kabir—the Great Devil. These names distinguish it from another pillar, the Wusta, or Central Place (of stoning), built in the middle of Muna, and a third at the eastern end, El-Aula, or the First Place.

The Shaytan el-Kabir is a dwarf buttress of rude masonry, about eight feet high by two and a half broad, placed against a rough wall of stones at the Meccan entrance to Muna. As the ceremony of Ramy, or Lapidation, must be performed on the first day by all pilgrims between sunrise and sunset, and as the fiend was malicious enough to appear in a rugged Pass,[1] the crowd makes the place dangerous. On one side of the road, which is not forty feet broad, stood a row of shops belonging principally to barbers. On the other side is the rugged wall of the pillar, with a *chevaux de frise* of Bedawin and naked boys.

The narrow space was crowded with pilgrims, all struggling like drowning men to approach as near as possible to the Devil; it would have been easy to run over the heads of the mass. Amongst them were horsemen with rearing chargers. Bedawin on wild camels, and grandees on mules and asses, with outrunners, were breaking a way by assault and battery. I had read Ali Bey's self-felicitations upon escaping this place with 'only two wounds in the left leg', and I had duly provided myself with a

[1] I borrow this phrase from Ali Bey, who, however, speaks more like an ignorant Catalonian than a learned Abbaside, when he calls the pillar *Le Maison du Diable*, and facetiously asserts that *le diable a eu la malice de placer sa maison dans un lieu fort étroit qui n'a peut-être pas 34 pieds de large.*

hidden dagger. The precaution was not useless. Scarcely had my donkey entered the crowd than he was overthrown by a dromedary, and I found myself under the stamping and roaring beast's stomach. Avoiding being trampled upon by a judicious use of the knife, I lost no time in escaping from a place so ignobly dangerous. Some Moslem travellers assert, in proof of the sanctity of the spot, that no Moslem is ever killed here: Meccans assured me that accidents are by no means rare.

Presently the boy Mohammed fought his way out of the crowd with a bleeding nose. We both sat down upon a bench before a barber's booth, and, schooled by adversity, awaited with patience an opportunity. Finding an opening, we approached within about five cubits of the place, and holding each stone between the thumb and the forefinger of the right hand, we cast it at the pillar, exclaiming, 'In the Name of Allah, and Allah is Almighty! (I do this) in Hatred of the Fiend and to his Shame.' After which came the Tahlil and the Sana, or praise to Allah.

The seven stones being duly thrown, we retired, and entering the barber's booth, took our places upon one of the earthen benches around it. This was the time to remove the Ihram or pilgrim-garb, and to return to Ihlal, the normal state of El-Islam. The barber shaved our heads, and, after trimming our beards and cutting our nails, made us repeat these words: 'I purpose loosening my Ihram according to the Practice of the Prophet, Whom may Allah bless and preserve! O Allah, make unto me in every Hair, a Light, a Purity, and a generous Reward! In the Name of Allah, and Allah is Almighty!'

At the conclusion of his labour, the barber politely addressed to us a 'Naiman'—'Pleasure to you!' To which we as ceremoniously replied, 'Allah give thee pleasure!' We had no clothes with us, but we could use our cloths to cover our heads, and slippers to defend our feet from the fiery sun; and we now could safely twirl our mustachios and stroke our beards—placid enjoyments of which we had been deprived by the Laws of Pilgrimage. After resting about an hour in the booth, which, though crowded with sitting customers, was delightfully cool compared with the burning glare of the road, we mounted our asses, and at eleven a.m. we started Meccah-wards.

This return from Muna to Meccah is called El-Nafr, or the Flight: we did not fail to keep our asses at speed, with a few halts to refresh ourselves with gugglets of water. There was nothing remarkable in the scene: our ride in was a repetition of our ride out. In about half an hour we entered the city, passing through that classical locality called Batn Kuraysh, which was crowded with people, and then we repaired to the boy Mohammed's house for the purpose of bathing and preparing to visit the Kaabah.

Shortly after our arrival, the youth returned home in a state of excitement, exclaiming, 'Rise, Effendi! dress and follow me!' The Kaabah, though open, would for a time be empty, so that we should escape the crowd. My pilgrim-garb, which had not been removed, was made to look neat and somewhat Indian, and we sallied forth together without loss of time.

A crowd had gathered round the Kaabah, and I had no wish to stand bareheaded and barefooted in the midday September sun. At the cry of 'Open a path for the Haji who would enter the House,' the gazers made way. Two stout Meccans, who stood below the door, raised me in their arms, whilst a third drew me from above into the building. At the entrance I was accosted by several officials, dark-looking Meccans, of whom the blackest and plainest was a youth of the Beni Shaybah family, the true-blue blood of El-Hejaz. He held in his hand the huge silver-gilt padlock of the Kaabah, and presently taking his seat upon a kind of wooden press in the left corner of the hall, he officially inquired my name, nation, and other particulars. The replies were satisfactory, and the boy Mohammed was authoritatively ordered to conduct me round the building, and to recite the prayers. I will not deny that, looking at the windowless walls, the officials at the door, and the crowd of excited fanatics below—

And the place death, considering who I was—

my feelings were of the trapped-rat description, acknowledged by the immortal nephew of his uncle Perez. This did not, however, prevent my carefully observing the scene during our long prayers, and making a rough plan with a pencil upon my white Ihram.

Nothing is more simple than the interior of this celebrated building. The pavement, which is level with the ground, is composed of slabs of fine and various coloured marbles, mostly however white, disposed chequer-wise. The walls, as far as they can be seen, are of the same material, but the pieces are irregularly shaped, and many of them are engraved with long inscriptions in the Suls and other modern characters. The upper part of the walls, together with the ceiling, at which it is considered disrespectful to look, are covered with handsome red damask, flowered over with gold, and tucked up about six feet high, so as to be removed from pilgrims' hands. The flat roof is upheld by three cross-beams, whose shapes appear under the arras; they rest upon the eastern and western walls, and are supported in the centre by three columns about twenty inches in diameter, covered with carved and ornamented aloe wood.

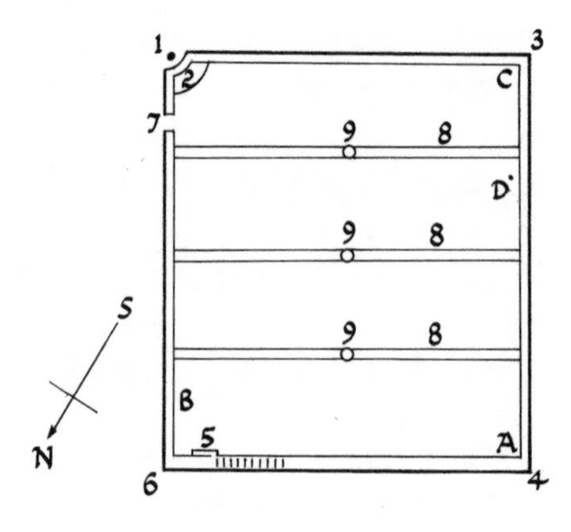

PLAN OF KAABAH

(1) Black Stone (exterior) and As'ad corner
(2) Wooden safe, in which key is kept
(3) Yemani corner (4) Shami corner
(5) Bab el-Taubah, dwarf door, leading to staircase, by which men ascend to the roof
(6) Iraki corner (7) Door
(8) Rafters (9) Columns
(A) First place of prayer (B) Second place
(C) Third place (D) Fourth place

At the Iraki corner there is a dwarf door, called Bab el-Taubah (of Repentance). It leads into a narrow passage and to the staircase by which the servants ascend to the roof: it is never opened except for working purposes. The Aswad or As'ad corner is occupied by a flat-topped and quadrant-shaped press or safe, in which at times is placed the key of the Kaabah. Both door and safe are of aloe wood. Between the columns, and about nine feet from the ground, ran bars of a metal which I could not distinguish, and hanging to them were many lamps, said to be of gold.

Although there were in the Kaabah but a few attendants engaged in preparing it for the entrance of pilgrims, the windowless stone walls and the choked-up door made it worse than the Piombi of Venice; perspiration trickled in large drops, and I thought with horror what it must be when filled with a mass of furiously jostling and crushing fanatics. Our devotions consisted of a two-bow prayer, followed by long supplications at the Shami (west) corner, the Iraki (north) angle, the Yemani (south), and, lastly, opposite the southern third of the back wall. These concluded, I returned to the door, where payment is made. The boy Mohammed told me that the total expense would be 7 dollars. At the same time he had been indulging aloud in his favourite rhodomontade, boasting of my greatness, and had declared me to be an Indian pilgrim, a race still supposed at Meccah to be made of gold. When 7 dollars were tendered, they were rejected with instance. Expecting something of the kind, I had been careful to bring no more than 8. Being pulled and interpellated by half a dozen attendants, my course was to look stupid, and to pretend ignorance of the language. Presently the Shaybah youth bethought him of a contrivance. Drawing forth from the press the key of the Kaabah, he partly bared it of its green-silk gold-lettered étui, and rubbed a golden knob quatrefoil-shaped upon my eyes, in order to brighten them. I submitted to the operation with a good grace, and added a dollar—my last—to the former offering. The Sherif received it with a hopeless glance, and, to my satisfaction, would not put forth his hand to be kissed. Then the attendants began to demand vails. I replied by opening my empty pouch. When let down from the door by the two brawny Meccans, I was expected to pay them, and accordingly appointed to meet them at the boy Mohammed's house; an arrangement to which they grumblingly assented. When delivered from these troubles, I was congratulated by my sharp companion thus: 'Wallah, Effendi! thou hast escaped well! some men have left their skins behind.'

All pilgrims do not enter the Kaabah; and many refuse to do so for religious reasons. Umar Effendi, for instance, who never missed a pilgrimage, had never seen the interior. Those who tread the hallowed floor are bound, among many other things, never again to walk barefooted, to take up fire with the fingers, or to tell lies. Most really conscientious men cannot afford the luxuries of slippers, tongs, and truth. So thought Thomas, when offered the apple which would give him the tongue that cannot lie:

> 'My tongue is mine ain,' true Thomas said;
> 'A gudely gift ye wad gie to me!
> I neither dought to buy nor sell
> At fair or tryst, where I may be:
> I dought neither speak to prince or peer,
> Nor ask of grace from fair ladye!'

Amongst the Hindus I have met with men who have proceeded upon a pilgrimage to Dwarka, and yet who would not receive the brand of the god, because lying would then be forbidden to them. A confidential servant of a friend in Bombay naïvely declared that he had not been marked, as the act would have ruined him. There is a sad truth in what he said: 'Lying to the Oriental is meat and drink, and the roof that shelters him.'

The Kaabah had been dressed in her new attire when we entered. The covering, however, instead of being secured at the bottom to the metal rings in the basement, was tucked up by ropes from the roof, and depended over each face in two long tongues. It was of a brilliant black, and the Hizam—the zone or golden band running round the upper portion of the building—as well as the Burka (face-veil), were of dazzling brightness.

The origin of this custom must be sought in the ancient practice of typifying the church visible by a virgin or bride. The poet Abd el-Rahim el-Bura'i, in one of his Gnostic effusions, has embodied the idea:

وعروس مكة بالكرامات تجلى

> And Meccah's bride (i.e. the Kaabah) appeareth decked with (miraculous) signs.

This idea doubtless led to the face-veil, the covering, and the guardianship of eunuchs.

The Meccan temple was first dressed as a mark of honour by Tobba the Himyarite when he Judaised. If we accept this fact, which is vouched for by Oriental history, we are led to the conclusion that the children of Israel settled at Meccah had connected the temple with their own faith, and, as a corollary, that the prophet of El-Islam introduced their apocryphal traditions into his creed. The pagan Arabs did not remove the coverings: the old and torn Kiswah was covered with a new cloth, and the weight threatened to crush the building. From the time of Kusay, the Kaabah was veiled by subscription, till Abu Rabi'at el-Mughayrah bin Abdillah, who, having acquired great wealth by commerce, offered to provide the Kiswah on alternate years, and thereby gained the name of El-Adil. The Prophet preferred a covering of fine Yemen cloth, and directed the expense to be defrayed by the Bayt el-Mal, or public treasury. Omar chose Egyptian linen, ordering the Kiswah to be renewed every year, and the old covering to be distributed among the pilgrims. In the reign of Osman, the Kaabah was twice clothed, in winter and summer. For the former season, it received a Kamis, or Tobe (shirt) of brocade; with an Izar, or veil; for the latter a suit of fine linen. Muawiyah at first supplied linen and brocade; he afterwards exchanged the former for striped Yemen stuff, and ordered Shaybah bin Usman to strip the Kaabah, and to perfume the walls with Khaluk. Shaybah divided the old Kiswah among the pilgrims, and Abdullah bin Abbas did not object to this distribution. The Caliph Maamun (ninth century) ordered the dress to be changed three times a year. In his day it was red brocade on the 10th Muharram; fine linen on the 1st Rajab; and white brocade on the 1st Shawwal. At last he was informed that the veil applied on the 10th Muharram was too closely followed by the red brocade in the next month, and that it required renewing on the 1st Shawwal. This he ordered to be done. El-Mutawakkil (ninth century), when informed that the dress was spoiled by pilgrims, at first ordered two to be given, and the brocade shirt to be let down as far as the pavement: at last he sent a new veil every two months. During the Caliphat of the Abassides this investiture came to signify sovereignty in El-Hejaz, which passed alternately from Baghdad to Egypt and Yemen. In

El-Idrisi's time (twelfth century AD), the Kiswah was composed of black silk, and renewed every year by the Caliph of Baghdad. Ibn Jubayr writes that it was green and gold. The Kiswah remained with Egypt when Sultan Kalaun (thirteenth century AD) conveyed the rents of two villages, Baysus and Sindbus, to the expense of providing an outer black and an inner red curtain for the Kaabah, with hangings for the Prophet's tomb at El-Medinah. When the Holy Land fell under the power of the Osmanli, Sultan Selim ordered the Kiswah to be black; and his son, Sultan Sulayman the Magnificent (sixteenth century AD), devoted considerable sums to the purpose. The Kiswah was afterwards renewed at the accession of each Sultan. And the Wahhabi, during the first year of their conquest, covered the Kaabah with a red Kiswah of the same stuff as the fine Arabian Aba or cloak, and made at El-Hasa.

The Kiswah is now worked at a cotton manufactory called El-Khurunfish, of the Tumn Bab el-Shaariyah, Cairo. It is made by a hereditary family, called the Bayt el-Sadi, and, as the specimen in my possession proves, it is a coarse tissue of silk and cotton mixed. The Kiswah is composed of eight pieces—two for each face of the Kaabah—the seams being concealed by the Hizam, a broad band, which at a distance looks like gold; it is lined with white calico, and is supplied with cotton ropes. Anciently it is said all the Koran was interwoven into it. Now, it is inscribed 'Verily, the First of Houses founded for Mankind (to worship in) is that at Bekkah; blessed and a Direction to all Creatures'; together with seven chapters, namely, the Cave, Mariam, the Family of Amran, Repentance, T. H. with Y. S. and Tabarak. The character is that called Tumar, the largest style of Eastern caligraphy, legible from a considerable distance. The Hizam is a band about two feet broad, and surrounding the Kaabah at two-thirds of its height. It is divided into four pieces, which are sewn together. On the first and second is inscribed the 'Throne verse-let', and on the third and fourth the titles of the reigning Sultan. These inscriptions are, like the Burka, or door curtain, gold worked into red silk, by the Bayt el-Sadi. When the Kiswah is ready at Khurunfish, it is carried in procession to the Mosque El-Hasanayn, where it is lined, sewn, and prepared for the journey.

After quitting the Kaabah, I returned home exhausted, and washed with henna and warm water, to mitigate the pain of the sun-scalds upon my arms, shoulders, and breast. The house was empty, all the Turkish pilgrims being still at Muna; and the *Kabirah*—the old lady—received me with peculiar attention. I was ushered into an upper room, whose teak wainscotings, covered with Cufic and other inscriptions, large carpets, and ample Diwans, still showed a sort of ragged splendour. The family had seen better days, the Sherif Ghalib having confiscated three of its houses; but it is still proud, and cannot merge the past into the present. In the 'drawing-room', which the Turkish colonel occupied when at Meccah, the *Kabirah* supplied me with a pipe, coffee, cold water, and breakfast. I won her heart by praising the graceless boy Mohammed; like all mothers, she dearly loved the scamp of the family. When he entered, and saw his maternal parent standing near me, with only the end of her veil drawn over her mouth, he began to scold her with divers insinuations.

'Soon thou wilt sit amongst the men in the hall!' he exclaimed.

'O, my son,' rejoined the *Kabirah*, 'fear Allah: thy mother is in years!'—and truly she was so, being at least fifty.

'A-a-h!' sneered the youth, who had formed, as boys of the world must do, or appear to do, a very low estimate of the sex. The old lady understood the drift of the exclamation, and departed with a half-laughing 'May Allah disappoint thee!' She soon, however, returned, bringing me water for ablution; and having heard that I had not yet sacrificed a sheep at Muna, enjoined me to return and perform without delay that important rite.

After resuming our laical toilette, and dressing gaily for the great festival, we mounted our asses about the cool of the afternoon, and, returning to Muna, we found the tent full of visitors. Ali bin Ya Sin, the Zem Zemi, had sent me an amphora of holy water, and the carrier was awaiting the customary dollar. With him were several Meccans, one of whom spoke excellent Persian. We sat down, and chatted together for an hour; and I afterwards learned from the boy Mohammed, that all had pronounced me to be an Ajami.

After their departure we debated about the victim, which is only a Sunnat, or Practice of the Prophet. It is generally sacrificed immediately after the first lapidation, and we had already been guilty of delay. Under these circumstances, and considering the meagre condition of my purse, I would not buy a sheep, but contented myself with watching my neighbours. They gave themselves great trouble, especially a large party of Indians pitched near us, to buy the victim cheap; but the Bedawin were not less acute, and he was happy who paid less than a dollar and a quarter. Some preferred contributing to buy a lean ox. None but the Sherif and the principal dignitaries slaughtered camels. The pilgrims dragged their victims to a smooth rock near the Akabah, above which stands a small open pavilion, whose sides, red with fresh blood, showed that the prince and his attendants had been busy at sacrifice. Others stood before their tents, and, directing the victim's face towards the Kaabah, cut its throat, ejaculating, 'Bismillah! Allahu Akbar!'[1]

The boy Mohammed sneeringly directed my attention to the Indians, who, being a mild race, had hired an Arab butcher to do the deed of blood; and he aroused all Shaykh Nur's ire by his taunting comments upon the chicken-heartedness of the men of Hind. It is considered a meritorious act to give away the victim without eating any portion of its flesh. Parties of Takruri might be seen, sitting vulture-like, contemplating the sheep and goats; and no sooner was the signal given, than they fell upon the bodies, and cut them up without removing them. The surface of the valley soon came to resemble the dirtiest slaughter-house, and my prescient soul drew bad auguries for the future.

We had spent a sultry afternoon in the basin of Muna, which is not unlike a volcanic crater, an Aden closed up at the seaside. Towards night the occasional puffs of Simoom ceased, and through the air of deadly stillness a mass of purple nimbus, bisected by a thin grey line of mist-cloud, rolled down upon us from the Taif hills. When darkness gave the signal, most of

[1] It is strange that the accurate Burckhardt should make Moslems say, when slaughtering or sacrificing, 'In the name of the most Merciful God!' As Mr Lane justly observes, the attribute of mercy is omitted on these occasions.

the pilgrims pressed towards the square in front of the Muna Mosque, to enjoy the pyrotechnics and the discharge of cannon. But during the spectacle came on a windy storm, whose lightnings, flashing their fire from pole to pole, paled the rockets; and whose thunderings, re-echoed by the rocky hills, dumbed the puny artillery of man. We were disappointed in our hopes of rain. A few huge drops pattered upon the plain and sank into its thirsty entrails; all the rest was thunder and lightning, dust-clouds and whirlwind.

XXXI

The Three Days of Drying Flesh

All was dull after the excitement of the Great Festival. The heat of the succeeding night rendered every effort to sleep abortive; and as our little camp required a guard in a place so celebrated for plunderers, I spent the greater part of the time sitting in the clear pure moonlight.

After midnight we again repaired to the Devils, and, beginning with the Ula, or first pillar, at the eastern extremity of Muna, threw at each seven stones (making a total of twenty-one), with the ceremonies before described.

On Thursday we arose before dawn, and prepared with a light breakfast for the fatigues of a climbing walk. After half an hour spent in hopping from boulder to boulder, we arrived at a place situated on the lower declivity of Jebel Sabir, the northern wall of the Muna basin. Here is the *Majarr el-Kabsh*, the Dragging-place of the Ram; a small, whitewashed square, divided into two compartments. The first is entered by a few ragged steps in the south-east angle, which lead to an enclosure thirty feet by fifteen. In the north-east corner is a block of granite (A), in which a huge gash, several inches broad, some feet deep, and completely splitting the stone in knife-shape, notes the spot where Ibrahim's blade fell when the archangel Gabriel forbade him to slay Ismail his son. The second compartment contains a diminutive hypogaeum (B). In this cave the patriarch sacrificed the victim, which gives the place a name. We descended by a flight of steps, and under the stifling ledge of rock found mats and praying-rugs, which, at this early hour, were not overcrowded.

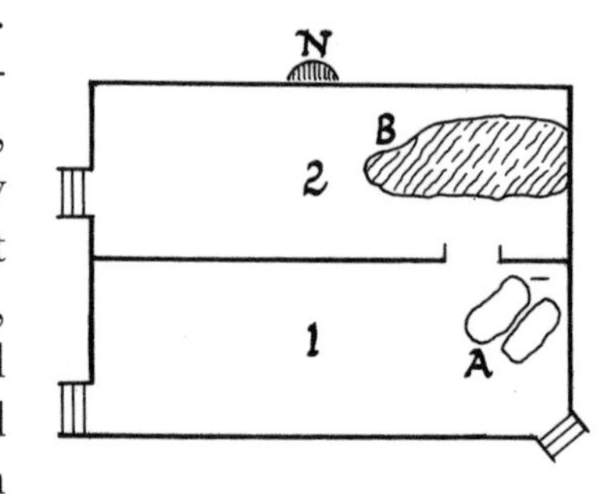

We followed the example of the patriarchs, and prayed a

two-bow prayer in each of the enclosures. After distributing the usual gratification, we left the place, and proceeded to mount the hill, in hope of seeing some of the apes said still to haunt the heights. These animals are supposed by the Meccans to have been Jews, thus transformed for having broken the Sabbath by hunting. They abound in the elevated regions about Arafat and Taif, where they are caught by mixing the juice of the Asclepias and narcotics with dates and other sweet bait.

The Hejazi ape is a hideous cynocephalus, with small eyes placed close together, and almost hidden by a disproportionate snout; a greenish-brown coat, long arms, and a stern of lively pink, like fresh meat. They are docile, and are said to be fond of spirituous liquors, and to display an inordinate affection for women. El-Masudi tells about them a variety of anecdotes. According to him, their principal use in Hind and Chin was to protect kings from poison, by eating suspected dishes. The Bedawin have many tales concerning them. It is universally believed that they catch and kill kites, by exposing the rosy portion of their persons and concealing the rest: the bird pounces upon what appears to be raw meat, and presently finds himself viciously plucked alive.

Throughout Arabia an old story is told of them. A merchant was once plundered during his absence by a troop of these apes; they tore open his bales, and, charmed with the scarlet hue of the Tarbushes, began applying those articles of dress to uses quite opposite to their normal purpose. The merchant was in despair, when his slave offered for a consideration to recover the goods. Placing himself in the front, like a fugleman to the ape-company, he went through a variety of manoeuvres with a Tarbush, and concluded with throwing it far away. The recruits carefully imitated him, and the drill concluded with his firing a shot; the plunderers decamped and the caps were recovered.

Failing to see any apes, we retired to the tent ere the sun waxed hot, in anticipation of a terrible day. Nor were we far wrong. In addition to the heat, we had swarms of flies, and the blood-stained earth began to reek with noisome vapours. Nought moved in the air except kites and vultures, speckling the deep blue sky: the denizens of earth seemed paralysed by the fire from above. I spent the time between breakfast and nightfall lying half-dressed upon a mat, moving round the tent-pole to escape the glare, and watching my numerous neighbours, male and female. The Indians were particularly kind, filling my pipe, offering cooled water, and performing similar little offices. I repaid them with a supply of provisions, which, at the Muna market-prices, these unfortunates could ill afford.

When the moon arose the boy Mohammed and I walked out out into the town, performed our second lapidation, and visited the coffee-houses. The shops were closed early, but business was transacted in places of public resort till midnight.

We entered the houses of numerous acquaintances, who accosted my companion, and were hospitably welcomed with pipes and coffee. The first question always was, 'Who is this pilgrim?' and more than once the reply, 'An Afghan,' elicited the language of my own country, which I could no longer speak. Of this phenomenon, however, nothing was thought: many Afghans settled in India know not a word of Pushtu, and even above the Passes many of the townspeople are imperfectly acquainted with it. The Meccans, in consequence of their extensive intercourse with strangers and habits of travelling, are admirable conversational linguists. They speak Arabic remarkably well, and with a volubility surpassing the most lively of our continental nations. Persian, Turkish, and Hindostani are generally known; and the Mustawwifs, who devote themselves to various races of pilgrims, soon become masters of many languages.

Returning homewards, we were called to a spot by the clapping of hands and the loud sound of song. We found a crowd of Bedawin surrounding a group engaged in their favourite occupation of dancing. The performance is wild in the extreme, resembling rather the hopping of bears than the inspirations of Terpsichore. The bystanders joined in the song; an interminable recitative, as usual, in the minor key, and—Orientals are admirable timists—it sounded like one voice. The refrain appeared to be—

Lá Yayhá! Lá Yayhá!

to which no one could assign a meaning. At other times they sang something intelligible. For instance:

نهار العيد فى منا شفت سيدى
غريب الدار عند كم فارحمو نى

That is to say—

> On the Great Festival-day at Muna I saw my lord.
> I am a stranger amongst you, therefore pity me!

This couplet may have, like the puerilities of certain modern and European poets, an abstruse and mystical meaning, to be discovered when the Arabs learn to write erudite essays upon nursery rhymes. The style of saltation, called Rufayah, rivalled the song. The dancers raised both arms high above their heads, brandishing a dagger, pistol, or some other small weapon. They followed each other by hops, on one or both feet, sometimes indulging in the most demented leaps; whilst the bystanders clapped with their palms a more enlivening measure. This I was told is especially their war-dance. They have other forms, which my eyes were not fated to see. Amongst the Bedawin of El-Hejaz, unlike the Somali and other African races, the sexes never mingle: the girls may dance together, but it would be disgraceful to perform in the company of men.

After so much excitement we retired to rest, and slept soundly.

On Friday, the 12th Zu'l Hijjah, the camels appeared, according to order, at early dawn, and they were loaded with little delay. We were anxious to enter Meccah in time for the sermon, and I for one was eager to escape the now pestilential air of Muna.

Literally, the land stank. Five or six thousand animals had been slain and cut up in this Devil's Punch-bowl. I leave the reader to imagine the rest. The evil might be avoided by building abattoirs, or, more easily still, by digging long trenches, and by ordering all pilgrims, under pain of mulct, to sacrifice in the same place. Unhappily, the spirit of El-Islam is opposed to these precautions of common sense—Inshallah and Kismat must take the place of prevention and cure. And at Meccah, the head-quarters of the faith, a desolating attack of cholera is preferred to the impiety of flying in the face of Providence, and the folly of endeavouring to avert inevitable decrees.[1]

Mounting our camels, and led by Masud, we entered Muna by the eastern end, and from the litter threw the remaining twenty-one stones. I could now see the principal lines of shops, and, having been led to expect a grand display of merchandise, was surprised to find only mat-booths and sheds, stocked chiefly with provisions. The exit from Muna was crowded, for many, like ourselves, were flying from the revolting scene. I could not think without pity of those whom religious scruples detained another day and a half in this foul spot.

After entering Meccah we bathed, and when the noon drew nigh we repaired to the Haram for the purpose of hearing the sermon. Descending to the cloisters below the Bab el-Ziyadah, I stood wonder-struck by the scene before me. The vast quadrangle was crowded with worshippers sitting in long rows, and everywhere facing the central black tower: the showy colours of their dresses were not to be surpassed by a garden of the most brilliant flowers, and such diversity of detail would probably not be seen massed together in any other building upon earth.

The women, a dull and sombre-looking group, sat apart in their peculiar place. The Pasha stood on the roof of Zem Zem, surrounded by guards in Nizam uniform. Where the principal Olema stationed themselves, the crowd was thicker; and in the more auspicious spots nought was to be seen but a pavement of heads and shoulders. Nothing seemed to move but a few dervishes, who, censer in hand, sidled through the rows and received the unsolicited alms of the Faithful.

Apparently in the midst, and raised above the crowd by the tall, pointed pulpit, whose gilt spire flamed in the sun, sat the preacher, an old man with snowy beard. The style of headdress called *Taylasan* covered his turban, which was white as his robes, and a short staff supported his left hand. Presently he

[1] NOTE TO THIRD EDITION. Since this was written there have been two deadly epidemics, which began, it is reported, at Muna. The victims, however, have never numbered 700,000, nor is 'each pilgrim required to sacrifice one animal at the *shrine of Mohammed*' (!) as we find in *Cholera Prospects*, by Tilbury Fox, MD (Hardwicke).

arose, took the staff in his right hand, pronounced a few inaudible words, and sat down again on one of the lower steps, whilst a Muezzin, at the foot of the pulpit, recited the call to sermon. Then the old man stood up and began to preach. As the majestic figure began to exert itself there was a deep silence. Presently a general 'Amin' was intoned by the crowd at the conclusion of some long sentence. And at last, towards the end of the sermon, every third or fourth word was followed by the simultaneous rise and fall of thousands of voices.

I have seen the religious ceremonies of many lands, but never —nowhere—aught so solemn, so impressive as this.

XXXII

Life at Meccah, and Umrah, or the Little Pilgrimage

My few remaining days at Meccah sped pleasantly enough. Umar Effendi visited me regularly, and arranged to accompany me furtively to Cairo. I had already consulted Mohammed Shiklibha—who suddenly appeared at Muna, having dropped down from Suez to Jeddah, and reached Meccah in time for pilgrimage—about the possibility of proceeding eastward. The honest fellow's eyebrows rose till they almost touched his turban, and he exclaimed in a roaring voice, 'Wallah! Effendi! thou art surely mad.' Every day he brought me news of the different caravans. The Bedawin of El-Hejaz were, he said, in a ferment caused by the reports of the Holy War, want of money, and rumours of quarrels between the Sherif and the Pasha: already they spoke of an attack upon Jeddah. Shaykh Masud, the camel-man, with whom I parted on the best of terms, seriously advised my remaining at Meccah for some months even before proceeding to Sanaa. Others gave the same counsel. Briefly I saw that my star was not then in the ascendant, and resolved to reserve myself for a more propitious conjuncture by returning to Egypt.

The Turkish colonel and I had become as friendly as two men ignoring each other's speech could be. He had derived benefit from some prescription; but, like all his countrymen, he was pining to leave Meccah. Whilst the pilgrimage lasted, said they, no *mal de pays* came to trouble them; but, its excitement over, they could think of nothing but their wives and children. Long-drawn faces and continual sighs evidenced nostalgia. At last the house became a scene of preparation. Blue china-ware and basketed bottles of Zem Zem water appeared standing in solid columns, and pilgrims occupied themselves in hunting for mementos of Meccah; ground-plans; combs, balm, henna, tooth-sticks; aloe-wood, turquoises, coral, and mother-of-pearl rosaries; shreds of Kiswat-cloth and fine *Abas*, or cloaks of camels' wool. It was not safe to mount the stairs without shouting 'Tarik' ('Out of the way!') at every step, on peril of meeting face to face some excited fair. The lower floor was crowded with provision-vendors; and the staple article of conversation seemed to be the chance of a steamer from Jeddah to Suez.

Weary of the wrangling and chaffering of the hall below, I had persuaded my kind hostess, in spite of the surly skeleton her brother, partially to clear out a small store-room in the first floor, and to abandon it to me between the hours of ten and four. During the heat of the day clothing is unendurable at Meccah. The city is so compacted together by hills, that even the Simoom can scarcely sweep it; the heat reverberated by the bare rocks is intense, and the normal atmosphere of an eastern town communicates a faint lassitude to the body and irritability to the mind. The houses being unusually strong and well built, might by some art of thermantidote be rendered cool enough in the hottest weather: they are now ovens.[1] It was my habit to retire immediately after the late breakfast to the little room upstairs, to sprinkle it with water, and to lie down on a mat. In the few precious moments of privacy notes were committed to paper, but one eye was ever fixed on the door. Sometimes a patient would interrupt me, but a doctor is far less popular in El-Hejaz than in Egypt. The people, being more healthy, have less faith in

[1] I offer no lengthened description of Meccah: Ali Bey and Burckhardt have already said all that requires saying. Although the origin of the Bayt Ullah be lost in the glooms of past time, the city is a comparatively modern place, built about AD 450, by Kusay and the Kuraysh. It contains from 30,000 to 45,000 inhabitants, with lodging room for at least treble that number; and the material of the houses is brick, granite, and sandstone from the neighbouring hills. The site is a winding valley, on a small plateau, half-way below the Ghauts. Its utmost length is two miles and a half from the Mab'dah (north) to the southern mound Jiyad; and three-quarters of a mile would be the extreme breadth between Abu Kubays eastward—upon whose western slope the most solid mass of the town clusters—and Jebel Hindi westward of the city. In the centre of this line stands the Kaabah.

I regret being unable to offer the reader a sketch of Meccah, or of the Great Temple. The stranger who would do this should visit the city out of the pilgrimage season, and hire a room looking into the quadrangle of the Haram. This addition to our knowledge is the more required, as our popular sketches (generally taken from D'Ohsson) are utterly incorrect. The Kaabah is always a recognisable building; but the 'View of Meccah' known to Europe is not more like Meccah than like Cairo or Bombay.

physic: Shaykh Masud and his son had never tasted in their lives aught more medicinal than green dates and camel's milk. Occasionally the black slave-girls came into the room, asking if the pilgrim wanted a pipe or a cup of coffee: they generally retired in a state of delight, attempting vainly to conceal with a corner of tattered veil a grand display of ivory consequent upon some small and innocent facetiousness.

The most frequent of my visitors was Abdullah, the *Kabirah*'s eldest son. This melancholy Jacques had joined our caravan at El-Hamra, on the Yambu' road, accompanied us to El-Medinah, lived there, and journeyed to Meccah with the Syrian pilgrimage; yet he had not once come to visit me or to see his brother, the boy Mohammed. When gently reproached for this omission, he declared it to be his way—that he never called upon strangers until sent for. He was a perfect *Saudawi* (melancholist) in mind, manners, and personal appearance, and this class of humanity in the East is almost as uncomfortable to the household as the idiot of Europe. I was frequently obliged to share my meals with him, as his mother—though most filially and reverentially entreated—would not supply him with breakfast two hours after the proper time, or with a dinner served up forty minutes before the rest of the household. Often, too, I had to curb, by polite deprecation, the impetuosity of the fiery old *Kabirah*'s tongue.

Thus Abdullah and I became friends, after a fashion. He purchased several little articles required, and never failed to pass hours in my closet, giving me much information about the country; deploring the laxity of Meccan morals, and lamenting that in these evil days his countrymen had forfeited their name at Cairo and Constantinople. His curiosity about the English in India was great, and I satisfied it by praising, as a Moslem would, their *politike*, their even-handed justice, and their good star. Then he would inquire into the truth of a fable extensively known on the shores of the Mediterranean and the Red Sea. The English, it is said, sent a mission to Mohammed, inquiring into his doctrines, and begging that the heroic Khalid bin Walid might be sent to proselytise them. Unfortunately, the envoys arrived too late—the Prophet's soul had winged its way to Paradise. An abstract of the Moslem scheme was, however, sent to the 'Ingreez', who declined, as the Founder of the New Faith was no more, to abandon their own religion; but the refusal was accompanied with expressions of regard. For this reason many Moslems in Barbary and other countries hold the English to be of all 'People of the Books' the best inclined towards them.

As regards the Prophet's tradition concerning the fall of his birthplace, 'and the thin-calved from the Habash (Abyssinians) shall destroy the Kaabah', I was informed that towards the end of time a host will pass from Africa in such multitudes that a stone shall be conveyed from hand to hand between Jeddah and Meccah. This latter condition might easily be accomplished by 60,000 men, the distance being only forty-four miles, but the citizens consider it to express a countless horde. Some pious Moslems have hoped that in Abdullah bin Zubayr's re-erection of the Kaabah the prophecy was fulfilled: the popular belief, however, remains that the fatal event is still in the womb of time. In a previous part of this volume I have alluded to similar evil presentiments which haunt the mind of El-Islam; and the Christian, zealous for the propagation of his faith, may see in them an earnest of its still wilder diffusion in future ages.

Late in the afternoon I used to rise, perform ablution, and repair to the Haram, or wander about the bazars till sunset. After this it was necessary to return home and prepare for supper—dinner it would be called in the West. The meal concluded, I used to sit for a time outside the street-door in great dignity, upon a broken-backed black-wood chair, traditionally said to have been left in the house by one of the princes of Delhi, smoking a Shishah, and drinking sundry cups of strong green tea with a slice of lime, a fair substitute for milk. At this hour the seat was as in a theatre, but the words of the actors were of a nature some what too Fescennine for a respectable public. After nightfall we either returned to the Haram or retired to rest. Our common dormitory was the flat roof of the house; under each cot stood a water-gugglet; and all slept, as must be done in the torrid lands, *on* and not *in* bed.

I sojourned at Meccah but a short time, and, as usual with travellers, did not see the best specimens of the population. The citizens appeared to me more civilised and more vicious than those of El-Medinah. They often leave

Home, where small experience grows,

and—*qui multum peregrinatur, raro sanctificatur*—become a worldly-wise, God-forgetting, and Mammonish sort of folk. *Tuf w' asaa, w' aamil el-Saba*—'Circumambulate and run (i.e. between Safa and Marwah) and do the seven (deadly sins)'—is a satire popularly levelled against them. Hence, too, the proverb *El-Haram f' il Haramayn*—'Evil (dwelleth) in the two Holy Cities'; and no wonder, since plenary indulgence is so easily secured. The pilgrim is forbidden, or rather dissuaded, from abiding at Meccah after the rites, and wisely. Great emotions must be followed by a reaction. And he who stands struck by the first aspect of Allah's house, after a few months, the marvel waxing stale, sweeps past with indifference or something worse.

There is, however, little at Meccah to offend the eye. As among certain nations further west, a layer of ashes overspreads the fire: the mine is concealed by a green turf fair to look upon. It is only when wandering by starlight through the northern outskirts of the town that citizens may be seen with light complexions and delicate limbs, coarse turbans and Egyptian woollen robes, speaking disguise and the purpose of disguise. No one within the memory of man has suffered the penalty of immorality. Spirituous liquors are no longer sold, as in Burckhardt's day, in shops; and some Arnaut officers assured me that they found considerable difficulty in smuggling flasks of *Raki* from Jeddah.

The Meccan is a darker man than the Medinite. The people explain this by the heat of the climate. I rather believe it to be caused by the number of female slaves that find their way into the market. Gallas, Sawahilis, a few Somalis, and Abyssinians are embarked at Suakin, Zayla, Tajurrah, and Berberah, carried in thousands to Jeddah, and the Holy City has the pick of every batch. Thence the stream sets northwards, a small current towards El-Medinah, and the main line to Egypt and Turkey.

Most Meccans have black concubines, and, as has been said, the appearance of the Sherif is almost that of a Negro. I did not see one handsome man in the Holy City, although some of the

Pilgrims at the Muzdalifah, near Muna

الجهة اليمنى للخارج من مكة
زيارة السيدة ميمونة

Pilgrim camp at the tomb of the Prophet's wife Maymunah, Sarif

The gate into Safa, Mecca

women appeared to me beautiful. In most families male children, when forty days old, are taken to the Kaabah, prayed over, and carried home, where the barber draws with a razor three parallel gashes down the fleshy portion of each cheek, from the exterior angles of the eyes almost to the corners of the mouth. These *Mashali*, as they are called,[1] may be of modern date: the citizens declare that the custom was unknown to their ancestors. I am tempted to assign to it a high antiquity, and cannot but attribute a pagan origin to a custom still prevailing, despite all the interdictions of the Olema. In point of figure the Meccan is somewhat coarse and lymphatic. The ludicrous leanness of the outward man, as described by Ali Bey, survives only in the remnants of themselves belonging to a bygone century. The young men are rather stout and athletic, but in middle age—when man 'swills and swells'—they are apt to degenerate into corpulence.

The Meccan is a covetous spendthrift. His wealth, lightly won, is lightly prized. Pay, pension, stipends, presents, and the Ikram, here, as at El-Medinah, supply the citizen with the means of idleness. With him everything is on the most expensive scale, his marriage, his religious ceremonies, and his household expenses. His house is luxuriously furnished; entertainments are frequent, and the junketings of his women make up a heavy bill at the end of the year. It is a common practice for the citizen to anticipate the pilgrimage season by falling into the hands of the usurer. If he be in luck, he catches and 'skins' one or more of the richest Hajis. On the other hand, should fortune fail him, he will

[1] The act is called *Tashrit*, or gashing. The body is also marked, but with smaller cuts, so that the child is covered with blood. Ali Bey was told by some Meccans that the face-gashes served for the purpose of phlebotomy, by others that they were signs that the scarred was the servant of Allah's House. He attributes this gashing, like female tattooing, to coquetry. The citizens told me that the custom arose from the necessity of preserving children from the kidnapping Persians, and that it is preserved as a mark of the Holy City. But its wide diffusion denotes an earlier origin. Mohammed expressly forbade his followers to mark the skin with scars. These beauty-marks are common to the nations in the regions to the west of the Red Sea. The Barabarah of Upper Egypt adorn their faces with scars exactly like the Meccans. The Abyssinians *moxa* themselves in hecatombs for fashion's sake. I have seen cheeks gashed, as in the Holy City, among the Gallas. Certain races of the Sawahil trace around the head a corona of little cuts, like those of a cupping instrument. And, to quote no other instances, some Somalis raise ghastly seams upon their chocolate-coloured skins.

feel for life the effect of interest running on at the rate of at least fifty per cent., the simple and the compound forms of which are equally familiar to the wily Sarraf, or money-changer.

The most unpleasant peculiarities of the Meccans are their pride and coarseness of language. Looking upon themselves as the cream of earth's sons, they resent with extreme asperity the least slighting word concerning the Holy City and its denizens. They plume themselves upon their holy descent, their exclusion of Infidels, their strict fastings, their learned men, and their purity of language. In fact, their pride shows itself at every moment; but it is not the pride which makes a man too proud to do dirty work. My predecessor did not remark their scurrility: he seems, on the contrary, rather to commend them for respectability in this point. If he be correct, the present generation has degenerated. The Meccans appeared to me distinguished, even in this foul-mouthed East, by the superior licentiousness of their language. Abuse was bad enough in the streets, but in the house it became intolerable. The Turkish pilgrims remarked, but they were too proud to notice it.

The boy Mohammed and one of his tall cousins at last transgressed the limits of my endurance. They had been reviling each other vilely one day at the house-door about dawn, when I administered the most open reprimand:

'In my country (Afghanistan) we hold this to be the hour of prayer, the season of good thoughts, when men remember Allah; even the Kafir doth not begin the day with curses and abuse.'

The people around approved, and the offenders could not refrain from saying,

'Thou hast spoken truth, O Effendi!'

Then the bystanders began, as usual, to 'improve the occasion'.

'See,' they exclaimed, 'this Sulaymani gentleman, he is not the Son of a Holy City, and yet he teacheth you—ye, the Children of the Prophet!—repent and fear Allah!'

They replied, 'Verily we do repent, and Allah is a Pardoner and the Merciful!'—were silent for an hour, and then abused each other more foully than before. Yet it is a good point in the

Meccan character, that it is open to reason, it can confess itself in error, and it displays none of that doggedness of vice which distinguishes the sinner of a more stolid race. Like the people of Southern Europe, the Semite is easily managed by a jest: though grave and thoughtful, he is by no means deficient in the sly wit which we call humour, and the solemn gravity of his words contrasts amusingly with his ideas. He particularly excels in the Cervantic art, the spirit of which, says Sterne, is to clothe low subjects in sublime language. In Mohammed's life we find that he by no means disdained a joke, sometimes a little *hasardé*, as in the case of the Paradise-coveting old woman.

The redeeming qualities of the Meccan are his courage, his *bonhommie*, his manly suavity of manners, his fiery sense of honour, his strong family affections, his near approach to what we call patriotism, and his general knowledge: the reproach of extreme ignorance which Burckhardt directs against the Holy City has long ago sped to the Limbo of things that were. The dark half of the picture is pride, bigotry, irreligion, greed of gain, immorality, and prodigal ostentation.

Of the pilgrimage ceremonies I cannot speak harshly. It may be true that 'the rites of the Kaabah, emasculated of every idolatrous tendency, still hang a strange unmeaning shroud around the living theism of Islam'. But what nation, either in the West or the East, has been able to cast out from its ceremonies every suspicion of its old idolatry? What are the English mistletoe, the Irish wake, the Pardon of Brittany, the Carnival, and the Worship at Iserna? Better far to consider the Meccan pilgrimage rites in the light of Evil-worship turned into lessons of Good than to philosophise about their strangeness, and to blunder in asserting them to be insignificant. Even the Bedawi circumambulating the Kaabah fortifies his wild belief by the fond thought that he treads the path of Allah's friend.

At Arafat the good Moslem worships in imitation of the Pure of Allah (Adam); and when hurling stones and curses at the three senseless little buttresses which commemorate the appearance of the fiend, the materialism of the action gives to its sentiment all the strength and endurance of reality. The supernatural agencies of pilgrimage are carefully and sparingly distributed. The angels who restore the stones from Muna to Muzdalifah; the heavenly host whose pinions cause the Kaabah's veil to rise and wave, and the mysterious complement of the pilgrim's total at the Arafat sermon, all belong to the category of spiritual creatures walking earth unseen—a poetical tenet, not condemned by Christianity.

The Meccans are, it is true, to be reproached with their open Mammon-worship, at times and at places the most sacred and venerable; but this has no other effect upon the pilgrims than to excite disgust and open reprehension. Here, however, we see no such silly frauds as heavenly fire drawn from a phosphor-match; nor do two rival churches fight in the flesh with teeth and nails, requiring the contemptuous interference of an Infidel power to keep around order. Here we see no fair dames staring with their glasses, *braqués* at the Head of the Church; or supporting exhausted nature with the furtive sandwich; or carrying pampered curs who, too often, will not be silent; or scrambling and squeezing to hear theatrical music, reckless of the fate of the old lady who—on such occasions there is always one—has been 'thrown down and cruelly trampled upon by the crowd'.

If the Meccan citizens are disposed to scoff at the wild Takruri, they do it not so publicly or shamelessly as the Roman jeering with ribald jest at the fanaticism of strangers from the bogs of Ireland. Finally, at Meccah there is nothing theatrical, nothing that suggests the opera; but all is simple and impressive, filling the mind with

> A weight of awe not easy to be borne,

and tending, I believe, after its fashion, to good.

As regards the Meccan and Moslem belief that Abraham and his son built the Kaabah, it may be observed that the Genesitic account of the Great Patriarch has suggested to learned men the idea of two Abrahams, one the son of Terah, another the son of Azar (fire), a Prometheus who imported civilisation and knowledge into Arabia from Harran, the sacred centre of Sabaean learning. Moslem historians all agree in representing Abraham as a star-worshipper in youth, and Eusebius calls the patriarch son of Athar; his father's name, therefore, is no Arab invention. Whether Ishmael or his sire ever visited Meccah to build the

Kaabah is, in my humble opinion, an open question. The Jewish Scripture informs us only that the patriarch dwelt at Beersheba and Gerar, in the south-west of Palestine, without any allusion to the annual visit which Moslems declare he paid to their Holy City. At the same time Arab tradition speaks clearly and consistently upon the subject, and generally omits those miraculous and superstitious adjuncts which cast shadows of sore doubt upon the philosophic mind.

The amount of risk which a stranger must encounter at the pilgrimage rites is still considerable. A learned Orientalist and divine intimated his intention, in a work published but a few years ago, of visiting Meccah without disguise. He was assured that the Turkish governor would now offer no obstacle to a European traveller. I would strongly dissuade a friend from making the attempt. It is true that the Frank is no longer, as in Captain Head's day, insulted when he ventures out of the Meccan Gate of Jeddah; and that our vice-consuls and travellers are allowed, on condition that their glance do not pollute the shrine, to visit Taif and the regions lying eastward of the Holy City.

Neither the Pasha nor the Sherif would, in these days, dare to enforce, in the case of an Englishman, the old law, a choice thrice offered between circumcision and death. But the first Bedawi who caught sight of the Frank's hat would not deem himself a man if he did not drive a bullet through the wearer's head. At the pilgrimage season disguise is easy, on account of the vast and varied multitudes which visit Meccah, exposing the traveller only to 'stand the buffet with knaves who smell of sweat'. But woe to the unfortunate who happens to be recognised in public as an Infidel—unless at least he could throw himself at once upon the protection of the government.[1] Amidst, however, a crowd of pilgrims, whose fanaticism is worked up to the highest pitch, detection would probably ensure his dismissal at once *al numero de' più*.

Those who find danger the salt of pleasure may visit Meccah; but if asked whether the results justify the risk, I should reply in the negative. And the vice-consul at Jeddah would only do his

[1] The best way would be to rush, if possible, into a house; and the owner would then, for his own interest, as well as honour, defend a stranger till assistance could be procured.

duty in peremptorily forbidding European travellers to attempt Meccah without disguise, until the day comes when such steps can be taken in the certainty of not causing a mishap; an accident would not redound to our reputation, as we could not in justice revenge it.

On the 14th Z'ul Hijjah we started to perform the rite of Umrah, or Little Pilgrimage. After performing ablution, and resuming the Ihram with the usual ceremonies, I set out, accompanied by the boy Mohammed and his brother Abdullah. Mounting asses which resembled mules in size and speed, we rode to the Haram, and prayed there. Again remounting, we issued through the Bab el-Safa towards the open country north-east of the city. The way was crowded with pilgrims, on foot as well as mounted, and their loud 'Labbayk' distinguished those engaged in the Umrah rite from the many whose business was with the camp of the Damascus Caravan.

At about half a mile from the city we passed on the left a huge heap of stones, where my companions stood and cursed. This grim-looking cairn is popularly believed to note the place of the well where Abu Lahab laid an ambuscade for the Prophet. This wicked uncle stationed there a slave, with orders to throw headlong into the pit the first person who approached him, and privily persuaded his nephew to visit the spot at night: after a time, anxiously hoping to hear that the deed had been done, Abu Lahab incautiously drew nigh, and was precipitated by his own bravo into the place of destruction. Hence the well-known saying in Islam, 'Whoso diggeth a well for his brother shall fall into it himself.' We added our quota of stones, and proceeding, saw the Jeddah road spanning the plain like a white ribbon.

In front of us the highway was now lined with coffee-tents, before which effeminate dancing-boys performed to admiring Syrians: a small whitewashed Bungalow, the palace of the Emir el-Hajj, lay on the left, and all around it clustered the motley encampment of his pilgrims. After cantering about three miles from the city, we reached the Alamayn, or two pillars that limit the Sanctuary; and a little beyond it is the small settlement popularly called El-Umrah. Dismounting here, we sat down on rugs outside a coffee-tent to enjoy the beauty of the moonlit night, and an hour of Kayf, in the sweet air of the Desert.

Presently the coffee-tent keeper, after receiving payment, brought us water for ablution. This preamble over, we entered the principal chapel; an unpretending building, badly lighted, spread with dirty rugs, full of pilgrims, and offensively close. Here we prayed the Isha, or night devotions, and then a two-bow prayer in honour of the Ihram, after which we distributed gratuities to the guardians, and alms to the importunate beggars. And now I perceived the object of Abdullah's companionship. The melancholy man assured me that he had ridden out for love of me, and in order to perform as Wakil (substitute) a vicarious pilgrimage for my parents. Vainly I assured him that they had been strict in the exercises of their faith. He would take no denial, and I perceived that love of me meant love of my dollars. With a surly assent, he was at last permitted to act for the 'pious pilgrims Yusuf (Joseph) bin Ahmed and Fatimah bint Yunus'—my progenitors. It was impossible to prevent smiling at contrasts, as Abdullah, gravely raising his hands, and directing his face to the Kaabah, intoned, 'I do vow this Ihram of Umrah in the Name of Yusuf Son of Ahmed, and Fatimah Daughter of Yunus; then render it attainable to them, and accept it of them! Bismillah! Allahu Akbar!'

Remounting, we galloped towards Meccah, shouting 'Labbayk', and halting at every half-mile to smoke and drink coffee. In a short time we entered the city, and repairing to the Haram by the Safa Gate, performed the Tawaf, or circumambulation of Umrah. After this dull round and necessary repose we left the temple by the same exit, and mounting once more, turned towards El-Safa, which stands about 100 yards south-east of the Mosque, and as little deserves its name of Mountain as do those that undulate the face of modern Rome. The Safa end is closed by a mean-looking building, composed of three round arches, with a dwarf flight of steps leading up to them out of a narrow road. Without dismounting, we wheeled our donkeys round, left shoulders forward, no easy task in the crowd, and, vainly striving to sight the Kaabah through the Bab el-Safa, performed the Niyat, or vow of the rite El-Sai, or the running.

After Tahlil, Takbir, and Talbiyat, we raised our hands in the supplicatory position, and twice repeated, 'There is no god but Allah, Alone, without Partner; His is the Kingdom, unto Him be Praise; He giveth Life and Death, He is alive and perisheth not; in His Hand is Good, and He over all Things is Omnipotent.'

Then, with the donkey-boys leading our animals and a stout fellow preceding us with lantern and a quarterstaff to keep off the running Bedawin, camel-men, and riders of asses, we descended Safa, and walked slowly down the street El-Masaa, towards Marwah. During our descent we recited aloud, 'O Allah, cause me to act according to the Sunnat of thy Prophet, and to die in his faith, and defend me from errors and disobedience by thy mercy, O most Merciful of the Merciful!' Arrived at what is called the Batn el-Wady (Belly of the Vale), a place now denoted by the Milayn el-Akhzarayn (the two green pillars), one fixed in the eastern course of the Haram, the other in a house on the right side, we began the running by urging on our beasts. Here the prayer was, 'O Lord, pardon and pity, and pass over what Thou knowest, for Thou art the most dear and the most generous! Save us from Hell-fire safely, and cause us safely to enter Paradise! O Lord, give us Happiness here and Happiness hereafter, and spare us the Torture of the Flames!'

At the end of this supplication we had passed the Batn, or lowest ground, whose farther limits were marked by two other pillars.[1] Again we began to ascend, repeating, as we went, 'Verily, Safa and Marwah are two of the Monuments of Allah. Whoso, therefore, pilgrimeth to the Temple of Meccah, or performeth Umrah, it shall be no Crime in him (to run between them both). And as for him who voluntarily doeth a good Deed, verily Allah is Grateful and Omniscient!'[2]

At length we reached Marwah, a little rise like Safa in the lower slope of Abu Kubays. The houses cluster in amphitheatre shape above it, and from the Masaa, or street below, a short flight of steps leads to a platform, bounded on three sides like a tennis-court, by tall walls without arches. The street, seen from

[1] Here once stood Asaf and Naylah, two idols, some say a man and a woman metamorphosed for stupration in the temple.

[2] Koran, chapter 2.

above, has a bowstring curve: it is between eight and nine hundred feet long, with high houses on both sides, and small lanes branching off from it. At the foot of the platform we brought right shoulders forward, so as to face the Kaabah, and raising hands to ears, thrice exclaimed, 'Allahu Akbar'. This concluded the first course, and, of these, seven compose the ceremony El-Sai, or the running.

There was a startling contrast with the origin of this ceremony—

> When the poor outcast on the cheerless wild,
> Arabia's parent clasped her fainting child—

as the Turkish infantry marched, in European dress, with sloped arms, down the Masaa to relieve guard. By the side of the half-naked, running Bedawin, they looked as if Epochs, disconnected by long centuries, had met. A laxity, too, there was in the frequent appearance of dogs upon this holy and most memorious ground, which said little in favour of the religious strictness of the administration.[1]

Our Sai ended at Mount Marwah. There we dismounted, and sat outside a barber's shop, on the right-hand of the street. He operated upon our heads, causing us to repeat, 'O Allah, this my Forelock is in Thy Hand, then grant me for every Hair a light on the Resurrection-day, O Most Merciful of the Merciful!' This, and the paying for it, constituted the fourth portion of the Umrah, or Little Pilgrimage.

Throwing the skirts of our garments over our heads, to show that our Ihram was now exchanged for the normal state, Ihlal, we cantered to the Haram, prayed there a two-bow prayer, and returned home not a little fatigued.

[1] The ceremony of running between Safa and Marwah is supposed to represent Hagar seeking water for her son. Usually pilgrims perform this rite on the morning of visiting the Kaabah.

XXXIII
Places of Pious Visitation at Meccah

The traveller has little work at the Holy City. With exceptions of Jebel Nur and Jebel Saur, all the places of pious visitation lie inside or close outside the city. It is well worth the while to ascend Abu Kubays; not so much to inspect the Makan el-Hajar and the Shakk el-Kamar,[1] as to obtain an excellent bird's-eye view of the Haram and the parts adjacent.

The boy Mohammed had applied himself sedulously to commerce after his return home; and had actually been seen by Shaykh Nur sitting in a shop and selling small curiosities. With my plenary consent I was made over to Abdullah, his brother. On the morning of the 15th Zu'l Hijjah (19th September) he hired two asses, and accompanied me as guide to the holy places.

Mounting our animals, we followed the road before described to the Jannat el-Maala, the sacred cemetery of Meccah. A rough wall, with a poor gateway, encloses a patch of barren and grim-looking ground, at the foot of the chain which bounds the city's western suburb, and below El-Akabah, the gap through which Khalid bin Walid entered Meccah with the triumphant Prophet.[2] Inside are a few ignoble, whitewashed domes: all are of modern construction, for here, as at El-Bakia, further north, the Wahhabis indulged their levelling propensities. The rest of the ground shows some small enclosures belonging to particular houses—equivalent to our family vaults—and the ruins of humble tombs, lying in confusion, whilst a few parched aloes spring from between the bricks and stones.

This cemetery is celebrated in local history: here the body of

[1] The tradition of these places is related by every historian. The former is the repository of the Black Stone during the Deluge. The latter, 'splitting of the moon', is the spot where the Prophet stood when, to convert the idolatrous Kuraysh, he caused half the orb of night to rise from behind Abu Kubays, and the other from Jebel Kayka'an, on the western horizon. This silly legend appears unknown to Mohammed's day.

[2] This is the local tradition: it does not agree with authentic history.

Abdullah bin Zubayr was exposed by order of Hajjaj bin Yusuf; and the number of saints buried in it has been so numerous, that even in the twelfth century many had fallen into oblivion. It is visited by the citizens on Fridays, and by women on Thursdays, to prevent that meeting of sexes which in the East is so detrimental to public decorum. I shall be sparing in my description of the Maala ceremonies, as the prayers, prostrations, and supplications are almost identical with those performed at El-Bakia.

After a long supplication, pronounced standing at the doorway, we entered, and sauntered about the burial-ground. On the left of the road stood an enclosure, which, according to Abdullah, belonged to his family. The door and stone slabs, being valuable to the poor, had been removed, and the graves of his forefathers appeared to have been invaded by the jackal. He sighed, recited a Fatihah with tears in his eyes, and hurried me away from the spot.

The first dome which we visited covered the remains of Abd el-Rahman, the son of Abubekr, one of the Worthies of El-Islam, equally respected by Sunni and Shiah. The tomb was a simple catafalque, spread with the usual cloth. After performing our devotions at this grave, and distributing a few piastres to guardians and beggars, we crossed the main path, and found ourselves at the door of the cupola, beneath which sleeps the venerable Khadijah, Mohammed's first wife. The tomb was covered with a green cloth, and the walls of the little building were decorated with written specimens of religious poetry. A little beyond it, we were shown into another dome, the resting-place of Sitt Aminah, the Prophet's mother. Burckhardt chronicles its ill-usage by the fanatic Wahhabis: it has now been rebuilt in that frugal style that characterises the architecture of El-Hejaz. An exceedingly garrulous old woman came to the door, invited us in, and superintended our devotions; at the end of which she sprinkled rosewater upon my face. When asked for a cool draught, she handed me a metal saucer, whose contents smelt strongly of mastic, earnestly directing me to drink it in a sitting posture. This tomb she informed us is the property of a single woman, who visits it every evening, receives the contributions of the Faithful, prays, sweeps the pavement, and dusts the furniture. We left 5 piastres for this respectable maiden, and gratified the officious crone with another shilling. She repaid us by signalling to some score of beggars that a rich pilgrim had entered the Maala, and their importunities fairly drove me out of the hallowed walls.

Leaving the Jannat el-Maala, we returned towards the town, and halted on the left side of the road, at a mean building called the Masjid el-Jinn (of the Genii). Here was revealed the seventy-second chapter of the Koran, called after the name of the mysterious fire-drakes who paid fealty to the Prophet. Descending a flight of steps—for this mosque, like all ancient localities at Meccah, is as much below as above ground—we entered a small apartment containing water-pots for drinking and all the appurtenances of ablution. In it is shown the Mauza el-Khatt (place of the writing), where Mohammed wrote a letter to Abu Masud after the homage of the Genii. A second and interior flight of stone steps led to another diminutive oratory, where the Prophet used to pray and receive the archangel Gabriel. Having performed a pair of bows, which caused the perspiration to burst forth as if in a Russian bath, I paid a few piastres, and issued from the building with much satisfaction.

We had some difficulty in urging our donkeys through the crowded street, called the Zukak el-Hajar. Presently we arrived at the Bayt el-Naby, the Prophet's old house, in which he lived with the Sitt Khadijah. Here, says Burckhardt, the Lady Fatimah first saw the light; and here, according to Ibn Jubayr, Hasan and Husayn were born. Dismounting at the entrance, we descended a deep flight of steps, and found ourselves in a spacious hall, vaulted, and of better appearance than most of the sacred edifices at Meccah. In the centre, and well railed round, stood a closet of rich green and gold stuffs, in shape not unlike an umbrella-tent. A surly porter guarded the closed door, which some respectable people vainly attempted to open by honeyed words: a whisper from Abdullah solved the difficulty. I was directed to lie at full length upon my stomach, and to kiss a black-looking stone—said to be the lower half of the Lady Fatimah's quern—fixed at the bottom of a basin of the same material. Thence we repaired to a corner, and recited a two-bow at the place where the Prophet used to pray the Sunnat and the Nafilah, or supererogatory devotions.

Again remounting, we proceeded at a leisurely pace homewards, and on the way we passed through the principal slave-market. It is a large street roofed with matting, and full of coffee-houses. The merchandise sat in rows, parallel with the walls. The prettiest girls occupied the highest benches, below them were the plainer sort, and lowest of all the boys. They were all gaily dressed in pink and other light-coloured muslins, with transparent veils over their heads; and, whether from the effect of such unusual splendour, or from the reaction succeeding to their terrible land-journey and sea-voyage, they appeared perfectly happy, laughing loudly, talking unknown tongues, and quizzing purchasers, even during the delicate operation of purchasing. There were some pretty Gallas, douce-looking Abyssinians, and Africans of various degrees of hideousness, from the half-Arab Somal to the baboon-like Sawahili. The highest price of which I could hear was 60*l*.

Passing through the large bazar, called the Suk el-Layl, I saw the palace of Mohammed bin Aun, quondam Prince of Meccah. It has a certain look of rude magnificence, the effect of huge hanging balconies scattered in profusion over lofty walls, *claire-voies* of brickwork, and courses of various-coloured stone. The owner is highly popular among the Bedawin, and feared by the citizens on account of his fierce looks, courage, and treachery. They described him to me as *vir bonus, bene strangulando peritus*; but Mr Cole, who knew him personally, gave him a high character for generosity and freedom from fanaticism. He seems to have some idea of the state which should hedge in a ruler. His palaces at Meccah, and that now turned into a Wakalah at Jeddah, are the only places in the country that can be called princely. He is now a state prisoner at Constantinople, and the Bedawin pray for his return in vain.[1]

[1] This prince was first invested with the Sherifat by Mohammed Ali of Egypt in AD 1827, when Yahya fled, after stabbing his nephew in the Kaabah, to the Beni Harb Bedawin. He was supported by Ahmed Pasha of Meccah, with a large army; but after the battle of Tarabah, in which Ibrahim Pasha was worsted by the Bedawin, Mohammed bin Aun, accused of acting as Sylla, was sent in honourable bondage to Cairo. He again returned to Meccah, where the rapacity of his eldest son, Abdallah, who would rob pilgrims,

The other places of pious visitation at Meccah are briefly these:

(1) Natak el-Naby, a small oratory in the Zukak el-Hajar. It derives its name from the following circumstance. As the Prophet was knocking at the door of Abubekr's shop, a stone gave him God-speed, and told him that the master was not at home. This wonderful mineral is of a reddish-black colour, about a foot in dimension, and fixed in the wall somewhat higher than a man's head. There are servants attached to it, and the street sides are spread, as usual, with the napkins of importunate beggars.

(2) Maulid el-Naby, or the Prophet's birthplace. It is a little chapel in the Suk el-Layl, not far from Mohammed bin Aun's palace. It is below the present level of the ground, and in the centre is a kind of tent, concealing, it is said, a hole in the floor upon which Aminah sat to be delivered.

(3) In the quarter Shaab Ali, near the Maulid el-Naby, is the birthplace of Ali, another oratory below the ground. Here, as in the former place, a Maulid and a Ziyarah are held on the anniversary of the Lion's birth.

(4) Near Khadijah's house and the Natak el-Naby is a place called El-Muttaka, from a stone against which the Prophet leaned when worn out with fatigue. It is much visited by devotees; and some declare that on one occasion, when the Father of Lies appeared to the Prophet in the form of an elderly man, and tempted him to sin by asserting that the mosque-prayers were over, this stone, disclosing the fraud, caused the Fiend to flee.

(5) Maulid Hamzah, a little building at the old Bab Umrah, near the Shabayki cemetery. Here was the Bazan, or channel

---

caused fresh misfortunes. In AD 1851, when Abd el-Muttalib was appointed Sherif, the Pasha was ordered to send Bin Aun to Stamboul—no easy task. The Turk succeeded by a manoeuvre. Mohammed's two sons, happening to be at Jeddah, were invited to inspect a man-of-war, and were there made prisoners. Upon this the father yielded himself up; although, it is said, the flashing of the Bedawi's sabre during his embarkation made the Turks rejoice that they had won the day by state-craft. The wild men of El-Hejaz still sing songs in honour of this Sherif.

NOTE TO SECOND EDITION. Early in 1856, when the Sherif Abd el-Muttalib was deposed, Mohammed bin Aun was sent from Constantinople to quiet the insurrection caused by the new slave laws in El-Hejaz. In a short space of time he completely succeeded.

down which the Ayn Hunayn ran into the Birkat Majid. Many authorities doubt that Hamzah was born at this place.

The reader must now be as tired of Pious Visitations as I was.

Before leaving Meccah I was urgently invited to dine by old Ali bin Ya Sin, the Zem Zemi; a proof that he entertained inordinate expectations, excited, it appeared, by the boy Mohammed, for the simple purpose of exalting his own dignity. One day we were hurriedly summoned about three p.m. to the senior's house, a large building in the Zukak el-Ḥajar. We found it full of pilgrims, amongst whom we had no trouble to recognise our fellow-travellers, the quarrelsome old Arnaut and his impudent slave-boy. Ali met us upon the staircase, and conducted us into an upper room, where we sat upon divans, and with pipes and coffee prepared for dinner. Presently the semicircle arose to receive a eunuch, who lodged somewhere in the house. He was a person of importance, being the guardian of some dames of high degree at Cairo or Constantinople: the highest place and the best pipe were unhesitatingly offered to and accepted by him. He sat down with dignity, answered diplomatically certain mysterious questions about the dames, and then applied his blubber lips to a handsome mouthpiece of lemon-coloured amber. It was a fair lesson of humility for a man to find himself ranked beneath this high-shouldered, spindle-shanked, beardless bit of neutrality; and as such I took it duly to heart.

The dinner was served up in a *Sini*, a plated copper tray about six feet in circumference, and handsomely ornamented with arabesques and inscriptions. Under this was the usual *Kursi*, or stool, composed of mother-of-pearl facets set in sandal-wood; and upon it a well-tinned and clean-looking service of the same material as the *Sini*. We began with a variety of stews—stews with spinach, stews with *Bamiyah* (hibiscus), and rich vegetable stews. These being removed, we dipped hands in *Biryani*, a meat pillaw, abounding in clarified butter; *Kimah*, finely chopped meat; *Warak Mahshi*, vine leaves filled with chopped and spiced mutton, and folded into small triangles; *Kabab*, or bits of *rôti* spitted in mouthfuls upon a splinter of wood; together with a *Salatah* of the crispest cucumber, and various dishes of water-melon cut up into squares.

Bread was represented by the eastern scone, but it was of superior flavour, and far better than the ill-famed Chapati of India. Our drink was water perfumed with mastic. After the meat came a *Kunafah*, fine vermicelli sweetened with honey, and sprinkled with powdered white sugar; several stews of apples and quinces; *Muhallibah*, a thin jelly made of rice, flour, milk, starch, and a little perfume; together with squares of *Rahah*,[1] a comfiture highly prized in these regions, because it comes from Constantinople. Fruits were then placed upon the table; plates full of pomegranate grains and dates of the finest flavour. The dinner concluded with a pillaw of boiled rice and butter, for the easier discussion of which we were provided with carved wooden spoons.

Arabs ignore the delightful French art of prolonging a dinner. After washing your hands, you sit down, throw an embroidered napkin over your knees, and with a 'Bismillah', by way of grace, plunge your hand into the attractive dish, changing *ad libitum*, occasionally sucking your finger-tips as boys do lollipops, and varying that diversion by cramming a chosen morsel into a friend's mouth. When your hunger is satisfied, you do not sit for your companions; you exclaim 'Al Hamd!', edge away from the tray, wash your hands and mouth with soap, display signs of repletion, otherwise you will be pressed to eat more, seize your pipe, sip your coffee, and take your Kayf.

Nor is it customary, in these lands, to sit together after dinner—the evening prayer cuts short the séance. Before we arose to take leave of Ali bin Ya Sin, a boy ran into the room, and displayed those infantine civilities which in the East are equivalent to begging for a present. I slipped a dollar into his hand; at the sight of which he, veritable little Meccan, could not contain his joy.

'The Riyal!' he exclaimed; 'the Riyal! look, grandpa', the good Effendi has given me a Riyal!'

[1] Familiar for Rahat el-Hulkum—the Pleasure of the Throat—a name which has sorely puzzled our tourists.

This sweetmeat would be pleasant did it not smell so strongly of the perruquier's shop. Rosewater tempts to many culinary sins in the East, and Europeans cannot dissociate it from the idea of a lotion. However, if a guest is to be honoured, rosewater must often take the place of the pure element, even in tea.

The old gentleman's eyes twinkled with emotion: he saw how easily the coin had slipped from my fingers, and he fondly hoped that he had not seen the last piece.

'Verily thou art a good young man!' he ejaculated, adding fervently, as prayers cost nothing, 'May Allah further all thy desires.' A gentle patting of the back evidenced high approval.

I never saw old Ali after that evening, but entrusted to the boy Mohammed what was considered a just equivalent for his services.

XXXIV
To Jeddah

A general plunge into worldly pursuits and pleasures announced the end of the pilgrimage ceremonies. All the devotees were now 'whitewashed'—the book of their sins was a *tabula rasa*: too many of them lost no time in making a new departure down south, and in opening a fresh account.

The faith must not bear the blame of the irregularities. They may be equally observed in the Calvinist, after a Sunday of prayer, sinning through Monday with a zest, and the Romanist falling back with new fervour upon the causes of his confession and penance, as in the Moslem who washes his soul clean by running and circumambulation. And, in fairness, it must be observed, that as amongst Christians, so in the Moslem persuasion, there are many notable exceptions to this rule of extremes. Several of my friends and acquaintances date their reformation from their first sight of the Kaabah.

The Moslem's Holy Week over, nothing detained me at Meccah. For reasons before stated, I resolved upon returning to Cairo, resting there for awhile, and starting a second time for the interior, via Muwaylah.

The Meccans are as fond of little presents as are nuns: the *Kabirah* took an affectionate leave of me, begged me to be careful of her boy, who was to accompany me to Jeddah, and laid friendly but firm hands upon a brass pestle and mortar, upon which she had long cast the eye of concupiscence.

Having hired two camels for 35 piastres, and paid half the sum in advance, I sent on my heavy boxes with Shaykh, now Haji, Nur to Jeddah. Umar Effendi was to wait at Meccah till his father had started, in command of the dromedary caravan, when he would privily take ass, join me at the port, and return to his beloved Cairo. I bade a long farewell to all my friends, embraced the Turkish pilgrims, and mounting our donkeys, the boy Mohammed and I left the house. Abdullah the Melancholy followed us on foot through the city, and took leave of me, though without embracing, at the Shabayki quarter.

Issuing into the open plain, I felt a thrill of pleasure—such joy as only the captive delivered from his dungeon can experience. The sunbeams warmed me into renewed life and vigour, the air of the Desert was a perfume, and the homely face of Nature was as the smile of a dear old friend. I contemplated the Syrian caravan, lying on the right of our road, without any of the sadness usually suggested by a parting look.

It is not my intention minutely to describe the line down which we travelled that night: the pages of Burckhardt give full information about the country. Leaving Meccah, we fell into the direct road running south of Wady Fatimah, and traversed for about an hour a flat surrounded by hills. Then we entered a valley by a flight of rough stone steps, dangerously slippery and zigzag, intended to facilitate the descent for camels and laden beasts. About midnight we passed into a hill-girt Wady, here covered with deep sands, there hard with gravelly clay; and, finally, about dawn, we sighted the maritime plain of Jeddah.

Shortly after leaving the city, our party was joined by other travellers, and towards evening we found ourselves in force, the effect of an order that pilgrims must not proceed singly upon this road. Coffee-houses and places of refreshment abounding, we halted every five miles to refresh ourselves and the donkeys. At sunset we prayed near a Turkish guard-house, where one of the soldiers kindly supplied me with water for ablution.

Before nightfall I was accosted, in Turkish, by a one-eyed old fellow, who,

> with faded brow,
> Entrenched with many a frown, and conic beard,

and habited in unclean garments, was bestriding a donkey faded as himself. When I shook my head, he addressed me in Persian. The same manoeuvre made him try Arabic: still he obtained no answer. He then grumbled out good Hindostani. That also failing, he tried successively Pushtu, Armenian, English, French, and Italian. At last I could keep a stiff lip no longer; at every change of dialect his emphasis beginning with 'Then who the d—— are you?' became more emphatic. I turned upon him in Persian, and found that he had been a pilot, a courier, and a servant to eastern tourists, and that he had visited England, France, and Italy, the Cape, India, Central Asia, and China. We then chatted in English, which Haji Akif spoke well, but with all manner of courier's phrases; Haji Abdullah so badly, that he was counselled a course of study. It was not a little curious to hear such phrases as 'Come 'p, Neddy', and '*Cré nom d'un baudet*', almost within earshot of the tomb of Ishmael, the birthplace of Mohammed, and the Sanctuary of El-Islam.

About eight p.m. we passed the Alamayn, which define the Sanctuary in this direction. They stand about nine miles from Meccah, and near them are a coffee-house and a little oratory, popularly known as the Sabil Agha Almas. On the road, as night advanced, we met long strings of camels, some carrying litters, others huge beams, and others bales of coffee, grain, and merchandise. Sleep began to weigh heavy upon my companions' eyelids, and the boy Mohammed hung over the flank of his donkey in a most ludicrous position.

About midnight we reached a mass of huts, called El-Haddah. Ali Bey places it eight leagues from Jeddah. At the Boundary, which is considered to be the half-way halting-place, Pilgrims must assume the religious garb, and Infidels travelling to Taif are taken off the Meccan road into one leading northwards to Arafat. The settlement is a collection of huts and hovels, built with sticks and reeds, supporting brushwood and burned and blackened palm-leaves. It is maintained for supplying pilgrims with coffee and water. Travellers speak with horror of its heat during the day; Ali Bey, who visited it twice, compares it to a furnace. Here the country slopes gradually towards the sea, the hills draw off, and every object denotes departure from the Meccan plateau. At El-Haddah we dismounted for an hour's halt. A coffee-house supplied us with mats, water-pipes, and other necessaries; we then produced a basket of provisions, the parting gift of the kind *Kabirah*, and, this late supper concluded, we lay down to doze.

After half an hour's halt had expired, and the donkeys were saddled, I shook up with difficulty the boy Mohammed, and induced him to mount. He was, to use his own expression, 'dead from sleep'; and we had scarcely advanced an hour, when, arriving at another little coffee-house, he threw himself upon the ground, and declared it impossible to proceed.

This act caused some confusion. The donkey-boy was a pert little Bedawi, offensively republican in manner. He had several times addressed me impudently, ordering me not to flog his animal, or to hammer its sides with my heels. On these occasions he received a contemptuous snub, which had the effect of silencing him. But now, thinking we were in his power, he swore that he would lead away the beasts, and leave us behind to be robbed and murdered. A pinch of the windpipe, and a spin over the ground, altered his plans at the outset of execution. He gnawed his hand with impotent rage, and went away, threatening us with the governor of Jeddah next morning.

Then an Egyptian of the party took up the thread of remonstrance; and, aided by the old linguist, who said, in English, 'by G—! you must budge, you'll catch it here!' he assumed a brisk and energetic style, exclaiming, 'Yallah! rise and mount; thou art only losing our time; thou dost not intend to sleep in the Desert!' I replied, 'O my Uncle, do not exceed in talk!'—*Fuzul* (excess) in Arabic is equivalent to telling a man in English not to be impertinent—rolled over on the other side heavily, as doth Encelades, and pretended to snore, whilst the cowed Egyptian urged the others to make us move. The question was thus settled by the boy Mohammed, who had been aroused by the dispute: 'Do you know', he whispered, in awful accents, 'what *that* person is?' and he pointed to me. 'Why, no,' replied the others. 'Well,' said the youth, 'the other day the Utaybah showed us death in the Zaribah Pass, and what do you think he did?' 'Wallah! what do we know!' exclaimed the Egyptian, 'What *did* he do?' 'He called for—his dinner,' replied the youth, with a slow and sarcastic emphasis. That trait was enough. The others mounted, and left us quietly to sleep.

I have been diffuse in relating this little adventure, which is characteristic, showing what bravado can do in Arabia. It also suggests a lesson, which every traveller in these regions should take well to heart. The people are always ready to terrify him with frightful stories, which are the merest phantoms of cowardice. The reason why the Egyptian displayed so much philanthropy was that, had one of the party been lost, the survivors might have fallen into trouble. But in this place, we were, I believe—despite the declarations of our companions that it was infested with Turpins and Fra Diavolos—as safe as if in Meccah. Every night, during the pilgrimage season, a troop of about fifty horsemen patrols the roads; we were all armed to the teeth, and our party looked too formidable to be 'cruelly beaten by a single footpad'.

Our nap concluded, we remounted, and resumed the weary way down a sandy valley, in which the poor donkeys sank fetlock-deep. At dawn we found our companions halted, and praying at the Kahwat Turki, another little coffee-house. Here an exchange of what is popularly called chaff took place.

'Well,' cried the Egyptian, 'what have ye gained by halting? We have been quiet here, praying and smoking for the last hour!'

'Go, eat thy buried beans,'[1] we replied. 'What does an Egyptian boor know of manliness!'

The surly donkey-boy was worked up into a paroxysm of passion by such small jokes as telling him to convey our salams to the Governor of Jeddah, and by calling the asses after the name of his tribe. He replied by 'foul, unmannered, scurril taunts', which only drew forth fresh derision, and the coffee-house keeper laughed consumedly, having probably seldom entertained such 'funny gentlemen'.

Shortly after leaving the Kahwat Turki we found the last spur of the highlands that sink into the Jeddah Plain. This view would for some time be my last of

> Infamous hills, and sandy, perilous wilds;

and I contemplated it with the pleasure of one escaping from it. Before us lay the usual iron flat of these regions, whitish with salt, and tawny with stones and gravel; but relieved and beautified by the distant white walls, whose canopy was the lovely blue sea. Not a tree, not a patch of verdure was in sight; nothing distracted our attention from the sheet of tur-

[1] The favourite Egyptian 'kitchen'; held to be contemptible food by the Arabs.

quoises in the distance. Merrily the little donkeys hobbled on, in spite of their fatigue. Soon we distinguished the features of the town, the minarets, the fortifications—so celebrated since their honeycombed guns beat off in 1817 the thousands of Abdullah bin Saud, the Wahhabi,[1] and a small dome outside the walls.

The sun began to glow fiercely, and we were not sorry when, at about eight a.m., after passing through the mass of hovels and coffee-houses, cemeteries and sand-hills, which forms the eastern approach to Jeddah, we entered the fortified Bab Makkah. Allowing eleven hours for our actual march—we halted about three—those wonderful donkeys had accomplished between forty-four and forty-six miles, generally of deep sand, in one night. And they passed the archway of Jeddah cantering almost as nimbly as when they left Meccah.

Shaykh Nur had been ordered to take rooms for me in a vast pile of madrepore—unfossilised coral, a recent formation—once the palace of Mohammed bin Aun, and now converted into a Wakalah. Instead of so doing, Indian-like, he had made a gypsy encampment in the square opening upon the harbour. After administering the requisite correction, I found a room that would suit me. In less than an hour it was swept, sprinkled with water, spread with mats, and made as comfortable as its capability admitted. At Jeddah I felt once more at home. The sight of the sea acted as a tonic. The Maharattas were not far wrong when they kept their English captives out of reach of the ocean, declaring that we are an amphibious race, to whom the wave is a home.

After a day's repose at the Caravanserai, the camel-man and donkey-boy clamouring for money, and I not having more than tenpence of borrowed coin, it was necessary to cash at the British vice-consulate a draft given to me by the Royal Geographical

[1] In 1817 Abdullah bin Saud attacked Jeddah with 50,000 men, determining to overthrow its Kafir-works, namely, its walls and towers. The assault is described as ludicrous. All the inhabitants aided the garrison: they waited till the wild men flocked about the place, crying 'Come, and let us look at the labours of the Infidel'; they then let fly, and raked them with matchlock-balls and old nails acting as grape. The Wahhabi host at last departed, unable to take a place which a single battery of our smallest siege-guns would breach in an hour. And since that day the Meccans have never ceased to boast of their Gibraltar, and to taunt the Medinites with their wall-less port, Yambu'.

Society. With some trouble I saw Mr Cole, who, suffering from fever, was declared to be not at home. His dragoman did by no means admire my looks; in fact, the general voice of the household was against me. After some fruitless messages, I sent up a scrawl to Mr Cole, who decided upon admitting the importunate Afghan.

An exclamation of astonishment and a hospitable welcome followed my self-introduction as an officer of the Indian army. Amongst other things, the vice-consul informed me that, in divers discussions with the Turks about the possibility of an Englishman finding his way *en cachette* to Meccah, he had asserted that his compatriots could do everything, even pilgrim to the Holy City. The Moslems politely assented to the first, but denied the second part of the proposition. Mr Cole promised himself a laugh at the Turks' beards; but since my departure, he wrote to me that the subject made the owners look so serious, that he did not like recurring to it.

Truly gratifying to the pride of an Englishman was our high official position assumed and maintained at Jeddah. Mr Cole had never, like his colleague at Cairo, lowered himself in the estimation of the proud race with which he has to deal, by private or mercantile transactions with the authorities. He has steadily withstood the wrath of the Meccan Sherif, and taught him to respect the British name. The Abbé Hamilton ascribed the attentions of the Prince to 'the infinite respect which the Arabs entertain for Mr Cole's straightforward way of doing business—it was a delicate flattery addressed to him'. And the writer was right; honesty of purpose is never thrown away amongst these people. The general contrast between our consular proceedings at Cairo and Jeddah is another proof of the advisability of selecting Indian officials to fill offices of trust at Oriental courts. They have lived amongst Easterns, they must know one Asiatic language, with many Asiatic customs; and, chief merit of all, they have learned to assume a tone of command, without which, whatever may be thought of it in England, it is impossible to take the lead in the East. The home-bred diplomate is not only unconscious of the thousand traps everywhere laid for him, he even plays into the hands of his crafty antagonists by a ceremonious politeness, which they interpret—taking ample care that the interpretation should spread—to be the effect of fear or fraud.

Jeddah has been often described by modern pens. Burckhardt (in AD 1814) devoted 100 pages of his two volumes to the unhappy capital of the Tihamat el-Hejaz, the lowlands of the mountain region. Later still, MM. Mari and Chedufau wrote upon the subject; and two other French travellers, MM. Galinier and Ferret, published tables of the commerce in its present state, quoting as authority the celebrated Arabicist M. Fresnel. These have been translated by the author of *Life in Abyssinia.* Abdulkerim, writing in 1742, informs us that the French had a factory at Jeddah; and in 1760, when Bruce revisited the port, he found the East India Company in possession of a post whence they dispersed their merchandise over the adjoining regions. But though the English were at an early epoch of their appearance in the East received here with especial favour, I failed to procure a single ancient document.

Jeddah, when I visited it, was in a state of commotion, owing to the perpetual passage of pilgrims, and provisions were for the same reason scarce and dear. The two large Wakalahs, of which the place boasts, were crowded with travellers, and many were reduced to encamping upon the squares. Another subject of confusion was the state of the soldiery. The Nizam, or Regulars, had not been paid for seven months, and the Arnauts could scarcely sum up what was owing to them. Easterns are wonderfully amenable to discipline; a European army, under the circumstances, would probably have helped itself. But the Pasha knew that there is a limit to man's endurance, and he was anxiously casting about for some contrivance that would replenish the empty pouches of his troops. The worried dignitary must have sighed for those *beaux jours* when privily firing the town and allowing the soldiers to plunder was the Oriental style of settling arrears of pay.

Jeddah displays all the licence of a seaport and garrison town. Fair Corinthians establish themselves even within earshot of the Karakun, or guard-post; a symptom of excessive laxity in the authorities, for it is the duty of the watch to visit all such irregularities with a bastinado preparatory to confinement. My guardians and attendants at the Wakalah used to fetch *Raki* in a clear glass bottle, without even the decency of a cloth, and the messenger twice returned from these errands decidedly drunk. More extraordinary still, the people seemed to take no notice of the scandal.

The little 'Dwarka' had been sent by the Bombay Steam Navigation Company to convey pilgrims from El-Hejaz to India. I was still hesitating about my next voyage, not wishing to coast the Red Sea in this season without a companion, when one morning Umar Effendi appeared at the door, weary, and dragging after him an ass more weary than himself. We supplied him with a pipe and a cup of hot tea, and, as he was fearful of pursuit, we showed him a dark hole full of grass under which he might sleep concealed.

The student's fears were realised; his father appeared early the next morning, and having ascertained from the porter that the fugitive was in the house, politely called upon me. Whilst he plied all manner of questions, his black slave furtively stared at everything in and about the room. But we had found time to cover the runaway with grass, and the old gentleman departed, after a fruitless search. There was, however, a grim smile about his mouth which boded no good.

That evening, returning home from the Hammam, I found the house in an uproar. The boy Mohammed, who had been miserably mauled, was furious with rage; and Shaykh Nur was equally unmanageable, by reason of his fear. In my absence the father had returned with a *posse comitatus* of friends and relatives. They questioned the youth, who delivered himself of many circumstantial and emphatic misstatements. Then they proceeded to open the boxes; upon which the boy Mohammed cast himself sprawling, with a vow to die rather than to endure such a disgrace. This procured for him some scattered slaps, which presently became a storm of blows, when a prying little boy discovered Umar Effendi's leg in the hiding-place. The student was led away unresisting, but mildly swearing that he would allow no opportunity of escape to pass. I examined the boy Mohammed, and was pleased to find that he was not seriously hurt. To pacify his mind, I offered to sally out with him, and to rescue Umar Effendi by main force. This, which would only have brought us all into a brunt with quarterstaves, and similar servile weapons, was declined, as had been foreseen. But the youth recovered complacency, and a few well-merited encomiums upon his pluck restored him to high spirits.

The reader must not fancy such escapade to be a serious thing in Arabia. The father did not punish his son; he merely bargained with him to return home for a few days before starting to Egypt. This the young man did, and shortly afterwards I met him unexpectedly in the streets of Cairo.

Deprived of my companion, I resolved to waste no time in the Red Sea, but to return to Egypt with the utmost expedition. The boy Mohammed having laid in a large store of grain, purchased with my money, having secured all my disposable articles, and having hinted that, after my return to India, a present of 20 dollars would find him at Meccah, asked leave, and departed with a coolness for which I could not account. Some days afterwards Shaykh Nur explained the cause. I had taken the youth with me on board the steamer, where a bad suspicion crossed his mind. 'Now, I understand,' said the boy Mohammed to his fellow-servant, 'your master is a Sahib from India; he hath laughed at our beards.' He parted as coolly from Shaykh Nur. These worthy youths had been drinking together, when Mohammed, having learned at Stamboul the fashionable practice of *Bad-masti*, or liquor-vice, dug his 'fives' into Nur's eye. Nur erroneously considering such exercise likely to induce blindness, complained to me; but my sympathy was all with the other side. I asked the Hindi why he had not returned the compliment, and the Meccan once more overwhelmed the Miyan with taunt and jibe.

It is not easy to pass the time at Jeddah. In the square opposite us was an unhappy idiot, who afforded us a melancholy spectacle. He delighted to wander about in a primitive state of toilette, as all such wretches do; but the people of Jeddah, far too civilised to retain Moslem respect for madness, forced him, despite shrieks and struggles, into a shirt, and when he tore it off they beat him. At other times the open space before us was diversified by the arrival and the departure of pilgrims, but it was a mere *réchauffé* of the feast, and had lost all power to please.

Whilst the boy Mohammed remained, he used to pass the time in wrangling with some Indians, who were living next door to us, men, women, and children, in a promiscuous way. After his departure I used to spend my days at the vice-consulate; the proceeding was not perhaps of the safest, but the temptation of meeting a fellow-countryman, and of chatting 'shop' about the service, was too great to be resisted. I met there the principal merchants of Jeddah; Khawajah Sower, a Greek; M. Anton, a Christian from Baghdad, and others.[1] And I was introduced to Khalid Bey, brother of Abdullah bin Saud, *the* Wahhabi. This noble Arab once held the official position of Mukayyid el-Jawabat, or Secretary, at Cairo, where he was brought up by Mohammed Ali. He is brave, frank, and unprejudiced, fond of Europeans, and a lover of pleasure. Should it be his fate to become chief of the tribe, a journey to Riyaz, and a visit to Central Arabia, will offer no difficulties to our travellers.

I now proceed to the last of my visitations. Outside the town of Jeddah lies no less a personage than Sittna Hawwa, the Mother of mankind. The boy Mohammed and I, mounting asses one evening, issued through the Meccan gate, and turned towards the north-east over a sandy plain. After half an hour's ride, amongst dirty huts and tattered coffee-hovels, we reached the enceinte, and found the door closed. Presently a man came running with might from the town; he was followed by two others; and it struck me at the time that they applied the key with peculiar *empressement*, and made inordinately low *congés* as we entered the enclosure of whitewashed walls.

'The Mother' is supposed to lie, like a Moslemah, fronting the Kaabah, with her feet northwards, her head southwards, and her right cheek propped by her right hand. Whitewashed, and conspicuous to the voyager and traveller from afar, is a diminutive dome with an opening to the west; it is furnished as

[1] Many of them were afterwards victims to the Jeddah massacre on the 30th June, 1858. I must refer the reader to my *Lake Regions of Central Africa* (appendix, vol. ii) for an account of this event, for the proposals which I made to ward it off, and for the miserable folly of the 'Bombay Government', who rewarded me by an official reprimand.

such places usually are in El-Hejaz. Under it and in the centre is a square stone, planted upright and fancifully carved, to represent the omphalic region of the human frame. This, as well as the dome, is called El-Surrah, or the navel. The cicerone directed me to kiss this manner of hieroglyph, which I did, thinking the while, that, under the circumstances, the salutation was quite uncalled-for. Having prayed here, and at the head, where a few young trees grow, we walked along the side of the two parallel dwarf walls which define the outlines of the body: they are about six paces apart, and between them, upon Eve's neck, are two tombs, occupied, I was told, by Usman Pasha and his son, who repaired the Mother's sepulchre. I could not help remarking to the boy Mohammed, that if our first parent measured 120 paces from head to waist, and eighty from waist to heel, she must have presented much the appearance of a duck. To this the youth replied, flippantly, that he thanked his stars the Mother was under ground, otherwise that men would lose their senses with fright.

Ibn Jubayr (twelfth century) mentions only an old dome 'built upon the place where Eve stopped on the way to Meccah'. Yet El-Idrisi (AD 1154) declares Eve's grave to be at Jeddah. Abdel-karim (1742) compares it to a parterre, with a little dome in the centre, and the extremities ending in barriers of palisades; the circumference was 190 of his steps. In *Rooke's Travels* we are told that the tomb is twenty feet long. Ali Bey, who twice visited Jeddah, makes no allusion to it; we may therefore conclude that it had been destroyed by the Wahhabis. Burckhardt, who, I need scarcely say, has been carefully copied by our popular authors, was informed that it was a 'rude structure of stone, about four feet in length, two or three feet in height, and as many in breadth'; thus resembling the tomb of Noah, seen in the valley of El-Bukaa in Syria. Bruce writes: 'Two days' journey from this place (Meccah or Jeddah?) Eve's grave, of *green sods*, about fifty yards in length, is shown to this day'; but the great traveller probably never issued from the town-gates. And Sir W. Harris, who could not have visited the holy place, repeats, in 1840, that 'Eve's grave of *green sod* is still shown on the barren shore of the Red Sea'. The present structure is clearly modern; anciently, I was told at Jeddah, the sepulchre consisted of a stone at the head, a second at the feet, and the navel-dome.

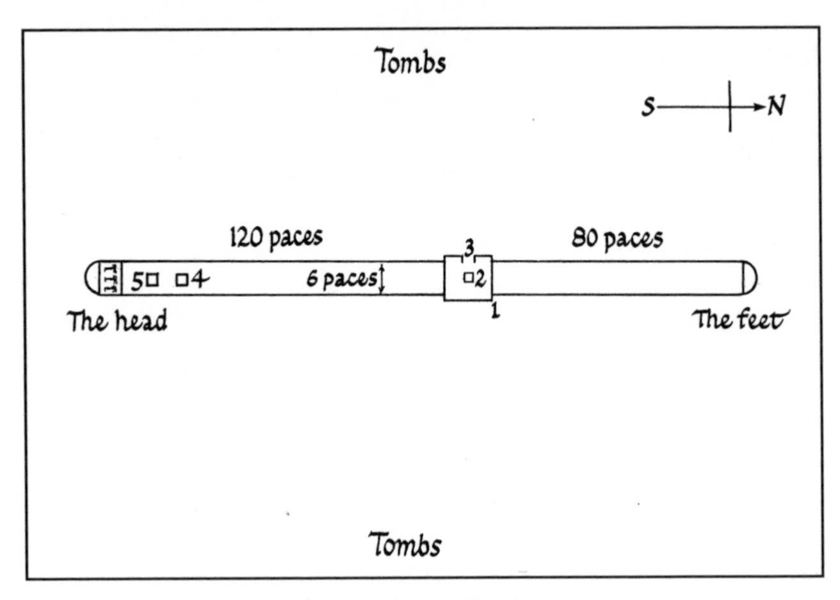

Plan of Eve's Tomb

The idol of Jeddah, in the days of Arab litholatry, was called *Sakhrah Tawilah*, the Long Stone. May not this stone of Eve be the Moslemised revival of the old idolatry? It is to be observed that the Arabs, if the tombs be admitted as evidence, are inconsistent in their dimensions of the patriarchal stature. The sepulchre of Adam at the Masjid el-Khayf is, like that of Eve, gigantic. That of Noah at El-Bukaa is a bit of aqueduct thirty-eight paces long by one and a half wide. Job's tomb near Hulah (seven parasangs from Kerbela) is small. I have not seen the grave of Moses (south-east of the Red Sea), which is becoming known by the bitumen cups there sold to pilgrims. But Aaron's sepulchre in the Sinaitic Peninsula is of moderate dimensions.

On leaving the graveyard I offered the guardian a dollar, which he received with a remonstrance that a man of my dignity should give so paltry a fee. Nor was he at all contented with the assurance that nothing more could be expected from an Afghan Dervish, however pious. Next day the boy Mohammed explained the man's *empressement* and disappointment—I had been mistaken for the Pasha of El-Medinah.

For a time my peregrinations ended. Worn out with fatigue, and the fatal fiery heat, I embarked (26th September) on board the 'Dwarka'; experienced the greatest kindness from the commander and chief officer (Messrs Wolley and Taylor); and, wondering the while how the Turkish pilgrims who crowded the vessel did not take the trouble to throw me overboard, in due time I arrived at Suez.

And here, reader, we part. Bear with me while I conclude, in the words of a brother traveller, long gone, but not forgotten—Fa-hian—this Personal Narrative of my Journey to El-Hejaz: 'I have been exposed to perils, and I have escaped from them; I have traversed the sea, and have not succumbed under the severest fatigues; and my heart is moved with emotions of gratitude, that I have been permitted to effect the objects I had in view.'

APPENDICES

I The Bayt Ullah

The House of Allah has been so fully described by my predecessors, that there is little inducement to attempt a new portrait. Readers, however, may desire a view of the great sanctuary; and, indeed, without a plan and its explanation, the ceremonies of the Haram would be scarcely intelligible. I will do homage to the memory of the accurate Burckhardt, and extract from his pages a description which shall be illustrated by a few notes.

'The Kaabah stands in an oblong square (enclosed by a great wall) 250 paces long, and 200 broad,[1] none of the sides of which run quite in a straight line, though at first sight the whole appears to be of a regular shape. This open square is enclosed on the eastern side by a colonnade. The pillars stand in a quadruple row; they are three deep on the other sides, and united by pointed arches, every four of which support a small dome plastered and whitened on the outside. These domes, according to Kotobeddyn, are 152 in number.[2] The pillars are above twenty feet in height, and generally from one foot and a half to one foot and three-quarters in diameter; but little regularity has been observed in regard to them. Some are of white marble, granite, or porphyry; but the greater number are of common stone of the Meccah mountains.[3] El-Fasy states the whole at 589, and says

[1] Ali Bey gives 536 feet 9 inches by 356 feet: my measurement is 257 paces by 210. Most Moslem authors, reckoning by cubics, make the parallelogram 404 by 310.

[2] On each short side I counted 24 domes; on the long, 35. This would give a total of 118 along the cloisters. The Arabs reckon in all 152; viz., 23 on the east side, on the north 36, on the south 36; one on the mosque corner, near the Zarurah minaret; 16 at the porch of the Bab el-Ziyadah; and 15 at the Bab Ibrahim. The shape of these domes is the usual *Media Naranja*, and the superstition of the Meccans informs the pilgrim that they cannot be counted. Books reckon 1,352 pinnacles or battlements on the temple wall.

[3] The 'common stone of the Meccah mountains' is a fine grey granite quarried principally from a hill near the Bab el-Shabayki, which furnished materials for the Kaabah. Eastern authors describe the pillars as consisting of three different substances, viz., Rukham, white marble, not alabaster, its general sense; Suwan, or granite (syenite?); and Hajar Shumaysi, a kind of yellow sandstone, so called from Bir Shumays, a place on the Jeddah road, near Haddah, the half-way station.

they are all of marble excepting 126, which are of common stone, and three of composition. Kotobeddyn reckons 555, of which, according to him, 311 are of marble, and the rest of the stone taken from the neighbouring mountains; but neither of these authors lived to see the latest repairs of the mosque, after the destruction occasioned by a torrent in AD 1626.[1] Between every three or four columns stands an octagonal one, about four feet in thickness. On the east side are two shafts of reddish grey granite in one piece, and one fine grey porphyry with slabs of white feldspath. On the north side is one red granite column, and one of fine-grained red porphyry; these are probably the columns which Kotobeddyn states to have been brought from Egypt, and principally from Akhmim (Panopolis), when the chief (Caliph) El-Mohdy enlarged the mosque in AH 163. Among the 450 or 500 columns which form the enclosure, I found not any two capitals or bases exactly alike. The capitals are of course Saracen workmanship; some of them, which had served for former buildings, by the ignorance of the workmen, have been placed upside-down upon the shafts. I observed about half a dozen marble bases of good Grecian workmanship. A few of the marble columns bear Arabic or Cufic inscriptions, in which I read the dates 863 and 762 (AH).[2] A column on the east side exhibits a very ancient Cufic inscription, somewhat defaced, which I could neither read nor copy. Some of the columns are strengthened with broad iron rings or bands,[3] as in many other Saracen buildings of the East. They were first employed by Ibn Dhaher Berkouk, king of Egypt, in rebuilding the mosque, which had been destroyed by fire in AH 802.[4]

[1] I counted in the temple 554 pillars. It is, however, difficult to be accurate, as the four colonnades and the porticoes about the two great gates are irregular; topographical observations, moreover, must be made under difficulties. Ali Bey numbers them roughly at *plus de 500 colonnes et pilastres*.

[2] The author afterwards informs us, that 'the temple has been so often ruined and repaired, that no traces of remote antiquity are to be found about it'. He mentions some modern and unimportant inscriptions upon the walls and over the gates. Knowing that many of the pillars were sent in ships from Syria and Egypt by the Caliph el-Mahdi, a traveller would have expected better things.

[3] The reason being, that 'those shafts formed of the Meccan stone are mostly in three pieces; but the marble shafts are in one piece'.

[4] To this may be added, that the façades of the cloisters are twenty-four along the short walls, and thirty-six along the others; they have stone ornaments, not inaptly compared

ALI BEY'S PLAN OF THE PROPHET'S MOSQUE AT MECCAH
(COMMONLY CALLED BAYT ULLAH OR GOD'S HOUSE)

(1) Bab Ali or Benu Hashim
(2) Minaret of Bab Ali
(3) Bab el-Zayt or Bab el-Asharah
(4) Bab el-Baghlah
(5) Bab el-Safa
(6) Bab el-Mujahid or El-Rahmah
(7) Bab el-Jiyad
(8) Bab Ujlan or Bab el-Sherif
(9) Bab Umm Hani
(10) Minaret of Bab el-Widaa
(11) Bab Ibrahim (Tailors' Gate)
(12) Bab Beni Saham or Bab el-Umrah
(13) Bab el-Ajlah or El-Basitiyah
(14) Bab el-Ziyadah or Bab el-Nadwah
(15) Minaret of Bab el-Ziyadah
(16) Minaret of Bab el-Salam
(17) Bab el-Salam or Bab Beni Shaybah
(18) Tomb of Ismail and his mother

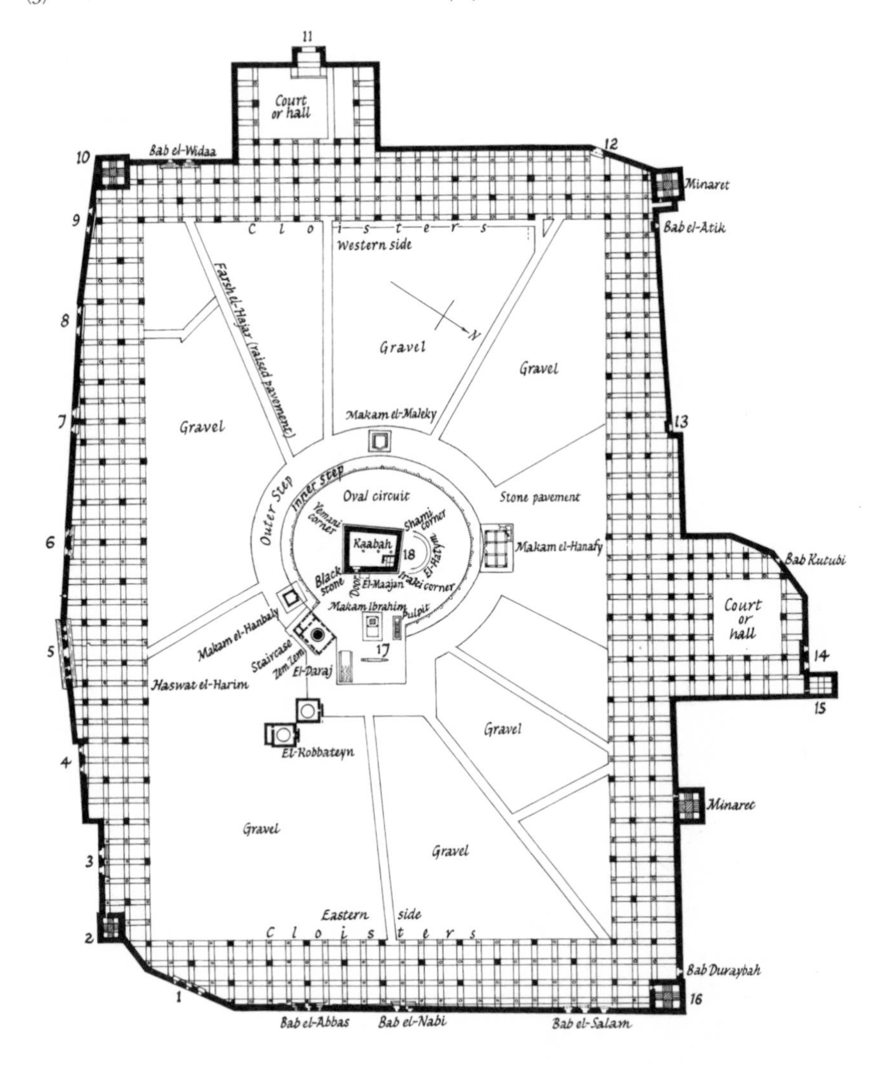

'Some parts of the walls and arches are gaudily painted in stripes of yellow, red, and blue, as are also the minarets. Paintings of flowers, in the usual Muselman style, are nowhere seen; the floors of the colonnades are paved with large stones badly cemented together.

'Some paved causeways lead from the colonnades towards the Kaabah, or Holy House, in the centre.[1] They are of sufficient breadth to admit four or five persons to walk abreast, and they are elevated about nine inches above the ground. Between these causeways, which are covered with fine gravel or sand, grass appears growing in several places, produced by the Zem Zem water oozing out of the jars which are placed in the ground in long rows during the day.[2] There is a descent of eight or ten steps from the gates on the north side into the platform of the colonnade, and of three or four steps from the gates on the south side.

'Towards the middle of this area stands the Kaabah; it is 115 paces from the north colonnade, and eighty-eight from the south. For this want of symmetry we may readily account, the Kaabah having existed prior to the mosque, which was built around it, and enlarged at different periods. The Kaabah is an oblong massive structure, eighteen paces in length, fourteen in breadth, and from thirty-five to forty feet in height.[3] It is constructed of the grey Meccah stone, in large blocks of different sizes, joined together, in a very rough manner, with bad cement.[4]

to the French fleur-de-lis. The capitals and bases of the outer pillars are grander and more regular than the inner; they support pointed arches, and the Arab secures his beloved variety by placing at every fourth arch a square pilaster. Of these there are on the long sides ten, on the short seven.

[1] I counted eight, not including the broad pavement which leads from the Bab el-Ziyadah to the Kaabah, or the four cross branches which connect the main lines. These Firash el-Hajar, as they are called, also serve to partition off the area. One space, for instance, is called Haswat el-Harim, or the 'Women's sanded place', because appropriated to female devotees.

[2] The jars are little amphorae, each inscribed with the name of the donor and a peculiar cypher.

[3] My measurements give 22 paces or 55 feet in length by 18 (45), of breadth, and the height appeared greater than the length. Ali Bey makes the eastern side 37 French feet, 2 inches and 6 lines, the western 38, 4, 6, the northern 29 feet, the southern 31, 6, and the height 34, 4. He therefore calls it a 'veritable trapezium'. In El-Idrisi's time it was 25 cubits by 24, and 27 cubits high.

[4] I would alter this sentence thus: 'It is built of fine grey granite in horizontal courses of masonry of irregular depth; the stones are tolerably fitted together, and are held by excellent mortar like Roman cement.' The lines are also straight.

It was entirely rebuilt, as it now stands, in AD 1627. The torrent in the preceding year had thrown down three of its sides, and, preparatory to its re-erection, the fourth side was, according to Asamy, pulled down, after the Olemas, or learned divines, had been consulted on the question whether mortals might be permitted to destroy any part of the holy edifice without incurring the charge of sacrilege and infidelity.

'The Kaabah stands upon a base two feet in height, which presents a sharp inclined plane.[1] Its roof being flat, it has at a distance the appearance of a perfect cube.[2] The only door which affords entrance, and which is opened but two or three times in the year,[3] is on the north side, and about seven feet above the ground.[4] In the first periods of Islam, however, when it was

[1] This base is called El-Shazarwan, from the Persian Shadarwan, a cornice, eaves, or canopy. It is in pent-house shape, projecting about a foot beyond the wall, and composed of fine white marble slabs, polished like glass; there are two breaks in it, one opposite and under the doorway, and another in front of Ishmael's tomb. Pilgrims are directed, during circumambulation, to keep their bodies outside of the Shazarwan; this would imply it to be part of the building, but its only use appears in the large brass rings welded into it, for the purpose of holding down the Kaabah covering.

[2] Ali Bey also errs in describing the roof as *plat en dessus*. Were such the case, rain would not pour off with violence through the spout. Most Oriental authors allow a cubit of depression from south-west to north-west. In El-Idrisi's day the Kaabah had a double roof. Some say this is the case in the present building, which has not been materially altered in shape since its restoration by El-Hajjaj, AH 83. The roof was then eighteen cubits long by fifteen broad.

[3] In Ibn Jubayr's time the Kaabah was opened every day in Rajab, and in other months on every Monday and Friday. The house may now be entered ten or twelve times a year gratis; and by pilgrims as often as they can collect, amongst parties, a sum sufficient to tempt the guardians' cupidity.

[4] This mistake, in which Burckhardt is followed by all our popular authors, is the more extraordinary, as all Arabic authors call the door wall Janib el-Mashrik—the eastern side—or Wajh el-Bayt, the front of the house, opposed to Zahr el-Bayt, the back. Niebuhr is equally in error when he asserts that the door fronts to the south. Arabs always hold the Rukn el-Iraki, or Irak angle, to face the polar star, and so it appears in Ali Bey's plan. The Kaabah, therefore, has no northern side. And it must be observed that Moslem writers make the length of the Kaabah from east to west, whereas our travellers make it from north to south.

Ali Bey places the door only six feet from the pavement, but he calculates distances by the old French measure. It is about seven feet from the ground, and six from the corner of the Black Stone. Between the two the space of wall is called El-Multazem (in Burckhardt, by a clerical error, 'El-Metzem', vol. 1, p. 173). It derives its name, the 'Attached-to', because here the circumambulator should apply his bosom, and beg pardon for his sins. El-Multazem, according to M. de Percival, following d'Ohsson, was formerly '*le lieu des engagements*', whence, according to him, its name. '*Le Moltezem,*' says M. Galland (*Rits et Cérémonies du Pélerinage de la Mecque*), '*qui est entre la pierre noire et la porte, est l'endroit où Mahomet se réconcilia avec ses dix compagnons, qui disaient qu'il n'était pas véritablement Prophète.*'

rebuilt in AH 64 by Ibn Zebeyr (Zubayr), chief of Mecca, it had two doors even with the ground-floor of the mosque.[1] The present door (which, according to Azraky, was brought hither from Constantinople in AD 1633) is wholly coated with silver, and has several gilt ornaments; upon its threshold are placed every night various small lighted wax candles, and perfuming pans, filled with musk, aloe-wood, etc.[2]

'At the north-east[3] corner of the Kaabah, near the door, is the famous Black Stone;[4] it forms a part of the sharp angle of the

[1] From the Bab el-Ziyadah, or gate in the northern colonnade, you descend by two flights of steps, in all about twenty-five. This depression manifestly arises from the level of the town having been raised, like Rome, by successive layers of ruins; the most populous and substantial quarters (as the Shamiyah to the north) would, we might expect, be the highest, and this is actually the case. But I am unable to account satisfactorily for the second hollow within the temple, and immediately around the House of Allah, where the door, according to all historians, formerly on a level with the pavement, and now about seven feet above it, shows the exact amount of depression, which cannot be due simply to calcation. Some chroniclers assert that when the Kuraysh rebuilt the house they raised the door to prevent devotees entering without their permission. But seven feet would scarcely oppose an entrance, and how will this account for the floor of the building being also raised to that height above the pavement? It is curious to observe the similarity between this inner hollow of the Meccan fane and the artificial depression of the Hindu pagoda where it is intended to be flooded. The Hindus would also revere the form of the Meccan fane, exactly resembling their square temples, at whose corners are placed Brahma, Vishnu, Shiwa, and Ganesha, who adore the Universal Generator in the centre.

The second door anciently stood on the side of the temple opposite the present entrance; inside, its place can still be traced. Ali Bey suspects its having existed in the modern building, and declares that the exterior surface of the wall shows the tracery of a blocked-up door, similar to that still open. Some historians declare that it was closed by the Kuraysh when they rebuilt the house in Mohammed's day, and that subsequent erections have had only one. The general opinion is that El-Hajjaj finally closed up the western entrance. Doctors also differ as to its size; the popular measurement is three cubits broad and a little more than five in length.

[2] Pilgrims and ignorant devotees collect the drippings of wax, the ashes of the aloe-wood, and the dust from the Atabah, or threshold of the Kaabah, either to rub upon their foreheads or to preserve as relics. These superstitious practices are sternly rebuked by the Olema.

[3] For north-east read south-east.

[4] I will not enter into the fabulous origin of the Hajar el-Aswad. Some of the traditions connected with it are truly absurd. 'When Allah', says Ali, 'made covenant with the Sons of Adam on the Day of Fealty, he placed the paper inside the stone'; it will, therefore, appear at the judgment, and bear witness to all who have touched it. Moslems agree that it was originally white, and became black by reason of men's sins. It appeared to me a common aërolite covered with a thick slaggy coating, glossy and pitch-like, worn and polished. Dr Wilson of Bombay showed me a specimen in his possession, which externally appeared to be a black slag, with the inside of a bright and sparkling greyish-white, the result of admixture of nickel with the iron. This might possibly, as the learned Orientalist then suggested, account for the mythic change of colour, its appearance on earth

building,[1] at four or five feet above the ground.[2] It is an irregular oval, about seven inches in diameter, with an undulating surface, composed of about a dozen smaller stones of different sizes and shapes, well joined together with a small quantity of

after a thunderstorm, and its being originally a material part of the heavens. Kutb el-Din expressly declares that, when the Karamitah restored it after twenty-two years to the Meccans, men kissed it and rubbed it upon their brows; and remarked that the blackness was only superficial, the inside being white. Some Greek philosophers, it will be remembered, believed the heavens to be composed of stones (Cosmos, *Shooting Stars*): and Sanconiathon, ascribing the aërolite-worship to the god Coelus, declares them to be living or animated stones. 'The Arabians', says Maximus of Tyre (*Dissert. 38*, p. 455), 'pay homage to I know not what god, which they represent by a quadrangular stone.' The gross fetishism of the Hindus, it is well known, introduced them to litholatry. At Jagannath they worship a pyramidal black stone, fabled to have fallen from heaven, or miraculously to have presented itself on the place where the temple now stands. Moreover, they revere the Salagram, as the emblem of Vishnu, the second person in their triad. The rudest emblem of the Bonus Deus was a round stone. It was succeeded in India by the cone and triangle; in Egypt by the pyramid; in Greece it was represented by cones of terra-cotta about three inches and a half long. Without going deep into theory, it may be said that the Kaabah and the Hajar are the only two idols which have survived the 360 composing the heavenly host of the Arab pantheon. Thus the Hindu poet exclaims:

> Behold the marvels of my idol-temple, O Moslem!
> That when its idols are destroy'd, it becomes Allah's House.

Wilford (*As. Soc.*, vols iii and iv) makes the Hindus declare that the Black Stone at Mokshesha, or Moksha-sthana (Meccah) was an incarnation of Moksheshwara, an incarnation of Shiwa, who with his consort visited El-Hejaz. When the Kaabah was rebuilt, this emblem was placed in the outer wall for contempt, but the people still respected it. In the Dabistan the Black Stone is said to be an image of Kaywan or Saturn; and El-Shahristani also declares the temple to have been dedicated to the same planet Zuhal, whose genius is represented in the Puranas as fierce, hideous, four-armed, and habited in a black cloak, with a dark turban. Moslem historians are unanimous in asserting that Sasan, son of Babegan, and other Persian monarchs, gave rich presents to the Kaabah; they especially mention two golden crescent moons, a significant offering. The Guebers assert that, among the images and relics left by Mahabad and his successors in the Kaabah, was the Black Stone, an emblem of Saturn. They also call the city Mahgah—moon's place—from an exceedingly beautiful image of the moon; whence they say the Arabs derived 'Meccah'. And the Sabaeans equally respect the Kaabah and the pyramids, which they assert to be the tombs of Seth, Enoch (or Hermes), and Sabi the Son of Enoch.

Meccah, then, is claimed as a sacred place, and the Hajar el-Aswad, as well as the Kaabah, are revered as holy emblems by four different faiths—the Hindu, Sabaean, Gueber, and Moslem. I have little doubt, and hope to prove at another time, that the Jews connected it with traditions about Abraham. This would be the fifth religion that looked towards the Kaabah—a rare meeting-place of devotion.

[1] Presenting this appearance in profile. The Hajar has suffered from the iconoclastic principle of Islam, having once narrowly escaped destruction by order of El-Hakim of Egypt. In these days the metal rim serves as a protection as well as an ornament.

[2] The height of the Hajar from the ground, according to my measurement, is four feet nine inches; Ali Bey places it forty-two inches above the pavement.

cement, and perfectly well smoothed: it looks as if the whole had been broken into many pieces by a violent blow, and then united again. It is very difficult to determine accurately the quality of this stone, which has been worn to its present surface by the millions of touches and kisses it has received. It appeared to me like a lava, containing several small extraneous particles of a whitish and of a yellowish substance. Its colour is now a deep reddish-brown, approaching to black. It is surrounded on all sides by a border composed of a substance which I took to be a close cement of pitch and gravel of a similar, but not quite the same, brownish colour.[1] This border serves to support its detached pieces; it is two or three inches in breadth, and rises a little above the surface of the stone. Both the border and the stone itself are encircled by a silver band,[2] broader below than above, and on the two sides, with a considerable swelling below, as if a part of the stone were hidden under it. The lower part of the border is studded with silver nails.

'In the south-east corner of the Kaabah,[3] or, as the Arabs call it, Rokn el-Yemany, there is another stone about five feet from the ground; it is one foot and a half in length, and two inches in breadth, placed upright, and of the common Meccah stone. This the people walking round the Kaabah touch only with the right hand; they do not kiss it.[4]

'On the north side of the Kaabah, just by its door, and close

[1] The colour was black and metallic, and the centre of the stone was sunk about two inches below the metal circle. Round the sides was a reddish-brown cement, almost level with the metal, and sloping down to the middle of the stone.

Ibn Jubayr declares the depth of the stone unknown, but that most people believe it to extend two cubits into the wall. In his day it was three 'Shibr' (the large span from the thumb to the little finger-tip) broad, and one span long, with knobs, and a joining of four pieces, which the Karamitah had broken. The stone was set in a silver band. Its softness and moisture were such, say Ibn Jubayr, 'that the sinner never would remove his mouth from it, which phenomenon made the Prophet declare it to be the covenant of Allah on earth'.

[2] The band is now a massive circle of gold or silver gilt. I found the aperture in which the stone is, one span and three fingers broad.

[3] The Rukn el-Yemani is the corner facing the south. The part alluded to in the text is the wall of the Kaabah, between the Shami and Yemani angles, distant about three feet from the latter, and near the site of the old western door, long since closed. The stone is darker and redder than the rest of the wall. It is called *El-Mustajab* (or *Mustajab min el-Zunub* or *Mustajab el-Dua*, 'where prayer is granted'). Pilgrims here extend their arms, press their bodies against the building, and beg pardon for their sins.

[4] I have frequently seen it kissed by men and women.

to the wall, is a slight hollow in the ground, lined with marble, and sufficiently large to admit of three persons sitting. Here it is thought meritorious to pray: the spot is called El-Maajan,[1] and supposed to be where Abraham and his son Ismail kneaded the chalk and mud which they used in building the Kaabah; and near this Maajan the former is said to have placed the large stone upon which he stood while working at the masonry. On the basis of the Kaabah, just over the Maajan, is an ancient Cufic inscription; but this I was unable to decypher, and had no opportunity of copying it.

'On the west (north-west) side of the Kaabah, about two feet below its summit, is the famous Myzab, or water-spout,[2] through which the rain-water collected on the roof of the building is discharged, so as to fall upon the ground; it is about four feet in length, and six inches in breadth, as well as I could judge from below, with borders equal in height to its breadth. At the mouth hangs what is called the beard of the Myzab; a gilt board, over which the water flows. This spout was sent hither from Constantinople in AH 981, and is *reported* to be of pure gold. The pavement round the Kaabah, below the Myzab, was laid down in AH 826, and consists of various coloured stones, forming a very handsome specimen of mosaic. There are two large slabs of fine *verde antico*[3] in the centre, which, according to Makrizi, were sent thither, as presents from Cairo, in AH 241. This is the spot where, according

[1] El-Maajan, the place of mixing or kneading, because the patriarchs here kneaded the mud used as cement in the holy building. Some call it El-Hufrah (the digging), and it is generally known as Makam Jibrail (the place of Gabriel), because here descended the inspired order for the five daily prayers; and at this spot the Prophet and the Archangel performed their devotions, making it a most auspicious site. It is on the north of the door, from which it is distant about two feet; its length is seven spans and seven fingers; breadth five spans three fingers; and depth one span four fingers.

The following sentence from Herklet's *Qanoon e Islam* (ch. xii, sec. 5) may serve to show the extent of error still popular. The author, after separating the Bayt Ullah from the Kaabah, erroneously making the former the name of the whole temple, proceeds to say, 'the rain water which falls on its (the Kaabah's) *terrace* runs off through a golden spout on a stone near it, called *Rookn-e-Yemeni.* or *alabaster-stone*, and stands over the grave of Ishmael'!

[2] Generally called Mizab el-Rahmah (of Mercy). It carries rain from the roof, and discharges it upon Ishmael's grave, where pilgrims stand fighting to catch it. In El-Idrisi's time it was of wood; now it is said to be gold, but it looks very dingy.

[3] Usually called the Hajar el-Akhzar, or green stone. El-Idrisi speaks of a white stone covering Ishmael's remains; Ibn Jubayr, of 'green marble, longish, in form of a Mihrab arch, and near it a white round slab, in both of which are spots that make them appear

to Mohammedan tradition, Ismayl the son of Ibrahim, and his mother Hajirah, are buried; and here it is meritorious for the pilgrim to recite a prayer of two Rikats. On this side is a semicircular wall, the two extremities of which are in a line with the sides of the Kaabah, and distant from it three or four feet,[1] leaving an opening which leads to the burial-place of Ismayl. The wall bears the name of El-Hatym,[2] and the area which it encloses is called Hedjer or Hedjer Ismayl,[3] on account of its being separated from the Kaabah; the wall itself also is sometimes so called.

'Tradition says that the Kaabah once extended as far as the Hatym, and that this side having fallen down just at the time of the Hadj, the expenses of repairing it were demanded from the pilgrims, under a pretence that the revenues of government were not acquired in a manner sufficiently pure to admit of their application towards a purpose so sacred. The sum, however, obtained proved very inadequate; all that could be done, therefore, was to raise a wall, which marked the space formerly occupied by the Kaabah. This tradition, although current among the Metowefs (cicerones), is at variance with history, which declares that the Hedjer was built by the Beni Koreish, who contracted the dimensions of the Kaabah; that it was united to the building by Hadjadj,[4] and again separated from it by Ibn Zebeyr.

'It is asserted by Fasy, that a part of the Hedjer as it now stands was never comprehended within the Kaabah. The law regards it as a portion of the Kaabah, inasmuch as it is esteemed

---

yellow'. Near them, we are told, and towards the Iraki corner, is the tomb of Hagar, under a green slab one span and a half broad, and pilgrims used to pray at both places. Ali Bey erroneously applies the words El-Hajar Ismail to the parapet about the slab.

[1] My measurements give five feet six inches. In El-Idrisi's day the wall was fifty cubits long.

[2] El-Hatim (lit. the 'broken'). Burckhardt asserts that the Mekkawi no longer apply the word, as some historians do, to the space bounded by the Kaabah, the Partition, the Zem Zem, and the Makam of Ibrahim. I heard it, however, so used by learned Meccans, and they gave as the meaning of the name the break in this part of the oval pavement which surrounds the Kaabah. Historians relate that all who rebuilt the House of Allah followed Abraham's plan till the Kuraysh, and after them El-Hajjaj, curtailed it in the direction of El-Hatim, which part was then first broken off, and ever since remained so.

[3] El-Hijr is the space separated, as the name denotes from the Kaabah. Some suppose that Abraham here penned his sheep. Possibly Ali Bey means this part of the Temple when he speaks of El-Hajar Ismail—*les pierres d'Ismail.*

[4] 'El Hajjaj'; this, as will afterwards be seen, is a mistake. He excluded the Hatim.

equally meritorious to pray in the Hedjer as in the Kaabah itself; and the pilgrims who have not an opportunity of entering the latter are permitted to affirm upon oath that they have prayed in the Kaabah, although they have only prostrated themselves within the enclosure of the Hatym. The wall is built of solid stone, about five feet in height and four in thickness, cased all over with white marble, and inscribed with prayers and invocations, neatly sculptured upon the stone in modern characters.[1] These and the casing are the work of El-Ghoury, the Egyptian Sultan, in AH 917. The walk round the Kaabah is performed on the outside of the wall—the nearer to it the better.

'Round the Kaabah is a good pavement of marble,[2] about eight inches below the level of the great square; it was laid in AH 981, by order of the Sultan, and describes an irregular oval; it is surrounded by thirty-two slender gilt pillars, or rather poles, between every two of which are suspended seven glass lamps, always lighted after sunset.[3] Beyond the poles is a second pavement, about eight paces broad, somewhat elevated above the first, but of coarser work; then another six inches higher, and eighteen paces broad, upon which stand several small buildings; beyond this is the gravelled ground; so that two broad steps may be said to lead from the square down to the Kaabah. The small buildings just mentioned which surround the Kaabah are the five Makams,[4] with the well of Zem Zem, the arch called Bab es-Salam, and the Mambar.

'Opposite the four sides of the Kaabah stand four other small

[1] As well as memory serves me, for I have preserved no note, the inscriptions are in the marble casing, and indeed no other stone meets the eye.

[2] It is a fine, close, grey, polished granite: the walk is called El-Mataf, or the place of circumambulation.

[3] These are now iron posts, very numerous, supporting cross rods, and of tolerably elegant shape. In Ali Bey's time there were *trente-une colonnes minces en piliers en bronze*. Some native works say thirty-three, including two marble columns. Between each two hang several white or green glass globe-lamps, with wicks and oil floating on water; their light is faint and dismal. The whole of the lamps in the Haram is said to be more than a thousand, yet they serve but to 'make darkness visible'.

[4] There are only four Makams, the Hanafi, Maliki, Hanbali, and the Makam Ibrahim; and there is some error of diction below, for in these it is that the Imams stand before their congregations, and nearest the Kaabah. In Ibn Jubayr's time the Zaydi sect was allowed an Imam, though known to be schismatics and abusers of the Caliphs. Now, not being permitted to have a separate station for prayer, they suppose theirs to be suspended from heaven above the Kaabah roof.

buildings, where the Imams of the orthodox Mohammedan sects, the Hanefy, Shafey, Hanbaly, and Maleky take their station, and guide the congregation in their prayers. The Makam el-Maleky on the south, and that of Hanbaly opposite the Black Stone, are small pavilions open on all sides, and supported by four slender pillars, with a light sloping roof, terminating in a point, exactly in style of Indian pagodas.[1] The Makam el-Hanafy, which is the largest, being fifteen paces by eight, is open on all sides, and supported by twelve small pillars; it has an upper story, also open, where the Mueddin who calls to prayers takes his stand. This was first built in AH 923, by the Sultan Selim I; it was afterwards rebuilt by Khoshgeldy, governor of Jeddah, in 947; but all the four Makams, as they now stand, were built in AH 1074. The Makam-es'-Shafey is over the well Zem Zem, to which it serves as an upper chamber.[2]

'Near their respective Makams the adherents of the four different sects seat themselves for prayers. During my stay at Meccah the Hanefys always began their prayer first; but, according to Muselman custom, the Shafeys should pray first in the mosque; then the Hanefys, Malekys, and Hanbalys. The prayer of the Maghreb is an exception, which they are all enjoined to utter together.[3] The Makam el-Hanbaly is the place where the officers of government and other great people are seated during prayers; here the Pasha and the Sherif are placed, and in their absence the eunuchs of the temple. These fill the space under this Makam in front, and behind it the female Hadjys who visit the temple have their places assigned, to which they repair

[1] The Makam el-Maliki is on the west of, and thirty-seven cubits from, the Kaabah; that of the Hanbali forty-seven paces distant.

[2] Only the Muezzin takes his stand here, and the Shafeis pray behind their Imam on the pavement round the Kaabah, between the corner of the well Zem Zem, and the Makam Ibrahim. This place is forty cubits from the Kaabah, that is to say, eight cubits nearer than the northern and southern Makams. Thus the pavement forms an irregular oval ring round the house.

[3] In Burckhardt's time the schools prayed according to the seniority of their founders, and they uttered the Azan of El-Maghrib together, because that is a peculiarly delicate hour, which easily passes by unnoticed. In the twelfth century, at all times but the evening, the Shafei began, then came the Maliki and Hanbali simultaneously, and lastly, the Hanafi. Now the Shaykh el-Muezzin begins the call, which is taken up by the others. He is a Hanafi; as indeed are all the principal people at Meccah, only a few wild Sherifs of the hills being Shafei.

principally for the two evening prayers, few of them being seen in the mosque at the three other daily prayers: they also perform the Towaf, or walk round the Kaabah, but generally at night, though it is not uncommon to see them walking in the daytime among the men.

'The present building which encloses Zem Zem stands close by the Makam Hanbaly, and was erected in AH 1072: it is of a square shape, and of massive construction, with an entrance to the north,[1] opening into the room which contains the well. This room is beautifully ornamented with marbles of various colours; and adjoining to it, but having a separate door, is a small room with a stone reservoir, which is always full of Zem Zem water. This the Hadjys get to drink by passing their hand with a cup through an iron-grated opening, which serves as a window, into the reservoir, without entering the room. The mouth of the well is surrounded by a wall five feet in height and about ten feet in diameter. Upon this the people stand who draw up the water in leathern buckets, an iron railing being so placed as to prevent their falling in. In El-Fasy's time there were eight marble basins in this room, for the purpose of ablution.

'On the north-east (south-east) side of Zem Zem stand two small buildings, one behind the other,[2] called El-Kobbateyn; they are covered by domes painted in the same manner as the mosque, and in them are kept water-jars, lamps, carpets, mats, brooms, and other articles used in the very mosque.[3] These two

[1] The door of the Zem Zem building opens to the south-east.

[2] This is not correct. As the plan will show, the angle of one building fronts the angle of its neighbour.

[3] Their names and offices are now changed. One is called the Kubbat el-Saat, and contains the clocks and chronometers (two of them English) sent as presents to the mosque by the Sultan. The other, known as the Kubbat el-Kutub, is used as a store-room for manuscripts bequeathed to the mosque. They still are open to Burckhardt's just criticism, being nothing but the common dome springing from four walls, and vulgarly painted with bands of red, yellow, and green. In Ibn Jubayr's time the two domes contained bequests of books and candles. The Kubbat Abbas, or that further from the Kaabah than its neighbour, was also called Kubbat el-Sherab (the Dome of Drink), because Zem Zem water was here kept cooling for the use of pilgrims in Daurak, or earthen jars. The nearer was termed Kubbat el-Yahudi; and the tradition they told me was, that a Jew having refused to sell his house upon this spot, it was permitted to remain *in loco* by the Apostle, as a lasting testimony to his regard for justice. A similar tale is told of an old woman's hut, which was allowed to stand in the corner of the great Nushirawan's royal halls.

ugly buildings are injurious to the interior appearance of the building, their heavy forms and structure being very disadvantageously contrasted with the light and airy shape of the Makams. I heard some Hadjys from Greece, men of better taste than the Arabs, express their regret that the Kobbateyn should be allowed to disfigure the mosque. They were built by Khoshgeldy, governor of Jeddah, AH 947; one is called Kobbet el-Abbas, from having been placed on the site of a small tank said to have been formed by Abbas, the uncle of Mohammed.

'A few paces west (north-west) of Zem Zem, and directly opposite to the door of the Kaabah, stands a ladder or staircase,[1] which is moved up to the wall of the Kaabah on days when that building is opened, and by which the visitors ascend to the door. It is of wood, with some carved ornaments, moves on low wheels, and is sufficiently broad to admit of four persons ascending abreast. The first ladder was sent hither from Cairo in AH 818, by Moyaed Abou el-Naser, king of Egypt.

'In the same line with the ladder and close by it stands a lightly built insulated and circular arch, about fifteen feet wide and eighteen feet high, called Bab es-Salam, which must not be confounded with the great gate of the mosque bearing the same name. Those who enter the Bait Ullah for the first time are enjoined to do so by the outer and inner Bab es-Salam; in passing under the latter they are to exclaim, "O God, may it be a happy entrance." I do not know by whom this arch was built, but it appears to be modern.[2]

'Nearly in front of the Bab-es-Salam, and nearer the Kaabah than any of the other surrounding buildings, stands the Makam Ibrahim.[3] This is a small building supported by six pillars about eight feet high, four of which are surrounded from top to bottom by a fine iron railing, while they leave the space beyond the two hind pillars open; within the railing is a frame about five feet square, terminating in a pyramidal top, and said to contain

[1] Called El-Daraj. A correct drawing of it may be found in Ali Bey's work.

[2] The Bab el-Salam, or Bab el-Naby, or Bab beni Shaybah, resembles in its isolation a triumphal arch, and is built of cut stone.

[3] 'The (praying) place of Abraham.' Readers will remember that the Meccan Mosque is peculiarly connected with Ibrahim, whom Moslems prefer to all Prophets except Mohammed.

the sacred stone upon which Ibrahim stood when he built the Kaabah, and which with the help of his son Ismayl he had removed from hence to the place called Maajen, already mentioned. The stone is said to have yielded under the weight of the Patriarch, and to preserve the impression of his foot still visible upon it; but no Hadjy has ever seen it,[1] as the frame is always entirely covered with a brocade of red silk richly embroidered. Persons are constantly seen before the railing invoking the good offices of Ibrahim; and a short prayer must be uttered by the side of the Makam after the walk round the Kaabah is completed. It is said that many of the Sahaba, or first adherents of Mohammed, were interred in the open space between this Makam and Zem Zem;[2] from which circumstance it is one of the most favourite places of prayer in the Mosque. In this part of the area the Khalif Soleyman Ibn Abd el-Melek, brother of Wolyd (El-Walid), built a fine reservoir in AH 97, which was filled from a spring east of Arafat;[3] but the Mekkawys destroyed it after his death, on the pretence that the water of Zem Zem was preferable.

'On the side of Makam Ibrahim, facing the middle part of

[1] This I believe to be incorrect. I was asked 5 dollars for permission to enter; but the sum was too high for my finances. Learned men told me that the stone shows the impress of two feet, especially the big toes, and devout pilgrims fill the cavities with water, which they rub over their eyes and faces. When the Caliph el-Mahdi visited Meccah, one Abdullah bin Usman presented himself at the unusual hour of noon; and, informing the prince that he had brought him a relic which no man but himself had yet seen, produced this celebrated stone. El-Mahdi, rejoicing greatly, kissed it, rubbed his face against it, and pouring water upon it, drank the draught. Kutb el-Din, one of the Meccan historians, says that it was visited in his day. In Ali Bey's time it was covered with *un magnifique drap noir brodé en or et en argent avec de gross glands en or*; he does not say, however, that he saw the stone. Its veils, called Sitr Ibrahim el-Khalil, are a green Ibrisham, or silk mixed with cotton and embroidered with gold. They are made at Cairo of three different colours, black, red, and green; and one is devoted to each year. The gold embroidery is in the Sulsi character, and expresses the Throne-verse, the Chapter of the Cave, and the name of the reigning Sultan; on the top is Allah, below it Mohammed; beneath this is Ibrahim el-Khalil; and at each corner is the name of one of the four Caliphs.

In a note to the *Dabistan* (vol. ii, p. 410), we find two learned Orientalists confounding the Black Stone with Abraham's Station or Platform. 'The Prophet honoured the Black Stone, upon which Abraham conversed with Hagar, to which he tied his camels, and upon which the traces of his feet are still seen.'

[2] Not only here, I was told by learned Meccans, but under all the oval pavements surrounding the Kaabah.

[3] The spring gushes from the southern base of Mount Arafat, as will afterwards be noticed. It is exceedingly pure.

the front of the Kaabah, stands the Mambar, or pulpit of the mosque; it is elegantly formed of fine white marble, with many sculptured ornaments; and was sent as a present to the mosque in AH 969 by Sultan Soleyman Ibn Selym.[1] A straight, narrow staircase leads up to the post of the Khatyb, or preacher, which is surmounted by a gilt polygonal pointed steeple, resembling an obelisk. Here a sermon is preached on Fridays and on certain festivals. These, like the Friday sermons of all mosques in the Mohammedan countries, are usually of the same turn, with some slight alterations upon extraordinary occasions.[2]

'I have now described all the buildings within the enclosure of the temple.

'The gates of the mosque are nineteen in number, and are distributed about it without any order or symmetry.'[3]

Burckhardt's description of the gates is short and imperfect.

[1] The author informs us that 'the first pulpit was sent from Cairo in AH 818, together with the staircase, both being the gifts of Moayed, Caliph of Egypt'. Ali Bey accurately describes the present Mambar.

[2] The curious will find a specimen of a Moslem sermon in Lane's *Modern Egypt*, vol. i, ch. 3.

[3] Burckhardt 'subjoins their names as they are usually written upon small cards by the Metowefs; in another column are the names by which they were known in more ancient times, principally taken from Azraky and Kotoby'. I have added a few remarks in brackets.

	Modern names	Arches	Ancient names
(1)	Bab el-Salam, composed of smaller gates or arches	3	Bab Beni Shaybah (this is properly applied to the inner, not the outer, Salam Gate)
(2)	Bab el-Neby	2	Bab el-Jenaiz, Gate of Biers, the dead being carried through it to the mosque
(3)	Bab el-Abbas, opposite to this the house of Abbas once stood	3	Bab Sertakat (some Moslem authors confound this Bab el-Abbas with the Gate of Biers)
(4)	Bab Aly	3	Bab Beni Hashem
(5)	Bab el-Zayt } Bab el-Ashra }	2	Bab Bazan (so called from a neighbouring hill)
(6)	Bab el-Baghlah	2	
(7)	Bab el-Szafa (Safa)	5	Bab Beni Makhzoum
(8)	Bab Sherif	2	Bab el-Djiyad (so called because leading to the hill Jiyad)
(9)	Bab Medjahed	2	Bab el-Dokhmah
(10)	Bab Zoleykha	2	Bab Sherif Adjelan, who built it
(11)	Bab Om Hany, so called from the daughter of Aby Taleb	2	Bab el-Hazoura (some write this Bab el-Zarurah)
(12)	Bab el-Wodaa (El-Widaa), through which the pilgrim passes when taking his final leave of the temple	2	Bab el-Kheyatyn, or Bab Djomah

On the eastern side of the Mosque there are four principal entrances, seven on the southern side, three in the western, and five in the northern wall.

The eastern gates are the Greater Bab el-Salam, through which the pilgrim enters the temple; it is close to the north-east angle. Next to it the Lesser Bab el-Salam, with two small arches; thirdly, the Bab el-Nabi, where the Prophet used to pass through from Khadijah's house; and, lastly, near the south-east corner, the Bab Ali, or of the Benu Hashim, opening upon the street between Safa and Marwah.

Beyond the north-eastern corner, in the northern wall, is the Bab Duraybah, a small entrance with one arch. Next to it, almost fronting the Kaabah, is the grand adit, Bab el-Ziyadah, also known as Bab el-Nadwah. Here the colonnade, projecting far beyond the normal line, forms a small square or hall supported by pillars; and a false colonnade of sixty-one columns leads to the true cloister of the Mosque. This portion of the building, being cool and shady, is crowded during divine worship, by the poor, the diseased, and the dying, and at other times by idlers, schoolboys, and merchants. Passing through three external arches, pilgrims descend by a flight of steps into the hall, where they deposit their slippers, it not being considered decorous to hold them when circumambulating the

(13)	Bab Ibrahim, so called from a tailor who had a shop near it	I	
(14)	Bab el-Omra, through which pilgrims issue to visit the Omra. Also called Benhi Saham	I	Bab Amer Ibn el-Aas, or Bab el-Sedra
(15)	Bab Atech (El-Atík?)	I	Bab el-Adjale
(16)	Bab el-Bastye	I	Bab Zyade Dar el-Nedoua
(17)	Bab el-Kotoby, so called from an historian of Mekka who lived in an adjoining lane and opened this small gate into the mosque	I	
(18)	Bab Zyade	3	(It is called Bab Ziyadah—Gate of Excess—because it is a new structure thrown out into the Shamiyah, or Syrian quarter)
(19)	Bab Dereybe	I	Bab Medrese
	Total	39	

Kaabah.[1] A broad pavement, in the shape of an irregular triangle, whose base is the cloister, leads to the circuit of the house. Next to the Ziyadah Gate is a small, single-arched entrance, Bab Kutubi, and beyond it one similar, the Bab el-Ajlah, also named El-Basitiyah, from its proximity to the college of Abd el-Basitah. Close to the north-west angle of the cloister is the Bab el-Nadwah, anciently called Bab el-Umrah, and now Bab el-Atik, the Old Gate. Near this place, an opening into the Kaabah, stood the Town Hall (Dar el-Nadwah), built by Kusay, for containing the oriflamme *El-Liwa*, and as a council-chamber for the ancients of the city.

In the western wall are three entrances. The single-arched gate nearest to the north angle is called Bab Beni Saham, or Bab el-Umrah, because pilgrims pass through it to the Tanim and the ceremony El-Umrah (Little Pilgrimage). In the centre of the wall is the Bab Ibrahim, or Bab el-Khayyatin (the Tailors' Gate), a single arch leading into a large projecting square, like that of the Ziyadah entrance, but somewhat smaller. Near the south-west corner is a double-arched adit, the Bab el-Widaa (of Farewell): hence departing pilgrims issue forth from the temple.

At the western end of the southern wall is the two-arched Bab Umm Hani, so called after the lady's residence, when included in the Mosque. Next to it is a similar building, Bab Ujlan, which derives its name from the large college Madrasat Ujlan; some call it Bab el-Sherif, because it is opposite one of the palaces. After which, and also pierced with two arches, is the Bab el-Jiyad (some erroneously spell it El-Jihad, of Religious War), the gate leading to Jebel Jiyad. The next is also double-arched, and called the Bab el-Mujahid or El-Rahmah (of Mercy). Nearly opposite the Kaabah, and connected with the pavement by a raised line of stone, is the Bab el-Safa, through which pilgrims now issue to perform the ceremony El-Sai. It is a small and unconspicuous erection. Next to it is the Bab el-Baghlah, with two arches; and, close to the south-east angle of the Mosque, the Bab Yunus, alias Bab Bazan, alias Bab el-Zayt, alias Bab el-Asharah, 'of the Ten',

[1] An old pair of slippers is here what the 'shocking bad hat' is at a crowded ball in Europe, a self-preserver. Burckhardt lost three pairs. I, more fortunate or less wealthy, only one.

because a favourite with the ten first Sahabah, or Companions of the Prophet.

'Most of these gates', says Burckhardt, 'have high pointed arches; but a few round arches are seen among them, which, like all arches of this kind in the Hejar, are nearly semicircular. They are without ornament, except the inscription on the exterior, which commemorates the name of the builder, and they are all posterior in date to the fourteenth century. As each gate consists of two or three arches, or divisions, separated by narrow walls, these divisions are counted in the enumeration of the gates leading into the Kaabah, and they make up the number thirty-nine. There being no doors to the gates, the Mosque is consequently open at all times. I have crossed at every hour of the night, and always found people there, either at prayers or walking about.[1]

'The outside walls of the Mosque are those of the houses which surround it on all sides. These houses belonged originally to the Mosque; the greater part are now the property of individuals. They are let out to the richest Hadjys, at very high prices, as much as 500 piastres being given during the pilgrimage for a good apartment with windows opening into the Mosque.[2] Windows have in consequence been opened in many parts of the wall on a level with the street, and above that of the floor of the colonnades. Hadjy living in these apartments are allowed to perform the Friday's prayers at home; because, having the Kaabah in view from the windows, they are supposed to be in the Mosque itself, and to join in prayer those assembled within the temple.

'Upon a level with the ground floor of the colonnades, and opening into them, are small apartments formed in the walls, having the appearance of dungeons; these have remained the property of the Mosque, while the houses above them belong to private individuals. They are let out to watermen, who deposit

[1] The Meccans love to boast that at no hour of the day or night is the Kaabah ever seen without a devotee to perform Tawaf.

[2] This would be about 50 dollars, whereas 25 is a fair sum for a single apartment. Like English lodging-house keepers, the Meccans make the season pay for the year. In Burckhardt's time the *Colonnato* was worth from 9 to 12 piastres: the value of the latter coin is now greatly decreased, for 28 go to the Spanish dollar all over El-Hejaz.

in them the Zem Zem jars, or to less opulent Hadjys who wish to live in the Mosque.[1] Some of the surrounding houses still belong to the Mosque, and were originally intended for public schools, as their names of Medresa implies; they are now all let out to Hadjys.

'The exterior of the Mosque is adorned with seven minarets, irregularly distributed: (1) Minaret of Bab el-Omra (Umrah); (2) of Bab el-Salam; (3) of Bab Aly; (4) of Beb el-Wodaa (Widaa); (5) of Medesa Kail (Kait) Bey; (6) of Beb el-Zyadi; (7) of Medreset Sultan Soleyman.[2] They are quadrangular or round steeples, in no way differing from other minarets. The entrance to them is from the different buildings round the Mosque, which they adjoin.[3] A beautiful view of the busy crowd below is attained by ascending the most northern one.'[4]

Having described at length the establishment attached to the Mosque of El-Medinah, I spare my readers a detailed account of the crowd of idlers that hang about the Meccan temple. The Naib el-Haram, or vice-intendant, is one Sayyid Ali, said to be of Indian extraction; he is superior to all the attendants. There are about eighty eunuchs, whose chief, Serur Agha, was a slave of Mohammed Ali Pasha. Their pay varies from 100 to 1,000 piastres per mensem; it is, however, inferior to the Medinah salaries. The Imans, Muezzins, Khatibs, Zem Zemis, etc., etc., are under their respective Shaykhs who are of the Olema.[5]

[1] I entered one of these caves, and never experienced such a sense of suffocation even in that favourite spot for Britons to asphixiate themselves—the Baths of Nero.

[2] The Magnificent (son of Selim I), who built at El-Medinah the minaret bearing his name. The minarets at Meccah are far inferior to those of her rival, and their bands of gaudy colours give them an appearance to tawdry vulgarity.

[3] Two minarets, namely, those of the Bab el-Salam and the Bab el-Safa, are separated from the Mosque by private dwelling-houses, a plan neither common nor regular.

[4] A stranger must be careful how he appears at a minaret window, unless he would have a bullet whizzing past his head. Arabs are especially jealous of being overlooked, and have no fellow-feeling for votaries of beautiful views. For this reason, here, as in Egypt, a blind Muezzin is preferred, and many ridiculous stories are told about men who for years have counterfeited cecity to live in idleness.

[5] I have illustrated this chapter, which otherwise might be unintelligible to many, by a plan of the Kaabah (taken from Ali Bey el-Abbasi), which Burckhardt pronounced to be 'perfectly correct'. This author has not been duly appreciated. In the first place, his disguise was against him; and, secondly, he was a spy of the French government. According to Mr Bankes, who had access to the original papers at Constantinople, Ali Bey was a Catalonian named Badia, and suspected to have been of Jewish extraction. He claimed from Napoleon a reward for his services, returned to the East, and died, it is

Briefly to relate the history of the Kaabah.

The House of Allah is supposed to have been built and rebuilt ten times.

The first origin of the idea is manifestly a symbolical allusion to the angels standing before the Almighty and praising his name. When Allah, it is said, informed the celestial throng that he was about to send a vicegerent on earth, they deprecated the design. Being reproved with these words, 'God knoweth what ye know not,' and dreading the eternal anger, they compassed the Arsh, or throne, in adoration. Upon this Allah created the Bayt el-Maamur, four jasper pillars with a ruby roof, and the angels circumambulated it, crying, 'Praise be to Allah, and exalted be Allah, and there is no God but Allah, and Allah is omnipotent!' The Creator then ordered them to build a similar house for man on earth. This, according to Ali, took place forty, according to Abu Hurayrah, 2,000 years before the creation; both authorities, however, are agreed that the firmaments were spread above and the seven earths beneath this Bayt el-Maamur.

There is considerable contradiction concerning the second house. Kaab related that Allah sent down with Adam[1] a Khaymah, or tabernacle of hollow ruby, which the angels raised on stone pillars. This was also called Bayt el-Maamur. Adam received an order to compass it about; after which he begged a reward for obedience, and was promised a pardon to himself and to all his progeny who repent.

Others declare that Adam, expelled from Paradise, and lamenting that he no longer heard the prayers of the angels, was ordered by Allah to take the stones of five hills, Libanus, Sinai, Tur Zayt (Olivet), Ararat, and Hira, which afforded the first stone. Gabriel, smiting his wing upon earth, opened a foundation to the seventh layer, and the position of the building is exactly below the heavenly Bayt el-Maamur—a Moslem cor-

supposed, of poison in the Haurán, near Damascus. In the edition which I have consulted (Paris, 1814) the author labours to persuade the world by marking the days with their planetary signs, etc., etc., that he is a real Oriental, but he perpetually betrays himself.

Some years ago, accurate plans of the two Harams were made by order of the present Sultan. They are doubtless to be found amongst the archives at Constantinople.

[1] It must be remembered that the Moslems, like many of the Jews, hold that Paradise was not on earth, but in the lowest firmament, which is, as it were, a reflection of earth.

ruption of the legends concerning the heavenly and the earthly Jerusalem. Our First Father circumambulated it as he had seen the angels do, and was by them taught the formula of prayer and the number of circuits.

According to others, again, this second house was not erected till after the 'Angelic Foundation' was destroyed by time.

The history of the third house is also somewhat confused. When the Bayt el-Maamur, or, as others say, the tabernacle, was removed to heaven after Adam's death, a stone-and-mud building was placed in its stead by his son Shays (Seth). For this reason it is respected by the Sabaeans, or Christians of St John, as well as the Moslems. This Kaabah, according to some, was destroyed by the deluge, which materially altered its site. Others believe that it was raised to heaven. Others, again, declare that only the pillars supporting the heavenly tabernacle were allowed to remain. Most authorities agree in asserting that the Black Stone was stored up in Abu Kubays, whence that 'first created of mountains' is called El-Amin, 'the Honest'.

Abraham and his son were ordered to build the fourth house upon the old foundations: its materials, according to some, were taken from the five hills which supplied the second; others give the names Ohod, Kuds, Warka, Sinai, Hira, and a sixth, Abu Kubays. It was of irregular shape: thirty-two cubits from the eastern to the northern corner; thirty-two from north to west; thirty-one from west to south; twenty from south to east; and only nine cubits high. There was no roof; two doors, level with the ground, were pierced in the eastern and western walls; and inside, on the right hand, near the present entrance, a hole for treasure was dug. Gabriel restored the Black Stone, which Abraham, by his direction, placed in its present corner, as a sign where circumambulation is to begin; and the patriarch then learned all the complicated rites of pilgrimage. When this house was completed, Abraham, by Allah's order, ascended Jebel Sabir, and called the world to visit the sanctified spot; and all earth's sons heard him, even those 'in their father's loins or in their mother's womb, from that day unto the day of resurrection'.

The Amalikah (descended from Imlik, great-grandson of

Sam, son of Noah), who first settled near Meccah, founded the fifth house. El-Tabari and the Moslem historians generally made the erection of the Amalikah to precede that of the Jurham; these, according to others, repaired the house which Abraham built.

The sixth Kaabah was built about the beginning of the Christian era, by the Beni Jurham, the children of Kahtan, fifth descendant from Noah. Ismail married, according to the Moslems, a daughter of this tribe, Daalah bint Muzaz bin Umar; and, abandoning Hebrew, he began to speak Arabic (*Taarraba*). Hence his descendants are called Arabicised Arabs. After Ismail's death, which happened when he was 130 years old, Sabit, the eldest of his twelve sons, became Lord of the house. He was succeeded by his maternal grandfather Muzaz, and afterwards by his children. The Jurham inhabited the higher parts of Meccah, especially Jebel Kaakaan, so called from their clashing arms; whereas the Amalikah dwelt in the lower grounds, which obtained the name of Jiyad, from their generous horses.

Kusay bin Kilab, governor of Meccah, and fifth forefather of the Apostle, built the seventh house, according to Abraham's plan. He roofed it over with palm-leaves; stocked it with idols, and persuaded his tribe to settle near the Haram.

Kusay's house was burnt down by a woman's censer, which accidentally set fire to the Kiswat, or covering, and the walls were destroyed by a torrent. A merchant-ship belonging to a Greek trader, called Bakum, being wrecked at Jeddah, afforded material for the roof, and the crew were employed as masons. The Kuraysh tribe, who rebuilt the house, failing in funds of 'pure money', curtailed its proportions by nearly seven cubits, and called the omitted portion El-Hatim. In digging the foundation they came to a green stone, like a camel's hunch, which, struck with a pickaxe, sent forth blinding lightning and prevented further excavation. The Kuraysh, amongst other alterations, raised the walls from nine to eighteen cubits, built a staircase in the northern breadth, closed the western door, and placed the eastern entrance above the ground, to prevent men entering without their leave.

When the eighth house was being built, Mohammed was in his twenty-fifth year. His surname of El-Amin, the Honest, probably induced the tribes to make him their umpire for the decision of a dispute about the position of the Black Stone, and who should have the honour of raising it to its place. Others derive the surname from this decision. He decided for the corner chosen by Abraham, and distributed the privilege amongst the clans. The Benu Zahrah and Benu Abd Manaf took the front wall and the door; to the Benu Jama and the Benu Sahm was allotted the back wall; the Benu Makhzum and their Kuraysh relations stood at the southern wall; and at the 'Stone' corner were posted the Benu Abd el-Dar, the Benu Asad, and the Benu Ada.

Abdullah bin Zubayr, nephew of Ayisha, rebuilt the Kaabah in AH 64. It had been weakened by fire, which burnt the covering, besides splitting the Black Stone into three pieces, and by the Manjanik (catapults) of Husayn bin Numayr, general of Yezid, who obstinately besieged Meccah till he heard of his sovereign's death. Abdullah, hoping to fulfil a prophecy, and seeing that the people of Meccah fled in alarm, pulled down the building by means of 'thin-calved Abyssinian slaves'. When they came to Abraham's foundation he saw that it included the Hijr, which part the Kuraysh had been unable to build. This house was made of cut stone and fine lime brought from Yemen. Abdullah, taking in the Hatim, lengthened the building by seven cubits, and added to its former height nine cubits, thus making a total of twenty-seven. He roofed over the whole, or a part; reopened the western door, to serve as an exit; and, following the advice of his aunt, who quoted the Prophet's words, he supported the interior with a single row of three columns, instead of the double row of six placed there by the Kuraysh. Finally, he paved the Mataf, or circuit, ten cubits round with the remaining slabs; and increased the Haram by taking in the nearer houses. During the building, a curtain was stretched round the walls, and pilgrims compassed them externally. When finished, it was perfumed inside and outside, and invested with brocade. Then Abdullah and all the citizens went forth in a procession to the Tanim, a reverend place near Meccah, returned to perform Umrah, the larger pilgrimage, slew a hundred victims, and rejoiced with great festivities.

The Caliph Abd el-Malik bin Marwan besieged Abdullah bin Zubayr, who after a brave defence was slain. In AH 74, Hajjaj bin Yusuf, general of Abd el-Malik's troops, wrote to the prince, informing him that Abdullah had made unauthorised additions to and changes in the Haram: the reply brought an order to rebuild the house. Hajjaj again excluded the Hatim, and retired the northern wall six cubits and a span, making it twenty-five cubits long by twenty-four broad: the other three sides were allowed to remain as built by the son of Zubayr. He gave the house a double roof, closed the western door, and raised the eastern four cubits and a span above the Mataf, or circuit, which he paved over. The Haram was enlarged and beautified by the Abbasides, especially by El-Mehdi, El-Mutamid, and El-Mutazid. Some authors reckon, as an eleventh house, the repairs made by Sultan Murad Khan. On the night of Tuesday, the 20th Shaaban, AH 1030, a violent torrent swept the Haram; it rose one cubit above the threshold of the Kaabah, carried away the lamp-posts and the Makam Ibrahim, all the northern wall of the house, half of the eastern, and one-third of the western side. It subsided on Wednesday night. The repairs were not finished till AH 1040. The greater part, however, of the building dates from the time of El-Hajjaj; and Moslems, who never mention his name without a curse, knowingly circumambulate his work. The Olema indeed have insisted upon its remaining untouched, lest kings in wantonness should change its form: Harun el-Rashid desired to rebuild it, but was forbidden by the Imam Malik.

The present proofs of the Kaabah's sanctity, as adduced by the learned, are puerile enough, but curious. The Olema have made much of the verselet: 'Verily the first house built for mankind (to worship in) is that in Bakkah (*Meccah*), blessed and a salvation to the three worlds. Therein (*fihi*) are manifest signs, the standing-place of Abraham, which whoso entereth shall be safe.' (Koran, chapter 3.) The word 'therein' is interpreted to mean Meccah, and the 'manifest signs' the Kaabah, which contains such marvels as the footprints on Abraham's platform, and the spiritual safeguard of all who enter the Sanctuary.[1] The other 'signs'—historical, psychical, and physical—are briefly these:

The preservation of the Hajar el-Aswad and the Makam Ibrahim from many foes, and the miracles put forth (as in the War of the Elephant) to defend the house; the violent and terrible deaths of the sacrilegious; and the fact that, in the Deluge, the large fish did not eat the little fish in the Haram. A wonderful desire and love impel men from distant regions to visit the holy spot; and the first sight of the Kaabah causes awe and fear, horripilation and tears. Furthermore, ravenous beasts will not destroy their prey in the Sanctuary land, and the pigeons and other birds never perch upon the house, except to be cured of sickness, for fear of defiling the roof. The Kaabah, though small, can contain any number of devotees: no one is ever hurt in it (this is an audacious falsehood; the Kaabah is scarcely ever opened without some accident happening); and invalids recover their health by rubbing themselves against the Kiswah and the Black Stone. Finally, it is observed that every day a hundred thousand mercies descend upon the house; and especially that if rain come up from the northern corner, there is plenty in Irak; if from the south, there is plenty in Yemen; if from the east, plenty in India; if from the west, there is plenty in Syria; and if from all four angles, general plenty is presignified.

[1] Makkah (our Meccah) is the common word; Bakkah is a synonym now used but in books. The former means 'a concourse of people'. But why derive it from the Hebrew, and translate it 'a slaughter'? Is this a likely name for a holy place? Dr Colenso actually turns the Makaraba of Ptolemy into 'Makkahrabbah', plentiful slaughter. But if Makaraba be Meccah, it is evidently a corruption of 'Makkah' and 'Arabah', the Arab *race*.

Again, supposing the Meccan temple to be originally dedicated to the sun, why should the pure Arab word 'Baal' become the Hebraised *Hobal*, and the deity be only one in the 360 that formed the Pantheon?

II The Meccah Pilgrimage

Having resolved to perform the Meccah pilgrimage, I spent a few months at Cairo, and on the 22nd May embarked in a small steamer at Suez with the Mahmal or litter, and its military escort, conveying the Kiswah or covering for the Kaabah. On the 25th the man at the wheel informed us that we were about to pass the village of Rabikh, on the Arabian coast, and that the time had consequently arrived for changing our usual habiliments for the Ihram or pilgrim-costume of two towels, and for taking the various interdictory vows involved in its assumption: such as not to tie knots in any portion of our dress, not to oil the body, and not to cut our nails or hair, nor to improve the tints of the latter with the coppery red of henna Transgression of these and other ceremonial enactments is expiated either by animal sacrifice, or gifts of fruit or cereals to the poor.

After a complete ablution and assuming the Ihram, we performed two prayer-flections, and recited the meritorious sentences beginning with the words 'Labbayk Allah huma labbayk!' 'Here I am, O God, here I am! Here I am, O Unassociated One, here I am, for unto Thee belong praise, grace, and empire, O Unassociated One!'

This prayer was repeated so often, people not unfrequently rushing up to their friends and shrieking the sacred sentence into their ears, that at last it became a signal for merriment rather than an indication of piety.

On the 26th we reached Jeddah, where the utter sterility of Arabia, with its dunes and rocky hills, becomes apparent. The town, however, viewed from the sea, is not unpicturesque. Many European vessels were at anchor off the coast; and as we entered the port, innumerable small fishing-boats darting in all directions, their sails no longer white, but emerald green from the intense lustre of the water, crowded around us on all sides, and reminded one by their dazzling colours and rapidity of motion of the shoals of porpoises so often seen on a voyage round the Cape.

On disembarking we were accosted by several Mutawwifs, or

circuit-men, so termed in Arabic, because, besides serving as religious guides in general, their special duty is to lead the pilgrim in his seven obligatory circuits around the Kaabah. We encamped outside the town, and, having visited the tomb of 'our Mother Eve', mounted our camels for Meccah.

After a journey of twenty hours across the Desert, we passed the barriers which mark the outermost limits of the sacred city, and, ascending some giant steps, pitched our tents on a plain, or rather plateau, surrounded by barren rock, some of which, distant but a few yards, mask from view the birthplace of the Prophet. It was midnight; a few drops of rain were falling, and lightning played around us. Day after day we had watched its brightness from the sea, and many a faithful Haji had pointed out to his companions those fires which were Heaven's witness to the sanctity of the spot. 'Al hamdu Lillah!' Thanks be to God! we were now at length to gaze upon the Kiblah, to which every Mussulman has turned in prayer since the days of Mohammed, and which for long ages before the birth of Christianity was reverenced by the Patriarchs of the East. Soon after dawn arose from our midst the shout of 'Labbayk! Labbayk!' and, passing between the rocks, we found ourselves in the main street of Meccah, and approached the Gateway of Salvation, one of the thirty-nine portals of the Temple of Al-Haram.

On crossing the threshold we entered a vast unroofed quadrangle, a mighty amplification of the Palais Royal, having on each of its four sides a broad colonnade, divided into three aisles by a multitude of slender columns, and rising to the height of about thirty feet. Surmounting each arch of the colonnade is a small dome: in all there are 120, and at different points arise seven minarets, dating from various epochs, and of somewhat varying altitudes and architecture. The numerous pigeons which have their home within the temple have been believed never to alight upon any portion of its roof, thus miraculously testifying to the holiness of the building. This marvel having, however, of late years been suspended, many discern another omen of the approach of the long-predicted period when unbelievers shall desecrate the hallowed soil.

In the centre of the square area rises the far-famed Kaabah, the funereal shade of which contrasts vividly with the sunlit walls and precipices of the town. It is a cubical structure of massive stone, the upper two-thirds of which are mantled by a black cloth embroidered with silver, and the lower portion hung with white linen. At a distance of several yards it is surrounded by a balustrade provided with lamps, which are lighted in the evening, and the space thus enclosed is the circuit-ground along which, day and night, crowds of pilgrims, performing the circular ceremony of Tawaf, realise the idea of perpetual motion. We at once advanced to the black stone imbedded in an angle of the Kaabah, kissed it, and exclaimed, 'Bismillah wa Allahu Akbar'—'In God's name, and God is greatest.' Then we commenced the usual seven rounds, three at a walking pace, and four at a brisk trot. Next followed two prayer-flections at the tomb of Abraham, after which we drank of the water of Zem Zem, said to be the same which quenched the thirst of Hagar's exhausted son.

Besides the Kaabah, eight minor structures adorn the quadrangle, the well of Zem Zem, the library, the clock-room, the triangular staircase, and four ornamental resting-places for the orthodox sects of Hanafi, Shāfī, Mālikī, and Hanbalí.

We terminated our morning duties by walking and running seven times along the streets of Safā and Marwā, so named from the flight of seven steps at each of its extremities.

After a few days spent in visiting various places of interest, such as the slave-market and forts, and the houses of the Prophet and the Caliphs Ali and Abubekr, we started on our six hours' journey to the mountain of 'Arifāt, an hour's sojourn at which, even in a state of insensibility, confers the rank of Haji. It is a mountain spur of about 150 feet in height, presenting an artificial appearance from the wall encircling it and the terrace on its slope, from which the Iman delivers a sermon before the departure of his congregation for Meccah. His auditors were, indeed, numerous, their tents being scattered over two or three miles of the country. A great number of their inmates were fellow-subjects of ours from India. I surprised some of my Meccah friends by informing them that Queen Victoria numbers nearly 20 million Mohammedans among her subjects.

On the 5th June, at sunset, commencing our return, we slept at the village of Muzdalifah, and there gathered and washed seven pebbles of the size of peas, to be flung at three piles of whitewashed masonry known as the Shaitans (Satans) of Muna. We acquitted ourselves satisfactorily of this duty on the festival of the 6th June, the tenth day of the Arabian month Zu'l Hijjah. Each of us then sacrificed a sheep, had his hair and nails cut, exchanged the Ihram for his best apparel, and, embracing his friends, paid them the compliments of the season. The two following days the Great, the Middle, and the Little Satan were again pelted, and, bequeathing to the unfortunate inhabitants of Muna the unburied and odorous remains of nearly 100,000 animals, we returned, 80,000 strong, to Meccah. A week later, having helped to insult the tumulus of stones which marks, according to popular belief, the burial-place of Abulahab, the unbeliever, who, we learn from the Koran, has descended into hell with his wife, gatherer of sticks, I was not sorry to relinquish a shade temperature of 120°, and wend my way to Jeddah *en route* for England, after delegating to my brethren the recital of a prayer in my behalf at the Tomb of the Prophet at Medinah.

In penning these lines I am anxious to encourage other Englishmen, especially those from India, to perform the pilgrimage, without being deterred by exaggerated reports concerning the perils of the enterprise. It must, however, be understood that it is absolutely indispensable to be a Mussulman (at least externally) and to have an Arabic name. Neither the Koran nor the Sultan enjoins the killing of intrusive Jews or Christians; nevertheless, two years ago, an incognito Jew, who refused to repeat the creed, was crucified by the Meccah populace, and in the event of a pilgrim again declaring himself to be an unbeliever the authorities would be almost powerless to protect his life.

An Englishman who is sufficiently conversant with the prayers, formulas, and customs of the Mussulmans, and possesses a sufficient guarantee of orthodoxy, need, however, apprehend no danger if he applies through the British Consulate at

Cairo for an introduction to the Amīrul Haj, the Prince of the Caravan.

Finally, I am most anxious to recommend as Mutawwif at Meccah Shaykh Mohammed 'Umr Fanāirjīzâdah. He is extremely courteous and obliging, and has promised me to show to other Englishmen the same politeness which I experienced from him myself.

1862	1278	الحاج عبد الواحد
AD	AH	(EL-HAJ ABD EL-WAHID)

INDEX